To
Reclaim
a
Divided
West

The Grand Canyon of the Colorado River, by William Bell.
(Courtesy, Library of Congress, Washington, D.C.)

To Reclaim a Divided West

Water, Law, and Public Policy, 1848–1902

Donald J. Pisani

Histories of the American Frontier
Ray Allen Billington, General Editor

Howard R. Lamar, Coeditor
Martin Ridge, Coeditor
David J. Weber, Coeditor

University of New Mexico Press
Albuquerque

333.91
P67t

Library of Congress Cataloging-in-Publication Data

Pisani, Donald J.
   To reclaim a divided west : water, law, and public policy, 1848–
1902 / Donald J. Pisani.
      p.   cm.
   Includes bibliographical references and index.
   ISBN 0-8263-1380-9
   1. Water-supply—Government policy—West (U.S.)—History—
19th century. 2. Irrigation—Government policy–West (U.S.)—
History–19th century. 3. Hydroelectric power plants—
Government policy—West (U.S.)—History—19th century.
4. Water—Laws and legislation—West (U.S.)—History—
19th century.   I. Title.
HD1695.A17P57   1992
333.91′00978—dc20   92-14161
                                                  CIP
TP

For Joey

Contents

Foreword

Perhaps the most enduring image of the American West is the vast arid landscape of the Southwest with its red bluffs, vacant mesas, and simmering heat. This image emerged from the narratives of early explorers and travelers who told tales of grueling journeys across naked wastelands, alkali deserts, and flint-hard barren mountains. Little wonder that historians began to describe the whole West as a land of semiaridity. In fact, one of the most distinguished scholars of the West, Walter Prescott Webb, asserted that the absence of sufficient rainfall established the basis for a unique and different culture beyond the 100th meridian. Webb's work validated the idea that the West was indeed a land of little rain, an idea so obvious to people who lived in the Southwest, the intermountain regions, and the high plains that it remains popular today. Although they have often described parts of the West as desert oasis, most scholars have long recognized that the West is far from a uniform region. Many areas—parts of the Great Plains and especially areas in the Southwest—are indeed arid, but others, like parts of the Pacific Northwest, have an abundance of rain, and still others contain lakes and rivers that are fed by melting mountain snow as well as monsoonal storms.

Diversity does not mean that water is not a problem in the West. Rainfall is scarce in many areas and it often occurs at times when grain farmers least need it. Moreover, in much of the West intense competition existed for the available water supply as farmers, miners, ranchers as well as town and city dwellers each struggled for a larger share.

Each tried to write rules for water distribution and use that best served its interests. Americans who came from the well-watered East had little experience in allocating and developing water resources in a dry region. In fact, throughout the nineteenth century Americans were still debating how to distribute the public lands, and it proved far more complicated to allocate water than many people at the time understood. The problems related to water allocation were compounded by the fact that virtually all political boundaries had been drawn with little regard to water use. Streams and rivers could flow through several communities, counties, and even states, and each could lay claim to the same water.

The subtleties involved in the American accommodation to the water issues of the West demonstrate how a democratic society with fragmented political power and competing economic traditions—mercantilism and liberalism—interacted at all levels of government in the West and in the nation's capital. That water questions are invariably local in origin, that they may be different because of various kinds of potential users, and that they are often infused with technical problems gives the study of water increased complexity.

Donald Pisani is uniquely prepared to address the problem of water in the West. He is an expert on western agriculture, and his book *From the Family Farm to Agribusiness: The Irrigation Crusade in California and the West, 1850–1931* identified him as a leader in the field. To complete this study, he consulted federal and state laws and court cases at many levels. He examines the history of water in the West in terms of law and public policy, which allows him both to tell the story of how water was distributed and to draw on the history of water in the West to explain an evolving debate over the whole issue of public resources and their use.

Donald Pisani confronted many genuine questions as well as myths surrounding the "arid West" in writing this splendid book. His research has been prodigious. He places the allocation of water within a national political and economic context, analyzes the organizations that advocated various national and state programs, and looks into the lives of men who promoted specific programs to deal with water as a resource. Most important of all, he explains the problem of water from the local level up rather than from the nation's capital down. In his fascinating account farmers, ranchers, engineers, businessmen, politicians, publicists, and even scientific frauds are important actors. The mysteries of the politics of water are exposed, and the reader comes away with a more profound understanding not only of the centrality of water to parts of the West but also of how water figured in national affairs. Unlike most earlier studies of water, Pisani's work is analytical and descriptive rather than narrative and prescriptive.

When the distinguished historian Ray Allen Billington initiated the *Histories of the American Frontier* series, he contemplated a set of well-written volumes in which each book would provide the general reader as well as the specialized student with an accurate summary of the available knowledge on a western subject. He was convinced that a full history of the frontier, this most American phase of the nation's past, would help the people of the United States better understand themselves and thus be better equipped to face the problems of the future. When Billington established the *Histories of the American Frontier* series, this book could not have been written because many of the ideas expressed in it were not yet fully explored, and much of the research at the grass-roots level had hardly begun. Yet, even if Billington could not have anticipated publishing a volume on water of this scope and complexity, he would doubtless have welcomed Pisani's book enthusiastically because it satisfies all of his goals for the series. Eminently readable, Pisani's modern account of water in the West establishes a proper basis for understanding many of the West's current problems.

To Reclaim a Divided West: Water, Law, and Public Policy, 1848–1902 testifies to how much the field of western American history has developed in the past thirty years and yet how persistent are the basic questions that historians ask of the past and how subtle is their search for answers. Simplistic theories about the economic development of the West, volatile ideological explanations, impressionistic treatments of victimization, and under-researched assertions of many kinds increasingly give way to careful studies and thoughtful analyses. This work joins earlier volumes in this series such as Rodman W. Paul's *The Mining Frontiers of the Far West* and Robert M. Utley's *The Indian Frontier of the American West* that have achieved near classic status as works in American history. The editors of this series invite the readers of this book into the best kind of western history, one that probes more deeply, searches more carefully, and examines more thoughtfully one of the most complex issues in the history of western America—the allocation of water.

Howard R. Lamar
Yale University

Martin Ridge
The Huntington Library

David J. Weber
Southern Methodist University

Preface

Since 1931, when Walter Prescott Webb published *The Great Plains*, many historians have considered the influence of aridity on the history of the western United States. Webb included most of the western half of the nation within the "Great Plains Environment," so his thesis extended far beyond the grasslands.[1] The absence of water, he argued, profoundly influenced the evolution of agricultural technology and institutions, ranging from the windmill to water law to irrigation. As if to underscore Webb's thesis, in the same year his book appeared, one of the nation's leading hydraulic engineers noted the marked differences in patterns of rainfall within the United States. Precipitation averaged forty-eight inches per year east of the 95th meridian, a line through central Minnesota and east Texas. The Great Plains—that band of prairie lying between the 95th and 103rd meridians—received an average of thirty inches, while the western two-fifths of the country captured only twelve.[2]

Webb regarded the "retreat" of the desert as the last, heroic chapter in the advance of American civilization. So did W. Eugene Hollon, a Webb student, whose *The Great American Desert, Then and Now*, appeared in 1966.[3] Both argued that aridity was a force for good in that it promoted ingenuity, resourcefulness, cooperation, and democracy. In 1985, however, Donald Worster published a much more somber appraisal of the relationship between water and western history.[4] Webb, he charged, had been too concerned with sectionalism and interregional conflict—especially the West's economic vassalage to the East—to see that even in 1931 the region showed signs of becoming an empire unto itself.[5] After 1945, in Worster's view, the "technological control of water," and the bureaucratization that control demanded, forged a new West that became the "principal seat of the world-encircling American Empire." This "hydraulic society" was dominated by undemocratic, rapacious elites. Aridity also resulted in the wanton abuse of nature, as dam-builders pushed economic development far beyond prudent environmental limits.[6]

Webb and Worster have had a substantial impact on Western history, but aridity is a shaky scholarly foundation. The *average* precipitation figures given above mask highly diverse conditions. There are obvious pockets of humidity in the West, including the "Great Pacific Rain Forest," and the frequency and duration of precipitation, along with seasonal variations, are just as important as the total volume. Moreover, westerners have shown a remarkable ability to circumvent or ignore arid and semi-arid conditions. Large parts of the West chose dry-farming over irrigation, and many farmers simply defied aridity. Nineteenth-century California, for example, became one of the nation's leading wheat-growing states despite precipitation that averaged only six to 22 inches a year in the Central Valley—far less than in other grain-producing regions. Crops lost to drought were more than offset by the productiveness of virgin soils. Finally, it is wrong to look at a West defined solely by desert because most of its states are also mountainous, and many of those mountains capture a large supply of water. Wyoming and Montana are favored by many substantial streams, and aridity has imposed far fewer limits there than in Nevada and Arizona.

Equally important, water management has been a *national* problem. Worster insists that the "water empire is a purely western invention."[7] Certainly, there is nothing in the East—with the possible exception of TVA—to match Hoover Dam, which stores more than an average year's flow of the Colorado River, or the California Aqueduct, which carries water hundreds of miles from northern California through the San Joaquin Valley to the Los Angeles basin. Nor do eastern water agencies rival the political power of southern California's massive Metropolitan Water District or Imperial Irrigation District. Nevertheless, nineteenth-century easterners built dams and canals, too, and they raised and spent huge sums of money to do so. From the 1820s through the 1840s, Massachusetts water and textile companies dammed the Merrimac River to provide factories with water power.[8] Other companies developed the technology to drain and fill swamps and dredge and straighten streams. Both private enterprise and the states built huge transportation arteries, such as the Erie Canal, and they constructed massive artificial waterways—such as the Croton Aqueduct that supplied New York City with water from the Catskills—to serve the needs of burgeoning cities. Moreover, along the Mississippi River and other streams, landowners and flood control districts erected massive levees to protect farms and towns in unusually wet years. Before historians can treat the West as exceptional, they will have to make direct comparisons between different regions and explain why irrigation is more important than flood control or the reclamation of wetlands. In short, the aridity model is too nebulous, and too subject to qualification and exception, to serve as a paradigm for the entire West.

This is not to say that aridity made no difference, or that in the second half of the nineteenth century the West was simply an extension of the East. Nevertheless, the differences that defined the two regions were more often of degree than of kind. In the West, rugged mountains, forbidding deserts, and diverse climates exacerbated the endemic American preference for localism. And in the absence of adequate transportation—much of the region was isolated even in 1902—state or territorial borders often mattered for little and many citizens showed scant attachment or allegiance to relatively inaccessible courts and legislatures. Thin and scattered populations, the presence of large numbers of Indians, and the fact that almost all land was owned by the federal government, rendered the West highly dependent on the central government for aid of all sorts, especially military protection. Westerners probably received more in benefits than they paid in federal taxes, but most of them thought that the flow of dollars moved East rather than West.

The nineteenth-century western economy moved in fits and starts, passing through even more severe boom and bust cycles than those experienced in the eastern states. As in most underdeveloped regions, shortages of capital forced westerners to depend heavily on nonresident investors. Not only was transportation much better developed in the humid half of the nation—where there were more rivers, canals, turnpikes, and railroads—but those rivers gave New England a cheap source of water power not available in the arid and semi-arid sections of the nation until the advent of hydroelectric power in the twentieth century. Western farmers usually escaped the labor and expense of clearing their land of forests, but many discovered that the wood they needed for houses, barns, fences, and fuel was far removed from where it was needed and often inaccessible. It was expensive, particularly on the Great Plains. Moreover, although some western states contained low-grade coal, they lacked the higher quality, easier to mine bituminous deposits of Pennsylvania, Kentucky, Tennessee, and West Virginia. In the nineteenth century, the eastern half of the nation also produced far more iron and petroleum—the building blocks of heavy industry. Little wonder that the West's image as the "Great American Desert" persisted. The region's almost pathological boosterism reflected insecurity as well as pride, fear as well as confidence.

All this has been well understood by American historians for generations. Nevertheless, these economic obstacles, to name just a few, help explain why water became a tool to build a "new West." In keeping with the format of the Billington Series, this is a narrative history. Throughout, I use *West* simply to denote the western half of the nation. The decision to study the region independently is, of course, arbitrary. I make no effort to answer the persistent question of whether the West is a distinct section, nor to provide a new theoretical model to direct future research. *To Reclaim a Divided West* is not even a comprehensive history of irrigation. (For example, there is little here about the Southwest, or the Pacific Northwest, or about the techniques of irrigation agriculture, or about the changing technology of dam and canal building, or about the lives of irrigation farmers, or about the society irrigation helped to produce.) Instead, I look at the relationship among water, law, and polity, and explore the development of irrigation as a private, public, and mixed enterprise. The focus is on Congress and four critical states—California, Colorado, Nevada, and Wyoming. I make several assumptions: first, that the West was made up of many diverse parts that were defined as much by American values, culture, and institutions, as by climate and geography; second, that local economic conditions mattered far more in the evolution of western water policy than aridity *per se*; and, third, that individuals mold history as history molds them.

There was no single West. The book's major theme is *fragmentation*, a word I use not just to represent the West's failure to achieve a unified, coherent water policy, but also to describe inconsistencies inherent in the law itself. Fragmentation resulted from a pervasive mercantilism that pitted community against community and state against state, from intense competition between regions within the West (such as the Great Plains and Rocky Mountain states), and from a decentralized system of government that encouraged the allocation of natural resources by users rather than by public officials. Within the arid and semi-arid West, conflict erupted between upstream and downstream states, between states that consisted almost entirely of public land and those whose arable land was in private hands, between older and newer states (which received different quantities of public land upon entering the Union), and between grazing and farming regions. The Reclamation Act of 1902 demonstrated that the western states and territories had learned to cooperate in matters of mutual concern. Nevertheless, that law also reflected persistent suspicions and irreconcilable differences. Most states competed among themselves just as strongly in 1902 as they had in the 1880s and 1890s, and they were reluctant to concede any real or imagined authority over natural resources to the government in Washington.

The book works from the particular to the general, from individual values to collective policies. After a brief introduction which describes some of the limits to American government in the nineteenth century, the scene shifts to the mining camps of California in the 1850s. There argonauts sharply disagreed over how water should be allocated and who should benefit. Chapter three discusses the spread of water law from mining to agriculture and subsequent attempts to reform a legal system that left the determination of water policy with individual users. Subsequent chapters deal with private irrigation ventures and with the attempt to find the proper level of government to plan and direct the expansion of western irrigation.

Acknowledgments

Many individuals and institutions helped make this book possible. I received indispensable financial support from the American Council of Learned Societies, the National Endowment for the Humanities, the American Bar Foundation, the American Philosophical Society, the University of Oklahoma Foundation, and the Texas A&M University Summer Grant and Mini-Grant programs. I would also like to thank the staffs of the Bancroft Library (University of California, Berkeley); the California section of the California State Library (Sacramento); the Boalt Law Library at the University of California, Berkeley; the National Archives; the Huntington Library (San Marino, California); the Federal Records Center, Suitland, Md.; the Wyoming Archives (Cheyenne); the California Archives (Sacramento); the Sterling Library (Yale University); the Nevada Historical Society (Reno); the Colorado Historical Society (Denver); the Louisiana Historical Center (New Orleans); the James J. Hill Library (St. Paul); the Minnesota Historical Society (Minneapolis); the Water Resource Library at the University of California, Berkeley; the Green Library (Stanford University); and the Special Collections Division at the University of California, Los Angeles and at Idaho State University, Pocatello. Special thanks are also due to the many helpful people in the interlibrary loan office of the Sterling C. Evans Library at Texas A&M University.

To list all the people whose work aided, inspired, and informed this book would be impossible, but I have tried to acknowledge my greatest intellectual debts in the notes. Above all, I have profited from the aid and encouragement of Robert Dunbar, Robert Kelley, Lawrence B. Lee, Douglas Littlefield, Richard Lowitt, Richard Orsi, and Harry N. Scheiber. Kelley, Lee, and Littlefield read an early draft of the manuscript and proposed many helpful revisions. Two scholars have had a particularly strong influence on this study. I regard Paul Wallace Gates as the greatest historian of natural resources this country has produced. His exhaustive and imaginative research, his meticulous craftsmanship as a writer, his commitment to democratic ideals and values, and his faith in the state's capacity to rectify social injustice, have heartened many scholars, but few more than me. His student, Harry Scheiber, has maintained the same high standards of intellectual inquiry, and no one has done more to define the relationship among government, the law, and economic development. His brilliant essays on federalism and the American economy have been especially illuminating. The editors of the Ray A. Billington Frontier Series, Howard Lamar, Martin Ridge, and David Weber, supported this work in many ways their modesty will not permit me to acknowledge. I have thanked them personally. Of course, all errors of fact, omission, or judgment remain mine alone.

Scholars also depend on friends and allies who are not professional historians, archivists, or librarians. David Holtby, editor at the University of New Mexico Press, was a model of geniality, tolerance, and understanding. My parents-in-law, Engel and Shirley Sluiter, provided comfortable accommodations and plenty of good cheer during many months of research at the Bancroft Library. No one could ask for more good-natured, hospitable in-laws. Diane Leach typed the bibliography with precision, good humor, and infinite patience; she also provided invaluable assistance as a proofreader. Special thanks are due to Mrs. Elizabeth Merrick Coe and her family, who have done so much to support higher education in Oklahoma, including the study of the American West. My wife, Mary Alice, knows her contribution. The dedication is to my fifteen-year-old son, who, as of this writing, shows little concern for scholarship, but exhibits a teenager's keen understanding of "pressure politics." He was always eager to pull me out of the nineteenth century and back into the present.

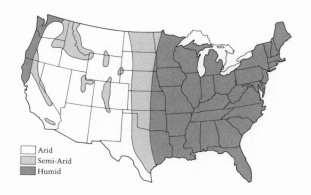

Arid
Semi-Arid
Humid

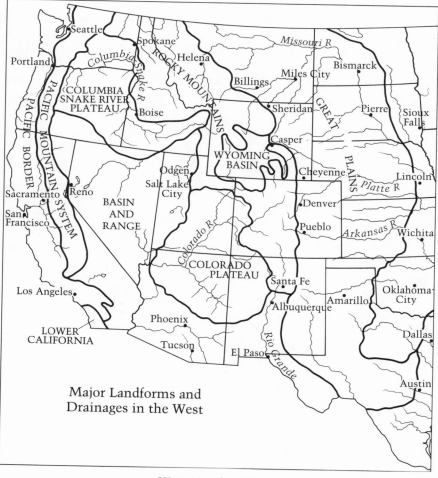

Seattle
Spokane
Portland
Helena
Columbia
Missouri R
Snake R
ROCKY MOUNTAINS
Bismarck
Miles City
Billings
COLUMBIA
SNAKE RIVER
PLATEAU
Boise
Sheridan
GREAT
Pierre
Sioux
Falls
Casper
PACIFIC BORDER
PACIFIC MOUNTAIN SYSTEM
WYOMING
BASIN
Odgen
Salt Lake
City
Cheyenne
PLAINS
Lincoln
Platte R
Sacramento
Reno
BASIN
AND
RANGE
Denver
San
Francisco
Colorado R
Pueblo
Arkansas R
Wichita
COLORADO
PLATEAU
Santa Fe
Los Angeles
Albuquerque
Amarillo
Oklahoma
City
LOWER
CALIFORNIA
Phoenix
Dallas
Tucson
El Paso
Rio Grande
Austin

Major Landforms and
Drainages in the West

Water in the West.

1
Introduction:
Government and Public Policy
in the Nineteenth Century

Τhis book is about the West, but it is also a study in American government. Westerners lived in a decentralized nation whose citizens harbored deep fears of the abuse of public power, fears reinforced by a strong preference for localism and economic individualism. Yet, like most other Americans, westerners expected public authorities at all levels to aid their quest for individual wealth and foster the economic development of their community, state, and region; they were unwilling to accept second-class citizenship or to live at a subsistence level for long. They looked at government in the same way as other Americans, though conditions in the West sometimes exaggerated their hopes and fears.

The United States was, of course, the "great exception" when compared to European nations. It was a fragment of European society, not a cross section. It lacked a monarch or monarchical class, a hereditary aristocracy, an established church, and a military caste or elite. It had escaped the revolt against feudalism that played such a vital role in the emergence of the nation-state. In Europe, centralized authority evolved as a tool to dismantle a traditional society dominated by the church and the landed artistocracy. State bureaucracies, standing armies, expanded public services, and high taxes symbolized modernization. But there was little need to centralize power in the United States, which lacked rigid social classes wedded to the economic status quo. The sheer size of the United States, its spectacular population growth, the federal system of government, the absence of a substantial military threat along the nation's borders, the lack of a self-conscious intelligentsia, the multiplicity of its ethnic groups and religions, the abundance of cheap land, and the widespread suffrage—all contributed to fragmentation. Government was expected to provide equal access to wealth, not to protect one class from another. The great reform

1

issues that dominated European politics in the early and middle nine-teenth century—manhood suffrage, annual representative assemblies, equal electoral districts, and the abolition of property qualifications to hold office—had long been settled in the United States.[1]

Nevertheless, the United States could not escape history. Both mercantilism and classical republicanism taught the value of an or-ganic or corporate society, the need to subordinate individual interests to a general good; the "common interest" was much more than the consensus of all individual and group concerns. Moreover, human so-cieties were believed to pass through inevitable cycles of birth, ma-turity, and death just like individual members of those societies. The United States might defer the final reckoning because of its rate of population growth, abundance of land, and superior institutions, but it was not immortal. The founding fathers' greatest fear was tyranny. In the eighteenth century, bureaucracy and patronage, arbitrary taxa-tion, standing armies, and established churches appeared as the insti-tutions most likely to undermine civic virtue. But in the following century, the mass of Americans worried even more that private inter-ests would capture government and establish monopolies that re-stricted or eliminated competition (for example, by chartering banks and incorporating transportation and manufacturing companies). Ec-onomic concentrations were artificial creations, which could not exist without the help of the state. Governmental favoritism, not fear of governmental intervention in the economy per se, caused the deepest concern.[2]

Under such circumstances, little wonder that the sovereignty of law replaced the sovereignty of the state. Americans believed that a fundamental higher law, a law declared rather than made, constituted a de facto governmental contract. The Aristotelian idea of higher law was embraced by such political theorists as Grotius, Bodin, Saurez, and, of course, John Locke. It largely disappeared in England during the civil wars of the seventeenth century; most members of Parliament were unwilling to recognize a body of law above both king and Parlia-ment that could not be altered or abridged. In the United States, how-ever, three transcendent principles survived: the idea that written constitutions embodied natural law and took precedence over both common and statutory law; the assumption that all legitimate legis-lative power derived from constitutions or other formal compacts; and the conviction that the courts or "the people," not legislative bodies, should determine the meaning and intentions of written charters of state. In England, which lacked a written constitution, Parliament, not the courts, emerged supreme, and the line between constitutional and statutory law was blurred. Even in France, which had a written constitution and a national government based on the separation of powers, courts accepted the acts of the legislature as final. But in the United States, judicial review became a fundamental feature of the rule of law.[3]

The legal system's contribution to the diffusion of power was matched by that of the nation's political parties. European parties embraced bold programs that sharply distinguished one from the other, but American parties were "constituent organizations"—nonideological, poorly suited to policy making, and highly responsive to local demands.[4] Government at all levels was small, so parties often served as an extension of the state. For example, they established procedures to fill government offices, mediated among contending groups, helped coordinate the work of the executive and legislative branches, and provided a mechanism for the transfer of power from one administration to another. Therefore, parties significantly reinforced the endemic American suspicion of centralized authority and, through their control of patronage, prevented or delayed the development of an independent, autonomous bureaucracy. (From 1816 to 1861, there was virtually no increase in the number of federal employees, except in the postal service.) The civil service became a highly politicized arm of the party in power. The power of these local institutions made centralized planning by either the national or state governments difficult, if not impossible. Wasteful and inefficient public works were the inevitable result.[5]

Not all Americans consistently favored "small government" and placed their faith in private enterprise. During the first decades of the nineteenth century, the United States lacked a "money class," and investment capital was scarce. Consequently, many states spent enormous sums to promote industry and commerce.[6] State and local governments provided 73 percent of the $188 million invested in canals before 1861 and 25 to 30 percent of the money spent on railroads. During the antebellum period over half the money invested in southern railroads came from government. Nevertheless, the five-year depression touched off by the Panic of 1837 left many states destitute and brought direct public works spending to a halt. The total state debt incurred to build canals exceeded $60 million. Pennsylvania led the parade with a deficit of $16,580,000, and New York was not far behind with one of $13,317,000. Both Ohio and Indiana owed more than $6 million.[7] By the early 1840s, eight states had defaulted on their bonds, and those whose transportation systems were still under construction could not borrow the money needed to complete them. Private companies bought most of the works for a fraction of their original cost.

By mid-century business entered a new phase, largely because the expansion of state banks and the use of incorporation permitted private companies to raise their own capital by tapping the nation's enormous pool of small savers. Local governments continued to "prime the pump" by granting loans, land, and other gifts to businesses, but immigration and industrialization eroded the simpler, more compact republican society that sustained the "commonwealth idea." Critics of state enterprise denied that government spending on internal improvements contributed to economic growth and prosperity. In the 1840s and after, when many of these states rewrote their constitutions, they prohibited state construction of public works, state ownership of stock in private companies, and even loans to private businesses.

The revulsion against public and mixed enterprise was only one symptom of the paralysis of state government in the second half of the nineteenth century. Most governers were figureheads. Executive bureaucracies were very small and staff functions were handled by legislative commissions or committees. No governor had the power to prepare the state's budget, and the executive's term of office was short—generally two years. The fear of concentrated power and attempts to democratize government limited executive authority.[8] Legislatures were more powerful but no more efficient. Since Americans demanded actual rather than virtual representation, electoral districts were small and representative bodies large. Lawmakers met seldom and turnover was great; they profited little from past experience. The sheer size of most legislatures contributed to a proliferation of committees—which encouraged localism as much as did the demand that the state's wealth be evenly distributed. As cities grew, legislators labored under an increasing burden of local or private bills that sought trolley, railroad, water, telephone, gas, and other franchises. These were widely recognized as, in Lord Bryce's words, "a perennial fountain of corruption."[9]

Legislatures created new agencies and boards upon the request of powerful interest groups, which knew it would be easier to control a discrete agency rather than a permanent state bureaucracy. Moreover, each profession wanted its own licensing board as a symbol of professionalization. Politicians also considered the creation of new boards and commissions as a method to increase patronage, and they feared that consolidating functions would enhance executive power. For example, New York had 10 executive agencies in 1800, 20 in 1850, and 81 in 1900. Illinois had 25 independent agencies in 1870 and over 110 in 1917.[10]

Nineteenth-century lawmakers kept commissions in line by limiting their life-span, restricting budgets and support staffs, and paying low salaries or no salaries at all, which forced appointees to hold other jobs. Typical was the California bank commission, created in 1878. It was responsible for overseeing the operations of all the banks in the state and for supervising those in receivership. Despite a dramatic increase in the state's financial institutions, the commission's modest staff remained unchanged for three decades. Such administrative bodies were preordained to inefficiency. The Erie Canal Commission was remarkably capable, but it was never perceived as a permanent state bureaucracy: "Every shift in political power in the state brought new engineers, collectors, weigh masters, boat inspectors, superintendents, and lock tenders to the entire line of the canal."[11]

Declining state budgets, a sharp reduction in the number of private bills introduced in the legislatures, and a renewed fear of unjust taxation characterized state governments in the second half of the nineteenth century. State constitutions adopted after the Civil War were much more detailed and restrictive than those drafted during the American Revolution. The U.S. Constitution contains six thousand words; Missouri's 1875 charter ran to about twenty-six thousand. Illinois's new constitution covered fifty pages and treated such narrow subjects as the mixing of two or more grades of grain in the same elevator. Twenty-eight constitutional conventions met in seventeen states from 1877 to 1887, and another seven convened in the new western states admitted in 1889, 1890, and 1896. Most exhibited a profound distrust of legislative power. They mandated short legislative sessions, usually sixty days or less, and biennial rather than annual legislatures; they prohibited special or local legislation (including individualized corporate charters); they increased the power of the courts; they limited state as well as city and county debts; they imposed limitations on the size of state property taxes; they increased the majorities needed to pass appropriation bills; they outlined new methods of calling and recording floor votes; they required that the title of bills pertain to their contents; and they forbade legislatures from discussing certain issues. The new debt limitations prevented states and municipalities from tackling comprehensive public works projects. "The corporation of Brooklyn was thus prevented from making all at once a great street which would have been a boon to the city, and more money had to be spent in buying up the land for it bit by bit," Lord Bryce wrote. "But the evils which have followed in America from the inmixture both of States and of cities in enterprises of a public nature, and the abuses incident to an unlimited power of undertaking improvements, have been so great as to make people willing to bear with the occasional inconveniences which are inseparable from restriction."[12]

The federal government was even less likely to undertake public works than the states. It did so with little vision, enthusiasm, or accountability. No state wanted to see its rivals achieve a competitive advantage. Moreover, southerners worried that internal improvements would drive up tariff duties and reduce their export trade, and most Americans assumed that any large increase in federal spending would make the states too dependent on the central government. During the 1820s, Congress invested $3,533,490 in four different canal companies. However, it was loath to dictate transportation policy. With one exception, the companies were not required to submit construction plans for approval, nor were they required to make annual reports to Congress, open their books to government inspectors, or submit their toll schedules for review.[13]

Despite the fact that the national government granted 125 million acres of land and millions of dollars in low-interest loans to private railroad companies from 1862 to 1871, it made little attempt to draft or implement a national transportation policy. For example, a historian of the Union Pacific Railroad characterized the federal government's "policy" as "a blend of neglect and unresolution." The Plains Indians had not been "subdued" when construction began, and there was little or no federal presence in Wyoming Territory. Although the government was represented on the company's board of directors, it made no effort to supervise construction, set tolls, regulate the issuance or sale of company stock, or administer the corporation's day-to-day operations. The Union Pacific and Central Pacific were the first private corporations chartered by the federal government (aside from the Bank of the United States). Subsequently, Congress incorporated the Northern Pacific (1864), the Atlantic & Pacific (1866), and the Texas & Pacific (1871). Federal incorporation might have inaugurated a new era of regulation. Instead, the federal courts and Supreme Court did far more than Congress to mold national markets. The government seemed quick to subsidize but slow to rule. "To say that the government created the robber barons," one historian concluded, "is to utter at least part of the truth." In short, the Union Pacific did not corrupt government, government corrupted the U.P., which was forced to create its own law in part because Congress would not. Business served as a surrogate for government, especially in the West where state and local government was often too poor and too weak to perform vital public services.[14]

To be sure, the federal government did much to encourage rapid settlement; it placed a high value on subduing the wilderness. In addition to railroad subsidies, it removed the Indians and confined them to reservations, constructed military forts, established territorial governments, and enacted a series of land laws—such as the Homestead Act (1862), the Free Mining Act (1866), the Timber Culture Act (1873), and the Desert Land Act (1877)—to transfer the public domain into private hands. But settlement occurred randomly and haphazardly, not systematically, and Americans paid a high price for the lack of planning. For example, the scattered population drove up the costs of transportation, marketing, education, and many other services, and a disproportionately heavy tax burden fell on developed rather than undeveloped land. Forest lands were denuded and not replanted; farmland was ruthlessly exploited and then abandoned; hydraulic mines left vast stretches of land pocked and eroded and rivers choked with silt and gravel. Such was the price of a government that refused to lead.

Nevertheless, institutions of the central state grew rapidly in size after the Civil War. In 1871, civilian federal employees numbered only 53,000, but that number increased five times to 256,000 employees by 1901. During the same three decades, the federal budget more than tripled. Two new cabinet posts were created, Agriculture and Justice, though Justice was merely an appendage of the Office of the Attorney General. Two new commissions appeared, the Civil Service Commission (1871, 1883) and the Interstate Commerce Commission (1887). In the Department of Agriculture, forestry and animal husbandry bureaus were organized in 1880 and 1884, along with an entomology bureau in 1885, a pomology bureau in 1886, an ornithology and mammalogy bureau in 1887, an Office of Experiment Stations in 1887, and a weather bureau in 1890. The department's budget increased from $199,500 in 1880 to $3,272,902 in 1898. Yet the growth of government reflected the need to gather and compile information more than the need to provide new services or planning. "An old-timer in Washington looking backward from the vantage point of the late 1890s," a historian has observed, "would have found the government establishment bigger but not much different from its essential nature in 1870."[15]

As early as the 1830s, Congress was a distributive—though not redistributive—institution. As annual proceeds from land sales increased from $1 million in 1811, to $5 million in 1834, to $15 million in 1835, and to $25 million in 1836, the treasury surplus became the paramount public policy issue, especially given powerful opposition to reducing the tariff. By parceling it out to the states, Congress sidestepped the issue of whether the money should be spent on transportation, colonization, education, or other policies that raised issues of class and ideology. Distribution also helped counter the persistent Jacksonian complaint that the central government served only the few.[16] Although the depression of the 1830s wiped out the surplus, post–Civil War tariff duties yielded a surplus every year from 1866 to 1893, even though federal spending increased from an average of $60 million in the 1850s, to $270 million in the 1870s, and to $400 million in the 1890s. Taxes on imports peaked in the years from 1886 to 1890, when nearly 58 percent of all federal income came from customs duties. The federal government might have spent this money on a national railroad or countless other worthy projects. Instead, pensions and river and harbor expenditures returned much of the surplus to the states.[17]

Government pensions were an early form of social security. An 1862 law compensated veterans for almost any disability; benefits were paid either to the veteran or to his survivors. Between 1861 and 1885, over 890,000 claims were filed, and nearly 60 percent were approved. Then, in 1889, Congress promised a pension to *any* veteran who had served for more than three years. The number of grantees soared—from 350,000 to 1,000,000 by the early years of the twentieth century—and pension expenditures almost doubled between 1889 and 1893. From 1890 to 1894, these benefits absorbed an average of 37 percent of the entire federal budget. By 1895, 63 percent of all Civil War veterans received federal grants. The commissioner of pensions, James Tanner, became known as "God help the Surplus" Tanner![18] Pensions left much to be desired as a distributive policy, not just because they encouraged and rewarded fraud and were expensive to administer but also because Confederate veterans were ineligible—which meant that the South reaped less than its fair share of the proceeds.

River and harbor bills were more equitable. They favored seaboard and well-watered states at the expense of arid and semi-arid states, but that was more acceptable because the latter states were thinly populated. Ostensibly, the purpose of this legislation was to improve navigation and reduce the cost of transportation by relieving pressure on overburdened rail lines. River and harbor appropriations averaged $370,000 a year during the 1850s but shot up to nearly $4 million in the decade after the Civil War. In 1880 they exceeded $8 million and by 1898 reached nearly $21 million. The annual bills were ingenious creations because they were self-perpetuating. The 1886 version launched over a hundred new projects, but it contained sufficient money to complete only five of sixty-three projects already under way.[19] In 1896, in the midst of hard times, Grover Cleveland vetoed the river and harbor bill, noting that the Corps of Engineers opposed many of the projects. Always protective of local interests, the House voted 219 to 61 to override, and the Senate, 56 to 5.[20]

All the major political issues of the Gilded Age had a local focus—civil service reform, civil rights, railroad rate regulation, and the "currency question," as well as the tariff. Nevertheless, congressional behavior resulted as much from structural problems as from any lack of courage or vision on the part of its members. Tremendous turnover characterized the House, both by modern standards and compared to the nineteenth-century English Parliament. Fifty-eight percent of the Congress that met in 1875–77 consisted of first-termers. During the 1880s, the average turnover from Congress to Congress fell to 30–40 percent, and it dropped to 20–30 percent in the 1890s—still very high compared to the 1980s. This, of course, translated into a lack of experience within key committees and a lack of continuity. It also forced ambitious congressmen to spend much of their time trying to secure renomination by finding offices for the friends and relatives of those who controlled nominating conventions. Congressmen were inundated with requests from constituents to help secure pensions, land patents, appointments, and many other favors. This was taxing enough, but Congress also suffered from antiquated rules. For example, chairmen of the forty-seven standing House committees had almost absolute power over what bills lived or died, and they jousted with each other to win favorable positions on the calendar for pet legislation. Party leaders had no authority to determine the order of business. Nevertheless, until 1890 the minority party could block bills by simply refusing to answer a roll call; no measure could be enacted unless a quorum was present *and voting.*[21]

The Senate was even less "efficient," and many of its members believed that "inefficiency" was a necessary part of the institution's character. Party regularity, caucus agreements, and the charisma of strong leaders mattered far less than the preservation of free debate and the maintenance of each member's independence. Party caucuses decided committee assignments and the legislative agenda. But as late as the 1880s, political affiliations mattered little within the Senate chambers. "It is immediately apparent," one historian of the late nineteenth-century Senate has written, "that on most legislation, party harmony was negligible." Nor did seniority or committee assignments impose discipline. In choosing committees, senate leaders paid more attention to balancing regions than to rewarding those with the longest service.[22]

Viewed from almost any angle, government in the late nineteenth century was weak, shortsighted, and inefficient, dominated by courts and managed by political parties. Moreover, Americans preferred it that way. Congress and the state legislatures refused to address major questions, and they were far less likely to do so after the 1840s than before.

Given the multiplicity of inconsistent programs for disposing of the public lands, and the lack of coherent transportation, banking, and currency policies, small wonder that those who offered comprehensive plans to solve the West's "water problem" invariably failed. By mid-century, classical republican thinking and the "commonwealth idea" had been seriously eroded. Little remained of the founding fathers' vision of a corporate society. Most western policy makers assumed that the discrete choices of individual economic actors should take precedence over the welfare of the community and long-range planning. Yet in California a fierce and often violent debate occurred over whether the gold within the public domain should primarily benefit the nation, the state, the largest number of miners possible, or those investors who would develop the new wealth most rapidly. Since water was essential to large-scale mining in California, it was at the center of that debate.

2
The Legal Context, 1848–66:
Water for Sale

One of the deepest conflicts in United States's law has been between the ideals of individual initiative, independence, and the promotion of new wealth on the one hand, and the protection of society from monopoly, special privilege, and anarchy on the other. One set of values has unified society by emphasizing common purposes and objectives, especially the need for community, while the other has tended to fragment and decentralize by liberating the diverse talents and energies of individuals and groups of individuals. Sometimes these values complement each other. Nevertheless, United States's law has never successfully amalgamated them into a stable compound. Rather, it has produced a mixture whose ingredients remain essentially the same but whose quantities change through time. The origins and nature of western water law, and the economy of the arid West, cannot be understood without recognizing the tendency of law to divide human beings as well as to bind them together. For example, western miners, who needed and used water in a variety of ways, conceived of certain legal principles as transcendent and immutable. Unfortunately, most miners also denied that any institution of government could be relied upon to interpret or protect those principles. Conflict was inevitable and, as we shall see, the same battles were fought repeatedly.

The greatest legal innovation in the history of the arid West was the doctrine of prior appropriation, which made water as much of a commodity as land, minerals, trees, crops, and livestock. In the humid half of the nation, the right to use water generally depended on the ownership of land adjoining a watercourse. Riparian (riverbank) owners could use a stream for any number of purposes from watering stock to turning millstones, but common law prohibited them from altering its course, substantially reducing its volume, or polluting it to the extent that it could not be reused downstream. Riparian owners did not hold title to specific quantities of water; their individual rights were "correlative"—that is, they existed only as part of a pool of rights—and could not be sold independent of the land. To be sure, in the early decades of the nineteenth century, some courts tempered the riparian doctrine so that capitalists could build canals to turn water from natural channels and erect dams to ensure a steady source of power. However, the advent of the steam engine and the railroad made these concessions temporary.

The California mining industry, and specifically its enormous need for capital, transformed water into a species of private property.[1] Walter Prescott Webb was the first historian to appreciate the full importance of this metamorphosis, and since the publication of his *Great Plains* in 1931, most western historians have assumed that California miners immediately rejected riparian rights as inadequate and unjust and wholeheartedly embraced prior appropriation as the most rational and equitable system of law. Yet when viewed from the ground up, the mining industry reveals a far different picture. This chapter builds on the wise observation that the "transfer of [financial] control from the working men in the foothills to the business and financial men in the cities" was "a gradual one and hardly reached significant proportions until the latter part of the fifties."[2] California water law mirrored that shift in power. During the 1850s, miners used water in many different ways and sharply disagreed over how it should be allocated. California was a frontier state with a decentralized economy rooted in individual communities, and there was little need for unified or comprehensive water laws. The different points of view represented in the mining camps became embedded in a system of jurisprudence which contributed mightily to the fragmentation that is the theme of this book.

As is so often the case, the problem originated with the paralysis of federal authority. For this reason, a review of national mineral policy is necessary for understanding the evolution of prior appropriation. The United States might have mined the mineral lands on its own, or chartered private companies to do the job, or delegated it to "mixed enterprises." Instead, it followed a vacillating and confused course. In 1807, the federal government approved the leasing of lead mines on the public domain in Indiana Territory, and in 1816 it extended the leasing principle to all the public lands. But trespassers ignored these laws, and the system cost more to administer than it brought in. It was retained for the copper mines of Wisconsin and Michigan, but in 1829 Congress authorized the outright sale of the lead mines and adjoining lands in Missouri for $2.50 an acre. In the early 1840s the rents returned only about six thousand dollars, less than one-fourth the cost of administering the mineral lands. Leasing also encouraged litigation between the federal government and individual citizens. In 1845, President James K. Polk called for abandoning the system, and in 1846 and 1847, all mineral lands containing lead, copper, and other common ores were put up for sale. Little wonder, therefore, that California miners persistently feared that the federal government would sell the gold fields to the highest bidders.[3]

Congress refused to confer territorial status on California in 1848, and the U.S. government was scarcely visible in the lands newly acquired from Mexico. The army in California had declined to 660 men in 1848; some soldiers fell victim to gold fever while others left the coast following their discharge at the end of the Mexican War. The main job of those who remained was to provide protection from Indians.[4] Colonel Mason, who commanded the U.S. forces, visited the mines in July 1848. He debated auctioning off the gold fields in parcels of twenty to forty acres, or charging each miner rent ranging from a hundred to a thousand dollars. But the sheer size of the mineral region, the limited number of troops available to police it, and the eagerness for self-rule exhibited by the miners together persuaded Mason not to interfere unless "broils and crimes" demanded it.[5] In the absence of specific instructions from Washington, he decided that the best policy was no policy.[6] Presidents Zachary Taylor and Millard Fillmore also favored selling or renting the mineral lands, but strident criticism from California demonstrated the necessity if not the wisdom of free mining. Thomas Butler King, whom the president sent to California in 1848 to survey conditions in the mines, confirmed that any alteration of the status quo would result in speculators acquiring the best claims. That, in turn, would lead to anarchy in the diggings. Not surprisingly, Congress even refused to authorize surveys of the mineral lands.[7]

In the late 1840s and early 1850s, California miners faced legal chaos. By proclamation, the military government of California abolished "all Mexican mining laws and customs" on February 12, 1848. The first legislature reaffirmed the inapplicablity of Mexican mining law on April 22, 1850,[8] and one year later the lawmakers legitimized the "customs, usages or regulations established and in force at the bar, or diggings,"[9] even though those customs varied from one mining district to another. The legislature acted not only because Congress had failed to respond, but also because many lawyers contended that California had, in the words of a later legal scholar, "succeeded to the sovereign rights which would have been possessed under the common law by the crown in England, and therefore was the owner of the royal metals in the public lands, of which it was contended the United States was trustee for the state until its admission into the Union, and therefore the regulations of the miners, authorized or adopted by a state statute, were an adequately authorized disposition of these minerals."[10] The California supreme court affirmed state control over the mineral lands in 1853, but the U.S. Supreme Court overturned that decision.[11] In the meantime, the state regularly passed laws pertaining to the mineral lands, including foreign miners' taxes—which provided for eviction from mining districts if the levies were not paid—and the Possessory Act (1850), which protected settlers who entered up to 160 acres of land against any subsequent trespassers, except miners.[12]

The legistature's most portentous decision also came during the first session, when it voted to adopt common rather than civil law as the foundation for the state's legal order.[13] Historians have long argued that the riparian doctrine sneaked in through the back door—that the legislature did not realize what it was doing.[14] That argument misreads the law and underestimates the knowledge of the lawmakers. Water laws were not an urgent matter in 1850 because both mining and agriculture were still in their infancy. The legislators, however, understood the nature of California's climate, especially those from south of the Tehachipi Mountains, who were well acquainted with the need to divert water for irrigation. Had it intended to abrogate the riparian doctrine, the legislature would have done so *explicitly*. That it did not testified to a faith in the ability of the common law to adapt to new circumstances and needs. The legislature did not enact its first major water law until 1854, and that statute specifically excluded the mining counties.[15] Meanwhile, miners acted on their own, shaping water law as the placer mining industry evolved.

One persistent myth in the history of California placer mining is that the industry evolved through distinct phases. Pan and rocker presumably gave way to long toms, sluices, and eventually large-scale hydraulic operations. As the technology of mining became more sophisticated, individual miners joined in informal groups, then formed joint-stock companies, and finally became employees of large corporations. The individual miner turned into a wage earner; the industry ceased being largely self-contained and became almost completely dependent on absentee owners and "foreign" capital. The myth contains many elements of truth: Technology and organization did change dramatically from the late 1840s to the 1860s. The phases overlapped, however, and the simplest forms dominated in one district while the most complex prevailed in the diggings next door.

The numbers of miners in California increased from about six thousand at the end of 1848 to at least forty thousand a year later. Almost all were placer rather than hard rock miners, but they worked different deposits.[16] At the time, many argonauts believed that the state's gold supply was virtually inexhaustible. (One popular theory held that the gold had been sprayed fairly evenly over the countryside by ancient volcanoes.)[17] This assumption reduced conflict because in those early months of the gold boom few doubted that the pie was big enough to serve all. Those who reached the diggings first usually took up claims along streams. There they enjoyed easy access to water and the flakes and chunks of gold concentrated in the bars and riffles. Those who came after the land adjoining a stream had been claimed worked "dry diggings" hundreds of yards from the water. They tunneled down to bedrock, poured the gravel into sacks, then used wheelbarrows, pack animals, or their own sturdy backs to carry it to the water.

There was also a third group, whose work involved extensive planning, organization, and coordination. Ironically, it was the need to get rid of water that motivated these miners to cooperate in formidable joint-stock ventures, pooling labor as well as capital. If rich gold deposits could be found adjoining a stream, they reasoned, then the bed of that stream would be even richer, perhaps solid gold. This assumption, and the fact that California streams all but dried up in the summer and gained volume and velocity so rapidly in the winter that they flooded many claims, prompted the construction of dams, ditches, and wooden flumes, the first attempts to turn rivers from their natural channels. In the days before high-powered explosives, digging ditches through granite took plenty of pick and shovel work, and with sawmills few and far between, the wood for dams and flumes had to be sawed and hewn by hand. Joint-stock ventures made such costly and labor-intensive efforts possible.

The first large projects, launched during the unusually dry spring of 1850, exposed riverbeds and bars on the American, Feather, Yuba, and other rivers. Timing was all important because the streams were manageable only in the summer months after the snowpack melted and before the first winter storms. Even then, some rivers were as much as twenty or thirty feet wide and ten feet deep. In the diggings around Jacksonville, miners formed fourteen companies which averaged 20 members apiece, but one outfit contained 50 and another 108. During the winter of 1852, twenty companies were organized on the Yuba within a stretch of four miles. They ranged in size from eight to thirty members. The diversion dams built on the Feather River—which was turned out of its natural channel for a distance of forty miles in 1850—cost from fifty to eighty thousand dollars, excluding the cost of flumes.[18]

From the beginning, miners showed a healthy fear of outside capital. For example, a group of argonauts from Jacksonville, in the southern mines, formed the Hart's Bar Draining and Mining Company and excavated a canal 638 feet long and 16 feet wide to turn the Tuolumne River out of its natural basin. The company's charter contained many provisions to guard against losing control to nonminers. All membership applications had to be voted on by the entire company, which originally contained twenty-one men. Admission was by secret ballot, and two negative votes were sufficient to block membership. Any miner who wanted to sell his stock had to offer the company the first right of purchase, and even if the company declined, he could sell only to a buyer it approved. Moreover, no member could hold more than one mineral claim, even by purchase.[19]

The founders of the Hart's Bar Company feared that rival miners might take control of their company, extend flumes into the dry diggings, and reduce the water supply available to those working close to the stream. In 1848 and 1849 miners who held nonriparian claims routinely dammed every available ravine to capture rainwater and avoid the arduous routine of moving gravel to water. The tension between these two groups of miners often prevented the construction of long diversion ditches. Many in both groups, though by no means all, accepted the principle of "first in time, first in right" that was the heart of prior appropriation, but they clashed over whether "first in time" meant the construction of a ditch, the actual diversion of water, or the use of the new supply by individual miners. The first mining ditch was cut at Yankee Jim's in Placer County in 1850, and a few weeks later a second was excavated near Nevada City. The Placer County canal provided five "tom streams" of water—enough to operate five long toms. The second ditch may well have provided the first water sold to miners in California. The owner rented long toms and water at the rate of sixteen dollars a day, though he retained the privilege of washing the tailings.[20] Because miners could afford to pay five dollars a day for water and still net a daily profit of five to seven dollars, the question of who owned the water was largely academic. Miners were happy to buy the water, and many supplemented their income by excavating ditches for private companies.

The earliest private companies, then, often appeared as benefactors. That changed as the supply of easily accessible gold declined and hydraulic mining became dominant. Hydraulic mining began with "ground sluicing" in 1850, and in some parts of the state—including Trinity County—this method survived into the late 1850s and beyond.[21] Virtually all historians give credit for the founding of "modern" hydraulic mining to Edward E. Mattison, who in 1853 at American Hill, near Nevada City, ran water under pressure through a rawhide hose connected to a wooden nozzle and conveyed the earth torn loose by the powerful spray into long sluices. The technique caught on rapidly, and a San Francisco newspaper reporter observed:

> The toughest clay dissolves like wax, thus disintegrating much fine gold, a greater part of which has hitherto been lost. The excellence of the plan and the wonderful celerity with which the work progresses must be seen to be appreciated. . . . The advantages of this important auxiliary to "sluicing" are—1st. The reduction of manual labor at least two-thirds; 2d. It opens to miners locations heretofore unremunerative, where they may now realize handsome returns, consequent on the great additional quantity of auriferous soil that may be washed within a given time; and 3d. the dangerous process of "undermining," with the fatal results which frequently attend it, may by this new invention be entirely obviated, as the operater can at all times be wholly out of reach of the overhanging embankments.[22]

Rawhide quickly gave way to canvas, tin replaced wood, and by the late 1850s iron pipe supplanted many of the hoses. Manufacturers of mining equipment experimented with an array of nozzles, and miners constructed larger and larger reservoirs and longer and longer flumes to ensure a steady year-round water supply and to build up the greatest "head" or pressure.[23] A Nevada City newspaper noted in 1853 that pans, long toms, and rockers were outmoded. "There is no longer a mere scratching over of the surface. One man now washes as much dirt as ten could then and saves more gold. . . . Tunnels, water ways through rock, perpendicular shafts an hundred feet deep, water conveyed for miles around through flumes, etc., etc., are the present achievements of miners in this region."[24] The cost of working a cubic yard of dirt was twenty dollars by pan, five by rocker, one by long tom, and twenty cents by the hydraulic method.[25]

Not surprisingly, California heard no more persistent cry during the 1850s and after than the demand for water. "We would direct the attention of capitalists to this means of employing money," the Stockton *Journal* editorialized in 1851, "with the certainty of realizing an immense percentage." A few months later the Nevada City *Journal* insisted that there was "certainly less risk in this kind of investment than in any other in this uncertain country."[26] Potential profits were enormous. As early as June 1852, the *Alta California* reported that "the attention of miners seems now to be almost entirely devoted to the construction of canals. . . . The owners of stock are now realizing large fortunes for the investment."[27] By 1852, money began to pour into the construction of diversion ditches, and argonauts began to recognize that water was more valuable than gold.[28] "Homer is speculating in water ditches," wrote one miner from Sonora concerning his former partner in October 1852, "He invests all his money and wants to borrow more but he doesn't work any."[29]

During the 1850s and 1860s, most water companies were partnerships and joint-stock ventures. In the richest diggings, however, private corporations began to appear in the early 1850s. They consolidated smaller ditches to increase profits, reach the largest number of potential customers, and reduce litigation. By 1870 nearly seven thousand miles of main and secondary ditches moved water to claims. In Nevada and Placer counties this process culminated following the drought of 1864. To supply miners at Badger Hill, Manzanita Hill, Birchville, and French Corral, the Milton Mining and Water Company built three dams—the highest 125 feet—and a ditch 80 miles long. The Eureka Lake Water Company, incorporated in New York in 1865, served a different part of the same ridge. It constructed a canal system that covered about 250 miles. By the early 1880s the reservoirs on the Feather, Yuba, Bear, and American rivers stored 50 billion gallons. The Spring Valley Mine at Cherokee Flat used 36 million gallons every twenty-four hours—three times the average daily consumption in the city of San Francisco—and the Sacramento *Daily Union* reported in 1888 that any one of Nevada County's five major ditch systems could supply the daily needs of the entire city of New York. These dams, canals, tunnels, and flumes were very expensive. In Butte County, the

Spring Valley Canal and Mining Company secured eleven thousand acres of mineral land at a cost of $240,527 and invested over $1 million in an elaborate and highly profitable water system. The North Bloomfield Company in Nevada County controlled over fifteen hundred acres and spent $2 million on its water system, which included two large reservoirs, one hundred miles of ditches and canals, and a work force of five to six hundred men. The company's largest dam was completed in 1872. Constructed of heavy cedar and tamarack, it created a lake 2.5 miles long that covered over 500 acres.[30]

Private investors had good reason to favor these companies. In 1854, the *Alta California* reported that the Gold Hill Water Company returned 42 percent *per month* to its investors and the Natoma Water Company 12 percent per month.[31] Large water companies appeared early in some districts, but came later or not at all in others. The transition depended on the quality of ore deposits, the availability of water, proximity to transportation, and many other considerations. In poorer districts, or in districts already abandoned by Euro-American miners, Chinese and Mexicans continued to use the rocker or cradle to work less attractive deposits.[32] Thus small-scale operations persisted in Mariposa and Trinity counties while large-scale enterprises dominated in Sonora, Nevada, and Placer counties.

Given the diversity of California placer mining, conflict was inevitable. Riverbed claims were often contested because variations in natural streamflow changed their size. This became even more of a problem once the stream was taken from its natural channel, because flumes often broke and diversion dams backed up water onto upstream diggings. For example, in 1850 eighty men tried to move a river, but their diversion ditch proved too small to contain it. The overflow submerged nearby claims, and the injured miners demanded indemnification. Their request was denied, whereupon they began digging in the riverbed—access to which was reserved by mining camp law to those who had exposed it. The diverters attempted to eject their rivals, and one neutral observer reported that in the ensuing melee knives, picks, rifles, and pistols were used. Hours later, upon returning to the field of battle, he was "horror-struck at the sanguinary atrocities which had been committed: some men lay with their entrails hanging out, others had their skulls smashed with the pickaze, and bodies lopt with the axe; while a few lay breathing their last, seemingly unscathed, but shot to death with bullets."[33] Most of the violence in 1850 arose because miners who turned streams either deprived other miners of water or gave them too much. All too frequently, unsuccessful negotiations, during which the injured parties were usually asked to join the company, culminated in attempts to tear down dams and flumes. Miners disagreed over which water rights were stronger: those senior in time, those used on land closest to the water, or those whose holders had invested the greatest amounts of money developing their claims.[34].

Tension increased as the decade wore on. The gold supply was finite, and the average daily income of individual miners declined from ten dollars a day in 1850 to about three dollars in the last years of the decade. The price of water also fell, but not as fast as income. Miners paid about 50 percent of their gross income for water, a percentage that increased dramatically in dry years.[35] Strikes and public protests against water prices and corporate monopolies became common. So did violence. For example, when a group of miners attacked the Table Mountain Water Company's ditch and flumes in Calaveras County in 1856, causing seven thousand dollars' worth of damage, the arrest of three of the leaders prompted three hundred sympathizers to march on the Mokelumne Hill jail and force the jailer to release the ringleaders on bond.[36] In the fall of 1856, the *California Mining Journal* reported that those holding river claims felt "great apprehension" because virtually the entire Mokelumne River had been diverted from its natural channel. "But few years will pass by," the paper ominously predicted, "ere every mountain stream will be lifted from its natural bed."[37]

Understandably, as water companies grew in size and number, and as ownership passed from the argonauts to investors in San Francisco and elsewhere, the new owners demanded that the legislature protect their capital. In the winter of 1852, the legislature considered a bill to grant private companies the right to all the water they could capture for fifty years. This increased public fears that powerful corporations had hatched a plot to take control of all the mineral lands in the state. Early in October 1853, representatives from thirty-one water companies that sold water for profit met in the back room of D. O. Mills's bank in Sacramento. Mills was a founder of the Tuolumne County Water Company, one of the largest in the state. The conferees noted that the diversion of water from natural channels was becoming much more common, and that private companies deserved "the encouragement and protection of all good citizens." The companies worried that "much doubt and uncertainty exist as to the rights of persons engaged in these pursuits." The meeting resulted in the formation of a "State Central Board of Mining Water Companies" to recommend state and national legislation. The board was appointed, but it made no headway in either Sacramento or Washington.[38]

Lawmakers in Sacramento, fearful that they were overstepping their authority by regulating the use of resources on the public domain, refused to do anything that might threaten congressional approval of a Pacific railway. As late as 1858, water companies urged the legislature to adopt a joint resolution asking Congress to grant "proprietors of water ditches, canals and flumes, constructed for mining purposes, the right of taking and diverting water from streams and lakes in this state, together with the right of way or easement over the public lands within this state for any and all ditches, canals or flumes, which now are or hereafter may be constructed for such purposes." The proposed resolution demonstrated that despite the California supreme court's endorsement of prior appropriation in 1855, miners continued to worry that Congress would ultimately reject priority rights.[39]

Nevertheless, the tyranny of private water companies became an obsession in the mining camps. In October 1853, angry miners at Yankee Jim's in Placer County informed the *Placer Herald* that

these ditches have been stretched from canyon to canyon, throughout the whole range of county, and the [water] companies have made it [the act of constructing ditches as opposed to delivering water] the foundation of a real right of property to all the water in the canyons, and are threatening to demolish every miner who dares to presume to go into a canyon . . . and get water to wash his claim.—They tell us that we are to be harassed and embarrassed with endless and perplexing law suits, that will cost more than all the claims are worth, and they further tell us, that the price of water will not be reduced. . . . Thus has crept into our midst a tyrant in the form of a lamb, and has gradually assumed the form of a two horned beast, whose right horn is bread, and the left horn water, and the community are gored into surfdom [*sic*].[40]

As the *Herald* suggested, the question of whether private water companies had the law on their side was irrelevant: The mere *threat* of lengthy lawsuits and bankruptcy was intimidating enough. Miners and "user companies" sold out to rival companies far more often than they took their grievances to court. The *Alta California* ackowledged that capital had to be protected and litigation avoided, but all that was needed, the paper editorialized, was a bill giving the right to *use* water, not to own it. How could private companies levy perpetual charges for water that had cost them nothing? How could the user-owners of small ditches protect themselves against these monopolies in the making? And how could the state give its blessing to the construction of large reservoirs when those structures often collapsed, causing irreparable harm to life and property?[41] Even miners who conceded the right to divert water from the natural channel of a stream and sell it to others usually argued that private companies had the right only to "surplus" water, not to *natural* streamflow.[42]

Few miners questioned the "inalienable right in the citizens of this State . . . to acquire, possess, and protect property."[43] When easterners moved west, they carried with them several interlocking assumptions: first, that in the absence of a formal legal structure, or when that structure broke down, "popular sovereignty"—in this case "squatter sovereignty"—should prevail; second, that "liberty" meant freedom from government interference in the individual search for wealth; third, that the right to pursue wealth was not a gift of the state, but, rather, derived from an individual's inalienable right to the product of his labor; fourth, that no person should be able to secure more land or water than he or she could make use of; and fifth, that the initiative and energy needed to develop a natural resource did more to create property than a formal title. Miners looked at the law in terms of self-interest, not protection of the "general interest." "Money is what we all want and came for," one miner wrote home in October 1852, "and when we get it and return [home we] will then perhaps look out for our country and see that she is not ruined."[44]

For all the praise Charles Shinn and other nineteenth-century historians heaped on the democracy, independence, self-sufficiency, and ingenuity of California's mining camps, those institutions were devoted almost entirely to making money, not to the establishment of social services or to the creation of stable communities. Shinn argued that the miners simply filled an institutional gap or power vacuum, but a far more perceptive observer, Josiah Royce, recognized that the districts sought to escape duly constituted authority as well as to fill an institutional void. Since they were created in large part to avoid the compromises essential to the democratic process, the law of the diggings represented institutionalized anarchy as much as a quest for order. Among the principles the district stood for were no outside interference; a reduction of the size of a community in the hope that homogenous values and expectations would minimize or eliminate conflict; a high level of member participation in the adjudication of disputes; and, above all, the protection of property. "In brief, the new mining camp was a little republic," Royce remarked over a century ago. It was "practically independent for a time of the regular State officers, often very unwilling to submit to outside interference . . . and well able to keep its own simple order temporarily intact."[45]

The mining codes reflected the self-interest of different groups of miners. The argonauts expected the law to serve their local community rather than far-off investors. They took pride in their autonomous "legal system," not just because they had created law where there was none, or because the system was quite responsive, but because it gave little opportunity for powerful legal castes to define rights. (Some districts attemped to exclude lawyers entirely.) Mining camp laws were a response to diverse climatic, geographic, and economic conditions, and the jumble of codes that resulted prevented the state legislature or Congress from enacting uniform legislation. Not only did rules differ from one county to the next—or even one ravine to the next—but since the influx of miners occurred in waves, the laws of the same district sometimes changed radically from one "generation" to the next. The Nevada City *Journal* remarked, "The great difficulty heretofore in such matters has been that the diversity of interests, phases of mining, etc., in the various counties and even townships, has prevented any harmonious action in general conventions, and always will upon any matters save of very general policy."[46]

Mining codes assumed that no rights existed without sanction from the miners themselves. They defined rights of discovery, the size and marking of claims, the length of the grace period before designating a claim and beginning to work it, and conditions of sale and abandonment.[47] They also regulated the use of water. Those placer mining camps that did not establish formal rules provided for the arbitration of disputes, and many forbade appeals to the courts.[48] The miners who reached the diggings in 1849 or 1850 found that the easiest way to resolve conflicts over mineral rights—such as the size of claims—was through migration. Moving on was a feasible solution when it required only a small financial sacrifice and when there were new diggings that promised greater wealth. But by the middle of the 1850s the state's mineral regions had been thoroughly explored. Mining had become more of a trade, and the growth of towns encouraged miners to put down roots. "Prospecting" gave way to the search for more efficient techniques to work and rework deposits that had already been claimed.

In the early 1850s, the effects of scarcity were felt throughout the mining camps, particularly following the unusually dry winter of 1852–

53. On June 24, 1853, the miners of Vallecito Camp, Calaveras County, California, proclaimed:

> Any individual or company turning the course of a running stream of water from its natural course, to the injury of any one miner, or miners, having claims or dirt to wash in the course of the stream, is deemed unjust, and ought not to be allowed. Therefore, we, the Miners of this Camp, in public meeting assembled, do authorize the Justice of the Peace of this district, upon the complaint of any Miner, to order the removal of any obstruction of the course of said stream; and if the same is not removed in twenty-four hours after such notice, to enforce the same by a suit at law.[49]

In the following year, miners at Diamond Springs, El Dorado County, publicly protested the grant to private companies of any permanent and exclusive water rights. They not only forbade companies from diverting water when it was needed to serve claims adjoining the natural channel, they also prohibited the construction of any dam that prevented the natural flow from reaching miners who worked the streambed below. They also required private companies to pay the enormous expense of fluming water across claims established prior to the construction of the company's ditches.[50]

Riparian rights were honored in many districts, although they varied from place to place. The Jamestown District in Tuolumne County restricted water claims to those who held land adjoining streams, but recognized chronological priority among this select group.[51] Miners in the Hungry Creek Diggings, in Siskiyou County, authorized the first claimant within a basin to divert water, but only when there were no claims downstream.[52] The Columbia District sanctioned diversions only when the miners who held riparian claims consented, and then only on condition that "when so diverted [the water] shall be held subject to a requisition of the parties interested [e.g., riparian claimants]." In other words, these miners demanded free water.[53]

By 1853 drought, the advent of hydraulic mining, and the availability of newly created district courts in some of the more remote parts of the state conspired to make sense out of the medley of mining-camp water laws. District courts did more to define the law of the West than did state or territorial supreme courts. The need to create a legal system de novo gave them far greater power than local courts exercised in more settled parts of the nation. So did the weaknesses of state and territorial legislatures in the West. Legislatures suffered from high turnover, which discouraged both planning and continuity in natural resource policies; from the overwhelming power of dominant interest groups, such as the railroads, which often rendered them impotent; and from infrequent and short sessions—usually once every two years for three or four months—which left power vacuums only the courts could fill. California's lower courts experienced pressure from both above and below. Unlike eastern courts, their presiding judges had to consider not just precedent, "doctrinal purity," or the logic of opinions, but the likelihood that rulings would be reviewed by Congress as well as the higher courts. Moreover, since district judges were elected rather than appointed, public opinion had a powerful influence on court decisions. Regardless of the training and sympathies of judges, juries consistently favored local miners over corporations with nonresident owners.[54]

A close reading of California mining-camp newspapers from the 1850s suggests that supreme court decisions attracted far less attention among miners than those of local courts. Since most mining camps were relatively isolated and autonomous, many miners questioned whether the state supreme court had jurisdiction over the public lands. In 1853, two years before the state supreme court made its first major statement on prior appropriation, Judge J. W. McCorkle of the Eleventh District Court (which included Yolo, Placer, and El Dorado counties) ruled that no system of water law other than priority rights could prevail on the public domain. He followed two lines of reasoning that the supreme court later pursued: First, riparian rights could not exist without landownership; second, if a riparian claimant could deny the right of a prior diverter to use water, then the mining industry would be crippled in its infancy. McCorkle had logic, if not justice, on his side. Sacramento's *Democratic State Journal*, however, referred to the case as "one of those difficult and doubtful cases regarding the right to use water by diverting it from its natural channel."[55]

In the following year, the same court, presided over by a new judge, reached the opposite conclusion in a classic contest between riparian and nonriparian miners. Judge J. M. Howell noted in his instructions to the jury hearing *Yankee Jim's Union Water Co.* v. *Smith* that "the right to the use of running water is a mere incident to the ownership of the soil.—Possession of the soil in good faith is presumptive evidence of ownership, and such possessor is entitled to all the privileges of the owner.—If the land thus possessed embraces a running stream, or threads upon it, the possessor is entitled to as much of the water as is necessary to the enjoyment of his estate, and no one can rightfully divert it."[56] As late as 1856, Judge Niles Searls, in the district court for Nevada County, instructed the jury that those who held claims on the margin of a stream had a paramount right to use water if they "so use it as to do the least possible injury to the prior [older] rights of a water company located below them." Apparently, most of the water these miners used returned to the natural channel, but Searls was careful to point out that "the use of water by the owners of mining claims is altogether irrespective of the question of priority of location." Time mattered far less than place.[57]

California's highest court attempted to remain true to the common law. Its bewildering trail of decisions was not just the result of judicial ignorance, inexperience, confusion, or the sheer complexity of the cases. Many other factors must be considered: the conflicting legal philosophies of individual judges, an absence of leadership until 1857,[58] the desire to balance contending economic interests, the fear that any radical change in the common law would threaten the stability of *all* property rights, the expectation that easterners would resent giving miners the common wealth of the nation without any compensation,[59] and the judges' desire not to convey the impression that the courts were usurping legislative power. (The legislature, after all, had formally adopted the common law, including riparian rights.) The best "rule" was to avoid rigid rules, and the court knew it. "In her [the State of California's] legislation upon this subject," the court noted in 1853, "she has established the policy of permitting all who desire it, to work her mines of gold and silver, with or without conditions; and she has wisely provided that their conflicting claims shall be adjudicated by the rules and customs which may be established by bodies of them working in the same vicinity."[60]

The first major water case, *Eddy* v. *Simpson,* reached the California supreme court in 1853. Like most disputes that got so far, it was complicated, since miners themselves or local courts resolved the more tractable conflicts. It involved the Shady Creek Water Company and Grizzly Water Company, both of which used Shady Creek in Nevada County—one carried water to French Corral, the other to nearby Cherokee Corral. The Grizzly Company was a miner-owned enterprise. The Shady Creek Company had begun that way, but it had eventually added outside investors interested in selling water for profit. It charged two-and-one-half times the price of its rival. Both sides accepted prior appropriation in principle. The issue was whether water transported over long distances by the Grizzly Creek Company through ditches and flumes still belonged to the company once the fluid had been used and drained back into the natural channel of Shady Creek and whether the other company had a right to reuse the water. In other words, did the act of diversion create an absolute property right or simply a right incidental to the act of mining? The Tenth District Court, which covered Sierra, Yuba, Nevada, and Sutter counties, upheld the older appropriation of the private company. "As a general principle, the party who first uses the water of a stream, is by virtue of priority of occupation entitled to hold the same," the judge ruled. "If a company or association of miners construct a ditch, to convey water from a running stream for mining or other purposes, and they are the first to use the water, locate and construct the ditch, they are legally entitled to the same as their property, to the extent of the capacity of the ditch to hold and convey water."[61]

As often happened in water cases, the local jury defied the judge by refusing to compensate the Shady Creek Company for damages. The company appealed, and a wide range of vexing issues fell into the lap of the California supreme court—especially the question of whether the delivery of water took precedence over actual use. When the judge of the Tenth District Court referred to "the party who first uses the water," he meant the party who "diverted water" rather than the one who first put it to use in mining. If the mere act of diversion conferred a right to water, private companies would quickly capture the entire water supply of the mineral region and charge whatever the market would bear.

On appeal, the attorney for the miners' company argued that water rights should be limited by more than the capacity of diversion ditches. The supreme court agreed, rejecting the strict doctrine of appropriation recognized in the district court as "a departure from all the [common law] rules governing this description of property" and also as "impracticable in its application." The high court considered it "much safer to adhere to *known principles* and well settled law, so far as they can be made applicable to the novel questions growing out of the peculiar enterprises in which many of the people of this State are embarked." As in so many of the early water cases, the court tried to accommodate rival interests just as the miners themselves did, but with a distinct preference for keeping the field open to the largest number of participants. "It is laid down by our law writers that the right of property in water is *usufructuary*," the court proclaimed, "and consists not so much of the fluid itself as the advantage of its use. The owner of land through which a stream flows, merely transmits the water over its surface, having the right to its reasonable use during its passage. The right is not in the *corpus* of the water, and only continues with its possession." In short, the court decided that all rights depended on actual use, not in making the water available for use.[62]

The court's effort to protect individual miners from monopoly persisted, despite the dramatic growth of large-scale hydraulic mining. In *Eddy* v. *Simpson* the contest was between two diverters. *Irwin* v. *Phillips* (1885), also a Nevada County case, turned on the question of whether, in the words of the supreme court, "the owner of a canal in the mineral region of this State, constructed for the purpose of supplying water to miners, has the right to divert the water of a stream from its natural channel, as against the claims of those who subsequent to the diversion take up lands along the banks of the stream, for the purposes of mining."[63] In other words, *Irwin* v. *Phillips* addressed the single most important water rights issue in the mining camps. Matthew Irwin had dammed the South Fork of Poor Man's Creek to convey water to Irwin's Diggings. He used part of the water on his claim and sold the remainder to other miners. Subsequently, Robert Phillips and seven partners cut the dam to permit the stream to flow past their claims, which had been taken up *after* the construction of Irwin's dam. They claimed riparian rights. A miners' committee ruled in favor of the channel miners; the district court judge favored the other side.

The supreme court sustained the lower court. "They had the right to mine where they pleased throughout an extensive region," it observed, "and they selected the bank of a stream from which the water had already been turned."[64] Irwin's lawyers argued that prior appropriation should promote the maximum production of gold and provide the greatest good to the greatest number. (The question, of course, was whether the "greatest number" should be defined as all the citizens of California, as all investors in San Francisco, New York, or London, as all the residents of the mining districts, or as all the residents of particular districts.) The high court agreed; if miners had an undoubted right to the protection of their claims, then the authority to work the land conferred corollary privileges, including prior appropriation. For the first time, the judges suggested that water was a separate commodity, the title to which was not entirely dependent on how it was used. The act of making it productive became the essence of the right.

Prior appropriation was on the verge of breaking free from the industry that gave it birth.[65]

Irwin v. *Phillips* seemed to separate water from the act of mining, but the court was not consistent. In the same year it also rendered two decisions that clashed with *Irwin*. In a suit questioning whether justices of the peace could prohibit unlawful water diversions, the court emphasized that water was not private property in the same sense as a mineral claim: "The right to running water is defined to be a corporeal right, or hereditament, which follows or is embraced by the ownership of the soil over which it naturally passes. . . . From the policy of our laws, it has been held in this State to exist without private ownership of the soil—upon the ground of prior location upon the land, or prior appropriation and use of the water. The right to water must be treated in this State as it has always been treated, as a right running with the land, and as a corporeal privilege bestowed upon the occupier or appropriator of the soil; and as such, has none of the characteristics of mere personalty."[66] In the second case, which pitted the owner of a sawmill against a water and mining company in Shasta County, the high court explained that it had rejected traditional riparian rights on the public domain not because the miners did not own the land, but because such rights were intrinsically monopolistic. Had they been permitted, "the entire gold region might have been enclosed in large tracts, under the pretence of agriculture and grazing and eventually, what would have sufficed as a rich [mineral] bounty to many thousands, would be reduced to the proprietorship of a few."[67]

The court's support for prior appropriation, ambiguous though it was, later won it the reputation of being in the service of large water companies. The charge was undeserved. The court's inconsistencies reflected a valiant effort to keep the mining industry open to the greatest number of participants despite changes in technology, organization, and capital requirements. To do so, it favored riparian rights in some mining districts and prior appropriation in others. *Irwin* v. *Phillips* was not as much of a turning point as it seems when studied in isolation. The district court judge in *Priest* v. *Union Canal Company* (1855) echoed the thinking on the high bench when he told the jury that "each case to a very great extent depends upon its own peculiar circumstances. No given rule can be laid down that will govern each controversy of this kind."[68]

During the late 1850s, the court continued to oppose the monopolization of water by private ditch companies when monopoly did not serve the needs of a majority of the miners in a particular locale. In 1857, the high court reiterated that it had considered the *"wants of the community,"* not just the rights or demands of capital.[69] In a case nearly as significant as *Irwin* v. *Phillips,* involving two groups of miners with claims adjoining a stream, the court acknowledged that those who used water to work riparian land had a right superior to those who carried the water to adjoining lands, even if the diverter was first on the scene.[70] Obviously, the court was still trying to balance inherently inconsistent rights long after it had accepted the *principle* of prior appropriation. The 1857 case did not sustain the distinction between titles to land and titles to water that *Irwin* had recognized. Quite to the contrary. "If the owners of the mining-claim, in the case of *Irwin* v. *Phillips,* had first located along the bed of the stream," the court noted, "they would have been entitled, as riparian proprietors, to the free and uninterrupted use of the water, without any other or direct act of appropriation of the water, as contra-distinguished from the soil."[71]

The state supreme court repeatedly qualified and restricted prior appropriation. Claiming water, it insisted, gave no right in itself. "Possession, or actual appropriation, must be the test of priority in all claims to the use of water, whenever such claims are not dependent upon the ownership of the land through which the water flows," the court noted in 1856.[72] Nor did the act of posting a claim or even cutting a ditch imply any right. The diversion had to be for a "useful object."[73] Moreover, no right could vest without diligence in the construction of diversion works, and the continuous use of water.[74] No rights were absolute and unqualified.

The first California lawyer to survey water rights, Gregory Yale, insisted that by the end of the supreme court's 1857 term, "the law upon [the] subject of prior appropriation must be considered as settled beyond controversy."[75] Whether he was right or wrong about the year, time was on the side of prior appropriation. Luckily for the hydraulic mining industry, when Stephen J. Field took his seat on the U.S. Supreme Court in 1863, after having served in the California legislature and on the California supreme court, the national court finally included a member who understood economic conditions in the arid West. In 1865 the court, speaking through Chief Justice Salmon P. Chase, formally acknowledged "the validity and binding force of the rules, regulations and customs of the mining districts." A year later, Congress followed the court's lead and formally accepted free mining, ending the threat that the mines would be sold or heavily taxed.[76]

By the 1860s, the basic features of prior appropriation were well established. The first claimant enjoyed an exclusive right, regardless of the amount of water used. His was the only "absolute" grant because all others depended on the size of the initial claim. The water could be used on any lands, at any distance from the source, not just on riparian land—even if the stream ran dry. Priority rights could be bought and sold, and they could also be lost or limited in a variety of ways. Yet prior appropriation was far from being a settled doctrine in 1866. Many issues remained unresolved. For example, did water rights belong to the company that provided the water, the ditch that delivered the water, the miner who used the water, or the claim upon which it was used? Did *ultimate* ownership reside with the federal government, the states, private companies, or individual users? How should "reasonable use" and "beneficial use" be defined? And since the California supreme court had ratified priority rights without abandoning riparian rights, at least on privately owned lands, which took precedence? The court left much unresolved.

There are many ways to allocate scarce resources, and the triumph of prior appropriation was not inevitable. Nevertheless, the priority system had several distinct advantages, at least in the short run. First, no value judgments had to be made about how or where the water was used. As long as the water was claimed for a "beneficial use," no one could overturn the original right—even if a subsequent claimant needed the water more or promised to produce greater wealth with it. Prior appropriation offered equal access to wealth, if not equal opportunity; it was consistent with American ideas of political liberty. It was familiar, embodying as it did the principle of "first in time, first in right," which had long prevailed on the public domain. It did not require an expensive bureaucracy to administer or maintain, a bureaucracy whose cost would have been prohibitive in frontier California and whose power might have encroached on that of the legislature. Finally, it was consistent with the cherished American ideal that individuals, not society, should control their destiny. The welfare of the community became the product of a multitude of discrete decisions made in the marketplace, with no sense of planning and little of collective responsibility.

Prior appropriation carried a heavy social cost. Because the system regarded water as "free," it returned no revenue to the state; water rights were property that could be bought, sold, and assigned, but because their value varied so much from place to place and time to time, they were difficult, if not impossible, to appraise or tax. Moreover, by encouraging rapid economic development, prior appropriation exacerbated the boom-and-bust mentality endemic to the mining industry, encouraging speculation and maximum production. Tragically, since the doctrine did nothing to preserve the quality of water and protect it for reuse—as riparian rights did—it permitted not just waste but environmental destruction on a vast scale. Large sections of the foothills were stripped of vegetation and topsoil; debris choked the Feather and Yuba rivers, rendering them unnavigable; and millions of tons of silt blanketed prime farmland in the Sacramento Valley.[77] Most of all, westerners soon discovered what many miners had feared from the beginning: Prior appropriation stimulated economic development at the price of creating powerful corporations, dangerous monopolies, and endless court contests among rival claimants. By the 1870s, when irrigation began to expand dramatically, so did the demands for a more equitable water system. As it spread, prior appropriation sowed the same seeds of conflict that it had planted in the mining camps.

3
The Legal Context, 1866–1902:
Localism and Reform

When the U.S. Supreme Court and Congress confirmed local customs and procedures pertaining to mining on the public domain in 1865 and 1866, they tacitly encouraged the states and territories to supervise the allocation of water. Consequently, western courts and legislatures became laboratories of public policy. Before the 1880s, the legislatures simply pasted one law over another rather than attempting to draft coherent, systematic codes. In the mining camps of California, water law reflected the fragmentation produced by inconsistent and discordant ideals, such as the simultaneous need to protect "vested rights" and develop new wealth. In the absence of a mediating authority, for example a strong state or ideologically committed political parties, no one exercised the power to decide just what kind of society the law should strive to produce. Because it could not reconcile different interests, the fledgling legal system pandered to localism in a vain effort to appease or balance them. Decentralized water laws suited the western economy of the 1860s and 1870s, an economy in which the needs of miners and stockmen were as important as those of farmers. Unfortunately, those laws were anachronistic by the 1880s and 1890s. They did not prevent conflict among individual water users; they did not help resolve disagreements between upstream and downstream states; and they did not promote stable communities. Legal diversity, localism, and fragmentation not only prevented states from modernizing their laws but also prevented the federal government from providing the leadership and coordination so desperately needed in the West.

The Tyranny of Prior Appropriation

As early as 1855, in a contest over water between miners and a sawmill operator, the California supreme court ruled that prior appropriation extended to water used for purposes other than mining. "The policy of this state, as derived from her legislation, is to permit settlers, in all capacities, to occupy the public lands," Judge Solomon Heydenfeldt proclaimed. "This policy has been extended equally to all pursuits, and no partiality for one over another has been evinced, except in the single case where the rights of the agriculturist are made to yield to those of the miner, where gold is discovered in his land. This exceptional privilege is of course confined to the public lands."[1] In the late 1850s and 1860s, the court repeatedly reaffirmed the applicability of prior appropriation to other industries, but always with the limitation that priority rights only applied within the public domain.[2]

For a variety of reasons, the California court did not fully explain the relationship between prior appropriation and riparian rights until the middle 1880s, when it heard the famous case of *Lux* v. *Haggin*.[3] It could not deny the validity of the priority system; Congress had sanctioned it in 1866, 1870, and 1877. Nevertheless, the California legislature had recognized the riparian doctrine in 1850, and settlers had taken up land along the state's streams long before Congress addressed the issue of water rights. Those citizens expected their titles to confer the traditional right to use water. Riparian rights had vested, and by 1886 a majority of the justices thought that no economic enterprise or public policy justified overthrowing those claims—no matter how ambiguous, complicated, inefficient, or expensive the resulting legal structure might be.

The California supreme court knew that reason and experience supported its decision. Many water users in the San Joaquin Valley engaged in both grazing and irrigation and claimed water under both the riparian and priority doctrines, depending on which better served their needs in a particular place at a particular time. Although California politicians and the popular press regarded the two systems as irreconcilable and antagonistic, the state courts had found ways to temper riparianism, just as they had qualified and limited priority rights. In 1850, with land titles in chaos and squatter riots common in San Francisco and Sacramento, California broke with common law tradition when it enacted a five-year statute of limitations, a remarkably short period considering that the English standard was twenty years and most of the newer states between the Allegheny Mountains and the Mississippi River prescribed a fifteen-year term. This statute of limitations had vast implications for titles to other forms of property, including water.

State courts subsequently ruled that if a farmer or stockman diverted water for five years without protest from downstream riparian owners, he thereby acquired a "prescriptive" right to that water, a right that could not be questioned thereafter. In addition, the courts sharply modified riparian rights as practiced in the eastern United States by permitting riparian owners to divert water for irrigation, thus reducing streamflow, and by permitting appropriators to purchase those rights and use the water anywhere within a river basin. This violated the basic principle of riparianism: that common law water rights could not be severed from the land. In 1886, the majority which handed down the *Lux* decision doubtless believed that once the dual system had been confirmed, rival groups of water users would settle their legal differences out of court.[4]

The supreme court had practical reasons for sanctifying a dual system, but it also found a theoretical justification. Since the Golden State and most of the rest of the arid West had been secured from Mexico by conquest and purchase, and since the U.S. Constitution gave Congress clear authority over the public lands, the central government stood as the "original proprietor," or the first riparian owner. Given the silence of Congress, and California's affirmation of common law rights in 1850, the California court assumed that common law rights prevailed on the national commons until they were abolished by the Desert Land Act in 1877. Sovereignty included the right to dispose of water as well as land, but the common law welded the two together. Therefore, until 1877 those who secured patents to government lands bordering streams also acquired common law water rights. That rationale, called the "California doctrine" in the twentieth century, ultimately prevailed in Montana, the Dakotas, Oregon, Washington, Oklahoma, Kansas, Nebraska, and Texas. Colorado, Wyoming, Nevada, Idaho, Utah, Arizona, and New Mexico recognized prior appropriation exclusively.[5]

The California doctrine was not just an intellectual justification; it was also an attempt to guard against the proliferation of priority rights. Montana justice C. J. Wade observed in 1872, before appropriation took firm root outside California, that if strict prior appropriation became the foundation of Montana water law, "long before one-tenth part of the tillable land in the Territory is subjected to cultivation the entire available water of the country will have been monopolized and owned by a few individuals . . . thereby repelling immigration thither." Those who watered farms at the mouth of a stream could forever prevent settlement in the valleys below, even if the soil downstream was richer and could support a larger population. "Surely," Justice Wade observed, "the climatic and physical conditions of this country cannot be such as to create a law so at variance with natural equity and so fatal to the improvement and prosperity of our best agricultural district." Moreover, because prior appropriation prevented the territorial government from reserving water for its own purposes, the doctrine would sharply reduce the selling price of school and railroad lands and thus hinder economic development. It would also limit the value of the federal lands. "And all these consequences, so disastrous in any view, are to be visited upon Montana, that a few individuals may have what does not now, and never did, belong to them," Wade concluded.[6]

There was more than a little truth to Justice Wade's warning, and it was later echoed by many of the West's leading hydraulic engineers. By 1889, California's first state engineer, William Hammond Hall, regretted that prior appropriation had become part of American law. "To 'appropriate,'" Hall fumed, "pre-supposes that the thing taken is without ownership, like a wild beast of the forest or of the plain; and it has been the curse of irrigation from time immemorial, that water has been treated like it was a beast—to be shot down and dragged out by the first brute that came in sight of it." Wyoming's state engineer, Elwood Mead, agreed: "It assumes that the establishment of titles to the snows on the mountains and the rains falling on the public land and the water collected in the lakes and rivers, on the use of which the development of the state in a great measure depends, is a private matter. It ignores public interests in a resource upon which the enduring prosperity of the community must rest. It is like A suing B for control of property which belongs to C." Finally, Frederick Haynes Newell, the first director of the Bureau of Reclamation, acknowledged that prior appropriation was "extremely simple and just," but only during the pioneer phase of settlement. Once the land was occupied, "there does not seem to be any good reason why a certain individual, who perhaps may be the poorest [worst] farmer of the community, should always have ample water simply because the man from whom he purchased or inherited his farm happened to take out and apply water a few days or months before his neighbors did. Ten men should not be deprived of the use of the life-giving fluid to satisfy the claims of a single individual." Prior appropriation was also inherently inefficient. In dry years, the last acre-feet of water used by profligate senior appropriators contributed far less to the production of crops, and hence to the wealth of a community, than the same amount of water granted to junior appropriators.[7]

What bothered engineers most was that during the 1880s no state or territory placed any *effective* restrictions on claims, a failure made all the more painful by the drought of the late 1880s and early 1890s. The vast majority existed only on paper. They were filed by land developers, water hustlers, or bona fide claimants who failed to raise sufficient money to begin or complete their water projects. Impractical projects lived on for decades, since courts accepted minimal work as evidence of "due diligence."[8] In Arizona, the Salt River was claimed twenty-five times over. By 1898, 151 claimants to the Boise River asserted rights to 6,361,800 miner's inches of water, although the river carried only 35,000 inches in September 1898. In California's Honey Lake Valley, sixty miles north of Lake Tahoe, the basin's water supply was sufficient to cover one hundred thousand acres, but claims had been filed for enough water to irrigate nearly 230 million acres, more than twice the total land area of California. And the Kern County Land Company owned about four hundred thousand acres of land but claimed enough water to serve two million acres.[9]

These claims—prompted as much by ignorance as by greed and speculation—produced unending litigation. "The same issues are tried over and over again," William Ellsworth Smythe, a leader of the western reclamation movement during the 1890s, noted in 1900 (see chapter 7). "When [water] decrees are rendered [by the courts], there is no power to enforce them save the tedious and costly process of another lawsuit, to be followed in time by another, and by still another."[10] In 1903, the journal *Forestry and Irrigation* estimated that in the dry year of 1899 every farmer in California "paid a tribute of 30 cents [per acre] to the courts and lawyers."[11] Western courts had little knowledge of hydrographic or soil conditions. Since most states lacked a state engineer's office, and since the federal government did not begin comprehensive studies of streamflow, soils, and irrigation techniques until the 1890s, the courts had nowhere to turn for impartial data; instead, they relied almost entirely on information provided by litigants. To be fair, they granted individuals and companies far more water than needed.[12] Latecomers, therefore, were often forced to file suit to reduce these overly generous grants.

To make matters worse, farmers practiced extravagant irrigation techniques and assumed that "more was better"—that abundant water would produce abundant crops.[13] Waste was also a way to "reserve" water, whether for later sale to newcomers, for use on land a settler hoped to buy in the future, or for the needs of thirstier crops he hoped to raise someday. Diversified agriculture required years to bring an entire tract of land under cultivation, so water rights had to be elastic. Moreover, courts could not define rights precisely when use varied dramatically from month to month and year to year. In wet years, farmers might not irrigate at all, and in dry years they often left part of their land fallow.

The major restrictions on prior appropriation were that water had to be diverted within a reasonable period of time following a claim; it had to be diverted "regularly," though not continuously; and most important, it had to be put to a "beneficial use."[14] Each of these requirements could be evaded. As for beneficial use, a leading scholar of water law has noted that in the nineteenth century "practically all of the farmers, miners, manufacturers, power companies, and cities of the West met this test when they took the water, since each had a practical wealth-producing use in mind. Each use advanced the development of the resources of the country."[15] Beneficial use was also difficult to define because nineteenth-century courts differed as to whether water rights should correspond to original claims; to the capacity of diversion canals; to the average amount of water used daily, monthly, or yearly (as measured over a long period of time); to the amount of land irrigated at the time of an inspection by the court; or to some arbitrary figure based on empirical studies of the amount of water needed to raise different crops in different soils.

The Legacy of Mexican Law and Community Irrigation Systems

Spanish and Mexican customs and tradition served as a temporary barrier to the spread of prior appropriation. They survived the nineteenth century in some southwestern states, although not in the leading irrigation states of California and Colorado. The "Plan of Pitic," drafted in Chihuahua in 1789 as a model for the new town of Pitic in Sonora, provided a blueprint for future settlements throughout Sonora and what would later become the southwestern United States. It closely resembled the "Regulations for the Government of California," issued by Governor Don Felipe De Neve on June 1, 1779. Both embodied principles that even antedated the *Recopilación* of 1681.

The Plan of Pitic acknowledged that irrigation was the "principal means of fertilizing the lands, and the most conducive to the increase of settlement." It provided for the common use of water *outside* as well as within each pueblo. The official who supervised the establishment of a new community was ordered to "distribute waters so that all land that may be irrigable might partake of them, especially during the spring and summer. He shall divide the territory into districts, marking out to each one a trench or ditch starting from the main source. Each settler shall know the *acequia* [community ditch] from which his plot shall be irrigated, and he cannot and shall not take the water of another or in a greater quantity than his share." The plan required the town council to appoint a watermaster to dole out water and to supervise maintenance of the ditch by the inhabitants. Each farmer contributed money or labor according to the amount of land he irrigated.[16]

Mexican water law differed radically from American law. With few exceptions, the Hispanic Southwest was settled through state-sponsored colonization, not by individuals. The Mexican government used land grants to attract settlers and reward service to the state. But water was too important to be regarded mainly as a tool to promote individual wealth and rapid economic growth. A deed to riparian land conferred the right to use water only for domestic purposes. A few western historians have mistakenly argued that prior appropriation was a legacy from Mexico.[17] Nothing could be further from the truth. Both Spain and Mexico made absolute grants of water to individuals, or groups of individuals, but only rarely. Although water rights could be bought, sold, and transferred from one parcel of land to another, they conveyed a right of *use*, not title to the water itself, or even to the use of a specific amount. When water was short, everyone suffered, regardless of how long they had irrigated or where their land was located. The main purpose of irrigation was to create a permanent community, not to encourage individual enterprise. And since formal ownership of the water remained with the state, water rights were far more adaptable than under Anglo-American law. The arbiter of such privileges might be a local alcalde, or the town council, or the watermaster, but the power of the state, exercised in the name of the community, always remained paramount.

This system sharply reduced litigation. When conflict occurred, judges tried to promote the greatest good for the greatest number. "Rights to the water were not permanent," Michael Meyer has observed, "as Spanish jurisprudence appreciated that few conflicts were resolved so wisely that future abuse could not stem from a decision at one time just." "In actual decisions," Meyer notes, "judges were at pains to indicate to their superiors that their verdicts had been rendered with the common good in mind." There was little resort to abstract principles beyond simple equity.[18]

Mexican water law was remarkably consistent, whether in California, where pueblos and presidios predominated, or in Texas, where private empresario grants characterized early colonization. Running water belonged to the king or the state and was common to all; irrigation could be practiced only with the consent of agents of the state; agriculture was a corporate endeavor, subject to community customs and traditions; and land adjoining a stream did not automatically possess water rights superior to nonriparian land. As a student of Texas water law has remarked, "to look at the Spanish system through the lens of individualistic property concepts is to miss its *raison d'être*."[19] In California, neither Spanish nor Mexican land grants automatically conferred a right to use water. Hence, even private grants were often required to conform to community customs and regulations.

No community irrigation system was more important than that of Los Angeles. In 1848, that pueblo covered nearly eighteen thousand acres, about one thousand of which were irrigated. The absence of accessible markets limited demand for the grapes (wine), oranges, peaches, and apricots raised there. Nevertheless, a gradual expansion of irrigation during the 1840s prompted city officials to enact laws regulating the construction, maintenance, and operation of the town's ditches. The watermaster became responsible not just for ensuring that the fluctuating supply was distributed fairly, and that the farmers maintained the ditches, but also for protecting the acequias from pollution.[20]

The water rights of southern California's irrigation farmers were in limbo from 1850 to 1854. When sovereignty over the American Southwest passed from Mexico to the United States, the Treaty of Guadalupe Hidalgo (1848) indirectly promised the survival of community water systems. The eighth and tenth articles of the treaty declared that "property rights of every kind" would be "inviolably respected" under American rule. Although Congress established a special commission to examine land titles in California, it did nothing to clarify the issue of water ownership. That task was left to the state. In 1850, the California legislature passed an act to incorporate Los Angeles, assuring that the town would "succeed to all the rights, claims, and powers of the Pueblo de Los Angeles in regard to property."[21] Two years later the state granted the city the power and responsibility to pass laws "providing for the proper distribution of water for irrigating city lands," a duty that was reaffirmed in 1854.[22] Since the population of the city doubled between the mid-1840s and 1853, administration of the irrigation system required the creation of a new department in the municipal government.[23]

When the legislature met in 1854, it confronted the question of what to do about water rights established *outside* the former pueblos. Given the large Hispanic population in southern California, and the absence of mining or other rival claims to water there, the lawmakers decided to extend the principles of community water use in force at Los Angeles to the other pastoral counties. In effect, they allowed custom and tradition to dictate the allocation of water for agriculture, as for mining.[24]

The new law permitted a majority of voters in any township within San Diego, San Bernardino, Santa Barbara, Napa, Los Angeles, Solano, Contra Costa, Colusa, and Tulare counties to form special boards to oversee water use. In incorporated cities within these counties, the mayor and city council could assume the commission's responsibilities without formal approval from the voters. The boards were required "to examine and direct . . . water courses, and apportion the water thereof among the inhabitants of their district, determine the time of using the same, and upon petition of a majority of the persons liable to work upon ditches, lay out and construct ditches." They could require each irrigator to work on the community ditches up to twelve days each year, and they could levy taxes to pay for repairing old or constructing new canals. They were also given the power to condemn land for rights-of-way. The 1854 act contained two important limitations: It did not apply in the mining counties—mining was given clear preference if, by some chance, the two industries clashed—and no diversions were permitted that violated riparian rights. The most important features of that law, in contrast to the system of priority rights slowly emerging in the mining camps, were community control over water and conditional grants dependent on month-to-month and year-to-year fluctuations in the water supply and the acreage under cultivation.[25]

By the mid-1860s, the legislature had fine-tuned the 1854 law to fit the needs of different counties. For example, in San Bernardino County those who took up land along a stream fully used for irrigation were treated as lawbreakers, as were farmers who lied to the overseer about the acreage they cultivated in order to get more water.[26] Unfortunately, in many river basins the prohibition against interfering with downstream riparian rights prevented the construction of community irrigation systems. In 1862 the legislature attempted to remove this obstacle by granting the commissions authority to condemn *all* water rights that interfered with public systems.[27] But many lawmakers questioned the constitutionality of condemning riparian rights, even for public purposes. Apparently, the 1862 law was never enforced, and the right to challenge riparian rights was dropped from legislation adopted in 1864 and 1866.[28]

Though riparian rights were a formidable obstacle to public water systems, in the 1860s they were too poorly defined to cripple the legislation. A more dangerous threat came from fledgling water companies bent on extending prior appropriation to land outside the mining districts. In 1862, the legislature, under pressure from two new irrigation companies in Yolo County, granted ditch and canal companies the right to condemn private land for rights-of-way, a privilege already enjoyed by railroads. One section of the act promised such companies the right to use "waters not previously appropriated." It specifically excluded eleven mining counties.[29] The 1862 law encouraged private water companies to enter those counties where, at least in theory, water had been reserved for public use under the 1854 law and its amendments. For example, following the first rush of settlers into Tulare County in 1866, the legislature emasculated that county's law by withdrawing the power of its water commission to survey ditches, dole out water, levy property taxes, and require farmers to maintain ditches. The commissioners could still appoint watermasters, but only from lists of candidates recommended by the water companies—and the companies were made responsible for paying their salaries! The law allowed the commissioners to reject proposed future diversions, ensuring that the first companies on the scene could monopolize most of the county's water.[30] Twenty years later the California supreme court wisely observed that the 1866 Tulare County law "seems to have been studiously prepared in the interest of the [water] companies then existing."[31]

The system of public control continued to erode. A severe drought in 1864 led to the subdivision of many large cattle ranches in southern California and introduced large-scale land speculation to the region. This, in turn, exposed the primary weakness of community water systems: They could not raise large sums of money to expand existing works or build new ones. They were suited to a relatively stable and concentrated population, not a rapidly expanding, dispersed one. In 1868, the legislature provided a formal procedure by which private companies in Tulare County could submit applications to the water commissions for permission to dig ditches. The new law specified that "nothing herein contained shall be so construed as to affect the right and privileges of those who, by prior appropriation, have secured the right to the use of water from the several rivers and streams in Tulare County." Within a decade, prior appropriation had also triumphed in Fresno County.[32]

Community control over water survived into the 1870s in San Bernardino County and even longer in Los Angeles, whose questionable "pueblo rights" were relatively immune to the demands of private companies. The city sold water to an increasing number of farmers within and without its formal boundaries, and the revenue paid for the construction and maintenance of public ditches, as well as for the salaries of the watermasters and other officials who ran the system. By 1877, community irrigation ditches served about forty-five hundred acres within the city and roughly the same acreage on the outskirts of town. The real estate boom that followed completion of the first rail line into the city, however, along with a major drought in 1876–77, made town lots more valuable for houses and businesses than for farming. The largest community ditch shut down in the late 1880s, though the last ditch operated until 1904.[33]

Southern California's community water systems had few admirers. State engineer William Hammond Hall charged that they were poorly constructed, wasteful, uncoordinated, and badly managed. Although public officials distributed water from the common ditches, there was little incentive to conserve it. Most southern California farmers flooded land instead of using more efficient irrigation techniques. Public control did not promote efficiency.[34] At the same time, large landowners regarded the ditches as relics of a primitive subsistence economy and as a limitation on speculative land profits; most Californians would have agreed with Nevada irrigation booster R. L. Fulton's observation in 1889: "We believe the Anglo-Saxon needs no example from Mexico, Spain or Lombardy, but will find in itself [sic] the intelligence, virtue, and grit to conquer this land as it has every country where it has ever set its foot." Given the assumed superiority of "Anglo-Saxon institutions," borrowing laws from Hispanic nations became a badge of weakness.[35] The West's leading jurists shared the public disdain for "alien legal principles." Champions of riparian rights were no more sympathetic to Mexican institutions than the advocates of prior appropriation.[36]

The California experience was replicated throughout the South-west, where community water systems survived the American take-over in 1848 only to fall before increasing populations and soaring land prices. In 1861, the Colorado territorial legislature gave its blessing to irrigation systems created in Costilla and Conejos counties during the 1840s. It provided for the election of watermasters and required each water user to help maintain the system. It also granted "public ace-quias, during the farming season . . . preference over all ditches used for any mills, machinery, or any other ditch that may not be exclusively used for farming purposes." This was not an important privilege, for little mining took place in southern Colorado. The law specified that "every one shall have the amount of water he is entitled to," but left the definition of community rights to local officials.[37] Colorado's com-munity ditches survived into the 1950s, administered by mutual water companies.[38]

New Mexico's territorial legislature was controlled by prominent Mexican-American families who favored stock raising and agriculture over mining.[39] In 1851, it reaffirmed the rights of communal water systems, but it also authorized all those who owned arable land the right to construct ditches, even across private property. Landowners served by public canals were required to maintain the ditches whether they used them or not. Moreover, no mill, whether erected for mining or manufacturing purposes, could "obstruct" (that is, dam) the flow of a stream "as the irrigation of the fields should be preferable to others [i.e., other uses]." A subsequent law confirmed the election of overseers to supervise the construction and maintenance of public ditches and the distribution of water. New Mexico's community water systems persisted well beyond 1887, when the legislature provided for the in-corporation of irrigation and colonization companies in an effort to attract the private capital needed to launch large-scale water projects.[40]

Early irrigation in Arizona was confined almost entirely to land along the Santa Cruz River between present-day Phoenix and Tucson. Arizona became a territory in 1863 and adopted its first water law in the following year. Understandably, given the prevailing excitement over mining, its water code was more complicated than New Mexico's. Unlike every other territory containing public ditches—where the over-seers or watermasters cut back farmers equally in dry years—the Arizona legislature insisted that the allocation of water correspond "to the dates of [farmers'] respective titles or their occupation of the lands." It also clouded the future of public water systems by granting those who built new ditches *exclusive* rights to all the water those ditches could carry. As in New Mexico, some community systems lasted well into the twentieth century, though they were clearly anachronistic. Given the desire of most politicians to force the pace of economic development, cooperative public works had little future in the arid West. Private water companies were much more attractive.[41]

Until the early twentieth century, irrigation in Texas was limited to the Pecos and Rio Grande valleys and the town of San Antonio. The mining industry was insignificant. Moreover, Texas contained no federal lands, and its wide range of climates militated against the adoption of any one system of water law.[42]

The state's largest community water system was constructed at San Antonio beginning in 1729, after the arrival of colonists from the Canary Islands. The irrigable land was divided into farms that could be flooded in one day, using the entire flow of the acequia for that period. One historian of water policy in Texas explained:

> The land units were given numbers and a drawing took place among the rightful applicants. The resulting award of chance was called a "suerte," meaning luck, and the land units themselves thereby became known as "suertes." They varied in area, depending upon the capacity of the ditch and the topography of the farms. Authorized inspectors studied each irrigable tract and determined what size it should be in order to fit the amount of water deliverable. Many old deeds warrant title to one day of water and its corresponding land. This system of distribution of water and land is of Moorish origin.

As in Spain, San Antonio's watermasters weighed dozens of criteria when they divided up the water, including topography, soil fertility, and the characteristics of various crops.[43]

Two stages marked the development of water rights at San Antonio. Originally, grants of water attached to the individual suertes, but during the second half of the eighteenth century, "the holder of a proportional right had his share made explicit in numbers of hours or days of water. Once this stage was reached, it then became possible to shift the rights around, and within a limited context to alienate them. The civil law tradition in Spanish Texas favored adscription, but Canarian custom favored a certain amount of privatization and encouraged the town fathers to regard the water of the creek increasingly as the patrimony of the town."[44] Nevertheless, in San Antonio water rights could not be transferred out of a canal's service area, and most were sold only for a limited time, usually no more than one year.[45] Farmers not only received water in proportion to the amount of land irrigated, but also alternated in using it. The *dura*, or "turn," was a basic feature of Spanish water law. When water was scarce, turns came less frequently. In effect, the *dura* became a measure of water as well as a principle of use. Above all, no rights were absolute.[46] Like other western states, Texas adopted prior appropriation in 1889 and 1895 to encourage the formation of private irrigation companies.

The Common Law Inheritance

Few westerners supported an expansion in community water systems as an alternative to prior appropriation. Some, however, thought that the riparian doctrine could be remodeled to suit new conditions— as it was refashioned in California. John Wesley Powell (see chapter 5), a close student of the arid lands and director of the U.S. Geological Survey from 1880–1894, repeatedly warned that the arid West's water supply was sufficient to serve only a fraction of its land, and that the superiority of alluvial soil dictated that riparian lands receive preference. Because that soil was more fertile, it generally required less water than land far removed from a stream; and much of the water used on riparian land seeped back into the source of supply and became available for reuse. Equally important, the irrigation of riparian lands was much cheaper because it required shorter and smaller ditches; the cost of condemning land for rights-of-way was lower; and shorter canals lost less water to seepage and evaporation. Because riparian rights did not confer an absolute title to water, they were more adaptable to river basins in which the water supply was inadequate to serve all the arable land. And since western streams varied enormously in volume from month to month and year to year, riparian rights were more flexible than specific grants.[47] Above all, by making rights correlative, the riparian doctrine encouraged landowners to resolve their own disputes informally rather than take them to court. It placed the peace and stability of the "community" first.

No devotee of the common law was more eloquent, and few were more perceptive, than the nineteenth-century legal scholar John Norton Pomeroy.[48] Pomeroy opposed prior appropriation partly because western legislatures had granted private companies an almost unlimited right to construct ditches across private lands, which he considered an unjustified abridgment of property rights. No law, he maintained, could "tend to the peace and prosperity of society which attempts to violate and override natural laws and natural rights—the immutable truths which exist in the regular order of nature."[49] Nature grants certain advantages to those who lived along streams, and legislation that ignores the fact "cannot work successfully . . . is essentially unjust, and can only produce wrong. Statutes, however elaborate and detailed, which [invade] natural rights, and [violate] the sense of natural justice, must be the occasion of unlimited confusion, strife, contention, and litigation; nothing can be settled and established by them."[50] Pomeroy argued that on small streams riparian rights should prevail exclusively; administrative commissions could apportion the water equally among riparian claimants. On larger streams, appropriative rights might be permitted, but only after the needs of all riparian owners had been satisfied.[51]

Pomeroy recognized that common law rights were subject to abuse. Some states allowed riparian landowners to sell water to nonriparian owners far removed from the stream, and since these rights were not limited to beneficial use, they could be even more wasteful than appropriative claims. Moreover, riparian owners who bought nonriparian land adjoining their estate often acquired the legal right to irrigate that land even when the previous owner had not done so.[52] The riparian doctrine might have been tempered by extending riparian status to all lands within a river basin, giving preference to those closest to water. Or states might have established priorities of use to rank different kinds of riparian users. Just as the courts granted preference to domestic uses over irrigation, they might have deemed the irrigation of crops a higher use than flooding pastureland. The problem was not the inflexible nature of riparian rights but rather the reluctance of most nineteenth-century courts to "legislate" and the unwillingness of legislatures to grant administrative commissions the power to regulate water users.

There was never a large-scale attempt to adapt riparian rights to western conditions, but the first water laws adopted in many states and territories contained many riparian or correlative elements. Utah is the best example. For years, the Mormons avoided or at least minimized the speculation in water and land endemic to the West and to the rest of the nation. The struggle to maintain group cohesion and to recapture the egalitarian spirit of early Christianity, and the church's dedication to stewardship over natural resources, helped to shape Utah's water law. Mormon leaders wisely chose to discourage mining, a pursuit that not only pandered to individualism and greed but also threatened to lure large numbers of "gentiles" into Utah. Instead, water law developed to serve agriculture exclusively. The legislature made some individual water grants, including grants to Ezra T. Benson, Heber Kimball, and Brigham Young, but all of them served a public purpose—such as promoting colonization or facilitating the erection of a flour mill. Most Mormons adhered to Young's famous declaration of September 30, 1848: "There shall be no private ownership of the streams that come out of the canyons, nor the timber that grows in the hills. These belong to the people: all the people." Individual awards were usually expressed as a percentage of streamflow rather than as a fixed quantity of water, and the legislature maintained the right to amend or rescind all grants.[53]

The first territorial legislature did not meet until 1851. In the meantime, the bishop in charge of each congregation supervised canal surveys and organized ward members into construction crews. All able-bodied men participated in excavating the ditches. When that was done, the church provided rules to govern water use and appointed a water-master to administer allocation and distribution. Water rights were "attached" to particular plots of land; no farmer received a property right apart from his farm. The first water statute, enacted in 1851, granted county judges the right to award water or timber, but only if "said privileges do not interfere with the rights of the community, for common uses, or irrigation, or any privileges heretofore granted by this legislative body."[54] The legislature's decision to rely on local courts to parcel out water and settle disputes ensured that control remained with the church. Usually, a bishop or a church-appointed arbitrator settled minor disputes, but the "bishop's court," composed of the local bishop and two counselors, heard more serious complaints. The next level of jurisdiction was the "council court," made up of a president and twelve other church officials chosen for their experience and judgment. This court was appellate, though it could exercise original jurisdiction in serious conflicts.[55]

Local courts and church officials maintained exclusive control over water until 1880. In that year, the Utah supreme court declared water and land open to appropriation by all.[56] The Mormon legislature's subsequent decision to embrace prior appropriation represented another chapter in the "Americanization of Utah," the substitution of "laissez-faire, individualistic institutions" for communism.[57] However, the 1880 law can also be interpreted as an attempt to protect Mormon property from expropriation by the federal government and from the increasing number of non-Mormons who had entered the territory. In fact, the change was more apparent than real; the 1880 law really restated the earlier statute. County selectmen now became ex-officio water commissioners to hear and determine claims, settle disputes, and appoint commissioners to distribute water. They issued certificates establishing claims. The church exercised de facto control over water until at least 1897, when Utah adopted an appropriation statute similar to Colorado's.[58]

Utah maintained strong control over those who took water by attaching water rights to the land. It sorted out water claims in two ways. One method divided the flow of streams into "primary rights" (the average volume) and "secondary rights" (floodwater). The other pooled rights according to dates of settlement. For example, those who took up farms within a certain river basin before 1860 had a "first right," those who settled between 1860 and 1880 a "second right," and those who arrived after 1880 a "third right." In dry years, holders of second or third rights might be cut off, but farmers *within* the same class shared water equally. "Division was not by measurement in miner's inches or cubic feet per second but by fractions of the stream flow, delivered by rotation. When the flow of the stream decreased, so did the delivery to each one. None were cut off, unless the stream went dry. All the 'brothers' within each category were treated alike; their rights were correlative."[59] Utah water law thus blended appropriation and riparian rights.

Even after Utah formally adopted prior appropriation, little changed. In 1901, one prominent Mormon noted in a letter: "The new theory that water is a commodity has not changed the character of our fundamental industry as much as might be supposed. Irrigation companies have been formed, and they have issued shares of water stock, but these are owned by the farmers themselves. . . . There is only one company in Utah that sells water to the farmers; all the other irrigation companies are composed of the land owners, and they make assessments only of the cost to keep the canals and ditches in repair. You will see by this that, while the theory has changed, the effects of the old idea of land and water unity are still felt for good in our commonwealth."[60]

Utah was exceptional: It was the only state or territory to use water law to *discourage* the inflow of outside capital and to *limit* settlement. Nevertheless, the legal experimentation that occurred in Colorado and Montana suggests that western courts everywhere initially considered the creation of stable communities to be just as important as the search for new wealth. Colorado's first territorial legislature (1861) limited diversions for irrigation to riparian owners and provided in times of scarcity for the appointment of special commissioners to apportion streams "in a just and equitable manner." A statute passed in 1862 extended the right to divert to nonriparian patentees, but it required that "there shall be at all times left sufficient water in said stream for the use of miners and farmers along said stream." This was reaffirmed in 1864, but only for miners, millmen, and others along the stream "who may have a priority of right."[61]

Montana's first territorial legislature (1865) modeled its water law after Colorado's. In both territories, the first farmers and ranchers took up land adjoining streams. They favored traditional riparian rights modified to permit diversions for irrigation, even if those diversions reduced the volume of water available to downstream users. The Montana law limited water use "to one who has riparian rights, either as owner of the riparian land, or through grant of the riparian owner." It also provided that when streamflow was insufficient "to supply the continued wants of the entire country through which it flows, then the nearest justice of the peace shall appoint three commissioners . . . whose duty it shall be to apportion, in a just and equitable proportion, a certain amount of said water, upon alternate weekly days, to different localities, as they may in their judgment think best for the interest of all parties concerned, and with a due regard to the legal rights of all."[62] The law was ruled unconstitutional in 1870 on grounds that it violated the territory's organic act, which granted the *judiciary* exclusive power to decide what was "just and equitable" in conflicts over property.[63] The legislature subsequently rescinded the 1865 statute and promised equal access to water to everyone who owned agricultural land in the territory, regardless of location. The problem posed by delegating judicial power to an appointive commission—an arm of the legislature— was avoided by requiring that all water controversies "shall be determined by the date of appropriation as respectively made by the parties."[64] This was yet another example of how the dominance of courts, and the lack of revenue, contributed to the spread of prior appropriation.[65]

Wyoming and Idaho also initially restricted agricultural water use to those who owned or occupied land adjoining streams. The Wyoming law allowed riparian owners to water any land, at any distance from the water source. It also provided for appointive commissions to resolve conflicts among water users and distribute water in dry years. The commissions were required to provide "a just and equitable proportion . . . to the different localities, as they may in their judgment think best for the interests of all parties concerned." Although the act protected the "prior vested rights of any mill, or ditch owner, or other person, to use the waters of any such water-course," it treated agricultural rights as correlative rather than absolute. The law recognized "prior rights," but it contained no provision for recording water claims or for establishing priorities of use. The rights of the most recent appropriator were not inferior to those of the oldest. The courts never overturned this law, though statutes passed in the late 1880s superseded it and the constitution of 1889 limited rights to prior appropriation.[66]

Idaho adopted its first water law in 1881, by which time private water companies already exercised considerable power in the territory. The legislation provided for the election of watermasters to distribute water in districts where farmers had constructed their own ditches, and to divide the water according to "respective rights and necessities." When the volume was "not sufficient to afford a full supply to those entitled or accustomed to use the same, according to the usage of the district, the water master and his deputies shall regulate the quantity to be used by each person, and the time at, and during which, each person may use the same." The law obviously tried to establish correlative rights. Nevertheless, private water companies were allowed to appoint their own watermasters, and the lawmakers promised that "nothing in this act shall be so construed as to interfere with the vested rights of individual companies or corporations."[67]

The first major water case decided after statehood resulted in a clean sweep for prior appropriation, but not without a dissent by Justice Charles H. Berry who warned that "a great majority of the cases relied on to establish this doctrine of absolute ownership and exclusive monopoly in streams do not relate to the use of water for agricultural purposes at all, but . . . relate to diversions or use for mining purposes only." Settlers would flee Idaho and its population would plummet if prior appropriation triumphed. "Is it reasonable to appropriate all the waters of a stream," Berry asked. "Is it reasonable to allow absolute and 'unrestricted' ownership in water diverted for purposes of irrigation, only, to be used, in this case, for sale to railroads and brickyards, or other purposes than irrigation, and still deny to others their natural, lawful, statutory rights in any of it? Where are the 'reasonable limits' of such a claim."[68] These questions haunted many westerners in the 1880s and 1890s.

Leaders in Reform:
California, Colorado, and Wyoming

The irrigation boom of the 1880s prompted the first large-scale efforts to draft more just and efficient water laws. In California, the inspiration for reform came mainly from three sources: those whose rights were threatened, land speculators and businessmen who thought that litigation over water hampered the sale of potential farmland and the development of rural markets, and advocates of modernization, such as state engineer William Hammond Hall.[69] It did not emanate from the public or from private water companies.

Article 14 of the state constitution adopted in 1879 stated that "the use of all water now appropriated, or that may hereafter be appropriated, for sale, rental, or distribution, is hereby declared to be a public use, and subject to the regulation and control of the State in the manner to be prescribed by law." The constitution mandated a new water code. The drought that afflicted many parts of the state in 1879, the hydraulic mining debris that filled streams in the Sacramento Valley, and lingering fears of land, water, and other monopolies added to the sense of urgency. There was also fear that if the lawmakers failed to clarify water rights the state supreme court would do so instead. At the beginning of the 1880 legislative session, Governor George C. Perkins warned that without reform, the state's agricultural and population growth would languish:

> Men of small means looking for homes are frightened away by this state of affairs, while large capitalists are offered a premium, as it were, to come in and control a whole colony or county. Thus it appears that the waters of our streams are being monopolized, and in some quarters irrigation is working as an ally to speculative farming to crush out the small land owners. I respectfully suggest that you so consider the question, that our laws on this subject will not be an impediment to the practical development of the lands of the State; and that the small homes will be encouraged to multiply and increase.

If the lawmakers could not rescind or abolish open-ended riparian rights, then the state would have to use its police powers to regulate diversions. The 1880 legislature asked William Hammond Hall to frame legislation for its consideration. He published two draft bills and the outline of a third.[70]

Litigation posed the most immediate problem. Contests were increasingly common: between appropriators and riparian owners, between rival appropriators, and between competing groups of users, such as shippers, miners, and irrigators. During the 1870s, a small but vocal minority of Californians, led by the Patrons of Husbandry, or Grange, an antimonopoly farmers' organization, campaigned for the condemnation of all water rights and the construction of a state irrigation system. They wanted cheap water, equal access to it, and direct government control over its distribution. Divisive questions, however, confronted the friends of state reclamation. Should the state eliminate private water rights entirely and assert formal control over *all* rivers and lakes, or should it simply reserve the state's surplus "flood" water—the supply capable of being stored in reservoirs—upon which the expansion of irrigation depended? Should it sell perpetual water rights or annual contracts? Should it restrict the use of "state water" to the best agricultural lands, which were often held by large nonresident farmers, land companies, and speculators, market it only to resident small farmers, or peddle it "first come, first served"? And, since even the state could not provide sufficient water to open all the irrigable land, would not such a policy be inherently discriminatory and hence unconstitutional?

Hall did not advocate a comprehensive, unified state water system. It would take too many years to build, its cost would be enormous, and its survival would depend on fickle legislators and uncertain appropriations. Moreover, augmenting the water supply would distract attention from the need to weed out bogus, extravagant, and monopolistic water claims, and from the need for farmers to practice economical irrigation techniques. Talk of a state system was premature. California had no inventory of claims, no record of the amount of water actually used, and no reliable data on the remaining supply. The legislature needed much more information before it could act.

Hall wanted to conduct soil tests, classify the public lands, and inspect potential reservoir sites, as well as measure the volume of the state's streams. As a first step, he recommended that California compile a list of diversions for each river basin. The burden of proof would be on users, not the state; those who refused to provide the required information would forfeit their water. The state engineer and county recorders would submit the data they collected to the state surveyor general, who would assume the job of maintaining and updating the list of diversions. The state attorney general, using information provided by the surveyor general, would then ask each county's district attorney to file in superior court to adjudicate the rights on each stream. The courts, however, would be prohibited from doing more than ruling on specific questions of fact submitted to them by state administrative officials.

The second part of Hall's reform package involved the distribution of water. He recommended that the governor, surveyor general, and state engineer serve as a "Board of Water Commissioners." Once the state engineer had divided California into hydrographic districts, each embracing from three to five counties, the governor would appoint a water board for each district, consisting of one representative from each county. These commissions would be subordinate to the state board and could not include any employees or agents of private water companies. The state board would establish uniform water measurements, assess the needs of different crops and soils, set water quality standards, and regulate all diversions from navigable streams. Local boards would be responsible for measuring streamflow and for allocating water, their decisions subject to review by the state. The boards could grant permanent or temporary rights, the latter in years of heavy runoff. A general tax levied on all district property would pay the salaries and expenses of board members.

Hall's proposals challenged established water users. He insisted that reform would not undermine existing water rights, but he also promised to free up a large quantity of water by eliminating waste and tying water rights to the land. His most radical proposition was to limit riparian rights to domestic purposes and watering stock. His logic was impeccable: Riparian rights made no sense in southern California, where streams often disappeared into porous sands only to reappear elsewhere. Why permit a stream to flow miles, and lose most of its volume, merely to satisfy a few riparian owners at its terminus? Hall wanted to limit riparian rights to existing uses *and* confine them to land within one quarter mile of a watercourse. No one could doubt that he wanted to centralize control over water and build a new administrative machine in Sacramento. Despite his sympathy for private capital and his desire to encourage investment by guaranteeing rights, he was deeply suspicious of the water and land monopolies so common in California. He anticipated most of the legal innovations later credited to Wyoming's state engineer, Elwood Mead, but his proposals won little support in the legislatures of 1881 and subsequent years.[71]

James B. Shanklin, California's surveyor general during the early 1880s and one of the state's largest speculators, also tried to temper prior appropriation. He made a determined effort to defend the customs and procedures inherited from Mexico, presumably in the hope of breaking the stranglehold of prior appropriation in parts of the state where he owned extensive tracts of dry land. He insisted that the 1862 law, which permitted private water companies to claim water "not previously appropriated," had used *appropriated* in its common usage, meaning "assigned or reserved to a particular use," not as shorthand for the doctrine of prior appropriation. The legislature would never have authorized the formation of local water commissions, he reasoned, without tacitly reserving a supply of water for those commissions to distribute. And had the 1862 law intended to expand prior appropriation to agricultural lands throughout the state, it would have contained a procedure for filing water claims, so that the courts could keep them in proper order. Instead, when the legislature codified the state's laws in 1872, and finally specified formal procedures for filing appropriative claims, it warned that the laws "creating or regulating Boards of Water commissioners and Overseers in the several townships or counties of the State" remained in force.[72]

In 1883 Shanklin, then a state legislator, introduced a bill to curb rights under prior appropriation. The legislation required each board of supervisors to distribute the county's water and give preference to "ditches built by public funds or acquired by the people of the district." Only when the water supply exceeded the needs of the community ditches would private companies and farmers beyond the reach of the public canals receive any water. Predictably, the bill won little support.[73] Whether Shanklin's interpretation of water rights was right or wrong, most lawyers and politicians construed the 1872 codification as formal recognition that prior appropriation applied to all industries and lands throughout the state.[74]

Colorado was watched closely by other states and territories because it was the first to enter the Union following adoption of the mining law of 1866. In that state, reform was favored by specific groups of irrigators seeking to protect their appropriative rights. Article 16, section 5 of the Colorado constitution (1876) stated: "The waters of every natural stream, not heretofore appropriated, within the state of Colorado, are hereby declared to be the property of the public, and the same are dedicated to the use of the people of the state, subject to appropriation as hereafter provided."[75] The constitution was, in part, a response to preexisting water problems. In 1874, a particularly dry year, farmers from the Greeley Colony on the Cache la Poudre River complained bitterly about new diversions twenty-five miles upstream at Fort Collins. The Greeley Colony had the oldest rights on the stream. Fort Collins farmers proposed dividing up the water according to the amount of land under cultivation, but downstream interests clung fast to their prior rights. Then, in 1878, the construction of a much larger canal financed by English capital alarmed both groups. Simultaneously, farmers in the St. Vrain and in other river basins began to worry about the security of their water supply. At the end of the year an irrigation convention in Denver appointed a committee to draft Colorado's first comprehensive water law.[76]

The committee's report urged the legislature to attach all water rights to the land, rather than to ditches, and to grant water commissioners the power to define rights (with appeal to the courts). The lawmakers, however, refused to grant that much power to administrative officials, and they also refused to abolish those legal incentives—such as the tax exemption on irrigation ditches—designed to encourage corporate investment. New laws divided the state into five drainage districts, each of which conformed to a hydrographic basin and was administered by a separate commissioner. Any water user could request a county court to rank all rights to a particular stream, and the commissioners were charged with distributing the water according to prior rights decreed by the courts.

There were fatal weaknesses in Colorado's new statutes. Neither the 1879 nor the 1881 laws provided for measurement of the state's rivers or for determining the volume of its canals, nor did they mandate a comprehensive public record of water rights. At no stage in the construction or operation of private irrigation projects did the state furnish direct supervision, and the state engineer—whose office was created in 1881—was not allowed to participate in adjudication proceedings, or even to provide the courts with streamflow data. (Indeed, the courts were not required to inform the state that a suit was under way!) The process of ordering claims was doomed from the start because many streams passed through two or more districts. In 1890, a state commission appointed to revise Colorado's water laws reported that in many cases "the whole volume of the stream was absolutely adjudged to the junior appropriators upon the upper parts of the stream in proceedings to which the senior appropriators in the lower parts of the stream were not parties, where they had neither right nor opportunity to be heard. The decrees, therefore, instead of affording, as was intended, a just, true and absolute measure of the rights of all appropriators for irrigation, are in fact false and misleading even as to those who participated in the inquiry upon which they are founded, and absolutely void as to all others."[77] Nor did the new laws help to conserve water. The courts granted more water than was needed—sometimes even more than ditches were capable of carrying—and in the absence of reliable information, different courts granted very different quantities of water to farmers who irrigated the same crops on the same number of acres. This, in itself, contributed to litigation. The "public interest" was never represented in these contests; adjudication suits tested and defined the relative rights of individuals exclusively.

There were many other pitfalls in the Colorado laws. For example, since water commissioners were paid by individual districts rather than by the state, the regulator was paid by the regulatee. Small wonder that commissioners often winked at illegal diversions. Moreover, neither the 1879 nor the 1881 law put any effective limit on the amount of water that could be granted by the courts. This omission was particularly important because after 1878, when the cultivation of alfalfa began in Colorado, agriculture in the state changed dramatically. Farmers who raised vegetables and grains diverted water during a growing season of about sixty days that coincided with the greatest flow of the state's streams, but alfalfa could be cultivated for as long as 180 days a year. Also, some farmers began to raise crops that matured later in the summer, such as potatoes and beets. As crops changed, farmers diverted the same amount of water over a much longer period, which provided a new source of litigation. Worst of all, the new laws did not regulate the construction or operation of storage reservoirs.[78]

The absence of effective legislation became more evident in the 1880s, when drought exacerbated the competition for water. The most powerful of many new companies formed in Colorado during the late 1870s and 1880s was the Colorado Mortgage and Investment Company. In 1879, it bought all the Kansas Pacific's land from the point at which the Platte River left the Rocky Mountains to below Denver, about one hundred twenty thousand acres in all. Late in 1879 it filed on water to serve land near Denver, and in the following year a subsidiary, the Northern Colorado Irrigation Company, began construction on the High Line Canal—or the "English Canal" as it was pejoratively called by critics who feared and resented the power of foreign investors. Unfortunately for the company's promoters, water rights on the Platte dated back to the 1860s, and the company promised far more water than it could deliver to those who bought land under its ditch. Although it sold water rights to thirty thousand acres, during the two decades from 1887 to 1906 the company served, on the average, only thirteen thousand acres a year; in a few dry years it delivered no water at all.[79]

Colorado's 1876 constitution dedicated all water not previously claimed or appropriated to the people of the state. The courts decided that the constitution prohibited all corporations, except those which provided water to their own stockholders (mutual or joint-stock companies), from owning water; the rest were merely "common carriers." This judgment had far-reaching implications. In dry years Colorado's private companies could not ask water users to share the burden equally, as companies did in California. Later settlers were left to bear water shortages alone because the courts required Colorado ditch companies to serve customers according to the strict priority of individual rights, even though the earliest users often wasted water and claimed far more than they actually used. Consequently, irrigation promoters sought to make money almost entirely from land sales, and irrigation projects in Colorado became even more speculative than in California. Companies built works with the intention of turning them over to the water users as quickly as possible, and construction standards suffered. Moreover, because the companies could not "reserve" a supply of water, they were prey to the extortionate demands of those who speculated in water rights with the sole intention of selling at a profit to bona fide companies. All this meant that private companies in Colorado had to offer very high rates of interest on their bonds—often 10 percent—to attract investors. As a result, water prices were also high, especially considering the value of the state's irrigated crops.

The High Line Canal was no exception. Water charges did not even pay maintenance costs, and in the middle 1880s the company imposed a surcharge or royalty of $10 to $30 an acre in addition to the customary annual toll of $1.75 an acre. This caused immense distress among the state's irrigation farmers, and not just those dependent upon the Northern Colorado Irrigation Company. The size of the High Line Canal project gave the company power to set legal precedents. For example, it charged farmers whose rights antedated the company for water and cut off those who refused to pay. This posed the possibility that senior rights would be preempted by private corporations throughout the state. Critics charged that the corporations intended to take possession of streams that carried no surplus by establishing a right to extend ditches under their original priority, thus preventing all future agricultural development except by large capital. As in Gold Rush California, the corporation needed the law to win. If farmers with older rights challenged the companies in court, they faced enormous legal expenses. If they did not, the company could acquire the right to water under the doctrine of adverse use or prescription, just by using it for four years in the absence of a formal legal complaint.[80]

The royalty came to symbolize the insolence of corporate power. As Denver's *Rocky Mountain News* editorialized in 1891:

> No Irish absentee landlord ever required his tenants to sign a more infamous contract than this company [the Northern Colorado Irrigation Company] forced on the farmers under their canal. Furthermore, the "royalties" or bonuses for water rights which have been demanded by many ditch companies . . . have repaid in many instances a large portion of the original or actual cost of the ditches. If they have put as much water in their stock as they can carry in their canal, they are not entitled to a single dollar of return on it. . . . To collect pay for water they do not carry, to demand six months' pay for two months' work, to require royalties and bonuses before they will sell water at all, to set themselves up as privileged individuals or organizations not subject to commercial losses like other people—all these assumptions are part and parcel of the arrogance which characterizes corporations, and which has been borne long enough. More than railroad legislation even, laws are demanded by which the rights of the people of Colorado shall be maintained as against corporations which, through the ownership or control of water, seek to absorb the farm lands of Colorado.[81]

In 1887, the Colorado legislature enacted an antiroyalty bill which prohibited surcharges for water, permitted county commissioners to fix rates charged by private companies, threatened corporations that violated the law with the loss of their charters, and warned guilty corporate officers, individually and jointly, to expect stiff fines and imprisonment.[82]

In 1888 the Colorado supreme court upheld the legislation.[83] Nevertheless, some companies continued to impose royalties under various guises, and the legislature failed to enact a comprehensive water code— partly because it split over whether the new laws should be drafted and enforced by a special legislative commission or by the state engineer, and partly because it could not decide whether reclamation ought to be the job of the state government, the federal government, quasi-public irrigation ditches, or private enterprise. After passage of the antiroyalty bill, a new code was needed to help the courts distinguish between appropriative rights, rights of carriage, and rights of use. Most Coloradans insisted that companies charge only for delivering water; the companies contended that their survival required them to charge for water, whether farmers under their ditches diverted it or not. Colorado water rights were no more secure in 1900 than in 1879, and the system of water allocation was no more just or efficient.[84]

Wyoming, which learned slowly from Colorado's mistakes, adopted its first comprehensive water law in March 1886. It simply copied Colorado's statutes of 1879 and 1881, including most of the defects. Elwood Mead later characterized the statute as "makeshift legislation," in part because the territory was too poor to fund the administrative positions needed to administer the law. By default, the work of determining, recording, and protecting water rights passed to existing county and state officers, including county clerks, district clerks, county surveyors, district judges, and the one new territorial officer, the territorial engineer.[85]

When the Wyoming constitutional convention met in 1889, the delegates knew that their state was unable to provide prospective settlers with the agricultural promise of Colorado or California. But Wyoming might be able to offer secure water rights immune to uncertainties and litigation. To achieve that objective, to give Wyoming a chance to survive and compete, its founding fathers imposed serious limitations on prior appropriation. During the constitutional debates, Judge Melville C. Brown of Albany County branded chronological rights as "pernicious and an outrage upon the people. . . . When we appoint a board of control to manage this water system, that we say belongs to the state, let us give them the authority to control it for the highest and best uses of the people of the state, and don't fix that control by saying that priority of appropriation shall settle the matter."[86] To Brown's disappointment, most delegates concluded that without some system of priority, all existing water rights would be thrown into the courts, resulting in chaos. Nevertheless, while Colorado's constitution declared that all water *not previously appropriated* belonged to the state, Wyoming's stated that *all* water belonged to the state. Moreover, although Colorado put no limits on the right to file appropriative claims, even on overappropriated streams, the Wyoming constitution provided that applicants for water could be denied "when such denial is de-manded in the public interest."

The Wyoming constitution went far beyond the existing water laws in any arid state or territory.[87] In theory, since all water was state property, diverters received a right of use, not absolute title. In addition, the new charter specified that water rights could be acquired only by prior appropriation; required that water rights attach to the land;[88] and provided that claims could be denied when "demanded by the public interests." It also divided the state into four water divisions that con-formed to major river basins; created the office of state engineer and vested it with "general supervision of the waters of the state"; and established a "board of control" composed of the state engineer and the superintendents from each district. The board supervised the ap-propriation, distribution, and diversion of water; its decisions were subject to review by the courts. A law passed by the first state legis-lature in December 1890 completed the water rights system by insti-tuting a formal administrative procedure to acquire rights and by granting responsibility for adjudication to the board of control, rather than the courts. The law also empowered the board to create water districts, each supervised by a water commissioner responsible for dividing up the water within that district. Before any adjudication began, the state engineer was required to measure the water supply of streams and diversion ditches and pass that data on to the board of control. The 1890 statute prohibited the board from granting more than one cubic foot per second (cfs) of water for each seventy acres of farmland. The new system's chief appeal to water users was that the state bore the cost of guaranteeing water rights. And since data gathered by state officials were more reliable than those collected by the courts, water rights settlements were more likely to last.[89]

The Wyoming system was designed to cure some of the most obvious weaknesses in the doctrine of prior appropriation. By the early years of the twentieth century, the Board of Control had issued more than five thousand certificates of appropriation. Each cost the state about twelve dollars (the claimants themselves paid one dollar for each certificate of appropriation and seventy-five cents to record it). Put another way, up to 1905, the water rights on fifty thousand ditches had been adjudicated at a cost to the state of about ten cents per acre. Only seven appeals were carried to the courts.[90]

Nevertheless, the new code did not repair all the defects in the Colorado system of water rights. For example, the Board of Control decided that an appropriation guaranteed only sufficient water to accomplish the purpose for which an application had been made, not the right to use a specific amount of water. But it did not have the staff to determine the actual amount of water each farmer or rancher used or needed, so waste continued. Moreover, while the constitution limited water users to a *maximum* of one cfs for each seventy acres, many applicants used that figure to calculate their claim, and the board could only accept it as the norm, rather than the upper limit. This was no trifling matter. When irrigation began in Colorado, the mean duty of water was one cfs for each fifty-four acres irrigated, but by the middle of the 1890s the same amount of water served from two to six times that acreage, owing to improvements in irrigation techniques and the fact that virgin land was far thirstier than land that had been irrigated for a few years. The same was true in Wyoming. To compound the problem, the constitution placed no absolute limit on the total amount of water that could be diverted during a growing season. If the owner of seventy acres took one cfs continuously, which was perfectly legal, the flow would cover that land to a depth of over ten feet in one year.[91]

Most of the Board of Control's problems were economic. Declining state revenue, particularly during the years from 1893 to 1900, limited what Wyoming's government could do. The first legislature failed to pass an appropriation bill to pay the salary of the state engineer or his assistant; Mead himself advanced the money that allowed his office to survive.[92] As a result, the board was compelled to adjudicate water rights before a systematic survey of the state's water supply had been completed. By 1900 only half the territorial water rights had been determined, and they covered much less than half the land served by those rights. No work at all had been done on the North Platte, Laramie, Sweetwater, Powder, and Big Horn rivers.[93]

The U.S. Geological Survey (USGS) came to the rescue in 1895 when it negotiated a cooperative agreement with the state to measure streamflow, but the Board of Control remained hard pressed just to keep up with surveys of new ditches and extensions of old ones. Since Wyoming had failed to attract many large water projects, state officials spent most of their time inspecting dozens of small canals no more than a mile or two in length. The number of applications to appropriate water increased from 645 during 1891 and 1892, to 824 in 1897 and 1898, 1,141 in 1899 and 1900, and 1,672 in 1901 and 1902. The legislature imposed a two-dollar fee on applicants for water rights to help defray administrative costs, but state appropriations consistently failed to keep pace with the growth of irrigation.[94]

Wyoming's new water laws had many other weaknesses. Most of the state's canals were built to tap spring "flood" runoff; when that disappeared in June or July, summer crops withered and died. While Mead and political leaders worried most about how to attract new residents to the state by developing virgin land, established ranchers and farmers demanded that the state first work to supplement existing water supplies. In the absence of conservation measures, which could not be imposed for a variety of reasons, the construction of storage reservoirs appeared as the most practical solution to this dilemma. Unfortunately, neither Wyoming nor any other western state had enacted a comprehensive law defining title to stored water; nineteenth-century laws concentrated on normal streamflow. Mead also asked the legislature to permit him to draft a state water plan to coordinate the construction of all private ditches and require state officials to regulate water rates and supervise the construction of dams and canals. He urged that the federal government grant no land before the state had approved a water right for that parcel. Unfortunately, the new administrative system did not alter the values of most Wyoming ranchers and farmers. Most had little sympathy for the "public interest." They believed that simply filing a claim with the county clerk created a property right and that appropriative rights depended more on the size of a ditch than the actual amount of water used.[95]

The use of experts to supervise the acquisition and adjudication of rights was a far-reaching reform, but the creation of a state bureaucracy to settle rights loomed as an enormous threat in the oldest western states. In Wyoming, there was no great fear of overturning vested rights, which helps explain why few water users there protested administrative adjudication. Moreover, in Wyoming the water was used to raise forage crops or natural grass, not high-value crops, so its value was far lower than in other states. Finally, California and many other western states honored riparian rights, which would have been impossible to adjudicate by a board of control because their very nature was indefinite.

Other states and territories culled parts of the Wyoming law, but only Nebraska copied it whole (in 1895). The establishment of state engineering offices constituted the single most important administrative reform. By 1907, Idaho, Utah, Nevada, Montana, the Dakotas, Oregon, and Oklahoma had state engineers, though their responsibilities varied. Everywhere, they measured streamflow and maintained a centralized record of claims. But as of 1910, only Wyoming, Nebraska, Nevada, and Oregon provided for administrative determination of water rights, and only Wyoming and Nebraska tied rights to the land. In Utah, the Dakotas, Oklahoma, and New Mexico, data collected by the state engineer were used as the basis for adjudications by the courts. Most state authorities acknowledged that water rights should be granted only through a formal procedure, but many states continued to recognize "prescriptive" rights, claims established through use rather than through a formal filing procedure. Only in Colorado and Wyoming had most water rights been confirmed by either court or commission. In sum, the "Wyoming idea" did not transplant easily. In large parts of the West, wholesale legal reform was infeasible, if not impossible.

The Specter of Federal Authority

Reform was designed in part to discourage the federal government from asserting or reasserting its own water rights and to prevent it from exercising administrative control over all rights. It was as convenient in 1880 or 1902 as it is today for students of western water law to assume that beginning in 1866, Congress gradually relinquished jurisdiction over western water to the states, if not the territories.[96] A large body of historical evidence, however, suggests that the states' rights arguments are twentieth-century creations and that politicians at both the state and national level seriously entertained the possibility of federal control during the late 1880s and 1890s—at least over interstate streams.

At the Wyoming constitutional convention in 1889, Judge Asbury B. Conway of Green River questioned the constitutionality of state ownership of water, remarking that the "United States, as the owner of public lands, is the owner of the water also." He wondered whether "our claim as a state to the ownership of all this water [will] not conflict with the rights of the United States."[97] A minority report of the U.S. Senate's Irrigation Committee published in 1890 insisted that the federal government had two strong claims to water on the public domain: first, it owned most of the land in the western half of the nation and deserved sufficient water to improve that land under the Constitution's property clause, and second, since it was responsible for keeping peace between the states, both the commerce and general welfare clauses justified federal control of interstate streams.[98] In 1889 the secretary of the interior noted that since a survey of irrigable lands then under way by the USGS would likely result in Congress reserving all the arid region's irrigable lands, Congress should also consider "what general laws it may deem best adapted to regulate the supply and use of water under Government control." And in the following year, he called for "comprehensive laws determining the National policy in this business . . . particularly guarding against such abuse of the powers granted as would allow upper lands to absorb the water continuously through the dry season." In 1891 the secretary conceded that the states and territories should exercise some control over private water companies, but he warned that "the United States Government, from whom these vastly important and far-reaching privileges emanate, should not release altogether its hold upon the water supply and its ultimate distribution."[99]

President Benjamin Harrison agreed that Congress had not relinquished control over water on the public domain. In his December 1891 message to Congress he warned that private companies threatened to monopolize western waters, making "the patentees of the arid lands . . . tenants at will of the water companies." "The United States should part with its ownership of the water sources, whether to the States and Territories or to individuals or corporations, only upon conditions that will insure to the settlers their proper water supply upon equal and reasonable terms," the president insisted. "In the Territories this whole subject is under the full control of Congress, and in the States it is practically so as long as the Government holds the title to the reservoir sites and water sources and can grant them upon such conditions as it chooses to impose." In 1896, the commissioner of the General Land Office called for a national commission to divide and administer interstate streams; he expressed no doubt that this was completely reasonable and constitutional. Two years later, a Kansas delegate to the National Irrigation Congress called for the creation of a public land commission to replace the medley of state water laws with a centralized, national system. The *Scientific American* magazine echoed the idea in a March 1900 editorial.[100]

Some members of Congress also supported an expansion of federal authority over water. Bills introduced in the late 1880s and after implied that, whatever temporary privileges had been granted to the states in 1866 and later, the central government might at any time take charge of at least the West's surplus water or interstate waterways.[101] Some proposals were very elaborate. For example, an 1890 bill provided for two commissions, one with jurisdiction east of the Rocky Mountains and the other west of the Divide, to supervise the acquisition and use of water. They would designate irrigation districts, appoint officials to supervise distribution, enforce existing court decrees, condemn property for reservoir and canal rights-of-way, and decide all claims to stored and flowing water. The secretary of interior would appoint survey engineers and foresters for each division, though the two commissions would be under a Division of Irrigation in the Department of Agriculture. Once that was done, all water users would be required to apply for a federal license. The commission would then hold public hearings and decide on what terms the water could be used. It would also serve as a court of appeals to hear protests against water rates charged by private companies. The bill earmarked proceeds from land and timber sales to pay for the new agencies. Such a system, which would have given an administrative tribunal control over land and forests as well as water, won little support in Congress.[102] Many westerners wanted the federal government to build reservoirs, but few trusted the central government to decide who would get the water. Still, for a variety of reasons, some system of federal control remained a potent possibility.

The drought of the late 1880s and early 1890s demonstrated that most of the West's smaller, intrastate streams had already been claimed; future growth depended on tapping the larger interstate rivers. State officials recognized that extending the principle of priority across state lines would challenge vested water rights by changing the relationship of rights to each other and, hence, the amount of water that could be turned into each ditch. In effect, the expansion of prior appropriation would have constituted an illegal seizure of property. Wyoming placed much more stringent restrictions on grants of water—as in its definition of what constituted a "beneficial use"—than its neighbors did. Therefore, although Wyoming and Colorado both recognized prior appropriation exclusively, Wyoming might reject claims acceptable under Colorado law. Moreover, Colorado and Idaho differed from Wyoming and most other states and territories in that they ranked appropriations for domestic uses above those for irrigation, regardless of chronological priority. While Wyoming had a centralized record of water claims, Utah's were scattered through four counties. And both Utah and Idaho permitted rights established by uncontested use without any formal application. Even if the federal government did not take direct control over the West's interstate streams, it was likely to pressure the states to enact model water codes to achieve consistency.

One example, the battle over the Rio Grande, speaks volumes. As early as 1873 and 1874, Mormon farmers took up land in Colorado's San Luis Valley, adjoining the Rio Grande. The valley was a geographical wonder, 40 to 60 miles wide and 150 miles long. At the end of the 1870s, the Denver & Rio Grande Railroad pushed into the region, prompting a scramble to build ditches. By 1892, Colorado canals watered about four hundred thousand acres in the basin. During the 1890s, irrigated acreage declined due to drought and the bankruptcy of the largest water companies, but it returned to about three hundred seventy-five thousand acres by 1906. Meanwhile, downstream in Texas and New Mexico, these upstream diversions exacerbated the effects of the drought. Irrigated acreage around El Paso declined from forty thousand to thirteen thousand acres, and over half the population on the Mexican side of the border abandoned their parched land. In two out of every three years from 1887 to 1908, the river ran dry during the irrigation season, including six straight years from 1899 to 1904. A private company promised to build a reservoir at Elephant Butte to alleviate the persistent shortage, but the federal government blocked the scheme. It wanted to divide the river with Mexico, and it had plans to build its own reservoir. Representatives of Texas and New Mexico complained that the oldest Texas water rights antedated those in San Luis Valley by a century and that the largest ditches serving New Mexico's Mesilla Valley had also been constructed before the first ditch in Colorado. There was, however, no way to enforce priority throughout the entire basin.[103] Similar conditions prevailed in many parts of the West, especially on the Arkansas River, shared by Kansas and Colorado; the Laramie River, shared by Colorado and Wyoming; the Bear River, shared by Utah and Idaho; and the Truckee and Carson rivers, shared by California and Nevada.[104]

Many solutions were proposed for the gap in sovereignty. The most famous, that offered by John Wesley Powell, sought to divide the arid West into 150 irrigation districts that conformed to natural drainage basins, each with its own water supply, timber, pasture, and as much irrigable land as could be watered. But since most reformers preferred either federal or state control over interstate rivers, this proposal—which might have encouraged the most efficient and equitable use of water—won little support.[105] Other schemes also ran into strong opposition. At least two bills required the adoption of uniform water codes and the preparation of comprehensive plans to divide interstate streams as preconditions to the cession of arid lands to the states.[106]

For these reasons, by the end of the 1890s, only two practical solutions to the management of interstate waters seemed open: joint state commissions, which might include some federal representatives, or direct national control by a quasi-judicial tribunal composed of federal bureaucrats, which might include some state representatives.[107] Of course, westerners feared that such a commission might draft a comprehensive federal code that would overturn state regulation of water rights and seriously threaten established property rights.[108]

One recent interpretation of the evolution of water law in the Rocky Mountain West insists that "although the creation of [economic] opportunity was a clear goal, law-makers channeled some behavior. In particular, water law promoted the efficient use of property."[109] The laws themselves may sustain that interpretation, but their consequences do not. At the close of the century, waste and inefficiency prevailed throughout the arid West, and water law had failed to produce peace and order between the central government and the states and territories, among the states and territories, or between different parts of individual states and territories. The value of administrative reform was more apparent than real. The private search for wealth still mattered far more than building stable communities—though, of course, most westerners thought the two objectives overlapped. Neither the nation nor the states had yet defined the "public interest" in water.

Water laws symbolized the West's fragmentation. As a California reformer wrote to Governor George Pardee in 1911: "At present we are going by the good old rule, the simple plan, that he may get who has power, and he may keep who can, and in the struggle, the people who are most vitally concerned, are absolutely ignored. They are compelled to sit by peaceably and quietly while more or less polite highwaymen squabble over the proper division of the goods of which they have despoiled them." Reclamation proponent William Ellsworth Smythe put it best when he observed that the arid West was "bound hand and foot by a system of illogical and antiquated laws and customs, born of the needs of other days and other countries, and wholly unsuited to this place and time."[110] By 1900, the law had contributed to the division of the West into rich and poor states and territories, upstream and downstream communities, and agricultural, mining, and stock-raising regions. Unity remained elusive.

4

Private Enterprise

"The pioneer's immediate concern was so focused on the accumulation of wealth," Ray Billington once observed, "that material values bulked larger in his life than in the lives of persons who lived in matured societies."[1] Whether this condition resulted from the West's attractiveness to greedy, adventurous risk takers, from the fluidity of its social classes, from the region's boom-and-bust economy, from high profits on capital, from a legal system very sympathetic to property, or simply from an abundance of natural resources, nineteenth-century westerners placed a premium on getting ahead, both individually and collectively. By the 1870s, irrigation became a way to wealth. Ironically, it was also a tool of social reform. Thus, the history of private irrigation development in the nineteenth century is the story of two conflicting forces, one communitarian and the other individualistic, one centripetal and the other centrifugal.

Reformers ranging from the Mormons to the Salvation Army embraced irrigation as a tool to build close-knit, unified, autonomous agricultural settlements. Such communities exhibited idealism, social planning, and centralized authority. They were not entirely altruistic, but for many promoters, profit took second place to the greater glory of man or God. These colonization schemes—with the exception of that of the Mormons—inevitably suffered from disunity and strayed from their original ideals. They closely resembed eastern antebellum communitarian experiments. Once groups of colonists arrived in the arid West, cohesion and the sense of mission decayed. Settlers simply refused to pull together. At the same time, while profit-oriented private companies opened millions of acres to cultivation, they too failed to live up to expectations. They constructed poorly planned, inefficient, and unprofitable projects. Two variations on private enterprise, mutual water companies and irrigation districts, attempted to blend elements of the communitarian and individualistic ethics, but they suffered from serious limitations as well.

Irrigation: The Financial Justification

Irrigation became popular only after certain assumptions and stereotypes concerning the West were challenged. Obviously, the first was the region's image as the "Great American Desert."[2] Many critics questioned whether the western half of the nation could or should harbor a large population. For example, in 1837 Washington Irving described the Rocky Mountain region in the bleakest terms:

> The great Chippewyan chain of mountains, and the sandy and volcanic plains which extend on either side, are represented as incapable of cultivation. The pasturage which prevails there during a certain portion of the year, withers under the aridity of the atmosphere, and leaves nothing but dreary waste. An immense belt of rocky mountains and volcanic plains, several hundred miles in width, must ever remain an irreclaimable wilderness, intervening between the abodes of civilization, and affording a last refuge to the Indian. Here roving tribes of hunters, living in tents or lodges, and following the migrations of game, may lead a life of savage independence, where there is nothing to tempt the cupidity of the white man.[3]

Nearly four decades later W. B. Hazen warned that all the land between the hundredth meridian and the Sierra Nevada was essentially uninhabitable: devoid of water, choked with poisonous alkali, and plagued with insects that destroyed "all vegetable life, many of the seasons." Hazen was disgusted with western boosters: "In this region there are many years of famine, and none of plenty. . . . Hereafter, let emigration to these places known not to be arable, be emphatically discouraged."[4] Although many early visitors to the region noticed the lush vegetation that skirted streams and lakes, and passed through oases of irrigated land cultivated by Mexican-Americans in California, New Mexico, and Colorado, they did not appreciate irrigation's power to transform desert into garden. It did not seem practical. Many of the largest streams had carved channels hundreds of feet below the tablelands, as in the Columbia basin of northeastern Washington, where potential farmland was as much as fifteen hundred feet above the river. Given the technology of the 1850s and 1860s, no pump or diversion dam could raise or lift water that high. Moreover, conditions had to be just right for irrigation to succeed: The surface had to slope gradually, and the soil had to be sandy and absorbent (otherwise the water would wash it away or render it like concrete in consistency). In addition, ditches were expensive to build and maintain. "The constant care and attention required," Myron Angel wrote in his 1881 history of Nevada, "make the cultivation of the soil by irrigation in large quantities nearly impossible."[5] Critics also warned that irrigation caused disease, particularly malaria; that it produced inferior crops; that it concentrated alkali and other contaminants that poisoned the soil; that it required the use of dams, which often collapsed; and that it invited the formation of water and land monopolies.[6]

Western promoters feared that the mere suggestion that farming was more expensive in the West would depress the price of land and drive away potential settlers.[7] Many boosters, particularly on the Great Plains, favored cheap alternatives to the construction of dams and canals. They were obsessed with artesian wells, and windmill irrigation became equally important, not just because of the steady breeze on the plains but also because in some places—such as the Arkansas River Valley—abundant supplies of water could be found within twenty feet of the surface. "The future of the semi-arid region," Denver's *Rocky Mountain News* proclaimed in 1895, "lies in the development of windmill pumps." It predicted that all the plains of Colorado and Kansas could be served by subterranean water and that the return from one year's crops would pay the cost of installing the pumps ten times over.[8] One enthusiast writing in 1904 promised that a windmill which cost one hundred fifty to two hundred dollars could provide sufficient water to irrigate as much as twenty acres, and that a diversified twenty-five-acre farm which raised strawberries, melons, sugar beets, onions, and cabbages would return as much as two thousand dollars a year.[9]

The search for cheap water also led to rain-making experiments, many prompted by the then common belief that explosives detonated during intense military battles often produced precipitation. On the evening of November 25, 1892, at a site in Texas, gigantic balloons filled with hydrogen and oxygen were exploded in the atmosphere, while four thousand pounds of gunpowder and one hundred fifty artillery shells were detonated on the ground. This display produced some clouds, according to the *Irrigation Age*, so another balloon was sent aloft and blown up in a huge cloud at about six thousand feet. The magazine reported that a drenching rain followed the blast, which after a few minutes gave way to a "slow drizzle" that kept up until five the following morning. Such experiments failed to impress the secretary of agriculture. "I have every reason to believe that, so far as the production of explosives is concerned, these experiments were eminently successful," he drolly concluded in his 1891 report. "As regards the object thereof, the production of rain, I have no data yet at hand which would justify me in expressing any conclusions on the subject."[10]

By far the most practical alternative to irrigation was dry farming, developed by Hardy Campbell during the Great Plains drought of the early 1890s. Campbell published his first pamphlet on this "new" agricultural method in 1893. Subsequently, with the support of the railroads, he conducted experiments in North and South Dakota, Nebraska, Kansas, and Colorado, which were publicized in his journal, *The Western Soil Culture.* He argued that moisture moved by capillary action from one soil particle to the next, much as kerosene soaked a lamp wick, and that mulching sharply reduced evaporation from cultivated land. Campbell's ideas were not entirely consistent, but his method generally included plowing land to a depth of about eighteen to twenty inches; using special moldboard plows, subsurface packers, and harrows; cultivating after every rain and spreading layers of dust to trap moisture; compacting the subsoil; "thin seeding" to produce smaller crops than those grown on the same size farm in the humid part of the country; and planting drought-resistant plants, such as alfalfa, clovers, beans, peas, Sudan grasses, and hearty strains of wheat—including Russian varieties adapted to cold weather—in place of corn, which had been the chief crop on the Great Plains before the drought.[11]

Dry farming preached the recognition of natural limits; irrigation emphasized the unlimited potential of western agriculture. The West's first travelers assumed that most of the region's land was sterile; the absence of trees, the parched grasslands of the late spring and summer, and the vast expanses of desert reinforced that impression. But the enormous productivity of California's wheat farms in the late 1850s and 1860s dispelled that impression, and by the 1870s, boosters bragged about the *superiority* of western soils. "In the humid regions, where there is greater precipitation," *The Forester* editorialized in 1899, "the soils have been leached of their soluble salts by the washings and percolations of ages of rainfall, and now lack fertility because of the loss of these elements which have been swept to the sea."[12] The West was different. The soils of Minnesota and Dakota's Red River Valley had produced as many as twenty-five crops of hard spring wheat in succession, and fields around Walla Walla, Washington, remained fertile after fifty years of cultivation. In California and many other parts of the West, the same farms had yielded abundant alfalfa crops for twenty-five consecutive seasons. Western farmers, boosters promised, could recover much of the cost of irrigation because they did not have to fallow land or apply fertilizers, as farmers did elsewhere. William Ellsworth Smythe asserted in 1900 that "the average arid soil is equal to the phenomenal soil of the East, while the soil of the arid West as a whole is beyond comparison with that of the humid East as a whole."[13]

"Water poured upon a rainless desert makes it blossom under the tropic sun as if some magician's wand had been waved over it," a writer in *Popular Science Monthly* observed in 1893.[14] In an age when prophesy often passed for science, this became an almost self-evident proposition, even though it was based on limited observations. Irrigation promoters assumed that water contained its own nutrients and liberated fertilizers already present in the land. They argued that water carried beneficial substances in suspension and solution, ranging from silt and decayed vegetation to carbolic acid and ammonia. Water also softened clay-choked soils and served as the medium by which *their* fertilizers reached plant roots. Irrigation had many other therapeutic values. It warmed the soil and kept it from freezing; it killed insect eggs and larvae; it drowned or at least discouraged burrowing pests that fed on crops; and it washed out dangerous substances, such as alkali and salts.[15]

In an age enamored with harnessing nature and achieving mastery over the earth, irrigation was an important part of "scientific agriculture." When the International Irrigation Congress assembled at Los Angeles in October 1893, the delegates gathered under a banner that read, "Irrigation: Science, Not Chance." In the arid and semi-arid regions, nature provided the perfect setting for agriculture. The sun shined far more often there than in humid sections, and crops matured more rapidly. Besides, rainfall was always uncertain, even in the wettest parts of the country, and in the East heavy storms were no less to be feared than long spells of dry weather. Irrigation turned a liability into an asset. "There is something fascinating in the idea of every man being his own rain-maker and being independent of shifting clouds and uncertain winds," a pamphlet issued by Colorado's Platte Land Company gushed in the early 1880s. "Irrigation in Colorado gives a security to the farmer, and a control over the results of his labor that nowhere else can be found in any State, east, north or south."[16] "Never a season goes by that he [the eastern farmer] does not hope and pray for rain at some time to save some partially matured crop, or fidget and stew about in impatience and fear lest his crop already made should be ruined before it can be harvested and cured," editorialized *Irrigation Age.*[17] Aridity made the West a perfect laboratory; water could be applied at precisely the proper times in precisely the proper quantities to *guarantee* the largest crops. Because the West also contained fewer insects and plant diseases, irrigated farms were akin to factories, with man in full control of the production schedule. In most parts of the West, wheat could be planted in November or December and harvested in April; then corn could be planted in April or May and harvested in August; then potatoes could fill the interval from August to November.

The ultimate value of science was to increase man's power over nature, and irrigation might even permanently transform the West's climate. Many nineteenth-century Americans believed that a humid, well-forested environment was nature's norm (deserts were an anomaly), and that human actions had a profound, if not determining, effect on the weather.[18] The Great American Desert was no different from the Sahara and other wastelands once heavily wooded, and irrigation could help nature return to normal. "A system of general irrigation in California," argued the Chicago *Tribune* in 1880, "would greatly increase the supplies of water by reason of the evaporation that would rise from the watered earth, which, borne by the winds against the lofty Sierra Mountain wall, would condense into rain and run down again in torrents to the rivers, and be spread by means of the canals. . . . The Mormons assert that the rainfall of their valley has doubled since irrigation has been adopted. The same effect on a vastly greater scale would unquestionably follow general irrigation in California."[19] The Union Pacific Railway's land commissioner promised Great Plains farmers that watering 10 in every 160 acres would cause drought and the severe storms that damaged crops to give way to frequent but gentle rains.[20] "It is a reasonable supposition," the commissioner of agriculture observed in 1887, "that ultimately some portion of the area now useless without irrigation may be productive with only the usual rainfall, which has proved insufficient heretofore."[21]

These arguments encountered considerable skepticism, but few boosters or promoters questioned irrigation's ability to augment crop yields and values. In the 1860s, the promised benefits were often modest, usually an increase of one fourth or one third. But by the 1880s many enthusiasts abandoned all caution. None was more optimistic than Richard J. Hinton, who headed the irrigation office in the USDA. "The evidence taken everywhere," Hinton declared, "shows that the production of grain can be doubled by means of irrigation within the arid region over equal areas within humid States; that the production of root crops and garden vegetables can be increased from five to ten fold over the same crops elsewhere, and that in the production of special products . . . the sections possessing constant sunshine, and soils laden with mineral elements, will have through irrigation an advantage and security no other region on the continent can possess."[22] John Wesley Powell, head of the USGS, made similar claims.[23] And a speaker at the 1906 National Irrigation Congress observed: "The average yield of wheat per acre in the United States for the past 10 years has been 13.4 bushels and under irrigation we can raise 40 to 60 bushels per acre; of oats 29.1, and we can raise 100 to 125; of barley 25, and we can raise 75 to 100; of corn 24.9, and we can raise 75 to 100 bushels."[24]

These wildly inflated production figures provided ammunition to a legion of westerners who argued for the agricultural superiority of their region over the rest of the nation. Some irrigated crops grew only in the West, or grew far better in the West; for example, in 1900 California's farms produced about twice the U.S. average dollar value in crops per acre. Stories of fabulous agricultural wealth tumbled from presses in an unending stream. During the first phase of southern California's horticultural development, one writer promised that a farmer's first crop of oranges would meet expenses, the second return a profit, and the third pay back the entire cost of the land, "allowing that nothing has been realized in the meantime from the space between the rows." Orange trees fifteen years old would net citrus tycoons from twenty to twenty-five dollars per tree, or from one to two thousand dollars per acre. An investment of twenty-five thousand dollars would double within five years and yield an annual income of seventy thousand dollars thereafter.[25] Nor were such returns restricted to California. In 1901, William Turner of Wenatchee, Washington, planted eighteen acres of apples. He sowed another fourteen acres the following year. To tide himself over until the trees started to bear, he grew strawberries in the rows between the trees. By 1907, his irrigated orchard generated an income of $585 an acre, and in the same part of the state farmers received as much as $2,500 an acre from seven- and eight-year-old trees. Such spectacular profits were very tempting.[26]

Those profits helped fuel the market for undeveloped land. The census of 1890 revealed that while the price of irrigated farms increased by 283 percent during the 1880s, the initial cost of providing water ran only $8.15 an acre compared to a per-acre crop value of $14.89. Moreover, the price of water rights, where separable from the land, averaged twenty-six dollars an acre, over three times the original cost of irrigation works.[27] No business venture offered greater returns to the prescient investor than speculation in land under ditch. Timothy Paige, a San Joaquin Valley developer, purchased between eight and nine thousand unimproved acres near Modesto in the early 1870s. Although he paid only sixty cents an acre, local residents warned that the land would never even pay his taxes. Little more than a decade later, after water became available, he sold fifteen hundred acres for $86.66 an acre. In the 1870s, the land on which Pasadena, California, now stands sold for about seven dollars an acre. Within a decade, it returned from five hundred to one thousand dollars an acre—as orchards, not town lots. In 1891, farmers at Greeley, Colorado, reported price increases ranging from 74 percent (for a farmer who had bought his land two years earlier) to 900 percent for some old-timers. In Yakima County, Washington, five thousand new irrigated farms were established from 1890 to 1910. The total value of agricultural products rose from $319,810 to $4,734,144, and the county's farmland increased in value from about $1,500,000 to $40,617,000. Irrigation played a large part in the creation of this wealth. In 1898, the former state engineer of Colorado estimated that land in his state worth $5 million before the construction of irrigation works was worth $60 million in 1898, an increase in value of more than 90 percent.[28]

As the foremost state in the number of acres irrigated (except in the 1890s when it briefly lost its lead to Colorado), California served as a bellwether. During the 1880s, the state's population increased about 39 percent. However, the population south of the Tehachapi Mountains, where irrigation was practiced extensively, more than tripled. In the major irrigation counties, taxable wealth increased by 340 percent as opposed to 50 percent in the eight foothill counties, where irrigation was limited.[29]

The benefits of irrigation were not limited to immediate profits. Boosters believed it would be a strong tonic to the entire western economy.[30] On the one hand, they touted irrigation as a way to restore a "natural balance" between agriculture, industry, and commerce, a method to make the West more like the East. Since many western cities, such as San Francisco and Denver, predated large-scale farming, and since many of the early residents were miners and ranchers, rather than farmers, the West's development seemed "out of order." Only agriculture could provide the foundation for a stable, diversified economy. On the other hand, by the 1880s and 1890s, after the most accessible mineral wealth had been exhausted, mining and agriculture began to appear complementary. Boosters believed the region contained an unlimited supply of low-grade ores. Traditionally, mining communities imported food from great distances, but irrigation would permit a wide variety of crops to be raised near the mines. By providing cheap forage, it might also lower the price of meat and allow mineowners to cut wages. Since mining profits had declined dramatically since the 1850s, a reduction in the cost of living could make the difference between success, or at least the industry's survival, and failure.[31]

Colonization

The main alternative to haphazard private land development was the irrigation colony, which built on communitarian impulses inherited from the Jacksonian period. The colonies extolled the moral welfare of the individual, emphasizing self-sufficiency and independence over personal gain. Most were promoted by idealists who shared Jefferson's faith that the moral strength of the yeoman farmer depended on freedom from tyranny of the market, and that limiting trade and commerce would prevent the emergence of sharply defined, rigid social classes.[32]

The irrigation colony had many advantages over settlement by individuals and families. It offered a method to pool money and talent and to cut out middlemen. The colonies bought land more cheaply because they purchased it in large unimproved tracts. In addition, they supplied coordinated management. Sponsors of colonies usually made some attempt to prepare land for settlement, though seldom more than clearing and grading. (Only rarely did they fence or seed farms, or construct barns, houses, roads, dairies, processing plants, or public buildings.) Moreover, the irrigation colony could resort to an element of coercion not available to communitarian experiments in the East: At least in theory, those who refused to cooperate faced a cutoff of their water, a severe penalty.

Nevertheless, colonies also faced some obvious problems. Most proponents of group settlement knew little about desert agriculture. Utopian ideals were no preparation to survey canal lines or find markets for agricultural products. Promoters of colonies also discovered that all too often those unhappy in their old homes were even more so in their new ones. Almost every colonial venture included a vocal minority of malcontents who would have had trouble fitting into any group. Finally, the colonies rested on the questionable assumption that farming was not merely a desirable way of life but also an occupation capable of supporting a family under the right circumstances. The promoters assumed that organization, cooperation, and efficiency could prevent or mitigate the financial problems faced by marginal farmers in the Midwest, East, or South.

The colonizers found a model in Utah. Spanish and Mexican settlers in the Southwest watered thousands of acres long before 1847, but the Mormons were the first English-speaking settlers to irrigate on a large scale. As early as 1850, Utah had ten to twenty thousand acres under irrigation, and that number swelled to one hundred fifty thousand acres by 1865, when about sixty-five thousand people lived on the reclaimed land. The vast majority of these farms, unlike those in California, were irrigated.[33] The Mormons demonstrated that irrigation could produce a society very different from that in the Midwest, where scattered families lived on quarter or half sections, widely separated from their neighbors. Salt Lake City's settlers surrounded the town with five- and ten-acre farms. Each received a town lot, chosen at random, along with a farm. The same pattern was repeated in other Mormon communities. To prevent land monopoly, the church forbade farms larger than twenty acres, and it also prohibited any farmer from owning more than one lot. "Village property rights were allocated and regulated under ecclesiastical leadership in accordance with certain specified principles which were thought to represent best the interests and welfare of the group as a whole," Leonard Arrington has observed. "This was made easier by the fact that [during the late 1840s and early 1850s] Congress had not yet passed laws under which the land in Utah could be privately owned." Unlike other parts of the West, particularly California, the first settlers in Utah had no advantage over latecomers, and church officials settled disputes over both land and water outside of court.[34]

The Mormon church planned irrigation systems for entire communities; settlers received shares in ditch companies according to the amount of labor they contributed toward construction and the number of acres they irrigated. (Utah residents were the first to experiment with joint-stock water companies—later called "mutual" companies—

which settlers owned and operated themselves.) If a proposed community contained one thousand acres of irrigable land that cost five dollars an acre to reclaim, the church, under the direct supervision of county courts, formed a water company to issue one thousand shares of stock with a value of five dollars a share. The stock could be bought with money or labor, and each share entitled the holder to a certain quantity of water and a proportional influence on company policies. The church also took shares for the money and materials it contributed. These were often distributed to later settlers so that their rights would be equal to those who built the ditches. Shares did not always attach to particular parcels of land, but the water rights they represented could not be sold or transferred outside the service area.[35]

Mexican-Americans established Colorado's first agricultural outposts during the 1850s. However, that state's colony boom did not occur until 1869–73, when communities were established at Longmont, Evans, Platteville, Green City, Sterling, Fort Collins, Manassa, and Ephraim. The history of the Greeley Colony, Colorado's most famous social experiment, is well known.[36] An offshoot of the Fourierist adventures of the 1840s, which included Brook Farm near Boston, the Union (later Greeley) Colony was the brainchild of Nathan Cook Meeker and Horace Greeley. In 1869, Meeker, who had lived in a Fourier phalanx at Trumbull, Ohio, in the mid-1840s, was agricultural editor of Greeley's New York *Tribune*. The two men pondered the failure of the Fourier communities and decided that such experiments could succeed only if they respected the sanctity of the nuclear family and private property. During the winter of 1869, Meeker cancelled a planned visit to Utah because of a fierce snowstorm. Instead, he toured Colorado territory and decided to plant a colony at the delta of the South Platte and Cache la Poudre rivers, about fifty miles north of Denver, not far south of the Union Pacific line then being built into Cheyenne. Denver and nearby mining camps were expected to provide ready agricultural markets.

Following Meeker's return to New York, the *Tribune* published a prospectus on December 14, 1869. Meeker and Greeley grappled with the problem all such communities encountered: how to gain the benefits of cooperation and group cohesion without sapping individual initiative. A committee selected about twelve thousand acres of private land in the Cache la Poudre Valley, most of which belonged to the Denver Pacific, and laid out the colony using the town plats of North Hampton, Massachusetts, and Painesville, Ohio. The townsite was surveyed in the spring of 1870, and the first fifty families—headed mainly by farmers, but including a substantial number of tradesmen and professionals—arrived in May on the new Union Pacific and Denver Pacific railroads. Each family was expected to live on a one-and-one-quarter-acre town lot adjoining farms ranging in size from five to eighty acres. To curb speculation, no resident was permitted to purchase more than 160 acres. Town lots were expected to soar in value, and the proceeds were set aside to pay for a church, meeting hall, school, public library, and other cooperative institutions. In effect, Meeker and his followers wanted to capture the "unearned increment" for the community and keep it out of the pockets of speculators. Members paid an average of three hundred dollars for town lots and an additional five dollars an acre for farms. By the end of spring, Greeley contained three general stores; two bakeries; two meat markets; a hotel and boardinghouse; a blind, sash, and paint shop; a bank; a post office; a telegraph station; and even an artists' studio.

Nevertheless, the colony did not prosper. Its secretary estimated the cost of canals needed to water one hundred twenty thousand acres at twenty thousand dollars, but the first ditch—which served less than three thousand acres—cost over fifty thousand dollars. Ultimately, the colonists spent more than four hundred thousand dollars on their irrigation system, and Greeley Colony water rights increased in value ten times from 1871 to 1882. The miscalculation came not from duplicity and deceit, as many colonists suspected, but from ignorance. Neither Meeker nor Greeley knew anything about irrigation.[37]

Not only did the cost of the ditch system absorb most of the revenue from town lot sales—money that might have been used to finance cooperative schemes including feed and hardware stores, banks, and sugar beet factories—but the company compounded its problems by selling too many water rights, which resulted in extensive litigation. Moreover, the exotic, high-profit tropical fruits the colonists expected to raise would not grow in the Cache la Poudre country, so settlers turned to the lowly potato as their principal cash crop. The colony foundered as much on the perversity of human nature as on immediate economic problems. For example, the colony's vice president wrote to Meeker in 1871 complaining about "sore heads and malcontents." "Some growl that we are so far from the mountains. Some think that the grass is too short, some that we cannot give [them] a quarter of a section next to the town. . . . Some complain that no lumber yards or lumber mills are provided, and some think the surveying is not done [fast enough] and the land [made] ready for occupation. Some are ready to return [home]."[38] The Greeley Colony survived and eventually prospered, but irrigation proved more expensive and less profitable than originally anticipated. As an experiment in social planning, the colony failed.

Many irrigation colonies were launched in California during the 1870s, most around Fresno or in southern California (Riverside, Redlands, Lompoc, and Pasadena, among the most notable). In each case small farms were created, and many of those farms raised high-value crops. Like Greeley, Riverside and Lompoc were originally temperance colonies, and some of the southern California communities pioneered in cooperative marketing. Most shared the objectives of Meeker and Greeley: organized rather than individual settlement; a community fund derived from land sales to finance public projects; prior planning to determine what crops could be raised and where they could be sold; cooperative institutions to reduce the cost of farming and make the communities relatively self-sufficient; shared values, such as temperance; and a planned social life to satisfy the instinct for human contact as well as to attract a well-educated, middle-class population.[39]

The depression of the 1890s gave new urgency to the formation of irrigation colonies. In the winter of 1894–95, William Ellsworth Smythe organized mass meetings in Boston and Chicago to enlist settlers and financial supporters for a five-thousand-acre colony in Idaho's Payette Valley, where an irrigation system constructed by a private company had gone bankrupt. Smythe launched "New Plymouth" in large part to show that irrigation agriculture could render communities immune to unpredictable business cycles. "There is an industrial system in Arid America which enables every family to obtain a generous living, regardless of panics, drouth, and political misfortunes," he promised, "and [it] guarantees this living for an indefinite period." Colonists were expected to produce what they consumed, thus realizing what Smythe called "industrial independence."[40] The *New York Times* reported: "Should the colony be a success, it is believed that there will be a heavy movement of population to the arid regions."[41]

Smythe recruited several dozen families. Most were from Chicago, drawn from "urban business and professional life." Each was required to hold at least a thousand dollars; there were to be no poor at New Plymouth. The land sold for thirty dollars an acre with an additional ten-dollar-per-acre assessment to pay for public works. Smythe originally intended to use the improvement fund to build a school and public library, cooperative creamery, cannery, slaughterhouse, fruit-processing plant, and other industries. As at Greeley, the New England village served as a model. The 5,000-acre tract included 320 acres for the town and a park 1 mile long and 240 feet wide. Everyone who bought a twenty-acre farm received a one-acre town lot free, and Smythe designed the community so that no farm would be farther than three miles from the center of the village. Unfortunately, the depression doomed Smythe's social experiment. When the anticipated migration from eastern cities did not materialize, there was little money to pay for public works. Moreover, the handful of colonists turned their backs on Smythe's social plan; most preferred to live on their farms, rather than in the village.[42]

The last great nineteenth-century colonization scheme was launched in 1898 by the Salvation Army. Officials in the army worried about the plight of the "worthy poor," who, through no fault of their own, suffered greatly during the depression. The head of the army, Commander Frederick Booth-Tucker, estimated that the $50 million to $100 million expended on poor relief in eastern cities could be better spent moving the poor onto irrigated farms. He, along with many other Americans of the 1890s, considered city life unnatural, debilitating, and corrupting. Irrigation agriculture promised a happy alternative. Colonization complemented irrigation because both required cooperation, reinforced the family farm ideal, increased the home market for the productions of eastern factories, and made good citizens.[43] Irrigation offered maximum returns with minimum risks. Army officials anticipated that the appreciation of land "under ditch" would pay for the colonies and turn a profit that would subsidize other charitable ventures as well. "An experience of nearly five years has shown that few outlets for capital are known [to be] so absolutely free from risk as colonization schemes of this kind," Booth-Tucker naively noted, "provided, of course, the enterprise be honestly and sensibly managed."[44]

The army established three colonies in 1898, two of them based on irrigation. Both recruited destitute families rather than individuals. Single men were more likely to drift away, and wives and children provided a source of labor that reduced the cost of family farming.[45] One colony was at Fort Amity, in the Arkansas River Valley of Colorado 267 miles east of Denver.[46] This community included over eighteen hundred acres adjoining the Santa Fe line and, according to Booth-Tucker, had "an almost unlimited opportunity for expansion." The three hundred settlers raised cantaloupes, sugar beets, and alfalfa. The army went much further than other colonizers by establishing an agricultural credit association and other mutual institutions. It provided each family with a house, livestock, and farm equipment, and made small weekly loans to get farmers started. It also established an orphanage in the hope that children brought from the cities would marry among themselves and take up farms once they became adults. A second colony, sponsored by San Francisco's chamber of commerce, was established at Fort Romie, near Soledad in California's Salinas Valley.[47] A benefactor sold 288 acres to the army, and eighteen "indigent" families were chosen from the San Francisco Bay area as the first residents. Again, the army provided cottages and prepared the land. Settlers raised potatoes, sugar beets, and alfalfa on ten-acre plots.[48]

Initially, the army's efforts received widespread support. Applications poured in from poor families, including one thousand from New York City and five thousand from Chicago. The governors of New York, Colorado, and Michigan—along with the mayors of Boston, Denver, and San Francisco—endorsed the colonization of poor urban families. (So convinced were these leaders that agriculture could transform society that the Salvation Army considered adopting a program hatched by a former mayor of Detroit, Hazen S. "Potato Patch" Pingree, to provide the poor with vacant downtown lots as sites for tiny farms.) But the three colonies established in 1898 were expensive. The cost of relocating each family—apart from the heavy investment in land, irrigation works, and buildings—was five hundred dollars. This money came from a bond issue of one hundred fifty thousand dollars and also from private donations. The transplanted poor were required to pay back the cost of land, livestock, and other expenses. They received wages of two dollars a day to build fences and perform other chores until the first crops were harvested.

Fort Amity and Fort Romie provided many success stories, such as that of the man who arrived at Amity in March 1899 with little more than household furniture and who four years later owned twenty acres of land and a neat stone cottage, having paid off his nine-hundred-dollar debt to the army in three years. But, as in every other colony scheme, individuals succeeded while the community languished. At the Amity colony the original population of 60 quickly swelled to 450, but the orphanage failed. In 1905, the orphans were returned to New Jersey, and the orphanage became a tuberculosis sanatorium. Moreover, frost and later hail destroyed the cantaloupe crop, and the Arkansas River flooded and waterlogged the land, bringing dangerous salts to the surface. In 1907 or 1908, a real estate developer bought out the army and the colony was abandoned. The Fort Romie colony was ruined by the California drought of the late 1890s, although the army sold the land for a hundred dollars an acre and ultimately turned a twelve-thousand-dollar net profit. The colonists themselves took over the water system in 1903. A historian of the Salvation Army has concluded that the colonies failed because "successful farming required skill and experience that the unemployed urban poor, worthy or not, did not possess."[49]

Commander Booth-Tucker hoped that his colonies would encourage the federal government to emulate New Zealand's elaborate colonization program, and Senator Mark Hanna of Ohio prepared a bill modeled on Booth-Tucker's suggestions. The legislation, introduced by Senator George F. Hoar after Hanna's death in 1904, called for the formation of a colonization bureau under the secretary of the interior to collect and distribute information regarding lands suitable for colonization; provide loans, building materials, and livestock; and grant each settler forty to eighty acres from the public domain. The national government would issue sixty-year bonds bearing 3 percent interest to raise the money. The legislation limited the total bond issue to $50 million, at a rate of no more than $5 million per year. Booth-Tucker assumed that this appropriation would permit the Salvation Army to settle 5 million poor on 25 million acres. The bill, however, clashed with the Reclamation Act of 1902 and died in the Public Lands Committee.[50] Subsequently, the army turned its attention to colonizing land in Canada, in the hope the British government might be willing to provide government aid to resettle the urban poor in that country. But neither the British nor the Canadian governments showed much interest. Between 1898 and 1904, the army moved a total of 530 people onto about three thousand acres at a cost of three hundred thousand dollars, and some of that number were former employees of the army, not urban poor. (For example, five of the twenty-eight colonists at Fort Romie were former Salvation Army officers who had suffered from "mental exhaustion" or bad health.) Even though a benefactor offered seventy thousand acres free as the site for additional settlements, the army fell far short of raising the seven hundred fifty thousand dollars needed to colonize that land. Colonization was beyond the means of private charities and philanthropic organizations.[51]

Colonization was too expensive, too paternalistic, and too regimented for the taste of most Americans. Moreover, it clashed with social Darwinism. A prominent official of the Southern Pacific Railroad, a strong friend of irrigation, attacked the idea of using reclamation to rid American cities of "social misfits," those, in his words, "incompetent to keep pace with their fellows in the race of life." He argued that concentrating the poor would produce an "incompetent community" and undermine social stability. If the Salvation Army's objective was simply to take people who were industrious and physically fit and give them greater opportunity, "it would be far better to leave such industrious and competent people associated with the successful life surrounding them. Such people do not need colonization."[52]

The irrigation colonies, a minor chapter in the history of communitarian experiments, were clearly a reaction to the complicated urban-industrial society that grew up in the last decades of the nineteenth century, and to the chronic social and economic problems created by the depression of the 1890s. But they had little influence on the irrigation crusade or on the law and economy of the American West, and they explain little about the values held by the mass of westerners. The direct impact of irrigation on the economy of the West is better reflected in the history of those private companies that regarded irrigation primarily as a business.

The Corporation

In 1860, in the western half of the nation, "extensive" farming was practiced only in Kansas, Texas, and California; the rest of the region included only about 7 million improved acres.[53] At that time, and for decades to come, many irrigators paid only a few dollars an acre to capture water and convey it to their land. The irrigated tracts adjoined streams and required only short canals and cheap diversion works; tablelands were largely ignored. Generally, the land was flood irrigated, a technique that did not require extensive grading or leveling. In the late 1880s, the average cost per acre to water virgin land ran $2.66 in Idaho and $4 in Utah.[54] And as late as 1919, 58 percent of Colorado's land was irrigated by over eight thousand ditches with an average length of 1.6 miles, and 60 percent of Wyoming's land was served by nearly forty-eight hundred ditches of roughly the same average length. The first farmers or ranchers wasted water and resisted replacing the dozens of tiny canals they had constructed with larger, more durable and efficient ditches. That lack of civic responsibility became one of the West's major sources of litigation.[55]

A second generation of ditches began to appear as railroads spread across the West and the federal government liberalized land laws. "As Henry Villard's construction crews approached," one historian of the Pacific Northwest has written, "farmers moved ahead of them into the Palouse country and the Columbia Basin, transforming a wide swath of bunch grass and plateau lands on either side of the right of way from cattle country into a highly productive wheat section."[56] The same thing happened in the San Joaquin Valley during the 1870s. The railroad companies identified and classified the best farmland, transported settlers and heavy agricultural equipment, planned cities, opened new markets, spurred investments and altered the economic environment in countless other ways. No matter how artful the promoter, irrigation projects could not succeed in regions far removed from rail lines. Proximity to transportation was more important than the quality of soil, the abundance of water, or even the nature of state and territorial water laws.

On rare occasions, railroads undertook irrigation projects on their own, as in the Yakima Valley. Construction of the Northern Pacific line at the end of the 1880s contributed to the formation of many private irrigation companies. The railroad sold unimproved land for about four dollars an acre, which fetched forty to fifty dollars an acre when irrigated. The cost of irrigation averaged about ten dollars an acre. In 1889 and 1890, the railroad's land department formed the Northern Pacific, Yakima and Kittitas Irrigation Company (later the Washington Irrigation Company). Railroad officials intended to water the entire Yakima Valley by building a canal in Kittitas County, two canals in Yakima County, and an extensive system of natural and artificial reservoirs at the headwaters of the Yakima River in the Cascades. They expected the largest ditch, the Sunnyside Canal, to traverse the entire valley, connecting the headwaters of the Yakima with the Columbia River. Construction began in 1891, and by the spring of the following year forty-two miles of aqueduct had been completed, covering about fifteen thousand acres. The main ditch was designed to serve eighty-five thousand acres. The railroad sold the land under ditch at from thirty to sixty dollars an acre, with one share of stock attached to each ten acres of land. Once it had sold the land, it planned to transfer control over the ditch to the farmers, who would then set their own water rates. However, the depression of 1893 cut off the flow of potential settlers, the canal was idle for most of the 1890s, and in the first decade of the twentieth century it was absorbed into the federal government's Yakima Project. The railroad had spent over $1 million on the irrigation system as of 1902; it was the largest water project in the Pacific Northwest.[57]

The Yakima project was unusual. Railroad leaders encouraged irrigation, but they were reluctant to own and operate their own water works. Many railroads held land in the humid Midwest as well as the arid West and feared that irrigating western lands would hurt land sales farther east. Then, too, national land laws prevented railroads from securing the unbroken tracts needed for comprehensive water projects, and many railroad directors refused to commit capital to ventures not directly related to transportation, especially during hard times. Land sales declined during depressions, and farmers who bought railroad land on credit often defaulted on their debt. How much more likely that farmers would renege if the railroads built canals and reservoirs and tacked the added expense onto land prices. Railroad officials also worried that if they took control of a region's land, water, and transportation, they would face even more strident antimonopoly sentiment. In any case, agricultural development was a mixed blessing. It drove up railroad taxes, threatened to reduce freight revenues from the livestock industry—because stockmen might move their herds elsewhere to avoid competition with farmers—and sometimes disrupted delicate factional balances in state legislatures. Most of all, railroad leaders recognized that water projects rarely made either money or friends. As Collis P. Huntington of the Southern Pacific wrote to Leland Stanford on June 1, 1874, "I think the ditch has yet to be built in California that paid 10% on all that it cost to build." He looked for surer, less controversial investments.[58]

Aside from the railroad, the most important spur to investment in land and ditch companies was the federal government. When Congress on July 26, 1866, formally recognized water rights established under local custom and procedure, it also authorized private ditch companies to carry water across government land, removing an important obstacle to investment. But by the middle 1870s, as more and more settlers swarmed onto the Great Plains, as the range cattle industry emerged as a major new enterprise, and as the depression of the 1870s deepened, calls came from many quarters to amend federal land laws to meet conditions in the arid West.[59] The commissioner of the General Land Office noted in 1875 that the Homestead Act had affirmed the principle, which was only implicit in the land laws adopted before the Civil War, that the greatest "profit to the Treasury and to the people at large was not to be found in largest measure in the consideration paid [for land], but rather in the productive forces which settlement and cultivation would necessarily bring into play." The reclamation of bench or mesa lands would involve much longer canals and ditches, he noted, but neither the Homestead nor the Preemption acts gave any security to potential investors. Consequently, the commissioner recommended that the bench lands should be sold at auction, and those not taken dumped on the market at $1.25 per acre:

> Persons desiring to acquire title ought to be relieved from the necessity of making questionable affadavits [lying] requisite under the homestead and pre-emption laws. Every hinderance to the fullest possible production in this region ought to be removed. The mining industry of the mountains, though in its infancy, demands of food products a large share of all that are raised within the contiguous country. Referring again to the particular matter of the pasture lands, the policy of such sale may be urged as necessary to the good order of the communities where the business is generally prosecuted, as well as on the ground of justice to the class engaged in the pasturage calling. The present policy compels them to use the public lands as their feeding ground, having no better right to their selected range as against another whose purposes or seeming convenience may lead to an attempted occupation of the same ground than they may be able to assert by forcible means. Conflicts and uncertainties necessarily follow upon this state of things, to the detriment alike of order and development.

While the commissioner acknowledged that a leasing system might also work, that was not "in consonance with the established methods of our land-system." Americans preferred rapid disposal of lands to actual settlers.[60]

Congress rejected the commissioner's proposal. In his annual message at the end of 1876, however, President Ulysses S. Grant noted that a recent visit to Wyoming, Utah, and Colorado had convinced him that the national land laws were "very defective" and that "land must be held in larger quantities to justify the expense of conducting water upon it to make it fruitful or to justify utilizing it as pasturage."[61] He urged Congress to appoint a special committee to reform the laws. Instead, the lawmakers dusted off a piece of legislation enacted in 1875, which pertained exclusively to Lassen County, California, and extended it to much of the arid West.[62]

There are many reasons why the Desert Land Act of 1877—which permitted individuals and companies to claim as much as 640 acres of arid land for $1.25 an acre—sailed through Congress with so little debate. The rush of settlers into Nebraska, Kansas, and Dakota in the middle and late 1870s helped undermine the persistent myths and distortions about the Great American Desert (or at least replaced one set of myths with another).[63] The Black Hills gold rush and the military campaigns of Custer, Crook, and Miles kept arid America in the news. Moreover, the depression of the 1870s rendered Congress more sympathetic to using the public domain as a "safety valve," just as the depression of 1893 paved the way for adoption of the Carey Act.[64]

Whatever its origins, the Desert Land Act had enormous significance.[65] Serious flaws were obvious from the beginning. No one in Washington knew how much "desert" land the West contained, or how much was close enough to water to be reclaimed.[66] A spread of 640 acres was too much land for one farmer to irrigate but not enough for a ditch company, unless it used fraud to acquire multiple sections. Moreover, Congress did not provide the General Land Office with the staff necessary to ensure that claimants complied with the act, and the new law allowed speculators to sell all or part of their holdings before obtaining final patents. Cattlemen often enclosed the land as pasture until the three-year "prove-up" period had elapsed. They refused to dig ditches and forfeited their claims. But since the legal eviction process often took a decade or more to complete, in the meantime they enjoyed the exclusive use of prime grazing land at little or no expense.[67]

Ditch companies, too, exploited weaknesses in the Desert Land Act. Their abuses were daring and even comical: "ditches" scratched a few inches into the soil to demonstrate "compliance" with the law; canals that began and ended miles from water; and cowboys herded to land offices to file on desert lands with the clear understanding that they would assign the claim to a stock, water, land, or bogus "improvement" company. For example, Wyoming's Union Cattle Company and Goshen Hole Ditching Company were both owned by investment syndicates headed by Thomas and Frank Sturgis. By using dummy entrymen—seven of whom resided in New Jersey, thirty in New York, and eleven in Massachusetts—they gained control of fifty-five parcels of desert land covering 35,200 acres. In southwestern Utah, one cattleman acquired riparian land for twenty miles on both sides of the Bear River and used the water to grow hay for livestock. On many western streams, including the Humboldt in Nevada and the Chugwater in Wyoming, the water supply was entirely monopolized by cattle companies, to the great regret of would-be farmers and rival stockmen.[68]

In 1884, the commissioner of the General Land Office charged that the Desert Land Act benefited stockmen far more than potential irrigators, but that was true only until the mid-1880s. By that time an increasing number of cattlemen recognized the need to produce forage if their industry was to survive, and the speculative profits from irrigated land began to look more appealing than those from livestock. In Wyoming, eleven irrigation companies were incorporated in 1882 and nine in 1883, but that number increased to nineteen in 1884 and thirty-six in 1885.[69] While both the commissioner of the General Land Office and the secretary of the interior argued for repeal of the Desert Land Act, it was very popular in most parts of the West. Despite many weaknesses, it did much to stimulate the formation of private water companies.[70]

Nevertheless, in California, where the corporate boom began in the 1870s, other conditions had as much of an impact on the formation of private water companies as did railroads and federal land policies. By the late 1860s, conditions in California were ripe for both swamp and arid land reclamation. The state's production of precious metals declined from an average $58 million per year during the 1850s, to $34 million a year during the first half of the 1860s, to about $18 million annually during the last half of the decade. That freed up capital for many fledgling industries, including railroad and canal companies. It could not have happened at a better time. The decline in mining coincided with a retrenchment in the San Joaquin Valley cattle industry brought about by overstocking the open range, a drought in the late 1860s, declining livestock prices, and, beginning in 1866, the advent of "no fence laws" which made cattlemen liable for crop damages. The number of miners declined from 83,000 in 1860 to 36,000 in 1870, but the number of farmers increased from 20,800 to 48,000 during the same decade.[71]

During the 1850s, wheat cultivation was largely confined to the valleys surrounding San Francisco Bay, but in the following decade it invaded the Central Valley. The crop expanded from 8,805,411 bushels in 1861, with a value of $9,069,573, to 21,000,000 bushels that returned $21,630,000 in 1868, to 28,380,000 bushels at $28,096,200 in 1874, to the banner year of 1878 in which 41,990,000 bushels sold for $43,249,700. Nevertheless, yields per acre varied dramatically from year to year, according to the vagaries of climate.[72]

During the 1860s, very little land in the Central Valley was irrigated. That changed as the Southern Pacific Railroad opened up the

San Joaquin Valley. Construction began just south of Stockton in 1869 and touched off a frenzy of land speculation. The line reached the Stanislaus River by September 1870, Oakdale in September 1871, Fresno in 1872, Goshen, Tulare, and Delano in 1873, and Bakersfield—at the south end of the valley—by 1874. New towns sprouted up along the line, including Modesto and Turlock. In 1872, the Southern Pacific completed a second line from the Salinas Valley through the Coast Range to Coalinga then on to Goshen, near present-day Visalia, where it intersected the principal north-south route. (The railroad down the west side of the San Joaquin Valley was not begun until 1888.) In 1865, the California Board of Agriculture conservatively estimated that about sixty-five hundred acres were irrigated in the state. The dramatic expansion of wheat cultivation in the valleys surrounding San Francisco Bay and on Central Valley lands near the Sacramento or San Joaquin rivers increased that acreage to as much as ninety to one hundred thousand acres in 1870, and the amount of irrigated land tripled during the 1870s.[73]

Since "unearned increment" was the primary source of profit for private irrigation companies, promoters appealed to Congress and the states for massive land subsidies. They argued that the sparseness of population in California, the lack of transportation, the shortage of investment capital, and local prejudices against irrigation justified such grants. During the 1850s, 1860s, and early 1870s, they pushed special bills rather than comprehensive legislation such as the Desert Land Act. As early as 1857, California granted the Tulare Land and Canal Company swampland to promote the construction of a thirty-four-mile ditch linking Tulare Lake and the San Joaquin River. Patents to nearly ninety thousand acres were approved in the early 1860s, even though the canal was never constructed.[74] In 1859, the state legislature petitioned Congress to grant the entire Colorado Desert (Imperial Valley) to the state so that it in turn could deed the land to a transportation and water company. That scheme was side-tracked by the Civil War.[75] Following the war, California congressman John Bidwell introduced legislation to subsidize a canal through the Sacramento Valley. However, few of the valley's wheat barons favored the scheme; on the average, the valley received more than twenty inches of rain annually, and most farmers there looked on irrigation as an expensive luxury.[76] Meanwhile, Ohio representative James M. Ashley introduced a bill on December 11, 1865, "to develop and reclaim public lands requiring irrigation" in Idaho, Colorado, Arizona, and Montana territories. This was probably intended as a reward to soldiers who had served in the war; the idea apparently originated with William N. Byers, editor of Denver's *Rocky Mountain News* from 1859 to 1878, and one of the West's first irrigation boosters.[77]

Congress ignored the Ashley bill, but in June 1870 the Sacramento *Daily Union* reported that "no less than ten" bills had been introduced in Congress to aid canal construction in California.[78] Following a severe drought in 1871, corporate irrigation in California expanded dramatically in the San Joaquin Valley, particularly in the Kings River basin around Fresno, where the Gould, Fresno, Fowler Switch, Peoples Ditch, Last Chance, Lemoore, and many other canals were constructed from 1870 to 1876.[79]

None of these projects matched the bold dream of John Bensley and William Ralston to reclaim the entire San Joaquin Valley with the largest private irrigation scheme projected in the nineteenth-century West.[80] No scheme better illustrated the problems encountered by private enterprise. Bensley, a San Francisco capitalist, formed the San Joaquin and Kings River Canal Company in March 1866, inspired by fields of irrigated grain and alfalfa he had seen on travels in Chile. Although he failed to attract investors, he began construction in 1868 using his own money.[81] Little was accomplished until the drought of 1871, when one of Bensley's partners in the California Steam Navigation Company, William Ralston, along with several other prominent San Francisco businessmen, joined the irrigation company. Ralston, California's best-known banker and entrepreneur in the early 1870s, was acclaimed for his sense of civic responsibility and admired for his commercial acumen. Writer Bret Harte honored Ralston for "the faith that soars, the deeds that Shine, above the gold that builds the shrine," and economist Henry George praised him as the ideal capitalist. Ashbury Harpending, a business associate, observed that the "most difficult problems of finance were as simple to him as the alphabet and his mind cut through all the perplexities and obstructions straight to the truth . . . he had an odd supplement to the cold boiled faculty of money making, a sort of richly oriental imagination that looked far beyond the mere acquisition of a pile of cash." Ralston's business ventures included silver mines, railroads, real estate, urban water companies, iron foundries, sugar refineries, the Mission Woolen Mills, the Kimball Carriage Factory, the Cornell Watch Factory, the West Coast Furniture Factory, the San Francisco Sugar Refinery, San Francisco's Grand and Palace hotels, and the dry dock at Hunter's Point in San

Francisco.[82] "For a decade . . . Ralston was the most spectacular, and perhaps the most trusted, figure in San Francisco's business and financial life," wrote a California historian. "He lived lavishly, gave generously, speculated on a grand scale, and initiated a dozen constructive enterprises in as many different fields."[83]

The Bensley-Ralston project reached public attention in the spring of 1871, at the same time that construction began in earnest. In the following winter, San Francisco's *Commercial Herald & Market Review* rhapsodized:

> The capital required to carry into effect this important enterprise can scarcely fall short of $26,000,000; but it will be one of the safest, most lucrative, and beneficial investments ever made on this coast. If it should be the means of rendering productive a fractional portion of the uplands now uncultivated, or partially cultivated, and subject to all the casualties of drought, it would enhance the export trade of this State in wheat alone more than $150,000,000 *per annum*. It would also be the means of encouraging the best class of immigration to California, to an extent that could scarcely be equaled, and certainly not surpassed, by any other public measure that could be devised.[84]

Anticipating the Central Valley Project by half a century, Ralston planned to irrigate the entire interior of California by moving water from the Sacramento to the San Joaquin Valley. Each side of the great valley would be served by a major canal, one skirting the eastern edge of the Coast Range and the other following the western flank of the Sierra Nevada. Together the aqueducts would cover about nine hundred miles, not including feeder lines. According to J. Ross Browne, Ralston's close friend and booster, the hydraulic network would irrigate 9,600,000 acres—nearly 10 percent of the state's total land area![85]

Construction began on the San Joaquin Valley aqueduct because that part of the state suffered most from drought, and far more support for irrigation existed there than in the Sacramento Valley. In addition, the best Sacramento Valley land was already in private hands, while large tracts in the San Joaquin remained part of the public domain. The engineer responsible for designing the San Joaquin system, Robert Brereton, estimated that a 160-mile canal from Tulare Lake (midway between present-day Fresno and Bakersfield) to Antioch (on the San Francisco Bay) could serve over 600,000 acres at an average cost of $4.33 an acre, or a total cost of $2,600,000. By charging farmers $1.25 per crop per acre, the company could raise $800,000 per year. That was only the beginning: Brereton calculated that 2,806,000 acres could be irrigated in the San Joaquin Valley, including 1,000,000 acres of marshland. He concluded a report to the company's directors on an optimistic note:

> I trust I have shown clearly enough that the development of an irrigation system in the drought-smitten plains and valleys of California is of the utmost importance and offers a splendid moral and financial reward for the outlay of capital and enterprise here contemplated. It is the only means you have of obtaining a permanent class of settlers. . . . With water, rich soils and heat combined, the productiveness of this country will be so great that the present wandering and never-settled class of cultivators, who are in the San Joaquin valley this year and next year in Oregon . . . will give place to settlers who will delight in making California their permanent abode.

Brereton also warned of several dangers. The project's fate hinged on winning support from the valley's large landowners, most of whom were speculators, and the company had to find inducements to lure farmers into the valley to take up the irrigated land. And if riparian owners insisted on keeping all streams in their natural channels, litigation would kill the project.[86]

While reclamation of the entire valley could proceed at a leisurely pace, the canal from Tulare Lake to Antioch had to be constructed as soon as possible; the success of the entire project hinged on its rapid completion. The promoters decided to begin work on the west side of the San Joaquin Valley where, in typical years, most of the land was incapable of raising crops without irrigation. Equally important, that land was not served by rail transportation. It was held in large blocks, and it sold for much lower prices than tracts on the other side of the valley. Since the western side of the valley was so thinly populated, the company needed a supplemental source of income to carry it through the first lean years. Consequently, the aqueduct was designed to double as a transportation artery. Once crops had been harvested in the spring, and the canal was no longer needed for irrigation, it could float grain-laden barges to San Francisco Bay for transshipment to Liverpool. Transportation tolls would provide a steady source of revenue until the anticipated settlers bought both land and water. Given mounting hostility to the railroad monopoly and Brereton's prediction that barges could carry freight for two dollars a ton—compared to the eight to ten dollars a ton charged by the railroad—the project's draftsmen felt confident that Californians in and out of the valley would welcome the San Joaquin and Kings River Canal and Irrigation Company as a public benefactor.

The first section of canal was constructed over land owned by the Miller & Lux Cattle Company, some of the best and most easily irrigable agricultural land in the valley. (The valley's prime agricultural land belonged to Miller & Lux, William S. Chapman, and Isaac Friedlander.) The company used its employees, tools, and horses to excavate the ditch. Miller had threatened to use his extensive riparian rights to block the project unless the company reached an understanding with him. In exchange for a right-of-way and the lease of 6,000 acres, the irrigation company promised in a contract signed on February 7, 1872, to provide the cattlemen with sufficient water to irrigate 16,667 acres in 1872, 33,334 in 1873, and 50,000 acres in 1874—at the price of $1.25 per acre per crop.[87]

Although Europe was his best potential source of capital, Brereton knew that Europeans would not buy stock without a substantial block of land to serve as collateral. Since the company could not afford to purchase that land from speculators, and since federal land laws offered few incentives to capitalists who wanted to launch irrigation projects, a special grant from the government was indispensable. Most investors had less confidence in the potential revenue from tolls and water sales than in the conviction that irrigated land "under ditch" would quickly advance in value from $2.50 an acre or less to $25 or $30 an acre, as it had near Fresno and in other irrigated communities.[88]

The San Joaquin and Kings River Canal and Irrigation Company first requested a land grant in January 1872.[89] At the time, the company had completed forty miles of ditch. Since much of the proposed grant was classified as "swamp" land, the company promised that its canals would provide flood control as well as cheap irrigation and transportation. The California legislature memorialized Congress to grant the even-numbered sections for five miles on either side of the canal, along with an indemnity strip, noting that it would be "many years before enough water could be sold from the irrigating canals to be constructed to pay a remunerative interest on the investment."[90]

Neither Ralston nor Brereton—nor any other of the company's chief boosters—anticipated the frosty reception their bill received in Congress; it was buried in committee. In 1870, the House of Representatives had adopted a resolution declaring that "the policy of granting subsidies in public lands to railroads and other corporations ought to be discontinued." The last railroad land grant was made on March 3, 1871, to the Texas Pacific, and in 1872 and 1876 both major national parties included planks in their platforms opposing further land subsidies to private businesses. Many westerners claimed that the railroads had been slow to market their lands, and that land subsidies violated the spirit of the Homestead Act—reserving the public domain for actual settlers. Land historians have noted that corporate grants challenged some of America's most cherished values: The Jeffersonian assumption that every man had a natural right to own land; the view that a nation of small farmers constituted the most stable and equitable society; the notion that the West existed as a "safety valve" for urban discontent in the East; the belief that the public lands belonged to all the people; and the faith that the central government existed to promote equal opportunity, not to encourage giant corporations. The San Joaquin and Kings River Canal and Irrigation Company fell victim to the same antimonopoly hysteria that was later directed against the railroads. It was California's first "octopus."[91]

Blocked in Congress, Brereton in 1872 traveled to England in search of capital. Unfortunately, English capitalists, having lost heavily in silver and railroad stocks, were doubly suspicious of gambling on such a novelty as irrigation. Brereton, who tried to peddle the irrigation company's stock at dramatically inflated prices, won the tentative promise of a handful of investors to visit California the following spring, but none was willing to invest in the project sight unseen.[92]

Meanwhile, in California, an unusually wet year in 1872 all but destroyed memories of the drought of 1871 and now, as most of the San Joaquin Valley yielded bumper wheat crops without irrigation, the company appeared superfluous. Only months before, the legislature had urged Congress to approve a land grant; now it debated countless proposals to strike down land monopolies, which many social critics considered the main source of the state's economic problems. Some called for land to bear all costs of government; others demanded constitutional restrictions on the amount of farmland that could be acquired. There were also plans to tax "unearned increment" to discourage speculation, plans to tax uncultivated land at the same rate as improved land, plans for graduated land taxes according to the quantity of land held, and plans to provide tax incentives to large landowners who sold to small farmers.[93] The press bristled with editorials directed against the state's rapacious corporations, which many editors assumed were owned or controlled by a single set of irresponsible plutocrats. As the

Fresno *Weekly Expositor* put it: "We have cursed railroad and steamboat monopolies long enough to have learned a lesson, and we must therefore strive to prevent a water monopoly."[94]

Since 1872 was a wet year, San Joaquin Valley farmers did not learn the extent of that monopoly until the spring of 1873, when the company announced its water rates. In February, the San Joaquin and Kings River Canal and Irrigation Company returned to Congress with another request for land—this time a more modest two sections per mile of canal, or 256,000 acres (the 1872 legislation had requested five sections per mile). The company also asked for an additional hundred acres for every ten miles of canal to pay for reservoirs.[95] To ensure a sufficient supply of water for both transportation and irrigation, the proposed legislation authorized the company to "appropriate and divert" *as much water as necessary* from Tulare, Kern, and other lakes, as well as from the Kings and San Joaquin rivers and tributaries. It also required *all* farmers within reach of the canal to pay a flat fee of $1.50 per acre in two annual installments, as well as one sixteenth the value of their crops for five years, whether they used water from the canal or not, and a perpetual charge of $1 per acre per year. On top of this, the bill authorized the company to charge "the usual" rates for water.[96]

Farmers and other critics bombarded Congress with petitions opposing the bill. Consequently, the company wrote Governor Newton Booth offering to sell the forty-mile stretch of canal already completed from Firebaugh to Los Banos. "Your Excellency has . . . expressed in official documents and otherwise the opinion that such enterprises ought not to be under the control of private corporations, but that all the inland waters of the State ought to be controlled by the State alone for the purpose of irrigation," the company observed. It requested the enactment of a law to condemn "the canal, surveys, water rights and lands, and all the property" of the company and the creation of a legislative commission to determine their value. "If there is any question of doubt about the power of the State to condemn our vested rights and property," the company's letter continued, "we will waive any legal rights we may have in the premises, and deed the same to the State for such sum as your commission may designate."[97] Booth and the legislature ignored the offer.

The company limped along for several more years. In 1874, Brereton put six thousand acres rented from the Miller & Lux Cattle Company under irrigation and took a party of thirty prominent California businessmen and politicians to view the experiment. The group included Governor Leland Stanford, B. B. Redding (chief of the Central Pacific Railroad's Land Department), G. H. Mendell of the Army Corps of Engineers, John S. Hittell, one of the state's leading boosters, and a host of businessmen and land speculators. The model farm produced five times more wheat per acre than unirrigated land. By this time, however, the depression of the 1870s had dried up investment capital. Subsequently, Brereton asked private landowners in the San Joaquin Valley to put up one hundred thousand acres of land in exchange for one hundred thousand shares of company stock (with a par value of twenty-five dollars a share). Holding the land as collateral, Brereton returned to London late in the year and formed a syndicate of investors, only to have the California landowners back out of the deal.[98]

The financial panic of 1875, and William Ralston's death in August of that year, drove the company's prime investors into bankruptcy. The canal project cost them over eight hundred thousand dollars.[99] Miller & Lux, the cattlemen through whose land the first ditch passed, and whose cooperation had been grudging at best, obtained the canal for less than one third of what it had cost to excavate. They extended it another twenty-seven miles during the drought of 1877–78, and sold water to wheat and alfalfa farmers at a substantial profit.[100] "Thus it came about that Henry Miller became the owner of the best canal system in the west, finally supplying water to over one hundred and fifty thousand acres of land, and he thus became a purveyor of water to the public," his adoring biographer has written. As was so often the case with canal projects, this one made money, but not for the original promoters and investors. By 1910, the fifty thousand acres of Miller & Lux land irrigated from the canal was worth five hundred dollars an acre, or $25 million.[101]

Alternatives to "Free" Enterprise: Rate Regulation, Mutual Companies, and Irrigation Districts

Western states granted extensive legal powers to private water companies. They could appropriate water for their own use and sell their rights to others. Some companies enjoyed an exclusive right to provide water within a "service area," and in a few states they could condemn as well as buy private rights. They could also acquire rights-of-way, through purchase or by using the state's power of eminent domain. American jurisprudence, however, had long assumed that corporate charters imposed responsibilities as well as privileges, particularly in the case of public utilities. The courts assumed that such companies tacitly accepted judicial supervision of their property when they applied for a franchise.[102]

California was the first western state to regulate private water companies. That effort demonstrated the pervasiveness of localism, the reluctance of the legislature to limit the power of fledgling corporations, and the difficulty in regulating public utilities. In 1862 the lawmakers conferred the responsibility for setting rates on the county boards of supervisors, but they also guaranteed private companies a minimum return of 1.5 percent per month on the money actually invested in a water project. Since the legislature refused to give public officials the right to examine the books of the companies, capitalization, expenses, profits, and net worth were impossible to determine. The two major goals of regulation—to ensure fair prices and equal treatment to all users within a service area—went unrealized. The boards of supervisors, which had no experience with rate making, left the job to the companies.[103]

The need to regulate rural water companies did not become pressing until the middle 1870s. At that time, a battle broke out in Riverside County between farmers and the Riverside Canal Company. The ditch business was the twin of a speculative land company. Initially, the company kept water prices artificially low to boost land sales, and a string of comparatively wet years permitted it to serve even those farmers who had not purchased their farms from the sister company. But when drought struck in the middle of the decade, the water company raised prices. Users had been promised a supply proportionate to the stock they held in the company, but the company had issued far more stock than the water supply warranted. As a result, it first cut off water users who had not bought land from its fellow company— even though many of these farmers had irrigated long before the companies came on the scene—then it began to discriminate among those who had. The farmers charged that the company's financial plight was irrelevant because the investors had already made more than enough money from inflated land prices. The controversy persuaded the 1876 legislature to enact a statute requiring irrigation companies to provide water on equal terms to all farmers whose lands could be reached by a ditch, though it said nothing about rates (which still fell under the dormant 1862 law). However, a new drought in 1877–78 demonstrated that the 1876 law was also inadequate because it did not authorize companies to reduce the amount of water they distributed to individual farmers in unusually dry years.

California's new state constitution, adopted in 1879, reaffirmed that "the use of all water now appropriated, or that may hereafter be appropriated, for sale, rental, or distribution, is hereby declared to be a public use, and subject to the regulation and control of the State in the manner to be prescribed by law." This authority remained with local officials, not the state, and the 1880 legislature limited the boards of supervisors to setting *maximum* rates. The proliferation and increasing political influence of private water companies during the 1880s further undermined regulatory efforts. In 1885, the legislature permitted companies to set their own rates unless twenty-five or more taxpayers asked their supervisors to do the job. Annual rates had to be more than 6 percent of the company's total value but less than 18 percent. Since those water users who appealed to local officials faced severe reprisals from the companies, this law was rarely used. In any case, the utilities were permitted to include the value of such nebulous assets as water rights and reservoir sites in their capitalization, all but nullifying a new requirement that they open their books to local officials.[104] Little was done to strengthen regulatory power until the Progressive Era.[105]

It is easy to interpret corporate opposition to regulation as open defiance of the public will and the public interest. Water companies, however, like railroads, often had logic if not justice on their side. For example, those that built canals during boom periods, when the cost of labor and materials was high, found that boards of supervisors and other local officials used "real value," rather than the actual cost of construction, in setting rates. Only by padding the value of their property were such companies able to recover their investment. Moreover, many companies argued that binding legal contracts, negotiated between company officials and the water users themselves, were a far more just and efficient way to set rates than leaving the job to local officials or special commissions.[106]

Despite the ineffectiveness of regulation in the nineteenth century, the law established a clear distinction between *public ownership* and *public control*. When Elwood Mead said of California that "nowhere else in the arid region has private enterprise gone so far nor public neglect been so pronounced,"[107] he ignored the distinction between control over water rights and control over water prices and service. By 1900 several basic principles had become widely accepted in the Golden State: that dependable service should be provided to all water users on equal terms; that water companies had to provide such service when a reasonable fee was paid; that no unreasonable requirements or conditions could be demanded of water users as preconditions to service; and that the courts were responsible for upholding these principles.[108] California courts consistently supported the idea that while ideally water rights should be attached to the land, until that could be done individual water users, rather than the private companies that provided water, should hold title to the resource.[109]

Many other states and territories, particularly Colorado, attempted to regulate water companies in the nineteenth century, but none was any more successful than California.[110] Since regulation was largely ineffective, many farmers attempted to manage the water themselves through institutional forms less subject to abuse than private corporations. In California, as in Utah, mutual companies became popular. They were formed by farmers or private irrigation companies to promote efficiency and democracy in the distribution and use of water. Farmers deeded their water rights to a company in exchange for shares of stock. The number of shares corresponded to the value of their property in relation to that of the whole community of water users; one share usually conferred the right to irrigate one acre. When a landowner sold his stock, the company had the responsibility to supply the buyer with the same amount of water, no matter where his land was located within a given service area. Usually, the stock could be rented or sold, but in many companies water rights attached to particular parcels of land. The guiding principles of mutual companies were, first, that rights to land and water should be inseparable, and, second, that water should be apportioned according to need rather than date of settlement, distance from a water source, or even variations in streamflow. The mutual company's greatest advantage was that by levying assessments against the stock, it forced water users to maintain and repair ditches. In effect, by becoming stockholders, farmers entered tacit contracts to pay for upkeep. And by using shares of stock as water rights, many of the problems inherent in the doctrine of prior appropriation were avoided and speculation was minimized. Equally important, mutual companies permitted groups of farmers to borrow money to pay for improvements to the water system.[111]

The mutal company's major weakness was its inability to raise the money needed to build the larger irrigation systems that began to appear during the 1880s and 1890s. Moreover, it lacked the power to condemn water rights or to consolidate existing systems. Consequently, the irrigation district emerged in the late 1880s and early 1890s as a second alternative to the traditional private water company.[112] Utah enacted district legislation as early as 1865, but it made no provision to issue bonds or to finance new irrigation works. The Wright Act, adopted by the California legislature in 1887, attempted simultaneously to reestablish public control over water and encourage private investment in water projects. When fifty or more freeholders decided to form a district, their county board of supervisors called a special election in which all eligible voters, not just landholders, participated. The law required a two thirds vote to form a district, but once it was established, a simple majority could approve the issuance of bonds. The irrigation district was a latter-day form of "mixed enterprise," a quasi-government district or municipal corporation. The cost of reclamation was assessed against *all* property within the district, including town lots, and the bonds constituted a first lien on that property. Taxes retired the capital and interest debt over twenty years.[113]

One of the most appealing features of the irrigation district was home rule, but it was attractive for other reasons as well. It promised to use the appreciation in value of *all* property within its borders to pay for irrigation—town lots and businesses as well as farmland. It was expected to reduce speculation because comparatively high taxes would discourage district residents from holding idle land. And because district bonds were secured by farmland, promoters hoped that those bonds would sell more easily and carry lower interest rates. Since interest was a very significant part of the cost of water projects, promoters expected the cost of irrigation to decline. Projects previously ignored by private capital would become economically feasible. Moreover, districts did not have to negotiate contracts with individual water users, which was very time-consuming, and, at least in theory, a minority of large landowners could not block projects favored by the majority.

In California, most districts were formed not to build entirely new hydraulic systems, but to upgrade and coordinate older ditches, canals, diversion dams, and headgates. They either purchased the irrigation works and water rights of bankrupt private water projects, or hired solvent companies to construct new systems. (In effect, the Wright Act provided a way to refinance arid land reclamation. Private water companies frequently quoted the price in bonds for their works even before a district was formed.)[114] Since large quantities of water were wasted by older ditches, consolidating them into more efficient systems increased the supply. Most important, the district held the power to condemn all water rights, riparian or appropriative, needed to produce a unified delivery system. In 1890, the chairman of the federal House Committee on Arid Lands echoed a widespread assumption among irrigation district promoters when he declared that the new law had largely overturned the riparian doctrine. Richard J. Hinton, head of the USDA irrigation office, also applauded the Wright Act's commitment to the public ownership and distribution of water. He believed that the law had "unquestionably caused a cessation of litigation over water rights and prior appropriations." The district offered the opportunity to put all water rights on an equal footing. District farmers held individual rights, but those rights also belonged to the community in that they had to be used within the district. The water was apportioned *by the district* according to the ratio of an individual's taxes to the combined district tax revenue.[115]

Few irrigation districts lived up to expectations. The Wright Act touched off a frenzy of speculation, but strenuous opposition from many large landowners, as well as the absence of state supervision over the construction or management of projects, reduced the value of the bonds. The law prohibited *sale* at less than 95 percent of par, so most were *traded* for water rights or irrigation works at a fraction of face value. Inflated construction costs, the isolation of many districts, the administrative inexperience of most directors (as they tried to manage large and complicated public works projects), their ignorance of irrigation, endless litigation over the constitutionality of the Wright Act, and the economic depression of the 1890s also helped to paralyze the districts. Of the fifty formed in California before 1893, only twelve remained solvent in 1910, and they served about 5 percent of the state's irrigated land. Only $2,000 of nearly $8 million in bonds had been paid off; most of the original investors ultimately settled for a few cents on the dollar. Nevertheless, the obvious weaknesses of private enterprise[116] inspired many states to copy California's district legislation, including Washington in 1890, Kansas and Nevada in 1891, Idaho, Nebraska, and Oregon in 1895, Colorado in 1901, Texas in 1905, Montana and Wyoming in 1907, New Mexico and Utah in 1909, Arizona in 1912, Oklahoma in 1915, and North and South Dakota in 1917. Each tailored the California legislation to suit its particular needs, but all embraced the principles of home rule and bonding the land.[117] Ultimately, irrigation districts became enormously successful, but not until the twentieth century.[118]

The Significance of Private Development

The census of 1890 reflected many of the triumphs of corporate irrigation. Irrigated acreage in the arid West had increased from about 250,000–300,000 acres in 1870 to 3,631,381 acres in 1890. California and Colorado were far in the lead with 1,004,233 and 890,735 acres respectively, but California's irrigation works had cost twice as much as Colorado's. Moreover, the average value of California's land under ditch, $150 an acre, was nearly double the value of irrigated land in its closest competitor, Utah, which averaged $84.25. California also had an edge in the value of crops grown, $19 per acre, compared to Utah's $18.03 per acre. In the percentage of farmland irrigated, however, California's 18 percent took fifth place behind Colorado's 31 percent, Idaho's 26 percent, Montana's 23 percent, and Utah's 22 percent.[119]

In 1889, Baring Brothers' financial house in England collapsed, depriving the West of a major source of foreign capital. Then, in 1891, Congress limited Desert Land Act entries to U.S. citizens, further reducing the interest of European investors in the West. Finally, the poor showing of bonds and securities issued by California's irrigation districts undermined faith in all water projects. The supply of irrigated land already greatly exceeded demand, but the surplus became all the more obvious as the depression of 1893 deepened.[120]

In 1907, agricultural economist Samuel Fortier estimated that "95 per cent of the capital invested in canal enterprises from 1885 to 1895 produced no dividends and much of it was entirely lost." For example, the Utah-based Bear Lake and River Canal Company's hydraulic works cost over $1,250,000 to construct, but, following its bankruptcy in 1894, sold for $125,000.[121] One writer described conditions in Colorado, where the depression had made the issue of public control over water rates moot:

> Many of these companies defaulted in the payment of interest, some not even paying the first semi-annual installment; liens were filed on nearly all of them for work and material furnished in their construction; the settlers under them were as a rule too poor to buy water rights outright, and often the source of supply of water was a sad disappointment, as no

previous gauging of the streams [by the state] had been made. In many instances the land owners took advantage of our constitutional provision empowering County Commissioners of the counties in which the principal headworks of the canal were located to fix rates of carriage for the water, which rates were often fixed so low as to amount to practical confiscation, as there was no means of appealing from such orders. Many of such companies soon became bankrupt, and what were then known as irrigation bonds became discredited.[122]

By the mid-nineties, most large private irrigation companies had collapsed, and the rest tottered on the edge of bankruptcy. Stockholders lost everything, and bondholders were asked to pay assessments to help their company survive until better days arrived. Although many defunct projects ended up in the hands of the farmers themselves (usually reorganized as mutual companies), individual property owners watched their land appreciate dramatically in value, and the tax rolls of irrigated counties soared. The public gained while investors lost.

Private water companies had no control over nature and served inherently unstable markets. Farmers in the Southwest and mountain West could not raise cash crops without irrigation; it was *essential*, year in and year out. But in many other parts of the arid West, irrigation was necessary only in unusually dry years; it was drought insurance. Private companies had two choices: they could sell water at enormous prices on demand and receive a return on their investment every second, third, or fourth year, or they could negotiate contracts that bound farmers to pay year in and year out, regardless of need. These companies usually demanded liens on the irrigated land because fixed costs required a relatively steady flow of revenue. Yet farmers deeply resented paying for water they did not need and sometimes, in unusually dry years, never saw. If a ditch company failed to provide water because of an act of nature, it lost nothing. But if drought caused a farmer to miss water payments, his land might be seized along with his water right.

Ditch companies bore an enormous number of expenses. The promoters expected a profit, and so did the investors and those who marketed and bought the company's stocks and bonds. In many cases, taxes had to be paid on improved land that remained uncultivated for years after a project opened. Once a project appeared feasible, the promoters applied to the state for a corporate charter. Then they could issue bonds to recover their original survey costs and to fund construction. One analyst of private irrigation ventures estimated that the cost of organization and promotion constituted about 10 percent of the total expenditure on a reclamation project, and the cost of administration during construction added another 10 percent. Interest on the bonds and miscellaneous expenses contributed as much as 30 percent more to the total outlay. Litigation over contested water rights was another major expense. In the years from 1891 to 1895, one Montana ditch company paid out 60 percent of the revenue it received from water sales in attorney fees and another 19 percent in court costs. By comparison, it spent only 14 percent on maintaining the canals. In short, the cost of constructing dams and canals was only a small part of the total cost of irrigation projects.[123]

Equally important, the private corporation did not attract sufficient farmers to its projects, nor did it institute rational settlement plans. Just as companies seldom paid adequate attention to markets and cooperative selling, few bothered to check whether there were buyers for the reclaimed land. No company could prosper if it watered only 20 or 30 percent of the land it opened to irrigation, or if it permitted settlers to scatter over a project, leaving great gaps between irrigated farms. When a corporation built a canal to irrigate a hundred thousand acres, the interest on its debt and the cost of maintenance could only be met if the land was settled relatively quickly and densely. Yet so many projects were launched in the 1880s and early 1890s that there were not enough farmers to go around. Consequently, charges for water rights and maintenance had to be increased, sometimes to the point of forcing the first wave of farmers to abandon their new homes. Otherwise, the company could not meet its expenses, let alone pay dividends on stock and interest on bonds.

Companies often waited years for settlers. By 1887, eight main canals had been constructed in Arizona's Salt River Valley at a cost of nearly $1 million. No more than fifty thousand acres—perhaps 20 percent of the land those ditches were capable of serving—was cultivated. Corporate greed compounded shortsightedness. There were not enough farmers to go around, but many companies exacerbated the problem by holding too much land for speculation, thus forcing bona fide settlers to bear a disproportionately heavy share of the cost of reclamation.[124]

Ironically, there is little evidence that private water companies charged all the maket would bear. Since most made their money from land speculation, irrigation agriculture was heavily subsidized long before the adoption of the Reclamation Act of 1902; western farmers could not or would not pay the full cost of reclaiming the land. Water rates were usually per acre per year; they did not vary according to the number of crops grown, the value of those crops, or the proximity of farms to main canals. Nor did companies adjust rates to fit demand—increasing the price of water during the late summer and early fall, when farmers were most likely to irrigate and when the supply was smallest.[125]

Private irrigation companies did try to monopolize water—they had to—and that led to baneful results. For example, since western water laws often limited appropriations to the size of a ditch, and since companies wanted to sign up as many farmers as possible as soon as possible, they built ditches much larger than needed. The companies assured settlers that they owned or controlled plenty of water. But they generally erred on the optimistic side, and they usually assumed that one or two acre-feet of water per acre—an amount sufficient to cover one acre a foot or two deep—was sufficient for most crops, when the actual "duty" of water ran several times that amount. Of course, companies that made their money selling water rights, rather than land, faced the greatest temptation to promise more than they could deliver and to sign up more farmers than they could serve—hoping for severe winters to increase the runoff during the growing season. As irrigation engineer Herbert M. Wilson of the USGS put it in 1892: "As a general thing water rights are now sold rather in proportion to the maximum capacities of canals than to their minimum discharges." The problem was compounded because a large ditch that carried only a fraction of its capacity exposed a proportionately greater volume of water to the sun than a smaller ditch filled to capacity. Speculative companies often learned too late that the longer and larger the canal, the greater the loss—from 1 percent of volume per mile if the canal carried a maximum of 100 cfs to over 5 percent per mile when the ditch carried only 25–50 cfs.[126]

The fate of private irrigation enterprise and the volatile economy of the nineteenth-century West were inextricably linked. The depression of the 1890s raised the prospect of perpetual economic adolescence. The region might become a lesson in arrested development, one vast pasture punctuated by declining farms, cities, and mines. The collapse of the irrigation boom raised the possibility that western agriculture had reached a dead end. There was little chance that the day would soon return when investors eagerly embraced irrigation projects. There were no more large tracts of first-class irrigable land near water;

there was insufficient public control over the feasibility and safety of projects; there was substantial hostility toward private companies on the part of water users; and, quite simply, irrigation projects did not pay. Private enterprise revived in the first decade of the twentieth century, but the ditch builders never recaptured the heady optimism of the 1880s and early 1890s.

William C. Ralston.
One of the nineteenth-century West's leading entrepreneurs and bankers, the fate of his bold project to water the entire Central Valley of California demonstrated many of the problems faced by private water companies in the 1870s and after. (Courtesy California Section, California State Library, Sacramento.)

William F. ("Buffalo Bill") Cody. This salesman and exemplar of the romantic, individualistic West hoped that irrigation would build a new commonwealth. But his Carey Act project at Cody, Wyoming—the nation's first—attracted few settlers. (Courtesy Library of Congress, Washington, D.C.)

William Hammond Hall.
The West's first state engineer, in the 1880s Hall attempted to reform and modernize California's anachronistic, inconsistent water laws. He was unable to win support from water users, the state legislature, or the public at large. (Courtesy the Bancroft Library, University of California, Berkeley.)

John Wesley Powell, scientist and bureaucrat. Head of the United States Geological Survey from 1881 to 1894, he administered the West's first "comprehensive" hydrographic survey in 1888–90. Both farsighted and naive, he was as much a victim of his own stubbornness and certitude as of divisions within the West or rapacious land, water, timber, mining, grazing, and transportation companies. (Courtesy National Archives, Washington, D.C.)

George Davidson.
Head of the U.S. Coast Geodetic Survey, member of the federal irrigation commission of 1873–74, and a close student of irrigation in foreign countries, Davidson was one of the leading scientists on the Pacific coast. Unlike John Wesley Powell, he recognized the dangers of leaving the allocation of water to local users and the courts. (Courtesy Bancroft Library, University of California, Berkeley.)

William Morris Stewart.
U.S. Senator from Nevada, 1864–75 and 1887–1905. Stewart, like Carey and Warren, saw irrigation as his state's main hope for diversified economic development. He demanded direct and immediate benefits from the Irrigation Survey of 1888–90, fearful that support in Congress for western expenditures would collapse if the survey dragged on for too many years. (Courtesy Nevada Historical Society, Reno.)

William Ellsworth Smythe.
Philosopher of irrigation, founder of the National Irrigation Congress (1891), editor of the journal *Irrigation Age* (1891–96), and promoter of agricultural colonies, he launched the irrigation crusade at the beginning of the 1890s but could not unite the West behind a coherent water policy or transform arid land reclamation into a national issue. (Courtesy California Section, California State Library, Sacramento.)

Joseph M. Carey.
U.S. Senator from Wyoming, 1890–96. Carey hoped that the 1894 bill he persuaded Congress to adopt would lure farmers onto land he owned around Wheatland, Wyoming, and offer his state a way out of the economic depression of the 1890s. (Courtesy Library of Congress, Washington, D.C.)

Francis E. Warren.
U.S. Senator from Wyoming, 1890–93 and 1895 to 1929. Because the silver issue was not as dominant in Wyoming as in other states, during the 1890s Warren emerged as the political leader of the reclamation movement. He assumed that for most of the arid West, no water policy could succeed without reconciling farming and grazing under state law. (Courtesy Library of Congress, Washington, D.C.)

Elwood Mead.
Wyoming Territorial and State Engineer, 1888–99, and head of the USDA Office of Irrigation Investigations, 1898–1907. Francis Warren's chief adviser on land and water policies, Mead drafted a model water code for Wyoming and wrote the most important irrigation legislation considered by Congress in the 1890s. However, he had serious doubts about the Reclamation Act of 1902. (Courtesy California Section, California State Library, Sacramento.)

Thomas Carter.
Commissioner of the General Land Office, 1890–92, and U.S. Senator from Montana, 1895–1901 and 1905–11, Carter paved the way for congressional approval of reclamation legislation in 1902 by talking the rivers and harbors bill to death at the beginning of 1901.
(Courtesy Library of Congress, Washington, D.C.)

Frederick Haynes Newell.
Appointed to the staff of the Irrigation Survey by John Wesley Powell in 1888, Newell remained with the USGS throughout the 1890s and became a leader in the movement for national forests as well as the campaign for federal reclamation of arid lands. He assumed the position of Chief Hydrographer in 1895 and subsequently measured the volume and condition of streams throughout the nation. Draftsman of the Reclamation Act of 1902, he became first director of the Reclamation Service.
(Courtesy Library of Congress, Washington, D.C.)

James J. Hill.
Railroad executive, financier, and builder of the Northwest. In the opening years of the twentieth century, Hill deeply feared a recurrence of the depression of the 1890s. He also wanted to drive up the value of railroad land and increase freight revenues. His Jeffersonian faith in the family farm as the foundation and salvation of the nation prompted him to organize and bankroll the publicity campaign that transformed arid land reclamation into a national issue. (Courtesy James J. Hill Library, St. Paul Minnesota.)

George H. Maxwell, water lawyer and publicist. Using funds provided by several large railroads, in the early years of the twentieth century he sidestepped the deep political and economic divisions within the West and sold reclamation as a moral imperative and a tool to reform American society. (From *Forestry and Irrigation*, 1902.)

Francis G. Newlands. Congressman from Nevada, 1893–1903, U.S. Senator, 1903–17. The quintessential "available man," Newlands sponsored Frederick H. Newell's irrigation bill because he saw it as economic salvation for his state and a vehicle by which he might achieve election to the United States Senate. (Courtesy Library of Congress, Washington, D.C.)

Theodore Roosevelt. President of the United States, 1901–9. Roosevelt feared the rapid disappearance of the public domain and the monopolization of land by large corporations, particularly livestock companies. Without his support, the 1902 Reclamation Act would not have reached the House floor. (Courtesy Library of Congress, Washington, D.C.)

Shoshone Falls, Snake River, by William Henry Jackson.
The West's problem was not just that water was scarce; it was often
inaccessible. Many streams ran in channels far below or far distant from
arable land, and much of the region could not be watered before the
construction of "high dams" in the 1930s and later. Other streams were too
swift, too steep, and too unpredictable in volume.
(Courtesy Library of Congress, Washington, D.C.)

Artesian well, Kern County, California.
Many westerners, particularly on the Great Plains, questioned the need to build expensive canals dependent on streams that originated in other states. They clung to the faith that underground water would provide an unlimited, cheap supply beyond litigation. This contributed to many conflicts among the friends of irrigation.
(Courtesy Library of Congress, Washington, D.C.)

Hydraulic mining in California.
Moving large quantities of water to placer deposits required substantial capital, and investors in mining and water companies demanded that this resource be treated as private property. Not all westerners, however, considered the legal principles that emerged from the 1850s and 1860s–laws later applied to irrigation agriculture—just, equitable, or efficient. (Courtesy Bancroft Library, University of California, Berkeley.)

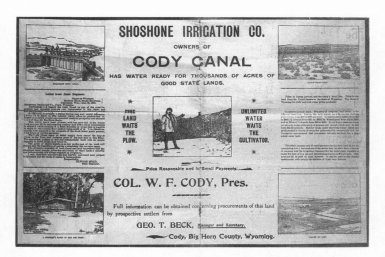

Advertisement for the Cody Canal from the *Cody Enterprise,* 1899.

Excavating a canal with plows and scrapers.
Many nineteenth-century ditches were no longer than a mile or two,
constructed by the farmers who used them.
(Courtesy National Archives, Washington, D.C.)

Steam shovel mounted on a barge.
Such tools were generally used for building large ditches that tapped
navigable streams.
(Courtesy Library of Congress, Washington, D.C.)

Ditch lined with concrete.
Few nineteenth-century canal builders were willing to pay the added
expense of lining ditches, even if they thereby prevented or reduced seepage,
erosion, and siltation. Most aqueducts were wide and shallow, which
increased evaporation and contributed to waste and litigation.
(From *Forestry and Irrigation,* 1902.)

Canal headgates, Imperial County, California.
In the nineteenth century, crude wooden curtains were used to separate the ditches of individual farmers from main canals. They frequently leaked, making precise measurements of diversions impossible. (Courtesy Library of Congress, Washington, D.C.)

Canal headgates, Arizona.
In dry years irrigators often cut off water to neighboring ditches or diverted more water than they were entitled to. Consequently, both individuals and private companies frequently used force to protect ditches and crops.
(Courtesy Salt River Project, Phoenix, Arizona.)

Flood irrigation.
The most common form of irrigation in the nineteenth century, it could be used on very uneven land and on low value crops, unlike furrow irrigation. By eliminating the need for leveling and grading, it reduced the cost of farming. But it also contributed to waste, inefficiency, and legal conflict.
(Courtesy National Archives, Washington, D.C.)

The Calloway Canal, Kern River, California.
One of the largest nineteenth-century enterprises.
(Courtesy Library of Congress, Washington, D.C.)

The High Line Canal, Platte River, Colorado.
Built mainly with English capital, this ditch became the most controversial in the entire West. It contributed to water law reform and the construction of reservoirs and canals by the state of Colorado.
(Courtesy Colorado Historical Society, Denver, Colorado.)

Political cartoons
from east coast newspapers
in support of federal reclamation (1902).

THE RIGHT KIND OF "WATER CURE."

5

Retreat from Nationalism

Irrigation in late nineteenth-century America posed challenging problems to both science and government. Western states and territories differed in their need for irrigation—and their need for state aid. The state governments could not agree on a common program, nor could the nation's intellectual leaders. In the 1870s and 1880s, many scientists became interested in irrigation, in part because it had a profound impact on nature, and in part because it involved so many fledgling disciplines, including soil science, forestry, and geology. But they disagreed sharply over the value and the dangers of irrigation, and over the role government should play in promoting it. In the debate over federal policy during the 1870s and 1880s, George Davidson and John Wesley Powell represented two different philosophies. The debate culminated in the Powell Irrigation Survey of 1888–90, which failed because of divisions both within the scientific community in Washington and within the West.

Irrigation in Congress During the 1870s

The event that first kindled interest in federal aid to irrigation agriculture was completion of the "transcontinental" railroad after the Civil War. Grenville Dodge supervised construction of the Union Pacific (1866–70), and while doing so he served one term as a congressman from Iowa (1867–69). He was doubtless interested in improving the value of arid and semi-arid lands granted to the railroad by the federal government. On May 7, 1868, the House approved his resolution calling for the commissioner of the General Land Office to advise Congress as to "the most approved method of irrigation, and also to obtain data illustrative of the national history and industrial and com-

mercial capacities of the public lands."[1] Apparently, Dodge had already
visited the land office, because three days earlier the commissioner
asked officers in the field to submit information about the "agricultural
resources" of the public lands, noting that "the latest indications are
that even the most unpromising portions of the public lands under a
proper system of cultivation may be made to support, in comfort, a
large population." The commissioner also wrote state department officials soliciting information about irrigation in other nations, including China and Egypt.[2]

Meanwhile, beginning in the late 1860s, the new U.S. Geological
Survey (USGS) called attention to the arid lands by surveying agricultural conditions in Nebraska, Wyoming, Colorado, and New Mexico.[3]
Reports on the travels and writings of Ferdinand V. Hayden, Cyrus
Thomas, and other members of the survey regularly appeared in the
columns of the eastern press. These expeditions drew President Grant's
attention to the Rocky Mountain West, and his interest became even
keener following the economic slump in 1873; he initially proposed
public works projects, including canals, to alleviate unemployment
and industrial distress. In his December 1873 message to Congress, the
president recommended statehood for Colorado and a partnership between the federal government and a private company that wanted to
build a six-hundred-mile-long gravity-fed canal from the South Platte
to the Missouri River, running from Denver to Kansas City along the
line of the Kansas Pacific Railroad, which had been completed three
years earlier. The Kansas Pacific favored the project to drive up the
value of its land, but Grant hoped that such a canal would link the
older states with the new through a line of settlements adjoining the
ditch.[4] Only weeks later, on January 24, 1874, Representative M. K.
Armstrong of Dakota Territory also proposed the reclamation of arid
lands through some form of mixed enterprise. "The natural lakes and
water-courses of the West," Armstrong declared, "are merely reservoirs
for the plains."[5]

The canal proposed by Grant was widely regarded as impractical,
and the pressure for some form of federal aid to irrigation came more
directly from California's San Joaquin and Kings River Canal and Irrigation Company. As mentioned in the last chapter, William Ralston
appointed Robert M. Brereton as chief engineer of the San Joaquin and
Kings River Canal and Irrigation Company, a position Brereton held
from 1871 to 1876. After the company lost its bid for a federal land
grant at the beginning of 1872, Brereton traveled to Washington at the

end of that year or the beginning of the next to appeal directly for aid. There he met, or renewed an earlier acquaintance with, Senator William Morris Stewart of Nevada, who had close ties to Ralston and to Nevada mining interests. Stewart also enjoyed a cozy relationship with the leaders of the Central Pacific Railroad. That company's subsidiary, the Southern Pacific, was busy building south through the San Joaquin Valley, acquiring millions of acres of public land that stood to appreciate greatly in value from the right federal reclamation program. Stewart may also have hoped that once he secured aid for California, Nevada would be next in line. But Brereton did not stop with Stewart. He enlisted Speaker of the House James G. Blaine and two famous generals, W. S. Hancock and George B. McClellan, in the cause of Ralston's project.[6]

"Big Bill" Stewart played as large a part in 1873 as he would in pushing through the Powell survey legislation in 1888, though his motives may only be inferred. That he knew Brereton very well can be seen in frequent letters exchanged by the two men after the Powell survey was authorized.[7] Equally important was the friendship between Stewart and Grant. During Grant's first term, Stewart took an active part in Radical Reconstruction, especially by helping to draft the Fifteenth Amendment. The two had met when Grant was a lieutenant stationed on the Pacific coast from 1852 to 1854. Years later, Stewart recounted that "night after night we would wander around the city [San Francisco] together, visiting games, and saloons and other sights. We had many adventures in those early days, and perhaps I would not stretch the truth in saying that we were a trifle wild. Young Grant drank considerably and he had no advantage of me in this respect." In 1871, Grant offered Stewart an appointment to the Supreme Court. Stewart declined, but visited the White House regularly during the president's first term. Stewart was not the only reason for the president's new interest in reclaiming the West, but clearly the Kings River Canal and Irrigation company profited from powerful friends in high places.[8]

Brereton quickly discovered that Congress was no more likely to approve a land grant in 1873 than it had been in the previous year.[9] Both Stewart and Senator Eugene Casserly of California, however, were on the Public Lands Committee, and George Gorham, the clerk of the Senate (and an unsuccessful Republican candidate for governor of California in 1867), confidentially promised Ralston that a comprehensive irrigation survey by the federal government would assure "to the most prudent that the future would bring all desired national aid to the noble enterprise [your] company has undertaken."[10]

In 1873, agriculture in the arid West was confined largely to California, Colorado, and Utah, and the West's population was too sparse and scattered to warrant a hydrographic survey of the entire region. Therefore, at the end of February 1873 Stewart introduced a bill authorizing an irrigation survey restricted to California. He carefully avoided tying the bill to the San Joaquin and Kings River Canal and Irrigation Company. It was sold as a compromise measure that both proponents and opponents of national irrigation could accept. The bill's friends hoped that a survey would justify land grants to private ditch companies, and that by demonstrating the increase in land values under irrigation, it might even pave the way for federal construction of dams and canals. In a depression year, however, when some members of Congress regarded public works as a way to ease unemployment, such a survey could also be used to delay or block more extreme action. It might even demonstrate that irrigation was impractical or dangerous. Nevertheless, when Stewart introduced the legislation, Senator Lyman Trumball of Illinois objected. "It is not the expense of the survey that I am looking to," he warned. "I merely want to give notice, that if this survey is allowed, and goes on, the time will come when you will be called upon for a very large appropriation to complete the work, if it should be recommended [by the special commission]."[11] Senators Cornelius Cole and Eugene Casserly tried to reassure Trumball, but he knew better.

The enabling legislation called for the formation of a commission consisting of two representatives from the Army Corps of Engineers, one from the Coast Geodetic Survey, the chief of the California Geologic Survey, and a consulting engineer—a slot doubtless created for Brereton. The commission was to "make a full report to the President on the best system of irrigation for said [Sacramento and San Joaquin] valleys, with all necessary plans, details, engineering, statistical, and otherwise, which report the President shall transmit to Congress at its next session, with such recommendations as he shall think proper." The cost of the survey, limited to five thousand dollars, included compensation for the two members not already employed by the federal government. The bill passed Congress on March 3, 1873.[12]

In the following month Grant appointed B. S. Alexander and G. H. Mendell as representatives from the army, and George Davidson as the Coast Geodetic Survey's agent. J. D. Whitney, head of California's

Geologic Survey, was unable to participate, so Clarence King took his place. Alexander, who became head of the commission, offered Brereton the position as consultant, but the latter refused (though he accompanied the group on most of its field trips).[13] Brereton rightly considered that if he participated directly, the strong opposition to his company within California would undermine the credibility of the survey. Stockton's *Daily Independent* warned that the commission was "appointed merely to aid in carrying out the designs of the company and to enable them to present their case before Congress in a manner to secure the passage of the act giving them the monopoly of the waters of these valleys."[14]

While the irrigation commission conducted its survey, excitement grew among irrigation enthusiasts, perhaps in anticipation of a large-scale federal reclamation program. "California, Colorado, and Wyoming are vigorously agitating the subject of irrigation," the *New York Times* editorialized, "and strong efforts will be made to induce Congress to grant aid to secure a general system of irrigation throughout the States and Territories lying on either side of the Rocky Mountains."[15]

The commission finished its cursory examination in November, after a scant six weeks in the field, and it completed the required report early in December, though the document was not forwarded to Washington until the end of February 1874.[16] The five-thousand-dollar appropriation was insufficient to gauge streams, test soils, run canal lines, or locate reservoir sites. Therefore, the report contained little in the way of hard data. Nevertheless, it concluded that irrigation on a large scale in the Central Valley was perfectly feasible; 12 million acres—more than 10 percent of the total area of California—could be watered, including land in the foothills. The average price of reclamation would be relatively low, at least as measured against the value of the improved land—about ten dollars an acre.[17]

Both the state and federal governments should promote irrigation, the report urged, beginning with "a complete instrumental reconnaissance of the country to be irrigated, embracing the sources from whence the irrigating-canals ought to commence, gauging the flow of the rivers and streams, and defining the boundaries of the natural districts of irrigation into which the country is divided."[18] Moreover, the state or nation should prepare a comprehensive reclamation plan. A project embracing the Central Valley could not be built all at once because settlement of the valley might take fifty years. Still, the irrigation works should be coordinated: "It is all-important that the works should be properly planned and located in the beginning, so that whatever is done to meet the present requirements of a sparse population may form a part of those that will be necessary to meet the demands of a population of millions by simply enlarging them."[19]

The report has sometimes been interpreted as a harbinger of federal reclamation. The commission did propose that the national government reclaim blocks of land entirely within the public domain, such as the land between Visalia and Bakersfield. But in California such unbroken tracts were scarce even in 1873. So "mixed enterprise," the old blend of private and public common in the East during the early decades of the nineteenth century, seemed a better alternative. The commission recommended that when private water companies were chartered to build irrigation works, the contract should provide for reversion of control to the state after a stipulated number of years, or at least give the state the right to buy out the company. These were common provisions in charters granted to banks and transportation companies before the Civil War.

In some ways the report anticipated the Central Valley Project (CVP) of the 1920s. It paid little attention to the construction of storage reservoirs because the San Joaquin River and other streams flowing out of the Sierra contained more than enough water to meet forseeable agricultural needs. Nevertheless, it contained the seed of the "multiple use" concept in its recognition that reservoirs in the foothills could serve miners there as well as farmers in the valley, and that storing floodwater would aid the reclamation of swampland. It also anticipated the CVP by publicizing the idea of using canals to transport water from the water-rich Sacramento to the water-poor San Joaquin Valley, by recommending a partnership between public and private enterprise, and by calling for a coordinated plan that recognized the interrelatedness of different water uses.[20] Paradoxically, the report questioned the simultaneous use of canals for both agriculture and commerce. The need for locks and other works would make the cost prohibitive and interfere with diversions for farming.[21] The report also questioned Ralston's plan to build two long canals, one on either side of the Central Valley. On the east side there were too many small streams to bridge, and their sheer number rendered a large canal unnecessary there.

Among the commission's more farsighted recommendations were that proper drainage facilities should be constructed along with irrigation canals, that farmers should be limited to a reasonable quantity of water per acre, that rights to land and water should be united, and that the success of any irrigation system depended on government control over water. In a letter on June 23, 1873, to the superintendent of the U.S. Coast Geodetic Survey, George Davidson declared that "the rights to the waters will demand the decision of the highest court: this . . . problem will form the most difficult to reconcile."[22]

The commission published its report in 1874, but the document did not prompt any discussion in Congress.[23] The brief flurry of excitement in 1873 had given way to lack of interest, skepticism, and disdain among federal officials. When Cyrus Thomas, an entomologist attached to the Hayden Survey, formally proposed the construction of an earthen levee two hundred miles long and thirty to forty feet high between the Arkansas and Platte rivers (expected to create a lake covering 768,000 acres that would irrigate between 8 million and 9 million acres), Hayden proclaimed that the scheme was "worthy to be ranked with the Chinese Wall and other expensive follies."[24] There was no immediate need for reservoirs, he assured readers in his report, and since the two streams would fill the reservoir to a depth of only two feet, the water would evaporate before it could do any good. In Hayden's words, "it would be difficult to keep the bottom of the reservoir moist."[25] In 1875, the commissioner of the General Land Office insisted that irrigation was "indispensable" in the arid West but that "the proportion of land . . . which, under the present system of disposals, can by this means be made productive, is insignificant." And Secretary of the Interior Carl Schurz observed that while there were "vast tracts of land which might be valuable for cultivation if properly irrigated . . . the water would have to be brought through canals for long distances, [so] the chances of their redemption are remote."[26]

George Davidson, Nationalist

George Davidson, who served on the irrigation commission and probably wrote the 1874 report, continued to study irrigation institutions in the middle and late 1870s. Davidson arrived in California in 1850 and joined the Coast Geodetic Survey, which was responsible for mapping the West Coast and preparing navigational charts. He became one of the West's most respected scientists and exhibited an amazing range of interests. He published scientific papers on geometry; geodetic survey instruments; Saturn, Jupiter, and Mars; comets and meteors; volcanoes; Sir Francis Drake; and even the origin and meaning of the name *California*. He served as president of the California Academy of Sciences from 1871 to 1885, and also as president of the Geographical Society of the Pacific, and he was elected a member of the National Academy of Sciences in 1874. He joined the faculty of the University of California as a professor of geodesy and astronomy in 1873 and taught full time as professor of geography after his retirement from government work in 1895. He sat on the university's board of regents from 1877 to 1884. His many achievements included building the first astronomical observatory on the coast in 1879 and persuading James Lick to establish his famous observatory; helping to design San Francisco's sewage system; recommending that San Francisco construct reservoirs throughout the city to prevent a total breakdown of the water supply system in the event of a major earthquake (he became the first president of the Seismological Society of the Pacific following the 1906 disaster); and spending many years on the board of directors of the Sierra Club.[27] Yet even his biographers have failed to catalogue Davidson's contributions to hydrology. No one in the nineteenth-century West—save perhaps California's state engineer during the late 1870s and 1880s, the brilliant, scholarly, arrogant, and irascible William Hammond Hall—knew more about the region's water problems.

From the early 1870s to the early 1890s, Davidson served as a consultant to many of California's largest irrigation companies. He also surveyed potential urban water systems, particularly for communities surrounding San Francisco Bay. His knowledge of hydrology won him appointments to two important commissions, the national irrigation survey of 1873 and the Mississippi River Commission (1888). He was also a charter member of the California Water and Forest Association, and at the end of the century he helped lead the crusade to build storage reservoirs in California. From the perspective of the development of the West, Davidson's most significant work came in 1875, when he visited Europe, the Middle East, and India to inspect irrigation and flood control works.[28] What he learned during these travels proved crucial when he returned home.

Brereton had provided the 1873 commission with information on irrigation in Europe and India, some of which appeared in the commission's report. Famine had long plagued India; for example, over 3 million people had died in 1769–70. Large-scale irrigation began in India in 1817, but before 1840 most hydraulic works were constructed by the British East India Company. After that year other private companies entered the field, but the government bought out the company in 1867,

as it tottered on the edge of bankruptcy, and launched a massive construction program which soon eclipsed in size and budget the few
remaining private projects. The network of aqueducts projected by the
British government stretched across India in a gigantic arc south of the
Himalayas from the delta of the Indus River in the west to the mouth
of the Ganges in the east. The Ganges Canal alone was 200 feet wide
and 348 miles long with three branches that aggregated 306 miles. This
system covered a land area exceeding 10,000,000 acres and actually
watered about 1,700,000 acres. There were also many large projects
farther south, including one on the Mahanuddy River along the south-
east coast.[29]

Initially, the British employed a form of mixed enterprise, not
because they considered it superior to direct action by the state, but
because demands on the government to construct public works exceeded available revenue. In 1858, the government asked the Madras
Irrigation Company to build a $5 million canal in exchange for a guar-
anteed annual return of 5 percent. The contract promised that all profits over 12 percent would be shared equally. But the company quickly
expended its $5 million and asked the government to bail it out. By
the time the canal was finished in 1871, the project had cost over $10
million, including interest. The government suffered a similar loss
when the East India Company tried to build a canal in the Orissa delta
soon after the Madras Irrigation Company began its work.

Not surprisingly, by the early 1870s the British concluded that
while private companies built good railroads, they should not be entrusted with irrigation projects. The prevention of private monopolies
and the equitable distribution of water took precedence over the cost
of works. The champions of national irrigation had discovered that
profits from water sales could help pay the cost of ruling India, not
just reward private investors.[30] Nevertheless, it took years for canals
to return a profit, and the 1873 U.S. commission concluded that *"as
a financial investment for private parties, irrigation-works have not
generally been favorable."* Clearly, only government had the capital,
time, and patience to make irrigation pay.[31]

The commission's report said little about the lessons Americans
should draw from the history of other nations. None of its members
had firsthand knowledge of irrigation outside the United States. However, when the U.S. Navy selected Davidson as chief astronomer on
an American expedition sent to Japan to observe the transit of Venus,
he expanded his itinerary to include an inspection tour of leading ir-

rigation projects in India and Egypt, as well as river and harbor improvements in western Europe. The trip was of more than academic
interest. His formal orders, issued in July 1874, only a few months
after the federal irrigation commission filed its report, noted that he
was being asked to investigate irrigation in India and Egypt in part
because "your services may probably be again required on that duty."[32]
The excursion may well have been arranged in the interest of the San
Joaquin and Kings River Canal and Irrigation Company. Senator Stewart later recounted that he had persuaded the Navy and Treasury departments to pay for Davidson's side trip, and after two months in
India Davidson wrote to Ralston from Cairo promising that he had "a
broad & comprehensive view of the results, present & prospective [of
irrigation]; with a vast amount of information that will interest you
in the development of California."[33]

In India, Davidson traveled five thousand miles and inspected
twelve large irrigation systems. In Egypt he explored the valley of the
Nile from the dams and canals at the delta to the first cataract, using
the khedive's steamer *Fayoum*. In Italy, the chief engineer of public
works showed him the public Cavour Canal as well as the great drainage project on the lower Po near Codijoro, where three hundred thousand acres were being reclaimed. Davidson was particularly impressed
by the size and efficiency of the British works in India and the boldness
of their design. His 1875 report went well beyond the 1873 irrigation
commission's conclusions. He paid far more attention to the weaknesses of private enterprise, and he insisted that vested rights could be
overturned using the power of the state. The British had solved the
great problem of reconciling private and public rights through the
Northern India Canal and Drainage Act of 1873, which gave the government full ownership and control over all water. Water conflicts were
resolved by the chief revenue officer of each district, without appeal
to higher authority.[34]

Davidson saw many similarities between the United States and
India. Both countries had large mountain ranges that provided excellent
reservoir sites, both had broad and fertile plains adjoining the mountains, and both possessed the qualities of the "English governing race."
There were also substantial differences. California posed fewer tough
engineering problems than did either Egypt or India. For example, the
Soane River at Dehrse was considerably more than two miles wide,
much larger than any stream in California. Moreover, in the arid West,
rainfall was scant at any time, save for summer thunderstorms. By

contrast, most parts of India regularly experienced six months of rain followed by six months of drought (in other places the land received twenty to thirty inches or more of rain each year, but all during a few torrential downpours). In the Ganges Valley, natural rainfall assured crops without irrigation two out of every three years.

The biggest difference between California and India was that India was very densely populated. Even in those parts of India where rainfall permitted raising crops without irrigation, the number of people who had to be fed made irrigation mandatory. One day, Davidson suggested, California would face the same imperative. Meanwhile, the sparseness of the state's population prevented water projects from paying for themselves and kept the supply of labor low and the cost of construction high. Furthermore, according to Davidson, residents of the arid West, if not Americans in general, exhibited a far different character from the inhabitants of other countries that practiced irrigation. "As a rule," he observed, "there is, among the people of India, Egypt, Italy, and Spain, an absence of self-reliance and assertion; but they have a stern plodding industry, an abiding faith in the modes of thought and actions of their forefathers; and they look to the governing powers for aid and comfort when the country is swept by pestilence and famine. These are to be borne in mind in deciding who shall plan, project, build, and control the works of irrigation in the United States." Davidson knew that the decision hinged as much on American attitudes toward government and the state as on the cost of reclamation, availability of labor, and population density. Nevertheless, he insisted that the federal government should exercise direct administrative control over the distribution of water and should create a bureaucracy large enough to render quick administrative decisions when canal laws and regulations were violated.[35]

By the time Davidson returned to the United States, the San Joaquin and Kings River Canal and Irrigation Company had collapsed, and William Ralston was dead. Those facts made it easier for Davidson to support the cause of national reclamation, but the depression had deepened the mood of retrenchment in Congress, and subsequently the scientist limited his attention to California. He lectured frequently on irrigation at institutions ranging from the California Academy of Sciences to the state legislature (which, when he addressed it in January 1878, was considering how to reform the state's water laws).[36] His message was always the same: California ought to adopt a comprehensive irrigation plan before water rights became too numerous and expensive for the state to condemn. Both riparian rights and prior appropriation should give way to a system that wedded the privilege of using water indissolubly to the land—the system that prevailed in most parts of Spain. All farmers, old and new, should be cut back equally during dry years. He acknowledged that vested rights were a barrier to future agricultural development, but he was not dismayed. "I would propose the condemnation of all the waters of the state, on the ground of a great public necessity," he boldly recommended, "and then reconstruct the whole fabric looking to the absolute rights of all, under the most intelligent views of a commission of arbitrators composed of engineers & statesmen, and representing the great interests involved." The commission would not include lawyers or judges. Tying water rights to the land would make the allocation of water an engineering problem rather than a legal issue. A comprehensive plan was imperative because the localized system of the 1870s would one day clash with the coordinated system that would be needed as the state's population increased. Science, not profit, should dictate the construction of hydraulic works. Only intelligent, systematic planning could ensure that discrete projects built over many decades would fit together.[37]

Davidson's warning went unheeded, and private water rights in California proliferated during the 1880s even faster than he had anticipated. The call for extensive federal aid first heard at the beginning of the 1870s was all but forgotten until the end of the 1880s and beginning of the 1890s. By that time the opportunities for government planning and control over water were much more limited than had been the case in the middle 1870s.

The Crisis of the 1880s

At the end of the 1880s, a series of events rekindled interest in federal aid to irrigation. Behind them lurked the land hunger that had long been part of the American character. In 1885, the commissioner of the General Land Office noted that the rapid disappearance of the humid public domain had "stimulated the exertions of capitalists and corporations to acquire outlying regions of public land in mass by whatever means, legal or illegal." The Oklahoma land rushes of 1889–90 and 1893, when millions of acres were claimed within a matter of hours, did not surprise the commissioner. "This unusual demand for land in Oklahoma did not arise because of any special preference for the climate or soil," he observed, "but because of the very limited area of public land remaining upon which a settler can raise crops without artificial irrigation." Increasing immigration and a high natural birth rate pointed to an inescapable conclusion not lost on proponents of irrigation. "The density of population is approaching, in parts of the country, the conditions of Europe," a writer in *Forum* warned, "and the child is now living who will perhaps see in the fertile portions of the United States a population almost equal in density to that of England or France. Our statesmen can find no greater field than this for the exercise of statesmanship."[38] In 1896 the secretary of the interior noted that while 620 million acres within the public domain had been disposed of in the century before 1883, in the thirteen years thereafter 325 million acres were taken. Settlers and speculators were filing on land at a rate of 25 million acres per year.[39]

The haunting fear that the United States was running out of farmland diverted attention to the hitherto ignored arid and semi-arid lands. So did the decline of the range cattle industry in many parts of the West. There had been plenty of hard winters before 1886, but in those years the ranges had not been overgrazed. Unfortunately, the "white winter" of 1886–87 followed a hot, dry summer which left pastures barren as winter approached. To compound the problem, a glutted market forced ranchers to keep an unusually large number of animals on the range as they waited for higher prices. In January 1887, blizzards hit the plains, driving temperatures to sixty degrees below zero. The effects of the harsh winter varied. Wyoming lost only about 15 percent of its cattle herd, though those that survived were in poor shape and produced a small calf crop. Losses in Montana were much greater, perhaps as much as 60 percent of the total.[40]

Drought followed hard upon the brutal winter, and in many parts of the West it lingered until the middle of the 1890s. Charles Irish, head of the irrigation office in the Department of Agriculture, recounted that "the greatest curiosity during those years [1887 and 1888] was a cloud; it was no uncommon thing to go ninety days consecutively without seeing one. . . . I have observed such conditions."[41] The combined effects of the white winter and the drought helped launch dozens of major irrigation projects, many on former grazing land.[42] For example, between 1888 and 1893 the Pecos Valley was transformed from open range to a flourishing agricultural region, with two towns and seventeen thousand people. The decline of the cattle industry raised new opportunities, and virtually all westerners, particularly investors, favored some kind of federal assistance—such as soil, stream, reservoir, artesian well, or canal surveys—to help tame the desert.[43]

The scarcity of water increased demands on reservoir sites and interstate streams. The pressure was severe in Nevada and Colorado, where the needs of stockmen combined with the ambitions of specu-lators to threaten the expansion of farming.[44] Stock raisers had a good knowledge of potential damsites. During the summer they grazed cattle and sheep in the high country near the headwaters of streams, and they often claimed likely reservoir sites simply to prevent the con-struction of irrigation projects in the valleys below that would interfere with the use of rangeland. "This is an emergency," Stewart warned the Senate in July 1888. "The places for reservoirs are being taken by private parties, and a person who locates where there ought to be a reservoir knows it very well."[45] The drought also touched off conflicts on vir-tually all the West's interstate streams. For example, on the Arkansas River, the construction of canals upstream in Colorado undermined irrigation agriculture in Finney County, Kansas, whose population de-clined from 5,200 to 2,900 during the 1890s, leading to the most famous water suit in the history of the American West.[46]

The impact of the drought was most severe on the Great Plains, whose population had greatly increased in the 1880s. There were 135,177 people in Dakota Territory in 1880, but its population nearly tripled from 1880 to 1885.[47] Western Kansas and Nebraska were settled be-tween 1883 and 1887 and eastern Colorado between 1886 and 1889. In 1885, the commissioner of the General Land Office reported that the rush for land in western Kansas was "unprecedented." "Every train brings in a crowd of land-seekers. For more than an hour before the [land] office opens a mass of humanity throngs the doorway, and it is a remarkable sight to see the press and excitement." These settlers, of course, carried dangerous assumptions about the agricultural potential of their new homes. "With the exception of some of the valleys in the Black Hills region," the governor of Dakota Territory blithely declared in 1881, "irrigation has not been deemed necessary or practicable in this Territory. The changing seasons seem to bring with them abun-dance of snow and rain, and as the country settles up and cultivation becomes general there is no apprehension of such droughts as would give the subject of irrigation any considerable importance." As late as June 1889, the *Denver Republican* noted that the line of aridity was inexorably moving west with the line of settlement. "It is now almost to be called doubtful," the editor proclaimed, "if there be any properly so-called arid region."[48]

Nevertheless, much of the Great Plains suffered the fate of the James (or "Jim") River Valley, where a partial crop failure in 1887 was followed by devastating losses in 1888 and complete famine in 1889 and 1890.[49] In eastern Colorado's Baca County, the 3,000 residents counted in the spring of 1888 had shrunk to 1,000 by the harvest of 1889. Although it lay just east of the hundredth meridian, Wichita, Kansas, the "Peerless Princess of the Plains," lost 13,000 inhabitants; its real estate business completely collapsed. In 1889, there were 81,279 people in Kansas west of that line, by 1895 only 49,850. Comanche County, Kansas, had a population of 5,004 in 1887 and 1,369 in 1898. Greeley County went from 4,646 to 502 during the same period, Stanton County from 2,864 to 326, Morton County from 2,560 to 255, and Stevens County from 2,663 to 519. In Nebraska, the populations of Blaine County and Perkins County fell from 1,146 to 300 and from 4,370 to 1,975 respectively during the 1890s.[50]

Ironically, those who fled were as likely to end up in Oklahoma or Colorado as back in the humid East, and those who stayed behind expected the federal government to make good on what they considered a tacit contract. The government had permitted, even encouraged, homesteaders to take up arid lands by designating them as "agricultural"; now it had an obligation to make those lands productive. The 1890 Trans-Mississippi Commercial convention, which met in Denver, urged that "the National Government shall make such appropriations as may be necessary to place under irrigation those lands which have been settled upon as agricultural lands and proven unfit therefor."[51]

On March 10, 1888, at the urging of William Morris Stewart and Henry M. Teller of Colorado, Congress approved the first large-scale hydrographic survey since 1873.[52] The enabling legislation, cast in the form of a resolution, declared that all the water in the West had been appropriated, but that the arid region was "capable of supporting a large population thereby adding to the national wealth and prosperity." By damming the many "natural depressions" within the watersheds of western streams, the agricultural future of the region would be assured and a demand created for then worthless public land. The law called for an inspection of potential storage sites, the preparation of construction plans, the measurement of the West's water supply, "and such other facts as bear on the question of storage of water for irrigating purposes." However, Congress did not make an appropriation for the survey until October 2, 1888.[53]

When the first appropriation bill came up for discussion in July, both sides were ready with a stockpile of arguments that would become familiar, if not hackneyed, by 1902. Senator Thomas M. Bowen of Colorado claimed that since 1789, Congress had appropriated about $150 million for river and harbor improvements and that it was about time the federal government spent some money to improve the arid West, which had few rivers and fewer harbors.[54] Representative Samuel R. Peters of Kansas argued that the rainbelt had moved 130 miles to the west since 1872 and implied that irrigation would speed up the process of turning arid to humid land. Others claimed that building reservoirs in the West would reduce flooding along the lower Mississippi River; that cheap lands would serve as a safety valve to avert a revolt by the working class; and that only a federal program could prevent private interests from snatching up the West's remaining land, water, and reservoir sites.[55]

In opposition, Representative William H. Forney of Alabama claimed that the farmland already available would provide homes for 300 million people, so there was no need for a reclamation program. Representative Hilary A. Herbert of Alabama worried that federal reclamation would bring 96 million acres of new wheatland into cultivation, about twice the acreage planted to that crop in settled parts of the nation. The threat to farm prices was obvious. The main objective of the Irrigation Survey, he insisted, was to get the central government to build projects that private enterprise was too smart to waste money on. If irrigation could be made to pay, he argued, private enterprise would have undertaken the task long ago. Besides, it was wrong to tax one section for the benefit of another. If 100 million acres cost ten dollars an acre to irrigate, the entire enterprise would require a billion dollars. Herbert articulated the fears of many who lived outside the arid region. Just as giant corporations grew from small companies, bureaus always sought to expand, both by absorbing other bureaus and by demanding ever larger appropriations. The $250,000 requested for the irrigation survey was only the beginning, these critics predicted. The USGS received $106,000 in fiscal year 1880, but over six times that amount in fiscal year 1888. Who was to say what the experiment in irrigation would ultimately cost?[56]

The debate over the Irrigation Survey suggested that Congress took the West far more seriously in 1888 than it had in 1873 or 1874.[57]

Directors of the natural resource bureaus shared the expectation that the survey would inevitably lead to a national reclamation program. Senator Teller told the Senate that once the irrigation survey had been completed, "it may be found desirable for the Government to take some steps to enhance the value of this land by building reservoirs and selling the land at an enhanced price."[58] Secretary of the Interior L. Q. C. Lamar agreed. "Although the cost may in the beginning be heavy," Lamar noted, "the promise appears trustworthy that the increased price at which the lands will be sold for agricultural uses will far more than re-imburse the outlay [for construction] and cost of maintenance. The advantage of thus enabling these, like other agricultural lands, to become the homes of a numerous and prosperous people, instead of falling in large bodies to the control of monopolies engaged in cattle raising, appears undeniable."[59] In the following year, the commissioner of the General Land Office noted that the Irrigation Survey had reserved land "that may be irrigated by the system of national irrigation." And early in 1890 he recommended that the secretary reject any bill to cede land to the arid states. "There are already upon the Statute books indications of a comprehensive plan of irrigation, to be prosecuted directly by the Federal Government in the arid regions of the west."[60] In 1896, the assistant commissioner of the General Land Office remembered the mood of Congress when it approved the irrigation survey on March 10, 1888: "There can be no doubt that it was contemplated at this time that this investigation would lead to the adoption of a system of irrigation to be carried on by the general government involving the construction of extensive irrigation works, and through this agency the reclamation of the lands to the extent that reclamation could be made possible."[61] Finally, at the end of the 1890s Secretary of the Interior Ethan Allen Hitchcock recalled that the reservoir sites set aside by the survey "were intended to be used in connection with a general plan of execution under the control and supervision of the United States."[62]

John Wesley Powell and the Irrigation Survey

Public expectations were very high when the Irrigation Survey began its work, far higher—and far different—from those of its leader, John Wesley Powell. Powell was one of the nation's best-known scientists in the nineteenth century.[63] His interest in irrigation dated to

1867, when he was sent to Colorado Territory by the Smithsonian Institution, the Illinois Natural History Society, and several other scientific societies to collect museum specimens. He later recalled:

> While in camp near Grand River a number of prominent gentlemen joined me and remained with me some time. . . . About the camp-fire on various occasions the problem of the future of the arid region was discussed. The central opinion expressed was that it would always be dependent upon mining industries, and that mining must necessarily, to some extent, be precarious. I took the ground that ultimately agriculture and manufacturing would be developed on a large scale, and to substantiate my opinion in relation to agriculture, I called attention to the vast agricultural resources of the arid regions of Egypt, Persia, India, China, and other countries of the world where agriculture was dependent upon irrigation, and I affirmed that in a very few decades all the waters of the arid region of the United States would be used in irrigation for agricultural purposes. During these conversations I became deeply interested in the problem.[64]

On his return to Washington, Powell launched a study of the climate of arid America, aided by Professor Joseph Henry, then secretary of the Smithsonian.

That study anticipated Powell's famous 1878 report on arid lands and his subsequent work on the public lands commission of 1879.[65] Powell decided that no revision of natural resource laws could succeed until the federal government classified the public lands so that irrigable land could be distinguished from mining, timber, and pasture lands. He also concluded that "every great stream with its tributaries found in the arid region presents peculiar problems of its own, and for that reason a general system of [water] laws for the entire country would be unwise." A five-month trip through the West in 1879, undertaken on behalf of the public lands commission, included several thousand miles of travel by stage to such remote places as Leadville, Colorado; Butte and Helena, Montana; the Salt Lake Valley of Utah; and California's Kern Valley. The trip reinforced Powell's prejudice against centralized control, and he remained faithful to his localized "system" of water use throughout his career in Washington. Like reclamation leader William Ellsworth Smythe, Powell was deeply influenced by communitarian ideals. The Mormon agricultural communities demonstrated the rewards of cooperation and close settlement; the western mining camps—which formed relatively autonomous, legally self-sufficient "districts"—also strongly influenced his thinking.

The famous second chapter of Powell's 1878 report contained

radical proposals to amend the West's land and water laws.[66] Powell assumed that only a small fraction of the West's land would ever be irrigable, and most of that was riparian. He proposed that each settler be permitted to file on 80 acres of irrigable riparian land and another 2,560 acres of grazing land back from the stream (twenty acres of which could also be irrigated). The irrigated land would produce mainly forage crops. When nine or more settlers agreed to take up land simultaneously, in adjoining parcels, they could form irrigation and grazing districts and make their own regulations and laws defining the use of natural resources. The one point Powell insisted on was that all water rights "attach" to the parcel of land irrigated to prevent the danger of "floating rights" and speculation in water. He predicted that his district system would have many benefits. Existing land laws encouraged settlers to scatter; these laws would encourage them to unite. Schools, churches, roads, and other public improvement missing in large parts of the "Old West" would be commonplace in these river-basin communities.[67]

Many historians have claimed Powell as the patron saint of federal reclamation, but he never favored a national program. On rare occasions he seemed to support federal construction of reservoirs at the headwaters of the Missouri. For each acre irrigated from tributaries of the Missouri, he insisted, another acre would be saved from flooding in the lower Mississippi basin.[68] However, Powell usually argued that national work should end with comprehensive surveys of the arid lands. In a letter to the secretary of the interior in 1888, Powell noted that nothing had changed since 1878, when he published his report on arid lands. "The conclusions therein set forth have not been materially modified by the developments of the last ten years," he noted, "although during this time agriculture has been greatly extended in the arid region, and the industrial problems involved have been seriously attacked by the State governments of Colorado and California."[69]

Nevertheless, many new water rights had vested since 1878, and that made the Irrigation Survey's job much more difficult. Powell originally estimated that the examination would take five or six years to complete with appropriations of $1 million per year and that he would merely designate reservoir sites, not prepare construction plans.[70] By May 1890, however, he insisted that even with an appropriation of $1 million a year, his survey would take a decade, and if appropriations were not increased beyond what he received in 1888 and 1889, it could take as much as thirty to forty years.[71] (Congress provided the irrigation survey with $100,000 for fiscal year 1889 and $250,000 for fiscal year 1890.) Nevertheless, Powell recognized that congressmen were unwilling to wait five or six years for results. "The exigencies of the service," Powell noted in a letter to his chief lieutenant, C. E. Dutton, "demand that the work of the engineers shall be commenced at an early date, in order that complete systems of irrigation can be projected and the plans reported to Congress at its next session."[72] This goal proved to be completely unrealistic, but Powell knew what Congress expected of him.

Powell organized three groups: one to expand the topographical surveys already under way, a second to look for reservoir sites, and a third to measure the volume of the West's largest streams. In addition to segregating irrigable lands and storage sites, he wanted to determine the maximum amount of water that storage would provide as well as the amount needed to water different crops in the various climates and soils of the arid West. Powell also promised that the irrigation survey would study rates of evaporation and seepage from canals and reservoirs; the clogging of reservoirs with debris, including silt; ways to prevent alkali buildup and flush away dangerous salts, and other matters.

At the end of 1888, less than 10 percent of the West had been mapped, so topographical work was the first priority. The survey, however, did little more than designate reservoir sites and gauge streamflow. The Arkansas, Rio Grande, upper Yellowstone, Snake, and a few smaller rivers—such as the Truckee and Carson in Nevada, the Bear and Sevier in Utah, and the Stanislaus, Tuolumne, Mokelumne, and Merced in California—received closest study. Powell well understood that he could succeed only by providing something for everyone—with particular solicitude for powerful friends in Congress. For example, his engineers, at least a few of whom got their jobs through Senator Stewart's influence, paid scrupulous attention to Nevada.[73] Senator Francis E. Warren of Wyoming, one of the most perceptive of western senators, appreciated Powell's political talents. "No Department or man," he wrote early in 1891, "understands better than [the] Geological Bureau with Maj. Powell, that success lies in keeping the distribution so adjusted as to receive support from all quarters."[74]

The first money appropriated for the survey did not become available until December 1, 1888, so little was accomplished during the winter of 1888–89, except for teaching newly hired engineers how to gauge streams at a camp on the Rio Grande near Embudo, New Mexico. By the summer of 1889, gauging stations had been established on the

Arkansas, Rio Grande, Carson, Truckee, Gila, and Snake rivers. To determine how much water was available for storage, the region's major streams would have to be measured for a decade or more; their flow was so erratic that any shorter period might give very misleading figures. During the same summer the first reservoir sites were designated—at Clear Lake in California, Bear Lake in Utah, and on the Rio Grande not far from Embudo.[75]

Hydraulic engineering involved choices between different theories and philosophies. For example, engineers sharply disagreed over where to build storage reservoirs. Powell preferred to dam high altitude natural lakes at the headwaters of major streams, such as Lake Tahoe in California and Nevada, Bear Lake in Utah and Idaho, and Yellowstone Lake in Yellowstone National Park. These lakes were cheap to plug and collected little sediment, and the water they captured was less subject to evaporation than that stored in foothill sites. They also presented less danger to downstream communities. (Floods exerted much more force on dams constructed at lower elevations, where the structures were usually larger than those erected at the outlet of mountain lakes.) Nevertheless, many engineers favored sites closer to arable land. The farther water had to travel before it reached its destination, the greater the chance of "pilferage," so downstream works posed fewer problems concerning the ownership of stored water. In addition, reservoirs close to the fields required shorter canals and captured water that entered rivers from tributaries in the foothills.[76]

Powell could impose his ideas on the engineers of the Irrigation Survey but not on Congress and western developers. "It is to be borne in mind that this survey is not primarily designed for the benefit of private parties who may contemplate the construction of works," Powell wrote his lieutenant, Dutton, in the spring of 1889, "though if they should incidently derive benefit therefrom it would be a matter for congratulation." Dutton informed the engineers he supervised that they "should take no account of works which are already constructed; nor should their judgment be swayed by any opinion on their part as to what works private enterprise and capital are likely to undertake in the next few years." The Irrigation Survey made a portentous decision: It would largely ignore the hydraulic works planned or in place and try to design *ideal* systems. Entrepreneurs soon discovered that the survey would not provide any direct aid to private enterprise, at least in the near future.[77]

Western boosters were confused and alarmed. They had welcomed the Irrigation Survey,[78] but by the summer of 1889 began to lose faith, some because Powell opposed federal construction of irrigation works,[79] others because the survey was perceived as unfriendly to private ditch and land companies, and still others because Powell was not enough of a cheerleader for western economic growth. The Irrigation Survey did nothing to make the withdrawn land and reservoir sites available to private enterprise, nor did it protect large companies against speculators.[80] To make matters even worse, Powell insisted that all water should be used within the basin of origin, limiting the opportunities for interbasin projects. Powell feared that water transfers would prevent the creation of the autonomous grazing and irrigation districts he was pushing in Congress.[81] But if water was not a commodity that could be transferred from place to place, Powell's critics charged, private companies had little future.

No better example of the conflict between the Irrigation Survey and private enterprise can be given than the plight of the Bear Lake and River Water Works and Irrigation Company, or Bothwell Irrigation Company. Bear Lake County in southern Idaho had been settled by Mormons in 1863. Its early inhabitants maintained closer ties to Utah than to Idaho; they imported most of their food and supplies from Utah's Cache Valley, about seventy-five miles away.[82] "Gentiles" in Idaho deeply feared—a fear that bordered on mass hysteria—that Mormons would take over the territory.[83] In 1889, the Bear Lake and River Water Works and Irrigation Company was created to divert water from that watershed south onto two hundred thousand acres of land between Corinne and Ogden in the Salt Lake basin. Bothwell, the company's president, was a New York financier, but the board of directors included many prominent Utah Mormons. The company's monopolistic claims to the Bear River and its tributaries, as well as Bear Lake, prompted Idaho's non-Mormon officials to petition the secretary of interior to block the scheme.[84]

On April 6, 1889, Bear Lake, an old furtrappers' rendezvous, became the first reservoir site set aside by the Irrigation Survey. The Bothwell Company, however, countered by filing on all the land and water rights within the basin. As the Cheyenne *Daily Leader* put it, "One corporation [based] outside of Idaho is attempting to own and control Boise lake for storage and the Bear river for a distance of 140 miles in Idaho that they may sell [water] to the lands and towns in Utah. Governor [George] Shoup has telegraphed the secretary of the interior stating the facts and asking that steps be taken at once to prevent this great wrong to Idaho."[85] Bothwell pointed out that the Powell survey had done no work at Bear Lake or along the Bear River, while his company had already expended as much as Congress had spent on the entire Irrigation Survey. The Idaho Constitutional Convention asked Secretary of Interior John W. Noble to kill the project. The contest between private enterprise and national planning had become a cause célèbre.

At this point a little-known provision of the Irrigation Survey enabling legislation came into play. In October 1888, Congressman George Symes of Colorado, responding to public hostility toward water companies and land speculators within his state, amended the Irrigation Survey's first appropriation bill to permit the secretary of the interior to withdraw from entry "all lands made susceptible of irrigation." At the time, most westerners shared the view of Denver's *Rocky Mountain News*: "The 'segregation' of irrigable lands provided for by the law is not intended in any way as a bar to their acquirement under the land laws. It is only designed to classify them as irrigable land, as other land is classified as pine, mineral or desert. The only reservation to be made is in the case of the sites for storage reservoirs. These are to be withdrawn from public entry to prevent their monopoly by speculators."[86] The Symes legislation, however, could be interpreted as authorizing the withdrawal of all land adjoining potential reservoir sites, all land that the survey decided was irrigable, or *all the potentially irrigable land in the entire West.* Powell had nothing to do with the legislation. Since the public lands had not been classified, since no one knew how much surplus water flowed in western streams, and since no one knew how much water could be captured by storage, he regarded such legislation as premature. Nevertheless, he was consoled by a second amendment which permitted the president to restore to entry any of the reserved land.[87]

Alarmed by Idaho's complaints against the Bothwell company, in August 1889 officials in the Interior Department, in close consultation with the president and Attorney General, decided to withdraw *all* public lands from entry, close the land offices, and suspend those claims filed after October 2, 1888. Much of the land was not irrigable, but their decision was both prudent and just. Stock growers often claimed grasslands or barren tracts to restrict access to prime agricultural land, and speculators often used such claims to blackmail bona fide settlers. Still, the withdrawal was grim news in the West. It was taken as an arbitrary change of government policy and as a warning that the Desert

Land Act would soon be repealed. Antonio Joseph, New Mexico's territorial delegate, charged that the wholesale withdrawal had thrown
land titles into chaos. "Immigration into the public land States and
Territories has been almost entirely stopped by the announcement that
the benefits of the homestead laws [are] no longer open," he proclaimed
in a July 1890 speech before Congress.[88] Two years later, in private
correspondence, Elwood Mead noted that the withdrawal "has so thoroughly frightened capitalists that the day of building large ditches across
Government land is at an end."[89]

The Bear River episode had disastrous consequencess for the Irrigation Survey. The withdrawal decision resulted in the suspension
of 134,000 filings and entries on 9 million acres.[90] The plans of the
Bothwell Irrigation Company were scuttled, but at a very high cost.
The Bear Lake controversy occurred during the last half of 1889. Apparently, Powell was oblivious to the political firestorm touched off
by closing the public domain. As late as the summer of 1890, he confidently predicted that "the appropriations made this year will be several times greater than they were last" and that the survey would need
"half a dozen new engineers who understand how to plan reservoirs
and other irrigation works."[91] His proposed budget of nearly eight hundred thousand dollars called for extending work to the Great Plains,
Oklahoma, Indian Territory, Texas, Oregon, Washington, and Wyoming.

Nevertheless, the Irrigation Survey was doomed. Westerners traditionally felt neglected or ignored by the government in Washington,
now they felt betrayed. The West was booming; never had it been more
attractive to foreign capital. The survey, many insisted, had killed
economic development. Little wonder that Senator Stewart of Nevada,
who had helped sponsor the survey and who represented the poorest
state in the arid West, savagely turned against Powell. One of Powell's
biographers has provided a vivid, if overdrawn, portrait of the Nevadan:

> In the story of Powell's fight against the dragons of error, backwardness,
> and unchecked exploitation it is fairly inevitable that Senator Stewart
> should get cast as one of the chief dragons. But he was a dragon of a
> classical frontier American breed. . . . Robust, aggressive, contentious,
> narrow, self-made, impatient of "theorists," irritated by abstract princi-
> ples, a Nevada lawyer, miner, Indian-killer; a fixer, a getter-done, an
> indefatigable manipulator around the whiskey and cigars, a dragon whose
> cave was the smoke-filled room, Big Bill Stewart was one to delight a
> caricaturist and depress a patriot. But he was also, in his way, a man of
> faith: he believed in Western "development" and he believed in the right
> of men—himself among them—to get rich by this "development."[92]

From 1875–87, Stewart practiced law in San Francisco. One of his leading clients was the Central Pacific Railroad. In 1887, he returned to the U.S. Senate as its agent. The railroad stood to gain in countless ways from an irrigation survey. Then, too, more than 90 percent of Nevada's streamflow ran to waste in the desert, and reclamation in the Silver State depended almost entirely on the construction of storage reservoirs.[93]

The Powell-Stewart rupture apparently happened in the late summer and fall of 1889, at the same time as the Bear River controversy. It took place during a western tour by Stewart's Senate Select Committee on the Irrigation and Reclamation of Arid Lands. This committee was charged with investigating the best methods to reclaim the arid West and with reporting its recommendations to the full Senate in December 1889. In all, the committee—which was represented much of the time only by Stewart and Powell—held 53 sessions, examined 382 witnesses, and traveled 14,000 miles, all in addition to several weeks of hearings in Washington, D.C. in January 1890.

No satisfactory explanation exists for the estrangement, but the trip highlighted deep differences that had always characterized the two men. Western politicians were boosters by their very nature, and as witness after witness painted the potential glory of the West, Powell refused to jump on the bandwagon. Instead, he was often arrogant and preachy, as during his address to the North Dakota Constitutional Convention on August 5, 1889, at one of the committee's stops. He urged the lawmakers to abandon the doctrine of prior appropriation— which many westerners, including Stewart, considered the only protection the states had from a system of federal control over water[94]— and he lectured them on the sins of the past:

> Years will come of abundance and years will come of disaster, and between the two the people will be prosperous and unprosperous, and the thing to do is look the question squarely in the face. . . . You hug to yourselves the delusion that the climate is changing. This question is 4,000 years old. Nothing that man can do will change the climate. . . . There's almost enough rainfall for your purposes, but one year with another you need a little more than you get. . . . There are waters rolling by you which are quite ample to redeem your land and you must save these waters. . . . You are to depend hereafter in a great measure on the running streams—in a small part on your artesian wells, and in part on the storage of storm waters [in ponds].[95]

It was not simply that Powell exploded myths, not simply that he was

a Washington bureaucrat, not simply that he proposed maps and surveys while most westerners demanded action, not simply that he was
often inconsistent in public statements, not even that he was perceived
as lordly and self-serving; his deepest sin was that he was a Cassandra
who questioned dreams without offering others to take their place.

By early 1890 Stewart saw Powell not just as a false prophet, but
almost as the Antichrist. In a May 26 letter, he attacked Powell's
justification for the preliminary topographical survey as "absurd." On
the same day he introduced a resolution calling for the secretary of the
interior to reveal how much money had been "diverted and used for
topographic surveys." He insisted that "the money has been squarely
misappropriated," and that "the whole legislation, which I was guilty
of inaugurating to some extent myself, has been an unmitigated evil
to the people of my part of the country. They can not make homes
there."[96] Early in June he declared that Powell had a "lobby force here
which is nearly overwhelming," and he implied that the director of
the USGS was holding the public lands hostage to blackmail Congress
into granting him larger appropriations for scientific projects. "He has
now the whole arid region under his control," Stewart warned, "and
is attempting to secure further legislation to strengthen his grasp and
increase his power." Later in the same month Stewart repeated the
charge in another letter, proclaiming that Powell was "drunk with
power and deaf to reason."[97] Stewart's public and private war of words
continued through the summer of 1890, and at one point he wrote to
former U.S. senator John Conness that he had "made some inquiry and
find that his [Powell's] habits with women are scandalous. . . . I thank
you for the hint you gave me."[98]

Stewart's political reputation was on the line. One historian has
remarked that the senator saw the Irrigation Survey as a necessary
prelude, perhaps even justification, for federal cession of arid lands to
the states. The surveys would show precisely what lands were irrigable,
and Congress would be more receptive to a limited than to a comprehensive grant.[99] There is plenty of evidence to support this conclusion.
Shortly before returning to the Senate, Stewart suggested that Congress
"either extend direct aid for the construction of the necessary hydraulic
works" or cede the public lands to Nevada on condition that the state
undertake the work, either directly or through private companies.[100]
Later, in March 1888, Stewart argued that once Powell had segregated
the irrigable land, then the land not suitable for irrigation could be
"disposed of to cattlemen and sheep men, and the proceeds used for

the construction of hydraulic works," presumably by the state.[101] He also recognized the value of California's Wright Act, by which farmers paid for their own irrigation works; the appeal to "home rule" was important in a state that contained few small farmers. In February 1889, he informed Nevada state senator Andrew Maute that he was "trying to get some provision inserted in the appropriation bill . . . whereby parties desiring to construct irrigation works may form themselves into districts and form co-operative associations to construct the works, and if need be, mortgage their claim to raise money for that purpose."[102]

Nevertheless, Stewart was not irrevocably committed to cession; like most western politicians he was eclectic, not doctrinaire. He did not oppose federal reclamation on principle. Instead, he thought that it would take too long for Congress to get construction started, that Nevada would inevitably be shortchanged, that the national government might overturn water rights established under state laws, that a national program might be ruled unconstitutional, and that it would depend too much on the whims of legislators unsympathetic to the West.

Science Divided

Stewart's views were not as rigid as some historians have claimed, and he alone was not powerful enough to kill the Irrigation Survey, which came to an end in August 1890.[103] There were deep divisions within the West itself. The Irrigation Survey lacked the money to pay equal attention to every state and territory. The Pacific Northwest, Great Plains, Arizona, and Wyoming were neglected and had little incentive to support Powell's work.[104] Moreover, with the exception of Colorado, the most populous and politically powerful western states had been left out. California, with the greatest need and potential for reservoirs, contained virtually no public lands capable of reclamation at a reasonable price, and most of its water and storage sites were already in private hands. Large parts of Oregon and Washington, including the Willamette Valley, required irrigation only every third or fourth year. And on the Great Plains, irrigation as practiced in the mountain West was simply impractical.

Powell never convinced residents of the Great Plains that the Irrigation Survey was anything more than the creature of a handful of politicians from the mountain states. In the late 1880s and 1890s, farmers on the plains feared that the expansion of agriculture in the Far West would further depress agricultural prices. For example, at an irrigation convention held at Oberlin, Kansas, on December 10, 1890, the eight hundred conferees adopted a resolution that declared: "We are unalterably opposed to the further opening of arid lands to settlement, and demand that the governmental experiment in irrigation . . . be confined, for the present, to occupied arid lands."[105] Moreover, the massive exodus following the drought of 1888 and 1889 suggested that any large program to reclaim the interior West might further deplete the shrinking populations of Kansas, Nebraska, and Dakota Territory. In 1892, *Irrigation Age* noted in an obituary for Senator Preston Plumb of Kansas that, as a member of the Senate Select Committee on Irrigation chaired by Stewart, "he was outspoken in his objection to any large scheme which might lead to an exodus of Kansas Farmers, to possibly more inviting fields."[106]

The Great Plains had few streams and no place to build large storage reservoirs. The handful of damsites were far removed from irrigable land and so shallow that any water stored there would have been subject to massive evaporation. Even if the plains had contained many rivers, the friable soil would have filled dams with silt far faster than in most parts of the arid West. And that soil, as the flow of the Arkansas River demonstrated, was so porous that much of the water would have simply disappeared. Ironically, that part of the West with the best soil, and where the cheapest ditches could be built, posed the greatest obstacles to irrigation. As of 1889, there were less than one hundred thousand acres watered on the Great Plains, including Texas.[107] Moreover, the construction of reservoirs on headwaters of the Platte, Arkansas, Republican, and tributaries of the Missouri, all of which originated in the mountain states, threatened to reduce the already scant supply that reached the plains. In Colorado and Wyoming, newspapers insisted that irrigated land was like a sponge: Once saturated, it returned virtually all the diverted water to the source.[108] But this argument had little appeal to residents of the Great Plains. They were keenly interested in irrigation, but not in storage reservoirs and long canals.

Midwestern farmers knew little about underground water, but they shared the belief of most westerners that artesian wells could provide an unlimited supply that was beyond litigation. It could supplement normal rainfall without committing farmers to the cost of building and maintaining ditches that might be needed only every three or four years. The 1870s saw many testimonials like that contained in a letter from a Nevadan appended to a report by Cyrus Thomas. "A sufficient supply of water for irrigation is the great want. This difficulty, however, can be obviated by artesian wells," the writer declared. "The time is not distant when hundreds of thousands of acres will be brought into subjection by this means, and now, where there is nothing seemingly but a desert waste, broad fields of the cereals and inviting meadows will delight the eye and relieve the present monotony."[109] In 1880, Congress appropriated twenty thousand dollars to sink two test wells. Supporters of the bill argued that only 3 percent of 500 million acres of potential farmland could be reclaimed from streamflow; the rest would remain unsold until some way could be found to supply it with water. Once the government had shown that subterranean water was available, the argument ran, settlers would purchase the land and private companies would drill the wells.[110]

Two government test wells on the plains east of the Rockies proved to be failures, but western boosters were not easily discouraged—or educated. For example, countless bills were introduced in Congress to pay for experimental wells in Nevada and two of its poor siblings, the territories of New Mexico and Arizona.[111] By 1883, towns, counties, territories, and states throughout the West had jumped on the bandwagon. Rush County, Kansas, asked for ten thousand dollars to sink an artesian well at a location to be decided by the secretary of the interior.[112] Another bill sought land grants of up to 1 million acres to subsidize the work of the "Western Well and Irrigation Company" in Colorado, Kansas, Arizona, and New Mexico. The city of Russell, Kansas, voted a bond issue of ten thousand dollars in the spring of 1883 to sink a well, but after digging one thousand feet without encountering water, appealed for a ten-thousand-dollar federal appropriation to continue the probe.[113] The flood of bills and petitions in favor of artesian wells contributed greatly to public interest in an irrigation survey.[114]

The drought of 1889 intensified the interest in underground water. In the spring of that year, *Scientific American* published an article on the James River Valley, which promised a limitless underground supply.[115] Artesian wells could guarantee abundant water for irrigation and also an ideal source of power that required little machinery or fuel. *"It is a Niagara Falls already harnessed for use,"* the *Aberdeen Daily News* declared. "All the textile fabrics could be manufactured here *cheaper than in any other part of the universe.* The time will come when this will be recognized, and [the use of] natural gas will be extinguished by *the giant gushing wells in Dakota.*" The *Daily News* predicted that the sinking of a multitude of shallow wells along the James River could reclaim 1 million acres of land, and the return flow or seepage from irrigation would render the stream navigable, eliminating the need for railroads to ship cattle and hogs to Sioux City, Omaha, and St. Louis.[116]

John Wesley Powell discounted this enthusiasm; he considered underground water, particularly artesian wells, an insignificant source.[117] Powell made his first public statements on groundwater during the Stewart committee's tour of the West in the late summer and fall of 1889. He surely winced as witness after witness presented ever bolder schemes to tap subterranean reservoirs. One popular theory held that all water hidden beneath the Great Plains originated in the Rocky Mountain snowpack and moved underground much as it did in streambeds on the surface. J. W. Gregory, one of Kansas's greatest boosters, insisted that there were two Arkansas Rivers, one aboveground and the other below. And since the underground stream had a slope of seven and a half feet per mile, horizontal tunnels could tap it and carry the water into canals and storage ponds adjoining the highlands on either side of the terranean stream. This done, he predicted, the Arkansas Valley could provide a home to 30 million people.[118] In other words, the supply of underground water was perceived as almost completely independent of local rainfall. And since the mountains were higher than the plains, the pressure in artesian wells would be constant. Water that fed into one end of an underground basin at a constant rate would come out elsewhere at that same rate.[119]

Powell had no patience with such arguments. Artesian wells could water stock, gardens, orchards, and vineyards, but they were inadequate to serve field crops. The porosity of soil on the Great Plains made it impossible to determine where water entered an underground pool, he pointed out, and it was also impossible to determine whether an artesian well was located above or below the inflow. Powell was one of the first Americans to recognize that the quantity of water drawn from the ground each year could not exceed the volume of water that reached the aquifer from the surface without depleting the supply—a lesson westerners have yet to learn. Any draft on subterranean water reduced the pressure; the more wells, the less pressure. The first were often gushers, but after a period of months or even weeks, most of the water had to be pumped. Once that happened, Powell predicted, legal conflicts would erupt between those who had sunk the first wells and those who came later, conflicts that resembled disputes over surface water.

"If all the artesian wells in the world which are used for irrigation were assembled in one county of Dakota," Powell testified before the Senate Committee on Irrigation early in 1891, "they would not irrigate that county." Like George Davidson, he tried to give Americans a history lesson based on the experience of other nations. No country in the world, he noted, had practiced extensive irrigation using artesian wells. Most used artesian wells as watering holes for stock. Algeria, with the largest acreage watered from this source, could reclaim only six thousand acres. The sheer cost of boring wells made this water too expensive for wheat and forage crops (far more expensive than the use of surface water in most parts of the West). The West had relatively few places where underground water could be tapped, and fewer still where the quantity obtained was commensurate with the cost.[120]

A minority report of the Senate Select Committee on Arid Lands echoed Powell, warning that it was particularly "unwise to create a new geological survey to discover artesian waters." Even locating underground water would raise false hopes and encourage the naive and gullible. Most Great Plains residents, however, adamantly rejected Powell's pessimistic message, and Powell finally bent to the pressure. In March 1890, he advised North and South Dakota's senators that "it is possible to place before the people of that country facts that will materially aid as a guide to the discovery of artesian fountains." An artesian survey could locate "important sources of water for irrigation . . . and the farmers of many districts could find relief thereby." Moreover, it would spare farmers in districts that could not be served by artesian wells "from making large and wasteful expenditures for this purpose."[121] Powell clearly hoped to administer any new survey.

Powell's enemies saw an entering wedge and took full advantage. His success at winning large appropriations for the Geological Survey had created considerable enmity in rival bureaus. Rumors had abounded for months that Powell's irrigation work would soon be taken from Interior and given to Agriculture, and that the Army Corps of Engineers would be asked to conduct the underground survey. Stewart had repeatedly asked the secretary of the interior to fire Powell and, when that effort failed, tried to have the entire Geological Survey abolished. Stewart's chief ally in these maneuvers was Senator Preston Plumb of Kansas.[122] In March 1890, Congress appropriated twenty thousand dollars for an emergency artesian well survey covering the land between the ninety-seventh meridian and the Rocky Mountains, but it entrusted the task to Richard J. Hinton in the Department of Agriculture, instead of giving the work to the Powell survey or creating a new bureau in the Interior Department. Hinton and Powell were arch-rivals, with Powell going so far as to suggest that Hinton had been part of John Brown's raid on Harper's Ferry. The senators from the two Dakotas, as well as Nebraska and Kansas, did most to push the appropriation bill through Congress, but Stewart also gave his hearty support because he saw the measure as an opportunity to undermine Powell's influence.[123] As the secretary of agriculture noted in his annual report for 1890: "It has been represented to me that the underflow waters can be made available for purposes of irrigation by means of pumping at a less expense than that entailed by the building and maintenance of extensive reservoirs, dams, and ditches."[124] The new Artesian Well Survey not only filled a gap left by the Irrigation Survey, it threatened to displace Powell's work altogether.

Richard J. Hinton and Edwin Nettleton conducted the artesian survey for the USDA and told Great Plains farmers what they wanted to hear. They devoted most of their attention to the Dakotas and those portions of Montana, Wyoming, Colorado, New Mexico, Texas, Nebraska, Kansas, and Oklahoma that had suffered most from the drought. They estimated that 98 percent of land in the James River Valley could be irrigated by groundwater, about 7 million acres. Though the cost of sinking each well would run from $2,800 to $7,300, drilling them as part of a coordinated plan promised to reduce the cost to $1,500 per well or less. Nettleton insisted that the depletion of underground water was nearly impossible; the water used to irrigate would eventually find its way back to its source, as would water that evaporated from fields and storage ponds. And farmers need not worry, the soothing report concluded, about any decrease in pressure; over one thousand wells in the Red River basin in northeast Dakota had flowed for years with no decline in the volume or rate of flow. Nettleton consciously appealed to those westerners most threatened or neglected by the Powell survey. For example, he took pains to show that many parts of California could tap underground water in lieu of streamflow. "The average Kern County [California] well will serve . . . one section of 640 acres of land," Nettleton promised. "If its continuous flow is properly stored, its service can be made as high as 3,500 acres. . . . So strong is the flow when the artesian supply is struck that the farmers find it difficult to control the same." Congress could help by finding the best sites.[125]

In September 1890, Nettleton's office received an additional forty thousand dollars to continue its survey during the next fiscal year, and it secured another ten thousand in March 1891.[126] Nettleton's survey ultimately established several important facts concerning subterranean waters: That underground water was not one massive pool, but many discrete bodies of water comparable to lakes and oceans on the surface of the planet; that underground water sometimes forced its way to the surface and augmented streamflow; and that the underground supply could serve only a small fraction of the West's arable land.[127] Nettleton's initial optimism soon evaporated, and his work left many questions unanswered. How large were the underground pools? What produced the pressure in artesian wells? And if underground waters were recharged from surface water, how quickly were they replenished? Of course, none of these questions mattered much to Great Plains boosters; they continued to report veritable gushers, like the well on the farm of Henry Risdon two miles north of Huron, which shot fifty feet into the air through an eight-inch pipe and could be heard and seen in town.[128]

Powell's support for artesian wells disappeared after Nettleton began work. The census of 1890 revealed that there were 3,930 of these wells in the arid West, which watered only 51,896 acres, an average of 13.21 acres per well. Over half were in California, where they served 38,378 acres. The average per-acre cost of irrigation from this source was $18.55, while it was only $8.15 for irrigation from surface flow.[129] Interest in artesian water lasted through the first half of the 1890s, but without the enthusiasm of the worst years of the drought from 1888 to 1891.[130] By 1891, Powell argued that where land could not be served from mountain storage reservoirs, capturing storm water in small ponds on each farm was the best alternative: "If every convenient depression and hollow were utilized to hold back the surplus rain water, and the same care were exercised in saving and using this that would be necessary in the case of storage and artesian waters, results far larger and surer could be obtained."[131]

The debate over artesian wells was not simply a struggle between Powell and his critics, between Interior and Agriculture, or even between the Great Plains states and the rest of the West; it represented an object lesson in the ways in which scientific differences affected public policy and congressional appropriations. Most historians have supported the thesis that "the West itself . . . beat him [Powell], the Big Bill Stewarts and Gideon Moodys [U.S. senator from South Dakota in 1890], the land and cattle and water barons, the plain homesteaders, the locally patriotic, the ambitious, the venal, the acquisitive, the myth-bound West which insisted on running into the future like a streetcar on a gravel road."[132] This view of history as an extended battle between good and evil, between the enlightened and ignorant, and between the selfless and the selfish obscures the fact that the Irrigation Survey would have collapsed even if it had won unanimous support in the West. With scientists so divided over fundamental questions, how could the West or the nation find a coherent water policy?

Conflicts over science extended far beyond such mundane questions as where to build reservoirs or the utility of artesian wells. Just as Stewart's Select Senate Committee on Irrigation finished its work, Professor E. D. Cope, paleontologist and editor of *American Naturalist,* who had lost his government job when Powell took charge of the unified Geological Survey, published a scathing attack on his rival. In an interview with the New York *Herald* on January 12, 1890, Cope and Professor W. B. Scott of Princeton charged Powell with stealing the work of others, with professional incompetence as a geologist, and with using his surveys to expand patronage and personal power instead of the frontiers of science. On the following day, the *Philadelphia Record* echoed the charge. "He has so thoroughly entrenched himself in the Geological Bureau by the arts of political management," it asserted, "that it would be hard for all the science in the country to dislodge him. He has done too many favors to members of Congress by making places for their relatives to dread any assault that may be made on him in the interests of learning." Although many westerners complained that the Irrigation Survey had not produced practical results, Powell suffered as much from charges of being too pragmatic as too theoretical. His enemies blamed him for putting topographical work before the mapping of dams and canals. But, ironically, Powell had beaten out Clarence King and Ferdinand V. Hayden for the directorship of the USGS by insisting—much to the delight of some members of Congress—that the federal government had no business supporting theoretical research in zoology and botany.[133]

One conflict over science did more to undermine Powell's following in Washington than any other. Given the widespread fear of floods and timber famines in the decades after the Civil War, the preservation of forests appealed to those from many different disciplines.

Debate raged during the 1880s and 1890s over whether forests increased rainfall or affected the climate. But most scientists assumed that deforestation—whether through fires, logging, or grazing—touched off a train of evil consequences including soil erosion, alternating cycles of flood and drought, the drying up of springs, the burial of prime agricultural land in valleys by topsoil and debris washed down from the mountains, and the permanent destruction of the land ("desertification," in nineteenth-century parlance). In the fall and winter, soil bacteria that lived on the forest floor converted organic vegetable mold into plant food; in the spring, rain and melting snow carried these nutritious nitrates onto farmlands in the valleys below.[134]

One of the first demands for a national forest came in 1883 and emphasized the intimate relationship between forestry and agriculture. *The Nation* supported creation of a preserve in northern Montana, at the headwaters of the Missouri and Columbia rivers. "Here, then, if the Government is to take any measure to protect the rivers of the country, and make agriculture possible west of the 100th meridian by means of irrigation, the experiment can best be tried."[135] Abbot Kinney, one of California's chief crusaders for irrigation and forest conservation, made the relationship between forests and streamflow even more explicit. "It is time that the farmers roused themselves and made a fight for their forest friends," he urged in 1891. "No forests, no farms. The pine tree sings in the Sierra a song that is echoed in the rich rustle of grain on the distant plain."[136]

By the turn of the century, a full-scale intellectual war had broken out among scientists over the relationship between forests and streamflow.[137] That debate had roots in the way conservationists viewed the Irrigation Survey of 1888–90. In 1889, with Powell's work well under way, the secretary of the American Forestry Association wrote to President Harrison warning that Congress should not "authorize any scheme of irrigation which does not recognize the indispensableness of the mountain forests, as *natural* storage reservoirs, and as auxiliaries to any artificial system."[138] To Powell, the great danger of forest conservation was that preservation of the trees would become sufficient in itself, eliminating the need for canals and artificial reservoirs. This was no less dangerous than the myth that forests increased rainfall.[139] Powell's ideas were already suspect. Those who supported the creation of national forests opposed his plan to grant autonomous grazing and irrigation districts carved from the public domain exclusive control over the forests within their borders.[140]

One of Powell's leading critics was Charles Sprague Sargent, professor of arboriculture at Harvard University, compiler of a lengthy report on the forests in the tenth census, editor of *Garden and Forest* (1888–97), and author of the epic *Silva of North America*, published in fourteen volumes between 1891 and 1902. Initially, Sargent strongly supported the construction of storage reservoirs, and Powell appeared equally sympathetic to forest conservation.[141] But Powell and many of his followers came to believe that forests deprived farmers of water, not just by imprisoning it in the soil, but by increasing evaporation through leaves and needles. Henry Gannett, chief geographer in Powell's Geological Survey, a founder and president of the National Geographic Society, may well have been speaking for his boss when he declared that "it is advisable to cut away as rapidly as possible all the forests, especially upon the mountains, where most of the rain falls, in order that as much of the precipitation as possible may be collected in the streams. This will cause, not a decrease in the annual flow of streams, as commonly supposed, but an increase. . . . It may be added that the forests in the arid region are thus disappearing with commendable rapidity."[142]

The Johnstown, Pennsylvania, flood in the spring of 1889, which killed twenty-two hundred people, alarmed Sargent and raised doubts in Congress about the wisdom of the reservoir survey. Now Sargent warned that something had to be done to stop a movement that seemed destined to end in government construction of "enormously expensive works, which all experience has shown to be inadequate for the purpose they are intended to accomplish, and fraught with serious danger to the lives and property of thousands."[143] Two months after Sargent published those words, Powell gave him more ammunition by publishing his own article on the significance of the Johnstown flood. Powell, like Gannett, challenged head-on the idea that forests were reservoirs. "In a treeless region the snows are accumulated in great drifts in the lee of rocks and cliffs and under the walls of gorges and canyons," he observed. "Such great drifts are themselves stupendous reservoirs of water, and artificial works are necessary only to control the flow properly and distribute the water at the places and times needed." In low mountains, forests were a useful tool to combat flooding precisely because they drained moisture from the soil and returned it to the atmosphere, reducing streamflow.[144]

To the champions of national forests, this was bad enough, but in the spring of 1890 Powell went further. He had already suggested that the forests would receive better protection under private rather than public ownership. Now he argued that the number of trees destroyed by man was insignificant compared to the number consumed by fire. Furthermore, 20–40 percent of the rainfall in a region was captured by vegetation and returned to the heavens. Research around the Wasatch Mountains had shown that denudation resulted in a "great increase" in the volume of streams. When water was stored in mountain lakes, the preservation of forests surrounding the reservoir was vital. In most places, however, trees and brush were just a nuisance. "For all these reasons," he proclaimed, "the forests of the upper regions are not advantageous to the people of the valleys, who depend on the streams for the fertilization of the farms."[145]

These words constituted a red flag to Sargent. "It is a matter of regret," he fumed, "that Major Powell and the admirable young men associated with him are not more vitally interested in the preservation of these important forests." Responding to Powell's article, Sargent criticized its "eccentric deviations from the teachings of experience in all times and countries," and characterized it as "a rhapsody rather than a sustained and coherent argument."[146] J. B. Harrison, secretary of the American Forestry Congress, echoed Sargent in arguing that the Johnstown tragedy compelled all conservationists to reassess the value of dams.[147]

Conclusion

By the end of June 1890, the Irrigation Survey had surveyed and requested the segregation of 147 reservoir sites—33 in California, 46 in Colorado, 27 in Montana, 39 in New Mexico, and 2 in Nevada. In addition, it had surveyed 335 miles of highline canals. In all, the reservoir sites covered 165,932 acres and, at the rate of 1.5 acre-feet to the acre—admittedly a very optimistic figure, but one widely used at the time—those reservoirs could have irrigated 1,898,544 acres. This was only a small fraction of the 30,000,000 acres designated as irrigable by the Irrigation Survey, yet it exceeded all the land then irrigated in Arizona, New Mexico, Utah, Wyoming, Montana, Idaho, and Nevada combined.[148] As a sop to private enterprise, Congress in 1891 passed a generous bill granting rights-of-way for canals and reservoirs on government land.[149] Although the 30,000,000 acres were restored to the public domain at the end of August 1890, the reservoir sites remained off limits until February 1897.[150] By that time, the value of many sites was impaired, if not destroyed, by the construction of reservoirs at alternate, inferior locations within the same watershed.[151]

Powell was in a corner, and when Congress cut off funds to the Irrigation Survey in August 1890, it performed a mercy killing. The rest of his career was a postscript to the events of 1888–90. In 1891, 1892, and 1893, appropriations for the geological and paleontological work of the USGS were slashed, and once again western politicians were at the vanguard of Powell's critics. He survived as director of the USGS until May 1894, though his reputation never recovered. The hydrographic survey taught him a sobering lesson: The best public land and virtually all the water had been claimed, so the value of future government aid would be very limited. If the federal government ever launched a reclamation program, it would have to serve private as well as public land, and assist existing farmers as well as new ones.

There were, of course, many other reasons for the failure of the Irrigation Survey. The 100 million acres that Powell promised could be reclaimed in the arid West represented half of the cultivated farmland in the United States in 1889. That terrified members of Congress from rural districts east of the Mississippi. Moreover, some allowance has to be made for party politics. As the Reno *Gazette* put it, Democratic members of the Senate Committee on Irrigation held "the ideas of the great party to which they belong: that the powers of the National Government are limited and restrained; that they extend only to matters relating to war, to commerce, and to police protection; that the Government is in no sense a paternal one, and that it has nothing whatever to do with the fostering of the great enterprises upon which the prosperity, the wealth and the progress of the country depend." A Democratic landslide in the fall of 1890 helped ensure that the Irrigation Survey's work would not be resurrected by the next Congress.[152]

Unfortunately, Powell's biographers, along with most western historians, have distorted the history of the Irrigation Survey. Powell has too often been portrayed as a rationalist and idealist battling the corrupt, perverted values of a sinister, materialistic age, or as one of the fathers of conservation preaching restraint to an audience of vandals. Either way, Powell has gotten considerably better press than his critics. He argued that the future of the West was limited by nature. He was certainly right, but historians cannot dismiss those who disagreed with him as simply selfish, venal, misguided, or blind. To a generation that deeply believed nature was malleable—for example, that human activities could modify the weather, that all desert soil was fertile under the right conditions, and that life in the arid West could be made to resemble that in the East—Powell was an arch-heretic. Westerners turned on him because he robbed them of the prospect of independence. He argued that aridity condemned the West to remain perpetually subordinate to the rest of the nation, a land of stockmen and small farmers, not of cities and industry. Westerners simply could not accept that view of their future.

Powell's contributions are not reduced by pointing out that he had plenty of blind spots. He thought that the underground water supply was insignificant, that an acre-foot of water was sufficient to water virtually any desert land, and that water would wash alkali and other impurities from the soil. All these assumptions were wrong.[153] So much of the literature on Powell has been uncritical that it is fair to consider the radically different portrait painted by historian Stanley Roland Davison. In Davison's pages, Powell appears as a fuzzy and impractical thinker given to bombastic purple passages, a man of colossal vanity obsessed with the desire to serve as spokesman for all of American science.[154]

Other criticisms are even more relevant. Paul Wallace Gates has noted that Powell failed to see the great agricultural potential of the land immediately west of the hundredth meridian, land that has produced much of the winter wheat raised in the United States since World War II. Nor did he see that his 2,560-acre "grazing homesteads"—which inevitably would have contained a great deal of potential farmland—invited tremendous abuse. Powell knew how cattlemen, land companies, miners, timbermen, and others twisted and distorted the Homestead, Timber Culture, and Desert Land acts. But he seemed oblivious to the ways his land system might have been perverted. As Gates puts it, Powell was insensitive "to the anti-monopoly movement in the West which . . . was trying to prevent the establishment of large estates through the adoption of rigid restrictions on the amount of land individuals could acquire from the government."[155] And although Powell appreciated the need for group settlement of the arid West,[156] he did not explain how or why Americans who had shown so little inclination to cooperate in other common endeavors would do so once they settled within one of his districts. Moreover, he seldom discussed how those districts might be organized or financed. By the late 1880s, the adoption of his scheme would have challenged an enormous number of long-established water rights. It was little more than a pipe-dream, so impractical that Congress never gave it serious consideration.[157]

There is no need to exalt George Davidson by demeaning John Wesley Powell, substituting one hero for another. As Donald Worster has pointed out, the "nationalists" had blind spots of their own.[158] Worster argues that the American engineers who inspected the irrigation systems of other nations were "classic studies in innocence abroad." They were technocrats interested in planning, efficiency, and modernization. They followed "the rule of instrumentalism: reason in the service of productivity, economic maximization, and domination, reason not about ultimate ends but about means." They were blind to the impact of large-scale irrigation on native cultures, blind to the sharp class differences that emerged between ruler and ruled, and blind to the "despotism" that destroyed all vestiges of self-government. Worster believes that irrigation engineers learned too much, not too little, from the experience of the British in India and Egypt. For the European dreams of imperial dominion ultimately infected the hydraulic engineers who helped to settle the American West. "The irrigation centralizers, whatever region they represented, were overwhelmingly an elite group promoting an elite program," Worster concludes. "Their overriding aim was to enlarge, for their own ends, the country's wealth and influence. To secure peace and stability at home. To earn profits at home and abroad. And to pursue power, always power."[159]

The relevance of Worster's ideas to the British experience warrants careful examination. It cannot be assumed that a "centralized" water system in the American West would have worked as it did in India or Egypt. Some allowance has to be made for imperialism independent of centralization; after all, the British were not just irrigators. Social and economic conditions in the West differed greatly from those in India. Moreover, the federal system of government that prevailed in the United States was far different from the structure of government in European nations and their colonies. One of the most important features of American government was that it permitted power to flow in two directions at once. For example, administration of the public domain was centralized, but it still catered to local interests. Consequently, many westerners who complained about irrational, impractical land laws also feared turning the public domain over to the states.

There is no certainty, of course, that the history of the arid West would have been any different had the recommendations of George Davidson and the "centralizers" been implemented. But it is clear that the rest of the world learned from America, particularly in water law. The Canadian equivalent of the Powell survey, undertaken in 1893–94, resulted in the enactment of a code that abolished riparian rights and vested complete control over water in the crown. As Lawrence B. Lee has pointed out, "since the Dominion owned the water, it could distribute this resource in the most equitable manner and did so through administrative procedures where water rights were granted on the basis of licenses to private parties. There was also the reservation by the government of an absolute right to take over and operate irrigation works set up under the statute." Although irrigation development was by private enterprise, the government kept a record of all water claims and limited them to the available supply.[160]

Australia followed a similar course. Beginning in 1886, the province of Victoria enacted water laws based on the recommendations of Alfred Deakin and later Elwood Mead. Deakin was the provincial attorney general in the 1880s. He toured the arid American West in the middle of that decade and witnessed the weaknesses of its irrigation laws firsthand. Mead, whose career is discussed in chapter 7, had served as Wyoming State Engineer and head of the Office of Irrigation Investigations in the Department of Agriculture before he became a consultant to the provincial government and Chairman of the Victoria Rivers and Water Supply Commission from 1907 to 1914. No American knew more about irrigation institutions.

In Australia, where the government owned the railroads, telegraph, and telephone, there was little opposition to national ownership of water. The province abolished riparian rights by purchasing the bed and banks of every major stream. In this way, it assumed absolute control over all canals at their source. In lieu of granting perpetual property rights, it issued licenses to use water for a specified number of years, usually 15. The license did not promise a particular quantity. Each year the water commission divided up the "normal" supply based on a number of variables including the size of farms and the crops each farmer grew. Any surplus was auctioned off to holders of regular water rights at an annual water sale. All grants were tied to individual farms and could not be bought, sold, or traded. (Deakin did this to prevent farmers from claiming more water than they needed in anticipation of selling the extra supply to newcomers, as was routinely done in California.) The state constructed, owned, and operated all irrigation works and permitted only groups to settle public lands (to prevent individual settlers from scattering and to limit speculation). State control was seen as the only rational system. Victorians trusted bureaucracy more than the courts; they had little fear of public power.[161]

Despite the fears of westerners, Elwood Mead knew that public ownership was not synonymous with tyranny, and that institutional anarchy posed a much greater danger than centralized authority. "When the reclamation of the Arid West becomes a matter of history," he wrote in 1897, "it will be seen that many of the arid States have wholly ignored the experience of other irrigated lands, and have enacted laws and customs which thorough and repeated trials have shown to be utterly pernicious and destructive." Victoria had all but eliminated conflict over water. "The thing that I keep asking myself," Mead mused in 1911, "is: Why could not the American States have adopted a plan of this kind?"[162]

These lessons were not learned in the United States until the 1920s and 1930s, if then. Meanwhile, the failure of the Powell survey, along with the depression of 1893–98, forced many westerners to look at other alternatives, particularly direct action by the states and a partnership between the states and private enterprise. Westerners would eventually return to federal reclamation, but only after the depression was over and a new wave of nationalism had swept across the nation. When that happened, few would remember George Davidson or his faith in centralized planning.

6
The Triumph of Sectionalism: State Enterprise in California, Nevada, and Colorado

In the 1880s and 1890s, three states—California, Nevada, and Colorado—attempted to escape the pitfalls of private reclamation by building their own irrigation works. All three failed. Inadequate budgets, insufficient knowledge of hydrography and irrigation agriculture, nonexistent or limited engineering staffs, defective water laws, and shortsighted legislatures all undermined ambitious pubic policies and planning. So did divisions among and within the western states. In all three states, the fear that one section might profit at the expense of another forced lawmakers either to abandon programs in their infancy or to engage in a futile effort to provide "something for everyone." The fate of state reclamation demonstrated not only the power of rival interest groups and the corruption and inefficiency of state officials but also structural weaknesses in the American system of governance.

Federalism, Mercantilism, and the American West

All societies exhibit tension between centralism—exemplified by unity, order, conformity, and rationality—and localism, characterized by diversity, individualism, and freedom. In the United States that tension has often manifested itself as a struggle between public and private values, the hinterland and the metropolis, or collectivism and individualism. Federalism flourished in the nineteenth century in large part because the United States managed to avoid major foreign wars. The nation did not require conscription or large expenditures for an army and navy, nor did it develop a military ruling caste. The twentieth century has demonstrated how exotic a plant nineteenth-century federalism really was. Two major wars, the depression of the 1930s, an increasingly interdependent economy, and the need to define such national values as "equality" (part of the civil rights revolution of the last few decades) have seriously modified the older decentralized system of rule.

Federalism diffused political power throughout society. It encouraged the formation of political parties, antislavery societies, nativist organizations, and temperance unions, among others. In effect, federalism made each town, county, and state a legal laboratory. No jurisdiction assumed *full responsibility* for economic development, and none was "locked out." The federal system increased the number of governmental forums entrepreneurs and interest groups could use to reach their goals, and economic actors played town, county, state, and nation against each other. For example, private companies that could not wrest land grants and loans from Congress often turned to the states or local governments for aid. Nevertheless, shared power came at a high price. It contributed mightily to sectionalism, in part because it did not adapt well to dramatic shifts in population. In a rapidly expanding nation, the demands of new towns and counties for increased representation in state legislatures and Congress generally encountered stiff opposition from established communities. Nothing did more to reinforce decentralization and localism.[1]

Federalism found a powerful ally in "rivalistic state mercantilism." The Constitution, it has been argued, was rooted in a medieval world view, specifically the organic relationship between lords and vassals. Elizabethan mercantilism, which grew out of this same world view, rested on several assumptions: that society was an interrelated system of conflicting, competing, and complementary interests; that only the state could promote wealth and the public good; that only the consciously active state would prosper; that trade was a major instrument of public policy; that a commercial empire was necessary to maintain prosperity at home; that only a "balanced economy," which recognized the interdependence of agriculture and trade, could flourish for long; and that in a finite world, where the supply of precious metals and basic natural resources was fixed or constant, one nation could succeed only by reducing the prosperity of rival nations—one nation's gain was another's loss. The idea of progress was largely absent from seventeenth-century England, but mercantilists exhibited a keen sense of its opposite: decay and degeneration.[2]

The English colonists learned that what was true of the British

Empire as a whole was also true of its parts. By regulating markets, they promoted allegiance to local institutions and used tariff duties to reduce internal taxes. Mercantilism became even more intense during the first decades of the nineteenth century. States along the eastern seaboard ruthlessly competed for access to the hinterlands in western New York, Ohio, Kentucky, Tennessee, and Alabama. Those that failed to build turnpikes and canals linking East and West faced the loss of existing or potential residents and capital to other states, and a possible decline in the value of their western lands. Despite the Supreme Court's efforts to create national markets, states found many ways to discriminate against each other. For example, New York's usury laws permitted an interest rate that was one percent higher than the rate allowed in Massachusetts. Consequently, in 1834 Boston merchants appealed to their legislature charging that "a constant drain is produced from our market, a vast amount of capital, which, if they were fettered by no law, would remain in circulation amongst our fellow citizens. . . . Were the present laws repealed, our own capital would remain in our own use, and the capital of the neighboring states would flow in upon us in such a manner that our business would be greatly extended and increased."[3]

Taxes on out-of-state corporations were also common. Chartering life insurance companies was one of the ways new states attempted to create a pool of investment capital and keep money at home. For example, California's Pacific Mutual Life Insurance Company was formed in 1861 to raise money to help build the Central Pacific Railroad. A year later, California followed the lead of many eastern states by imposing a 2 percent gross premium tax on out-of-state companies, though it permitted the state comptroller to waive the charge for any insurance company that invested at least $150,000 in state, county, or city bonds, or in California real estate.[4] States also tried to prohibit contracts between their residents and out-of-state businesses, imposed special license fees on interstate traveling salesmen, and limited the property rights of nonresident and alien landowners.[5]

These examples merely hint at the inventiveness of the states. State constitutions sometimes required that a majority of corporate boards of directors reside within that state, and occasionally they prohibited nonresidents from owning stock in home companies. Legislatures favored state over national banks—manipulating banking regulations in an attempt to drive out notes issued by "foreign" banks—and they levied discriminatory freight rates on through traffic carried over their state's turnpikes, canals, and railroads. Nevertheless, most of these restrictions and limitations were ephemeral. State legislatures feared trade wars and discrimination against their own companies, and preferential laws divided the business community. For example, bankers and railroad executives often favored discriminatory taxes while retail merchants opposed them.

If anything, state mercantilism was even stronger in the West than back East. By 1850 most of the eastern half of the nation (excluding the South), and especially New England, was served by an elaborate transportation network. Therefore, eastern cities and states had access to far more markets than did most western cities and states. Equally important, the size of western states and territories, and the arbitrary way their boundaries were drawn, exacerbated competitive tensions and invited realignments. For example, during the 1880s many residents of northern Idaho wanted to become part of Washington State. The mountains separating northern and southern Idaho were nearly impassable, even in the summer, and there was little communication between the two sections. The journey to Boise required taking a stage to Spokane, then riding the Northern Pacific to Butte, then transferring to the Utah Northern for passage to Blackfoot, then catching the stage to Boise. Western Washington was much more accessible than southern Idaho.[6] The western states also varied enormously in economic potential. The poorer states and territories stood at a great disadvantage, particularly because two of the wealthiest states, California and Colorado, were among the first to be settled. Those who moved west after the 1860s had to be given good reasons to pick Arizona, Idaho, or Wyoming over the older, more established, more promising commonwealths. In a region where capital was scarce and tax revenue even scarcer, boosters knew that their job was to hold onto old residents as well as to capture new ones. The dilemma was how to raise the revenue needed to provide the public services (such as fire protection and public education) expected of a prosperous and growing town or city without frightening off new businesses.

In a region where the most common, if not always the most profitable, investment was land, everyone from local businessmen to members of state legislatures gambled on the growth and prosperity of their towns and cities, along with the surrounding hinterland. As a consequence, political factions followed geography more than party; every politician struggled to see his community prosper so that he could prosper himself. Nowhere was this more apparent than in the contest for county seats. Land speculators knew that getting their town designated as a county seat dramatically increased land sales. Because the urban population was so mobile, and the western economies so subject to boom and bust, county boundaries changed rapidly. Therefore, rival towns were not just rival towns, but potential nuclei of new political subdivisions, and the process of carving smaller counties out of larger ones inevitably reduced the tax base and power of older centers of authority. This competition became even more intense than battles over the location of state capitals and state institutions because, theoretically, the number of counties was unlimited.

Western newspapers carefully tracked population migrations—though seldom from within the communities that lost residents. During the 1850s and 1860s, mining strikes from British Columbia to Mexico persuaded many Californians to abandon their new home. Similarly, when the southern California land boom of 1887 and 1888 collapsed, the tide of immigration turned away from California to Oregon and Washington, where land was cheaper and often did not require irrigation. These new settlers were joined by Kansas farmers fleeing the drought of the late 1880s. At about the same time, Colorado newspapers worried that residents of its parched eastern counties would forsake their farms and head for Oklahoma.[7]

Western state mercantilism did not constitute a coherent, well-integrated program. For example, during the 1890s it manifested itself in U.S. senator Francis Warren's valiant efforts to maintain the high national tariff on wool to protect Wyoming's sheep industry, in the passion for free silver within the mining states, and in the opposition to national forests within the timbered states. But no issue fitted state mercantilism better than irrigation. To flourish, states and territories had to become independent and self-sufficient. In 1887, Colorado's state engineer complained that his state had spent nearly $5 million to import oats, corn, lard, and fruit. "The question thus becomes an important one," he insisted. "Can we not stop this fearful drain upon our capital and turn it into a channel by which our own people are to be benefited, and not those of other commonwealths?" Elwood Mead, Wyoming's state engineer, raised the same question in 1894. In 1893 residents of his state paid about $1 million for imported food. All of it, Mead insisted, could have been grown locally. "That amount of money . . . goes out never to return again," Mead concluded. "We have no reciprocal trade relations with our neighbors. We buy from them, but they buy not a dollar from us in return. Suppose now that this million dollars went annually to the grangers of our own state." In the late 1880s, Nevada imported virtually all the food it consumed, except potatoes and beef, and more than half the food used in Idaho was grown outside its borders.[8]

Since many western cities, such as San Francisco and Denver, developed long before large-scale agriculture appeared, western economic development seemed "out of order." Irrigation became not just a method to secure independence, self-sufficiency, and economic growth, but also a way to restore an assumed "natural" balance between farming, commerce, and industry that transplanted easterners had known in their former homes. "The mainstay of Wyoming at this time is in the utilization of the waters of the state for irrigating the arable land," Cheyenne's leading newspaper proclaimed in September 1895. "This is the foundation upon which our people must build. Wyoming has other material resources, such as oil, soda, coal, iron ore, asbestos, etc., but they will not be available until we cease to import agricultural products. So long as we send out money for grain, hay and vegetables, just so long the state will be poor and unable to develop its mineral resources." In many parts of the West, irrigation represented the best hope for escape from what was then perceived as "colonial subordination" or perpetual dependence on mining and grazing. Thus it had great potential to unify the West. At the same time no issue was more divisive, as the efforts of California, Nevada, and Colorado to build irrigation works demonstrate.

California

From the 1850s on, California was a state plagued by persistent competition among its communities for settlers, capital, and trade. These struggles pitted Sacramento against San Francisco and Stockton, San Francisco against Los Angeles, and Los Angeles against San Diego, to name just a few. In addition, there were strong rivalries between northern and southern California, between the Sacramento and San Joaquin valleys, and between coastal and foothill farming districts. At the end of the 1870s, the state created the office of state engineer and attempted to draft a comprehensive water plan, only to find that these differences were irreconcilable.

By the middle of the 1870s, hydraulic mining in California was two decades old. Year after year, mining debris had washed down from the Sierra foothills into the river channels of the Sacramento Valley, and many streams were strangled with silt. Marysville, at the confluence of the Feather and Yuba rivers, originally stood twenty feet above water. In the 1850s it had been the third largest city in the state; now it was a walled city surrounded by levees as high as rooftops. Flood-wary investors looked elsewhere. River traffic gradually disappeared on the Feather, and only small boats could navigate the Sacramento, which forced wheat farmers to rely mainly on railroads to carry their crops to market. Critics of hydraulic mining feared that the debris would eventually fill in San Francisco Bay, thus imperiling the economy of the entire state. During spring floods silt covered thirty to forty-five thousand acres of bottomland adjoining the Yuba, Bear, and Feather rivers. And since some of the foothill canyons contained debris deposits as thick as one hundred feet, residents of the Sacramento Valley feared that the worst was yet to come.[9]

Valley farmers turned to the courts in 1876, insisting that the mines were far less valuable to the state's economic future than its farms. Moreover, river transportation—about sixty steamers and forty barges plied California's inland waters in the late 1870s—offered the only feasible alternative to the railroad. But the state supreme court, federal courts, and U.S. Supreme Court proved unsympathetic.[10] In its zeal for hydraulic mining, the state legislature had tacitly decided that society as a whole should shoulder the cost of damages, not just the industry. In effect, farmers were asked to subsidize mining. On the other hand, the miners responded that their dams decreased flooding in the winter and that mining debris was a fertilizer, particularly valuable in raising potatoes. Mining had been the state's first major industry, the defense argued, and valley farmers had taken up land with full knowledge that hydraulic mining was going on upstream. There was plenty of cheap land in the San Joaquin Valley, but no more gold fields. Besides, not only did the miners produce greater wealth than the farmers, but farming would have been impossible without the markets that mining provided.[11]

California's size and range of climates, the immensity of its floods, the ineffectiveness of the swampland districts created in response to those floods, and the intense competition for water among miners, shippers, farmers, and others all demanded coordinated action. If flood control, drainage, and irrigation were left entirely to private enterprise and local government, the state would end up with the uncoordinated and wasteful network of canals and dams that scientist George David-

son had warned against (see chapter 5). Moreover, by the end of the
1870s, many Californians had seen enough prolonged, intractable suits
over water rights to convince them that the state should build and
operate irrigation works. The extent of public support for state enterprise is unclear, in part because many proponents of a state program
called for comprehensive hydrographic surveys as a first step, a measure that the champions of private enterprise also supported. In addition, many supported state reclamation in the hope that large canals
could be used for transportation as well as irrigation, freeing the state
from the tyranny of both rail and water monopolies. "It is certain,"
Sacramento's *Record-Union* editorialized in 1881, "that this State must
have a system of irrigation, and that this system must be wholly free
from the control of corporations. These two essentials must be held
to under all circumstances."[12]

The state's water problems were so vast and complicated that the
legislature refused to act on its own. Instead, in March 1878 it created
the office of state engineer, "to provide," in the words of the law, "a
system of irrigation, promote rapid drainage, and improve the navigation of the Sacramento and San Joaquin Rivers." The job involved
locating water sources and mapping land that could be irrigated; measuring the volume of streams; preparing plans for hydraulic works; defining natural drainage districts; and providing "opinion and advice"
to private irrigation companies and would-be investors. This was a bold
step, not only because California was the first state in the Union to
turn its water problems over to experts—in effect diverting authority
from standing legislative committees—but also because it anticipated
the doctrine of "multiple use," which did not come into its own until
the New Deal, half a century later. Ironically, it was the hydraulic
mining industry, not private irrigation or river transportation companies, that insisted that water problems could not be solved piecemeal
and that waterways had to be considered almost as living organisms:
What happened upstream could not be separated from what happened
downstream.[13]

In the spring of 1878, the new state engineer, William Hammond
Hall,[14] sent four parties of men into the field to gauge streams, map
river channels and levee systems, survey potential irrigation canals,
and inspect the damage caused by mining debris. Debris was the most
immediate problem, and Hall recommended building dams in the deep
canyons to capture rocks and uprooted vegetation, and "settling basins"
at the base of the foothills to trap silt. He estimated that less than

three hundred thousand acres were irrigated in California at the end of the 1870s, but the transition from wheat and barley to diversified agriculture would increase demands for water, as would the state's growing population. "Irrigation in California means immigration," Hall noted in his 1880 report to the legislature, "and it means not only cultivation of crops, but also cultivation of irrigators."[15]

Hall's initial report was comforting to the mining industry. When the legislature met in 1880, the mining delegation, assisted by its powerful allies in the San Francisco financial community, pushed through a bill that committed the state to build dams to impound the debris. Since the mid-1870s, representatives of the industry had argued that dredging rivers was a waste of money. They embraced and popularized the theory that streams deposited silt only when they moved at a sluggish pace. Confining watercourses within steep levees would increase the velocity, permitting the water to scour out the channel and transport the debris to San Francisco Bay. Eventually, Sacramento Valley rivers would return to normal. This plan, however, required dykes and levees as well as a network of reservoirs in the deep canyons of the foothills to trap boulders and uprooted trees. When the Joint Committee on Mines, Mining Debris, and Water Rights held its first meeting on February 16, 1880, Marysville's *Daily Appeal* noted that both Hall and Colonel G. H. Mendell of the Army Corps of Engineers had "stated that the reclamation of the lands of the valleys were all interconnected in such a way that this reclamation ought to be under the control of one direction, and that the treatment of this detritus is the first step in the reclamation of these lands." Significantly, the legislature spent little time debating either the constitutionality of state involvement in river-basin planning or the proper role of state government. Neither farmers nor miners questioned the state's right to undertake large-scale internal improvements.[16]

The "Debris Law" or "Drainage Act"of 1880 created a "drainage commission" consisting of the governor, state engineer, and surveyor general. It was responsible for dividing the state into flood districts and providing plans for improvements. The law included an elaborate system of taxation: a general tax of .05 percent on all taxable property within California, proceeds from which were dedicated to a "drainage fund" that could be spent anywhere in the state; a district tax of the same amount on all property within a particular drainage district, to be spent exclusively within that district; a tax on reclaimed swampland, not to exceed three dollars per acre, to be paid into the district reclamation fund; and an annual tax of half a cent for each miner's inch of water used in hydraulic mining, which money would be paid into the district construction fund, to be used exclusively for dams to impound debris or improve river channels.[17]

In 1904, Hall recalled that he had opposed the Drainage Act of 1880 because it committed the state to unknown expeditures and did not coordinate the construction of drainage and debris works:

> Before the Legislature met [in 1880], the State Engineer represented to those who were framing this State Drainage measure that it was premature, that in his opinion, the people of the State were not ready for such legislation, and that certain irrigation interests would demand like State construction of works, which would immediately make trouble through opposition by other and more powerful irrigation interests, and that the General Government should be called upon to pay half of the cost of debris storage and river improvement works.

Since his advice fell on deaf ears, Hall then tried to persuade the legislators to frame the law so that no money could be spent until Congress matched the state's appropriation. That plan failed because the ranking Corps of Engineer official in California, Colonel G. H. Mendell, refused to support it (presumably because Mendell did not think Congress would expand the responsibilities of the Corps of Engineers to include drainage and flood control, as well as navigation).[18]

Whatever his later reservations, in 1880 Hall was confident that a combination of dams and levees would solve the debris problem. The Sacramento Valley became the first drainage district designated by the Debris Commission. Work began in the fall of 1880, as two crews of about eight hundred men constructed brush and log dams on the Bear and Yuba rivers, tributaries of the Sacramento that carried immense quantities of sand and gravel. The dam on the Yuba River cost $105,000, and the structure on the Bear $74,000. This was a small part of the half million dollars spent by the commission, most of which went for levees and other channel work rather than dams.[19] The dams themselves, designed by Hall, were also approved by the Debris Commission's consulting engineer, Captain James B. Eads, who was already famous as designer of the jetty system at the mouth of the Mississippi River.[20] They consisted of brush mattresses stacked one on top of the other, to a height of fourteen feet on the Yuba River. "The intention," Hall explained to Governor George Perkins in October 1881, "was to build a series of low brush dams, over these great sand and gravel deposits [in the places where the stream was most likely to deposit debris], which are resting over the beds of the tributary streams, at intervals of several miles from the main rivers up to the foothills, thus forcing the floods to spread from levee to levee, in their passage down the slopes, and preventing that channeling down [scouring] which is to be feared." In other words, while Hall wanted to speed up the flow of the Sacramento to restore its normal channel, he also wanted to slow down the streams in the foothill canyons. The settling action would render the dams useless in a few years at most, but then the crest could easily be raised, using the same foundation.[21]

In January 1881, in a special message to the legislature on the debris question, Governor George Perkins predicted that the total cost of debris work would run between $5 million and $10 million, but that this expenditure would prevent $66 million in property damage and permit the continuance of hydraulic mining, which he claimed was worth $100 million to the state's economy.[22] Although Hall's board had reviewed all plans prepared by the new drainage district, the state engineer later claimed that district directors built too tall a dam on the Yuba too far downstream, at a site where there was no suitable foundation.[23] Whoever was at fault, in February 1881 a major flood swept away parts of the dams, and other sections settled, rendering Hall's plan useless. The failure of the dams occurred only days after the entire assembly had inspected the Bear River restraining works. Then, in the fall, fire—perhaps set by farmers—destroyed what remained of the Yuba dam. To compound these problems, the unusually wet winter of 1880–81 washed an enormous quantity of new debris into the upper channels of the Bear, Yuba, and Feather rivers.[24]

On February 10, 1881, Stockton's *Independent* called the debris issue "the all-absorbing topic of the day." Critics of the state program fell into three camps: those who argued that the miners should have paid for the work entirely on their own, those who said the federal government should have paid, and those who maintained that all hydraulic mining should cease. A fierce fight occurred in the assembly over a bill to repeal the 1880 legislation; it lost by a vote of 39 to 36. The *Kern County Californian* reported that the mining block paid up to a thousand dollars a vote to block repeal.[25]

It is impossible to predict how much money would have been spent on debris work, and perhaps even irrigation, had the courts not overturned the 1880 law. State senator W. W. Camron of Alameda County[26] put together a suit challenging the act's constitutionality. He argued that the law embraced many subjects not mentioned in the title; that it improperly delegated the power to tax to a special commission; that it attempted to confer the power of eminent domain upon a body not competent to exercise it; that it circumvented the requirement that the state Board of Examiners audit all claims against the state treasury; that it discriminated against Chinese and "Mongolian" labor and violated the equal protection clause of the Constitution; and that it was a general law that applied only to a few rivers, thus favoring part of the state even though it imposed a system of statewide taxation. Supreme Court justice Robert F. Morrison issued a writ suspending the Debris Act in March 1881, and on September 26, 1881, the Supreme Court formally disallowed it. The court held that debris dams and channel improvements did not, strictly speaking, constitute "drainage works;" that the legislature could not delegate the power to collect state taxes to local districts; and that the law violated the principle of equal taxation.[27]

The early 1880s were wet in California, and the debris or "slickens" question commanded more public attention than irrigation. Originally, the state engineer's office was divided into an irrigation section and a debris section, but the 1880 legislature slashed funds available for the agricultural work. Thereafter, the irrigation staff spent most of its time compiling published information, not conducting field surveys. No drainage investigation was conducted in the San Joaquin Valley or south of the Tehachipis, let alone any practical work useful to land and water companies. Nevertheless, the state's most prominent agricultural journal, the *Pacific Rural Press,* predicted that the settling dams were just the start of a major state water program. After all, dams might also be used to reduce flooding and store water for irrigation. "There is also a feeling among the dwellers in those [agricultural] counties," the *Press* noted in January 1881, "that they will not be fairly dealt with, unless the State, which orders them to pay taxes for the impounding of mining debris, shall also spend public money to aid them in the development of their interests. There seems to be pure justice in the claim." The legislature considered many bills to create drainage and irrigation districts. Some were designed, at least in part, to pave the way for state construction of irrigation works.[28]

Nineteenth-century westerners complained bitterly about corrupt legislatures, but sectionalism, localism, mercantilism, and parochialism left little alternative to vote buying. In November 1880, Sacramento's *Record-Union* lamented that southern Californians wanted to repeal the debris bill even before the legislation had been given a fair chance. "The idea that the State is not an entity, but merely a sort of confederation of independent sections, underlies all such talk," the newspaper concluded. "The truth is that the State is one and indivisible, and that whatever is done to benefit a part of it is done for the good of the whole." The *Record-Union* claimed that there was no such thing as a tax that applied equally to all. For example, residents of the East Coast were taxed to pay for lighthouses, breakwaters, and military posts on the other side of the country, while people in the West paid for river and harbor improvements in the East. The *Record-Union*, which was subsidized by the Central Pacific, insisted that complaints of unequal taxation under the Debris Act missed the point that reducing damages from mining would increase the amount of land under cultivation in the Sacramento Valley and conceivably *reduce* the tax burden in southern California by broadening the tax base in the north. In any case, improvements in river transportation would benefit the entire state.[29]

None of the *Record-Union*'s arguments carried much weight in the San Joaquin Valley or south of the Tehachipis. There the debris bill became a potent symbol of the legislative overrepresentation of the sparsely settled Sacramento Valley and the mining counties. "It is a positive outrage—the way all the public institutions of the State have been made to cluster within a short radius of the Bay of San Francisco," the Los Angeles *Herald* grumbled. (In 1880, southern California's representatives pushed a bill through the state senate to establish a teacher's college in Los Angeles only to see it shelved in the assembly.) Given the way southern California had been treated, there was no justice to the drainage legislation: "It would be just as logical to tax the whole State to pay for a failure of the crops and fleece which have been ruined by . . . drouth in the southern counties [in past years]," the *Herald* fumed. A few days later, after the debris bill passed, the *Herald* implored the governor to veto it. "No more iniquitous measure ever passed a California Legislature," it proclaimed. In the middle of April 1880 the legislation prompted new demands to divide the state, the most serious since the 1850s.[30]

Many southern California residents feared that a strongly centralized water system would require confiscation of existing water rights and result in wholesale transfers of water from one area to another. Equally important, the Debris Act exposed rivalries *within northern California*. The statewide tax underscored the competition between one set of San Francisco investors committed to a dying industry and another that favored land and water projects. For example, many northern California boosters believed that foothill lands offered the only hope of attracting a large number of small farmers to their part of the state. Since wheat farmers monopolized the Sacramento Valley's land, the foothills contained the state's last large blocks of arable government land—along with an elaborate, if decaying, system of dams, ditches, and flumes. Until hydraulic mining was shut down completely, however, few farmers would risk taking up land in the foothills.[31]

This is not to say that sectionalism alone explains the fate of the Debris Act. There was hostility toward the mining industry even in San Francisco. Miners were often portrayed as nomads who burrowed in the ground or washed it away, leaving behind sterile deserts incapable of generating new wealth. Westerners deeply believed that societies passed through stages. Mining contributed to the settlement of "virgin land," but not to long-term growth; that depended on agriculture. The Debris Act posed a fundamental question that had deep meaning to Californians who had just passed through the depression of the 1870s: If the state used general tax revenue to bail out troubled industries, was there any limit to taxation? Would the railroad be next? The failure of the debris dams also raised new doubts about the feasibility of large-scale water projects. One critic wrote to the *Bear River News*: "This damming business will do about the same proportion of good to our farms and river channels as putting your finger into the strait of the Golden Gate to stop the flow of the tide into San Francisco bay." If the debris problem was beyond the grasp of such master engineers as William Hammond Hall, James B. Eads, and George Mendell, perhaps there was no solution save shutting down hydraulic mining completely. Moreover, in the minds of many critics the perception remained that public works inevitably cost far more than they were worth and fed corrupt "rings." In April 1880, the Fresno *Expositor* announced passage of the debris bill with the prediction that the money would be "fiddled away by a lot of leeches. . . . If this appropriation is finally made it will afford rich pickings for the civil engineers who are fortunate enough to get their fins into the pudding."[32]

Finally, after the mid-1870s many opponents of state hydraulic work insisted that the federal government, not the state, was responsible for protecting the Sacramento River, as it guarded the navigability of rivers elsewhere. In early 1882, Colonel Mendell of the Army Corps of Engineers recommended that Congress appropriate a half million dollars to repair the existing debris dams and construct new ones on the Yuba, Bear, and American rivers. But strident opposition to hydraulic mining helped block Mendell's plan. Not until 1890 did California secure any return from the river and harbor bills.[33]

The failure of the debris dams crippled state water policy. In 1881 the legislature slashed the irrigation section's appropriation from fifty to twenty thousand dollars.[34] At the time, Hall had done little more than locate a few reservoir sites. The state engineer's work was criticized both for having no practical or immediate value to farmers and investors and for being the creature of powerful special interests. During the 1880s, Hall managed to alienate most of his supporters, perhaps unavoidably, and in 1889 he resigned to take a job with the Powell Irrigation Survey. The office of state engineer was abolished soon thereafter. The Wright Act of 1887 convinced many Californians that state reclamation was unnecessary and a dead issue. Meanwhile, in January 1884, Justice Lorenzo Sawyer of the U.S. circuit court in San Francisco granted a perpetual injunction against hydraulic mining. The industry briefly revived during the 1890s but never again posed a threat to agriculture.[35]

At the end of the 1890s, drought again visited California. That condition, combined with the failure of the Wright Act, the low price of wheat grown in the Sacramento Valley, the region's declining land values, and southern California's continued population growth, revived the crusade for state reclamation. Northern California businessmen—many of whom owned land in the Central Valley—were joined by politicians, engineers, and lawyers eager to see northern California regain its competitive edge. By 1900, however, southern California had the political power to checkmate the north. Its leaders feared that any state program would mainly benefit northern California communities. Southern California still contained some arable public lands, which, it was assumed, the federal government would eventually reclaim. Northern California had no such lands.[36]

Nevada

Boosters in all parts of the West predicted a glorious future for the region. But Nevada tested the hope and faith of even its most ardent champions. By the early 1880s it became the butt of cruel jokes. Widely

Irrigated Areas
of California, 1900

Total Irrigated Area
1,446,114 Acres

California irrigation map.

perceived as an economic and political colony of California, Nevada, the wags said, was a defunct mining camp represented by two U.S. senators. California, they said, was especially favored because it had four U.S. senators and an extra congressman: Nevada ought to become a county in eastern California. The humor had a bitter core. The jokes implied that the state should be dismembered and divided up among its neighbors, or returned to a territorial form of government. In 1885, after a California congressman introduced legislation to permit California to annex three Nevada counties, a western Nevada newspaper remarked that his state's congressional delegation was "considerably annoyed answering the questions put to them about the possible extinction of Nevada as one of the States of the Union, as the entire press of the East is seriously discussing the effect of a State being taken out of the Union, as if such a thing was possible and probable. They [Nevada's senators and representative] say this kind of talk will have a bad effect on the material interests of Nevada unless it can be stopped soon, for it is creating the impression that the State is drying up and is about to blow away."[37]

By the late 1880s, Nevada's economic "vital signs" were indeed alarming. In the presidential election of 1876, about 20,000 voted; in the election of 1888 little more than 12,000. Nevada's population declined from 62,266 in 1880 to 47,355 a decade later, and to 42,335 in 1900—even less that the 42,491 enumerated in 1870. During the 1880s, when most western states enjoyed substantial increases in population, only one Nevada county, Washoe—which included Reno and much of the state's best farmland—showed an increase. Storey County, the home of Virginia City and Gold Hill, lost half its residents during the same decade. Whether or not a state could be returned to territorial status if its population fell below the fifty thousand required for statehood was a moot question. Far more serious, declining state revenues threatened the survival of basic state institutions. Nevada received $217,509 from its bullion tax in 1876, but only $18,983 in 1888. Storey County paid $194,509 in bullion tax in 1876, but only $4,492 in 1888. "All of us know the Comstock will fail very soon as a source of revenue to the State," Carson City's *Appeal* predicted in 1889. "And when it fails Western Nevada will in a great measure, go with it."[38]

The *Appeal*'s editorial was misleading. The constitution of 1864 prohibited mines from being taxed directly and limited indirect taxes on "net proceeds" to 1 percent. Even that rate was seldom reached, and except for the boom years from 1871 to 1875, mining contributed only a small fraction of state tax revenue, and levies on railroads and other businesses did not pick up the slack. Agriculture and ranching paid most of the cost of government, and three centers of power emerged in Nevada: Reno (agriculture), Winnemucca and Elko (grazing), and Virginia City and Carson City (mining and milling). Like California, Nevada was deeply divided, and social critics resented not just the mining industry's disproportionate and unjust power in the legislature, but also its corrosive influence on public opinion and civic responsibility.[39]

The state's two leading railroads, the Virginia & Truckee and the Central Pacific, had as much of a stake in keeping the state's population small as did the mining companies—if only to make it easier to look out for their interests in the legislature. It should be no surprise, given the close alliance between the Central Pacific and Southern Pacific railroads—the latter of which held millions of acres of prime agricultural land in the San Joaquin Valley—that Nevada would be slighted. Agricultural prospects were far better in the Golden State. "Whenever they have advertised their [Nevada] lands at all," one irrigation engineer reported, "it has been simply as a stock range." This sharply contrasted with the Union Pacific in Colorado and the Southern Pacific in California, both of which worked hard to market agricultural land and attract permanent residents. The relative unimportance of Nevada was apparent in the fact that the Central Pacific persistently refused to provide that state with a general manager, vice president, or other official who could speak directly for upper management. The local land agent was often as much in the dark about the railroad's plans as the mass of Nevadans.[40]

Nevada faced almost insurmountable obstacles as it tried to compete with other states. It had no spectacular scenery, save for Lake Tahoe; no large forests; no substantial banks; a poor transportation network; and no commercial center to rival San Francisco, Denver, Salt Lake City, or Seattle. Worst of all, it had very little water. "Perhaps no other part of the earth's surface is as destitute of rivers as Nevada," one writer observed in 1876. "And the few streams which she does possess would not, in most countries, be called rivers at all."[41] No state's future depended more on irrigation, but during the 1860s and 1870s, the political power of the railroad-mining syndicate, based in western Nevada, and the livestock industry, located in central and eastern Nevada, ensured that agriculture received little attention.

Nevada agriculture got its start in the Carson Valley in June 1851, when John Reese and a handful of Mormons from Salt Lake City planted crops to sell to California-bound emigrants. Then, in 1858, California cattlemen began to drive stock across the Sierra to winter pastures in the Carson and Eagle valleys and the Truckee Meadows.[42] The first major water project in Nevada involved the Humboldt River, in the center of the state. In 1862, the Humboldt Canal Company announced plans to divert the entire flow of that stream at present-day Golconda and carry it ninety miles across the desert to Mill City, the principal ore reduction center for northern Nevada. The promoters hoped to sell water to both mills and farmers, but the first section of aqueduct exhausted the company's treasury, and its stock did not sell, in part because the desert's thirsty soil absorbed most of the water before it reached the end of the ditch. The canal provided irrigation water to ranchers below Golconda for several years, but the property was sold at a tax sale in 1868.[43]

In 1865, Nevada's surveyor general predicted that "many millions" of Nevada's acres "would be valuable if irrigated," and in 1872 he called for a comprehensive *state* water system, including storage reservoirs to eliminate water conflicts between miners and farmers. The Desert Land Act (1877) spawned a handful of important water projects, but most of them failed.[44] Nevada's population was too small, and the barriers to successful agriculture too great, to attract private capital.[45] Yet without storage, there was scarcely enough water to irrigate thin strips of land adjoining the streams, and by 1880 much of that land had been claimed by cattlemen.[46] In that year Nevada's congressman persuaded Congress to permit his state to swap its 4 million acres of unsalable school lands—the sixteenth and thirty-sixth sections in each township—for 2 million acres anywhere in the state. However honorable his intentions, the trade permitted livestock interests to acquire thousands of additional acres adjoining rivers, lakes, and springs, an extremely important concession given the fact that in 1880 the riparian doctrine still prevailed in Nevada.

In 1886, Nevada's surveyor general, C. C. Powning, bluntly declared that the only demand for land in the state came from the stock industry, "or those who desire to engage in it, poor as well as rich, and who find creeks and springs sufficient to provide water for their stock, and possibly allow them to irrigate enough land to raise alfalfa hay to furnish the cattle or sheep with feed during a hard Winter. This State affords no attractions for the 'settler.' There is not a dozen quarter sections in it worth settling upon. Eleven men out of twelve would die of starvation trying to make a living." The 2-million-acre grant did nothing to attract new settlers and little to help the schools—the land sold for as little as twenty-five cents an acre. In 1890, less than a dozen men owned more than one quarter of the 4 million acres privately held in Nevada. The census of that year indicated that Nevada's farms were the largest in the West. In 1870 the state contained 1,036 farms which averaged 201 acres. A decade later the number had increased by almost half, to 1,404, but the acreage had nearly doubled, to 378 acres. The impact of the 1880 law and the drought of the late 1880s could be seen in the statistics for 1890, when Nevada's 1,277 farms averaged 1,301 acres each, nearly three and one half times the average of a decade earlier. Since stockmen had claimed virtually all the state's water, irrigation promoters had to challenge powerful vested rights before agriculture could flourish.[47] The limited supply of surface water increased interest in artesian wells. In 1879, the Nevada legislature approved an act requiring the counties to subsidize companies drilling for artesian water at the rate of two dollars for every foot beyond five hundred, but there is no evidence that the counties complied or that any wells were sunk.[48]

The state legislature did not seriously consider the reclamation issue until 1881, following congressional approval of the special 2-million-acre grant mentioned above. The lawmakers had many precedents for aiding private companies, including the half million dollars Storey and Ormsby counties had provided to the Virginia & Truckee. Only the most speculative water companies, however, were willing to take a chance in Nevada when California and Colorado offered much better financial opportunities. Consequently, Senator P. N. Marker of Washoe County, which included the Truckee River, introduced legislation to authorize direct state construction of irrigation works. His bill was clearly designed to benefit his own county, which contained thousands of acres of potentially irrigable land adjoining the river. It provided for a state board to decide where the first project would be built, on land selected as part of the 2-million-acre grant. A loan of one hundred thousand dollars from the school fund would pay for construction—the loan to be retired through an annual tax of one dollar an acre on all irrigable land within the reach of state canals.

It was significant that the legislation originated in western Nevada rather than in the Humboldt region. The insecurity of water titles on the Truckee and Carson rivers, both of which began in California, had dissuaded cattlemen from taking up as much land in the Truckee,

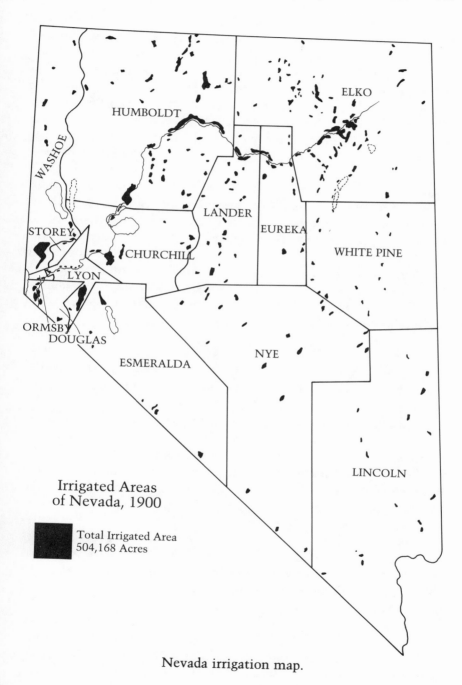

Irrigated Areas
of Nevada, 1900

Total Irrigated Area
504,168 Acres

Nevada irrigation map.

Carson, and Walker river basins. (The Humboldt was the only substantial stream located entirely within the state. Moreover, while stock
growers had the Humboldt largely to themselves, by 1881 the Carson
River was used by silver mills, and the Truckee was used to raise crops
for forage and for sale in the mining camps.) By driving up the price
of state lands, the Marker bill promised to increase the school fund—
which was derived from the sale of state lands—and the perpetual
dollar-an-acre fee might even pay part of the cost of government. The
legislation appeared to be antimonopoly and antispeculation because
landowners would have to pay for water whether or not they irrigated.
This, Marker hoped, would attract actual settlers to the state and dis-
suade large cattle companies from acquiring the reclaimed land. Nevertheless, opponents of the bill charged that Marker, who owned land
in Washoe County, stood to gain personally. And since any new state
project would tap the Truckee or Carson rivers *above* many existing
irrigation ditches, critics of the legislation also feared interference with
older water claims downstream. They insisted that since Nevada had
virtually no laws regulating the use of water, legislation providing
formal procedures for filing new rights and adjudicating old ones should
precede the construction of state works. The bill also threatened the
school fund. Once the first project had been built, would not other
counties demand ditches of their own? And how many other worthy
state public works projects would ask for aid in the future?[49]

The bill reappeared in 1883 and 1885, each time winning considerable public support, but it never came close to adoption. Defenders
of the status quo considered any state action as potentially disruptive.
Humboldt River and Comstock Lode communities deeply feared the
growth of Carson City and Reno. Reno enjoyed important advantages
because it was located on the Central Pacific line, because it commanded large areas of potential agricultural land in the valleys to its
north, because the Truckee River carried twice as much water as either
the Carson or Walker rivers, and because Lake Tahoe at the headwaters
of the Truckee was the largest natural storage reservoir in the American
West. Washoe County's population increase during the 1880s prompted
it repeatedly to call for reapportionment, only to find itself checkmated
by the stock and mining interests. H. M. Yerington, manager of the
Virginia & Truckee Railroad and overlord of the legislature, used all
his considerable political influence to block the flow of power to Washoe.
In 1889 he notified Senator William Morris Stewart that a Washoe
representative was trying to secure two more seats in the legislature

at the expense of the grazing counties. "Of course," he noted, "we would not stand any such foolishness & knocked him out." In an 1891 letter to Francis G. Newlands, a close business associate (see chapter 8), Yerington fretted that if the Washoe delegation succeeded in getting reapportionment, it would "cinch every railroad out of its boots, and also down any bill likely to aid any other portion of the state." He feared that a Washoe-dominated legislature would vote massive appropriations, which would require a dramatic increase in railroad taxes.[50]

Marker and the rest of Reno's champions did not take defeat easily. In 1887, when Senator E. D. Boyle of Storey County proposed the construction of a four-mile tunnel from Lake Tahoe to Carson City, which he claimed would water 150,000 acres along the Carson River, Washoe County's delegation got its chance to retaliate and killed the legislation.[51] Although many lawmakers thought that large-scale reclamation could not be undertaken without extensive hydrographic surveys, which only the federal government was capable of conducting, the 1887 legislature authorized a state lottery, the proceeds from which were earmarked for a state canal and reservoir fund. The governor, however, vetoed the legislation on grounds that the state constitution required the voters to approve such a scheme. All that the 1887 session managed to accomplish was the adoption of another ineffective bill to encourage the drilling of artesian wells.[52]

Nevertheless, the Powell Irrigation Survey, the land boom in southern California,[53] the Wright Act—which threatened to divert even more potential settlers from Nevada—and above all the drought of the late 1880s made the 1889 session different. "Never in the history of Nevada," the Reno *Gazette* observed in the fall of 1888, "has there been such a dry season as the present one. Water is short in every river in the State, and in many valleys stockmen have had to sink wells to procure water enough for stock."[54] By the fall of 1889, Carson City's *Morning Appeal* reported that "cattle in the ranges, maddened with thirst, wander aimlessly in search of drink and in some places, hundreds have met and fought to the death for the possession of some little muddy pool." In eastern Nevada, the range was littered with carcasses. Forest fires raged through the Sierra and covered western Nevada with a thick haze.[55] The drought also reopened old disputes over water.[56]

The worst conflict erupted on the Carson River. The high price of cordwood in barren western Nevada, along with the cost of buying and maintaining steam-powered ore reduction machinery, made water power a necessity, especially in the reduction of low grade ores. The first mills dated to 1858. By the 1870s, the largest, scattered from Carson City to Dayton, had been consolidated into the Union Mill and Mining Company, which held some of the oldest water rights on the river. Upstream, in Douglas County, fledgling communities such as Genoa served a ranching population of about one thousand. As early as 1861, Douglas County ranchers near Nevada's western border irrigated forty-seven hundred acres from the East Fork of the Carson and another thirty-nine hundred from the West Fork.[57] The first legal contests between ranchers and the mills occurred in 1864 and 1871, but the most protracted dispute came during the dry summer of 1887 and persisted, with periodic truces, well into the 1890s. The Carson River posed the classic contest between upstream and downstream communities, as well as between a "new" use of water and an old.[58]

Nevada's financial crisis made the 1889 legislature's job even tougher. As Governor C. C. Stevenson explained to the lawmakers in March:

> It is bad indeed for a State or individual to have to borrow funds to defray current expenses, especially so when there is no prospect of an early income to meet such humiliating liability. . . . But our borrowing limit is almost reached, and our revenue, through a vicious, unjust and unconstitutional system of assessment, is decreasing—not that we have not the property from which to raise all we need. We have it, but we do not assess it honestly; and this vicious system, which is growing worse and tending rapidly to ruin, you might have killed and buried, but have countenanced and encouraged. The inevitable result must be that, during the current two fiscal years, our borrowing capacity will be exhausted to run the Government, and when the Legislature shall meet in 1891, there will be little, if any, money in the treasury to meet [even] the expenses of the session.[59]

In 1889, the state debt stood at $175,815.10, not far from the $300,000 limit set by the state constitution, and revenue had declined by 24 percent in the three years from 1883 to 1886.[60]

Rather than raise taxes, the legislature again debated authorizing a lottery and tapping the school fund (which, under the state constitution, could be invested only in U.S. bonds or the bonds of other states). One lottery company promised that, in return for an exclusive franchise, it would pay the state from forty to seventy-five thousand dollars a year—one sixth to one third of the total expenses of operating Nevada's government. However, in February the voters overwhelmingly rejected constitutional amendments to authorize a lottery and to increase the debt ceiling from $300,000 to $1,500,000.[61]

The rejection of the constitutional amendments forced the friends of reclamation—an odd and fragile alliance of newspaper editors, businessmen, land speculators, and political opportunists—to look elsewhere for revenue. One alternative was local funding and construction. Washoe County formed a citizen's committee that debated two possible solutions: a general tax on all property within the county and a tax levied exclusively on irrigated land. Carson City's *Appeal* proposed that Douglas, Ormsby, Lyon, Storey, Esmeralda, and Churchill counties, through which the Carson River flowed, join together, issue two hundred thousand dollars in twenty-five-year bonds carrying 6 percent interest, spend fifty thousand dollars to build a big reservoir upstream and expend the rest on canals. Property taxes would pay interest on the bonds, and water rentals would pay the principal.[62]

The Virginia & Truckee and the mining and milling interests wanted to maintain a steady flow in the Carson River, but they had no desire to increase their taxes. So they concocted a plan to make the farmers and ranchers pay most of the cost of storage. The Ormsby (Carson City) and Storey (Virginia City and Gold Hill) delegations rammed a reservoir bill through the legislature despite strong opposition from Washoe County.[63] The new law provided for a hundred-thousand-dollar loan from the school fund. A board named in the legislation—whose members were clearly sympathetic to the mining industry—was responsible for selecting the reservoir site and preparing construction plans. The loan would be redeemed by proceeds from sales of thirty-year bonds, and the bonds would be paid off by water user fees and, after January 1, 1891, a tax of two cents per hundred dollars on all taxable property in Nevada. Proponents of the legislation promised that if the remainder of the 1880 land grant was selected within range of the new hydraulic works, revenue from the sale of that land would rapidly fill the state treasury to overflowing.[64]

Not surprisingly, Washoe County papers railed against the project, noting that it imposed water charges on farmers and ranchers, but not on the mills. "The whole thing, from beginning to end, has an unsavory cast," Washoe County's Reno *Evening Gazette* remarked, "and it looks very much like a large sized job put up in the interest of the mills on the Carson river." Winnemucca's *Silver State* branded the irrigation bill as a "raid on the School Fund." Carson City's *Morning Appeal* conceded that the legislation had been framed to benefit one section of the state and one industry. But, it countered, Reno had played the same game. Reno had "stolen" the state university from Elko and was trying to steal the state prison from Carson City. Its voters had rejected the lottery, the *Appeal* charged, mainly because the added revenue would have made Carson City the largest town in the state. "During the past ten years Ormsby has over and over refused alliance with Storey's ten votes and coquetted with Washoe's three votes, and Washoe has invariably deceived, tricked and bulldozed us." "Whatever keeps the stamps of the mills in operation," the *Appeal* insisted, "helps the entire State, Washoe county included," and "the experiment will prove of such benefit to the State that this appropriation will only be a beginning to what will follow." State reclamation had to begin some-place, and it was important that the first project meet well-defined needs. The *Appeal* urged ranchers and miners on the Carson River to join hands. If the silver industry collapsed, it warned, the value of ranches would decline by 50 percent. "The senseless fight between the leading industries of the State is keeping Nevada dead, and in a little while, unless the two interests pull together, Nevada will be not only dead but buried." "The present condition of the State is due more than anything else, to the disposition of one locality to fight improvements in another," the *Appeal* concluded in September.[65]

Such appeals for unity had no greater effect than the Sacramento *Union*'s able defense of the California Debris Act in 1880 and 1881. In April 1889, L. A. Blackslee, a member of the new state reclamation board, blithely predicted that if the "experiment" proved successful, "as it is bound to be, in my judgment, there will be other appropriations made every two years and gradually the entire State will be using a system of storage reservoirs."[66] Nevertheless, even friends of the leg-islation recognized that it raised difficult questions. Was it legal to use the school fund for public-works projects? Could the board use money raised in Nevada to purchase and improve damsites and other property in California, property which would be subject to taxation in the latter state? Was the reclamation board required to charge $1 an acre for water—the price specified in the act—even if the owner chose not to use the water? Was the $100,000 appropriation adequate to complete a storage project? Was a general state tax used to pay for regional im-provements constitutional? Above all, could the state reclaim one val-ley without creating claims for public works in every other valley? Once the state began its work, there would be no stopping. Thereafter, critics of the 1889 law charged, no private corporation, county, or district would be willing to tackle the job. The entire financial burden would fall on the state.[67]

To compound problems, Nevada's Reclamation Board began work when federal construction of storage reservoirs or the cession of public lands to the states appeared imminent. Powell's lieutenant in Nevada, Lyman Bridges, arrived at the beginning of July 1889 and predicted that the national work would "practically revolutionize Nevada" and double its population "in an exceedingly short time." A Carson River storage reservoir would serve as the foundation for "an empire of 50,000 people" in the Carson Valley, he proclaimed. It would provide plenty of water for both the mills and the ranches. He suggested that the state use the hundred-thousand-dollar appropriation to build a reservoir in the Carson basin's Long Valley, which was located entirely within Nevada, "even if I could not make it more than five feet high with the available funds." It could be completed with subsequent appropriations, leaving to the national government the construction of a second dam upstream in California's Hope Valley. Congress would "take hold of the matter with much greater interest" if Nevada's government demonstrated a financial commitment to reclamation. There was "no doubt of getting material aid [from Washington]." Bridges met with the Nevada Reclamation Board on August 13, but the board refused to commit the state to build a reservoir that Bridges predicted would cost two hundred thousand dollars—twice the amount appropriated by the legislature. Meanwhile, the visit to Reno by the Senate Select Committee on Irrigation (Stewart committee) at the end of August kept interest in federal aid at white heat.[68]

Lyman Bridges's bubble burst in September. By that time, he had finished preliminary reservoir surveys on both the Carson and Truckee rivers, but the Genoa *Courier* reported that "the [federal] money allotted to this division has been expended much more rapidly than was expected, and . . . the season's work here must soon be closed." Such was the official reason the USGS gave for firing the engineer, but the real reason was a conflict of interest. Bridges had invested in a private land company that tried to buy state land in Long Valley, near the site of the proposed reservoir. In effect, the school fund was being raided, and the USGS was providing hydrographic information, to enrich land speculators. Bridges's relationship to the ranching and milling interests was and is unclear. However, by reinforcing the popular assumption that the reclamation crusade was simply the creature of selfish special interest groups, his actions contributed to the paralysis of the Reclamation Board.[69]

The board also suffered from the uncertainty of water rights, especially the inability of Carson River users to resolve their differences. When the 1889 legislature met, there were virtually no laws regulating the acquisition or use of water in Nevada, and riparian rights had not yet been disallowed by the state supreme court, as they would be later in the year. On both the Humboldt and Carson rivers, water users demanded a cheap way to protect their rights. Consequently, the legislature enacted a law modeled on Colorado's, which designated the state's four major river basins as irrigation districts and turned adjudication within those districts over to local courts.[70]

The law resulted in a rush to county recorder's offices by water users attempting to legitimize extravagant claims. It neither limited the amount of water that could be claimed nor required that water be put to an immediate "beneficial" use. Nor did it establish a state agency to supervise water use. Nevertheless, many stockmen considered *any* adjudication as tantamount to confiscation. By reducing extravagant claims, the courts might shift the balance of power on the state's major streams to a multitude of newer claimants, possibly even from ranching to farming. In June 1890, the district court for Humboldt County ruled the law unconstitutional. Opponents of the statute charged that it violated the state's prohibition on special legislation because it applied only in designated irrigation districts, not throughout the state; because it confiscated rights without due process; and because it delegated too much law-making power to the governor by permitting him to create water districts and thus decide where the law would apply. The legislature followed the court's lead in 1893, when it rescinded the law. Nevada returned to the pre-1889 era when there was no state control over water rights.[71]

Meanwhile, the drought continued and on September 11, 1889, the Union Mill and Mining Company filed suit against upstream ranchers on the Carson River.[72] The millowners argued that they had older water rights than most of the ranchers and that the mills generated much more income than the ranches and supported a much larger community. Moreover, they charged that the ranchers wasted water. The ranchers demanded that the mills shut down in summer, or else install steam stamps to break up the ore-bearing rock.[73] Francis G. Newlands, who had just moved to Nevada and served as a legal representative for the estate of Nevada silver-baron William Sharon, tried to mediate the dispute. He knew that a protracted suit would all but eliminate support for comprehensive water projects in western Nevada, and that the money wasted on litigation could better be used to build reservoirs. Newlands suggested that the farmers hire an engineer to design a comprehensive water system to reduce waste upstream. If the ranchers could persuade the state to invest the hundred-thousand-dollar appropriation in a reservoir, and if they could come up with an additional seventy-five thousand dollars themselves, then the mining and milling companies would match that amount.[74] But, he warned, the mills would not tolerate the diversion of the entire stream during the summer and early fall. After July 4 or 5 of 1889, the mills had been forced to shut down completely, and many farms downstream from the mills had also suffered.[75]

In October, the millowners proposed a new compromise. They promised to drop the suit and invest between twenty-five and seventy-five thousand dollars in a new reservoir, depending on the amount raised by farmers and ranchers. Until the structure was completed, the mills would permit *all* upstream diversions from the beginning of the growing season through July 15. In return, they asked the farmers and ranchers to acknowledge their superior water rights. The upstream interests refused. They worried about their ability to finance an adequate dam, particularly because the millowners wanted 7 percent interest on the money they provided, which meant that the stored water would have to sell at a very high price. And since the millowners insisted that their rights were paramount, if the reservoir did not capture as much water as expected, the farmers might be worse off than before it was built. Douglas County water users preferred to wait until the next legislature met, in 1891, so that they could secure permission to issue county bonds to pay for the dam.[76]

The Union Mill and Mining Company's suit was dormant during the wet year of 1890, and the sharp reduction in mining operations during the 1890s reduced the number of mills. The declining quality of Comstock ore, however, made cheap water power all the more necessary. Newlands urged restraint in letters to William Sharon. "I have always looked with regret, as you well know," he wrote in January 1891, "upon litigation which would create antagonism between the agricultural and mining interests." He saw no sense in fighting to the bitter end to protect the rights of a doomed industry. Newlands chastised those unwilling to admit that mining was dying as well as those who thought that if the mines gave out there would be no local markets for farmers and ranchers. Even though the mills had the law on their side, the enormous cost of litigation would not add a drop of water to the summer supply. Newlands had opposed the suit in 1889, and he still opposed it in 1891.[77]

By the end of 1889, only a few months after Bridges completed his hasty surveys on the Carson and Truckee rivers, Newlands concluded that neither the state nor federal government would build reservoirs in western Nevada.[78] Hungry for public acclaim and eager to move to Washington, he enlisted the support of Robert L. Fulton, William Hammond Hall, and others to secure the property needed for comprehensive irrigation projects on both the Carson and Truckee rivers.[79] Given the speculative fever that swept through the West in the wake of the Powell surveys, Newlands had to move fast. Unless he did so, speculators would acquire the best land and reservoir sites, driving up the cost of reclamation in western Nevada—whether undertaken by government, private, or mixed enterprise. On July 1, 1889, Newlands formed the Occidental Land and Improvement Company "to buy, lease, improve, cultivate and sell lands, and to buy and sell cattle, in the States of California, Oregon and Nevada, and in the Territory of Arizona."[80] In the fall of 1889, Newlands secured control of the outlet of Donner Lake, which emptied into the Truckee River in California. (The eighteen thousand dollar price was nearly three times what the land had sold for earlier in the year.) He hoped eventually to purchase all the land along the rim of the lake and raise its level twenty feet. In November, Newlands bought 160 acres at the outlet of Lake Tahoe, where he hoped to build a new dam. Subsequently, he also purchased half interest in a damsite at Long Valley in the Carson basin, 13,000 acres of agricultural land near the Truckee River, and another 15,000 acres near the Carson River. In all, he spent one hundred thousand dollars on seven dam and reservoir sites and another hundred fifty thousand dollars on 28,160 acres of land.[81]

By the fall of 1890, Newlands was ready to unveil his comprehensive reclamation plan. He did so in a widely distributed pamphlet entitled *Address to the People of Nevada on Water Storage and Irrigation,* published serially in the Reno *Gazette* in early October.[82] The time had come for Nevadans to demonstrate self-reliance. According to Newlands, they had been crippled by an almost pathological lack of initiative and by the assumption that the federal government would come to the rescue.[83] What Nevada needed most was planning and foresight. Newlands explained:

Dams, main canals and distributing ditches have been multiplied by the desire of every landowner, or of a few landowners associated together, to control the entire system of supply, whereas a scientific system of distribution would only require a single dam and a large main canal, with distributing ditches, to control an area now covered by many such canals and dams. By the present method the expense of maintenance is increased and a great loss of water results through evaporation and seepage. . . . It is believed that by remodeling our present system of irrigation according to some intelligent and scientific plan much of the present loss by evaporation will be stayed and greater economy in the use of water secured. If this is done the area of irrigation cultivation can be largely increased apart from the construction of storage reservoirs.[84]

In the absence of a larger design, he believed, augmenting the existing supply would do little good.

Nature dictated very different water systems in the Truckee and Carson basins. The Truckee basin was devoted largely to farming and the Carson to ranching. The Truckee offered many locations for cheap storage, including Lake Tahoe, but delivering the water promised to be expensive because the remaining irrigable lands were in valleys higher in altitude than the river. Long and expensive highline canals would be necessary. In the Carson basin good storage sites were far less common, but the irrigable lands were flat and nearer the level of the stream. And because the Carson River was twice as long as the Truckee, its water was subject to use over and over again. Unfortunately, there was virtually no good public land left within that basin except in the Carson Sink, at the end of the stream. Of the forty thousand acres of land irrigated within the Carson watershed, twenty-five thousand lay in the upper valley in Douglas County and another fifteen thousand downstream, well beyond the mills in Churchill County.

Newlands predicted that the cost of reclaiming the arid lands of western Nevada would run from $7.50 to $20 an acre, but he did not say who should do the job. Watering seventy-five thousand acres would cost about $1 million, but if the reclaimed land sold at a modest $40 an acre, reclamation would turn a $2 million profit. If the state did the work, "it is readily seen that from the profits on the lands and the income derived from the reservoirs and canals, a fund for reclamation could be established which would ultimately reclaim every acre of land capable of reclamation in the State." Still, private reclamation taught one great lesson: To make money from irrigation, you had to *own* the arable land. The state might acquire some valuable tracts if the central government ceded the arid lands to the states, or if private landowners joined Newlands in selling their excess holdings to the state at cost, but as of 1890 virtually all the reclaimable land was in private hands. Newlands expected either the counties or special irrigation districts to tackle the job. Since the Truckee River flowed entirely within Washoe County, the legislature could simply grant that county the right to issue bonds up to a specified limit. But because the Carson River passed through several counties, any comprehensive project in that basin would require a special district.[85]

Newlands observed that he was providing "food for reflection" to encourage the forthcoming legislature to adopt "a broad and comprehensive [reclamation] policy." If it did not, he warned, "I shall then hold myself free to pursue such a course (as a matter of private enterprise and profit), as I may deem proper, either to secure the reimbursement of my expenditures or the development of my purchases."[86] Newlands echoed this note in a letter to his land agent, R. L. Fulton, at the end of the year: "Should I conclude to go into the Carson River matters as a matter of profit, we may arrange something to your profit advantage in speculation."[87]

Newlands, like Powell, feared that reclamation by the federal government or states would sacrifice home rule for large, expensive, arbitrary, remote, and unwieldy bureaucracies. Nevada, he thought, needed far more than irrigation. He wanted to kindle the same kind of "community spirit" that he had seen in San Francisco. With that done, reclamation would take care of itself. In the winter of 1889 he helped create the Nevada Board of Trade. The organization's specific objectives were to break up the large tracts of land held for pasture, and to publicize the state's agricultural potential.[88] Preaching unity and optimism, the board of trade served as a forum for boosters who believed that only irrigation could increase the state's population. Newlands tried desperately to get water users along the Truckee and Carson to act in concert. He urged Truckee basin residents to file applications on good public land near the river and hold it in trust to preserve what little remained of the 2-million-acre grant of 1880. On the Carson River, he acquired an interest in the ditches used by large ranchers, such as Henry F. Dangberg, W. C. Noteware, and D. R. Jones, to limit their water monopoly in the upper Carson basin.[89]

Newlands knew that neither private philanthropy nor public spirit was enough. Winning the Central Pacific Railroad's support for reclamation was vital. If that company showed tangible faith in Nevada's future, private land and water companies would "discover" the state and private water users would begin to organize. The railroad still owned thousands of acres along the Truckee and Carson rivers, and a subsidiary company—the Donner Boom and Logging Company—owned the dam at Lake Tahoe's outlet to the Truckee. In 1889 and 1890 that dam was used largely to regulate the river's flow to float logs downstream to mills around the town of Truckee. Newlands thought that a dam capable of raising the lake's level ten feet would capture sufficient water to irrigate millions of acres in western Nevada and could be constructed for ten thousand dollars.[90]

Late in September 1889—several months before his *Address to the People of Nevada* appeared—Newlands wrote to Charles F. Crocker, one of the founders and chief executives of the Central Pacific, asking that the railroad sell the existing Tahoe damsite or build a new structure and lease it to Nevada's Truckee River water users. In either case, he explained, the railroad would benefit from increased rail traffic and land sales. At first, Crocker seemed sympathetic, so Newlands formed a delegation of prominent Nevadans to carry a formal appeal to corporate headquarters in San Francisco. The group included Senator Stewart, who had long been an agent and ally of the Central Pacific. When it reached San Francisco, however, the figurehead of the Big Four, Leland Stanford, raised probing new questions. What, he asked, had Nevada done to help itself? It had refused to launch an artesian well survey, gauge its streams, or determine how much water was needed to irrigate its lands. Even worse, in the absence of effective state water laws, what was to prevent the monopolization by *existing* ditch owners of any new water supply stored at Tahoe or in other reservoirs? Stewart responded that the state would reserve as much land as it could adjoining the river (the remainder of the 2-million-acre grant), attach water rights directly to the land, and limit farms to twenty or forty acres. The Nevada Reclamation Board created by the 1889 legislature could supervise operation of the dam and sales of land; monopoly would be impossible. Unfortunately, as Stanford well knew, the 1880 grant limited the selection of land to *individuals*; the state had no power to select land on its own, nor could it limit the size of parcels sold.[91] Stanford remained unmoved, even after Newlands, in November 1889, wrote to W. H. Mills, the railroad's land agent in California and one of the West's leading proponents of irrigation, asking Mills to persuade Huntington, Crocker, and Stanford to turn control of the Tahoe dam over to the Nevada Board of Trade and grant stopover privileges to prospective Nevada settlers, as the Southern Pacific did in both Arizona and California.[92]

Newlands soon lost patience with the Central Pacific. On July 9, 1890, he wrote to Crocker bluntly noting that "the most discouraging outlook in the situation is the apparent indisposition of the Central Pacific railroad to co-operate with us."[93] A special committee of the Board of Trade agreed:

> Most of the States have four or five [railroad] systems, all trying constantly to build up the territory so as to increase their revenues from it. They carry cheap fuel almost for nothing in order to encourage the growth of manufactories. They give free passage to immigrants who will buy homesteads in their land grants; contribute money to surveys for systems of irrigation and storage; for the establishment of factories; for opening timber tracts, etc. They scatter annual passes among stock buyers, grain dealers, lumbermen, etc., to stimulate trade. They grant low rates for seed and stock when misfortune has attacked either the agricultural or cattle interest. Where any district shows a capacity to produce an article of commerce every effort is made to encourage its production, and special rates, even free transportation, have been granted for that purpose. Everywhere agents are kept constantly on the watch for such opportunities . . . yet we feel the Southern Pacific Company have shared the impression held by people further away, that there is nothing in Nevada, and instead of watching foropportunities to benefit her industries, they have taken each bit of traffic as if it were the last they would ever get, and as if any attempt to stimulate growth would be an unfruitful benevolence.[94]

The board asked the railroad to appoint a special agent for Nevada who would reside in the state and speak directly for the company. It also requested that all second-class ticket holders be granted stopover privileges and that the railroad organize a colonization bureau to advertise and market railroad land in the Silver State.

The railroad balked at giving up control over the Tahoe dam and the land it still owned in western Nevada, and it refused to contribute to the Board of Trade. The Central Pacific did push reclamation in the Humboldt basin, where it paid for the survey of an irrigation project in 1890 and urged construction of a dam near Humboldt House. This was much safer than reclamation on the Truckee because resort owners at Lake Tahoe insisted that holding back water in the spring for subsequent use in the summer would flood beaches and ruin Tahoe's value as a summer resort. Many of Tahoe's summer residents were wealthy, powerful Nevadans whom the railroad was very reluctant to antagonize. Ultimately, however, the Central Pacific encountered the same problem in the Humboldt basin that it faced in western Nevada. Its directors refused to give up the Humboldt damsite without some assurance that the water stored there would be used to provide small farmers with homes rather than strengthen the existing monopoly of large cattlemen.[95]

The railroad's caution strengthened Newlands's conviction that Nevada water users had to rely on themselves and not just wait for outside assistance. So did the appearance of the first and only report of the fledgling Nevada Board of Reclamation, created by the legislature in 1889. That document advised the incoming 1891 legislature that, given Nevada's limited resources, reclamation by the state was impossible.[96] Governor R. K. Colcord reinforced that conclusion in his speech to the legislature. As an alternative, he proposed that Nevada follow California's Wright Act (1887) by extending assistance "to associations of individuals who engage in this very laudable undertaking [reclamation], even to the extent of loaning her credit, with proper safeguards, by investing in the bonds and securities" of districts.[97] Fulton, on the advice of political boss Yerington, asked Trenmore Coffin—the head of the Union Mill and Mining Company and the architect of the company's suit against Douglas County ranchers and farmers—to draft a district bill.[98] Newlands's motives are unclear. One historian maintains that he supported district legislation "primarily to enable Washoe County to purchase his properties along the Truckee River . . . a financial crisis beginning in 1890 forced him to seek a more liquid cash position by disposing of all or part of his investments in irrigable lands."[99] That answer is too simple. Every other practical alternative had fallen flat; the irrigation district was a last resort.

As a former Californian and investor in irrigation projects in that state, Newlands recognized the dangers faced by irrigation districts, particularly the bonding and taxing of property not directly benefited by irrigation. The California districts drove up land prices and attracted private capital, but they also encountered serious problems, including suits pressed by ranchers and farmers who did not want to be included and slow bond sales. More to the point, what worked in California might not work in Nevada. Could a district succeed, Newlands wondered, where there was such a small population and tax base? Could it create a sense of community despite the fragmented nature of Nevada's economy and society?[100] How would the Central Pacific Railroad react to having its land taxed, given its record of resisting projects to improve Nevada lands at the expense of its holdings in California? And could any district succeed on the Humboldt River, where the railroad was the largest landowner? The idea that districts should include entire river basins clashed with the notion that such institutions could work only where they served compact, concentrated populations. Any Carson or Humboldt river district would have to include several counties and would be harder to govern as a consequence.[101]

Economy and retrenchment dominated the 1891 legislature as the state's newspapers debated plans to reduce the number of counties from fourteen to eight, cut the length of the legislative session from sixty to forty days, abolish various state agencies, and sharply reduce the number of legislators and state employees.[102] Always one terrible question lurked in the background of legislative deliberations: Why would anyone want to move to Nevada? Even to acknowledge the question was to encourage defeatism, but it kept popping up at awkward moments. For example, early in 1891, at a meeting of the Nevada Board of Trade, a guest scandalized the gathering by suggesting that, under the circumstances, a fair-minded jury would vote to hang or imprison anyone responsible for luring prospective farmers into the state.[103]

All the major reclamation legislation proposed in 1889 and 1891 was paid for by special-interest groups, such as the Union Mill and Mining Company and the Board of Trade. Reclamation never became a broad-based public movement. The leading journal in central Nevada, Winnemucca's *Silver State,* charged that the Board of Trade "are and have been working in the interest of Reno, hence the lack of interest [in irrigation districts] taken by the citizens of the outside counties."[104] Even the ranchers who stood to gain from the expansion of irrigated forage crops showed little interest.[105] "I pumped Baker today," Fulton wrote to Newlands, "and asked him what the Legislature would do this Winter. He said it would do nothing unless it was paid for it." Fulton estimated it would cost ten thousand dollars to secure a comprehensive irrigation district bill.[106] In the middle of February, Yerington informed Newlands that while the legislature had shown no real enthusiasm for the district bill, it would be approved, "and then if the people refuse to act under its provisions we cannot help it."[107]

The act itself provided for the formation of districts empowered to issue bonds at 6 percent against all the property within their borders. Unlike the Wright Act, the petition to organize had to be signed by a *majority of taxpayers* within the proposed boundaries. Then, in a general election, two thirds of all voters had to approve formation of the district. The law also differed from California's in that it granted no right to condemn existing property rights. While it gave each district the right to use "flood water," no one knew how much was available. Interestingly, within the district the board of directors could in times of scarcity distribute water as it saw fit; it was not bound by the doctrine of prior appropriation.[108]

Some proponents of the legislation hoped to use the hundred thousand dollars authorized in 1889 as seed money. As always, Newlands tried to reconcile his vision of the agricultural future of western Nevada with his paramount commitment to serve the Carson River milling interests. He wanted the voters to authorize the legislature to invest seven hundred thousand dollars from the school fund in the bonds of four proposed districts (on the Humboldt, Carson, Truckee, and Walker rivers). This would "prime the pump" so that the districts could sell their bonds to outside investors. The Carson River would be first. Newlands suggested that agents of the state select one hundred thousand acres of school land within easy reach of that stream and turn it over to the district at $1.25 an acre with ten years to pay. The state could purchase one hundred fifty thousand dollars in bonds and the mills one hundred thousand dollars' worth to pay for a dam.[109]

In one way, Nevada's irrigation district legislation was more of a model to the arid West than California's. California was an anomaly. In many parts of that state, wheat farms had replaced the open range long before the irrigation boom of the 1870s and 1880s. Nevada was far more "typical" in that it attempted to make the jump to irrigation agriculture *before* any substantial number of farmers arrived in the state and before the hold of the stock industry had been broken. In California, one major purpose of the irrigation district was to break up wheat farms that numbered in the thousands of acres and replace them with family farms and diversified agriculture. The Wright Act was far-reaching. The district would own *all* irrigation works, not just storage reservoirs, and control *all* water rights, not just those established after the district was formed. In Nevada, the family farm would exist side by side with the stock industry, except in scattered oases of intensive agriculture, such as the Truckee Meadows outside Reno. The Nevada district law recognized the two land uses as compatible.

The Nevada law languished until the summer of 1891, but Newlands was hopeful: "We find our sister State, California, actively engaged in the formation of irrigation districts. Eleven districts are in process of formation, and the total bonded indebtedness about to be created will exceed eleven million dollars. Public attention is everywhere being called to the matter; the people are moving; the newspapers are active, and California seems to be upon the eve of a great development, the wave of which may reach Nevada, if she now takes advantage of her opportunities."[110] At an irrigation convention held in Carson City on October 9, Senator Stewart maintained that large landowners would have plenty of incentive to sell part of their property at reasonable prices once they saw how a district would drive up the value of land. Yet the meeting reflected that Nevadans still had not reached a consensus as to who should be responsible for expanding irrigation. Some speakers insisted that *all* water should be owned and controlled by the state and that the district law was too timid; others argued that the new law was a substantial threat to established rights. There was little room for compromise between those who believed that if private entrepreneurs had no incentive to undertake a project it was not worth doing and those who believed in a "public interest" that only strong state control could protect. Since water rights on Nevada streams had not been adjudicated, and since claims were invariably extravagant, districts would have to purchase *all* rights to a stream to be on the safe side.[111]

The papers of the Fulton family contain an undated "Freeholder's Petition for Organization of an Irrigation District to be known as the Carson Irrigation and Water Storage District, Including Lands in the Counties of Churchill, Lyon, Ormbsby, and Douglass [*sic*], State of Nevada," which contains sixty-three signatures headed by those of Newlands and Douglas County's most prominent ranchers. But the district was never formed. Fulton and Newlands could not secure the support of a majority of taxpayers within the proposed district, in part because the early 1890s were unusually wet years in western Nevada. Once again, the legislature had failed to unify the state's water users and rival industries.[112]

In the spring of 1892, Newlands turned one last time to the Central Pacific. He asked it to join him in selling the prime land and reservoir sites each held within the Truckee basin to a private ditch company in exchange for stock. Tahoe, Donner, Webber, and Independence lakes in the Sierra would provide storage. If Newlands put up sixteen thousand acres and the Central Pacific twenty thousand, he conjectured, other large landowners might provide additional land. The land would sell quickly for ten to twenty-five dollars an acre, and a highline canal to Lemmon Valley and other arable land north of Reno could be financed from the profits. The company would charge a flat fee of two dollars an acre a year for water. Newlands cared little about how the arrangement was carried out. The real question was "not what *I* am willing to do," Newlands explained in a letter to Fulton, "but what *others* are willing to do. I am willing to meet any proposition made by the Railroad people and the people of Truckee [Meadows] in which they show their confidence by investing their money."[113]

In the fall of 1892, Newlands finally won a seat in Congress. His interest in water development persisted because the smoldering Carson River litigation often threatened to burst into flames once again.[114] His new responsibilities, however, along with the economic depression and growing importance of the silver issue, forced him to acknowledge privately in July 1893 that he had "failed utterly" to attract capital, and he ordered Fulton to "curtail all expenses in connection with these enterprises." He conceded that with Fulton's help he had "collected together a very valuable amount of property," but correctly predicted that years might elapse before the work of reclaiming western Nevada could be resumed.[115]

With Newlands's attention diverted to a larger stage and state revenue shrinking, the 1893 legislative session was anticlimactic. Legislators debated a bill to copy the "Wyoming Plan"—the adjudication of rights and distribution of water by a state engineer and "board of control" rather than through the courts. Given the cost of litigation on the Carson and Humboldt rivers, and the damage it had done to the state's economy by limiting the price of land and the tax base, Nevada was too poor to afford the proposed state engineer's three-thousand-dollar annual salary, let alone those of his assistants. L. H. Taylor, who drafted the bill, asked rhetorically in a letter to the *Morning Appeal* on February 5, 1893: "Is it better for the farmers of our State to continue under the present system with insecure and undefined water rights, and consequent low and uncertain values of land, or to have those rights definitely determined and fixed as are their titles to the land and thus the value of both at least doubled?" Nevada's farmers and ranchers paid little attention to Taylor's argument, and the legislature once again failed to provide a way to sort out the state's water rights.[116] A good example of the impact of litigation on irrigation in Nevada came two years later when William Ellsworth Smythe examined potential sites for his irrigation colonies. Smythe considered buying some of Newlands's land in Churchill County, at the end of the Carson River, but anxiety about upstream water claims forced him to turn elsewhere.[117]

Just before the legislature adjourned in 1893, Dan De Quille informed the Salt Lake City *Tribune:* "Were big irrigation works started in the State at this time there would be made an outlet for a considerable amount of surplus labor on the Comstock. But nobody comes near us for the purpose of undertaking any such enterprise. Nevada appears to be a stench in the nostrils of those who have robbed and plundered her. They do not want to hear of her or come near her. . . . No State in the Union is more hated and sneered at by bankers and capitalists than Nevada." Newlands had to live with the fact that, whatever Nevada's bad luck, he had not been able to convince its citizens that they could control their own destiny.[118] "There are no irrigation laws in Nevada to-day," Fulton observed sadly in June 1894, "and the detriment which this condition of things is to the State, and the extent of its check on her future prosperity if it be not speedily remedied, is beyond appreciation."[119]

Colorado

The gentle grade of the eastern slope, excellent soil, relatively abundant water supply, and fine reservoir sites provided by the Rocky Mountains made Colorado ideal for irrigation. Americans first watered Colorado land in 1839, near present-day La Junta, five miles above Fort Bent on the Arkansas River. Irrigation may also have been practiced near Pueblo, farther upstream on the Arkansas, after that town was settled in 1842. The first ditch of any size—the San Luis Valley's "People's Ditch"—was not completed until 1852, when southern Colorado was still part of New Mexico. Settlers near the Santa Fe Trail tapped the Culebra River, a tributary of the Rio Grande, just north of the present-day border between the two states. Two years later, on the west side of the Rio Grande, another group established the town of Guadalupe and diverted water from the Conejos River. Later, these and other early agricultural settlements in the San Luis Valley provided grain and vegetables to settlers who moved into Colorado to escape the political conflicts in Kansas and the severe business depression of 1857–58. Of course, the largest new markets were provided by the Pike's Peak gold rush in 1859.[120]

From 1865 to 1870, Colorado's population grew by 60 percent, and during the following decade its farmers increased from 3,406 to 16,389, most of whom practiced irrigation. The first railroad reached Denver in 1870, bringing with it a substantial number of agricultural colonists. By 1868, four large ditches had tapped the Arkansas River near Canon City. Two ran north of the stream and two to the south; in all they covered twenty miles, served about forty-three hundred acres, and cost over twenty thousand dollars. During these years Colorado became agriculturally self-sufficient and shipped surplus crops to military posts in Montana. By 1870, the commissioner of the General Land Office estimated that the value of agricultural products produced in Colorado nearly equaled the value of its mineral output.[121]

During the 1870s and 1880s, the eagerness of railroads to sell their land and the markets provided by the mining communities tributary to Denver shifted the locus of agriculture north to the Platte and Cache la Poudre river basins. By 1881, farmers had taken up land along the Platte for a distance of fifty or sixty miles above and below Denver, and most of the normal streamflow had been claimed. The first ditches were excavated by individual farmers or groups of farmers, but at the end of the 1870s and beginning of the 1880s, Colorado entered its corporate phase of water development. While the economic growth of Wyoming, Montana, and Nevada was impeded by inadequate transportation, the railroad favored Colorado above all western states. The Santa Fe reached Pueblo by 1876, then built south to the New Mexico state line by 1878, and north to Denver by 1887; the Denver & Rio Grande laid an average of three hundred miles of new track in Colorado each year from 1880 to 1882; the Denver & South Park line connected Denver and the Arkansas Valley below Leadville in 1880; and the Denver & New Orleans Railroad linked those communities eight years later. Meanwhile, the Burlington entered the state from Nebraska and reached Denver in 1882; the Missouri Pacific built along the Arkansas Valley and reached Pueblo in 1887; and the Rock Island Railroad entered Colorado Springs in 1888, the same year the Denver, Texas & Fort Worth completed a line to the Gulf of Mexico. By the end of the 1880s, Colorado was served by six eastern lines—the Union Pacific, Burlington, Rock Island, Kansas Pacific, Missouri Pacific, and the Santa Fe. Boosters portrayed Denver as a hub city similar to Chicago. They projected lines to Duluth, Puget Sound, and Galveston, and to other parts of a Rocky Mountain empire. The length of rail lines increased from 1,570 miles in 1880 to 4,176 miles in 1890.[122]

Simultaneously, capital discovered irrigation. The High Line Canal symbolized the new era. Completed in 1882–83, it covered about forty-four miles and cost $640,000, most of which was raised in England. The canal-building mania reached its peak in the middle and late 1880s; four hundred miles of ditch were constructed in 1884 alone. By the end of the decade, every stream flowing east from the Rockies—with the possible exception of the Arkansas River—had been overappropriated. Still the investment orgy continued. The *Colorado Farmer* reprinted an editorial from western Colorado's *Grand Valley Star* in February 1890, which complained that "one would think from reading accounts of new canals projected in Eastern Colorado that the Platte and Arkansas were—like the Grand—inexhaustible as to water supply. . . . A study of the priority appropriations on file in the State Engineer's office would be interesting reading to people who propose to put money into new canals in the Platte valley."[123]

Since ditch companies usually made far more money by selling land through confederate companies than by selling water, the canal boom coincided with vast new claims to Colorado's remaining arable land. When the state entered the Union it received nearly seven hundred fifty thousand acres from the federal government (in addition to school sections) to help pay for the construction of public buildings and an agricultural college. This land was far more valuable than the sixteenth and thirty-sixth sections because it could be selected anywhere within what remained of Colorado's public domain. In 1883, the legislature offered for sale alternate quarter sections selected by state officials, in the hope that over the years the construction of private canals would drive up the price of the land retained by the state. Meanwhile, the rest of Colorado's holdings were leased. Unfortunately, the pressure to transfer *all* the land to private parties proved too great. By January 1891, 343,416 acres had been sold and another 186,662 acres were under lease for the bargain price of from two and a half to five cents an acre per year. Of course, the leased land returned no tax revenue at all.[124]

Colorado's best land was quickly claimed, except that located beyond the reach of canals in the eastern quarter of the state. According to the Colorado state engineer, over 1,300,000 acres of federal, railroad, and state land were taken in his state in 1885 and over 2,900,000 acres in the following year. During 1886, the largest number of new migrants followed the Julesburg and Burlington lines into eastern Weld County (today's Pawnee National Grassland). "It has within the past eighteen months been discovered," the Denver *Republican* naively announced at the beginning of 1887, "that crops can be grown there without irrigation."[125] The northeastern counties grew most rapidly in 1887, but the settlers who arrived in 1888 preferred Bent and Las Animas counties and the San Luis Valley. Seven new counties were created in eastern Colorado in 1889 alone. The state's population roughly doubled between 1885 and 1889, and 1 million more acres were assessed as agricultural land in 1890 than in 1889. Many of the new counties were established by fraud against the wishes of a majority of their residents. The promoters—generally speculators—often drew county boundaries in the hope that property taxes on railroads would pay all or most of the cost of local government.[126]

Private irrigation development played a large part in the state's economic prosperity, and by 1890 Colorado boosters knew their state was on the verge of overtaking California in the contest for new farmers. At the beginning of 1891, the Colorado state engineer reported that his state contained 10,000 miles of irrigation ditches, 4,000,000 acres "under ditch" (within reach of canals), and 1,500,000 acres actually irrigated. The latter figure was probably closer to 1,000,000 acres, slightly less than the area watered in California. Colorado's growth during the 1890s, however, permitted the mountain state to take the lead briefly at the turn of the century.[127]

As in every other western state, rapid growth was a mixed blessing. No one could deny that the railroads and irrigation were largely responsible for the state's exuberant economic upswing during the 1880s. Yet the transportation and irrigation booms provoked the same antimonopoly cries that had been heard in California since the 1870s. "How many hundreds of thousands of dollars they have wickedly taken from their victims during the seven years of its life nobody but the company knows," the *Colorado Farmer* remarked in an editorial on the history of the High Line Canal. "Every dollar it got was obtained upon false pretenses. It has no water to carry. It never had any, and it is not entitled to have." Or as the Farmers' Protective Association—an organ of the Colorado Grange created in 1886—charged in a memorial to the legislature in 1887: "For whoever owns the waters of an irrigating country thereby owns the country; and if one set of proprietors own the water and another the soil, without the intervention of the State by the arm of the laws, the latter class can only be land serfs of the former."[128]

No single type of legislation grew faster during the years from 1879 to 1891 than bills pertaining to water rights and water companies,

Irrigated Areas of Colorado, 1900

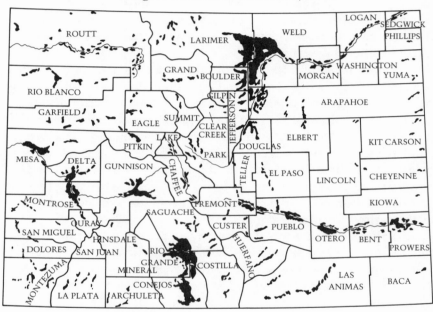

Total Irrigated Area
1,611,271 Acres

Colorado irrigation map.

and 76 percent of them were introduced during the legislative sessions of 1887, 1889, and 1891.[129] At the beginning of the 1887 session, the *Rocky Mountain News* proclaimed: "The time has come when it must be determined whether or not the people have any rights which the corporate creatures of their own creation are bound to respect. The contest is at hand." The *News* demanded three reforms: the creation of a railroad commission that could set transportation rates; a reduction in fees charged by state, county, and local officials; and a new irrigation law "to prevent the stealing of the water by the powerful foreign or domestic corporations, and [to prevent] the levying of so-called 'royalties' on the land owners, for the right to use that which the constitution declares shall be forever the property of the people."[130]

In Colorado, as in every other arid state, legal uncertainty served as the primary justification for greater state involvement in the allocation and distribution of water. Indeed, many reformers assumed that the state would inevitably displace private enterprise through a natural evolutionary process. Road building and mail delivery, once reserved largely to private companies, had increasingly been taken over by government. The same thing would happen with irrigation; corporate control of water was only a phase. As Elwood Mead noted, corporations were considered individuals under the law, hence any statutes that granted absolute water rights to corporations were anachronistic, throwbacks to the age of monarchy in Europe, when kings and queens granted entire streams to the nobility. In the spring of 1888, Governor Alva Adams called together representatives of the state's water districts, boards of trade, and labor unions to discuss the water question and decide on a state policy. The convention coincided with Congress's approval of the Powell Irrigation Survey and revealed a deep rift between the proponents of state and federal reclamation, a division also evident in California and Nevada. Adams and the Colorado State Grange, however, saw the two as complementary. They assumed that the federal government would build storage reservoirs but leave the construction of canals and the administration of water rights to the states.[131]

State reclamation got a strong boost from the drought that afflicted large parts of Colorado, particularly the eastern plains, from 1889 to 1895. The newspapers were filled with stories like that of Julius Thimjau and his family. They had fled Nebraska in 1889 and settled on a preemption claim in eastern Colorado between Sterling and Fleming. At the time, Thimjau had four hundred dollars in cash, which he quickly spent breaking the prairie sod and erecting a house. He planted corn, but nothing came up, and in the following year lost his barley, oats, and corn. During the winter of 1889–90, Thimjau found work in Denver and sent food and clothing to his wife and six children, who remained on the claim, but the second crop failure left the family destitute, along with thousands of others. "It is a fact which can scarcely be realized, and yet it is a fact," the *Rocky Mountain News* observed at the end of 1890, "that within one hundred miles of our city, men, women and children are starving and going half clad on the wintry plains. They are suffering for food, for fuel, for clothes to wear, for the commonest necessities of life. Their condition is pitiable in the extreme."[132] The legislature frequently considered relief bills, but most failed, often because they touched off intense sectional rivalries. For example, early in 1891, the Pueblo *Chieftain*, published in the Arkansas River basin, protested a bill for fifty thousand dollars to provide seed to farmers in eastern Colorado, on grounds that the state should spend the money moving the farmers to those parts of the state—such as the Arkansas Valley—served by irrigation.[133]

Nevertheless, in 1889 and for some years thereafter many members of the legislature thought that the state had a responsibility to stem the flow of small farmers from drought-afflicted counties into other states. They were encouraged by the fact that the state's Internal Improvements Fund—a legacy of Congress's 1841 decision to grant new states five hundred thousand acres on condition they use the proceeds to pay for internal improvements—contained over four hundred thousand dollars.[134] Congress had consistently rejected appeals from the states to permit them to turn this revenue into their general treasuries. (Colorado's state debt was over $1 million in 1889, and it had increased by $327,000 during 1887 and 1888.) Consequently, most of the money had been spent on roads. But the fund grew rapidly as the state disposed of its land during the 1880s, and early in 1889 the state supreme court ruled that the money could also be spent on reservoirs and canals. Although many Coloradans hoped the state would use the fund to buy up ditches owned by private corporations, rather than to build new ones, the former state engineer estimated that that would cost $15 million, and the current state engineer pegged the cost at $7 million—far more than the four hundred thousand dollars available. Moreover, the condemnation of existing canals was expected to involve years of litigation.

When the state legislature convened in 1889, the *Rocky Mountain News* predicted that because of the extensive topographical mapping program Powell favored, the construction of federal reservoirs could not begin in less than five or six years.[135] Within a few weeks, the legislature found itself swamped by canal and reservoir bills.[136] The supporters of state reclamation divided into two groups: those who wanted to construct a handful of reservoirs fairly evenly spaced along the eastern base of the Rockies, where they would do the most good, and those who wanted to spread the benefits among the largest possible number of communities. The latter won out in the waning days of the 1889 session, after a conference committee recommended a package of twenty-five bills, which allocated $185,000 from the internal improvements fund for reservoirs, $124,500 for bridges, $66,500 for roads, and $25,000 for straightening streams. The package constituted a bundle of trade-offs between different parts of the state as well as between those who wanted to spend the money entirely on transportation and those who favored spending it exclusively on irrigation. It contained everything from a few thousand dollars to straighten the Cucharas and Las Animas rivers to seventy-five thousand dollars to build a bridge across the Rio Grande linking Conejos and Costilla counties.[137] When the legislature adjourned, the Denver *Republican* remarked that "every bill that contemplated a raid on the Treasury, and every new county scheme that was well backed up with corner [town] lots and boodle, found hearty supporters."[138]

Almost overlooked in the cascade of internal improvement legislation was a ten-thousand-dollar appropriation to use convict labor to dig a canal out of the Arkansas River, yet this was destined to become the most controversial part of the state reclamation program approved between 1889 and 1893. The question of how to provide meaningful work to convicts had long weighed on officials at the isolated state prison at Canon City. The prison contained no workshops. Inmates found occasional work burning lime, manufacturing brick, raising hogs, and cutting stone, but they spent most of their time in idleness, confined one man to a cell, a solitary condition that drove some to insanity. Many private companies, including ditch enterprises, had offered to put the men to work; for example, in 1889 a textile company sponsored legislation to build a factory at Canon City so that Colorado wool could be processed entirely within the state. Such schemes promised "work therapy" for the convicts, and held out the hope that the prisoners would pay part of the annual cost of maintaining the prison. As early as 1886, the board of prison commissioners recommended that inmate labor be used to excavate two large ditches from the Arkansas

River to serve tracts of state land near the penitentiary. The commissioners estimated that the sale of water from these canals would bring in fifty thousand dollars a year—a figure the warden increased to one hundred thousand dollars a year in 1889. (That, perhaps not coincidentally, was the prison's annual budget.) The 1889 legislature appropriated sufficient money to begin preliminary work on the ditch and designated the penitentiary commissioners as a Board of Construction, granting it the power to lease water rights to private landowners.[139]

State Canal Number One, as it came to be called, was clearly an experiment. As the *Rocky Mountain News* noted in 1893, if the canal was successfully completed, "its operation may furnish an unanswerable argument in favor of as many state irrigating canals as it shall be possible for the state to construct." Governor Davis H. Waite, a Populist, predicted that the ditch would "add greatly to the value of some of the state lands and will also be a source of revenue by supplying with water lands of private citizens in the vicinity."[140] The popularity of State Canal Number One reflected the increasing power of Populists in the legislature, reformers who used public works as a weapon against private monopolies. It also mirrored the legislature's inability to reform the state's water laws; the state had to move fast to create its own water rights, in effect to reserve a water supply, and the Arkansas was the last major stream on the eastern slope which carried any unappropriated water.

In June 1889 the state engineer surveyed twenty-five miles of aqueduct, but construction did not begin until 1891, when the legislature appropriated fifty thousand dollars to build a canal from Canon City to Pueblo to serve about thirty thousand acres of state land west of the latter city. Even though an average of over one hundred inmates from the state prison worked on the project each day, the appropriation was inadequate. By the time the 1893 legislature met, only 2 of 40 miles had been completed, along with 270 feet of tunnel. Consequently, the lawmakers made an end run around the internal improvements fund by authorizing the sale of land in the vicinity of the canal line even before the aqueduct was completed, using the proceeds to pay for construction. In the meantime, the state issued certificates of indebtedness bearing 5 percent interest in payment for supplies and construction materials. Proponents of this scheme pledged that land and water sales would easily raise the six hundred fifty thousand dollars needed to complete construction, but critics feared that the policy would result in a massive "raid" on the treasury and heavy new taxes.[141]

By 1895, the canal still had not been completed, but the cost had reached one hundred ten thousand dollars, with no end in sight. The high price of reclamation raised the prospect that once the state's irrigation system had been completed, the charges for water would be so high that no one would buy it. To ensure an adequate supply, proponents of the Canon City–Pueblo ditch now talked about constructing an auxiliary reservoir at Twin Lakes, one hundred miles upstream at the headwaters of the Arkansas. A legislative commission inspected state irrigation works during the summer of 1894 and filed an alarming report. The cost of state reclamation was running four times that of private ditch companies for comparable work; State Canal Number One would cost as much as $1,300,000 to complete; and farmers below Pueblo had already claimed all the stream's water.[142] The Senate Finance Committee agreed. It warned that completion of the ditch and reservoir would touch off new water wars, especially since 1895 was a dry year. Moreover, the committee insisted that the financial condition of the state did not warrant large expenditures for public works.[143] To make matters even worse, when the 1895 legislature debated a fifty-thousand-dollar bill to begin work on the Twin Lakes reservoir, it discovered that the Colorado Water and Power Company, formed in 1892, claimed both the reservoir site and all the surplus water it could contain. Lengthy condemnation proceedings, or a large outlay to buy the company's rights, would be necessary before a dam could be constructed.[144]

State Canal Number One was a trade-off. Tension had always existed *among* the proponents of state reclamation, especially among speculators who hoped state efforts would drive up the price of virgin land and actual farmers who wanted to relieve chronic water shortages on land already cultivated, particularly in the Platte, Clear Creek, Cache la Poudre, St. Vrain, and Boulder Creek watersheds.[145] The Arkansas Valley project survived as long as it did only because the 1891 legislature authorized the construction of a second major canal in Mesa County, at the western edge of Colorado, where a new wave of immigrants took up land around Grand Junction in the early 1890s in the hope of raising apples, peaches, and other high value fruits. (Eastern Colorado, by contrast, produced mainly field crops.[146]) The Grand River was particularly attractive because it contained plenty of unappropriated water.

Of course, irrigation boosters in eastern Colorado feared any project that might divert the stream of settlement away from the Arkansas

and San Luis valleys. They also knew that the two canals would compete for limited state funds. Because it appropriated one hundred fifty
thousand dollars for State Canal Number One, the 1891 legislature
refused to spend more than fifteen hundred dollars on the canal in
western Colorado—barely enough to begin surveying an aqueduct sixty
miles long, capable of serving seventy-five to one hundred thousand
acres. Nevertheless, on the mere promise of state reclamation, hundreds of farmers and speculators swarmed into the Grand River Valley.
The legislature promised that if Grand Valley residents could raise fifty
thousand dollars, form a cooperative irrigation company to bond their
irrigable land, and construct secure barracks, the state would provide
convict labor to excavate the ditch. Although the biennial harvest from
the internal improvements fund was dwindling with each new legislature, boosters anticipated that if State Canal Number One proved
successful, the lawmakers might vote money from the general fund or
authorize certificates of indebtedness to pay for State Canal Number
Two, as they had for the first canal.[147]

Much of the support for the two state ditches came from Populist
legislators. By 1893, the drought and tight money had undermined both
the effectiveness and the popularity of private water works. Therefore,
reformers in the legislature hoped that if the state canals proved successful, Colorado would be able to take over *all* the ditches in the state
for a price much lower than in the late 1880s. The largest private canal
on the Grand River went bankrupt in late 1892 or early 1893, raising
the possibility that the state could assert control over all the water
used within that basin by purchasing the ditch. Unlike the Arkansas
Valley, where there were many private companies and individual water
users, the Grand offered a test case, a chance to "start over" and show
what the state could do.[148]

Since 1889, the *Rocky Mountain News* had consistently criticized
the legislature for frittering away internal improvement money on a
multitude of small projects. "A county that cannot take care of its
roads and construct its bridges," the newspaper proclaimed, "has no
excuse for existence."[149] The *News* attributed opposition to State Canal
Number Two to a private syndicate that hoped to build the ditch in
exchange for state land. However, the requested $150,000 appropriation
to begin construction came at a time when the entire internal improvement fund contained only $157,000 or $159,000, when over $1
million worth of public works bills had been introduced, and when
many proponents of reclamation thought that the state should finish

the first ditch before beginning a second.[150] Governor Waite appealed to the legislature to approve the use of certificates of indebtedness to pay for State Canal Number Two, but opponents of the Mesa County work defeated the bill after amending it into uselessness. The *News* suggested that the senator who led the floor fight against the appropriation had been bought off by a "combine of capitalists" who wanted to steal the Grand River, but the friends of State Canal Number One also played a part in its defeat, as did the economic slump.[151] Nevertheless, before it adjourned the legislature revived the 1891 law, which permitted the people of Grand Valley to build the canal themselves, using convict labor, if they could raise the money.[152]

The depression of 1893 hit Colorado particularly hard because it coincided with a steep decline in the prices of silver and sheep. By 1895 the internal improvement fund contained little more than one hundred thousand dollars, one fourth the amount available in 1889. The goose that laid the golden eggs was dead.[153] Some state officials urged an expansion of state reclamation to relieve unemployment, but a legislative committee appointed in January 1894 to inspect the state works recommended against state construction of the Mesa County ditch. It noted that transporting convicts from the Canon City state prison to the Grand Valley, 250 miles away, would impose substantial costs on the state for special guards as well as for transportation. It estimated the cost of State Canal Number Two, and the pumps needed to raise the water from the Grand River into the ditch, at seven hundred thousand dollars. The committee concluded that if a private company was willing to do the work for half the land under ditch, in effect paying $11.67 an acre for raw prairie, that translated into a very good deal for Grand Valley residents. As the antimonopoly hysteria of the early 1890s abated, the Grand Junction *News*, and even the *Rocky Mountain News*, came out in favor of this plan. The legislature abandoned the state reclamation program, sold State Canal Number One, and refused to appropriate sufficient money to maintain the dams already built.[154] In 1899, the state turned over control of these structures to the counties.

The fate of State Canal Number Two was the last act in a comedy of errors.[155] In 1891, the legislature had appropriated money to build reservoirs in Custer, El Paso, Saguache, Chaffee, and Las Animas counties, and between 1892 and 1895 the state constructed seven dams at a cost of well over a hundred thousand dollars. Collectively, these stored no more than three thousand acre-feet, about enough water to irrigate one thousand acres and only a small fraction of the volume stored by the largest dam on the Cache la Poudre. In two cases the structures were so badly designed and constructed that they could not hold water. They were never regularly used by irrigators. The poor quality of the works and the fact they were often built in the wrong place were compounded by a basic legal problem. The normal flow in some of the streams chosen for reservoirs had been appropriated even before the state began work, but in every case the beginning of construction prompted so many new claims that there was no water left when the project was completed. In fact, the state works increased rather than decreased conflicts over water.[156] Nevertheless, individual communities invariably blamed their rivals for undermining the state program. For example, in 1893 the Pueblo *Chieftain* insisted that the main source of opposition to State Canal Number One was Denver, which dominated the trade of northern Colorado and whose leaders feared that their city and older irrigation districts would lose power as new settlers streamed into the Arkansas Valley. Two years later, the *Chieftain* bitterly charged that a bill to complete the canal "would certainly have been passed had no sectional prejudices interfered."[157]

The failure of state reclamation did not surprise most Coloradans. History and experience taught that government was an easy prey for rings and gangs. In 1889, the Denver *Republican* cautioned that the state should build reservoirs only after adequate hydrographic surveys. It charged that many of the internal improvement bills "cover disgraceful jobs and steals, and not one of them should become a law unless the Governor is certain that it is a necessity and that the money will be properly applied." The Colorado Springs *Gazette* urged the governor to appoint a board of engineers to choose the reservoir sites. "In the present bills, the place to try the experiment is fixed by logrolling," it correctly observed, "every community trying to get something out of the internal improvement fund. As a necessary result of such a course, most of the money will be lost." Some members of the legislature freely admitted that they had no idea whether reclamation schemes proposed by their fellow legislators were practical or not, and some friends of state reclamation worried that wasteful expenditures would hurt their cause more than help it. But most lawmakers were intent on getting as much as they could for their constituents; questions of waste and efficiency were irrelevant. *All* the dams built from 1891 to 1894, and many that never got off the drawing board, were impractical. For example, the 1889 legislature approved the construction of a reservoir on Clear Creek, above Golden, even though the accumulation of silt would have quickly rendered it useless. The governor vetoed the bill, despite severe criticism from local farmers and speculators. And had the internal improvement fund not run dry, the legislature would have approved a dam at Twin Lakes in 1893 or 1895, despite evidence that the structure was likely to wash out every year (because bedrock was so far beneath the surface) and despite the fact that the porous sand-and-gravel bed of the river was likely to soak up all the stored water long before it reached the headgate of State Canal Number One.[158]

Many of the reclamation bills required the Colorado state engineer to prepare plans and supervise construction. But he had little or no influence on the amount of money appropriated for each job—which was usually far too little to pay for first-rate work—and he was also limited by a small staff and the legislature's persistent refusal to provide sufficient money to survey Colorado's water supply and reservoir sites. Had he tried to block all impractical schemes, he would have alienated politicians and boosters throughout the state, making the rest of his job impossible. Nevertheless, he did eliminate a few of the more outrageous schemes—bridges and roads as well as canals—by estimating that they would cost far more than the legislature had appropriated. As a result, while the 1889 legislature appropriated $209,560 for irrigation work, but $96,387.07 remained unspent when the 1891 legislature convened.[159]

As a political strategy, the legislature lumped irrigation projects together with roads and bridges. Then, as now, omnibus bills had a power all their own. The construction of dams, canals, roads, and bridges had this much in common: they could be built as separate works or part of much larger systems, all at once or in sequence. At the end of the nineteenth century, the state engineer pointed out some of the weaknesses in the state's network of roads. It was time, he thought, "to take up the matter of state thoroughfares in a systematic manner. Heretofore much money and energy have been expended at random and without beneficial returns commensurate therewith. I think it advisable to have a general plan of state roads, embracing every section of the state, so that when completed it will form a complete and connected whole, giving communication for distant and remote districts with each other and with the more thickly settled portions and the principal cities."[160] This, of course, was doubly true of reclamation.

In conclusion, Colorado suffered from two clashing definitions of "commonwealth." The legislature followed the democratic precept that public funds belonged to the entire state, hence each section deserved its fair share of benefits. Yet that conflicted with the assumption that the state had the responsibility to *increase* wealth, not just parcel out the existing supply. In many ways, this latter vision was equally damaging because it prompted Colorado farmers and boosters to demand that the state give away its water. There was never any serious attempt to charge for it, even though friends of state reclamation originally promised that the program would pay for itself—just as the champions of federal reclamation would do later. As the state engineer noted, "the idea has generally prevailed that the waters stored are to be free, or will be distributed pro rata among all ditches having established rights on the stream below."[161] It was this clash of ideals—more than the inflated cost of public enterprise, or logrolling and corruption, or the inefficiency of the hydraulic works themselves—that doomed Colorado's public irrigation program.

Conclusion

For all the wealth of the nineteenth-century West, it was also a land of limits, and its residents harbored many anxieties. The states, territories, counties, and towns in the western half of the nation railed against the dominance of eastern capital and elites, but they were equally worried about the mercantile imperialism followed by their close neighbors. They were locked in a struggle for growth and commercial supremacy in which failure was far more common than success. "We [the people of California] must adopt that line of policy which will increase our population, if we mean to be great, and progress in wealth," a Stockton newspaper editorialized in 1856. If the state did not, property values would stagnate, "and in the end she must retrograde."[162] That, of course, was the lesson Nevada taught the West. A state bright with promise in the 1870s did not profit from the income generated by mining, and by the 1890s it had regressed to pastureland. It joined many other losers. For example, during the boom decade of the 1880s, when the West grew in population faster than the rest of the nation, the population of Tucson declined by 27 percent, that of Santa Fe by nearly 7 percent, and that of Silver Cliff, Colorado, a mining town, by over 50 percent.[163] The breakdown of state reclamation was another example of the broader failure of public policy in a nation dominated by provincial instincts. Most western states tried to promote economic growth through private reclamation schemes, which worked until the 1890s, albeit at a very high price. A few also tried state reclamation, though timidly, with inadequate appropriations and inadequate water laws. Federal reclamation remained a lively option, but for many in the arid West, the best hope of future growth was cession of part or all of the public lands to the states and territories.

7

Wyoming, Land Cession, and the "Terrible Nineties"

In the 1890s, Wyoming had much in common with its poor relative, Nevada. Both were large states inadequately served by rail transportation; both had small populations; both lived in the long shadow of successful agricultural states; both had volatile economies; both feared a possible return to territorial status; and in both, politics was a highly personal affair, dominated by a handful of men. Nevertheless, there were significant differences between the two. For example, while the state of Nevada had land to sell but no water to make it productive, Wyoming had just the opposite problem. Wyoming's leaders worried that divided control over land and water inhibited the spread of irrigation agriculture, and most called for the cession of all or part of the public domain to the states. Cession was not the West's only option during the 1890s; the irrigation district had enthusiastic supporters, especially in the more populous states, and even after the demise of the Powell Irrigation Survey federal reclamation had its share of friends. Still, the campaign for cession had broad appeal, particularly in the grazing states at the headwaters of the West's major rivers. It culminated in the Carey Act of 1894—yet another unsuccessful attempt to transcend the diverse economic, geographic, and climatic conditions in the arid and semi-arid West.

Troubled Wyoming

Wyoming was a child of the Union Pacific Railroad. The line reached Cheyenne in 1867, only a few months after the town's founding. In less than a year Wyoming became a territory. Gigantic Indian reservations in the northern two thirds of the territory covered its best potential farmland, and a short growing season, combined with inadequate transportation and limited local markets, rendered large-scale agriculture impractical. In 1880, the territory's population was less than 21,000, half of whom lived in seven towns strung along the Union Pacific line: Cheyenne, Laramie, Rawlins, Evanston, Rock Springs, Carbon, and Green River City. Colorado's spectacular growth during the 1870s left Wyoming far behind and raised the prospect that Wyoming might be dismembered, with the southeastern part, including the railroad line, added to Colorado.[1]

The confinement of Wyoming's Indians to reservations during the 1870s opened up the immense grasslands north of the Platte River and east of the Big Horn Mountains. A relatively brief cattle boom followed, reaching its peak in the years from 1878 to 1884. "A man with some capital that will stick to the business for five years, with but ordinary luck can be worth a hundred thousand dollars," Joseph M. Carey, soon to become one of the territory's leading politicians and entrepreneurs, wrote to his brother in 1869. "I believe it to be a sure road to a fortune." Although the average elevation of Wyoming is six thousand feet, its many valleys (which protected cattle herds from storms and high winds), its streams, and its lush grasses provided a congenial home for livestock. Unlike pastures at lower elevations, the forage was tall, thick, succulent, and present all year long—and it had far less sagebrush to compete against. In addition, Wyoming had a strategic advantage over Montana, Idaho, Washington, and Oregon in its proximity to markets and supplemental feed. As the governor of Wyoming remarked in 1878, "it is no small advantage to be at the very back-door of those great corn-growing states of the Missouri Valley, whose grain can be had at a very low price and turned to such excellent account as a means of improving the quality of our beef." Between 1882 and 1886, Wyoming incorporated ninety-three cattle companies capitalized at more than $51 million. These included the Union Cattle Company, the Swan Land and Live Stock Company, the Powder River Cattle Company, and the Luke Voorhees Cattle Company. As in California during the heyday of the mining industry, high profits in cattle initially discouraged investments in irrigation agriculture.[2]

The end of the cattle boom came several years before the notorious "white winter" of 1886–87. Thousands of animals died during the winter of 1884–85 and the unusually dry summer that followed. The number declined from as many as 1,500,000 in 1885, to 900,000 in 1886, to 300,000 a decade later. In 1886, the assessed value of Wyoming's cattle was $14,651,125. That amount had shrunk to $3,732,558 a decade later, and a $2,000,000 increase in the assessed value of sheep only partly offset the $9,000,000 decline in the value of cattle. Animals that had sold for as much as fifty or sixty dollars at the peak of the boom returned little more than ten dollars in 1892.[3]

In 1890, Wyoming was the nation's fourth largest state in area but the second smallest in population (ahead of Nevada). Although the railroad line ran through the least promising agricultural section of the state, in 1895 almost 85 percent of Wyoming's nearly 6 million taxable acres belonged to the Union Pacific. Newspapers frequently complained that the railroad took far more interest in the growth of Nebraska, Kansas, Colorado, and Utah than in that of Wyoming. They repeatedly criticized the company's refusal to build spur lines into the northern part of the state. Economically, the ranches, farms, and towns of northern and eastern Wyoming—which had grown up in part to provide for the needs of forts Washakie and McKinney—were tied more closely to Billings and Omaha than to Cheyenne. Moreover, critics charged that the absence of feeder lines limited farming to hay and root crops used as winter feed for stock, increasing the state's dependence on the cattle industry.[4]

The problems of poor transportation were compounded by Wyoming's limited tax base. Sales and rentals of state lands returned some revenue, but most state money came from land taxes, and almost all land was part of the public domain. The constitution prohibited taxes higher than four mills per dollar and restricted the state debt to 1 percent of taxable property, except in time of war or domestic insurrection. Unless put to a vote, no debt could be incurred that exceeded the current year's taxes. Consequently, Wyoming rarely used bonds to pay public expenses (though a fifteen-thousand-dollar issue helped erect the insane asylum in 1887 and a ninety-thousand-dollar issue in the following year created a public building fund). The state's population increased by almost 48 percent during the 1890s, but tax revenue expanded very little.[5]

To make matters worse, Congress stipulated that none of the land granted to Wyoming could be sold for less that $10 an acre, or leased at an annual rate of less than 5 percent of its assessed value—this at a time when federal lands rarely sold for more than $2.50 an acre. In 1895 the Wyoming legislature bitterly complained:

An experience of four years in the selection and management of these lands has shown beyond question that such minimum selling price is an unwise and injurious condition. It is unwise because it is arbitrary and has no relation to the actual value of the land it affects. Although a minimum price it is far above the maximum value of unimproved land in this state. So long as the best lands of adjoining states can be had under Federal land laws for a nominal price, it is useless to attempt to secure the occupancy or improvements, much less sale, of state land to which this condition attaches. That this is true is shown by the history of the past four years, in which the state has sold only 720 acres of a total grant of over three million acres.[6]

Whatever the intentions of Congress, many Wyoming residents thought that it had severely impaired their state's ability to attract new residents. Given the artificially high price of state lands, and Congress's delay in appropriating money to survey them, politicians worked hard to get additional grants with no strings attached.

Wyoming's harsh climate limited the growing season to 90–150 days, and cattlemen fenced off the region's most accessible rivers. Still, those streams carried plenty of water, they ran through the best agricultural lands in the state, and their "fall" (grade) made the construction of short ditches easy. Most canals were less than a mile long, and the average cost of irrigating Wyoming land at the beginning of the 1890s was $3.62 an acre, far less that the $8.15 average for the entire arid region.[7] In the 1890s the Platte, Big Horn, and Green rivers were practically untouched. In most parts of the West, irrigation was a major source of friction between farmers and stockmen, but Wyoming promised to unite the two. The winter of 1886–87 demonstrated the need to supplement natural grasses with irrigated pasture, and it paved the way for the investment of profits from the range cattle industry in irrigation projects. It heralded the transition from a highly speculative industry to a more stable business characterized by smaller herds maintained on privately owned ranches and pastures, with summer grazing in the state's forests. Selective breeding required separating the herds, and that meant fencing the land. "Agriculture and stock-raising combined will surely give birth and impetus to a degree of development that will produce many a thickly settled, prosperous district," one writer observed in 1893, "where now there is little else than the magic soil itself."[8]

The irrigation of native grasses for hay cost little in labor or money, served a large home market, and yielded crops relatively immune to Wyoming's frequent wind and hail storms. Moreover, in most parts of the West high value crops—such as sugar beets, potatoes, or-

Irrigated Areas of Wyoming, 1900

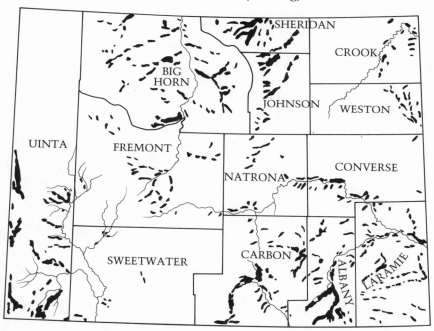

Total Irrigated Area
605,878 Acres

Wyoming irrigation map.

chard fruits, and even alfalfa—required late season irrigation in September or even October, when streams carried their smallest volume of water. Those crops could not be raised without expensive supplemental water storage. In Wyoming, on the other hand, most streams outside the Powder River Basin carried an adequate year-round flow that eliminated the need for large storage reservoirs. Nevertheless, the state faced a clouded future. In 1890, it contained 470,000 irrigated acres, 240,000 of which produced natural grasses and another 207,000 planted to forage crops. Only 23,000 acres—5 percent of the total—generated field crops such as oats and wheat. And while the census indicated that almost as many residents worked in agriculture as in stock raising, that number lagged far behind any state or territory in the Rocky Mountain region.[9] To make matters worse, Wyoming's abundant water supply was worthless without the construction of highline canals. "The extension or irrigation . . . has about reached its limit," Wyoming state engineer Elwood Mead wrote in 1892. "Nearly all the small streams in the eastern half of the State have been fully appropriated. Many have more ditches diverting water than can be supplied. On practically all there is a shortage during the latter part of the irrigating season . . . the principal extension of the irrigated area in the future, must be made by means of large and expensive canals."[10]

Land Cession Through 1891

The crusade to cede the "surplus" lands to the states was as old as the nation itself. Frontier states like Missouri and Kentucky resented the fact that Virginia, Massachusetts, and other members of the original Union had been allowed to retain and sell large tracts of unoccupied land within their borders. Western and southern politicians often argued that economic needs on the frontier should dictate land policy, not the date a state entered the Union or the size of its population. On May 16, 1826, one of the early proponents of cession, Senator Thomas Hart Benton of Missouri, predicted that "the public lands will soon either be transferred, upon equitable terms, to the States in which they lie, or divided into classes; the first to be sold out for the payment of public debt; the second to be given to the States for the promotion of education, the construction of roads and canals, and for gratuitous distribution among the poor."[11]

Benton's cession plan drew substantial criticism in the East and even on the frontier. Henry Clay claimed that cession was, as one historian put it, "robbing the Original States of a share in valuable property which they had created. Free land or a reduction in the price of government land would likewise rob the older states of some of the benefits they hoped to receive from sharing the proceeds of the public lands."[12] Cession threatened to depopulate the Atlantic states, drive down the value of eastern farms, encourage speculation, contribute to the growth of land monopolies, cheat those who had purchased land from the government at the minimum price, and undermine nationalism by making the states far less dependent on the central government. Equally important, the policy was inherently inequitable: Missouri, with a much smaller population, would receive much more land than Ohio. And if the states dumped all the ceded land on the market at once, the benefits would be limited and ephemeral. "Whose imagination can paint the scenes of confusion and rivalry that must result from establishing in the West a number of independent and contending vendors of the public lands?" one of Benton's critics asked. "Each State would immediately bid for the migrating population of the Union. The Federal plan, which has resulted in such uniformity and security of [land] titles, could not be sustained by the States; and the scenes of land-litigation of Kentucky and Tennessee, under the defective land laws of Virginia and North Carolina, would be reenacted upon the theatre of the West."[13]

In 1841, John C. Calhoun entered the debate on the side of cession. He asked that all government land in Alabama, Louisiana, Mississippi, Arkansas, Missouri, Illinois, Michigan, Ohio, and Indiana be ceded to those states on condition that they return 65 percent of all proceeds to Washington. If this was done, Calhoun promised, "you will at once take away one-third of the business of Congress; shorten its sessions in the same proportion, with a corresponding saving of expense; lop off a large and most dangerous portion of the patronage of the Government; arrest these angry and agitating discussions, which do so much to alienate the good feelings of the different portions of the Union, and disturb the general course of legislation, and endanger ultimately the loss of the public domain. Retain them [the public lands], and they must continue, almost without mitigation, apply what palliatives [such as the distribution of proceeds from land sales and pre-emption] as you may." Calhoun worried as much about how the land issue diverted congressional attention from other vital issues as he did about the threat to states' rights. Since nearly half the public domain had been disposed of during the speculative frenzy of 1835–37, and since squatters posed an increasing problem, he predicted that the public domain would soon be exhausted and the new states would have nothing to show for it.[14]

Sectional tensions, the disappearance of the budget surplus, the Preemption Act of 1841, and the debate over homestead legislation and railroad grants all stiffened opposition to cession as northerners increasingly identified the policy with disunion. Nevertheless, cession took on new life in the arid West after the Civil War. In the early 1870s, its most vocal advocates lived in Colorado. Drought hit that territory at the beginning of the decade, along with a boom in railroad construction. "Hundreds have . . . turned away from Colorado during the last year, baffled in their efforts to secure a home within our borders," Colorado's governor S. H. Elbert remarked. "The agricultural domain of the United States subject to the operation of the Homestead and Pre-Emption laws, outside of this region, is comparatively exhausted."[15] In its October 15 issue the *Rocky Mountain News* observed that "unless our extended plains and uplands can be placed under water, agriculture will come to a sudden standstill."[16]

Members of the Colorado Farmers' Union met many times during the spring and summer of 1873 in response to the drought, which they feared would cut off immigration to Colorado and reduce the value of their land. These meetings paved the way for the West's first major irrigation convention, which gathered in Denver in mid-October 1873.[17] Governor Elbert, who held out little hope that Congress would grant any additional *land* to the states or private companies, proposed that half the *proceeds* from federal land sales in each state or territory be set aside in a special fund controlled by the states to pay for reclaiming that land. To prevent monopoly, title to each tract would pass directly from the national government to the individual settler. The Elbert plan drew considerable criticism from the conferees. Many thought that the land itself should be granted to the states and territories, especially since none of the states represented in Denver had received any floodland under the Swamp Land Act of 1850. Others grumbled that settlers should not have to pay anything for land; that $1.25 or even $2.50 an acre would not pay the cost of reclamation; that the states and territories should receive *all* the revenue produced by public land sales, not just half; that reclamation ought to be left to private enterprise rather than the state or territorial governments; or that the federal government should do the job. In short, the fragmentation that characterized the "irrigation movement" in the 1890s was already evident in the early 1870s. The convention endorsed Elbert's plan, with the understanding that if Congress refused to grant the states land or money, the central government should build the irrigation works. A bill to that effect appeared in Congress at the end of 1873, but it died in committee.[18]

Cession did not win broad-based support until the drought of the late 1880s.[19] The Powell survey's anticipated reservation of damsites and irrigable lands, the expected admission of the "omnibus states" into the Union, and the abundance of private ditch companies willing to build irrigation works in exchange for state lands gave cession distinct advantages over both federal reclamation and irrigation districts. There was little agreement, however, on what form the policy should take. Some supporters called for unconditional grants of *all* arid lands, others wanted only the grazing and farmland. And while some preferred legislation covering the entire West, others favored grants to individual states and territories.[20] In the late 1880s, Colorado provided the greatest popular support for cession, but during the 1890s the most effective congressional leadership came from Wyoming. To a large extent, the movement depended on the talents and ambitions of three men: Francis E. Warren, Elwood Mead, and William Ellsworth Smythe.

When Warren first reached Cheyenne, it was a collection of covered wagons, shacks, and tents, still part of Dakota Territory. At a time when few residents expected the town to survive, he pushed for permanent improvements, including water and sewer systems and brick buildings. Largely through his efforts, Cheyenne became one of the first American cities to provide electric lighting and a centralized heating plant for its business district. Warren fought to develop the capital city just as he would later fight for the entire state. As Cheyenne prospered, so did Warren. In 1871, he bought a half interest in A. R. Converse's drygoods business and six years later took it over. He purchased houses, apartment buildings, hotels, and entire city blocks of lots in the business district, and he invested in a wide range of business ventures, including mines and railroads along with electric, carriage, telegraph, phonograph, streetcar, and irrigation companies. The Warren Land and Livestock Company, which acquired between two hundred fifty and three hundred thousand acres in Wyoming and Colorado, became the keystone of his economic empire.

Warren sat on Cheyenne's city council in 1872–73 and 1883–84 and also served as the town's mayor. He was elected to the territorial legislature and was appointed territorial treasurer and territorial governor (twice). In 1889, Warren became the state's first governor, but he resigned in 1890 when the legislature selected him and former territorial delegate Joseph M. Carey as U.S. senators. He served in the Senate continuously until his death in 1929, except for a break from 1893 to 1895. Warren was known for a phenomenal memory and prodigious energy, but he exhibited few qualities of statesmanship. "Trapped in this never-ending round of patronage disposal, appropriation decisions, and lobbying sessions," Lewis Gould has written, "Warren, in his long tenure, left scant positive imprint on American life. He rarely looked up from his pursuit of influence for himself and riches for his state to consider the pressing questions of his time. That was true of most senators from the West. This attitude reflected Warren's accurate appraisal of the mood of his constituents, who preferred the concrete rewards of federal projects to the ephemeral satisfaction of having a representative in Washington with direct influence on national politics." Whether in the form of a military fort or a postmastership, a new road in Yellowstone or a federal judgeship, the fruits of Warren's labor could be seen throughout the state. In the 1890s and the early years of the twentieth century, his support for the sheep industry—especially his success in maintaining high tariff duties on imported wool—earned him recognition as "the greatest shepherd since Abraham."[21]

Elwood Mead lacked Warren's political ambition and canny political instincts, but he well understood irrigation's potential to transform the society and economy of Wyoming and the West. He was born in 1858 on a nine-hundred-acre Indiana farm about forty miles south of Cincinnati. As a boy, Mead witnessed a metamorphosis in rural life as owner-operated farms fell into the hands of speculators who, in turn, leased them to tenants. The renters cared little for maintaining the vitality of the soil; they used it ruthlessly, with little thought for the future. Inevitably, community spirit languished. The tenant farmers had no interest in local affairs, attended church rarely if at all, and seldom sent their children to school. Mead learned a bitter lesson, and the ideal of the family farm, and of farmers working together to solve common problems and build a better world, never left him.

Mead ended up in the arid West quite by chance. He married in 1882 and honeymooned in Colorado, where one of his former teachers from Purdue University presided over the fledgling agricultural college at Fort Collins. That connection, and his brief experience working for the Army Corps of Engineers on Wabash River navigation projects, served him well. He became assistant to Colorado's state engineer, parceled out water to farmers in the Fort Collins area, and taught a course at the college. In 1883, Mead returned to Purdue to finish work on his civil engineering degree. He then earned master's degrees from both Purdue and Iowa Agricultural College at Ames. Undecided whether to practice engineering, read law, teach, or farm, Mead returned to Colorado in July 1885. At age twenty-seven, he became the first professor of irrigation engineering in the United States (serving simultaneously as assistant state engineer). In 1888, he moved to Wyoming as its first territorial, and subsequently state, engineer.[22]

Mead's personality was far different from that of the West's first state engineer, California's William Hammond Hall (see chapter 6).[23] Hall was combative, self-righteous, arrogant, doctrinaire, and often pompous; Mead was unassuming, conciliatory, loyal, and deferential. He survived in the political fishbowls of Colorado and Wyoming precisely because he removed himself from politics.[24] Yet the two men had much in common. Both were "social planners" as well as engineers; both recognized that the laws regulating the allocation of water would profoundly shape the "New West"; both had strong scholarly instincts; and neither saw any conflict between the greater glory and good of their states and the greater glory and good of those private land and water companies they represented or bought stock in. Following the drought of the late 1880s, Mead found many opportunities to pad his income as a consultant and investor.[25] He was the chief engineer of several major irrigation companies, including Utah's Bear Lake and River Water Works and Irrigation Company. He gave up his outside practice in October 1890 but resumed it in 1894—if not before—when he became engineer for William F. Cody's Shoshone Land and Irrigation Company. These ties strongly influenced his views on water policy. He was convinced that while the state should control the allocation of water, private enterprise should construct all irrigation works, with encouragement and supervision from government. He doubted that land and water policies set in Washington could be either efficient or just.[26]

A third major figure in the crusade for cession in the early 1890s was William Ellsworth Smythe. For a few years, Warren, Mead, and Smythe made a formidable team, though both Warren and Mead considered Smythe hopelessly impractical. Warren's political skills, Mead's broad knowledge of hydraulic engineering and irrigation agriculture, and Smythe's zeal, facile pen, and organizational skills fitted together well. Smythe, simultaneously the puppet of large land and water companies and a prophet of the "New West," remains one of the most fascinating characters in the history of arid America.

Smythe was born in Worcester, Massachusetts, in 1861 and never escaped his New England past. To him, irrigation was a social tool, a way to recapture the democracy, cooperation, order, and unity of village life. That it was also a more profitable and dependable method of farming came second. A born publicist and a gifted, if unoriginal, writer, Smythe became the editor of the Medford (Massachusetts) *Mercury* at the age of nineteen. At the end of the 1880s, as the great drought descended on the plains, he assumed the editorship of the Kearney (Nebraska) *Enterprise*. He later joined the editorial staff of the Omaha *Bee*, and in January and February 1891 he prepared a series of editorials pleading for money, food, seed, and other supplies to help the drought victims. Smythe traveled through California and New Mexico during the summer of 1889, and he marveled at how irrigation had transformed the Las Animas and Vermejo valleys. The happy scenes there contrasted starkly with the tales of crop failures, abandoned farms, and even starvation that filled the columns of Great Plains newspapers. In his mind irrigation heralded a new American civilization, and it promised a cure for most of the social and economic ills associated with the "terrible nineties."

Early in 1891, Smythe helped organize and orchestrate irrigation conventions which met at McCook, Nebraska, at the end of January, and at Lincoln in February. Such assemblies, which usually called for federal or state aid, were common in the darkest months of the drought. At about the same time, he decided to leave the *Bee* and launch a new monthly periodical, *Irrigation Age*, which he edited until 1895. During the same years, he dominated the executive committee of the annual national irrigation congress. A quintessential booster publication, heavily subsidized by the West's land, water, and farm machinery companies, *Irrigation Age* became the voice, conscience, and pulse of the new movement. Its pages beguilingly described the immense profits offered by western lands and irrigation bonds, and it chronicled the activities of water companies and irrigation districts in great detail. Smythe spoke almost exclusively to promoters and investors, not to actual farmers; the magazine neglected the actual techniques, methods, and problems of cultivating arid land. Nevertheless, its circulation grew rapidly, with most readers concentrated in Utah, Colorado, and California.[27]

Smythe embraced cession because it left reclamation in the hands of private enterprise and control over water in the hands of the states. Private enterprise had done its job well: he estimated that irrigated acreage in the West had more than doubled between 1886 and 1891, with a particularly rapid increase in orchards.[28]

Many residents of the grazing states supported cession long before Smythe transformed it into an icon in his crusade to water the West. In July 1889, in anticipation of the visit to Wyoming of the U.S. Senate Select Committee on Irrigation, Elwood Mead called a meeting at his office in Cheyenne to discuss what reclamation policy territorial officials should recommend to the committee. A year earlier, he had insisted that national reclamation was "the only sound public policy." Wyoming, he argued, needed a federal program because it could not afford to conduct hydrographic surveys on its own and could not compete for residents with Kansas, Nebraska, and Iowa—states where farmers did not have to pay for water. "The government can well afford . . . to extend aid to enterprises of this character," Mead noted, "since the permanent addition to the productive wealth of the country and the consequent return in taxation makes the outlay a wise one from a business standpoint."[29]

By the summer of 1889, federal reclamation seemed far less likely or desirable. Participants in the Cheyenne conference included such Wyoming notables as Francis E. Warren and Joseph M. Carey. The group concluded that the Powell survey would lock up the public domain for at least ten years, perhaps a generation. Cheyenne's *Daily Leader* reported that "everybody [at the meeting] realized that this meant the almost total cessation of emigration to the territory and a paralysis in development which would have fallen little short of annihilation."[30] Mead now insisted that officials in Washington knew little or nothing about conditions in Wyoming, though he still hoped that Powell would locate irrigable lands and reservoir sites so that they could easily be assigned to the states and territories.[31] Had the territory controlled all the irrigable lands within its borders, it could have provided, in Mead's words, "such protection to canal companies as would have given our agriculture four times its present importance and more than doubled our population; instead of this, there have been repeated instances where arbitrary and unreasonable rulings have subjected our people to heavy and wholly unnecessary expense and cause the whole land policy to be regarded as oppression."[32]

In late 1889 and early 1890, Congress considered a number of general cession bills, all of which died in committee.[33] But when Congress reconvened at the end of 1890, Francis E. Warren took his seat in the Senate and went to work for Wyoming. The cancellation of the Powell survey in the summer of 1890 created substantial sympathy for cession as a permanent solution to the problem of the central government's proper role in western economic development.[34] The admission of the "omnibus states" made the region's appeals for aid more frequent, more shrill, more irritating, and potentially more obstructive. By granting the arid lands, Congress could cast off an albatross. Moreover, a few months after Warren took office, the 1890–91 Congress passed an omnibus land reform bill that authorized creation of the first national forests, abolished the Preemption and Timber Culture laws, and plugged loopholes in the Desert Land Act and Homestead Act. Many westerners thought that these reforms narrowed their economic horizon, and cession assumed new significance as a way to guard against future revisions and to prevent the selection of new national forests. The national forest provision was criticized for driving up the price of lumber, interfering with grazing, and cutting off access to reservoir sites.[35]

At Warren's urging, Mead sifted through the cession bills introduced in previous Congresses and produced a very general plan to divide the public domain into natural irrigation districts that included timber and grazing lands.[36] His plan required the states to designate the districts and set the maximum size of farms. All forests and reservoir sites within the districts would remain inalienable *state* property. No individual could own more than 1,280 acres of pasture (in addition to his irrigable tract), and proceeds from land sales could be used only to build storage reservoirs. Mead promised Warren that his bill would "quadruple the area of land now under cultivation" in Wyoming by encouraging the use of streams as yet almost untouched, including the North Platte, Green, Wind, Big Horn, and Snake, and he predicted that the construction boom in irrigation works would "stimulate all branches of trade and industry."[37]

Warren's bill was not the only cession legislation to come before the Fifty-first Congress in 1890–91,[38] but it won the support of many prominent western politicians, especially Senator Stewart and the commissioner of the General Land Office, Thomas Carter of Montana.[39] Moreover, public support for cession grew rapidly in 1890 and 1891.[40] The irrigation convention held at Lincoln, Nebraska, in February 1891 called for an interstate meeting, and its presiding officer, Nebraska governor Furnas, appointed Smythe chairman of the arrangements committee. Denver was the first site proposed, but opposition from Colorado's bitter agricultural rivals, Kansas and Nebraska, persuaded Smythe to pick Salt Lake City instead.[41]

The spirit of voluntary association that had long prevailed in the United States often gave rise to quasi-governmental organizations, such as claims clubs, squatter governments, and vigilance committees. The "national" irrigation congresses, held almost every year from 1891 to the end of World War I, were good examples of this impulse. They were attempts not only to influence government but also to forge a policy consensus that Congress and the state legislatures had been unable to provide. The first irrigation congress, held September 15–18, 1891, at Salt Lake City's great exposition building, was clearly rigged. Over 350 delegates, from all the arid states and territories except Washington and Arizona, attended.[42] Warren, Stewart, and Francis G. Newlands were active participants and spoke for business interests.[43] Those interests included cattle companies, water and ditch companies, and railroads. Any fair debate over the alternatives open to the West in 1891 would have included a full discussion of both federal reclamation and irrigation districts. Virtually every speaker at the conference, however, favored cession. In fairness to Smythe, the convention had been called to unify the West behind one policy and to advertise irrigation to the "nation"—that is, to help make irrigation "respectable" to untutored eastern investors.[44] Western disunity, Smythe insisted, gave Congress the perfect excuse to ignore the region's needs. The resolutions adopted at the end of the congress did not oppose federal reclamation on principle. Instead, they reiterated arguments based on practicality: Congress would never appropriate funds from the general treasury to pay for internal improvements in the West; the Powell Irrigation Survey's slow rate of progess demonstrated the major weakness of government work; and geographic and climatic variations, as well as many other differences among the states, would always prevent the federal government from treating the states and territories fairly and equally.[45]

The convention appealed for cession, but it also anticipated the Reclamation Act of 1902 by requesting that a share of the proceeds from public land sales in the Dakotas, western Nebraska, Kansas, and Oklahoma be set aside in a special fund to provide irrigation for that land. This fund, designed to bail out drought-stricken farmers, was a sop to the western states that contained little public land.[46] The fate of the Powell Irrigation Survey demonstrated the need to pacify politicians from the Great Plains.

Introduction of the Warren bill in 1891 coincided with orchestrated pro-cession appeals to Congress from the Wyoming and Idaho
legislatures.[47] Warren's cattle empire and "general odds and ends for
my constituency," however, occupied most of his attention during the
early months of 1891, and the senator admitted privately that he regretted "every day my inability to give this particular subject [recla-
mation] the attention it deserves."[48] Meanwhile, *Irrigation Age* and
many local newspapers publicized the bill,[49] and when Congress reconvened at the end of 1891, it was flooded with petitions for cession.
They included appeals from the irrigation congress; the city councils
of Leadville, Pueblo, and Durango, Colorado, and Tombstone, Arizona;
the Denver Chamber of Commerce; the Denver Real Estate and Stock
Exchange; the Omaha Board of Trade; and groups of residents from
Utah, Nevada, Wyoming, and California.[50] The same Congress received
a much smaller number of petitions *against* cession—most from Colorado, but a handful from humid agricultural states, including New
York.[51] Granges and Farmers' Alliances in the Atlantic states opposed
any policy designed to create new farms.[52] Cultivated land within the
United States had increased from 81 million acres in 1865, to 113
million in 1874, to 195 million in 1884, and 211 million in 1890. Wheat
production soared from 148,500,000 bushels in 1865 to 612 million
bushels in 1892; the corn crop increased from 700 million bushels in
1865 to 2 billion in 1891. Farm organizations in the East blamed the
rapid opening of the Great Plains for many of their woes. What would
happen if Warren had his way?[53]

The Populist Backlash

The political climate in the West was equally damaging to Warren's legislation. The Populist tide rose quickly in 1890 and 1891, and
nowhere more quickly than in Colorado and Wyoming. Earlier studies
have portrayed Populism in the Rocky Mountain states as the insti-
tutionalization of the crusade for free silver,[54] but more recently Robert
Larson and Karel Bicha have shown that Rocky Mountain Populism
comprised many issues that varied from state to state. Populists were
eclectic; they were not slaves to theory. Some considered the "money
question" as paramount. They claimed that a handful of plutocrats
kept the money supply artificially small and, in this way, monopolized
the nation's natural resources. Others argued that the corner on land

itself was the father and mother of economic injustice. Local economic conditions frequently dictated political philosophies. In many parts of the West, silver held center stage. But political rings and "elitism," the quest for good government, railroad rates and practices, "alien" land-ownership, the working conditions of miners, high taxes, banking policies, mortgage foreclosures, the protective tariff, and monopolies of land, water, and cattle also received serious attention. Bicha argues that "the true bases of Populism were the restoration of the classical market and the atomized polity, and the diminution of the dimensions and responsibility of government." This can be questioned, but he is on firmer ground when he describes the party as "self-consciously rooted in old, traditional and conservative values." Bicha and Larson agree that antimonopoly sentiment was the fountainhead of dissent; Larson goes so far as to say that hostility toward combinations was the glue that held Rocky Mountain populism together. "Indeed, it seems evident," Larson concludes, "that at least in Wyoming, the essence of opposition to the status quo was antimonopolism."[55] Bicha and Larson largely ignore conflicts over natural resources, but nothing illustrates the antagonism to monopoly better than the controversy over cession.

Warren's political foundation had been shaky long before he entered the U.S. Senate. Since territorial days, Democratic newspapers had portrayed Warren and Carey as leaders of the "Cheyenne Ring" and criticized them for monopolizing public offices as they monopolized grazing land. For example, after his appointment as territorial governor in 1889, Warren selected the Warren Mercantile Company's manager as territorial treasurer.[56] The *New York Times*, in a piece widely reprinted in Wyoming and Colorado, branded the stockman as "notoriously unfit," charging that he had "fitted up the executive office in regal style, and through the lavish display of whisky and cigars made it more of a resort of men of leisure than a place for the transaction of matters of state." It also criticized him for traveling in a special Pullman car provided by the Union Pacific, for contributing to the death of Chinese miners during the riot at Rock Springs, and for serving as an unofficial lobbyist for the Wyoming Stock Growers' Association.[57] The Cheyenne *Daily Leader*, Wyoming's most popular Democratic paper, struck hard at the Carey-Warren alliance, or "Me and F.E." as it came to be called derisively. "I have watched the thing for a good many years," one prominent Cheyenne resident reported in the summer of 1890. "It finally began to dawn on me that the same man had a happy faculty of always bobbing up serenely. The thing began to grow monotonous. If it wasn't Warren and Carey, it was Carey and War-ren. . . . It is a curse to see any country . . . owned politically by one or two men."[58]

Warren was elected Wyoming's first governor in the fall of 1890, and the state constitution declared the chief executive ineligible for "any other office during the term for which he was elected." This restriction was designed in part to prevent a governor from using his legislative influence to gain election to the U.S. Senate. Therefore, when the lawmakers selected Warren and Carey as the first two U.S. senators, the air was thick with stories of political intrigue.[59] To make matters worse, the legislature violated an unwritten rule by selecting two senators from the same part of the state—indeed from the same town, Cheyenne—and who represented the same industry.

Once in Washington, both Warren and Carey underestimated the strength of Populist and "Popocrat" sentiment back home. They sup-ported the omnibus land reform act in March 1891, and in July they were the only western senators outside the Dakotas to vote against the inflationist Sherman Silver Purchase Act. Wyoming was not a silver producer, but the state's leading Democratic newspaper declared that "the price of silver affects the price of every product of human industry, and . . . involved in this fight is the supreme question of whether the rich man's possessions are to be increased in value . . . and the debtors' and poor man's correspondingly decreased."[60] This assault was a warn-ing, but Warren ignored it. Most of the state's newspapers were dom-inated by the Republicans and remained solidly under his influence.

Warren became chairman of the Senate Committee on Irrigation (formerly a select committee) in late 1891 or early 1892, and when Congress reconvened he put much more energy into land legislation than in 1891.[61] A few days before he introduced a new cession bill on March 9, 1892, Warren informed William Ellsworth Smythe that it was very important to show

> good faith as to our intent to irrigate and reclaim lands instead of opening them to speculation. On this account, as well as some others, I think it better to first propose about all the restrictions that others might propose, and in putting them in, arrange them so they may not be unduly for-midable and so they will not kill the usefulness of the bill. . . . Then cut out the useless restrictions later. My experience is, that if you can once get a man to discuss and consider the cession of lands, if you show a willingness to restrict, the more the new man talks on it and thinks of it the less necessity he sees for restrictions and quite often they exclaim,

"cede the lands without restrictions." So I am satisfied that the introduction of the restrictions in the first instance will work out faster
towards a good bill than to introduce the raw proposition of simply ceding
and get antagonism started before a reasonable consideration is given.[62]

"My bill is a feeler," he explained in a letter to Wyoming's governor,
"trimmed down to a conservative standard so as to be able to get the
eastern and southern people to concede that it isn't high-way robbery
in itself. As the bill reads, it is also intended to guarantee in some
regard, the 'afraids' of the west who think they are going to be swin-
dled."[63] Privately, Warren and Mead favored unconditional cession.[64]

The 1892 legislation, also drafted by Mead, was much more detailed than Warren's 1891 proposal.[65] As in the first bill, the states
would divide the ceded land into irrigation districts and mortgage,
pledge, or conditionally sell all or any portion of it to accomplish
reclamation. Each settler would be limited to 160 acres of irrigable
land and an additional 160 acres of nonirrigable land. The first would
be sold at the pro rata cost of reclamation, the latter for no more than
$1.25 an acre. The bill contained two very daring features. First, if after
ten years the president was dissatisfied with a state's efforts to irrigate
the ceded land, then the United States could resume title to the unoccupied land—but only if the central government agreed to water it.
Second, the legislation permitted the states to lease *unlimited* amounts
of pastureland adjoining the irrigated tracts.[66]

Not surprisingly, the Select Committee on the Irrigation of Arid
Lands reported the bill favorably. "It is not in keeping with the progress
of the age, the growth and dignity of our country, and the wants of our
people that it [the arid public domain] should remain in its present
unproductive condition," the committee concluded. "It must be rendered habitable. It can not, and ought not to, remain a perpetual wilderness and destitute of useful results." The committee promised that
Warren's bill would prevent the arid states from making "enormous
and unpredictable" claims on the treasury for federal reclamation and
also save the nation the cost of administering essentially worthless
lands. But the minority report of John L. Bretz of Indiana and Jerry
Simpson of Kansas—the fact that they represented midwestern agricultural states was significant—invoked the equally hallowed argument that the public domain was "the common heritage of all the
people alike." Bretz and Simpson pointed out that although "mineral
lands" were excluded, there was no way of knowing what minerals

might *become* valuable in the future or where they were located. The bill would open the door "to a never-ending dispute and contention between the Government and the State or Territory wherein these newly discovered mineral lands lie as to their ownership." Similarly, since the arid lands had never been classified, the Warren bill might well deed away agricultural tracts that did not require irrigation. Moreover, the legislation contained no mechanism to enforce the 160-acre limitation; once the land had been deeded to the states and territories, nothing would prevent them from granting any amount to individuals or companies. Past experience—particularly the school and swampland grants—demonstrated that ceded lands invariably fell into the hands of speculators, who became rich "at the expense of the very persons intended to be benefited by the grants." "Who can give that positive assurance," Bretz and Simpson asked, ". . . that these same inexcusable frauds will not be repeated in this instance? Had we not better profit by our past experience in similar cases. . . ?"[67]

By the time Warren took the floor of the Senate to explain his bill on July 21, 1892, it was already too far down the list to receive formal consideration, and even the congressional delegation from the grazing states was deeply divided.[68] Montana's senator Thomas C. Power publicly charged that cession was the child of railroads and large mining companies. Once the land was donated to the states, he warned, the railroads would use their stranglehold over the legislatures to create land monopolies unprecedented in American history. An irrigation convention held in Montana at the beginning of January 1892 called for Congress to donate *proceeds* from arid land sales to the states rather than the lands themselves, and urged the next state legislature to adopt a law modeled on California's Wright Act.[69]

Protests in Montana and Colorado were mild compared to the firestorm in Wyoming. In the winter of 1891–92, Mead had reported widespread support for cession as a general proposition, except in tiny Uinta County in the southwestern corner of the state.[70] By March, however, the tide of public opinion had changed, especially in Sheridan and Johnson counties, the stronghold of the "granger element." "There is a wave sweeping over the rural districts in Wyoming against the ceding of the arid lands," Warren wrote Wyoming's governor in the middle of the month. "I think it has been systematically started by the kickers and growlers who play upon the farmers . . . leading them to believe that any change in the land laws is necessarily 'all agin the working man.'" According to Warren there were "kickers" everywhere, "one class kicking because they cannot get control of all God's creation, another class kicking because they are afraid some body will get too much, another class kicking because they are afraid of something and do not know what."[71]

Several weeks later, vigilantes rode into Johnson County to teach its inhabitants a lesson. The large livestock companies, represented by the Wyoming Stock Growers' Association, had long been popular targets in the state's newspapers. They had engaged in massive land frauds by using their employees as surrogates to secure hundreds of thousands of acres. They had persuaded lawmakers to assess private grazing lands at lower tax rates than farmland. Even worse, they treated the public domain as their own fiefdom, fencing off the best land and blocking access to streams. The "invasion" was a premeditated response to the growth of communities of small farmers and ranchers in and around such agricultural towns as Buffalo, Sheridan, Casper, and Douglas during the 1880s and early 1890s. The flood of new residents—many of whom had moved to Wyoming to escape the drought in western Nebraska and South Dakota—threatened the political power of the cattle barons and the dominance of southern Wyoming in state affairs. There were rustlers in Johnson County, but their "crimes" were far more modest than the cattle companies claimed. Farmers often neglected to fence their land; the cost of fencing was a big expense, especially for new settlers. Instead they killed the cattle that wandered onto planted fields and used them for food, or simply added "strays" to their own herds. In the new agricultural counties, where the stock laws were considered unrealistic and unjust, it was nearly impossible to convict "rustlers."

The Johnson County War brought the worst fears of Wyoming residents to life. The "invasion" took place with the full sympathy of the Wyoming Stock Growers' Association; with the complicity of one of the Cheyenne Ring's leading members, Joseph M. Carey; and with the acquiescence of the state's largest corporation, as the Union Pacific provided special cars to carry the twenty-two hired gunmen and their associates from Cheyenne to Casper. Moreover, the law offered little protection. The Cheyenne *Daily Leader* lamented that "in no American community has the law been used as such an engine of oppression on the one side or proven so elastic to shield on the other, as in this, the youngest state in the American union. . . . It is not idle speech to say that the people this year are fighting for their lives and liberties."[72] The vigilantes killed two residents of Johnson County, but justice was cheated. Carey and Warren arranged for the accused murderers to be tried in Cheyenne, rather than in Buffalo, Sheridan, or some other community in northern Wyoming. The case wore on, month after month. Defense counsel persuaded two key prosecution witnesses to leave the state, and Johnson County finally abandoned the suit when the cost of the trial became prohibitive. County officials also faced considerable pressure from local businessmen and real estate promoters who feared that a long trial would drive away potential settlers and investors by reinforcing the impression that Wyoming—particularly north-central Wyoming—was a lawless frontier where neither property nor human life was safe.[73]

Now Warren's arid land bill assumed larger meaning as part of a conspiracy to perserve the power of a cruel and arrogant elite. As the *Cheyenne Daily Leader* noted in September, "there are thousands of people in the state who cannot be convinced that Warren's arid land bill is anything but the biggest scheme of them all to corral all the land in sight, portion out the state into big tracts among members of the ring and thus make of Wyoming a pocket borough safe to return Warren to the United States senate as long as he wants to go there."[74] The evidence seemed irrefutable. The Warren Livestock Company controlled about 285,000 acres, but it owned only a third of that land. Its domain included a fenced tract twenty-five miles long and eleven miles wide on the south side of the Union Pacific tracks near Cheyenne, much of which was public domain.[75] In 1892, the *Leader* printed many stories describing the tactics used by Warren to harass small competitors and force them to sell out at low prices. In March, the newspaper editorialized:

> When they [the public] hear him talking about protecting the small settler or cattle owner and consider that for years he has pillaged and ridden rough shod over them in the might of his tyrannical power, is it any wonder that they have at last grown suspicious and construe his meaning by the rule of contraries? When they consider his vast domain with its thousands of acres of government land indiscriminately fenced with the railroad land to which he is acquiring title—when they reflect that all others are arbitrarily barred from these lands and that his herds desolate a vast scope of the open country during the summer months, destroying the feed upon which the smaller ranchmen are forced to depend and driving them either into bankruptcy or forcing them to remove to more favored localities so that he may be able to protect his enclosed government and railroad land for fresh winter ranges, is it to be wondered that

they grow suspicious of any movement which he may inaugurate for alleged public benefit?[76]

Warren's behavior in the 1891 Congress now seemed all the more deceitful and self-serving. According to the *Leader*, he had voted for the omnibus land reform bill for selfish reasons. That legislation rescinded the Preemption and Timber Culture acts, and crippled the Desert Land Act, placing the public lands "off limits" until Warren could push his monopolistic cession bill through Congress.[77]

Whatever Warren's intentions—and they were certainly less selfish than his critics realized—his 1892 land bill lacked sufficient safeguards to protect against fraud and concentrated ownership. There were no restrictions on the terms of leases and no description of the responsibilities of lessees to the land. "The great stretches of grazing and agricultural lands will be lumped off to this baron and that potentate until the public domain will become the private preserves of the wealthy," the *Buffalo Bulletin* declared, "and the emigrant will be forced into a vassalage or serfdom like unto his European brother."[78] Once the state took possession of the land, how could the federal government force compliance with terms of the act? The president could restore control over unreclaimed lands only in the unlikely event that Congress appropriated the money to reclaim them. Moreover, since Wyoming had reached the constitutional limit of its bonded debt, state reclamation might drive away more settlers than it attracted by requiring a dramatic increase in taxation. In any case, entrusting reclamation to the legislature would create vast new opportunities for graft and corruption and exacerbate the sectionalism already so pronounced in Wyoming. "We believe the matter to be the biggest kind of a white elephant that Wyoming cannot feed and protect," charged the *Bulletin*; far better to leave the public domain under national control.[79]

The election of 1892 proved disastrous for the pro-cession forces. In June 1892 the Republican National Convention met in Minneapolis and—doubtless at the urging of Warren, Carey, and Commissioner Thomas Carter of the General Land Office (the latter two sat on the Republican National Committee)—adopted a pro-cession plank. This prompted William Ellsworth Smythe to editorialize: "No great cause ever made a more rapid advance in popular favor. We believe its final triumph is near at hand."[80] In Wyoming the Democrats and Populists joined hands, and their state platform flatly rejected Warren's bill and insisted that Wyoming voters be permitted to approve or reject any

cession scheme.[81] In November, Wyoming elected a Popocrat congressman, Henry Coffeen, and a Popocrat governor, John Osborne. Warren
was the biggest casualty. The Wyoming legislature failed to elect a U.S.
senator, and for two years Joseph M. Carey was Wyoming's sole representative in the upper house. Cession had helped unseat Warren and
exposed the Cheyenne Ring. At a critical hour, the reclamation movement lost its most effective political leader. Moreover, the election left
a potent legacy. The fear of being tarred as a hireling of the cattle barons
persisted for years, and most Wyoming politicians refused to discuss
needed land law reforms for fear that they would be driven from office
as Warren had been.

The irrigation crusade received a second major blow six months
after the election. In March 1893 the Philadelphia and Reading Railroad
failed, touching off the worst depression the country had experienced.
In the darkest months of 1894, unemployment approached 20 percent,
and strikes, farm mortgage foreclosures, and large numbers of tramps
suggested an economy out of control.[82] The depression of 1893 stalled
western economic development. The casualties included the Union
Pacific Railroad, which went bankrupt in October 1893, and the Warren
Livestock Company which fell into receivership during the summer
of 1894, two hundred thousand dollars in debt.[83] No longer did private
land and water companies and railroads see cession as an opportunity
to profit from reclamation, and, faced with large deficits, Congress
proved unwilling to provide any direct aid to the arid states.[84] In 1897,
after almost five years of depression, Nevada congressman Francis G.
Newlands insisted that until the treasury showed a surplus, there would
be no appropriation "save for the absolutely necessary expenditures of
government."[85]

The economic depression also damaged the irrigation movement
by making silver the paramount political question in the West. Senator
Stewart argued that only silver coinage would revive the economy and
permit federal expenditures for hydrographic surveys and irrigation
works,[86] and many western politicians insisted that land prices would
remain low until monetary inflation ensured that farmers got fair prices
for their crops. As Newlands put it: "The best assistance the National
Government could give the arid west is the coinage of silver—agricultural and irrigation development could follow in its train."[87]

William Ellsworth Smythe thought that the West's obsession with
reviving the mining industry placed the cart before the horse. Only
irrigation could provide the region with a stable society and sustained

economic growth. "The mining of silver makes a few men rich and they give employment to a few thousand laborers in the intervals between strikes, lockouts and shutdowns," Smythe observed. "Occasionally the man who has acquired wealth in the mine puts up a fine building or residence in a western city. But usually he spends his money elsewhere."[88] Smythe loved to deliver jeremiads, and by the end of 1893 his editorials began to take on a strident quality as his influence crumbled. In 1891, the first irrigation congress had lined up fairly quietly behind cession. The October 1893 meeting was much harder for Smythe to control.[89] The depression and the Populist crusade diverted public attention from reclamation, and the meeting was held in Los Angeles, California, where cession had few sympathizers. Stretched across the stage of the Grand Opera House was a banner bearing the motto of the Congress: "Irrigation: Science, Not Chance." The convention, however, paid little attention to science, efficiency, or the practical needs of irrigators. William Ellsworth Smythe believed that the future of American civilization was at stake, and he used his considerable oratorical talents to their limit. "This assembly will have a place in the history of human progress," he promised the delegates. "We meet not merely to extend our country's frontiers, but to widen the boundaries of civilization itself. The seed which we shall plant in the soil of the desert will bear the flower of industrial independence for millions of the freest men who ever walked the earth." Although Smythe spoke for economic interests with a large and immediate stake in land development schemes, he took the high ground:

> We are laying today the corner-stone of the Republic of Irrigation. It shall not be laid on avarice and cemented with greed. That would not be fitting for a people living in sunlit valleys guarded by eternal mountains, for the men of the mountains have ever been the defenders of liberty. We will lay the superstructure of this edifice by the plumb-line of justice and equity. (Applause) We will write upon its white cornerstone, "Sacred to the Equality of Man." (Applause) We will inscribe upon its massive arch those two synonymous terms, "Irrigation and Independence" (Applause).

As if to underscore the gravity of the moment, at the end of the congress the assembled delegates adopted an "Address to the American People," which lamented the disappearance of the humid public lands, the "pressure of surplus population," and "the alarming increase of the class of homeless people within the borders of the United States."[90]

Smythe's attempt to galvanize western opinion failed, and his religious fervor alienated many hardheaded engineers and politicians whose support was vital to the success of the irrigation movement. "The truth is," Mead wrote privately less than a year after the Los Angeles meeting, "that Mr. Smythe has nothing in view except his own interests and the interests of *Irrigation Age*, and is besides a visionary enthusiast who, if left alone would make the whole movement ridiculous." Mead characterized the 1893 congress as "a sort of love feast between Kansas and California." Few who attended the meeting knew much about irrigation, water law, or practical politics. The delegates constituted a strange collection of dreamy idealists like Smythe, "sagebrush rebels" interested in using irrigation to assert states' rights, representatives and bondholders of California irrigation districts who wanted the state or federal government to assume district debts, and the agents of a wide assortment of land and water companies and related enterprises. The 1891 Salt Lake City conference had attracted a handful of prominent western politicians and engineers; the Los Angeles meeting was entirely the creature of boosters and promoters.[91]

These boosters and promoters preferred irrigation districts to federal reclamation, and they had nothing but scorn for cession. One of the most forceful declarations against cession was presented by Abbot Kinney, a southern Californian, who introduced a resolution declaring that cession "will result in waste, inefficiency and corruption . . . it will result in nothing but evil. We believe this question to be not narrow or sectional, but one of the deepest interest to the whole American people."[92] Ultimately, the Los Angeles meeting endorsed the Wright Act, deemed it unsuited to the needs of sparsely populated parts of the West, and accepted Smythe's recommendation that each governor appoint a commission "to enter upon a careful investigation of the conditions existing in each of their States or Territories, and then formulate plans looking to the adoption of a national policy." Smythe wanted the 1894 congress to use the state reports as the basis for legislation that would serve all of arid America.[93]

Neither Smythe nor his supporters anticipated the seriousness of the depression. There were thirteen hundred strikes during the winter of 1893–94, culminating in the massive Pullman Strike and Coxey's army.[94] Labor unions in Cincinnati, Chicago, St. Louis, and Denver, along with the St. Paul Chamber of Commerce, demanded that the nation put idle men to work digging canals, then give them homes on the reclaimed lands. The Seattle *Telegraph* went so far as to suggest that workers be paid in scrip redeemable in irrigated land. Although the irrigation congress had splintered into warring factions, Smythe crowed: "The future belongs to Arid America. There alone can population safely expand; there alone can labor win independence; there alone can a new and a better civilization be erected under the impulse of the new century about to be born."[95]

The Carey Act

If Joseph M. Carey read Smythe's words, he must have smiled. To Carey, irrigation was a business, one that could contribute to his wealth and the wealth of Wyoming, and not a social experiment. The agricultural West would be built by inventive engineers, canny investors, and practical politicians—men who knew the "lay of the land." Publicists like Smythe could help mold public opinion and apply pressure to lawmakers, but their mercurial zeal made them appear impractical, unpredictable, and at times positively silly to entrepreneurs.

Carey helped Ulysses S. Grant in his first campaign for the presidency and, as a reward, became Wyoming's first U.S. attorney in 1869, when he was twenty-five. In 1872, his friendship with the president won him a seat on the territorial supreme court, where he served until 1876. In that year he was appointed to the Republican National Committee (a position he held for twenty years). He was elected mayor of Cheyenne in 1880 and in 1884 became territorial delegate to Congress, a post he held until 1890, when the state legislature chose him as the new state's first U.S. senator. Meanwhile, Carey organized the J. M. Carey and Brothers Livestock Company—the "C Y" was one of Wyoming's oldest recorded brands—and in the middle 1870s he became active in the Wyoming Livestock Association, an affiliation he kept throughout his political career.[96]

Carey's first exposure to irrigation agriculture came when, along with Warren, Andrew Gilchrist, and Thomas Sturgis, he organized the Wyoming Development Company to reclaim fifty to sixty thousand acres of public land near Wheatland, sixty-five miles north of Cheyenne. In the mid-1880s, the company completed one hundred miles of main canals, but it could not secure title to the public land served by the ditches. This was the largest irrigation scheme in Wyoming, but the first settlers did not arrive until early 1894, nine years after completion of the project. The Wyoming Development Company's story illustrated the need to unify control over land and water so that private companies could use large blocks of public land as collateral for their investments. Carey's land bill was tailored to meet this need.[97]

The Carey Act (1894) was adopted in lieu of a bolder bill approved by the western congressmen in caucus. That legislation, introduced by Congressman Willis Sweet of Idaho, called for a $325,000 appropriation to pay for hydrologic surveys and the preparation of plans for one irrigation project in each arid state and territory, at locations specified in the bill. Wyoming Congressman Henry Coffeen of Sheridan opposed the Carey Act,[98] and convinced Sweet to designate the North Platte basin as the site of Wyoming's project. In Coffeen's words, that region was "central to the state and contains a large area of especially fine land on which thousands of farmers could become thrifty and independent if that great valley could be reclaimed." Coffeen doubtless realized that the long drought in Nebraska represented a fine opportunity for water-rich Wyoming. Farmers in the Platte Valley needed to move only a short distance to escape nature's curse.[99]

Among eastern congressmen, the Sweet bill was perceived as too expensive and as the foundation for a massive federal public works program. The more conservative Carey Act provided that each state containing desert land (as defined in the Desert Land Act) could select up to 1 million acres for reclamation, though it could not receive patents to the land until the individual tracts had been irrigated and occupied by actual settlers. In effect, the state would not own the land at all; it would merely serve as trustee for the settlers. The states could either construct hydraulic works on their own or negotiate contracts with private companies. The companies had to reclaim the land for a price per acre fixed by the state. Once the company received its money, all additional proceeds from land sales belonged to the state, but they could be used only for reclamation. The law also required companies to submit project plans to the secretary of the interior, and the land was closed to entry after the secretary decided that the works were feasible and the promoters in earnest. Construction and settlement of all projects had to be completed within ten years from the date of the act. No person could acquire more than 160 acres; none of the land could be leased; and at least 20 of the 160 acres had to be cultivated by actual settlers.[100]

Given the antimonopoly assault that had driven Warren from the senate, little wonder that the Carey legislation made no provision for the leasing of grazing lands, as Warren's bills had. It was designed to serve the needs of those states whose largest streams still carried plenty of unclaimed water, such as Wyoming, Montana, and Idaho. The law contained nothing that would encourage private companies to build expensive *storage* projects, and it assumed a very low per-acre cost for water. It was, in effect, a conservative compromise between unconditional cession, autonomous state reclamation programs, private reclamation under strong state supervision, and a centralized federal program.[101] In theory it had four great advantages over earlier land laws. First, since no one could file on the segregated land except actual settlers, theoretically the land could not be monopolized by nonresidents and speculators. Second, because the landholders were, in effect, shareholders in the canal company, they could look forward to the day when they would control the operation and maintenance of the water system. Third, since the state guaranteed the price of water rights both to the settler and to the company, there was no danger that arbitrary county commissioners would intervene and set confiscatory rates, nor any danger that the company would arbitrarily increase its rates. Finally, since the law required settlers to apply for a water right at the same time that they filed for land, it welded land and water titles together, reducing the threat of litigation.

Although simple, the legislation responded to many of the criticisms of earlier reclamation laws. Critics of California's Wright Act charged that that legislation failed to provide for state supervision of the formation of districts, the construction of works, the process of settlement, and the distribution of water. For example, since state officials exercised no control over land prices, those who bought farms within a district several years after it opened paid far more for their land and water than the first settlers. That was a "tax" delivered to speculators. Under the Carey Act, the state not only supervised construction, it also set land and water prices. The Carey Act was not a halfway point between private and public enterprise, as some historians have argued, or even a compromise between the two. It was a mixture. The state chose both the land and the settlers. Whether individual states or private companies built the irrigation works, the central government had to review and approve the plans and procedures. The law attempted to create a practical federalism in arid land reclamation by blending state and national control over the most valuable arid lands.

The Carey Act was a crossroads in the history of western reclamation. Those who opposed federal reclamation liked the fact that the conditional 1-million-acre grant did not commit the nation to spend any money. In fact, the law transferred part of the cost of classifying the arid lands to the states by making them responsible for locating the best potential farms. The legislation was perceived as an experiment. As the New York *Sun* editorialized:

> Congress may still authorize surveys for setting apart reservoir sites or for similar purposes; but it is quite safe to say, as to the ditching of lands, it will wait to see what the states and territories do with the areas thus ceded to them. If these states should do nothing . . . under this act, it will show that Congress certainly ought not to undertake what the communities so intimately concerned do not attempt. On the other hand, should the grant of these lands be heartily welcomed and used, it will be easy to procure the similar cession of other millions of acres.[102]

The modest grant might, as William Jennings Bryan recognized, lead either to the unconditional cession of all the arid lands or to federal reclamation.[103] "When we have made the experiment," Bryan observed, "we may find that this work of irrigation must be attempted on a larger scale than can be carried out by a single state." If the West could show that reclamation was more than a pipe dream, it might even be able to tap into the rivers and harbors fund.[104] Oddly, the most obvious question about the Carey Act—how it could manage to lure farmers west in the midst of a depression—was never asked.

The state might have added additional restrictions to Carey's legislation, such as an 80-acre rather than 160-acre limitation, but it did not.[105] Mead predicted that "the land bill is going to greatly stimulate settlement in this state. The number of inquiries coming in already makes us very sanguine as to the future." Governor William A. Richards anticipated that the legislation would "witness a larger investment of money in irrigation works, a greater increase in our agricultural population, a greater improvement in the general welfare and prosperity of our people during the next five years than has been witnessed under the public-land laws during the past twenty-five."[106]

One of the first companies to take advantage of the Carey Act, the Shoshone Land and Irrigation Company, was headed by the western promoter, William F. "Buffalo Bill" Cody. In the 1870s and 1880s, Cody helped to define and glamorize the "Old West" on stage, in print, and in his Wild West Show. But by the 1890s, as if to compensate for the indelible image of the Wild West he had sold to adoring American and European audiences, he decided to help civilize the region. Cooperation and interdependence counted for more than individualism and autonomy, and nothing demanded greater cooperation or promised to build stronger communities than irrigation agriculture. As one of his biographers has written, Cody dreamed of "sharing the wide open spaces of his beloved West with people from the crowded areas of the world. . . . As he saw it, irrigation was the means by which he could bring this about." Cody first tried to water land adjoining his ranch in North Platte, Nebraska. In January 1884 he purchased two hundred acres and acquired clear access to the North Platte River, which he tapped in 1894 with a twelve-mile-long canal. Unfortunately, the drought and depression of 1893 killed Cody's scheme to settle Quakers from the East on forty- to eighty-acre irrigated farms.[107]

Simultaneously, Cody launched an irrigation scheme in Wyoming's Big Horn Valley. In 1874 and 1876, he led military expeditions into the basin, and in 1888 he accompanied Wyoming's territorial engineer, Elwood Mead, on a reconnaissance mission to assess the region's agricultural potential.[108] The Big Horn country had once been an inland sea, so its soil was extremely fertile. It contained an abundance of irrigable land and, unlike many parts of Wyoming, its ample water supply had not been monopolized by cattlemen. "The valleys of the Green and Big Horn offer today the best opportunities for the construction of a system of irrigation works . . . of any section [of Wyoming] with which I am familiar," Elwood Mead wrote in his report for 1888. "To a large water supply and immense tracts of valuable public land, there is added the total absence of vested rights to interfere with the construction of necessary works."[109] In the early 1890s, the Burlington and Missouri pushed into northeastern Wyoming from Nebraska. By the early months of 1893 tracks stretched to the Powder River in Sheridan County and the roadbed had been graded all the way to Sheridan. During the spring of 1893, this touched off the first large-scale migration into the Big Horn basin as several hundred Mormons took up homes on the Greybull River, thirty to sixty miles due east of present-day Cody.[110]

Cody became interested in Wyoming irrigation through George T. Beck, a well-known Sheridan entrepreneur, irrigation promoter, and politician.[111] In the spring of 1893, Jerry Ryan, a stonecutter, and Labin Hillsberry, a sometime prospector, surveyed a ditch from the south fork of the Shoshone or Stinking Water River. That fall they applied for a water right. Subsequently, in May 1894, Beck and Sheridan banker H. C. Alger bought out Ryan and Hillsberry for two thousand dollars. Soon thereafter Elwood Mead surveyed a thirty-two-mile-long aqueduct covering four hundred thousand acres between the Shoshone and Grey-bull rivers. He predicted that the ditch would be enormously profitable because the cost of reclamation would average only five dollars an acre, far less than the value of the reclaimed land. He also anticipated that it would produce collateral investment opportunities by creating new towns and generating electricity. But to avoid the danger of opening up too much land too soon, he recommended that the promoters begin by irrigating twenty-five thousand acres near the confluence of the south and north forks of the Shoshone, using a canal which he esti-mated would cost about $110,000. The ditch could be extended as the region was settled.

When the Wild West Show's 1894 summer season ended, Cody decided to winter in Sheridan, where he owned the Sheridan Inn. His son-in-law, who managed the hotel, had accompanied the survey party and enthusiastically recommended the project. Alger and Beck sub-sequently enlisted Cody as president of the company, hoping he could recruit investors from his wide circle of wealthy and influential friends. He did so. The group included businessmen from Buffalo, New York, and Omaha, Nebraska, notably George Bleistein, Bronson Rumsey, and H. M. Gerrans. Cody's business partner, Nate Salsbury, also joined up, along with Beck and Alger. Each contributed five thousand dollars as seed money.[112]

Cody expected that either the Burlington and Missouri, or the Fremont, Elkhorn, and Missouri Valley railroad, would soon link his isolated valley with the markets of the world. After Wyoming's leg-islature ratified the Carey Act at the beginning of 1895, Beck and Cody selected a block of land at the foot of the Shoshone Mountains, about thirty-five miles from the border of Yellowstone National Park and sixty miles from the railhead at Red Lodge, Montana. Between four thousand and five thousand feet above sea level, one of the lowest parts of Wyoming, the land received little snow or wind, and it com-prised a series of terraces left by the receding waters of a prehistoric lake. The soil was rich, and the terraces were so uniform, and their contours so close to the ideal gradient for irrigation ditches, that the cost of excavating the main ditch and laterals was relatively low. The Shoshone River carried an abundance of water, roughly twenty times the volume of the South Platte in June and three times the volume of the North Platte in July. Whatever the motives of the New York and Nebraska investors lured into the venture, Buffalo Bill was looking for more than profit. "I propose to leave a monument of my work for the

West by founding a colony in the Big Horn basin," Cody told Mead, "which shall be to Wyoming what the Greeley Colony is to Colorado."[113] Early in 1896, Mead noted in a letter that Cody was "becoming more noted as a builder of canals than you ever have been in your previous enterprises no matter how great their success."[114]

The Shoshone Land and Irrigation Company was organized in March 1895 with a principal office in Chicago and a branch office in New York City. Canal construction began in September. "If settled in small tracts [the project] will support twice the present population of the entire State," Mead promised. "If half is placed under cultivation it will be six times the cultivated area of the entire state in 1890."[115]

The first phase of construction included twenty-eight miles of ditch. By February 1896 nine miles had been completed, and the twenty-eight thousand acres deeded by the federal government to Wyoming in March 1896 was the first land transferred to any state under the Carey Act.[116] Nevertheless, 1896 was not a happy year for the Shoshone Land and Irrigation Company; the company had spent eighty thousand dollars on fifteen miles of ditch, but only a dozen farmers purchased land and they watered only about four hundred acres.[117] Even worse, as the company's application made its way through the General Land Office and Department of Interior, speculators filed on about one thousand acres of the best tracts in the Lander land office.[118] The company quickly exhausted its capital, and the economic depression prevented the Burlington and Missouri from expanding its line into the valley.[119] Cody's partners refused to pour more money into the project, and the shortage of capital forced the company to sell thirty thousand dollars in bonds to heiress Phoebe Hearst, at a 10 percent discount.

In 1897, the promoters did their best to revive the languishing enterprise. They attempted to "prime the pump" by telling reporters that hundreds of farmers had bought land in the Big Horn basin, that hundreds more were on the way, and that the valley's population would soon reach twenty-five thousand.[120] A promotional pamphlet, *Homes in the Big Horn Basin*, announced the sale of twenty-five thousand acres at the stipulated Carey Act price of fifty cents an acre, with an additional charge of ten dollars per acre for a perpetual water right. Those who waited too long, the circular warned, would pay as much as fifteen dollars an acre for water. To ensure that the farmers would control their own destiny, the purchase of each forty acres included one share of stock in the company. When all the land had been sold, the farmers would own the hydraulic works.

The company promised that ultimately its aqueduct would reach a length of 150 miles at a cost of $1,750,000. Even though the basin averaged about forty-five hundred feet above sea level, "all the vegetables, cereals, grasses, small fruits, with all the meat products and those of the dairy, can be successfully grown." Promised crop yields were spectacular, including a minimum of thirty-eight bushels of wheat per acre. And since the basin was surrounded by mountains, subject to frequent chinook winds and on the same latitude as Madrid, residents could expect mild and pleasant weather. "It is hardly possible to describe the charms and health-giving qualities of the climate of this region without indulging in what would seem to be extravagance," the promotional pamphlet gushed. "Life and activity are prolonged by a residence here, and almost perfect freedom from all forms of ill health is enjoyed."[121]

The company's land agent, D. H. Elliott, hoped to lure agricultural colonies into the Big Horn basin. He approached many individuals and organizations, ranging from Eugene V. Debs to the Salvation Army, but nothing came of his efforts.[122] In the summer of 1897, the board of directors fired Elliott and slashed company salaries, including those of Beck (the company's manager) and Alger (treasurer).[123] The Shoshone Irrigation Company survived only because Cody repeatedly bailed it out using profits from the Wild West Show. In 1899, he put up $2,100 to pay the interest on the bonds held by Phoebe Hearst. If the other corporate directors did not follow suit, he threatened to let the bondholders attach the company's property. Cody frequently questioned the business acumen of his partners and Beck's administrative abilities.[124]

Even though work on the canal ceased in 1897, Buffalo Bill constructed a two-story house at Cody along with a hotel, general store, and school; subsidized publication of the town's first newspaper; organized and led hunting parties composed of wealthy potential investors; and announced his intention to retire in the Big Horn basin.[125] The Burlington and Missouri finally extended its line to Cody in November 1901, and the tracks ran directly through a large block of land the company owned on the north side of the river between that town and Garland, twenty-five miles to the northeast.[126] But the directors could not or would not raise the money needed to maintain the original canal, let alone build another. They shared the sense of weariness and hopelessness exhibited by Bronson Rumsey, one of the original investors, in his May 1904 letter to Beck: "Please George push this through for all your worth & let's get the d—— thing turned over to the state or settlers."[127]

Despite these setbacks, Buffalo Bill never lost confidence in the Big Horn basin. "Yes, Cody will be a western metropolis and no mistake," he told a reporter for the *Cheyenne Daily Leader* in 1900. "Why, nature has given us everything we could desire."[128] It was a testament to his naivete that he supported the company as long as he did. The settlers showed little gratitude. The Shoshone Land and Irrigation Company sold most of its water rights for ten dollars an acre, but it cost the company twenty-two dollars an acre to provide the water. To add insult to injury, in 1906, when a break in the canal interrupted service, disgruntled settlers sued the company in a sympathetic local court and won. Others threatened to do the same until the directors canceled all remaining debts.[129] Following passage of the Newlands Act in 1902, Cody sold the land north of the river to the federal government, which began construction in 1904 on a ditch to water that land. The basin's population more than tripled between 1900 and 1910, when the Reclamation Service completed the Buffalo Bill Dam, a 328-foot-high structure that plugged the Shoshone River eight miles southwest of Cody. By 1920, the Shoshone Project served sixty-five thousand acres. Ultimately the Bureau of Reclamation spent nearly $26 million to serve less than one hundred thousand acres.[130]

In his will, Cody asked to be buried not at "Scout's Acres," his North Platte ranch, but on a mountain overlooking the Big Horn basin and the town that bore his name. He hoped, his will explained, that the town of "Cody should not only grow in prosperity and become a populous and influential metropolis, but that it should be distinguished for the purity of its government and the loyalty of its citizens to the institutions of our beloved country."[131] He requested that a huge buffalo carved from Wyoming's native red stone serve as a grave marker— tribute to a man who helped destroy the buffalo and undermine the culture of the Plains Indians but who also embraced an agricultural innovation that came to epitomize the twentieth-century West. He closed the last of his autobiographies, published in 1920, on a poignant note that testified to his efforts to bridge the old and the new. "All my interests are still with the West—the modern West," he insisted. "I have a number of homes there, the one I love best being in the wonderful Big Horn Valley, which I hope one day to see one of the garden spots of the world."[132]

The Shoshone Land and Irrigation Company's experience was

fairly typical.[133] The Carey Act companies quickly ran out of money; the expected wave of new farmers never materialized; and those who came had too little capital to carry them through the lean months and years before their farms began to pay. Moreover, the projects were far removed from rail lines and major markets. Worst of all, the 1894 law did not provide adequate protection against speculators. The Carey Act could work only if the land to be reclaimed was segregated and reserved *immediately*. The first applications for Carey Act land sent to the General Land Office received no response for months, which prompted Elwood Mead and Idaho state engineer F. J. Mills to visit Washington in June 1895 and January 1896 in an attempt to speed up the review process.

Initially, the General Land Office insisted that the companies and the states submit elaborate and expensive maps and construction plans, including contour lines and the location of lateral as well as main ditches. In addition, the Interior Department demanded that duplicate maps and plans be filed with local land offices as well as with the General Land Office in Washington. This was an open invitation to fraud. Survey parties were easy to track, and interlopers had little trouble gaining access to the files of regional land offices. Mead and Mills suggested that the federal government reserve the land upon the presentation of a simple report from state officials pledging that the contemplated project conformed to the law. That document would include a sketch showing the land to be reclaimed, the approximate line of the ditch, and the location of any other works. Then, once the land was protected from entry, the state could provide accurate, detailed maps and field notes. State officials desperately needed the power to withdraw land temporarily while formal surveys were under way.[134]

The pleas of Mead and Mills fell on deaf ears. Secretary of the Interior Hoke Smith held fast to the stringent survey requirements. He insisted on reviewing each application personally, and he routinely referred applications to the land division in the attorney general's office, which further delayed the process of segregating the land. For example, the tracts served by the Globe Canal Company were not reserved until July 1896, nearly two years after work began on its ditch.[135] A Georgian, Secretary Smith knew little about the public domain, let alone irrigation, when he took office. He never gave the new law a fair chance. In his annual report issued in November 1895, he insisted that the Carey Act was a failure—more trouble than it was worth. He urged an *unconditional* grant of 1 million acres to each western state along with the reservoir sites placed off limits by the Powell Irrigation Survey.[136] According to Senator Warren, the secretary was preoccupied with illness in his family, the currency question, and the 1896 election. In private correspondance, Mead assailed "official inertia" and predicted that the Department of the Interior's policy was "so indefinite that there will be no end to what might be required and so expensive that all investors will look elsewhere." He recommended that the state engineers of Montana, Washington, Idaho, Colorado, and Wyoming—those states which had passed legislation to take advantage of the Carey Act—stand together to fight senseless federal requirements.[137] By February 1896, however, Mead had become convinced that opposition within the department had crippled the legislation. "They [federal officials] not only refuse to amend their original regulations but have added others," he fumed in a letter to the Idaho state engineer. "My conclusion is that you can't draft a law that will not be distorted by . . . [federal] regulations and . . . there is only one satisfactory solution to this question, the absolute cession of the land to the states."[138]

These problems were compounded by persistent flank attacks from Grangers and other dissidents within Wyoming. When the legislature met at the beginning of 1895, the only substantial opposition to the Carey Act and its enabling legislation came from Populists in Johnson County. It was organized by state senator Robert Foote, a Buffalo merchant who was also president of the state's immigration board. In August 1895 Foote wrote to Hoke Smith charging that a "Land Ring" consisting of F. E. Warren, Congressman F. W. Mondell, Governor W. A. Richards, State Treasurer Henry G. Hay, State Engineer Elwood Mead, Omaha bankers, William F. Cody, and "a combine of Eastern wire-pullers" had taken control of the state's water and its best potential farmland with the intention of creating "a system of peonage, or tenantry-at-will, along all of our rich valleys where honorable and independent manhood should be found." The Carey Act was, according to Foote, "one of the most glaring and gigantic frauds of the age." He charged that the Arid Land Board responsible for selecting the 1 million acres was just a front for State Engineer Mead, an "absolute Dictator" who distorted and construed Wyoming water laws "so as to give him the right to assign all of the waters of the several streams to one man, or to a coterie of friends, whether they have, or have not, lands upon which to use it, thus depriving the actual settler, upon the public domain, of the use of water running idly by his home."

According to Foote, Mondell, as an agent of Yellowstone Park

Land and Irrigation Association, or Globe Canal (a Carey Act project), had filed for enough water from the Shoshone River to irrigate 150,000 acres. Yet neither Mondell nor the company owned lands along that stream at the time of application, and the land selected for reclamation was not desert. Cottonwood trees grew along the Shoshone, lush native grasses often reached three feet in height, and the rich alluvial soil could be irrigated without corporate aid. The Yellowstone Park Land and Irrigation Association wanted eight dollars an acre to water this land; the settlers could do it themselves, Foote maintained, for less that one dollar an acre. Furthermore, he charged that in May and June 1895 the Yellowstone company had imported dummy entrymen from Nebraska to file on the lands covered by its ditch, furnishing free round-trip tickets from Omaha to Billings. This was done to prevent honest settlers from entering the land. "All of the land asked to be withdrawn from settlement [under the Carey Act] . . . in Johnson, Sheridan, and Fremont counties, is similar to that under the Globe Canal," Foote insisted, "open to successful settlement by poor, but industrious, home-seekers, and [it] should be reserved to this large class of honest men." He asked that no land be reserved in Wyoming until the Department of the Interior sent a special agent to investigate his charges.[139]

The accusations were largely fanciful, but they appeared in Chicago, Denver, and Salt Lake City newspapers. Governor W. A. Richards responded by pointing out that no title to water in Wyoming could be secured without a beneficial use. Of the thousand permits granted by the Wyoming Board of Control, not one had been appealed to the courts. And in the Big Horn basin, where Foote charged that bona fide settlers had been deprived of water, only five applications had been turned down by the board—all because they threatened prior appropriators or asked to use water within the Shoshone Indian Reservation. Nor did the Carey Act constitute class legislation; only one member of the state legislature besides Foote had voted against the bill to accept the grant. This hardly sustained the charge that the legislation was cooked up by a "Land Ring."[140]

If Foote's charges were insubstantial, they still expressed the fears of many Wyoming farmers and small ranchers. In late 1894, one critic of the new cession law began publishing a populistic newsletter in Cheyenne, the *Big Horn Basin Savior*, to expose the activities of the Cheyenne Ring, defrock land and water monopolies, discredit Carey in his bid for reelection, and block acceptance of the new law in the legislature. "If the legislature soon to meet makes the Carey law operative in this state," the *Savior* editorialized in November 1894, "a home in the Grey Bull valley will cost the future settler anywhere from 22 to 50 times as much in cash as a home costs there now." "The country people of this state want no arid land law," the editor proclaimed.[141] Like Foote, the editor assumed that the farmers themselves could build ditches much more cheaply than private companies, *if* they could get water.[142]

By the end of 1895, the Populist tide had receded in many parts of Wyoming, and some newspapers criticized Foote for condemning the state to economic stagnation. Cheyenne's *Leader*, which in 1892 had seen rings and political conspiracies everywhere, charged that "nothing has been more injurious to the west than the Populist craze"; only when Populism disappeared would private companies resume reclaiming the land. "Wyoming is now behind every state that surrounds it in agricultural development," the *Leader* lamented on September 24, 1895, "and this is not due to a lack of agricultural resources or opportunities, but to the action of persons like Mr. Foote, who make war upon all investments. The trouble about the letter of Mr. Foote is that it goes outside of the state, where the pessimistic character of this fanatic is not known." Usually—and 1892 was decidedly not a "usual" year in Wyoming—few acts won such public censure as tarnishing the bright state image that newspapers and boosters worked so hard to project. "If the immediate future of Wyoming is to brighten," the Denver *Republican* noted in an editorial on Foote, "at least her own citizens must be true to her interests. . . . The demand in the west at the present time is for men who will build up instead of tearing down." The loss of *prospective* settlers and investors was only half the problem. Since Colorado, Montana, and Idaho had also taken advantage of the Carey Act, those who had launched Wyoming's projects might decide to move their money elsewhere.[143]

The damage had already been done. The Wyoming Arid Land Board received no new requests for Carey Act land in 1897, and three of the original applications were abandoned. The remaining projects were unable to attract settlers. As if conditions were not already bad enough, sheepmen drove their flocks onto some project land and, in Mead's words, held them there "until every vestige of vegetation has been eaten off in order to make the land as unattractive to intending settlers as possible. . . . [T]hey have discouraged a great many visitors from filing on the land." Neither Mead nor Warren thought that the 1894 law's defects could be repaired. "The cost of building ditches and getting settlers seems to be greater than the value of both land and water," Mead observed.[144] Warren estimated that ten dollars had disappeared in Carey Act canals for every dollar returned to investors. "So it is clearly proven," the senator concluded, "that if we are to reclaim land under still costlier projects far more liberal legislation must be had." The law could not work when there was so little demand for irrigated land, and when the market for irrigation bonds was so weak.[145]

Colorado, Idaho, and Montana encountered problems similar to Wyoming's, including the persistent localism and sectionalism that had crippled state reclamation. For example, Montana's legislature voted to accept the Carey Act in March 1895, but only following a heated debate over whether the projects should be restricted to the best agricultural land or divided up among all the counties. On April 6, 1897, the Billings *Gazette* attacked the "Helena Hog" because three of five members of the arid lands board—which was responsible for selecting the land to be reclaimed—were from Helena. It noted that "eastern and northern Montana, which naturally present the most inviting field for irrigating enterprises, are left entirely without representation." The *Gazette* charged that one Helena member wanted to bail out a defunct, half-finished irrigation project he owned near the capital city, and the other two Helena representatives were expected to go along.

Montana, however, was no more willing than Wyoming to reclaim land on its own, as the Carey Act permitted. When its legislature accepted the new law, it also forbade the assumption of any new debt by the state. Moreover, it reduced the cost of maintaining the arid lands commission by appointing business and professional men who already held full-time jobs; in that way, it did not have to pay their salaries. One historian of the Carey Act in Montana has concluded that "there should have been provision for fulltime state employees, at least one of whom should have been an engineer. The value of construction work was consistently over-estimated, and the value placed on the land was quite unrealistic for those times. . . . In short, the work of the Arid Land Grant Commission was a complete fiasco." By 1903 only one project had been launched in Montana. Eleven thousand acres had been segregated and the promoters built nineteen miles of ditch, but there were no settlers. Clearly, local conditions were as much responsible for the Carey Act's failure as were weaknesses in the act or the Department of the Interior's delay in approving land applications.[146]

Other western states did no better.[147] By 1898, the attempt to establish a partnership between state and nation had ended, at least for the time being. Only one third of the arid states had passed legislation accepting the Carey Act donation; only two had had any land selections approved; and only one, Wyoming, had carried a project through to completion. By 1902, 669,476 acres had been segregated in four of the ten states covered by the Act. But only about 12,000 acres had been reclaimed in the entire arid West.[148]

Aftermath

Any appraisal of the Carey Act must consider its impact on the irrigation movement as well as on the actual reclamation of arid lands. Initially, Smythe characterized the bill as "an imperfect and abortive measure" that served "neither one side nor the other of the old controversy between those who favored and those who opposed the absolute control of the public lands by the several states." He resented the fact that Carey had not consulted him or announced his plan at the 1893 Los Angeles meeting, and he promised to use all the irrigation congress's influence to defeat it. He did not embrace the new law until the fall of 1894, by which time the congress had lost much of its support in the Mountain West.[149]

Smythe hoped that the 1894 irrigation congress meeting in Denver would be able to forge a coherent reclamation policy that suited the entire West. The 1891 and 1893 congresses focused attention on many of the West's most pressing problems, including the inadequacy of land and water laws, the need to determine the volume of the West's streams, and the necessity for concerted action to attract investors. But they never spoke for "the West," nor did they provide it with much leadership. In Denver, Smythe asked his executive committee to prepare a series of bills for consideration by Congress. He wanted legislation to identify and segregate the irrigable lands, to release the reservoir sites reserved by the Powell survey for use in conjunction with the Carey Act, to extend the new law to the territories, and to repeal the Desert Land Act. He also wanted Congress to create a national irrigation commission to recommend solutions to interstate water conflicts, draft a comprehensive reclamation plan to be submitted to the irrigation congress before it went to the U.S. Congress, and supervise the construction of all national irrigation works.[150]

The Los Angeles meeting seriously eroded Smythe's image as statesman of the irrigation crusade; the 1894 Denver congress destroyed what little faith remained in his leadership. It convened amid charges that Smythe was nothing more than a pawn of the water, land, railroad, and cattle companies; that he had packed the convention with delegates who favored cession; and that the irrigation congress had only one reason for being—to increase public pressure on Congress to achieve unconditional cession. Bitter debates erupted between friends of cession and friends of federal reclamation. In a heated exchange between Congressman Henry Coffeen and Senator Joseph Carey, Coffeen charged that the Carey Act would prevent would-be farmers and small ranchers from securing land in Wyoming and would transform those already in the state into serfs or peons; he warned that it would extinguish any federal responsibility for aiding or directing western economic development.[151] The recommendations of the state irrigation commissions mandated at the 1893 meeting were contradictory. For example, Arizona and Oregon declared for unconditional cession, Oregon for a 4-million-acre grant, and Kansas and North Dakota for federal reclamation. Washington was willing to accept either cession or a federal program.[152] The majority report issued at the end of the Denver meeting endorsed many of Smythe's ideas, but the sheer mass of resolutions it contained indicated failure to reach consensus on the big issues. The West was no closer to a unified reclamation program than it had been in the late 1880s.[153]

Smythe not only failed to unify the West, he also failed to make irrigation an important issue in Washington. Secretary of Agriculture J. Sterling Morton, who understood the potential menace large-scale irrigation posed to crop prices, refused to permit Agriculture's Office of Irrigation Inquiry to send a representative to Denver. "The questions considered by these Irrigation Conventions have nothing to do with practical irrigation," Morton informed one delegate. "They amount simply to the coming together of a body of citizens for the purpose of petitioning Congress for grants of land, and a cession of whatever control or ownership the General Government may have of the waters of the arid regions."[154] And several months after the Denver meeting, the head of the Office of Irrigation Inquiry, Charles Irish, proclaimed that "it is really singular that the people of the arid regions will permit a small band to continually harass Congress for laws which will take the lands of those regions entirely out of the hands of the settlers, and put them completely under the control of corporations and monied men."[155]

Smythe knew that the speculative bubble had burst and that his lobbying efforts had reached an impasse. In February 1895 he sold *Irrigation Age*[156] and returned to his native New England to preach the gospel of irrigation to enthusiastic audiences in Boston. There and in Chicago, as discussed in chapter 4, he formed colonization clubs to recruit middle-class settlers for his own Carey Act project, the "Plymouth Colony" in Idaho's Payette Valley. "The startling fact about existing conditions in the East," Smythe observed in a lecture in Reno, "is not that a comparatively few are standing on the verge of starvation, but that the whole body of our middle classes, which constitute the bone and sinew of our people, is in a gradual process of decadence."[157] He wanted middle-class men and women to lead America out of the chaos and uncertainty of the depression. With their success to serve as a lesson and testimonial, Smythe hoped to raise the money to resettle the genuinely needy—he estimated that 19 million Americans were homeless—from overcrowded eastern cities onto western lands.[158]

Smythe no longer participated actively in the irrigation congresses,[159] and by August 1896 even *Irrigation Age* had soured on them.[160] The magazine insisted that a large number of states had been excluded from the irrigation movement, particularly those that had not taken advantage of the Carey Act.[161] That charge was echoed at the 1896 irrigation congress in Phoenix, where Arizona and Kansas expressed renewed interest in federal reclamation.[162] Nevertheless, Utah, Idaho, and Wyoming still championed cession—though they could not agree on whether to modify the Carey Act or hold out for an unconditional grant—and California still hoped to refurbish the Wright Act by creating a state commission to regulate the formation of districts, by limiting voting in district elections to actual landowners, and by depositing proceeds from bond sales in the state treasury until actually disbursed. The states that supported federal reclamation did so for very different reasons. For example, Arizona resented the fact that the territories were not included in the Carey legislation, and Kansas did so in part because it feared Colorado's control over the interstate streams the two states shared. The resolutions adopted in Phoenix revealed the new influence of George Maxwell and other proponents of national reclamation, but they came no closer to a consensus on principles than did those adopted in Los Angeles or Denver.[163]

The 1896 Phoenix conference has often been portrayed by historians as the fountainhead of federal reclamation, but few of its participants had much confidence in the future. George Maxwell later recounted that "at Lincoln, Nebraska, [at the end of September 1897] the Irrigation Congress came as near flickering out and passing into 'innocuous desuetude' as any organization ever did in the world."[164] Only "the loyal determination of a little handful of not more than a dozen of the old war horses and stalwarts of the irrigation movement" kept it limping along. The Lincoln meeting attracted few delegates from outside Nebraska. As the *Irrigation Age,* now a bitter critic of the congress, concluded: "The West, as a whole, no longer worked in harmony; unity of purpose and effort was abandoned. The northwest and the Southwest were pitted against each other. . . . those who were directly interested in irrigation cared but little what the congress might or might not do, and the general public cared nothing. The recent congress [at Lincoln] was the culmination of the spirit of sectionalism and personal aggrandisement."[165] Elwood Mead complained that he was "utterly sick and disgusted with the cheap crowd who have been running the Irrigation Congress for the past two years. None of them know the first thing about irrigation, [or] have any interest in the development of the west but are simply concerned in the pickings which come from these Congresses." According to Mead, the formal irrigation movement had been captured "by a lot of wind mill agents, cheap John lawyers and real estate fakers." That delegates from Illinois, Kentucky, and Tennessee had an "equal vote and more voice" than delegates from the arid states made the meetings "a regular farce."[166]

Meanwhile, economic conditions in Wyoming had never looked worse. The Carey Act's failure; increasing conflicts between cattle and sheep owners, small and large livestock companies, and stockmen and farmers; and the inability or unwillingness of Congress to open the national forests created since 1891 to mining, grazing, and lumbering all begged for a new land policy. National forest boundaries had been carelessly drawn and included land not actually forested. The designation of reserves had stalled mining, road building, and reservoir and ditch construction—without doing anything to protect the forests from their chief enemy, fire. Those who opposed the creation of forest reserves in the 1890s were not just plunderers of the public domain. Some believed that the greatest danger to the reserves was President Grover Cleveland's obsession with economy. Better to have no reserves at all than to lock away land without first preparing a plan for its management and use. To many Wyoming residents, the reservations were made to be forgotten, and as such they represented a conscious attempt to limit western economic development. Opposition became even more shrill after Cleveland designated thirteen additional reserves on February 22, 1897, including the 1.2-million-acre Big Horn Reserve.

Throughout Wyoming sheep, which were more profitable and survived much better on exhausted land, invaded ranges once reserved for cattle. Cattlemen reacted by consolidating pastures, which further limited access to water. "During the past few years the hiring of men to file on the land around springs and water holes has been a conspicuous feature of the effort to devise a substitute for [open] range rights," Mead reminded the National Stockgrowers' Association in January 1898. "The buying out of settlers to get possession of water front along streams has been another. Along many streams stockmen's conflicts have temporarily set back the advance of reclamation; settlers have either been bought out or compelled by loss of outside range to move out and many areas of land once irrigated have gone back to aridity." Fencing the commons was illegal, but necessity knew no law, especially law made two thousand miles away.[167] The range wars of the 1890s underscored the fact that reclamation was just one part of the West's complex "land problem." "Whether we like it or not," Mead warned the Stockgrowers' Association, "more settlers are coming to occupy the irrigable lands and more flocks and herds will each year dispute for possession of the pasture lands. The injury from overstocking is destined each year to become more marked until the profits from the free use of this land will be more than offset by the uncertainty, contentions and losses which this unrestricted competition creates."[168]

At the same meeting of the Stockgrowers' Association, Governor W. A. Richards demonstrated that the proponents of cession had gone back on the offensive, this time in favor of unconditional cession.[169] The strongest arguments against a complete transfer of title were that it would encourage speculation and monopoly; increase the power of entrenched elites; retard settlement by small farmers; commit the states to expensive reclamation programs; burden them with the cost of maintaining a vast bureaucracy to sell, lease, and administer the public lands; and contribute to corruption in the legislatures. Critics of cession consistently argued that since the states had squandered most of the land they had received in the past, such as the swamp[170] and school grants, they could scarcely be expected to administer a more comprehensive award honestly and wisely. The opponents of cession turned this argument on its head. The failure of Congress to adopt a policy regulating the use of the national forests, they reasoned, was evidence enough that the central government was no better suited to administer natural resources than were the states.

Cession had already reappeared as an issue in Congress.[171] On May 3, 1897, the Senate debated Alabama senator John T. Morgan's proposal to transfer all the public lands to the states and territories in which they were located by 1900 to pay for education or irrigation.[172] Francis E. Warren was caught in a dilemma. By late 1896 he had decided that the nation should build reservoirs as part of the River and Harbors program.[173] Cession, however, still appeared to be the most practical way to secure peace on the range and protect state control over water. Moreover, the depression had paralyzed Wyoming's government, and Mead now argued that the public lands could as easily be used to pay for essential state services as to build canals and reservoirs. Wyoming might lease 5 million to 10 million acres and use the proceeds to survey its water supply, supervise distribution, and litigate water rights. Nevertheless, such a policy would reduce the federal government's incentive to build dams.[174]

In 1897, Warren did not introduce any cession bills that pertained directly to irrigation, but he asked that every state be assigned one hundred thousand acres for each seat in Congress it held. He also requested several special grants for Wyoming: sixty thousand acres for a soldier's home, three hundred thousand acres to build a normal school, and an unconditional 5-million-acre grant.[175] "I am not as particular what I get the land for as I am to get it," Warren wrote Mead. He needed propositions that would win votes in Congress and keep his constituents happy. He admitted that "the fact that we want a lot of land in order to rent it and accommodate our stock men and farmers and reimburse our [state] treasury . . . does not draw many votes from the Senators and Members from some other parts of the country." Still, his bills were a warning that western congressmen and senators would be much more aggressive and demanding in the future.[176]

In the last years of the 1890s, Warren devoted relatively little attention to irrigation. He was preoccupied with tariff questions in 1897 and, as a member of the Military Affairs Committee, with the Spanish-American War and Philippine uprising in 1898 and 1899. In 1898, he revived and amended his 1892 cession bill, but he remained torn between home rule and state's rights on the one hand, and the glittering prospect of federal construction of dams and canals on the other.[177] Congress was inundated with cession bills in 1898.[178] Binger Hermann, commissioner of the General Land Office, insisted that the

Carey Act would not receive a fair trial as long as westerners could hope for a complete, unconditional grant.[179]

At the end of 1898, Warren rewrote a bill prepared by Stewart to give each state and territory 5 million acres.[180] For some supporters of cession, a limited grant had far more appeal than a complete transfer because it would allow the states to select the choice lands and spare them the expense of administering worthless lands; prevent Congress from using cession as an excuse to cut off or sharply reduce future appropriations to the West; and create less opposition in the General Land Office and Department of the Interior. Congress routinely solicited reports from the executive departments on pending legislation, and Interior consistently filed negative reports on cession bills, partly because the legislation threatened to eliminate the land office. Stewart's private secretary informed Nevada's governor that such a bill would undoubtedly pass at the next session of Congress because "all during the debate on the River and Harbor bill, where money was sought to be obtained to construct reservoirs, many senators stated that they were willing to give the arid lands for that purpose."[181]

Nevertheless, even Wyoming could not present a united front in favor of cession. As a formal political movement Populism had abated, but deep differences among stock growers remained. In 1900 strong protests against both cession and leasing appeared in Natrona and Converse counties. The Carbon County Wool Growers' Association opposed "any further public land being ceded to the state and . . . the present system of leasing state land, on the ground that such a system tends to build up a monopoly of said lands in the hands of a few wealthy individuals and corporations, against the interests of the great majority of wool growers of Carbon county and of the state of Wyoming." In parts of the state, the spectacular increase in the number of sheep made cession even less attractive than it had been in 1892. Under the existing "free grazing" system, when the animal stripped the vegetation from one tract of government land, shepherds simply moved them to "fresh" pasture. Sheep growers favored the open range even more than cattlemen. Small and large operators who opposed the existing lease policy worried that most federal land ceded to the state would be rented on the same terms.[182] In 1900, Congressman Frank W. Mondell resurrected one of Mead's cession-leasing bills (see next chapter), but by that time attention had shifted to federal reclamation.[183]

Cession failed for many reasons. Opposition in the East was significant but not decisive. After all, the Warren legislation and most other cession bills could be interpreted as an aid to the grazing industry and a *limit* on western agriculture, and cession was widely perceived as a method to pacify the West without spending any money and without giving up anything of real value. Most bills failed because of divisions *within* the West, not because of opposition from outside the region. The western obsession with monopoly, and the nature of the region's governing elites, made any comprehensive land legislation suspect. So did the assumption that agriculture and grazing were incompatible and that what aided the grazing industry would inevitably weaken or cripple agriculture. Some critics insisted that the federal government had a moral responsibility to develop the public lands. They opposed any policy that rewarded the livestock industry—big operators or small, sheepmen or cattlemen—because they considered it an obstacle to the intensive use of land. To them, grazing was a relic of the "Old West," an impediment to economic progress and industrial diversification. Others were more concerned that cession would result in a transfer of sovereignty over the West's water to Colorado, Wyoming, and Montana, to the detriment of downstream states.[184] In any case, the increasing willingness of many members of Congress from the eastern half of the nation to give up the public lands in 1899 and 1900 suggested that they might be willing—under artfully applied pressure—to do much more than that to aid the West. By the end of the nineties, the depression had lifted. The future looked much brighter for both Wyoming and its neighbors.

8

The Reclamation Act of 1902

The Reclamation Act of 1902, one of the most anomalous laws ever passed by Congress, promised to unify the West, but it also reflected many political and economic divisions within the region. It held out the hope of centralizing control over land and water, but it perpetuated nineteenth-century concepts of limited government. It embodied twentieth-century ideals of rational planning, efficiency, and government by experts, but it alo constituted a bundle of compromises that inevitably undermined those ideals. It was the product of many historical currents that converged at the close of the nineteenth century, including the depression of 1893, a new American nationalism, pervasive doubts that the vast numbers of "new" immigrants could be made into responsible citizens, rapid population growth, anxiety over the future of rural America, the increasing influence of industry and labor as opposed to agricultural interests, the new strength of the West in the U.S. Senate, the desire of railroads to sell their land, the political ambitions of Francis G. Newlands, and the accession to the presidency of Theodore Roosevelt. After trying unsuccessfully to tap appropriations for rivers and harbors, the friends of federal reclamation—who disagreed strenuously over what form their program should take, both before and after passage of the act—found a new tactic. They sold federal reclamation as a national rather than regional measure—one that would pay for itself.

Rivers and Harbors

The admission of the "omnibus states" in 1889–90, and of Utah in 1896, had little effect on the U.S. House of Representatives, where the entire western half of the nation had fewer seats than New York, but it gave the region 30 percent of the votes in the Senate. Some writers concluded that the national balance of power was shifting. "Ten or twenty years will probably witness the West in control of the government," one confidently predicted. "The West has been accustomed to have its wishes and demands for justice in the apportionment of appropriations disregarded, . . . [but] the time approaches when the West will not pay tribute to New York or the railroad kings. There is growing a West that can not be trifled with."[1] Western politicians quickly learned that they could strengthen their political muscle by allying with the South. For example, in January 1891 Nevada's William Morris Stewart, aided by other western senators, prevented the consideration of a new force bill, which had been approved by the House. The legislation authorized the president to use federal election supervisors and troops to protect the voting rights of black citizens. In return, southern Democrats supported opening debate on silver coinage legislation. Senator John C. Spooner of Wisconsin fumed: "The Confederacy and the western mining camps are in legislative supremacy."[2] In the following year, western politicians eager to cripple the U.S. Geological Survey—then under John Wesley Powell's leadership—enlisted southern support to slash the agency's appropriation from $541,000 to $335,000.[3] Southern Democrats consistently supported cession, partly in the hope that the West would join in their campaign against high protective tariffs.

Nothing better illustrated the West's new power than congressional debates over federal reclamation. National expenditures for river improvements dramatically expanded after the Civil War. From Jefferson to Tyler, the federal government spent $17,200,000 on improving river channels, excluding levee work. But from 1870—when river and harbor bills became an annual affair—to 1886 that amount soared to $126,600,000.[4] As early as 1852, a congressional report proposed the use of storage reservoirs to ensure year-round navigation on the Ohio and Mississippi rivers and to protect and reclaim the flood lands of Mississippi, Arkansas, and Louisiana. Twenty-five years later, Congress ordered the Department of War to investigate the possibility of damming the headwaters of the Mississippi River.[5] That paved the way in 1880 for congressional approval of a plan to plug the main stem of the Mississippi and its tributaries in Minnesota and Wisconsin, including the Chippewa, St. Croix, and Wisconsin. The House Commerce Committee predicted that by capturing debris and reducing the erosion of riverbanks, reservoirs could save much of the cost of dredging the Mississippi. The estimated cost for eleven dams was $1,380,791.09.[6]

The first appropriation was a modest $75,000, but Congress voted additional money biennially for a decade. By 1899, it had spent more than $1,800,000 to build forty-one impoundment structures in Minnesota and Wisconsin. The four largest—at Lake Winnibigoshish, Leech Lake, Pokegama Falls, and Pine River—were completed in 1884 and 1886, and a fifth at Sandy Lake was finished in 1895.[7]

The experiment failed. These crude timber dams, the most elaborate reservoir system in the world at the time, had very little influence on navigation or floods on the lower Mississippi. They were too small, too flimsy, and too far upstream.[8] Their ineffectiveness played a large part in the Corps of Engineers' later reluctance to build dams for any purpose. Nevertheless, they had great symbolic significance. If Congress was willing to build dams to serve Missouri or Louisiana, then how could it ignore the needs of Wyoming and Colorado?

For all the money spent on the Mississippi River, the Missouri had been entirely neglected. On May 12, 1896, Senator Francis E. Warren of Wyoming offered a successful amendment to the rivers and harbors bill calling for the survey of one or more reservoir sites in Wyoming or Colorado. He argued that storage reservoirs on tributaries of the Missouri River would prevent floods, reduce the erosion of riverbanks, improve navigation in dry years, stimulate mining and milling, and reclaim arid lands. He also promised that "the presence and use of this additional water would, according to accepted theories, greatly increase rainfall in those high, dry regions, thus reproducing and increasing itself."[9] The federal government was justified in undertaking the work, he reasoned, because the Missouri was an interstate stream, because most of the land adjoining that stream was still part of the public domain, because allowing flood water to run unused into the ocean was a great waste, and most of all because Wyoming, Colorado, New Mexico, Arizona, Utah, and Nevada had been completely excluded from river and harbor appropriations. "It is no more than fair and just," Warren told the Senate, "that these arid-land States shall participate hereafter in the deliberations, emoluments, and perquisites of river and harbor bills. If money is to be distributed with some little regard for local benefits, then give us our share."[10] If the Senate killed his amendment, he promised to vote against all future river and harbor bills.

Warren's ploy was all too familiar. First an investigation, then two years later an appropriation to launch construction, then a long string of annual or biennial expenditures. As the senator confided to a friend: "My object was to get a place—a footing, as I may express it, . . . for Wyoming and the western states, so that after establishing this fulcrum we can use our lever across it, in prying out appropriations and work within our lines hereafter." He won approval for his amendment only by leaving out the word "irrigation," and Warren predicted it would be "slow, tedious work . . . to get the Government and the country interested."[11] "Please think it out and get up the data and argument as to what site we will have examined in Wyoming, if the bill passes," he requested of Elwood Mead. "My motto is, we either want money for improvement or we want the lands. I am going to look to you for arguments, plans, schemes and general information and constant help." Two weeks later, Warren requested Mead to provide him with a "multitude" of small feasible reservoir projects if he could not find a big one. "We have got to keep this reservoir and irrigation business red hot all the time and as fast as we discard or wear out old schemes we must have new ones, for we must rivet and retain public attention and opinion to the matter."[12] Since there was little grass-roots support for Warren's efforts, he also urged Mead to encourage friendly newspapers in Wyoming to publicize the work.[13]

The senator recognized that the future of his state and region might well depend on the results of the reservoir survey, so he considered carefully who should take charge of it. He had known Captain Hiram Martin Chittenden of the Army Corps of Engineers since the early 1890s.[14] Chittenden had laid out roads in Yellowstone National Park, and no army engineer knew Wyoming better. Moreover, he headed the Missouri River Commission, also created in 1896, which was responsible for surveying that stream from its mouth to Sioux City, Iowa. In August 1896, at Warren's request, the army ordered Chittenden to conduct the reservoir survey. Warren and Mead had already decided on the damsites they wanted to have investigated, and Mead provided the engineer with topographical maps and other information from his files.[15]

The Chittenden survey was orchestrated by Warren, although Chittenden tried to maintain a measure of independence even while he remained loyal to the senator. On August 7, he informed his military superior that the survey would involve an inspection of reservoir sites and preparation of a map of "the western country" that would show all possible reservoir sites "and all other matters necessary to elucidate the report."[16] In December 1896, at the annual meeting of the American Society of Irrigation Engineers in Denver and the irrigation congress meeting in Phoenix, Chittenden met many prominent figures in the reclamation movement, including F. H. Newell, George Maxwell, C. C. Wright, and James D. Schuyler. He then visited southern California, where Wright, Schuyler, and Maxwell gave him a guided tour of irrigated small farms near Los Angeles, San Diego, and Escondido. In May 1897, he examined potential reservoir sites on the South Platte in Colorado and on the Laramie and Sweetwater rivers in Wyoming. In August and September, he traveled with Mead through remote sections of Wyoming and northeastern Colorado. Mead prepared the itinerary.[17]

Chittenden's report to Congress in December 1897 contained bad as well as good news. The negative message was that reclamation would have to stand on its own, independent of flood control and navigation. It was a "common error," he concluded, to link flooding on the lower Mississippi with melting snow at the headwaters. Since drainage from the Ohio River caused most Mississippi River floods, storage reservoirs on the Missouri would provide little benefit to the most populous parts of the Mississippi basin. To tame the Ohio, the government would have to build more than fifty reservoirs the size of the one at Lake Winnebigoshish in Minnesota, which Chittenden claimed was the largest storage reservoir ever built. Chittenden admitted that reservoirs might have some effect on the Missouri's navigability, but he assumed that the heyday of river transportation had passed.[18]

On the positive side, Chittenden proposed that the national government construct reservoirs at three locations in Wyoming and two in Colorado. The sites in Colorado were fifty miles southwest of Denver at the junction of the two forks of the South Platte, and at Boyd Lakes near Loveland, between the Big Thompson and Cache la Poudre rivers. The sites in Wyoming were on the Sweetwater, about twenty miles above that stream's junction with the North Platte; on the Laramie, about five miles southwest of the town of Laramie; and on the Big Piney near Buffalo. The Sweetwater site was the best, but there was no pressing need for water in that part of the state. At about 4,600 feet, the country around Buffalo was much lower in elevation than other parts of Wyoming, and it was one of the few places where there were small farmers who needed more water. Warren favored this region above all others; it was no coincidence that Buffalo had been the center of Populist and "Popocrat" opposition to the Cheyenne Ring in the years from 1891 to 1895. The existing ditches out of Piney and Rock creeks covered four times the amount of land under cultivation and were idle half the summer because of water shortages late in the irrigating season.[19] "In no part of Wyoming has the water of streams been more fully used in irrigation than in the section of country along Clear and Piney creeks and their tributaries," Chittenden observed. "The resources of these streams in their natural condition have been exhausted, yet there is [an] abundance of land in their immediate valleys to utilize the flow which now goes to waste." About thirty thousand acres could be added to the ten thousand regularly cultivated and the ten thousand that received sufficient water only in the late spring and early summer. Chittenden urged the construction of three reservoirs on Piney Creek that would collectively store 85,448 acre-feet of water at an average per-acre cost of only $2.51.[20]

Although Chittenden's report recommended reservoirs only in Wyoming and Colorado, it had many implications for reclamation in the rest of the West. "Reservoir construction in the arid regions of the West is an indispensable condition to the highest development of that section," he concluded. "It can properly be carried out only through public agencies. Private enterprise can never accomplish the work successfully." He predicted that the average cost of sufficient storage to reclaim all the West's arid land would run $5.37 an acre, or about $1,430,031 per year for a century. Unlike many pork-barrel appropriations, reservoirs would generate new wealth. Therefore, Chittenden recommended that all water stored in government reservoirs "should be absolutely free to the people forever, just as the canals, harbors, and other public works are free for general use without toll or levy of any kind." With the exception of interstate ditches, which only the central government should build and administer, the delivery system should be constructed by the states, water users, or private companies under state laws. He dodged the question of how the nation could "build, own, maintain, and operate" storage works without encroaching on states' rights.[21]

The war with Spain absorbed most of Warren's energy in 1898, but he returned to the irrigation issue—at least briefly—in the following year. National reclamation was a very old idea in 1899. Journalists had proposed it,[22] settlers had pleaded for it,[23] and Congress had considered countless bills to implement it, especially after 1888. Legislation proposed paying for irrigation works from general revenue and through the issuance of federal bonds, through loans to the states, through lending the nation's credit in support of state bond issues, and through the use of lease proceeds from grazing or mineral lands or the sale of public lands.[24] None of these schemes won widespread support, even in the West, but the ineffectiveness of the Carey Act demanded a new policy. On February 4, 1899, both Francis Warren and Montana senator Thomas Carter offered amendments to the rivers and harbors bill. Carter asked for $2 million to build reservoirs and canals in all the arid states, Warren for $250,000 to construct the reservoirs on Piney Creek in Wyoming, along with dams on a tributary of the Yellowstone River near present-day Williston, and on the South Platte River in Colorado.[25] Subsequently, Warren, Carter, and other western senators united behind a $215,000 scheme to build the Piney Creek structures, along with $50,000 to survey one or more dams in each arid and semi-arid state.[26]

Warren and Carter knew only too well that many easterners thought that tapping the river and harbor bills for arid land reclamation was unconstitutional. That explains why they placed so much emphasis on flood control and navigation. Chittenden had argued that reservoirs would provide little flood control to communities along the lower Mississippi, so Warren devoted most of his attention to the Missouri. Piney Creek fed into the Powder River, which, in turn, emptied into the Yellowstone, the Missouri's largest tributary. Warren boldly promised that the three reservoirs on Piney Creek would help open to navigation as much as fifteen hundred miles of the Missouri River above Sioux City and mark "the possible beginning of the end of destructive floods on the Missouri River." The only way to secure a uniform stream-flow, he argued, was with reservoirs. "In practice every acre-foot of flood water stored in these reservoirs will cause another acre-foot to be taken from the flood flow of these rivers by irrigation ditches and canals." True, the Ohio River contributed far more volume to the Mississippi than the Missouri, but its flood stages were impossible to predict and no levees or reservoirs could tame that river at flood stage. The Rocky Mountain snowpack, however, melted at a predictable time and rate, which meant that the Missouri could be managed much more effectively.[27]

Warren, who interpreted the commerce clause of the constitution as authority to *create* commerce as well as improve navigation, also justified the national construction of reservoirs "on the line of the United States taking care of its own." The Constitution conferred clear authority over the public domain, the proposed reservoirs were on the public domain, and they were surrounded by what was left of the public domain. The land was worthless without irrigation, and existing land laws were not adapted to the arid region. The government had sold arid land on the pretext it was agricultural; now it had the responsibility to make that land productive. Railroad land grants had been rationalized in part by the assumption that the land retained by the federal government would appreciate dramatically in value. Warren used the same argument to support federal reclamation.[28] He carefully placated senators from established agricultural states, assuring them that there was no danger that the new land brought into agricultural production would contribute to the agricultural glut. The high cost of transportation would forever bar western farmers from eastern markets. In any case, western farmers had no desire to compete directly with the farms of the East. "We desire an opportunity to raise some forage for the pack mules that are bringing the sacks of ore out from behind the mountains," Warren explained disingenuously. "We must have certain food and forage products raised near our mines." Carter added that the vast markets of China and Japan would one day absorb all the agricultural products the West could export, anyway.[29]

These arguments were beside the point; Warren knew that river and harbor bills were simply a method to share the wealth. "There is not a single dollar in all the twenty-eight or thirty million dollars carried in the bill . . . that we can not get along without expending," the Wyoming senator proclaimed. "It [the rivers and harbors bill] is simply a dividend declared by this nation and distributed over it for the benefit of trade and commerce. That is all there is of it, and there need be no concealment." Of the money appropriated in the bill, the western half of the nation received $2 million and the eastern half $28 million, despite the fine harbors on the Pacific coast. In effect, one half of the country was being taxed to support the other. The West had asked for a "trifling sum," as Carter put it, but he put the Senate on notice—as Warren had during earlier floor debates—that this was merely the beginning. "If in the end it requires $50,000,000 to complete the contemplated system, well and good," Carter remarked in the debate on March 3, 1899.[30]

These arguments did not go unchallenged. There was one major difference between appropriations for flood control, navigation, and irrigation: The national government retained title to navigable streams—an individual could not even build a bridge across such a watercourse without congressional approval—but water stored for irrigation became the property of the individuals who used it. Senator Spooner of Wyoming pointed out that the *primary* purpose of the proposed reservoirs was reclamation, not navigation or flood control. The Constitution gave the government the responsibility to encourage commerce, but not to create it; therefore, there was no implied power to aid agriculture. The Warren Amendment would ultimately cost the government hundreds of millions of dollars. "When you boil it down it is . . . a proposition to turn the United States . . . into a great water company," Spooner insisted."I think there would be just as much sense in the Government spending vast sums of money to sink oil wells throughout the country on Government land." The measure was both unconstitutional and inequitable. It would create one and a quarter million farms of eighty acres each using the taxes of already hard-pressed eastern farmers. The same object could be achieved by ceding the arid lands to the states, an alternative Spooner claimed to support.[31]

Francis Warren had been a U.S. Senator for nearly a decade, save for the two-year interruption caused by the Johnson County War and the Populist uprising (see chapter 7). He relished the challenge of winning money, influence, and offices for his home state, but he also lamented the West's impotence in Washington. Since the great increase in western states did not come until 1889–90, western senators had not been able to accrue the seniority needed to dominate key committees, as they would do in the twentieth century. And with notable exceptions—such as Henry M. Teller as secretary of the interior in the early 1880s and Thomas Carter as commissioner of the General Land Office in the early 1890s—top posts in the Interior Department did not go to westerners.

When Warren took the floor of the Senate at 8:30 A.M. on March 3, 1899, it was with a strong sense that the West had been betrayed again. There would be no money for dams. Despite unanimous Senate approval for his February 24 amendment to the river and harbor bill, it had been scrapped by a conference committee of seventeen that did not include a single member from west of the Mississippi. Aware that the committee had cast aside many other pet projects, Warren launched an attack on the issue of prerogative rather than of western rights. The House had defied the will of the Senate, he argued, and his reservoir scheme had been killed by one particularly vociferous member of the conference committee. This was an act "more dangerous than any page ever recorded in legislative doings, i.e., that conference committees need not confer, that majorities can not rule, but that the House portion of a conference committee may arbitrarily dictate and proclaim that certain matters shall not go to conference but can be foreclosed against without even [a] reading."[32]

Warren knew that a filibuster was risky. If the ponderous bill went back to committee for reconsideration, it might not make it back to the floor before adjournment; the reservoir appropriation could not be reconsidered without debating the merits of many other public works that had been deleted in conference. And despite the fact that many senators shared Warren's outrage, they worried more about protecting their pet projects than protecting the honor of the Senate. Nevertheless, Warren plunged on. Once he had the floor, he read from Army Corps of Engineers reports at excruciating length and repeatedly attacked the "spirit of intolerance" that the West encountered in its quest for what he considered a fair share of the public treasure. He railed against the notion that Congress had no responsibility to aid in the economic development of the arid region. "Only the few who kept track of affairs under the surface knew that the feeling of indignation [of the western senators] was so great as to threaten the defeat of the entire [rivers and harbors] bill, carrying $45,000,000," the *Washington Post* commented."It was the biggest 'barrel of pork' . . . which has been in Congress for a long time." The *Post* continued:

> [Warren] knows more about irrigation than Bryan knows about silver—which is saying a great deal. . . . Minutes and hours went by and still Senator Warren . . . let his words pour forth. . . . Meanwhile, it was quite evident that the flow of oratory was not to stop if Warren should suddenly fall by the wayside. Mills, of Texas, angry because . . . his pet project for a canal to Houston, for which $4,000,000 had been appropriated [was cut], held himself in readiness. . . . One o'clock [in the morning] came . . . and he [Warren] was still telling the Senate more about arid lands than any one had ever suspected that one man could know.[33]

The Senate finally agreed to send the bill back to conference, but it returned to the floor unchanged. Warren gave up at 3 A.M. on March 4, during the last hours of the Fifty-fifth Congress. He did so in deference to sympathetic colleagues who feared losing their projects, and because he did not want to kill the sundry civil bill and other important pending legislation along with the rivers and harbors bill. He submitted "this one time, under duress and protest, to the other features of the imposition, as I term it, and [to] the arrogance of the House."[34] Yet Warren's warning shot had been heard. On March 6, 1899, he informed Mead: "I had them on the tender hooks all the day and night of the 3rd of March & early morn of fourth and it was brought to the attention and consideration of every member of the House as well as of the Senate that I had them where they were short. . . . [I]t has set up a devil of a thinking over there [in the House] and the arid land cessionists are in dozens and scores where they did not appear as units before." In other words, the "scare" Warren had thrown into the House transformed discussion into a debate between the champions of direct federal appropriations and cession; in the mid-1890s it had been between those who favored cession and those who favored doing nothing.[35]

Although Warren led the 1899 filibuster, Carter was, if anything, even more truculent and less compromising. Like many western politicians, he was "shrewd, cautious, but courageous, he was a man of great power, although his ability to obtain something for Montana and the West in all types of legislation, and the way in which he strove to reconcile opposing principles laid him open to charges of insincerity."[36] In 1900, Carter lost his bid to return to the Senate for a second term. That defeat gave him the greatest opportunity of his political career, and he made the most of it. In 1901 as in 1899, the Senate approved a rivers and harbors bill that called for the construction of several reservoirs at the headwaters of the Missouri—essentially the Warren/Chittenden plan. Yet, once again, the bill was emasculated in conference.[37] The Senate conferees, led by Knute Nelson of Minnesota, put up a strong fight, but they could not persuade key House members to restore the appropriation. In floor debate, Warren noted bitterly that over $4 million in proceeds from the sales of western lands poured into the treasury each year, and since the late 1880s those sales had raised more money than the entire rivers and harbors appropriation for 1901. Since the rivers and harbors bill aimed to improve land by keeping it dry, why not improve land by making it wet? As in 1899, Warren suggested that the East had *consciously* tried to keep the West in a dependent condition and block its agricultural and industrial development.[38]

At 11:40 on the night of March 3, 1901, the age of the "New West" dawned: Senator Carter began talking and, with brief breaks, continued for twelve hours straight, ending within half an hour of the inauguration of President William McKinley. The *New York Times* called Carter's filibuster "one of the most notable occurrences in the history of Congress."[39] The rivers and harbors bill approved by the Fifty-sixth Congress promised over $60 million; it was the second largest on record. Carter probably killed it as much to save McKinley an unpopular veto as to protest congressional neglect of the West. The rivers and harbors bill was, he insisted, "vicious and entirely contrary to just and equitable principles of legislation." It had been constructed on the

principle of "division and silence." The bill ran 135 pages and constituted nothing less than a wholesale raid on the treasury. "To rush upon
the river and harbor bill has become a current mania," Carter lamented.
". . . [A] foot of water in an unheard of stream becomes the basis of a
$25,000 appropriation in this bill."[40]

In many parts of the East—even on the Mississippi—railroads
could move most goods more cheaply than barges or ships. Moreover,
river improvements had gone far beyond channel dredging to include
pulling stumps and even trimming trees that leaned over small streams.
Appropriations in Pennsylvania were promised for Murder Kill River
and Raccoon Creek. North Carolina received money to improve Pagan
River, the Scuppernong, and both the Little Pedee and Great Pedee.
Then there was the Cocheco River in New Hampshire, which carried
six inches of water, and Mattituck Harbor on Long Island—"unknown
to anybody outside of postal authorities"—whose outlet was one to
two feet in depth.[41] State by state, Carter lectured the Senate about
streams and harbors most of its members did not know existed. He
encountered more than a little hostility and testiness. "I sympathize
with the Senator," Senator Ben Tillman of South Carolina remarked,
"for I have been out through this country [Montana], and I could never
see what it was made for except to hold the world together. (Laughter)."
Edmund W. Pettus of Alabama insisted that he had supported aid to
the arid region in the past, but that Carter had made that cause "odious
in the eyes of all mankind." "How can I go along with a set of men,"
he wondered aloud, "who are conducting themselves in the way the
business of the Senate has been conducted this morning?" Still Carter
continued, and when Senator Pettigrew moved to adjourn the Senate
at 8:55 A.M.—at a time when Carter had held the floor for more than
nine hours and only eight or ten senators were left in the Senate chambers—Carter objected, insisting that he be allowed to finish his speech.[42]

There was no rivers and harbors bill in 1901, and in a speech
delivered a decade later George H. Maxwell reflected on the significance of Carter's act:

> You all remember, no doubt, an event which is very clear in my memory,
> because I sat all night long in the gallery of the United States Senate
> watching it being done; you no doubt remember the time when Senator
> Carter of Montana talked the River and Harbor bill to death, and they
> did not get any River and Harbor bill at that session, because the West
> had decided to show its teeth and satisfy the people of this country that
> it meant business. And in the next session of Congress those who had

opposed our measures came to us and said, "For God's sake take an irrigation bill or any kind of bill that will keep you off our River and Harbor bill," and we got our irrigation bill.[43]

Senator Warren publicly predicted that "before another River and Harbor bill passes and becomes a law, there will be reservoirs built and provided for by this nation, either in the River and Harbor bill or by some other appropriation bill, or in an independent measure."[44] His judgment was vindicated.

George Maxwell, James J. Hill, and the Ideology of Reclamation

While Warren and Carter kept reclamation before the Senate, the irrigation crusade found a new champion in George H. Maxwell. A decade after passage of the Reclamation Act of 1902, Frederick Haynes Newell, the first director of the Reclamation Service, observed in a letter to Theodore Roosevelt that "very few people appreciate how thoroughly the ground was prepared in advance [of the 1902 legislation] and what a large amount of thankless labor was performed by a few men, notably by George H. Maxwell."[45] Little has been written about Maxwell, but he played a vital role in the history of the American West.[46]

Maxwell was born in Sonoma, California, in 1860. His father died when he was fifteen, which forced the young man to take employment as a field hand at seventy-five cents a day and board. Sometime during the next few years, Maxwell devised a new shorthand system, and by 1880 he was the official court stenographer for four courts: the U.S. circuit court at San Francisco, Department Five of the San Francisco superior court, and the superior courts of San Mateo and San Luis Obispo counties. He was, in his own words, "the fastest shorthand writer in the world."

Having observed the legal process at close range, Maxwell enrolled at Hastings Law School in San Francisco. Within a year he was admitted to the bar—at the age of twenty-three—and his first year's income was twenty-five thousand dollars, an enormous income in the 1880s. His prosperity as a lawyer derived from complicated water rights cases.[47] In 1889 he was hired by a group of large California landowners who wanted to overturn the Wright Act. To be sure, many of the reclamation projects launched under that legislation were wildly speculative, but

Maxwell made no effort to distinguish between good and bad districts. The same man who would later champion the small family farm had enlisted on the side of stockmen and wheat barons, many of whom strongly opposed irrigation. "That was some War," he recalled in 1935, "and in one way or another it involved about every engineering and legal problem that ever grew out of the existence of water." Maxwell also served briefly in 1890 as editor of *California—A Journal of Rural Industry*. As a lawyer and a publicist, no one could sell reclamation better than Maxwell.[48] He did not speak with the engineering authority of F. H. Newell or Elwood Mead, but he managed to avoid William Ellsworth Smythe's reputation as an impractical dreamer and visionary.[49] The *Los Angeles Express* editorialized in 1902: "Modest in his deportment, untiring in his zeal, tactful, cultured, so thoroughly versed in his subject that he is a veritable encyclopedia of facts without ever becoming a bore, a brilliant and forceful speaker of the logical and argumentative type, George H. Maxwell is an ideal executive leader."[50]

Maxwell first achieved national prominence in December 1896, at the Fifth National Irrigation Congress at Phoenix, where he restored the gospel of federal reclamation to respectability. He favored the construction of storage reservoirs by the federal government and declared that the "ultimate aim [of reclamation] is that we may become a nation of rural homes, rather than a nation of large cities."[51] The first priority of William Ellsworth Smythe and many other leaders of the irrigation movement had been to rally the West behind a common policy so that the region could present a united front in Congress (see chapter 7). Maxwell, however, reasoned that if the proponents of national reclamation could show how the needs of East and West complemented each other, then the East might provide far more effective political support than the West. Indeed, a comprehensive irrigation program might be adopted in spite of western fragmentation. Of course, this would require the leaders of the movement to work harder to win over industry and labor, rather than to placate eastern and midwestern farmers. "The wage-earners of the East want wider fields for labor," Maxwell wrote in 1899. "The manufacturers of the East want new markets for their wares. Where can either get what they want so fully as by the development of the great arid West which is capable, with irrigation for its irrigable lands, of sustaining a greater population than the whole United States holds to-day."[52] The East and Midwest could sell machinery and manufactured goods to the arid West; the South could provide the West with cotton; and what the West produced beyond its own needs could be sent to the burgeoning markets of Asia.

In the early 1890s, Smythe spoke mainly to speculators and investors who hoped to profit directly from the growth of western agriculture. He also appealed to potential settlers by insisting that communities built on a foundation of irrigation offered all the advantages and none of the disadvantages of urban life; they would have good schools and churches; modern conveniences, such as gas, electricity, and telephones; and such amenities of life as theater and opera as well as literary guilds and public lectures. Irrigation would produce an ideal democracy, perhaps even serve as the foundation for a new ethical code and a higher civilization. That was the bright side of the dream. Maxwell, however, sold reclamation through fear more than hope. His greatest fear was that labor-saving machinery would dramatically reduce the need for industrial workers and drive down their wages, lessening their ability to purchase the products of farm and factory. Work had become increasingly routinized, regimented, and degrading, and unemployment and strikes had become commonplace. Where would the surplus workers go? What would they do? How would they feed their families? These were questions of the utmost urgency. Maxwell also played on such fears because he knew that irrigation could not pay for itself: It *had* to be justified as a social reform because the collapse of private reclamation had already demonstrated that water projects could no longer be regarded as profitable business ventures.[53]

The memory of the depression of 1893 aided Maxwell's efforts in countless ways. He courted eastern boards of trade, chambers of commerce, labor unions, and civic organizations. He also published several magazines devoted to irrigation and social reform, notably the *California Advocate, National Advocate,* and *National Homemaker.* Labor unions were easy converts to his national program because they favored cheap lands as a source of economic opportunity and perceived the West as a safety valve to drain off surplus labor and keep up wages. The West could perform a vital service to the nation because economic downturns occurred with amazing regularity, and many social critics feared that industry would never be able to provide enough jobs for the vast numbers of immigrants who entered the work force each year. In 1899 Maxwell formed the National Irrigation Association (later the National Reclamation Association), and he convinced the National Board of Trade to form a Committee on Irrigation (with members from Pittsburgh, Cincinnati, St. Louis, Chicago, and New Orleans). The committee recommended that Congress "provide for the supervision and direction of all irrigation enterprises in the hands of United States authorities, where such work is undertaken upon waterways affecting interstate navigation." Over the next few years, Maxwell's policies won endorsements from the Chicago Federation of Labor, the American Federation of Labor of Rochester, New York, the Missouri Press Association, the National Business League, the National Association of Manufacturers, the United Mine Workers, and the St. Louis Manufacturers' Association. As a result, by the early months of 1902, many prominent eastern newspapers supported federal reclamation, including the Boston *Transcript, Boston Globe,* New York *Tribune, New York Times,* New York *World,* Philadelphia *Inquirer,* Philadelphia *Ledger,* and Detroit *Tribune.*[54] Maxwell then used eastern support to enlist the aid of western bankers and businessmen.[55]

When he went off to Washington in January 1899, Maxwell included in his program federally financed storage reservoirs from river and harbor appropriations, and locally financed canals and other delivery works (in effect, the Chittenden plan). However, by the end of that year or the early months of 1900, he decided reclamation should be paid for with the proceeds from public land sales.[56] He drew a clear distinction between public and private lands. Federal reclamation would be restricted to improving the public lands, something the Constitution authorized. The states would redeem privately held lands, using revenue generated by leases on the grazing lands. And where landowners had the financial ability to help themselves, the job could be done by mutual water companies.[57]

Maxwell's greatest triumph was nationalizing the irrigation issue—something Smythe, Warren, and Newlands had been unable to do. He began by approaching the directors of the West's railroads. In 1913, railroad baron James J. Hill of the Great Northern and Northern Pacific took personal credit for the Reclamation Act of 1902, pointing out that it had been his idea to hire Maxwell as a lobbyist.[58] Hill, a Jeffersonian with a deep faith in the family farm, was convinced that one day Montana and the Dakotas would be the granary of the world. The Great Northern and Northern Pacific would carry the region's crops to harbors on the Pacific coast for transport to China and the Far East.[59] Crop surpluses were temporary, Hill reasoned, because the nation's agricultural production had not kept pace with population growth. From 1882 to 1907, the wheat supply increased little more than 25 percent while the population grew by 63 percent.[60]

Hill shared Maxwell's fear that the dramatic increase in America's industrial work force and its shrinking farm population boded ill for the future. As Hill noted in June 1901, both farmers and industrial workers claimed that they were not receiving a fair share of the nation's new prosperity. Consequently, he feared revolution. "At the present time there is a widespread and general feeling of dissatisfaction," he warned, "which will I think increase as we go on and will by 1903 be in full blast."[61] The West was a potential safety valve, but in many parts of the region stable agricultural communities depended heavily on the spread of irrigation.[62] Hill's interest in reclamation was not entirely altruistic. In 1900, the Northern Pacific still held nearly 13,500,000 acres in Montana, and he did everything possible to increase the value of this land and to promote sales.[63] The federal government could help by instituting a national reclamation program that served private (that is, railroad) as well as public lands and by repealing all land laws besides the Homestead Act (which would stimulate railroad land sales).[64] In May 1902, about a month before passage of the Reclamation Act, Hill observed that the "largest area for cheap irrigation in the United States" was along the line of the Great Northern in northeastern Montana, where there were four or five million acres that could easily be opened to cultivation. "These lands now bring no revenue," he remarked, "and are occupied by cattle men as ranges. If there was a good supply of water for irrigation, they would be rapidly settled upon at from ten to twenty dollars an acre." The lack of feeder railroads, the state's enormous Indian reservations, and the dominance of the livestock industry had sharply limited the growth of agriculture in Montana.[65]

Hill had an immediate cause for concern. From 1898 to 1901 much of the West experienced a severe drought; the Red River Valley's wheat crop declined by 50 percent in 1899, and freight revenues plummeted. On April 17, 1899, George Maxwell and Elwood Mead met with representatives of the Great Northern, Northern Pacific, Southern Pacific, Union Pacific, and Santa Fe railroads. According to a report prepared by the representative of the Northern Pacific, the conferees discussed legislation to lease federal grazing lands and grant the proceeds to the states, which, in turn, could use the money to construct reservoirs (Mead's scheme), as well as legislation that would permit the railroads to consolidate their holdings by swapping some sections for government land. Widespread hostility to the railroad grants and the fear that the railroads would pervert or abuse any land reform or reclamation measure persuaded those present at the meeting to maintain a low profile. "It was the concensus [*sic*] of opinion," the railroad executive wrote, "that the railroad companies could accomplish little or nothing . . . appearing in it for themselves, but that they would have to furnish the sinews of war for at least the first year." Each of the five lines promised to contribute five hundred dollars a month to Maxwell's campaign, a total of thirty thousand dollars each year. (They continued to subsidize him until 1904 or 1905.) It was a small price. As the Northern Pacific agent wrote to his president, "We believe that if the single bill could be passed by which Government lands would be leased that this company would be benefited many times annually the expense incurred."[66] Maxwell's affiliation with the railroads convinced him to abandon his cooperative state and national reclamation program for a more centralized national system that would serve private as well as public lands.[67]

Not all the lines shared the enthusiasm of the Southern Pacific and Great Northern. Other railroads contributed to the war chest more out of deference to Hill and Collis P. Huntington, head of the S.P., than from any expectation of gain. Charles S. Manderson, director of the legal department of the Burlington and Missouri Railroad, called Maxwell a "paid advocate of the impossible."[68] Nevertheless, Hill was a shrewd judge of character; he knew that Maxwell understood economic conditions and public opinion in all parts of the nation. In the West, federal reclamation drew its strongest support from large landowners and established irrigation farmers. Maxwell, however, knew that his job was not just to court those with an immediate interest in irrigation. He could succeed only by linking irrigation to other issues that dominated public attention from 1897 to 1902. For example, the U.S. war with Spain raised many vexing questions about empire. What was the status of the new subject peoples? Could they become useful American citizens? Was imperialism consistent with American ideals of freedom and democracy, let alone those of self-sufficiency and independence? Westerners had fought side by side with southerners and easterners in Cuba, and, at least temporarily, war effaced sectional differences. But where would the lust for empire lead? San Francisco's *Call* editorialized in 1898:

It is the question whether [Americans] shall employ their energies and their surplus wealth in irrigating the desert lands of the Great West or in conquering, civilizing and supporting some millions of mongrels in the tropic islands of the Orient. There can be no question as to which of the two would be the cheaper. It will cost us more time, more money and more labor to establish order in the Philippines than to irrigate the 70,000,000 acres of Western land. The land when irrigated will maintain not only itself, but a thrifty population of Americans, and pay a revenue to the Government. The Philippines, when once subdued, will continue to be an expense. The issue is one of home development against foreign imperialism, and every argument of economy is on the side of home.[69]

Americans could enjoy the glory of empire without the burdens. They could multiply citizens rather than subjects and populate the vast interior of arid America before turning outward. "It is better and cheaper to reclaim land than to reclaim Filipinos," a small newspaper in western Nevada editorialized, "and the people will yet find it out."[70] Irrigation held out the promise of a more homogeneous "empire," and it posed a clear alternative to the "white man's burden." Moreover, home markets would be more stable and predictable—an important consideration in a nation that had just passed through a major depression.[71]

Urban problems also came to the aid of national reclamation. The depression had been strongly identified with the city. Those who immigrated to the United States during the 1890s were far less likely to take up farms than earlier settlers had been; most were absorbed into the burgeoning industrial work force, or else joined the masses of homeless, whose numbers dramatically increased during the darkest years of the 1890s. The city had always symbolized vice and crime, disease and poverty; it was the very antithesis of rural life. The concentration of people in cities, George Maxwell wrote, made "our politics an engine of corruption and oppression."[72] In the closing decades of the nineteenth century, cities also became identified with "new" institutions that provoked deep anxiety among Americans, including gigantic manufacturing corporations, trusts, and industrial labor unions. Many social critics charged that these fed on the poor and trampled the middle class. The city sapped such basic American virtues as independence and autonomy, and it concentrated "disorderly" and "lawless" citizens.

Worst of all, the city had, in the minds of many Americans, crippled the American family, whose health weighed heavily on the minds of many reformers. In 1902, the president of the National Irrigation Congress lamented "the narrow limitations of city life." "I am thinking . . . of the family unit—of the father and mother and little children. . . . I am thinking how their horizon is to be broadened, and how their daily lives are to be enriched, by the transition from paved streets and crowded tenements out under the blue sky and into the sweet, pure air. . . . The man who rears his sons and daughters in the rural life of our irrigation empire will give them a better chance to become useful men and women than boys and girls will have when raised in the city." Or as Commander Booth-Tucker, head of the Salvation Army, put it: "The pivot of true social reform appears to me to turn upon the preservation, and if necessary, the restoration of the *family unit*. Destroy the home and you destroy the nation. We must show the poor man how he can afford to get married and can bring up his family in decency and comfort, and become a home-owner."[73] Nor was city life beneficial to the middle class. As one popular writer remarked in 1900, many of the brightest urban women "give their time and their strength to society rather than to home and maternity. The husbands think first of business, next of the Club, and lastly of home. Aversion to matrimony increases among the marriageable . . . the result being that the types that should [reproduce], do not, while those that should not, do, multiply too abundantly. Hence, we say that city life tends to deteriorate the race physically." Urbanization led to a weakening of moral fiber as well as the decay of "manly virtues."[74]

Yet what was the alternative? Outside the arid West, the United States had no more cheap virgin land; reasonably priced farms in the East were often worn out and in many cases abandoned. Late in the 1890s, Canadian provinces began granting free land to private irrigation companies, which, in turn, offered it at low prices—usually five to eight dollars an acre—to settlers from the United States. In 1900, five thousand Americans—most from Utah, Idaho, and Montana—left for Saskatchewan, and the exodus to Canada continued in the following year. While thousands of new settlers flooded into Montana and Washington, James J. Hill also reported "quite a movement from Iowa, Michigan and Wisconsin, and some from Southern Minnesota, into Western Manitoba, for cheap grain lands along the railway. I should not be surprised if this reached ten thousand settlers for the current year. When you and I came to St. Paul we never supposed that the time would come when 'Uncle Sam would not have Land enough to give us all a Farm,' but the country is growing faster than we ever supposed it possibly could." Apparently fifty thousand Americans crossed the border to obtain cheap lands in 1902. They were people who, under the right circumstances, might have settled on railroad land in Montana, South Dakota, or Washington.[75] The secretary of the American Beet Sugar Association noted that "while the East is being inundated by a million immigrants a year, largely the vicious, ignorant pauper scum of southern Europe, a single state [Iowa] is annually sending 15,000 of her brightest flowers to a foreign land whose immigration agents openly state that they expect an immigration of 300,000 people from the United States during 1903."[76]

Hill, Maxwell, and other irrigation boosters hoped that federal reclamation would stop this migration and serve as a safety valve in other ways as well. Writers who addressed the "land problem" in the late nineteenth century clung to the long-cherished assumption that democratic institutions depended on widespread property ownership. Rome fell because its aristocracy had absorbed all the best land, and European feudalism had subverted crude but effective democratic institutions. The Civil War had been fought, one popular theory ran, to protect the homestead ideal from the "slaveocracy." Statistics were not comforting; farm tenancy increased from 25.5 percent to 35.3 percent from 1880 to 1900, and the increase was nearly uniform throughout the nation. Tenancy became one of the most widely discussed social problems in late nineteenth-century America. In Massachusetts, however, between 70 and 80 percent of the state's residents were landless tenants, as contrasted with Utah, an irrigation commonwealth, where 90 percent of all agriculturalists owned their own farms.[77]

Time and again, irrigation promoters pledged that the efficient use of the public domain would mitigate those class conflicts that seemed to threaten the nation during the 1890s. Rural homes were the nation's ballast or gyroscope. The greater the number of property owners, the stronger such republican values as independence and equality would become. In a gushy 1898 address to the irrigation congress, one friend of irrigation explained its greatest value:

But, my friends, the grandest of all would be the hundreds of millions of true, loyal American yeomen who would plant that glorious emblem of brotherly love, the stars and stripes, so deep and firm in that irrigated soil, that all the foes of human liberty, both at home and abroad, could never tear it down; thus insuring to our beloved children when we are gone, and to their posterity for all time to come, a treasure ten thousand times more precious than all the jewel-bedecked crowns ever worn by all the kings, queens, princes and potentates this world ever saw; a treasure they could, and surely would, share with suffering humanity in any quarter of the world where the tyrant's blood-stained treasure is freedom, civil and religious liberty, secured by a government of the people, by the people and for the people, a true democracy.[78]

Following the coal strike of 1902, Hill noted in a letter to Elwood Mead that when "the conservative agricultural element . . . is not dominant in this country, the end of the Republic is rapidly approaching." Yet open the door to the arid West, and most of the nation's fundamental problems would settle themselves. "The man who lives upon the farm is never an anarchist; he is never a communist; he is never a revolutionist," Senator Henry Teller of Colorado proclaimed in a speech before the U.S. Senate in 1888.[79] During floor debate on the Newlands Act, Senator Thomas M. Patterson promised that "the addition of a new county of agricultural lands to this country is better than a regiment of soldiers for the purpose of preserving the peace. The addition of a new State . . . is better than a standing army." Put the landless man on a farm of his own, Congressman Wesley L. Jones of Washington maintained, and "the seeds of anarchy and lawlessness will shrink and die, while love for family and country will . . . grow stronger and stronger from day to day."[80]

Hill and Maxwell took advantage of many ideas that were "in the air." They played on an amazing range of American hopes and anxieties—not the least of which was the suspicion that the depression of 1893–98 would soon return, that the economy was so "out of balance" that hard times had become a chronic affliction. Nevertheless, Congress could be remarkably resistant to public opinion, and the very breadth of Maxwell's appeal was also its weakness. For all of Maxwell's lobbying, arid land reclamation never captured the eastern press like the debate over tariff policies, civil service reform, or the war with Spain.

Irrigation and the Western Livestock Industry

The persistent fear of monopoly in the West reached its peak in the late 1890s and early years of the twentieth century, at the same time the corporate merger movement was transforming the American economy. Strangely, given the amount of land and timber they owned, the railroads caused far less concern than livestock companies. In 1901, Congressman Oscar Underwood of Alabama predicted dire consequences if the nation did not launch a reclamation program soon: "If this policy is not undertaken now, this great Western desert will ultimately be acquired by individuals and great corporations for the purpose of using it for grazing vast herds of cattle. They will acquire the waterways and water rights for the purpose of watering stock and become land barons. Then it will be impossible to ever convert it into the homestead lands for our own people or to build up the population of this Western country." A dramatic increase in the land owned by livestock companies underscored Underwood's warning. Grazing land entries increased from 5 million acres in 1898 to over 16 million acres in 1901–2.[81]

Of course, to talk about a "grazing industry" is to suggest a uniformity of interests and objectives that never really existed among stock growers. For example, in 1878 the Colorado Stock Growers' Association asked Congress to identify the grazing lands and lease or sell them. The Wyoming Stock Growers Association, however, opposed outright sale, even at the modest price of five cents an acre. Its members feared that state land taxes would cut deeply into profits. Besides, they insisted, the question of whether overgrazing would destroy the range was "unsettled." The association also rejected a plan to lease the land for twenty years at half a cent per acre per year with an option to buy at five cents an acre anytime within the contract period. Thomas Sturgis, secretary of the association, explained that the cattle industry was in its infancy and many members of his organization were deeply in debt; that the increasing size of herds indicated that the existing land system was working; that under private ownership the land would have to be fenced, which would dramatically increase costs; and that five cents an acre, added to the cost of barbed wire, would run as much as 20 percent of the value of the stock itself. Historians have often assumed that nineteenth-century land laws were unrealistic if not irrational, but many livestock interests regarded the Desert Land Act, Homestead Act, and Timber Culture Act as perfect complements to the open range.[82]

During the 1880s, most legislation pertaining to grazing land was rejected because the Constitution had only empowered Congress to *dispose* of the public lands, not lease them. Moreover, the disposal of any land in large tracts was premature, given that the irrigable lands had not been classified and reserved and given the persistent fear of land and water monopolies. As the acting commissioner of the General Land Office remarked in 1883, even if the irrigable land could be placed off limits, "the leasing of actually arid lands would result in so surrounding cultivable lands as to bring all such lands in the region of country subject to leasing within the practical control of the lessees to the exclusion of agricultural occupants."[83]

The conflict between agriculture and grazing faded during the 1890s, or, more precisely, it was absorbed into the campaign for cession. The stock industry, in serious trouble, hit rock bottom by the middle 1890s. The number of range stock declined by two thirds during the same period. Even though the sheep count more than tripled, F. V. Coville, chief botanist for the USDA, estimated their value in 1898 as less than $6 million, only about 40 percent of the value of Wyoming's cattle in 1886. And governor William A. Richards lamented that in many parts of the state "ten acres will not furnish the feed supplied by one acre a decade ago."[84]

As noted in the last chapter, in the 1890s Elwood Mead and Francis Warren tried to forge a policy linking grazing and reclamation in the Mountain West. In their minds, one could not succeed without the other. Since the central government had refused to enact comprehensive policies regulating use of the public domain, the states had to find some way to unify authority over land and water. The two regarded the Carey Act as the only option available during the mid-1890s. But they hoped that the new law would pave the way for outright cession, or at least an unconditional grant of several million acres. In his report for 1897, state engineer Mead supported a 5,000,000-acre grant to each western state and territory—which Warren introduced in Congress at the end of 1898. The legislation provided that stockmen could lease up to 2,560 acres from the state if they also took up a 160-acre irrigated farm. Mead promised that such a policy would "prevent the [further] destruction of the native grasses, now taking place, reduce taxes, provide ample revenue for county and state government, increase the profits of farmers, [and] put an end to range conflicts."[85]

Mead won support for his cession-leasing plan from the state engineers of Utah, Colorado, Nebraska, and Kansas,[86] but many members of Congress thought that the revenue from leasing should belong to *all* the states, not just those in the West, and when the governors of the western states met in Salt Lake City in April 1900, they adopted a resolution which favored unconditional cession but opposed leasing on principle.[87] A plan similar to Mead and Warren's proposed by the USDA's Coville won no greater support.[88]

During the opening years of the twentieth century, prosperity returned to the cattle and sheep industries. Syndicates, such as Swift & Company, consolidated many of the old livestock companies and competed with each other to secure good waterfront property and make the most of the open range. The dream of blending farming and stock raising began to fade. In January 1902 Mead noted in a letter to Ray Stannard Baker of *McClure's* that "the range industries proper are more and more passing into the hands of corporations and capitalists who are trained business men . . . and are working free grazing for all it is worth while it lasts without any regard to what follows, and who work on the prejudices . . . of the small ranchman whenever any reform in land laws is proposed [that would break up the open range]."[89]

Consolidation gave the debate over grazing policy new urgency in the Fifty-seventh Congress. Early in 1902, Secretary of the Interior Ethan A. Hitchcock decided to enforce the 1885 law that prohibited enclosing public lands; he promised to send Interior Department agents to tear down the fences of ranchers who refused to comply voluntarily. The Wyoming Cattle Growers' Association appealed to President Roosevelt to stay the order until Congress could adopt appropriate leasing legislation. Only leasing, it now insisted, could protect stock from theft and from wolves, eliminate the infection of healthy by diseased animals, allow ranchers to secure watering holes and windmill ponds, prevent "the tramping of thousands of hoofs" from destroying the range, and permit those in debt to borrow against their herds. The association predicted that Hitchcock's decision would result in "the calling of loans, and hence financial panic, thereby not only ruining countless home makers of the Arid West, but in the time of its prosperity will wipe out large portions of a great industry."[90] Grazing legislation also seemed imperative because Congress appeared likely to authorize a comprehensive reclamation plan in 1902.

In 1902, the leading leasing bills provided for national, rather than state, control over the public grazing lands. The most publicized bill, sponsored by Senator J. D. Bowersock of Kansas, was drafted during the summer of 1901 by a committee representing the West's largest cattle breeders' association. It called for leasing the 525 million acres of vacant public lands for two cents an acre per year. Leases were to run ten years with a right to renew for another ten-year term. Freeholders had priority, and they could claim ten acres of contiguous pasture for every acre they owned. Any remaining land could be rented for the same price to nonresident stockmen in proportion to the size of their herds in 1901. The secretary of interior could cancel any lease at any time, with no compensation, and the government could reassert control over tracts it subsequently chose for reclamation. Moreover, livestock owners were held liable for damages to irrigation works, artesian wells, and other agricultural improvements. All proceeds, save for the cost of administering the leases, would be paid into a reclamation fund, but under *federal* rather than state control.[91]

The Bowersock bill offered a way to pay for reclamation—a sop to agricultural interests—but it was riddled with weaknesses. The rent was too low, far below the interest rate of private grazing land purchased on credit. Moreover, the preference granted to freeholders was a ruse because few of that class held farms adjoining large tracts of vacant public land; the act would work mainly to the advantage of large stockmen. And since the Bowersock bill permitted leases to be bought, sold, and assigned, it raised the prospect of extensive speculation by nonresidents. Finally, there was no provision for a land classification survey before leasing and no limitation on the acreage any individual or company could acquire. The secretary of the interior was required to rent *any* tract of unclaimed nonmineral land, even if that land was valuable for timber or agriculture.

Even the provisions ostensibly included to protect farmers were dangerous. For example, the bill made lessees liable for all damages done by their livestock. Nominally, that was to protect crops from being eaten or trampled, but since few small ranchers could afford to fence their land on entry, the cost would weigh much more lightly on large cattle companies. The commissioner of the General Land Office called Bowersock's plan a "fraud," an outright attempt to steal the public domain. The Colorado and Montana legislatures submitted protests to Congress against both cession and leasing. Colorado's lawmakers declared that "the present laws pertaining to the public land . . . [are] equitable to all, allowing the home seeker and homesteader yet to come amongst us all the rights, privileges and favors that a free Government can bestow."[92]

The Bowersock bill failed, as did all the other schemes to regulate grazing on the public domain considered by Congress in 1901 and 1902.[93] But the legislation had an unintended and ironic result. While it further divided the West's stock growers, it helped to unify the supporters of federal reclamation by inciting the primal fear of monopoly that had so often motivated reform movements in the American West.

The Reclamation Bill and
Its Friends and Critics

Many reclamation bills appeared in Congress in 1900 and 1901, but no single piece of legislation was able to win support throughout the West.[94] Some proposals pertained to the entire region, others to individual states and territories. Some promised each state and territory an irrigation project, others required the secretary of the interior to choose the best sites. Some limited the cost of reclaimed land to a flat $2.50 or $5 per acre, others called for pro-rata repayment according to the acreage served and the total cost of construction. Some designated the revenue from water sales as a permanent or perpetual source of revenue to the federal government, most required the nation to turn the completed works over to the states or water users. Some contemplated control of the hydraulic works by the federal government, some by the states, and some by the irrigators themselves. Some wanted the cost of reclamation to be paid from the federal treasury, others through sales of public lands. Some restricted benefits to states with adequate water laws. Some confined reclamation to dams, others to both dams and canals, and some also included artesian wells. Most limited each settler to 80 acres of reclaimed land, but some promised 160 acres, and a few imposed no limit at all. Some confined reclamation projects to public lands, others were drawn mainly to benefit private lands.

Obviously, what the West most needed was someone to reconcile or at least smooth over these differences, and it found the quintessential "available man" in Nevada's congressman, Francis G. Newlands. Born in Mississippi in 1848 and educated at Yale University and Columbia Law School, Newlands moved to San Francisco in 1870 and four years later married the daughter of Comstock silver baron William Sharon. That gave him both wealth and influence. Newlands managed Sharon's property while the latter served in the U.S. Senate from 1875 to 1881, and following Sharon's death in 1885 he became one of two trustees for a vast estate, which included Carson River silver mills and the Virginia & Truckee railroad, along with Comstock silver mines. In the same year, Newlands launched a campaign for the Senate. He had inherited his wife's fortune when she died in 1882 and, following Sharon's death, he used his benefactor's fortune to build a political base in the Golden State. However, in 1887 the California legislature gave the Senate seat to George Hearst. Newlands's political future in California seemed clouded. The following year brought another severe disappointment. He had gained notoriety as Sharon's defense attorney in a famous adultery and divorce case against Sarah Althea Hill, a suit that captivated public attention from 1880 to 1888. However, in 1888 the California supreme court upheld Hill's claims and Newlands moved to Carson City and rented a house owned by William Morris Stewart. A few months later, he decided to build a permanent home in Reno, overlooking the Truckee River.[95]

Barbara Richnak has remarked that the California refugee burst on the Nevada scene "like a peacock in a chicken yard." (When he persuaded his new wife, the European-educated Edith McAllister, to leave her New York brownstone and visit Carson City, wags still described Nevada's capital as "wire grass on the alkali flats.") Through Sharon, Newlands had already forged alliances with some of the most powerful men in Nevada, including Henry M. Yerington and Stewart, a fellow Yale alumnus. Stewart considered Newlands a protégé, and Newlands accompanied the Senate Select Committee on Irrigation on part of its swing through the West in 1889.[96]

Newlands came to Nevada looking for a cause and an office. Stewart had used irrigation to return to the U.S. Senate in 1887, and Newlands had invested heavily in irrigation projects in the San Joaquin and Owens valleys.[97] It is easy to portray Newlands as simply a politician hungry for power and profit. But clearly he was more. During his San Francisco years, as one historian has observed, Newlands "manifested a fondness for the discussion of questions involving the legal and political rights of the community." In Reno and Washington, no less than in San Francisco, Newlands engaged in countless projects to improve the beauty and efficiency of those cities. Common themes ran through his plans to improve Golden Gate Park in San Francisco, construct reservoirs in western Nevada, and later build model suburbs in Chevy Chase, Maryland. He believed in harmonious development, comprehensive planning, thorough systems, and consolidation of power. Newlands was dedicated to civic improvement long before he developed political ambitions.[98]

For most of the the 1890s, Newlands was silent on irrigation. Soon after he took his House seat in 1893—which he held until winning election to the Senate in 1903—he proposed that the war department spend twenty-five thousand dollars on reservoir and canal surveys in each arid and semi-arid state, including Nevada's Humboldt basin, but nothing came of that scheme.[99] From 1894 until 1898, Newlands favored cession and reclamation by the states. "The National Government is unwilling to undertake the work," he explained during debate over the Carey Act, "though the States in the arid region desired it to do so, and thought it ought to do so."[100] The irrigation issue languished in Nevada until 1898, the driest year in a decade. In that year, the Truckee River ran dry in mid-July and carried no water for several months. (The drought continued into the summer of 1900, at which time the Truckee River's flow was insufficient to generate electricity for Reno.) In mid-July 1900, the *Reno Evening Gazette* predicted that by the end of the month "there won't be water enough running past Reno to give a jackrabbit a drink."[101] The drought coincided with a split between Newlands and Stewart which resulted from Newlands's abortive bid for Stewart's Senate seat in 1898. As part of their campaigns, both men introduced irrigation bills—a sure sign that the worst effects of the depression had passed.[102]

Competition between Newlands and Stewart for recognition as Nevada's patron saint of irrigation continued in 1899 and 1900. In 1899, Congress approved Newlands's bill authorizing reservoir surveys on Nevada's four largest streams, though a year later it rejected a request for $285,000 to build dams in the Humboldt basin. The latter bill provided for the settlement of government land under the Homestead Act in tracts no larger than forty acres for $2.50 an acre down and an additional $7.50 per acre paid over ten years.[103] Then, at a dinner in Denver hosted by Wyoming congressman Frank Mondell at the end of the year—attended by twelve congressmen from California, Colorado, Wyoming, Nebraska, South Dakota, Idaho, Washington, Oregon, Nevada, and Montana—Newlands proposed a federal appropriation of one hundred thousand dollars for each western state to construct an experimental storage reservoir.[104] He also tried to revive interest in the comprehensive private water project he had launched in 1889, but western Nevada's water users remained uncooperative despite the drought. Finally, in the summer of 1900, as a member of the national Democratic party's platform committee, Newlands secured a plank in support of federal reclamation by invoking a common Democratic argument: that the arid West would add far more wealth to the nation than a thousand insular possessions.[105]

November 1900 marked a turning point in Newlands's career. He longed to escape the little world of Nevada politics, along with his vassalage to the silver issue, and to exhibit on a larger stage those qualities of vision and statesmanship he had shown in his campaign to make San Francisco the Paris of American cities. He had not attended an irrigation congress since 1891, but he was a featured performer at the 1900 Chicago meeting, along with Frederick Haynes Newell, Hiram Martin Chittenden, and other champions of federal reclamation.[106] To shatter the image of reclamation as a western issue, George Maxwell—who now held sway over the irrigation congress much as Smythe had in the early 1890s—chose Chicago (the city that straddled East and West) as the convention site. Coming as it did in the wake of war, the 1900 congress was unabashedly nationalistic,[107] and Newlands delivered the keynote address to thunderous applause. The conference gave him the opportunity to renew his friendship with Newell, head of the USGS Hydrographic Branch, whom he had first met in 1898. Newell worried that relying on river and harbor bills to pay for reservoir construction would result in the Army Corps of Engineers taking charge of federal reclamation rather than the USGS. If that happened, he would lose the opportunity to direct potentially the greatest public works program in American history. He also feared that the army engineers would build wasteful, inefficient, and poorly coordinated water systems.[108] A week after the convention ended, Newlands visited Newell at the Geological Survey's office, and subsequently Newell prepared a bill introduced on December 17 (H.R. 12844) pertaining to water storage on the Humboldt River.

Early in 1901, Maxwell rented the house next to Newell's, and in his unpublished memoirs the engineer remembered that "we talked over the situation most every evening. Mr. Newlands got into the habit of dropping into my office late in the afternoon and I put into shape many suggestions for bills which he later introduced."[109] On January 8, 1901, Newlands hosted the first of a series of formal dinners, which included speeches and Newell's lantern slide show. The speakers included the secretary of the interior, the director of the USGS, Newell, and Maxwell. The slides depicted the startling transformation of land "under the ditch"; Newell's show included many "before and after" scenes. It also showed potential reservoir sites and major streams in drought and flood. The secretary of the interior and sixteen western politicians attended the first banquet. On January 17, Newlands hosted the House Public Lands Committee and outlined a new plan to free national reclamation from bondage to the river and harbor bill by dedicating the proceeds from public land sales to reclamation. That scheme won a warm reception, and after extended conversations with Maxwell and Newlands, Newell drafted a formal bill which Newlands introduced in Congress as H.R. 13846 on January 26, 1901. Senator Henry C. Hansbrough sponsored similar legislation in the Senate.[110]

The bill introduced on January 26, 1901, as "amended" on February 6 and March 1,[111] borrowed freely from legislation introduced in 1900 and 1901. It restricted the size of homesteads to eighty acres and limited farmers to the water needed to irrigate that tract. Any surplus could be sold outside government projects, but the eighty-acre limitation would apply there as well. Farmers would have ten to twenty years to repay the cost of irrigation, and the secretary of the interior could cut off the water supply and cancel the homestead entry of those more than one year in arrears on their payments. All reservoirs constructed by the nation would be "perpetually operated and maintained by the Government as public works."[112]

The legislation sought to pacify two groups: easterners who feared a western raid on the river and harbor bills, and the proponents of cession. If Congress refused to grant the public lands to the states, the next best thing was to secure the *proceeds* from those lands. And by creating a perpetual "revolving fund," replenished by the payments of farmers for irrigation works, Newell freed reclamation from the annual river and harbor free-for-all and the need to appeal to Congress for yearly appropriations.

The Newell/Newlands scheme was also revolutionary in that it broke with the cherished western assumption, embodied in the Chittenden Plan, that the federal government should build storage reservoirs and permit the states to dispose of the land and water. The legislation assigned the disposal of lands to the General Land Office under the Homestead Act and bypassed state water laws, at least to the extent of restricting the size of farms and attaching water rights to the land benefited. Congress adjourned on March 4, 1901, before the legislation could be debated in the House and Senate. Newlands and Hansbrough had agreed that, if House leaders refused to permit the bill to be discussed on the floor, Hansbrough would tack the legislation onto the "sundry civil" bill to force consideration in the Senate. The crush of legislation in the upper house, however, prevented use of that tactic, setting the stage for Carter's filibuster.[113]

In the House, Charles H. Grosvenor of Ohio, John Dalzell of Pennsylvania, and Joseph Cannon of Illinois, chair of the House Appropriations Committee, were particularly hostile toward the Newell/Newlands measure. Cannon's opposition was one of the main reasons that senators Warren and Carter favored tapping the river and harbor bill. The House leadership consistently blocked irrigation legislation, and many House members regarded Newlands's bill as one man's ploy to revive a dying state and prevent the elimination of his seat in Congress; they knew little about the West and had no desire to learn more.[114] House opposition, however, was not the only problem. While George Maxwell's propaganda mill ground out plenty of favorable press, many agricultural publications, led by the venerable *Country Gentleman* and *Irrigation Age*, vigorously attacked the reclamation bill.[115] And while Newlands enjoyed the full support of Newell, the USGS, and the secretary of the interior, the Commissioner of the General Land Office expressed serious reservations about the legislation and the Agriculture Department condemned it outright.

Opposition from the Agriculture Department was particularly strident. As discussed in chapter 5, in 1888 Congress gave John Wesley Powell and the USGS the responsibility for locating reservoir sites and canal lines, but it abruptly cut off the Irrigation Survey's funding in 1890. Meanwhile, the Agriculture Department had beaten the USGS into the field by appointing journalist Richard J. Hinton to compile information on irrigation in 1886. Hinton's first report appeared in 1887, and his last was published in 1892. He also directed the Artesian Well Survey of 1890–92 (see chapter 5), which was perceived in many parts of the West—particularly on the Great Plains—as an alternative to the work of the Irrigation Survey. When Congress terminated the underground water investigation, the secretary of agriculture made Hinton the first director of the Office of Irrigation Inquiry, with the responsibility "to collect and publish information as to the best methods of cultivating the soil by irrigation" as well as to continue the surveys of underground water. From the beginning, however, Hinton's office suffered from meager appropriations and from the limited fact-gathering mission it had been given.[116] Secretaries of agriculture J. Sterling Morton (1893–97) and James Wilson (1897–1913) were keenly aware that eastern farm organizations opposed opening new farmland in the West. Consequently, they prohibited USDA employees from attending meetings of the national irrigation congress and from lobbying for bills pertaining to land and water.

Despite occasional efforts to upgrade the Irrigation Office into a bureau, it remained small and steered clear of politics.[117] Nevertheless, its leaders consistently feared that Congress would resurrect the Irrigation Survey in Interior—even as they recognized the need for centralized planning and coordination. In 1893, Hinton noted that "[t]his whole irrigation inquiry has been characterized by a wasteful scramble to get in on it. The State Department has published a volume thereon; the Treasury's Bureau of Statistics has dabbled therein in its volume on 'Internal Commerce'; . . . the Weather Service is discussing 'Earth Moisture,' etc., and the Army Engineer Office got in a little one on [irrigation in] Egypt. The Department of Agriculture only did what it was ordered and of late months not all of that." One of Hinton's successors, Charles W. Irish, privately expressed deep frustration with his office's inability to compete for appropriations with the politically entrenched USGS:

> You speak of the half million, or more, dollars wasted by the Geological Survey. I have seen this waste going on from year to year ... and I am satisfied that it will be found hereafter, that all which they have done in the field [of irrigation] will be worthless, perfectly useless, but then, the Geological Survey has such a character for *scientific work* that they can obtain any amount, whatever they ask, while this department, making an effort to bring out practical matters on the subject of irrigation, and place in the hands of those most needing the information thus obtained, is barely allowed an existence.[118]

In March 1895, Congress created a Board of Irrigation to coordinate national reclamation policies. The Interior Department's General Land Office, Indian Office, and USGS had an immediate interest in the spread of this new mode of agriculture as did the Office of Irrigation Inquiry, Weather Bureau, Forestry Office, Division of Soils, and Division of Physiology and Pathology within the Agriculture Department. The board consisted of six members, including two from the Geological Survey and one from the Office of Irrigation Inquiry. Its basic goal was to prevent duplication of efforts. It met frequently but did little to transcend or surmount bureaucratic rivalries or to formulate comprehensive policies.[119]

One reason for the lack of success was that the deepening agricultural depression eroded support for the Office of Irrigation Inquiry within the Agriculture Department. In the wake of the economic collapse of 1893, shrinking federal revenues, slumping crop prices, and Secretary Morton's heroic opposition to opening new farmland further undermined the agency's support. In 1895, it was abolished, in part so that the money saved could be allocated to the USGS. F. H. Newell had assumed the responsibility of measuring western streams after the Irrigation Survey ended in 1890, but Congress did not make a specific appropriation for that purpose until 1894. In the following year, the demise of the Office of Irrigation Inquiry allowed the Survey to create a Hydrographic Department to study the nation's rivers and Newell was appointed director. He quickly set up over 100 gauging stations on the Upper Missouri, Platte, Arkansas, Rio Grande, Colorado, Columbia, Sacramento, San Joaquin, and many streams in the eastern United States.[120]

Francis E. Warren worried about the growing power of the USGS. In 1898, he sought to create a bureau more responsive to Wyoming's needs and he turned to Mead for leadership. He considered the restoration of Agriculture's irrigation bureau as a prelude to national reclamation, not an end in itself. "Of course the matter of government construction of reservoirs and cession of lands have to follow along a little in the rear," Warren observed in a March 1898 letter to his protégé.[121] The senator hoped that the new office would survey and construct the reservoirs proposed by Hiram Martin Chittenden in his famous 1897 report, discussed at the beginning of this chapter. Moreover, there had never been a thorough study of the soils of the arid region. Westerners, Warren thought, deserved a bureau that would provide practical advice to farmers. Above all, something had to be done to quiet titles to water. "We need to know exactly what land laws and what water laws are required to make canal building a success," Warren wrote in a memorandum. "To do this we must know why some have been a success and why some have failed in the past. We should, therefore, authorize the Secretary of Agriculture to make such investigations as will show what part inadequate laws have contributed to create the present stagnation [in western economic conditions]."[122]

On February 2, 1898, Warren offered an amendment to the Agricultural Appropriation Bill to create a "Division of Irrigation and Reclamation of Arid Lands" charged with a wide range of responsibilities. He encountered strong opposition from senators Stewart, Teller, and Carter—who opposed the creation of any bureau that might threaten state administrative control over water—and from critics who branded the legislation as an "entering wedge" for a public works program.[123] A conference committee slashed the appropriation he had requested to $10,000, sharply limiting the initiative of the new agency, but Warren was not dismayed. "Now, my dear Mead, the water melon is about ready to cut," Warren wrote to his friend on March 4. "I do not know whether the amount is going to be enough; whether the certainty of continuance of appropriation is sufficiently assured, or whether the way in which the Secretary is to appoint or employ is satisfactory so that you will have the interest in this that you once thought you might have. . . ." Mead jumped at the chance but retained the job of Wyoming state engineer for a year following his July 1898 appointment to the federal post.[124]

Newell's position as head of the Hydrographic Department, and Mead's new job, put the two ambitious young men on a collision course. Twice Mead had been offered positions with the Irrigation Survey; he was highly respected by both Powell and Powell's chief lieutenant in the survey, C. E. Dutton.[125] Mead corresponded frequently with Newell during the early 1890s. As noted in chapter 3, when Wyoming entered the Union, its first legislature provided for administrative adjudication of all water rights at state expense. Mead decided to begin work in the region Chittenden had paid closest attention to—Sheridan and Johnson counties, particularly Clear Creek and other tributaries of the Powder River. By the beginning of 1891 there were 500–600 irrigation ditches in the Big Horn basin and most of its streams were overappropriated. Mead informed Powell that "[i]t is [our] intention to begin the adjudication this summer and as a part of the work to keep a record of the discharge of each stream and make a gauging of each ditch. . . . This will give a complete record of the water supply and of the capacity of the distributing works, but we should have in addition a topographical survey, showing the route of each ditch and the amount of land it waters or is capable of watering. The state has not the [financial] means of undertaking this work. . . ." During the 1890s, state appropriations for the engineer's office averaged only about $1,500 a year above salaries. Half that amount went for office supplies, so there was little money left for stream gauging and the administrative adjudication of water rights—let alone for surveying reservoir sites and canal routes, another responsibility the 1890 legislature had imposed on the state engineer.[126] Mead thought that assistance from the USGS could cut the state's cost of adjudication in half.[127]

In 1891, the USGS loaned Wyoming the instruments needed to measure streamflow. At the end of that year, Mead forwarded the records compiled by his office to Newell and thanked him for the "valued assistance provided by the U.S.G.S."[128]

Understandably, Mead had mixed feelings toward the USGS and its work. Early in 1892, while under consideration for appointment as head of an expanded irrigation office in Agriculture, Mead urged that the entire Geological Survey be transferred to the USDA.[129] In the fall, however, following Benjamin Harrison's unsuccessful bid for reelection, Mead realized that if he accepted the position, he would likely lose it when the Cleveland Administration assumed power. Consequently, he turned it down.[130] He had met F. H. Newell in 1889 or 1890. "I know Mr. Newell personally," he wrote to U.S. Senator Joseph M. Carey in 1890. "He is an excellent man but has no practical knowledge of irrigation."[131] In the first half of the 1890s, Mead consistently supported congressional efforts to expand Newell's stream-gauging work, and in a private letter to Wyoming's U.S. Senator C. D. Clark in 1895 he described the USGS official as "a level-headed, common sense sort of person. . . ." However, he testily informed Newell that "the topographic work heretofore done [by the USGS] is of no value whatever in assisting in the laying out of irrigation works." The maps were drawn to a different scale from those prepared by the General Land Office, and government surveyors left no monuments to designate township boundaries. Thus there were no fixed points that could be used as reference points in laying out canals.[132]

As the crusade for federal reclamation revived at the end of the 1890s, the tension between Mead and Newell increased. It erupted into open conflict in early 1898, when Congress created the Office of Irrigation Investigations in Agriculture. Not surprisingly, Newell saw the Chittenden Survey and Mead's new office as part of a carefully orchestrated plan to cripple the Geological Survey. Mead insisted that he had always supported the work of the USGS, but, simultaneously, he arranged a meeting between the state engineers of Wyoming, Utah, Colorado, Kansas, and Nebraska to enlist their support for his plan to have Congress grant 5,000,000 acres of grazing land to each western state, the proceeds from which would allow the states to create autonomous irrigation departments.[133]

By the summer of 1898 the rift was complete. Mead angrily asked Newell to return a paper he had prepared for publication in the USGS Water Supply and Irrigation Series. "I make this request because some of your recent statements concerning me have been so unfriendly and, in my opinion, so uncalled for that I cannot consent to your publishing the bulletin which I have prepared. . . . I do not think the co-operation and assistance you have received from this office is meeting with the response it deserves and as I have not interfered with your work, nor do I intend to, I will greatly appreciate a similar attitude on your part with respect to my own." When Newell complained to the secretary of agriculture that Mead was trying to lure engineers away from the USGS to staff his new office, Mead responded: "I do not expect [that] we can agree about the wisdom or expediency of the projected investigation of the Agricultural Department but we ought to be of one mind in realizing that ill feeling or personal bickering can only result in harm to us and the cause we are endeavoring to promote." Francis E. Warren was no less concerned about the feud than Mead. "I don't know what is the matter with that fellow," he confided to Mead, "perhaps we magnify him too much by paying any attention to him?"[134]

In 1900, Mead's office began a comprehensive survey of water rights in California.[135] That work permitted the Department of Agriculture to forge alliances with California irrigation promoters, politicians, and business leaders, alliances that promised to serve Elwood Mead well if a federal reclamation program was launched by Congress. It also resulted in a 43 percent increase in the appropriation for his office.[136] Given the power of California's congressional delegation, Newell had plenty of cause for worry. As always, Mead insisted that the USGS knew little about western water law and desert agriculture. "In constructing reservoirs," he wryly observed, "it is as necessary to know whether they will be filled in a few years by silt as to know that the dam rests on a solid foundation. . . . In planning diversion works it is as necessary to know how much water it takes to irrigate an acre of land as to know how much water is available for such irrigation."[137]

In 1901, with the help of Warren and other political allies, Mead tried in vain to persuade Congress to turn his office into a "Bureau of Rural Engineering," with varied responsibilities ranging from laying out roads to reclaiming eastern swamplands. He also lobbied for transferring the census of irrigation—which had been conducted by Newell in 1890 and 1900—to his jurisdiction. This generated as much hostility within the Department of Agriculture as within Interior. Both the Forestry and Soils offices wanted to wrest the hydrographic work away from Irrigation Investigations. By 1902, Mead's office had a staff of 46 "who were," in the words of historian Paul W. Gates, "well prepared to assist in planning any reclamation program Congress might adopt."[138]

Mead's office won particularly strong support in the Rocky Mountain West, where the "state party"—proponents of a decentralized federal reclamation program—had several major fears. First, since most national storage reservoirs would be located at the headwaters of the West's streams, and since most of the available public land was far downstream from the damsites, the nation would have to assert control over entire watersheds to protect the new water supply from pilferage by established farmers. Second, most western states lacked adequate laws to protect established rights, let alone the new rights that would be created by federal water projects. Finally, the wide variation in state and territorial laws ensured that only the central government would be able to decide which claims to recognize and which to disallow, especially on interstate streams.[139]

Mead went so far as to charge that the federal reclamation program envisioned in the offices of the USGS had been designed in large part to reassert federal authority over water in the arid West. "The abuse of western States and western irrigation authorities which has been so liberally indulged in recently by the agitators for National control," Mead wrote in December 1901, "shows that this is their ulterior purpose." Once the USGS began building dams under the Newlands bill, and once it had secured firm control of western water rights, a massive and tyrannical new bureau would be required to maintain national control. The arid states would virtually cease to exist as independent entities. Take away the water, or even threaten to take it, and land values would collpase—with devastating effects on the western economy. If federal reclamation was launched in such an uncertain legal climate, the program would be nothing short of confiscatory. Whatever *ideal* system the fertile imaginations of government engineers and scientists could envision, water rights had *vested* and deserved protection as well as respect.[140]

Both Mead and Idaho state engineer D. W. Ross also questioned whether there was much water left. Idaho contained about 550,000 acres of irrigated land, but this was only one third of the land "under ditch" (capable of irrigation from existing works). One legacy of the boom period of private reclamation was hundreds of thousands of acres of vacant land that could easily be watered—if not from existing ditches, then from relatively cheap extensions of those ditches. Federal reclamation would prevent the full development of partially completed as well as future private projects. Even the Snake River did not furnish sufficient water to fill all the canals that tapped it. "Therefore, in my judgment," Ross informed Mead, "we are interested at this time in protecting the interests of the users of water of these streams and [in] carrying out the plans already entered into to a happy conclusion rather then [sic] diverting water from these streams onto other [virgin] lands. In my opinion, it would be practically impossible for the Government to engage in the work of either reservoir or canal building in this state with a view of utilizing the water on public lands without coming into conflict with the rights of those who are interested in works partially constructed."[141] The Denver *Republican* put the matter succinctly. Any federal program "would doom many a farmer now trying to cultivate his land to a perpetual shortage, and no one should advocate a policy which would thus render it possible to place the seal of inefficiency upon existing irrigation systems for all time to come."[142]

On June 10, 1901, the state engineers of Idaho, Utah, Colorado, and Nebraska met in the Wyoming state engineer's office at Cheyenne to discuss their objections to the Newell/Newlands legislation. At a second meeting ten days later they were joined by seven or eight congressmen from the same states. As a basis for discussions, Fred Bond, the Wyoming engineer, revised a bill prepared by Elwood Mead a month or two earlier. The legislation provided, in the words of Francis E. Warren, that "construction, supervision, control or sale of irrigation works [erected by the federal government] and storage, division, disposal and distribution of stored water, shall be in the engineer's office of each state or territory accepting the benefits of Government aid; the feasibility of all plans subject, however, to the Secretary of the Interior." One of Mead's friends noted that while such a bill stood little chance of adoption, "it may result in a movement to give us the lands and let us work out our own salvation without further help from the government which, of course, would be a very satisfactory solution of the problem."[143]

The major issues discussed at the meeting included whether a new federal bureau should be set up to supervise the construction of reservoirs, whether the secretary of agriculture (meaning Mead's office) should be allowed to pass on plans submitted by the state engineers, and whether construction should remain exclusively in the hands of the secretary of the interior (meaning the USGS). The second meeting was attended by George Maxwell who, according to Warren, did "a good deal of scrapping" with Wyoming's congressman, Frank Mondell, so much so that "it got tedious at times. Of course, he differed with about all of us, but fortunately he pressed his differences with the Nebraska people, and got into quite a 'mix-up' by antagonizing them." The conferees agreed to meet again in Washington after Congress reconvened in December.[144]

Meanwhile, in many parts of the arid West, the summer of 1901 continued the drought that had begun in 1898, and in the fall Theodore Roosevelt assumed the presidency, following the assassination of William McKinley. Roosevelt's interest in conservation long antedated his presidency. In his *Autobiography*, he recalled that as a rancher in Dakota Territory (1884–86) he came to appreciate the value of irrigation and became "amused and irritated by the attitude of Eastern men who obtained from Congress grants of national money to develop harbors and yet fought the nation's power to develop the irrigation work of the West." Even before he took office as vice president, Roosevelt called for "[federal] government construction and control of great irrigation plants."[145]

Roosevelt later described reclamation as the "first work I took up when I became President."[146] Gifford Pinchot, soon to be chief forester, had been one of his advisers while Roosevelt served as governor of New York (1898–1900), and, through Pinchot, Roosevelt met Frederick Haynes Newell. The new president asked Pinchot, Newell, and Mead to make suggestions for his first message to Congress, delivered on December 3, 1901. In that address, Roosevelt appealed for national reclamation but urged that the distribution of water be left to the settlers themselves under state laws, "and without interference with those laws or with vested rights. The policy of the National Government," Roosevelt declared, "should be to aid irrigation in the several States and Territories in such a manner as will enable the people in the local communities to help themselves, and as will stimulate needed reforms in the State laws and regulations governing irrigation." For example, the ownership of water and land should go hand in hand, one and inseparable. Roosevelt pledged to uphold state laws, but only if they conformed to his vision of what those laws should be.[147]

Roosevelt was widely perceived as a "nationalizer." Following the convocation of the new Congress in December 1901, that image, as well as the state party's earlier objections to the Newell/Newlands legislation, prompted the formation of a seventeen-member conference committee, composed of one congressman or senator from each state and territory west of the Missouri River, with Francis E. Warren presiding and Newlands as secretary. The group first met on December 3, 1901, at Warren's home and appointed a subcommittee to draft a new reclamation bill. Senator Fred Dubois of Idaho presided over many meetings of the conference committee and later noted: "The conditions and necessities of the different states and territories were so at variance that it required the utmost patience, liberality and yielding of views on the part of all to harmonize the conflicting interests."[148]

The drafting committee consisted of two strong proponents of a centralized national reclamation program (Newlands of Nevada and Hansbrough of North Dakota) and three advocates of a decentralized program (Warren and Mondell of Wyoming and Congressman James Shafroth of Colorado). Despite the social events that competed for their attention during the opening days of Congress, the five men met for three or four hours almost every evening. They tried to reconcile the bills previously introduced by Newlands, Hansbrough, and Shafroth, along with Warren's revision of the "State Engineers' Bill," originally prepared in June 1901 by Fred Bond.[149] (The Warren legislation, never introduced in Congress, would have required the secretary of the interior to build irrigation projects from plans provided by the state, and it would have restricted federal control over water to those states and territories that had not enacted legislation to regulate appropriation and distribution on their own.) Initially, the only point of agreement within the drafting committee was that reclamation ought to be paid for with revenue generated by public land sales. By the middle of the month Warren informed the president of the Burlington and Missouri that he did not expect "to get a measure framed that will be very satisfactory to me or that will entirely meet your views, but the desire has been very great to get united action on something. It looks just now as if the bill would be very much nearer what we have desired than I feared in the commencement of our work." By the end of January 1902 the legislation was ready for introduction, but it was amended many times in succeeding weeks.[150]

The modified Newell/Newlands bill drafted in December and early January was introduced in both the House and Senate on January 21, 1902.[151] It differed from the 1901 legislation in several ways. The original Newlands legislation limited settlers to eighty acres to discourage speculators, but the new version allowed the secretary of the interior to lay out farms ranging from 40 to 160 acres (depending on whether the reclaimed land would be used to raise high or low value crops). Second, the new legislation required a majority of the revenue derived from land sales to be spent in the state where the land was located. This was a throwback to cession, except that the states would receive the proceeds from land sales rather than the land itself. Finally, the bill contained much stronger language defending the primacy of state water law than had the earlier Newell/Newlands bill.[152]

Recognizing the likelihood that a reclamation bill would be adopted in 1902, many midwesterners rallied behind rival legislation proposed by the chairman of the House Public Lands Committee, John F. Lacey of Iowa. By doing so, they hoped to forestall Newlands's more ambitious program. Lacey proposed that the secretary of the interior design and build *one* experimental water project containing up to 1 million acres of public land. This "national irrigation district" would allow Congress to safely assess "the cost and feasibility of such a proposition." The reclaimed land would be opened to entry under the Homestead Act at $2.50 an acre, but the national government would retain own-

ership of the water, renting it on long-term contracts to individual
users. The secretary could set the size of homesteads at less than 160
acres where appropriate. Lacey's bill appropriated $1 million for the
model project.[153] It met strong opposition in Wyoming and many of
the poorer states and territories in the West.[154] They stood little chance
of being selected as the site for the inaugural project.

The appearance of the Lacey bill was evidence that the revised
Newell/Newlands legislation would face many of the same criticisms
encountered a year earlier. The legislation's most articulate critic was
Congressman George Ray of New York, chairman of the House Judiciary Committee. In March 1902 Ray wrote the minority report for
the House Arid Lands Committee.[155] That document echoed criticisms
of the bill that had appeared in many eastern newspapers and magazines.[156] Ray fretted about future crop surpluses and a new agricultural
depression.[157] He also pointed out that since proceeds from land sales
had fed into the general treasury, and would no longer do so if the
Newlands measure was adopted, the scheme would not pay for itself
as proponents promised. Federal reclamation was just another method
to tax the many and reward the few—in this case, speculators and
railroads that hoped to inflate land values. Moreover, Ray predicted
that the sale of public lands would prove an inadequate source of revenue, so future assaults on the treasury could be expected. The general
government was undertaking work that had bankrupted a large number
of private reclamation companies. Why should it be any more
successful?[158]

Ray also raised important constitutional questions. Congress, he
charged, had no authority to undertake reclamation, especially if it
benefited private lands. The Constitution did not grant the central
government power to condemn land or water in one state to improve
land in another state, even when the land benefited was part of the
public domain. Would California freely submit as the central government stored water, in reservoirs within the Golden State, to nourish
western Nevada? Without the clear authority to build dams in one
state to benefit lands in another, the nation was opening itself to
tremendous legal challenges and expenses. Ray repeated Mead's warning: To be on the safe side the federal government would have to
purchase or condemn "every foot of soil and every water right for
hundreds of miles from the source to the mouth of such streams ex-
cepting only those now owned by the Government." And since large-
scale irrigation might sharply reduce the volume of water in streams

like the Missouri, the questionable right to divert water for irrigation might extinguish the central government's unquestioned right and responsibility to protect navigable waters. Furthermore, Congress was being asked to give up the power of the purse because the secretary of the interior would be granted almost dictatorial powers under the proposed legislation.[159]

Given frequent estimates that the federal government would reclaim as much as 100 million acres—nearly 20 percent of the remaining continental public domain—these were significant warnings. They reinforced the secretary of agriculture's ominous prediction that under Newlands's bill the cost of setting up a farm in the arid West would be "prohibitive for all except men of considerable means." The federal government would have to provide far more than irrigation works if it wanted to increase the number of western farms and farmers. The construction of dams and canals would be only the beginning; other acts, providing even greater assistance to western farmers, were sure to follow. In addition, the secretary reflected Mead's thinking when he insisted that no reclamation act could succeed unless it was part of a wholesale revision of public land laws that acknowledged the intimate relationship between agriculture and grazing.[160]

The most surprising opposition came from George Maxwell, who knew that a centralized reclamation program would benefit the railroads much more than one administred by the states.[161] Originally, he favored using *direct* federal expenditures to pay for irrigation rather than a revolving fund, and he feared that the Newell/Newlands legislation would not give the federal government adequate power to control the water it stored and made available to farmers. The committee bill would play into the hands of land and water sharks, and the states would have no power to prevent it. The legislation did not prohibit filing on government land before the construction of works began; therefore, he reasoned, nothing would prevent speculators from using the Desert Land Act or even land scrip to acquire potential project land marked off by government survey parties. Since the surveys would precede by months the formal announcement of a project, this was a major loophole. And since the proposed law did not suspend existing land laws, settlers could parlay various claims into huge estates regardless of the size of project farms subsequently specified by the secretary of the interior. True, they could receive cheap water for no more than 160 acres, but private landowners limited to that supply might still secure two to four times the water granted to farmers who took up their land later because the secretary of the interior might set farms as small as 40 acres. In any case, the 160-acre limitation could easily be evaded, and the provision that state or territorial laws would govern the distribution of water would prevent the construction of interstate projects. In lieu of the Newlands bill, in February and March 1902, Maxwell called for legislation to construct four reclamation projects already investigated and approved by the secretary of the interior: the Gila River project in Arizona, the Humboldt and Truckee projects in western Nevada, and the St. Mary's River project in Montana. Not surprisingly, each was on the line of a major railroad.[162]

President Roosevelt shared Maxwell's doubts. When he first took office, he favored the construction of a test project before the nation committed itself to a comprehensive program.[163] Newlands, however, convinced the president that the public domain was disappearing so rapidly that delay would be fatal to a comprehensive program. In addition, if the experimental project failed, Congress might use it as an excuse to reject all future appropriations for irrigation, rather than a way to learn from mistakes.[164] At the end of March and beginning of April, Roosevelt called leading western members of the House and Senate to the White House, along with Pinchot and Maxwell, and insisted he would veto the legislation, which had passed the Senate on March 2, unless basic changes were made. He demanded that the secretary of interior be given the power to withdraw from entry *all* lands within a project, not just those needed for reservoirs and ditches, and that the land should be reserved *before* formal canal surveys were made. Project land should be subject to entry only under the Homestead Act shorn of the commutation clause. And to prevent speculation in water rights, no water should be sold except to those who lived on the land. Finally, Roosevelt asked that the part of Section 8 which provided that "State and Territorial laws shall govern and control in the appropriation, use and distribution of the water rendered available by the works constructed" be replaced with the words "and the Secretary of the Interior in carrying out the provisions of this act, shall proceed in conformity with such [state] laws, and nothing herein shall in any way affect any right of any State, or of the Federal Government, or of any land owner, appropriator, or user of water in, to or from any interstate stream or the waters thereof." This wording, he hoped, would protect national rights at the same time it reassured downstream states, such as Nebraska, which worried that Wyoming would claim exclusive control over the Platte River, and Kansas, which feared that Colorado would do the same with the Arkansas.[165]

The Hansbrough bill—the Senate equivalent of the Newlands legislation—passed the Senate at the beginning of March 1902 with only one dissenting vote. It won enthusiastic support from New England senators George Hoar and Jacob Gallinger, and from Ben Tillman, Augustus O. Bacon, and Alexander S. Clay from the South. However, the House bill faced tough opposition from Speaker David B. Henderson, from the chairman of the House Appropriations Committee, Joseph G. Cannon, and from the same House leaders who had opposed the measure in 1901, particularly C. H. Grosvenor, John Dalzell, and Sereno Payne. Elwood Mead informed the president of the University of California that "I do not believe any of the irrigation bills now before Congress will pass. The foolish talk about hundreds of millions of acres of land and hundreds of millions of dollars of money has scared the eastern farmer until he lies awake nights thinking about the new peril." Senator Paris Gibson of Montana considered the chances for the conference bill as "hopeless" because no western senator seemed willing to talk the rivers and harbors bill to death. And in a letter to William M. Stewart, George Maxwell predicted that the Hansbrough/Newlands legislation had "no possible chance of passage in the House."[166]

In April the reclamation bill was amended to meet some, but not all, of Maxwell and Roosevelt's reservations. Then, in exchange for a promise from the western congressmen not to hold the appropriation bills hostage to irrigation, Henderson and the House Committee on Rules promised to give the bill a hearing if time remained at the end of the session, after Congress passed the appropriation bills and finished its other routine business.[167] They were true to their word. From April through early June, Congress was preoccupied with legislation to provide civil governments for the Philippines and Cuba and with the Panama Canal. But on June 12, the House began a two-day debate on the Newell/Newlands bill.

The formal discussion added nothing to the stock of arguments, pro and con, nor did it change many minds. The opposition raised all the old doubts about constitutionality, potential cost overruns, interstate complications, the inadequacy of western water laws, and farm surpluses. The small western delegation in the House heroically denied that federal reclamation would undermine the new agricultural prosperity of the East and Midwest. Six months earlier, Newlands had observed that the nation's population growth had been more than a match for territorial expansion. The 70 million acres he hoped the nation would water was only twice the size of Iowa, and because the construction of hydraulic works and the preparation of arid lands for the plow took time, that land would come into production much more gradually than had the farmland of the humid Midwest. Even if 1,000,000 acres of virgin desert land were added to the nation's stock of farmland each year, that was far less than the average 3,500,000 acres brought into cultivation annually during the last three decades of the nineteenth century. "Why, gentlemen, you have opened up in Oklahoma within the last few years more land capable of being watered from the heavens than can by any possibility under this bill be reclaimed in the arid region in many years," he observed.[168]

Yet for all the concern with crop surpluses, westerners in Congress thought that there was a larger issue at stake: White Americans still had a mission to extend their civilization across the continent. The critics of national reclamation should have been born a century earlier, Congressman W. A. Reeder of Kansas remarked, so that they could have "set up bars or guards all along the Allegheny Mountains. They should have prevented the people from coming West at all. . . . If they are right now, it would be better for the country lying east of the Mississippi River if we could destroy everything between the Mississippi River and the Pacific Ocean."[169]

Those who spoke against the irrigation bill were all Republicans, including George W. Ray of New York, James M. Robinson of Indiana, Joseph G. Cannon of Illinois, John Dalzell of Pennsylvania, J. A. Hemenway of Indiana, and W. P. Hepburn of Iowa. The great threat remained that Cannon would prevent the bill from coming to a vote. Roosevelt lobbied him personally. Explaining that he had never before interceded on behalf of a particular bill, the president asked his fellow Republican "not to oppose" the irrigation measure:

Believe me this is something of which I have made a careful study, and great and real though my deference is for your knowledge of legislation, and for your attitude in stopping expense, I yet feel from my acquaintance with the far West that it would be a genuine and rankling injustice for the Republican party to kill this measure. I believe in it with all my heart from every standpoint. I am just about to sign the River and Harbor bill. . . . Now this is a measure for the material benefit of your State and mine and of the other states with harbors and navigable rivers. Surely it is but simple justice for us to give to the arid regions a measure of relief, the financial burden of which will be but trifling, while the benefit to the country involved is far greater than under the River and Harbor bill. I cannot too strongly express my feeling upon this matter.[170]

Roosevelt's veiled threat to veto the river and harbor bill, and his appeal for party unity, cleared away the last major obstacle. Cannon and Grosvenor left the House early on June 13, 1902, before the formal vote was taken. On that date the House adopted the reclamation bill by a vote of 146 to 55. The margin was overwhelming, but 132 members did not vote—an unusual number given the significance of the measure—and another 18 simply answered "present" at the roll call. Much to Roosevelt's embarrassment, the bill won stronger favor from Democrats than from Republicans. Seventy-six Democrats approved the bill and only thirteen opposed it, while the Republican count was sixty-eight for and forty-two against. Strong support from the South, whose delegation approved the measure by a nearly four-to-one margin (37 for, 10 against), helped explain the Democratic edge.[171] The West voted 38 to 0 in favor, and the North and Midwest supported the legislation, 71 to 45. Nevertheless, the number of members who abstained suggested both lack of interest and an appreciation of the tremendous risks any federal reclamation program would face—as well as a fear of western reprisals.[172]

Conclusion

Editorial comment on the new law was mixed. *Harper's Weekly* proclaimed that "the bill aims at substantial and enduring effects upon the broader economic development of the nation. There was and still is in some quarters an ill-judged disposition to regard it as of merely sectional interest; but in the true analysis its significance is national, not local. . . . A hundred million acres [reclaimed] will give homes for a million families, and afford sustenance for many times that number." New York City's *Christian Work* pronounced reclamation as "one of the stupendous tasks of the opening century. . . . The first year of the Roosevelt administration has been rendered not more notable by the determination to build the Isthmian Canal than by the passage of the bill to water the dry lands of the great American West." Philadelphia's *Inquirer* announced that "millions of now sterile acres will be converted and the only ultimate regret will be that so beneficent a work was not sooner undertaken." And the *New York Times*, commenting on opposition to the Reclamation Act in Indiana, celebrated national

markets: "When the United States government paid the first install-
ment toward opening up the territory, then a wilderness, from which
the Indiana representative is now elected, it made free competition
throughout the entire continent inevitable. And it is precisely that
freedom that has made the country the most powerful and wealthy of
the world. The irrigation plan is but adding to the general resources of
the nation in furtherance of the impulse which has carried our vigorous
race from the little fringe along the Atlantic to the shores of the Pacific
and far into Asian waters."[173]

Of course, the new law also elicited plenty of editorial criticism,
even in the West. The Charlottesville, Virginia, *Progress* charged that
"the measure is to improve private lands, lands owned by giant corporations, and henceforth to be worked and sold as strictly private
property! An outrage indeed upon the farmers of the country—their
money to be used for the benefit of corporate interests in turn, to
develop an enormous source of competition! The measure is the most
vicious and outrageous piece of class legislation we have ever known."
The Lawrence, Kansas, *Journal* insisted that there was already too
much unused farmland and that the cost of reclamation would reach
at least a hundred dollars an acre, many times the early estimates. The
New York *Sun* warned that "as soon as the vast scheme of local improvement at the general cost is well under way, we shall have an
annual irrigation bill which will make the river and harbor bill or the
public building omnibus bill of past experience seem insignificant."
The *Denver Republican* warned that there were no large projects available in Colorado, and that the federal government should not "take
upon itself all the future work of reclaiming the arid lands." The tiny
Genoa Weekly Courier in western Nevada admitted that "the moment
we get a little appropriation, we will like it very much, and get very
mad if we don't get another soon, and a little bigger each time, as once
a person enjoys a 'good thing,' it makes him furious to be made to let
go. It looks now as though we will finally get on the pay roll of the
government, and that we will be pulling on the table cloth as well as
the rest of the States." Then there were journals that expressed disappointment that *more* had not been accomplished: "It is a very modest
beginning, by no means adequate to the necessities of the case," the
Salt Lake Tribune argued. "Hereafter we hope to see appropriations put
in the river and harbor bill for the reclamation of the public arid lands,
on a scale commensurate with the very great importance and magnitude of the work to be done."[174]

Meanwhile, Francis G. Newlands struggled to turn passage of the legislation to political advantage as he looked forward to a hard campaign for the U.S. Senate. As early as December 1901 Newlands had fretted that "the press very frequently gives the credit of this bill to Senator Hansbrough," fearing that his work would go unrewarded because the 1901 Newell/Newlands bill now carried the trademark of a conference committee.[175] "I hope the new irrigation bill will be of service to our State," Newlands wrote to a confidant three days after the act passed. "I feel quite done up after the strain and heat of the contest. I have been working on this night and day since Congress met. Even those who were with me had no expectation that the bill would finally pass. Senator Teller assured me that he knew that the attitude of the leaders of the House was such toward it that it would never pass and a Democratic member from Georgia told me yesterday that he regarded the irrigation fight as the best organized Congressional fight that he had ever seen."[176] F. H. Newell and George Maxwell quickly acknowledged Newlands's role in securing the new law. "I doubt whether any one else realizes as well as I do," Maxwell wrote in July, "how much the great results achieved for irrigation in this session of Congress were due to your personal efforts and influence."[177]

Nevertheless, Newlands, nominally a Democrat, suffered as Roosevelt heaped praise on his own party and warned both Secretary of Interior Ethan Hitchcock and Secretary of Agriculture James Wilson to ignore Newlands: "Interviews that I am sure are faked have appeared in which you are represented as stating that Mr. Newlands was entitled to the credit of passing the irrigation measure. Now, as a matter of fact, I never consulted with him or said a thing to him about my message, although I did consult Senators Stewart and Warren and Congressmen Mondell, Long, and Burkett. If the interviews are not true, I should think that a brief statement from you to that effect might be good, as Newlands is evidently trying to use your interviews as a campaign document."[178] After the Nevada legislature elected him to the Senate that winter, Newlands took little direct interest in the work of the new Reclamation Service. He moved on to other issues, ranging from antitrust legislation to comprehensive river basin planning. He became more and more impatient with local concerns, more and more detached from Nevada politics. Nevertheless, like Francis E. Warren, who was in many respects Newlands's antithesis, he never attained the stature of a George Norris or Hiram Johnson—western politicians who used natural resource issues to build national reputations.

That was ironic because the Reclamation Act of 1902 was certainly the boldest piece of legislation ever enacted pertaining to the trans-Mississippi West.[179] In June 1902 neither friend nor critic of the legislation could have predicted how little impact it would have during the next few decades—until Hoover Dam ushered in the "high dam era" and multiple-purpose projects. The thirty irrigation projects created during Theodore Roosevelt's two terms contained only about 3 million acres, and much of that land had been irrigated before 1902. This was a far cry from the 60–100 million acres irrigation boosters had promised would transform the arid West into a region of small farms. It was not an auspicious beginning. Within a decade, critics of federal reclamation in the Department of Agriculture pointed out that the U.S. Reclamation Service served less than 3 percent of the irrigated acreage in the arid West, and about 30 percent of the project land was unsettled. To officials in Agriculture the message was clear: There was no need for a federal program and there never had been.[180]

These critics forgot that in 1902 one of the prime justifications for national aid was that only the nation could build irrigation works *in advance of actual need*. The whole enterprise would have been impossible if the federal government had waited until settlers were on the ground. Nevertheless, Congress did exhibit many blind spots in 1902. For example, it ignored an important lesson from the history of nineteenth-century land policy. Every attempt by the government to sell land on credit had been a disaster—an object lesson in naivete, bad luck, selfishness, and greed that did not bode well for the Reclamation Act. As one writer warned in 1899: "The [credit] system [of the early nineteenth century] engulfed large numbers in hopeless debt and called for the repeated intervention of the government, to save men from the consequences of their own acts. Laws for this purpose were in force during nearly half the lifetime of the credit system; and even then, reversions and forfeitures were not uncommon."[181] The 1902 law gave farmers ten years to repay the cost of dams and canals, but Congress had not resolved the problem of what to do with those who defaulted on payments, except to cancel or extend the debt. Its failure to address this matter was all the more important because the prospect of a "tenant class" on the public domain was much greater in 1902 than it had been in the early decades of the nineteenth century. The cost of farming had soared, and the price of unimproved land and the expense of irrigation constituted a small part of the typical outlay for fencing, grading, seed, farm machinery, livestock, and barns and houses.

Worse still, the centralization and planning promised by the new law were largely illusory. Since 1803 the states had fought to gain access to the proceeds of public land sales, if not to the lands themselves. They received millions of acres from the public domain before 1902, but very little revenue. The Newlands Act not only pledged 51 percent of the proceeds from land sales to reclamation within the state where the land was sold, it set the precedent for later grants of the proceeds from rentals of grazing and mineral lands and the licensing of hydroelectric power sites. The Reclamation Act was the father of "revenue sharing."[182] Moreover, as the Reclamation Act disbursed money to the states, it also prevented coordinated or unified water resource management in Washington. It vested enormous power in the secretary of the interior, ensured that the Reclamation Fund and the River and Harbor Fund would be forever separate, and guaranteed that neither the secretary of war nor the secretary of agriculture would play any part in the selection, construction, and operation of irrigation projects.

Under the 1902 law, reclamation was largely self-contained and self-sufficient. The West secured what appeared to be a continuing source of revenue independent of changes in political leadership in Washington, and of good or bad economic times. As the *Genoa Weekly Courier* proudly declared: "It is perhaps the only bill ever passed which furnishes so complete, comprehensive and automatic a plan of action." Newlands predicted that through land sales and the repayment of construction costs, at least $150 million would become available to the Reclamation Fund over the ensuing thirty years.[183] However infeasible or unnecessary a water project was, once started it could be carried to completion. This increased the power of local water users, who recognized that in the absence of annual reviews by Congress, getting a project approved was the big hurdle. In any case, project feasibility was difficult to determine. The Reclamation Act acknowledged—by its offer of "free" land and interest-free loans—that reclamation could not pay for itself. Projects had to be evaluated as much for "intangible benefits" as for direct economic returns.[184]

The most important feature of federal reclamation was that it reflected diversity in unity. The West had learned to act in concert, to use its power to achieve common goals, but localism had not been surmounted. Within the West, old fears remained. The forest reserve policy was widely regarded as a failure; why should federal reclamation be any different? Washington was too remote, the West was too large and diverse, and easterners were too unsympathetic for the program to live up to expectations. The Reclamation Act did not unify the West, it simply provided something for everyone. "By looking at the bill you will find a lame, bungling effort to accomplish an impossible blending of the views of the President for national control and the contrary view of platforms and constitutions for State control," Congressman James M. Robinson of Indiana correctly observed.[185] A good example was the contrast between the secretary of the interior's absolute freedom to select project sites and the requirement that he spend 51 percent of the proceeds of land sales within the state where the lands were located. The reasons for support of federal reclamation varied dramatically within the region. However, most westerners saw it mainly as a benefits program, a way to stimulate local economic development. Supporting the construction of irrigation projects was no different from supporting the construction of state prisons or hospitals; each expanded the economic horizon.

This should remind us that the Reclamation Act was revolutionary, but not "radical." The 1902 law has been portrayed as a sharp departure from nineteenth-century land policies, which emphasized individualism and self-reliance; as a challenge to the power of state legislatures in the West as well as the power of Congress; and as the substitution of a rational process of screening public works projects (as opposed to the river and harbor free-for-alls). Such interpretations are open to question. So is the idea that Theodore Roosevelt's conservation policies were motivated primarily by the ethics of order and efficiency. According to William Henry Harbaugh, Roosevelt blended "the scientific outlook and his moralistic conception of the public interest. . . . And though he was repeatedly criticized, rebuffed, and insulted, he refused to be thwarted or even to compromise significantly."[186] Yet by encouraging pet bureaus and special commissions, Roosevelt did as much to discourage as to promote coordinated water resource planning. It is also important to remember that he played an important role in defining the *limits* of reclamation legislation. He applauded nationalism and the family farm, but not paternalism. In 1900 Newlands publicly suggested that as part of its homemaking function the central government should prepare the public lands for settlement as well as build reservoirs. But Roosevelt despised any program that threatened the "moral fiber" of Americans. Under his leadership, federal reclamation would be a form of "demographic planning," a policy to redress a population imbalance, not an experiment in socialism or community building.[187] In the end, the Reclamation Act simply expanded the Homestead Act—a decidedly nineteenth-century measure—to suit the new conditions of the arid West. It reaffirmed that, in spite of the vast economic changes that had taken place since the Civil War, the self-sufficient, independent family farm should remain the linchpin of American society, free from centralized planning and control.

In 1902 there were plenty of justifications for tightening federal control over water, but the Reclamation Act pandered to home rule and institutionalized fragmentation. Section 8 of the act ratified a medley of state and territorial water laws that crippled coordinated planning in its infancy. It gave the U.S. Supreme Court the perfect excuse to rule in *Kansas* v. *Colorado* (1907)[188] that the central government had no undefined or hidden water rights of its own, even on interstate streams. The conflict between the states' rights and nationalist interpretations of western water law continued well into the twentieth century, but the chance of asserting effective federal control steadily shrank.[189] Contrary to appearances, the decentralizers won a signal victory in 1902, one destined to have a profound influence on water policy in the twentieth century.

9

Conclusion:
The Fragmented West

In 1931, John Ganoe became the first professional historian to survey the evolution of federal water policy in the nineteenth century. In a brief article, "The Origin of a National Reclamation Policy," he argued that Congress followed a logical, predictable course from 1877 to 1902 and that the 1902 law was an appropriate response to a real need. The Desert Land Act (1877) and Carey Act (1894) demonstrated that neither private enterprise nor the states could reclaim the West alone. Before 1894, the year when private capital dried up in the region, support for federal construction of hydraulic works was "insignificant." Yet by 1897, when the Chittenden report was published, national involvement appeared inevitable—not only because most arid states were poor and faced interstate conflicts over shared lakes and streams, but because of the need to develop each storage site to its full potential and coordinate the operations of competing works. George Maxwell based his publicity campaign on Chittenden's report, and Francis G. Newlands and Theodore Roosevelt provided the necessary political leadership to secure a national program. Ganoe anticipated later writers in several ways: He claimed that the irrigation movement passed through logical phases; he suggested that federal reclamation was the result of the inability of private enterprise and the states to respond to the massive drought of the late 1880s and early 1890s and the depression of the 1890s; he implied that the dictates of science and efficiency played an important part in the reclamation movement; and he intimated that reclamation was an elitist rather than a broad-based reform, one in which western farmers played little part. The Reclamation Act of 1902, according to Ganoe, was a mature, deliberate, well-conceived measure that resulted from years of policy experimentation.[1]

Ganoe performed a valuable historical service by piecing together a complicated story, but he looked mainly at events in Washington rather than the arguments or leadership of the reclamation movement at the local, state, or territorial level. This oversight was partially remedied by Stanley Roland Davison in a provocative dissertation belatedly published in 1979.[2] *Leadership of the Reclamation Movement, 1875–1902* was a diatribe against federal reclamation that anticipated later criticisms by "free market economists." There was nothing heroic or praiseworthy about the events leading up to the Reclamation Act, Davison insisted, because in 1902 neither the West nor the nation needed any additional irrigated land. The depression of 1893 was a great blow to the West, but it followed years of frenzied private construction. By that year, the most feasible irrigation projects were already complete, and they included millions of acres of unsettled land. The market for irrigated farms was saturated. Until the middle 1890s, the leaders of the reclamation movement only asked for "legislation to clarify the question of ownership of water, to permit private acquisition of the necessary lands for reservoirs and canals, and to encourage settlement by individuals of small means. Government surveys were welcome, and government studies of stream flow; some public agency might even work out the plans for dams and other structures"—but no direct federal involvement was contemplated.[3]

To Davison, the leaders of the reclamation movement were a rag-tag band of explorers, military officers, writers, land speculators, railroad barons, and impractial dreamers who knew little about agricultural conditions in the arid West. They were obsessed with subduing and peopling the region, and to them it really did not matter whether reclamation was economically feasible or not. They were men and women looking for a cause, and they transformed the irrigation movement into a panacea for all the nation's problems. The turning point came in 1893, when, in a speech at the Los Angeles irrigation congress, John Wesley Powell pointed out that there was not sufficient water left in the West's streams to serve all the land already under ditch, let alone to launch entirely new projects. That sobering thought was not well received. Once the high priest of the movement, Powell now questioned a basic article of faith, and for that he was excommunicated. In the following years, as practical businessmen lost interest in reclamation, the movement became ever more detached from economic conditions in the West. "Realizing the necessity of convincing the country that the benefits would be nationwide," Davison observed, "the reclamationists made full use of all the emotional appeals that could be wrung out of the situation, and followed by a misrepresentation of many of the facts involved."[4] In short, a program that had dubious value to potential farmers was sold as a boon to the whole society. Emotion triumphed over reason; the promise that reclamation would pay for itself mocked the lessons of history.

Davison argued that the Reclamation Act of 1902 represented the failure of democracy itself. He noted that slavery, prohibition, and immigration restriction had all become emotionally charged issues, and he pondered whether "a wave of sentimentalism has to precede congressional action on many matters where it might seem that reason should be the controlling faith." Nevertheless, he emphasized that the Reclamation Act of 1902 was not a logical culmination of past policies—quite the contrary. It came about not just because of the social problems the nation faced, but because of "rising sentimentalism toward Indians, cowboys, and western life in general" during the 1880s and 1890s—a reaction to the perceived closing of the frontier.[5]

Davison's work had little influence compared to that of Samuel P. Hays. Hays's *Conservation and the Gospel of Efficiency: The Progressive Conservation Movement, 1890–1920* is probably the most influential history of conservation and natural resources ever published.[6] Much more than a book about conservation, it represented the first flowering of the "organizational synthesis," and it anticipated themes later explored by Robert Wiebe in *The Search for Order, 1877–1920.*[7] The new organizational society was built on rapidly changing technology, the bureaucratization of government and business, professionalization, and the transition of American society from relatively small, independent communities to larger regional and national associations and identities. Most of all, power became increasingly concentrated in the new society.[8] The organizational revolution touched every aspect of American life, from the structure of the corporation to the unionization of labor, from the growth of unified school districts to the rise of metropolitan newspapers, and from the nationalization of markets to reform movements such as Populism and Progressivism.

Natural resource policies interested Hays because they reflected bureaucratization and "modernization," changes in both the structure of government and in American society as a whole. He rejected earlier views of the Progressive movement, which pitted "the people" against "the interests," or democracy against corporate monopoly.[9] The conservationists were an elite, not a mass movement; they were not anticorporation or antimonopoly; and they did not attempt to redistribute the nation's wealth. Conservation was, instead, the child of specialists from a wide variety of newly emerging fields, such as hydrology, agronomy, forestry, and geology, and it transferred many decisions about how natural resources should be allocated and used from the marketplace or the floor of Congress to new resource bureaucracies, such as the Reclamation Service (after 1907, the Reclamation Bureau). Foresters decided how much timber to cut each year; agronomists decided how many livestock the public grazing lands could support; and hydrologists decided how much water was available and where to build reservoirs. The "gospel of efficiency" replaced the gospel of political expediency.[10]

Hays argued that the reclamation movement was rooted in a deep faith in the ability of science and technology to improve human lives and reform society. That movement "gave rise to the term 'conservation' and to the concept of planned and efficient progress which lay at the heart of the conservation idea." It did so by introducing new concepts of resource management, including comprehensive river-basin planning and "multiple use." The arguments for and against reclamation offered in the years from 1898 to 1902, Hays implied, were little more than window dressing. The movement began with the Powell Irrigation Survey, which Hays insists "anticipated direct federal financing" of reclamation projects. After the demise of the Irrigation Survey, Frederick H. Newell—an engineer trained at MIT—continued as chief hydrographer of the USGS to gather the streamflow data he hoped would one day become the foundation for a federal program. Unlike the leaders of the more traditional Army Corps of Engineers, he placed the standards of his profession before the dictates of Congress. As secretary of the National Geographic Society in 1892–93 and 1897–99, and as secretary of the American Forestry Association, Newell demonstrated a keen understanding of the related uses of natural resources. For example, he recognized the importance of protecting forests to preserve water flows. In 1902, he succeeded in removing reclamation from the political arena. Newell was lucky to win the support not only of Francis G. Newlands, but also of Theodore Roosevelt, who favored federal reclamation partly to strengthen the family farm, partly because of his "love for the out-of-doors," and partly because he admired "organization and efficiency in economic affairs."[11]

Hays suggested that the 1902 law was enacted in spite of the West rather that because of it, a theme explored at greater length in William Lilley and Lewis Gould's "Western Irrigation Movement, 1878–1902," published in 1966.[12] Lilley and Gould claimed that from the late 1870s on, westerners recognized the need to "create the agricultural base necessary for a stable society and to substitute the promise of a viable economy for the burden of a colonial one." Unfortunately, the region was led by "political amateurs and economic innocents" who failed to recognize that irrigation was too complex and expensive for private enterprise; only the federal government could do the job. Westerners discarded one scheme after another to prop up and encourage private enterprise. The Powell Survey, Wright Act, cession, and Carey Act were examples of the tenacity with which they clung to a laissez-faire economy. Finally, the region was saved from itself by Newlands and Roosevelt, both easterners by birth: "Newlands was the rarest kind of Westerner. In contrast to his colleagues, he regarded rational planning, orderly economic development, and stronger political institutions as components essential to any 'thoroughly organized [irrigation] system.'" The Nevada congressman had broken with western "laissez-faire traditions" in 1889, but he found no help within his own state. His 1902 bill represented a "deliberate obliteration of private enterprise.... With the Newlands Act in operation, no possible phase of reclamation remained open to private enterprise." According to Lilley and Gould, westerners generally opposed the Newlands bill, and only when the illness of his wife forced Francis Warren to leave Washington in March 1902 was Newlands able to push the legislation through Congress. When Warren returned, he found solid support for the bill in other parts of the nation. Consequently, he and the other members of the "state party" threw their support behind the legislation, hoping it could be amended later.[13]

Lilley and Gould, as well as Hays, saw great advantages to centralized power; Donald Worster did not. Worster argued that the Reclamation Act of 1902 was the foundation of a "hydraulic society," an empire similar to those of the ancient world. In all times and all places, he maintained, irrigation eventually leads to the emergence of powerful elites that undermine democratic government and values. In the twentieth-century West, the power of those elites was reinforced by the dominant capitalist ethos. Reclamation produced a managed landscape, and it destroyed the region's democratic promise. Worster was mainly concerned with the period since World War II—when "the two forces of government and private wealth achieved a powerful alliance, bringing every major western river under their unified control and perfecting a hydraulic society without peer in history"[14]—but the turning point came in the last decade of the nineteenth century and the first decade of the twentieth. "By the 1890s, the West had gone as far as it could on its own hook," Worster contended. "It had tried partnerships, theocracy, foreign and local capital—and still most of the rivers ran on freely to the sea. . . . So they [westerners] raised their voices in one loud, sustained chant that could be heard all the way to Washington, D.C.: 'We need the state!'" Thereafter, the "federal government took firm charge of the western rivers, furnishing the capital and engineering expertise to lift the region to a higher plateau of development."[15] Implicit in his view of the stages of reclamation development—even though Worster admitted that the stages overlap and that they are punctuated by "plateaus"—is the persistent myth that state action largely displaced private enterprise after 1902,[16] and that it produced an autocratic elite that sharply reduced the independence and autonomy of western water users.

The Ganoe, Davison, Hays, Lilley and Gould, and Worster interpretations have much in common. Most are presentistic. Davison looks backward from the massive welfare program national irrigation had become by the 1950s; Hays searches for the origins of modern American society and the bureaucratic state; and Worster sees environmental degradation, social injustice, and the perversion of democratic ideals in the modern American West. Davison and Worster, in particular, reduce complicated history to little more than a morality play. With few exceptions, their "players" are one-dimensional: fools, innocents, and victims pitted against self-serving technocrats, politicians, and predatory capitalists. Occasionally a hero, such as Powell, struts across the stage, but believable men—let alone good ones—are hard to find. However satisfying this view is to many modern readers who are disenchanted with American society, it ignores the context of reclamation: local political and economic conditions, the legal structure, the depression of 1893, the Populist movement, and many other forces that impeded planning and coordinated action.

The study of the West must begin from the ground up, rather than from the top down; the parts must be understood before sense can be made of the whole. Most of these authors find a stages-of-development theory attractive because they look at the West as a whole—or in Worster's case generalize about the West based largely on California's experience—and fail to appreciate the region's diversity. As early as the 1870s, support for federal reclamation was strong in some parts of the West, particularly California, and it coexisted with rival policies, such as irrigation districts and cession. Even in 1902, it was only one alternative, not the inevitable by-product of earlier policy failures.

The asssumption that the 1902 law was the only or even best remaining policy option does not square with the facts. The choice in that year was not private versus public control, or state versus national development. As mentioned in the last chapter, in the years from 1898–1902 the state party in Wyoming, Idaho, and other Rocky Mountain states argued that the federal government should build dams, leaving the construction of main canals and the allocation of water to the states. While the Reclamation Act nominally concentrated power over national irrigation in the hands of the secretary of the interior, many western politicians thought that the letter of the law was far less important than how it would be administered. Congress might not control the Reclamation Fund, but federal reclamation could not prosper without strong politial support from the western states. The amount of power that had shifted to Washington remained to be seen. Moreover, in 1902 many westerners hoped that reclamation would progress on many levels. If the central government restricted itself to the construction of interstate projects, the states could tackle intrastate projects on private land or on land ceded by the federal government, and private companies could construct smaller projects which appeared infeasible in 1902 but might become more attractive as federal reclamation lured potential settlers into the West.

An even larger theme raised by the Reclamation Act is that of fragmentation, a theme that has been largely ignored by western historians.[17] That there was centralization during the Progressive era is undeniable, but most of it derived not from a quest for efficiency or professionalization, but rather as a response to industrialization and rapid population growth. As Morton Keller has pointed out, the federal system did much to protect the power of individual states, which retained almost complete control over education, civil rights, and public health. A strong argument can be made that the "modernization" of the West in the early decades of the twentieth century resulted far more from the rapid expansion of secondary education and state highways than from national resource policies.[18]

More to the point, the evidence that reclamation went hand in hand with rational planning or efficiency is scant. Although the Powell survey responded to the ethics of efficiency when it reserved reservoir sites and public lands in the late 1880s, it was also responding to insistent appeals from local developers. And even though the Reclamation Act was designed in part to shield the Reclamation Service from the grass roots, it did not and could not do so. The new agency may have managed to escape graft and waste, but it could not escape federalism. To protect its turf, the service was, from the beginning, forced to seek allies in Congress. Most were from western states and demanded a payoff for their constituents in exchange for their votes. As for efficiency, the engineers who staffed the Reclamation Bureau certainly had an expertise not shared by the officers of the General Land Office, who had supervised the Carey Act projects. But their professional training did not lead to comprehensive project planning, let alone accountability. F. H. Newell, the bureau's first director, was a first-rate hydraulic engineer, but he knew little or nothing about agronomy, psychology, or "rural sociology." He built good, strong dams, but specialization, if not professionalization, militated against seeing the whole problem of reclaiming the arid West. Under the circumstances, it is not surprising that no coherent water or land policy emerged from Washington.

Moreover, the mere creation of new federal agencies did not centralize power. Rival bureaus often worked at cross purposes, and their functions overlapped. For example, from 1898 to 1905, the Forest Service under Gifford Pinchot and the General Land Office squabbled over control of the national forests and grazing policies, and the Reclamation Bureau fended off frequent attacks from the Office of Irrigation Investigations in the USDA and from the Army Corps of Engineers. Both Newell and Pinchot sought to coordinate the activities of their two agencies, particularly in the creation of national forests to protect watersheds and streamflow, but their bureaucratic relationship was always tense. Officials in the Reclamation Service thought that the Forest Service's sympathy for large cattle and sheep growers would imperil the West's water supply, and, by the end of the Roosevelt Administration, Newell wanted to divert money from the sale of timber and grazing leases into the Reclamation Fund. On the other hand, Pinchot, who as early as 1903 had sought to consolidate the work of the USGS, General Land Office, and Forest Service in the USDA, eventually favored the creation of a new cabinet post, a Department of Natural Resources, to coordinate virtually *all* natural resource policies. Of course, he hoped to head the new department.[19]

Many changes in natural resource policies during the "Progressive Era" were more apparent than real. Thus the Inland Waterways Commission (1907–8), which is often taken as the highwater mark of conservation during the Roosevelt presidency, was symptomatic of the fact that Roosevelt had not been able to break down the barriers between rival federal bureaus and agencies. In his *Autobiography*, Pinchot concluded that in 1907 and 1908,

> every separate Government agency having to do with natural resources was riding its own hobby in its own direction. Instead of being, as we should have been, like a squadron of cavalry, all acting together for a single purpose, we were like loose horses in a field, each one following his own nose. Every bureau chief was for himself and his own work, and the devil take all the others. Everyone operated inside his own fence, and few were big enough to see over it. They were all fighting each other for place and credit and funds and jurisdiction. What little co-operation there was between them was an accidental, voluntary, and personal matter between men who happened to be friends.[20]

At the state level, the diversity of western water laws was potent evidence of the power of localism.[21] In fact, virtually all water law reforms were undertaken not in the name of rationality and bureaucratic order, but, rather, because one group of water users sought dominance over another, or one community, region, or state sought to gain a competitive advantage over another. In California, the Wright Act—which was strongly supported in southern California and just as strongly opposed in the Sacramento Valley—was entirely beyond state regulation in the nineteenth century. After 1889, California had no state engineering office, and Wright Act projects were administered by local farmers, speculators, and businessmen, not experts. The Golden State was not unusual. Everywhere in the arid West, engineers complained that private enterprise produced poorly constructed, inefficient canals, but no state gave an administrative commission the power to supervise the construction of public works. And while Wyoming attempted to expand state control over water rights and established an arid lands board to supervise the construction of Carey Act projects, its state legislature never provided the money to create the bureaucracy necessary to centralize authority.

If any part of the nation ever contained the relatively autonomous "island communities" Robert Wiebe wrote about, it was not the West. The region was always aware of its dependence on distant markets and financial centers. This was as true of the California wheat industry as of silver mining in Nevada or cattle ranching in Wyoming. Nevertheless, mercantile thinking, the persistent fear of private and public monopolies, and regional and intercommunity rivalries resisted centralization. The assumption that one community's gain was, inevitably, another's loss defined the West as much as aridity. The water story illustrates the way institutions resist change and the ways people find to preserve their autonomy. Everywhere in the nation, the transition to the "modern state" has been uneven and irregular, but in many ways it is more appropriate to see "modern" institutions grafted onto anachronistic ones than to see one set inexorably replacing another.[22] Whether any "rational" or "efficient" water policy could have been adopted for the entire West is problematical given the size, limited tax base, and divisions within the arid states. Federalism created many Wests, and that legacy persists.

Notes

Preface

1. Walter Prescott Webb, *The Great Plains* (Boston, 1931). In particular, see the map of the "Great Plains Environment" following page four.
2. F. H. Newell, "Water," in Louis Havemeyer, ed., *Conservation of Our Natural Resources* (New York: Macmillan Co., 1931), p. 117.
3. W. Eugene Hollon, *The Great American Desert, Then and Now* (New York, 1966).
4. Donald Worster, *Rivers of Empire: Water, Aridity, and the Growth of the American West* (New York, 1985); also see Worster's "New West, True West: Interpreting the Region's History," *Western Historical Quarterly,* 18 (April 1987), pp. 141–56.
5. See, for example, Walter Prescott Webb, "The West: A Plundered Province," *Harper's,* 169 (Aug. 1934), pp. 355–64, and *Divided We Stand: The Crisis of a Frontierless Democracy* (New York, 1937).
6. Worster, *Rivers of Empire,* p. 15.
7. Worster, "New West, True West," p. 152.
8. See, for example, Theodore Steinberg, *Nature Incorporated: Industrialization and the Waters of New England* (Cambridge, Mass., 1991).

Chapter 1

1. Louis Hartz, *The Founding of New Societies: Studies in the History of the United States, Latin America, South Africa, Canada, and Australia* (New York, 1964), pp. 3–48; Samuel P. Huntington, *Political Order in Changing Societies* (New Haven, 1968), pp. 93–139; J. Rogers Hollingsworth, "The United States," in Raymond Grew, ed., *Crises of Political Development in Europe and the United States* (Princeton, N.J., 1978), pp. 163–95; Morton Keller, "Social Policy in Nineteenth-Century America," in Donald T. Critchlow and Ellis W. Hawley, *Federal Social Policy: The Historical Dimension* (University Park, Pa., 1988), pp. 99–115; Daniel Bell, "The End of American Exceptionalism," *The Public Interest,* 41 (Fall 1975), pp. 193–224; Charles C. Bright, "The State in the United States During the Nineteenth Century," in Charles Bright and Susan Harding, eds., *Statemaking and Social Movements: Essays in History*

and Theory (Ann Arbor, Mich., 1984), pp. 121–58; Charles Tilly, "Reflections on the History of European State-Making," in Charles Tilly, ed., *The Formation of National States in Western Europe* (Princeton, N.J., 1975), pp. 3–83.

2.   J. G. A. Pocock, *The Machiavellian Movement: Florentine Political Thought and the Atlantic Republican Tradition* (Princeton, 1975); Gordon S. Wood, *The Creation of the American Republic, 1776–1787* (Chapel Hill, N.C., 1969); Gerald Stourzh, *Alexander Hamilton and the Idea of Republican Government* (Stanford, Calif., 1970); Arthur M. Schlesinger, Jr., "The Theory of America: Experiment or Destiny?" in *The Cycles of American History* (Boston, 1986), pp. 3–32.

3.   Charles G. Haines, *The American Doctrine of Judicial Supremacy* (New York, 1914); Huntington, *Political Order in Changing Societies*, pp. 98–100.

4.   For analyses of political parties that place greater emphasis on ideology, see Daniel Walker Howe, *The Political Culture of the American Whigs* (Chicago, 1979); Robert Kelley, *Battling the Inland Sea: American Political Culture, Public Policy, and the Sacramento Valley, 1850–1986* (Berkeley, 1989); and Kelley, *The Cultural Pattern in American Politics: The First Century* (New York, 1979).

5.   Arthur M. Schlesinger, Jr., "The Short Happy Life of American Political Parties," in *The Cycles of American History*, pp. 256–76; Theodore J. Lowi, "Party, Policy, and Constitution in America," in William Nisbet Chambers and Walter Dean Burnham, *The American Party Systems: Stages of Political Development* (New York, 1967), pp. 238–76; Stephen Skowronek, *Building a New American State: The Expansion of National Administrative Capacities, 1877–1920* (Cambridge, Mass., 1982), pp. 24, 29; James Q. Wilson, "The Rise of the Bureaucratic State," *The Public Interest*, 41 (Fall 1975), pp. 81–82.

6.   For an introduction to a vast literature, see Harry N. Scheiber, "Government and the Economy: Studies of the 'Commonwealth' Policy in Nineteenth-Century America," *Journal of Interdisciplinary History*, 3 (Summer 1972), pp. 135–51; and Robert A. Lively, "The American System: A Review Article," *Business History Review*, 29 (March 1955), pp. 81–96.

7.   Carter Goodrich, "Internal Improvements Reconsidered," *Journal of Economic History*, 30 (June 1970), pp. 296–97; E. C. Kirkland, *A History of American Economic Life* (New York, 1969), pp. 164–65, 131–70; Stuart Bruchey, *The Wealth of the Nation: An Economic History of the United States* (New York, 1988), pp. 43–47.

8.   Loren P. Beth, *The Development of the American Constitution, 1877–1917* (New York, 1971), p. 74; Arthur N. Holcombe, *State Government in the United States* (New York, 1916), p. 106; Leslie Lipson, *The American Governor from Figurehead to Leader* (Chicago, 1939), pp. 9–30.

9.   James Bryce, *The American Commonwealth* (New York, 1915), vol. 1, p. 542.

10.   William R. Brock, *Investigation and Responsibility in the United States, 1865–1900* (Cambridge, 1984), pp. 47–48; Beth, *The Development of the American Constitution*, p. 79; Lipson, *The American Governor from Figurehead to Leader*, pp. 22–30; Arthur F. Bentley, *The Process of Government* (Cambridge, Mass., 1967), pp. 360–81.

11.   Gerald D. Nash, *State Government and Economic Development: A History of Administrative Policies in California, 1849–1933* (Berkeley, 1964), pp. 179, 181, 185; Ronald E. Shaw, *Erie Water West: A History of the Erie Canal, 1792–1854* (Lexington, Ky., 1990), p. 253.

12.   Morton Keller, *Affairs of State: Public Life in Late Nineteenth Century America* (Cambridge, Mass., 1977), pp. 112–14, 319, 423; Bryce, *American Commonwealth,* vol. 1, pp. 496, 527, 530–32, 532 (quotation), 565–66; Beth, *Development of the American Constitution,* pp. 74, 92. Keller notes that the debt carried by all levels of government declined from 11 percent per $100 of wealth in the United States in 1870 to little more than 3 percent in 1890 (p. 329).

13.   Leonard D. White, *The Jacksonians: A Study in Administrative History, 1829–1861* (New York, 1954), pp. 479–80. Also see Matthew A. Crenson, *The Federal Machine: Beginnings of Bureaucracy in Jacksonian America* (Baltimore, 1975).

14.   Wallace D. Farnham, "'The Weakened Spring of Government': A Study in Nineteenth-Century American History," *American Historical Review,* 68 (April 1963), pp. 662–80, esp. 675–76. Also see Farnham, "Railroads in Western History: The View from the Union Pacific," in Gene M. Gressley, ed., *The American West: A Reorientation* (Laramie, Wyo., 1966), pp. 95–109. Just as Congress was reluctant to use its constitutional power to incorporate, it rejected countless other opportunities to direct economic development. For example, although it enacted a national bankruptcy act in 1867, which might have increased the regulatory power of the federal government and decreased the power of the states, it rescinded the law in 1878, abdicating all authority over that aspect of economic life. See Kermit Hall, *The Magic Mirror: Law in American History* (New York, 1989), p. 93.

15.   Leonard White, *The Republican Era, 1869–1901* (New York, 1958), p. 2 (quotation); Keller, *Affairs of State,* pp. 102–4, 314.

16.   Robert Harrison, "The 'Weakened Spring of Government' Revisited: The Growth of Federal Power in the Late Nineteenth Century," in Rhondri Jeffreys Jones and Bruce Collins, eds., *The Growth of Federal Power in American History* (Dekalb, Ill., 1983), p. 63; Richard L. McCormick, "The Party Period and Public Policy: An Exploratory Hypothesis," *Journal of American History,* 66 (Sept. 1979), pp. 279–98; Lowi, "Party, Policy, and Constitution in America," pp. 273–74; Sidney Ratner, *American Taxation: Its History as a Social Force in Democracy* (New York, 1942), pp. 39–40.

17.   Keller, *Affairs of State,* pp. 309–10; Richard Franklin Bensel, *Sectionalism and American Political Development, 1880–1980* (Madison, Wis., 1984).

18.   Maris A. Vinovskis, "Have Social Historians Lost the Civil War? Some Preliminary Demographic Speculations," *Journal of American History,* 76 (June 1989), pp. 51–55; Bensel, *Sectionalism and American Political Development,* pp. 63–67, 70; Fred A. Shannon, *The Centennial Years: A Political and Economic History of America from the Late 1870s to the Early 1890s* (New York, 1967), pp. 151–52.

19.   Keller, *Affairs of State,* pp. 167, 381–82; Bryce, *American Commonwealth,* vol. 1, p. 179; Shannon, *Centennial Years,* pp. 88–90, 148.

20.   Daniel McCool, *Command of the Waters: Iron Triangles, Federal Water Development, and Indian Water* (Berkeley, 1987), pp. 29–30.

21.   Bryce, *The American Commonwealth*, pp. 197–98; White, *The Republican Era*, pp. 72–76; Keller, *Affairs of State*, pp. 300, 305–7; John Garraty, *The New Commonwealth, 1877–1890* (New York, 1968), p. 234; Beth, *The Development of the American Constitution*, pp 32–34.

22.   David Rothman, *Politics and Power: The United States Senate, 1869–1901* (Cambridge, Mass., 1966), pp. 4, 19, 39–42, 54, 71–72, 88, 260.

Chapter 2

1.   I have examined the origins and historiography of nineteenth-century western water law in "Enterprise and Equity: A Critique of Western Water Law in the Nineteenth Century," *Western Historical Quarterly*, 18 (Jan. 1987), pp. 15–37. For a sampling of the historical literature on the origins of water law in California during the 1850s, see Douglas R. Littlefield, "Water Rights During the California Gold Rush: Conflicts over Economic Points of View," *Western Historical Quarterly*, 14 (Oct. 1983), pp. 415–34; Donald J. Pisani, "The Origins of Western Water Law: Case Studies from Two California Mining Districts," *California History*, 70 (Fall 1991), pp. 242–57 and 324–25; Gordon R. Miller, "Shaping California Water Law, 1781–1928," *Southern California Quarterly*, 55 (Spring 1973), pp. 9–42; and Donald J. Pisani, "The Crucible of Western Water Law," in *From the Family Farm to Agribusiness: The Irrigation Crusade in California and the West, 1850–1931* (Berkeley, 1984), pp. 30–53. I have profited enormously from Littlefield's thoughtful and provocative article, which traces three leading water cases in Nevada and El Dorado counties from miners' arbitration committees to the California supreme court. Water, of course, had long been a subject of litigation in the East, particularly during the 1820s–1840s. Large textile mills in Massachusetts dammed streams as a source of power, and New England courts anticipated prior appropriation. See Theodore Steinberg, *Nature Incorporated: Industrialization and the Waters of New England* (Cambridge, Mass., 1991); Joseph K. Angell, *A Treatise on the Law of Watercourses* (Boston, 1874); and Morton Horwitz, *The Transformation of American Law, 1780–1860* (Cambridge, Mass., 1977).

2.   Rodman W. Paul, *California Gold: The Beginning of Mining in the Far West* (Cambridge, Mass., 1947), p. 166.

3.   Benjamin Hibbard, *History of the Public Land Policies* (New York, 1924), pp. 512–15; Gerald D. Nash, *State Government and Economic Development: A History of Administrative Policies in California, 1849–1933* (Berkeley, 1964), pp. 31–34.

4.   John R. Umbeck, *A Theory of Property Rights with Application to the California Gold Rush* (Ames, Iowa, 1981), pp. 71–73.

5.   Neal Harlow, *California Conquered: War and Peace on the Pacific, 1846–1850* (Berkeley, 1982), pp. 297–98.

6.   John F. Davis, *Historical Sketch of the Mining Law in California* (Los Angeles, 1902), p. 12.

7.   Joseph Ellison, *California and the Nation, 1850–1869: A Study of the*

Relations of a Frontier Community with the Federal Government (Berkeley, 1927), pp. 55–57, 61–62, 74.

8. Charles E. Haas, "Early California Courts," *The State Bar Journal* (California), 10 (July 1935), p. 175.

9. *California Statutes* (1851), p. 51.

10. Charles J. Hughes, "The Evolution of Mining Law," in *Report of the Twenty-Fourth Annual Meeting of the American Bar Association Held at Denver, Colorado, August 21, 22, and 23, 1901* (Philadelphia, 1901), p. 337.

11. *Hicks* v. *Bell,* 3 Cal. 219 (1853). Also see *Stoaks* v. *Barrett,* 5 Cal. 39 (1855).

12. *Cal. Stats.* (1850), p. 203; (1852), p. 158; Gregory Yale, *Legal Titles to Mining Claims and Water Rights in California, under the Mining Laws of Congress of July, 1866* (San Francisco, 1867), pp. 44, 52–57; Nash, *State Government and Economic Development,* p. 36.

13. *Cal. Stats.* (1850), p. 219.

14. For example, see Miller, "Shaping California Water Law, 1781–1928," pp. 28–29.

15. Pisani, *From the Family Farm to Agribusiness,* pp. 41–45. Also see the discussion of the 1854 law in the next chapter.

16. J. S. Holliday, *The World Rushed In: The California Gold Rush Experience* (New York, 1981), p. 300.

17. For example, see Lauson B. Patterson, *Twelve Years in the Mines of California* (Cambridge, Mass., 1862), pp. 54–85; *Alta California* (San Francisco), April 2, 1850.

18. A. Delano, *Life on the Plains and among the Diggings* (Buffalo, 1854), pp. 280–81; S. Weston, *Four Months in the Mines of California: or, Life in the Mountains* (Providence, 1854); Daniel B. Woods, *Sixteen Months at the Gold Diggings* (New York, 1851), pp. 123–24, 133–35, 143–53, 171–75. Also see the *Alta California* (San Francisco), Dec. 16, 1851, Feb. 18, 1852, Feb. 10, 1853.

19. Woods, *Sixteen Months at the Gold Diggings,* pp. 145–48.

20. *Evening Bulletin* (San Francisco), March 1, 1859; *Alta California,* Jan. 29, 1859.

21. Ground sluicing involved the excavation of small ditches through gravel deposits. Water turned into the ditch peeled away layers of soil in the banks, and the gold settled to the bottom along with the heavier sands. Once the water was cut off, the "pay dirt" could be removed and panned. This technique flourished during the wet years of 1850–52.

22. *Alta California,* June 7, 1853.

23. The best survey of early hydraulic mining in California is Rossiter W. Raymond, *Mining Industry of the States and Territories of the Rocky Mountains* (New York, 1874), pp. 390–424. Also see W. W. Jenkins, "History of the Development of Placer Mining in California," *Publication of the Historical Society of Southern California, 1906* (Los Angeles, 1907), pp. 69–77; Paul, *California Gold,* pp. 147–70; Otis Young, *Western Mining* (Norman, Okla., 1970), pp. 125–31; Robert L. Kelley, *Gold vs. Grain: The Hydraulic Mining Controversy in California's Sacramento Valley* (Glendale, Calif., 1959), pp. 21–56; Philip Ross May, *Origins of Hydraulic Mining in California* (Oakland,

Calif., 1970); and Robert M. Wyckoff, *Hydraulicking: A Brief History of Hydraulic Mining in Nevada City, California* (Nevada City, Calif., 1962).

24.   *Nevada Journal* (Nevada City, Calif.), Jan. 7, 1853.

25.   George Black, *Report on the Middle Yuba Canal and Eureka Lake Canal, Nevada County, California* (San Francisco, 1864), p. 8.

26.   The *Stockton Journal* editorial is as reprinted in the *Nevada Journal*, Nov. 29, 1851. The second quotation is from the *Nevada Journal*, Jan. 3, 1852.

27.   *Alta California* (San Francisco), June 15, 1852.

28.   John Steele, *In Camp and Cabin: Mining Life and Adventure in California During 1850 and Later* (Lodi, Wis., 1901), p. 30; Louise Amelia Knapp Smith Clapp, *The Shirley Letters* (Santa Barbara, Calif., 1970), p. 122.

29.   Enos Christman, *One Man's Gold: The Letters & Journal of a Forty-Niner* (New York, 1930), p. 272.

30.   *Sacramento Daily Union*, Sept. 10, 1888; Rodman Paul, *Mining Frontiers of the Far West, 1848–1880* (New York, 1963), pp. 90–91; J. B. Hobson, "Nevada County," in *Tenth Annual Report of the [California] State Mineralogist* (Sacramento, 1890); Titus Fey Cronise, *Agricultural and Other Resources of California* (San Francisco, 1870), p. 28; Ralph Mann, *After the Gold Rush:, Society in Grass Valley and Nevada City, California, 1849–1870* (Stanford, Calif., 1982), p. 136; Raymond, *Mining Industry of the States and Territories of the Rocky Mountains*, p. 68; May, *Origins of Hydraulic Mining in California*, pp. 10–11; "Precious Metals," in *Tenth Census of the United States* (Washington, D.C., 1885), vol. 13, p. 202; Kelley, *Gold vs. Grain*, pp. 45–46; Wyckoff, *Hydraulicking*, p. 13; Hittell, *Mining in the Pacific States of North America*, p. 80; Paul, *California Gold*, p. 164; *Prospectus of the Eureka Lake and Yuba Canal Company* (New York, 1866), pp. 5; Black, *Report on the Middle Yuba Canal and Eureka Lake Canal, Nevada County, California*, pp. 5, 30.

31.   *Alta California*, Feb. 15, Feb. 27, and June 14, 1854. Outside Nevada County, the stronghold of hydraulic mining in the 1860s and after, most water companies quickly lost their profitability. In 1869, J. Ross Browne noted ruefully that while many of the state's smaller ditches paid "very well," the large aqueducts had "almost without exception . . . proved unprofitable." At least $20 million was invested in the canals, but Browne estimated their worth at no more than 10 percent of that figure (*Resources of the Pacific Slope*, pp. 180–81). Browne discusses the mining ditches of California in detail on pp. 179–206.

32.   See, for example, the *Alta California*, April 30, 1854.

33.   William Shaw, *Golden Dreams and Waking Realities: Being the Adventures of a Gold-Seeker in the California and Pacific Islands* (London, 1851), pp. 84–85.

34.   Steele, *In Camp and Cabin: Mining Life and Adventure in California During 1850 and Later*, pp. 34–35; Helen S. Giffen, ed., *The Diaries of Peter Decker: Overland to California in 1849 and Life in the Mines, 1850–1851* (Georgetown, Calif., 1966), pp. 225–28; Holliday, *The World Rushed In*, p. 379.

35.   May, *Origins of Hydraulic Mining in California*, p. 25.

36.   *Weekly Placer Herald* (Auburn, Calif.), Aug. 9, 1856.

37.   *California Mining Journal* (Grass Valley, Calif.), Sept. 1, 1856.

38.   *San Francisco Herald* and *Daily Alta California*, Oct. 6, 1853. Also see the account of the August 1857 meeting of mining ditch owners held in Sacramento, as reported in the *Herald*, Aug. 30, 1857.

39.   *Shasta Courier*, Feb. 6, 1858.

40.   Letter from "The Committee" in the *Weekly Placer Herald*, Oct. 29, 1853.

41.   *Alta California*, April 7, 1852; also Nov. 14, Dec. 9, and Dec. 17, 1853.

42.   See, for example, the reports and resolutions of Placer County miners at Ophir and Dutch Ravine concerning the destruction of a dam erected by the Bear River Water Company, in the *Weekly Placer Herald*, Dec. 23, 1853, and Jan. 28 and Feb. 11, 1854. Also see the *Sacramento Daily Union*, Dec. 20, 1853, and the *Weekly Placer Herald*, Sept. 2, 1854.

43.   From foreign miners' tax, as quoted in Harry N. Scheiber and Charles McCurdy, "Eminent-Domain Law and Western Agriculture, 1849–1860," *Agricultural History*, 39 (Jan. 1975), p. 121.

44.   As quoted in Earl Pomeroy, "California, 1846–1860: Politics of a Representative Frontier State," *California Historical Quarterly*, 32 (Dec. 1953), p. 296.

45.   Josiah Royce, *California: From the Conquest in 1846 to the Second Vigilance Committee in San Francisco, a Study in American Character* (Boston, 1886), p. 280.

46.   *Nevada Journal*, April 22, 1853; *Alta California*, July 4, 1853.

47.   Charles H. Shinn, *Land Laws of the Mining Camps* (Baltimore, 1884), and *Mining Camps: A Study in American Frontier Government* (New York, 1885). If many mining camps were reluctant to make water private property, they were no less reluctant to authorize the buying and selling of the mineral land itself. "That mining-claims should become a subject of speculation, of sale and purchase, of transfer from owner to owner," Shinn wrote, "seems to have been foreign to the views of the earliest placer miners of California; and in some camps a man who sold his claim could not take up another." On the same page Shinn noted that "probably every man in the gold-region had been educated in the doctrine of individual ownership of land; yet this instructive return to first principles, this adoption of the ancient idea of 'free mining lands,' common to all as once the woods and fields and pastures of England were common, will ever prove an attractive theme for students of historical and social subjects" (*Mining Camps*, p. 235).

48.   The Saw Mill Flat District in California, organized in 1850, provided for a special committee, elected by the miners in general assembly, to arbitrate each dispute. In the Brown's Flat District miners appointed a panel of arbitrators who held their positions on good behavior. In other districts, arbitrators were chosen by the disputants themselves. See Shinn, *Land Laws of Mining Districts*, p. 21.

49.   As reprinted in Jane Bissell Grabhorn, *A California Gold Rush Miscellany* (San Francisco, 1934), facing p. 34. Many districts passed similar laws. See, for example, the code adopted at the Jacksonville diggings in 1850, as reprinted in Woods, *Sixteen Months at the Gold Diggings*, pp. 126–30, and the 1855 code adopted in the Oregon Gulch Mining District in Butte County and

the 1856 laws enacted by the Little Humbug Creek District in Siskiyou County, in "Mining Laws," *Tenth Census of the United States,* pp. 286, 291. Also see the resolutions of the Columbia and Ophir districts in the *Alta California,* Oct. 12 and Dec. 21, 1853.

50.   *Alta California,* Feb. 14, 1854.

51.   Tyrrell Martinez and Frank J. Drummond, "Early Mining Laws of Tuolumne and Calaveras Counties," p. 16, undated manuscript in Bancroft Library, University of California, Berkeley.

52.   "Mining Laws," *Tenth Census of the United States,* p. 297.

53.   Hittell, *Mining in the Pacific States of North America,* pp. 192–95; Shinn, *Land Laws of Mining Districts,* pp. 56–57; John Heckendorn and W. A. Wilson, *Miners & Business Men's Directory for the Year Commencing January 1st, 1856* (Columbia, Calif., 1856), p. 9.

54.   Haas, "Early California Courts," pp. 126–30, 172–75.

55.   The *State Journal's* editorial was reprinted in the *Columbia Gazette,* June 10, 1854. Apparently, this case was not appealed to the supreme court. The *Journal* did not identify it by name.

56.   Judge J. M. Howell's instructions to the jury were reprinted in the *Shasta Courier,* Aug. 19, 1854. Also see the *Weekly Placer Herald,* May 20, 1854. Even after the California supreme court handed down its 1855 decison in *Irwin* v. *Phillips,* discussed below, a judgment generally regarded as the first unequivocal statement of that court in favor of prior appropriation, Howell refused to accept the opinion as dictum. In his instructions to the jury in *Bear River and Auburn Water and Mining Co.* v. *Little York Mining Co.* (1856), a contest between two appropriators, Howell acknowledged the reasoning of the higher court but insisted that there were no absolute rights to water. Any attempt to create them, he charged, was "at utter variance with all of the adjudicated cases, subversive of the best interests of the country, and inconsistent with the law of nature." See the *Weekly Placer Herald,* Oct. 4, 1856, and the *California Mining Journal* (Nevada City, Calif.), Sept. 1, 1856.

57.   *Placer Herald,* July 26, 1856.

58.   Charles McCurdy has portrayed a California supreme court whose authority was weakened by "a rapid turnover in personnel and frequent reversals of prior decisions." Only when Stephen J. Field took charge of the high court in 1857 did it achieve "stability and doctrinal symmetry." Unfortunately, McCurdy looked at the law from the top down and failed to appreciate the depth of disagreements over water rights among the miners and district courts. See McCurdy, "Stephen J. Field and Public Land Law Development in California, 1850–1866: A Case Study of Judicial Resource Allocation in Nineteenth-Century America," *Law and Society Review,* 10 (Fall 1975), pp. 235–66, esp. pp. 236–37, 254.

59.   S. C. Wiel, "The Water Law of the Public Domain," in *American Law Review,* 43 (July–Aug. 1909), p. 484; Wiel, "'Priority' in Western Water Law," *Yale Law Journal,* 18 (Jan. 1909), p. 190; and Wiel, "Theories of Water Law," *Harvard Law Review,* 27 (April 1914), pp. 530–44. Also see Wiel's magnum opus, *Water Rights in the Western States* (San Francisco, 1905).

60.   *Hicks* v. *Bell,* 3 Cal. 219 (1853), at p. 227. The court reiterated this

dictum often in the next two decades. For example, in 1860 it insisted that "the custom of miners is entitled to great if not controlling weight" (*Brown* v. *'49 and '56 Quartz Mining Co.*, 15 Cal. 152 [1860], at p. 161).

61.   The decision of the lower court is reprinted in *Eddy* v. *Simpson*, 3 Cal. 249 (1853), at p. 250. Also see the *Daily Alta California*, Aug. 4, 1853, and the *Sacramento Daily Union*, Dec. 20, 1853.

62.   *Eddy* v. *Simpson*, 3 Cal. 249 (1853), pp. 252, 253; Littlefield, "Water Rights During the California Gold Rush," pp. 427–29.

63.   *Irwin* v. *Phillips*, 5 Cal. 140 (1855), at p. 145.

64.   Ibid., at p. 146.

65.   Ibid., pp. 146–47. For the details of this case in lower courts, see Littlefield, "Water Rights During the California Gold Rush," pp. 429–31.

66.   *Hill* v. *Newman*, 5 Cal. 445 (1855), at p. 446.

67.   *Tartar* v. *Spring Creek Water and Mining Company*, 5 Cal. 395 (1855), at p. 398.

68.   The judge's instructions are as quoted in Littlefield, "Water Rights During the California Gold Rush," p. 426.

69.   *Hoffman* v. *Stone*, 7 Cal. 47 (1857), at p. 48.

70.   *Crandall* v. *Woods*, 8 Cal. 136 (1857). *Irwin* v. *Phillips* had argued that traditional riparian rights could not exist on the public domain, but in this case between parties who both occupied land adjoining the same stream, the supreme court remarked: "The property in the water, by reason of riparian ownership, is in the nature of a usufruct, and consists, in general, not so much in the fluid as in the advantage of its impetus. This, however, must depend on the natural as well as the artificial wants of each particular country. The rule is well settled that water flows in its natural channels, and should be permitted thus to flow, so that all through whose land it passes may enjoy the privilege of using. A riparian proprietor, while he has the undoubted right to use the water flowing over his land, must so use it as to do the least possible harm to other riparian proprietors" (p. 141). Claims along the bed of a stream took precedence over subsequent diversions, even if the first party had not filed for a water right (p. 143).

71.   *Crandall* v. *Woods*, 8 Cal. 136 (1857), p. 143. Also see *Hill* v. *King*, 8 Cal. 336 (1857), at p. 338.

72.   *Kelly* v. *Natoma Water Company*, 6 Cal. 105 (1856), at p. 108.

73.   *Maeris* v. *Bicknell*, 7 Cal. 261 (1857).

74.   *Thompson* v. *Lee*, 8 Cal. 274 (1857), at p. 280. This case was a perfect example of how the court balanced rival interests. No water right could be perfected without use, but once established, rights dated from the posting of the claim, not from the beginning of ditch construction or the date of completion. This protected large water companies from blackmail by those who came on the scene after construction began, filed on water, and dug useless, small "token" ditches in the hope the company would buy them out. "If it [the right] does not commence until the canal is completed," the court had wisely observed a year earlier, "then the license is valueless, for after nearly the whole work has been done, any one, actuated by malice or self-interest,

may prevent its accomplishment; any small squatter might effectually destroy it" (*Conger* v. *Weaver,* 6 Cal. 548 [1856], at p. 558).

75.   Gregory Yale, *Legal Titles to Mining Claims and Water Rights in California under the Mining Law of Congress of July, 1866,* p. 177.

76.   *Sparrow* v. *Strong,* 70 U.S. 97 (1865), at p. 104. Section 9 of the Act of 1866 specified that "whenever by priority of possession, rights to the use of water for mining, agricultural, manufacturing, or other purposes, have vested and accrued, and the same are recognized and acknowledged by the local customs, laws, and decisions of courts, the possessors and owners of such vested rights shall be maintained and protected in the same; and the right of way for the construction of ditches and canals for the purposes herein specified is acknowledged and confirmed. . . ." U.S., *Statutes at Large,* v. 14 (1866), p. 253.

77.   For a recent survey of the environmental impact of mining, see Duane A. Smith, *Mining America: The Industry and the Environment, 1800–1980* (Lawrence, Kans., 1987).

Chapter 3

1.   *Tartar* v. *Spring Creek Water and Mining Co.,* 5 Cal. 395 (1855), at p. 398.

2.   *Hill* v. *King,* 8 Cal. 336 (1857); *McDonald & Blackburn* v. *Bear River and Auburn Water and Mining Company,* 13 Cal. 220 (1859); *Boggs* v. *Merced Mining Co.,* 14 Cal. 279 (1859); *Rupley* v. *Welch,* 23 Cal. 452 (1863); and *Ferrea* v. *Knipe,* 28 Cal. 340 (1865).

3.   *Lux* v. *Haggin,* 4 Pacific Reporter 919 (1884). The supreme court reheard the case in 1886 (*Lux* v. *Haggin,* 69 Cal. 255 [1886]). For the story and significance of this famous suit, see Donald J. Pisani, *From the Family Farm to Agribusiness: The Irrigation Crusade in California and the West, 1850–1931* (Berkeley, 1984), pp. 191–249; and Eric T. Freyfogle, "*Lux* v. *Haggin* and the Common Law Burdens of Modern Water Law," *University of Colorado Law Review,* 57 (Spring 1986), pp. 485–525.

4.   Arthur Maass, *Water Law and Institutions in the Western United States* (Boulder, Colo., 1990), pp. 11–12.

5.   *Lux* v. *Haggin,* 69 Cal. 255 (1886), at pp. 336–40. Two early Nevada cases anticipated this argument: *Vansickle* v. *Haines,* 7 Nev. 249 (1872), at p. 280; and *Union Mill & Mining Co.* v. *Ferris,* 2 Sawyer 176 (1872), at pp. 179–80. The Nevada court reversed itself in *Jones* v. *Adams,* 19 Nev. 78 (1885), which built on *Coffin* v. *Left Hand Ditch Company,* 6 Colo. 443 (1882). The rationale in the latter case—which came to be called the "Colorado doctrine" by twentieth-century legal scholars—was diametrically opposed to that in *Lux* v. *Haggin.* The Colorado court insisted that when Congress created new territories and states, those legal entities inherited full sovereignty over water. Two major arguments were cited to justify this position: first, that Congress had *implied* a transfer of control when it gave the states administrative control over the acquisition of water rights in 1866 and after; second, that it had explicitly accepted state sovereignty when it admitted Colorado and Wyoming to the Union, both of which proclaimed state ownership of water in their constitu-

tions. For a summary of the California and Colorado doctrines, see C. S. Kinney, *A Treatise on the Law of Irrigation and Water Rights and the Arid Region Doctrine of Appropriation of Waters* (San Francisco, 1912), vol. 2, pp. 1093–1124.

6.   *Thorp* v. *Freed*, 1 Mont. 651 (1872), at pp. 654, 686, amd 687; John D. W. Guice, *The Rocky Mountain Bench: The Territorial Supreme Courts of Colorado, Montana, and Wyoming, 1861–1890* (New Haven, 1972), pp. 127–28.

7.   William Hammond Hall to Elwood Mead, Oct. 4, 1889, in "Elwood Mead, Territorial & State Engineer: Incoming Correspondence from Federal Government Officials, 1888–1890," Mead Papers, Wyoming State Archives, Cheyenne; Elwood Mead, *Irrigation Institutions* (New York, 1903), pp. vi–vii, 207; F. H. Newell, *Irrigation in the United States* (New York, 1902), pp. 291–92.

Many other federal and state officials recognized the dangers of prior appropriation. See, for example, E. S. Nettleton (Colorado state engineer) to Elwood Mead, July 24, 1888, in "Elwood Mead . . . Incoming Correspondence . . . 1888–1890," Mead Papers; C. E. Dutton (John Wesley Powell's chief lieutenant on the Irrigation Survey), in "Ceding the Arid Lands to the States and Territories," H. Rep. 3767, 51st Cong., 2d sess., serial 2888 (Washington, D.C., 1891), pp. 169, 185, 186; John Wesley Powell, "Report on the Lands of the Arid Region of the United States, with a More Detailed Account on the Lands of Utah," H. Ex. Doc. 73, 45th Cong., 2d sess., serial 1805 (Washington, D.C., 1878), pp. 40–41.

8.   "Diligence" went hand in glove with beneficial use. It required the construction of water projects within a reasonable period of time, which varied from state to state. Most courts, however, were quick to grant extensions and permitted modest periodic work to keep claims alive.

9.   Mead, *Irrigation Institutions*, p. 277; Mead, *Report of Irrigation Investigations in California*, USDA Office of Experiment Stations Bulletin 100, S. Doc. 356, 57th Cong., 1st sess. (Washington, D.C., 1902), pp. 84, 85, 88, 94–95; Paul L. Murphy, "Early Irrigation in the Boise Valley," *Pacific Northwest Quarterly*, 44 (Oct. 1953), p. 178; *Eleventh Annual Report of the Director of the United States Geological Survey [1889–90], Part 2: Irrigation* (Washington, D.C., 1891), p. 236.

10.   William E. Smythe, "The Struggle for Water in the West," *Atlantic*, 86 (Nov. 1900), p. 648.

11.   *Forestry and Irrigation*, 9 (Nov. 1903), p. 524.

12.   Samuel Fortier, a leading student of agriculture in the arid West, observed in 1910: "All over the arid region individuals, associations and corporations composed of farmers have received from the courts two, three and even four times more water than their crops require under economical use. Until such evils are remedied, this region can never hope to possess that extent of irrigated land which its available water would furnish if equitably apportioned" (Samuel Fortier, "The Agricultural Side of Irrigation," in *Official Proceedings of the Eighteenth National Irrigation Congress Held at Pueblo, Colorado, Sept. 26–30, 1910* [Pueblo, Colo., n.d.], p. 335).

13.   Secretary of Agriculture James Wilson estimated that, on the average,

irrigation farmers used twice the water required. See *Eleventh National Irrigation Congress Held at Ogden, Utah, September 15–18, 1903* (Ogden, 1904), pp. 165–66.

14.   For a statement of the restrictions on prior appropriation, see *Sowards v. Meagher*, 37 Utah 212 (1910).

15.   Frank J. Trelease, "Uneasy Federalism—State Water Laws and National Water Uses," *Washington Law Review*, 55 (Nov. 1980), pp. 752–53.

16.   On the Plan of Pitic, see Michael C. Meyer, *Water in the Hispanic Southwest: A Social and Legal History, 1550–1850* (Tucson, 1984), pp. 30–37, 117, 126; John A. Rockwell, *A Compilation of Spanish and Mexican Law* (New York, 1851), pp. 445–50; Leonidas Hamilton, *Hamilton's Mexican Law* (San Francisco, 1882), pp. 110–27; Richard E. Greenleaf, "Land and Water in Mexico and New Mexico, 1700–1821," *New Mexico Historical Review*, 47 (April 1972), p. 3; Francis F. Guest, "Municipal Government in Spanish California," *California Historical Society Quarterly*, 46 (Dec. 1967), p. 307. For the plan itself, see Addendum 7 in John W. Dwinelle, *The Colonial History, City of San Francisco* (San Francisco, 1867), pp. 11–17.

17.   See, for example, Walter Prescott Webb, *The Great Plains* (Boston, 1932), p. 440; and Robert V. Hine, *The American West: An Interpretive History*, rev. ed. (Boston, 1984), p. 131.

18.   Meyer, *Water in the Hispanic Southwest*, pp. 92, 163.

19.   Betty Eakle Dobkins, *The Spanish Element in Texas Water Law* (Austin, 1959), p. 98.

20.   William Hammond Hall, *Irrigation in [Southern] California* (Sacramento, 1888), pp. 535–70; Vincent Ostrom, *Water and Politics: A Study of Water Policies and Administration in the Development of Los Angeles* (Los Angeles, 1953), pp. 27–40.

21.   *Cal. Stats.* (1850), p. 155.

22.   The 1852 law is as reprinted in Hall, *Irrigation in [Southern] California*, p. 559; *Cal. Stats.* (1854), p. 205.

23.   Lewis Publishing Company, *An Illustrated History of Los Angeles County, California* (Chicago, 1889), p. 262.

24.   *Alta California*, May 14, 1854; *Los Angeles Star*, Feb. 18, 1854.

25.   *Cal. Stats.* (1854), p. 76. In 1857, the 1854 law was expanded to include two additional counties outside the mining districts, Santa Cruz and San Luis Obispo. At this time the extent of riparian rights in California was very uncertain. The titles to 13–14 million acres of prime agricultural and grazing land granted by Spain and Mexico before 1846 remained to be adjudicated. For overviews of land policies in the 1850s, see Paul W. Gates, "California's Embattled Settlers," *California Historical Quarterly*, 41 (June 1962), pp. 99–130; and Gates, "The California Land Act of 1851," *California Historical Quarterly*, 50 (Dec. 1971), pp. 395–430.

26.   *Cal. Stats.* (1859), p. 217; (1864), p. 87.

27.   *Cal. Stats.* (1862), p. 235.

28.   *Cal. Stats.* (1864), pp. 87, 375; (1866), pp. 609, 777.

29.   *Cal. Stats.* (1862), p. 540; *Report of the California State Board of Agriculture for the Years 1864–1865* (Sacramento, 1866), app. 2, pp. 19–20; Paul

Gates, *California Ranchos and Farms, 1846–1862* (Madison, 1967), p. 81; Gerald D. Nash, *State Government and Economic Development* (Berkeley, 1964), p. 78; *Sacramento Daily Union*, Jan. 30, 1866.

30.   *Cal. Stats.* (1866), pp. 313–14.

31.   *Lux v. Haggin*, 69 Cal. 255 (1886,) at p. 365.

32.   *Cal. Stats.* (1868), p. 113; (1876), p. 547.

33.   Richard J. Hinton, *Irrigation in the United States*, 49th Cong., 2d sess., 1887, S. Misc. Doc. 15, serial 2450, pp. 95–97; Ostrom, *Water and Politics*, p. 40. In the late nineteenth century and after, Los Angeles, San Diego, Albuquerque, San Antonio, and some other communities created before the Treaty of Guadalupe Hidalgo claimed "pueblo rights" to water, rights independent of state law. See Wells A. Hutchins, *The California Law of Water Rights* (Sacramento, 1956), pp. 256, 259; Ira G. Clark, *Water in New Mexico: A History of Its Management and Use* (Albuquerque, 1987), pp. 9–23; Robert E. Clark, "The Pueblo Rights Doctrine in New Mexico," *New Mexico Historical Review*, 35 (Oct. 1960), pp. 265–83; and Richard E. Greenleaf, "The Founding of Albuquerque, 1706: An Historical-Legal Problem," *New Mexico Historical Review*, 39 (Jan. 1964), pp. 1–15. Norris Hundley, Jr., argues persuasively that the Spanish pueblo right, if it ever existed, was not the absolute grant that the courts took it to be. See his *The Great Thirst: Californians and Water, 1770s–1990s* (Berkeley, 1992), especially Chapter 2, "Hispanic Patterns: Community and Authority." Also see Daniel Tyler, *The Mythical Pueblo Rights Doctrine: Water Administration in Hispanic New Mexico* (El Paso, 1990).

34.   Hall, *Irrigation in [Southern] California*, pp. 301–2, 442.

35.   *Report of the Special Committee of the United States Senate on the Irrigation and Reclamation of Arid Lands* (Washington, D.C., 1890), serial 2707, vol. 2, p. 148.

36.   See, for example, John Norton Pomeroy, *Treatise on the Law of Water Rights* (St. Paul, 1893), p. 327.

37.   *General Laws, Joint Resolutions, Memorials, and Private Acts, Passed at the Fifth Session of the Legislative Assembly of the Territory of Colorado [1866]* (Central City, Colo., 1866), pp. 61–64. Although this statute is included with the 1866 collection, it is dated Feb. 5, 1861.

38.   Raphael J. Moses, "Irrigation Corporations," *Rocky Mountain Law Review*, 32 (1959–60), p. 528.

39.   Howard R. Lamar, *The Far Southwest, 1846–1912: A Territorial History* (New Haven, 1966), p. 91.

40.   *N.M. Stats.* (1851), p. 188; (1851–52), p. 276; Clark, *Water in New Mexico*, pp. 100–108; F. C. Barker, *Irrigation in Mesilla Valley, New Mexico*, Water Supply and Irrigation Paper 10 (Washington, D.C., 1898).

41.   *The Howell Code Adopted by the First Legislative Assembly of the Territory of Arizona* (Prescott, 1865), pp. 422–26; R. H. Forbes, *Irrigation in Arizona*, USDA Office of Experiment Stations Bulletin 235 (Washington, D.C., 1911), p. 57.

42.   Dobkins, *The Spanish Element in Texas Water Law*, p. 139.

43.   Edwin P. Arneson, "Early Irrigation in Texas," *Southwestern Historical Quarterly*, 25 (Oct. 1921), p. 128; William F. Hutson, *Irrigation Systems in*

Texas, USGS Water Supply and Irrigation Paper 13 (Washington, D.C., 1898), pp. 41–50.

44.   Thomas F. Glick, *The Old World Background of the Irrigation System of San Antonio, Texas* (El Paso, 1972), p. 53.

45.   The Texas legislature formally acknowledged rights acquired under Spanish and Mexican law in 1852. See A. A. White, "The Flow and Underflow of *Motl* v. *Boyd,"* *Proceedings, Water Law Conference, June 17–18, 1955* (Austin, 1955), p. 54. The 1852 statute was not repealed until 1913.

46.   Glick, *Old World Background of the Irrigation System of San Antonio, Texas,* pp. 4, 8, 38, 41, 42. Also see Hans W. Baade, "The Historical Background of Texas Water Law—A Tribute to Jack Pope," *St. Mary's Law Journal,* 18 (1986), pp. 1–98, esp. pp. 60, 95–96.

47.   Elwood Mead noted that the volume of the North Platte River in Wyoming reached its peak in June; the July flow was only one third that of June, and the September flow was less than 10 percent of the maximum. The North Platte was a fairly typical western stream. See *Second Biennial Report of the State Engineer to the Governor of Wyoming, 1893 and 1894* (Cheyenne, 1894), p. 131.

48.   There is no full-length biography of Pomeroy. The best introduction is Phillip S. Paludan, "John Norton Pomeroy, States Rights Nationalist," *American Journal of Legal History,* 12 (July 1968), pp. 275–93.

49.   Pomeroy, *Treatise on the Law of Water Rights,* p. 329.

50.   Ibid., p. 331.

51.   For a summary of Pomeroy's conclusions, see ibid., pp. 346–47.

52.   As of the 1880s, western courts still had not settled such fundamental questions as whether all riparian lands subdivided by the original patentee carried riparian rights, or only those immediately adjoining the stream. See Wells A. Hutchins, *The California Law of Water Rights* (Sacramento, 1956), p. 200; and Ralph H. Hess, "An Illustration of Legal Development—The Passing of the Doctine of Riparian Rights," *American Political Science Review,* 2 (Nov. 1907), pp. 15–31.

53.   Robert G. Dunbar, *Forging New Rights in Western Waters* (Lincoln, 1983), p. 13; Dale Morgan, "The State of Deseret," *Utah Historical Quarterly,* 8 (April, July, Oct. 1940), pp. 197–99; Leonard Arrington, *Great Basin Kingdom: An Economic History* (Cambridge, Mass., 1958), pp. 52–54, 241–44; George Thomas, *The Development of Institutions under Irrigation: With Special Reference to Early Utah Conditions* (New York, 1920), pp. 48, 54–58, 88–89.

54.   Morgan, "The State of Deseret," p. 225; Moses Lasky, "From Prior Appropriation to Economic Distribution of Water by the State—Via Irrigation Administration," *Rocky Mountain Law Review,* 1 (April 1929), p. 2.

55.   William R. Palmer, "Utah's Water Courts," *Reclamation Era,* 33 (Nov. 1947), pp. 233, 240, 246.

56.   *Monroe* v. *Ivri,* 2 Utah 535 (1880).

57.   Dunbar, *Forging New Rights in Western Waters,* p. 17.

58.   Gordon Bakken, *The Development of Law on the Rocky Mountain Frontier: Civil Law and Society, 1850–1912* (Westport, Conn., 1983), pp. 36–38.

59.   Dunbar, *Forging New Rights to Western Waters*, p. 82; Arthur Maass and Raymond Anderson, *". . . and the Desert Shall Rejoice": Conflict, Growth, and Justice in Arid Environments* (Cambridge, Mass., 1978), pp. 337–51; *Report of the Special Committee of the United States Senate on the Irrigation and Reclamation of Arid Lands*, vol. 2, p. 59. Apparently, Idaho courts defined some appropriative rights in the same way as Utah, perhaps because southern Idaho was first settled by Mormons. Under the "Stewart Decree" of 1906, later rights to the Boise River were shut off in dry years, and, if necessary, earlier rights were then reduced to 75 or 60 percent of decreed rights. This principle was also followed on other Idaho streams. See Murphy, "Early Irrigation in the Boise Valley," p. 184.

60.   Joseph F. Smith to William E. Smythe, Dec. 14, 1901, RG 8, Records of the Bureau of Agricultural Engineering, Box 1, "General Correspondence, 1898–Dec. 31, 1902," Federal Records Center, Suitland.

61.   *General Laws, Joint Resolutions, Memorials, and Private Acts, Passed at the First Session of the Legislative Assembly of the Territory of Colorado . . . [1861]* (Denver, 1861), pp. 67–69; *General Laws . . . [1862]* (Denver, 1862), p. 48; *General Laws . . . [1864]* (Denver, 1864), p. 58; Alvin T. Steinel, *History of Agriculture in Colorado* (Fort Collins, 1926), pp. 177–78; Dunbar, *Forging New Rights to Western Waters*, pp. 75–76; *Yunker v. Nichols*, 1 Colo. 551 (1872), at p. 566.

62.   *Acts, Resolutions and Memorials, of the Territory of Montana, Passed by the First Legislative Assembly* (Virginia City, Mont., 1866), pp. 367–69. The statute is also reprinted in *Basey v. Gallagher*, 87 U.S. 670 (1874), at pp. 674–75.

63.   *Thorp v. Woolman*, 1 Mont. 168 (1870). See also *Smith v. Denniff*, 24 Mont. 20 (1900).

64.   Mont. Stats. (1870), p. 57. This law is also reprinted in *Basey v. Gallagher*, 87 U.S. 670 (1874), at p. 675.

65.   In *Mettler v. Ames Realty Co.*, 61 Mont. 152 (1921), the Montana high court ruled that the common law doctrine of riparian rights had never prevailed in that state, but in *Thorp v. Freed*, 1 Mont. 651 (1872), at p. 688, Justice C. J. Wade observed that "the whole purpose of the [1865] statute was to utterly abolish and annihilate the doctrine of prior appropriation, and to establish an equal distribution of the waters of any given stream in the agricultural districts of the Territory. . . . If this section of the law [Section 4] does not mean that there shall be an equal distribution of the waters of a stream among all the parties concerned in such water, without any regard whatever to the date of location or appropriation, then we are utterly unable to comprehend the language used."

66.   *The Compiled Laws of Wyoming . . .* (Cheyenne, 1876), pp. 377–79.

67.   *General Laws of the Territory of Idaho Including the Code of Civil Procedure, Passed at the Eleventh Session of the Territorial Legislature* (Boise, 1881), pp. 273–75.

68.   *Drake v. Earhart*, 2 Ida. 750 (1890), at pp. 763–64.

69.   For a more thorough discussion of William Hammond Hall and water

law reform in California, see Donald J. Pisani, *From the Family Farm to Agribusiness*, pp. 154–90.

70.   See the "Annual Message of George C. Perkins to the [California] Legislature, December, 1880" and "The Irrigation Question in California: Appendix to the Report of the State Engineer to His Excellency, George C. Perkins, Governor of California, by Wm. Ham. Hall, State Engineer, October, 1880," in *Appendix to the Journals of the California Senate and Assembly*, 24th Sess., vols. 1 and 3 (Sacramento, 1881).

71.   In addition to his October 1880 report, see William Hammond Hall, "The View of the State Engineer as Contrasted with Those of the Surveyor General," in *Report of the Surveyor General, August 1, 1880 to August 1, 1882* (Sacramento, 1883), pp. 37–38; *Sacramento Daily Record-Union*, Aug. 2, 1882; Hall to Gov. George Perkins, Jan. 29, 1880, and Hall to Gov. George Stoneman, Nov. 19, 1882, in State Engineers' Papers, California State Archives, Sacramento.

72.   *Report of the Surveyor General of California, August 1, 1880 to August 1, 1882*, app. 1, pp. 30–37.

73.   *Visalia Weekly Delta* (Visalia, Calif.), Aug. 11, 1882, and Jan. 26, 1883.

74.   Sections 1410–22 of the 1872 civil code required claimants to post notice at the point of their diversion specifying the amount of water claimed, the size of their ditch, where the water would be used, and the purpose of use. Within ten days the claim had to be filed with an appropriate county recorder, although the right itself dated from the announcement of intent to divert. Work had to begin within sixty days of filing, and the claimant had to "prosecute the work diligently and uninterruptedly to completion." All those who had claimed water in the past, but had not begun construction, had twenty days to begin, on pain of forfeiting their right. The legislature did not intend to give any new sanction to prior appropriation; it simply ratified principles established by the courts. Its main purpose was to help sort out contested claims by establishing precise dates for the inception of rights. Section 1422 read: "The rights of riparian proprietors are not affected by the provisions of this title." The supremacy of riparian rights on private lands remained unquestioned. See *California Civil Code* (1872), Title VIII, Sec. 1410–22, pp. 268–70; *Palmer v. Railroad Commission*, 167 Cal. 163 (1914); and the *Biennial Report of the [California] Divison of Water Rights, November 1, 1924* (Sacramento, 1925), pp. 26–27.

75.   *Proceedings of the Constitutional Convention of Colorado, 1875 and 1876* (Denver, 1906), pp. 44, 374.

76.   Dunbar, *Forging New Rights in Western Waters*, pp. 86–98; Dunbar, "The Origins of the Colorado System of Water Right Control," *Colorado Magazine*, 27 (Oct. 1950), pp. 241–62; Dunbar, "The Significance of the Colorado Agricultural Frontier," *Agriculture History*, 34 (July 1960), pp. 119–26; and Dunbar, "History of Agriculture [in Colorado]," in Le Roy Hafen, ed., *Colorado and Its People* (New York, 1948), vol. 2, pp. 127–28. Also see Mead, *Irrigation Institutions*, pp. 222–23, 143–79.

77.   *Report of the Commission Appointed by His Excellency the Governor of the State of Colorado to Revise the Laws of the State Regulating the Appropriation, Distribution and Use of Water* (Denver, 1890), p. 7.

78.   Dunbar, *Forging New Rights in Western Waters*, p. 98; *Ninth Biennial Report of the State Engineer to the Governor of Colorado, for the Years of 1897 and 1898* (Denver, 1899), pp. 19–21; *Tenth Biennial Report of the State Engineer to the Governor of Colorado, for the Years 1899 and 1900* (Denver, 1901), p. 15; *Eleventh Biennial Report of the State Engineer to the Governor of Colorado, for the Years 1901 and 1902* (Denver, 1902), p. 25; Frank C. Goudy, "Benefits and Dangers of Private Irrigation," in *Official Proceedings of the Eighteenth National Irrigation Congress Held at Pueblo, Colorado, Sept. 26–30, 1910*, p. 42; John E. Field, "Development of Irrigation [in Colorado]," in *History of Colorado* (Chicago, 1918), vol. 1, p. 505.

79.   James E. Sherow, "Watering the Plains: An Early History of Denver's Highline Canal," *Colorado Heritage*, 4 (1988), pp. 3–13.

80.   *Denver Republican*, March 3, 1887; *Rocky Mountain News* (Denver), Feb. 12, 1891.

81.   *Rocky Mountain News*, Feb. 9, 1891.

82.   *Denver Republican*, March 8, 1887. Also see the *Republican*, Feb. 16, 1887, and the *Rocky Mountain News*, Jan. 7 and 30, Feb. 16, 24, 26, and 28, and March 3, 1887.

83.   Steinel, *History of Agriculture in Colorado*, pp. 207–8; *Colorado Farmer and Live Stock Grower*, Jan. 12 and 19, 1888.

84.   *Denver Republican*, Feb. 7, 9, 24, and 26, March 10 and 25, 1891; *Rocky Mountain News*, Jan. 16, Feb. 16 and 24, March 5, 7, 14, and 25, and April 3, 1891.

85.   *Second Biennial Report of the State Engineer to the Governor of Wyoming, 1893 and 1894* (Cheyenne, 1894), pp. 14–15; Francis Beard, ed., *Wyoming: From Territorial Days to the Present* (Chicago, 1933), vol. 1, p. 387.

86.   *Journals and Debates of the Constitutional Convention of the State of Wyoming* (Cheyenne, 1893), p. 503. Also see Brown's comments on pp. 289 and 498 of the same volume and W. E. Chaplin, "Reminiscences of a Member of the Wyoming Constitutional Convention," *Annals of Wyoming*, 12 (July 1940), pp. 176–77, 191–92, 196. Delegate Henry Coffeen of Sheridan County echoed Brown's attack on prior appropriation (*Journals and Debates*, p. 535).

87.   Dunbar, *Forging New Rights in Western Waters*, pp. 99–112. The objectives of Elwood Mead, who drafted the section of the constitution pertaining to water rights and subsequently became Wyoming's first state engineer, can be found in his "Letter to Irrigation Committee of the Constitutional Convention" (n.d. [probably fall 1889], Mead Papers). Also see Elwood Mead to Joseph Nimmo, Aug. 21, 1889, and Mead to Calvin Cobb, Sept. 30, 1889, in Mead Letterbook, Apr. 23, 1888–Aug. 16, 1890, Mead Papers.

88.   Both California and Colorado permitted the sale of water rights, even those that had not been defined by the courts. Mead recognized that titles to water could never be quieted in those states because the purchasers of rights often changed the point of diversion and even the purpose for which the water was used. He cited the simple example of three appropriators on a stream, "A" (upper), "B" (middle), "C" (lower), to illustrate the dangers of "floating rights." Assume that B has enough water, but A wants to sell to C. Any system that permitted the transfer of rights was manifestly unjust. If the water was not

being used by A, he should not be allowed to levy tribute on C for something he had obtained for nothing; the water should belong to the public. Moreover, Mead charged that it was unfair to transfer water rights from one part of a basin to another. As much as 50 percent of any diversion returned to the stream and became available for reuse downriver. Therefore, if A sold to C, part of B's supply might be taken inadvertently. For these and other reasons, Mead feared that if water rights were allowed to float on large streams, "it would be absolutely beyond the power of human effort or human intelligence to sort them out" (*Second Biennial Report of the State Engineer to the Governor of Wyoming, 1893 and 1894*, pp. 45–46).

89.   Dunbar, *Forging New Rights in Western Waters*, pp. 108–11; Beard, *Wyoming*, vol. 1, pp. 448–50.

90.   Elwood Mead defined the basic principles of the new code of laws in "Irrigation," in *Report of the Industrial Commission, 1901* (Washington, D.C., 1901), vol. 10, p. ccv. Also see Clarence T. Johnston (Wyoming state engineer), "State Progress in Irrigation, Wyoming," in *Official Proceedings of the Eleventh National Irrigation Congress Held at Ogden, Utah, September 15–18, 1903*, pp. 402–4.

91.   *Third Biennial Report of the State Engineer to the Governor of Wyoming, 1895 and 1896* (Cheyenne, 1897), pp. 40–46; *Seventh Biennial Report of the State Engineer to the Governor of Wyoming for the Years 1903 and 1904* (Laramie, 1905), p. 67.

92.   Elwood Mead, unpublished "Report of the State Engineer," dated Oct. 30, 1890, in "Elwood Mead, State Engineer: Correspondence, Observation of River Heights, Various Reports, 1889–1897," Mead Papers.

93.   *Fourth Biennial Report of the State Engineer to the Governor of Wyoming for the Years 1897 and 1898* (Cheyenne, 1898), p. 12; *Sixth Biennial Report of the State Engineer to the Governor of Wyoming for the Years 1901 and 1902* (Laramie, 1902).

94.   Beard, *Wyoming*, pp. 504–5; *Third Biennial Report of the State Engineer to the Governor of Wyoming, 1895 and 1896*, pp. 74–75, 161, 164–65; *Sixth Biennial Report of the State Engineer to the Governor of Wyoming for the Years 1901 and 1902*, p. 16; *Cheyenne Daily Leader*, Feb. 24, 1895.

95.   *First Biennial Report of the State Engineer to the Governor of Wyoming, 1891 and 1892*, pp. 60–61; *Second Biennial Report of the State Engineer to the Governor of Wyoming, 1893 and 1894*, p. 29; *Fifth Biennial Report of the State Engineer to the Governor of Wyoming for the Years 1899 and 1900* (Cheyenne, 1901), pp. 73–74, 77–78, 165–71.

96.   For an overview of this question in the late nineteenth and early twentieth centuries, see Donald J. Pisani, "State vs. Nation: Federal Reclamation and Water Rights in the Progressive Era," *Pacific Historical Review*, 51 (Aug. 1982), pp. 265–82.

97.   *Journal of the Constitutional Convention of the State of Wyoming* (Cheyenne, 1893), p. 291; Dunbar, *Forging New Rights in Western Waters*, p. 108.

98.   *Report of the Special Committee of the United States Senate on the Irrigation and Reclamation of Arid Lands*, vol. 1, p. 130.

99.   *Report of the Secretary of the Interior, 1889* (Washington, 1890), p. xxvi; *Report . . . 1890* (Washington, D.C., 1890), p. xiii; *Report . . . 1891* (Washington, 1891), pp. xi–xii.
100.   James D. Richardson, *A Compilation of the Messages and Papers of the Presidents, 1789–1897* (Washington, D.C., 1900), vol. 9, p. 205; *Report of the Commissioner of the General Land Office, 1896* (Washington, D.C., 1896), p. 60; *Proceedings of the Seventh Annual Session, National Irrigation Congress [1898]* (Cheyenne, 1899), p. 144; "Our Rapidly Growing Irrigation Areas," *Scientific American,* 82 (March 3, 1900), p. 131.
101.   See, for example, S. 2104, 51st Cong., 1st sess., introduced Jan. 16, 1890 (Plumb); S. 2740, 52d Cong., 1st sess., introduced March 28, 1892 (Perkins); and H.R. 5954, 52d Cong., 1st sess., introduced Feb. 13, 1892 (Pickler).
102.   H.R. 7504, 51st Cong., 1st sess., introduced Feb. 26, 1890 (Peters).
103.   Ira Clark, "The Elephant Butte Controversy: A Chapter in the Emergence of Federal Water Law," *Journal of American History,* 61 (March 1975), pp. 1006–33; "Equitable Distribution of the Waters of the Rio Grande," S. Doc. 229, 55th Cong., 2d sess., serial 3610 (Washington, D.C., 1898), pp. 47–177; W. W. Follett, "Irrigation on the Rio Grande," *Proceedings of the Sixteenth National Irrigation Congress [1908]* (Albuquerque, n.d.), pp. 136–52; Follett, "The Interstate Uses of Water," in *Official Proceedings of the Eighteenth International Irrigation Congress, 1910,* pp. 315–25.
104.   Clarence T. Johnston and Joseph A. Breckons, "Water-Right Problems of Bear River," USDA Office of Experiment Stations Bulletin 70 (Washington, D.C., 1899); Elwood Mead, "The Influence of State Borders on Water-Right Controversies," *Independent,* 57 (Dec. 8, 1904), pp. 1302–3.
105.   John Wesley Powell, "Ceding the Arid Lands to the States and Territories," pp. 112, 135; *Congressional Record,* 52d Cong., 1st sess., July 21, 1892, pp. 6499–6500; and undated statement to the press from the early 1890s in RG 57, Records of the United States Geological Survey, Powell Irrigation Survey, Box 1, D-121, National Archives, Washington, D.C. Also See Orren M. Donaldson, "Irrigation and State Boundaries: A Problem of the Arid West and Its Solution," *Irrigation Age,* 8 (Feb. 1895), pp. 47–53.
106.   H.R. 1, 52d Cong., 1st sess., Jan. 5, 1892 (Herbert); H.R. 433, 52d Cong., 1st sess., Jan. 7, 1892 (Lanham).
107.   As early as 1889, Senator William Morris Stewart of Nevada introduced a bill to permit federal circuit courts to hear disputes over interstate water rights. In 1901, he proposed a special federal board to adjudicate all water rights from source to terminus of interstate streams. However, Senator Henry Teller of Colorado, a staunch proponent of states' rights, argued that there was no need to debate the plan because most arid states would flatly reject it. *Pacific Rural Press,* 37 (Feb. 9, 1889), p. 128; *Congressional Record,* 57th Cong., 1st sess., Dec. 4 and 9, 1901, pp. 130, 216–18; *Forestry and Irrigation,* 8 (Feb. 1902), p. 76.
108.   *Official Proceedings of the Third International Irrigation Congress, Held at Denver, Colorado, Sept. 3rd to 8th, 1894,* pp. 64, 65, 91; "An Address to the People of the United States by the National Irrigation Congress, Fourth Annual Session, at Albuquerque, N. Mexico, September 16–19, 1895," S. Doc.

253, 54th Cong., 1st sess., serial 3354 (Washington, D.C., 1896), p. 3; *Annual Report of the Commissioner of the General Land Office for the Fiscal Year Ending June 30, 1896* (Washington, D.C., 1896), pp. 60, 81; *Proceedings of the Seventh Annual Session, National Irrigation Congress [1898]* (Cheyenne, 1899), pp. 143–44.

109.   Bakken, *The Development of Law on the Rocky Mountain Frontier: Civil Law and Society, 1850–1912,* pp. 129–30. Also see Bakken's chapter, "Rocky Mountain Water Law," pp. 69–89.

110.   L. L. Dennett to George Pardee, Nov. 25, 1911, Dennett file, George Pardee Collection, Bancroft Library, University of California, Berkeley; William E. Smythe, "The Struggle for Water in the West," *Atlantic,* 86 (Nov. 1900), p. 650.

Chapter 4

1.   Ray A. Billington, *America's Frontier Heritage* (Albuquerque, 1974), p. 165.

2.   Ralph C. Morris, "The Notion of a Great American Desert East of the Rockies," *Mississippi Valley Historical Review,* 13 (June 1926), pp. 190–200; Eugene Hollon, *The Great American Desert: Then and Now* (New York, 1966).

3.   Washington Irving, *The Adventures of Captain Bonneville, U.S.A., in the Rocky Mountains and the Far West* (Norman, Okla., 1961), p. 372.

4.   W. B. Hazen, *Our Barren Lands: The Interior of the United States* (Cincinnati, 1875), p. 52.

5.   Myron Angel, *History of Nevada* (Oakland, 1881), p. 135.

6.   For a fuller discussion of the perceived limitations of irrigation, see Donald J. Pisani, *From the Family Farm to Agribusiness: The Irrigation Crusade in California and the West, 1850–1931* (Berkeley, 1984), pp. 61–70. George Perkins Marsh, the American ambassador to Italy and the author of *Man and Nature; or Physical Geography as Modified by Human Action* (New York, 1864), published one of the best discussions of the dangers of irrigation based on his travels in North Africa, India, the Middle East, and Europe. See Marsh, "Irrigation: Its Evils, the Remedies, and the Compensations," S. Misc. Doc. 55, 43d Cong., 1st sess. (Washington, D.C., 1874), serial 1584, pp. 3–12.

7.   For example, John S. Hittell, in *The Resources of California* (San Francisco, 1863), devoted eighty-seven pages to agriculture (pp. 151–237) but none to irrigation. He insisted there were 40 million acres of arable land in the state, about 40 percent of California's total area.

8.   *Rocky Mountain News* (Denver), March 9, 1895. Also see the *News* for Feb. 24, 1895, and the *Daily Territorial Enterprise* (Virginia City, Nev.), March 5, 1889.

9.   A. Bower Sageser, "Editor Bristow and the Great Plains Irrigation Revival of the 1890s," *Journal of the West,* 3 (Jan. 1964), p. 84; Sageser, "Windmill and Pump Irrigation on the Great Plains, 1890–1910," *Nebraska History,* 48 (Summer 1967), pp. 107–18; B. A. McAllister, "Irrigation by the Use of Windmills," *Irrigation Age,* 6 (Jan. 1894), pp. 18–20; J. W. Gregory, "Irrigation in Southwest Kansas: Experience Teaches Practicability of Pump Irrigation," *Irrigation Age,*

8 (Jan. 1895), pp. 13–17; W. C. Fitzsimmons, "The Wind-Mill in Irrigation," *Irrigation Age*, 11 (Jan. 1897), pp. 15–16; C. C. Hutchinson, "Irrigation by Pumping in Kansas," *Irrigation Age*, 8 (June 1895), p. 175; "Pumping Water for Irrigation," *Forestry and Irrigation*, 8 (March 1902), pp. 130–33; Philip Eastman, "Windmill Irrigation in Kansas," *Review of Reviews*, 29 (Feb. 1904), pp. 183–87.

10.   "Texas," *Irrigation Age*, 3 (Jan. 1893), p. 247; *Report of the Secretary of Agriculture, 1891* (Washington, D.C., 1892), p. 58. Also see Clark Spence, *The Rainmakers: American 'Pluviculture' to World War II* (Lincoln, 1980).

11.   Mary Hargreaves, "The Dry-Farming Movement in Retrospect," *Agricultural History*, 51 (Jan. 1977), pp. 152–54; James C. Malin, *The Grassland of North America: Prolegomena to Its History with Addenda and Postscript* (Gloucester, Mass., 1967), pp. 227–42; Walter Prescott Webb, *The Great Plains* (Boston, 1931), pp. 366–74; John A. Widtsoe, *Dry-Farming* (New York, 1911), pp. 351–81; L. E. Hicks, "Storage of Storm-Waters on the Great Plains, *Science*, 19 (April 1, 1892), pp. 183–84; F. L. Kent, "Value of Drought Resistant Crops," in *Official Proceedings of the Fourteenth National Irrigation Congress Held at Boise, Idaho, Sept. 3–8, 1906* (Boise, 1906), pp. 198–203.

12.   "The Protection of Irrigation Works," *The Forester*, 5 (Feb. 1899), p. 44.

13.   William Ellsworth Smythe, *The Conquest of Arid America* (New York, 1905), p. 39. For earlier statements see, *First, Second and Third Annual Reports of the United States Geological Survey of the Territories for the Years 1867, 1868 and 1869* (Washington, D.C., 1873), p. 236, and *Tenth Annual Report of the U.S. Geological and Geographical Survey, 1876* (Washington, D.C., 1878), p. 319.

14.   Charles Howard Shinn, "Irrigation in the United States," *Popular Science Monthly*, 43 (June 1893), p. 159.

15.   E. Goodrich Smith, "Irrigation," in *Report of the Commissioner of Patents, for the Year 1860* (Washington, D.C., 1861), pp. 204 and 215; Charles D. Poston, "Irrigation," in *Report of the Commissioner of Agriculture, 1867* (Washington, D.C., 1868), p. 199; "Report of the Commissioner of the General Land Office," in *Report of the Secretary of the Interior, 1868* (Washington, D.C., 1868), p. 140; *Report of the Commissioner of Agriculture, 1873* (Washington, D.C., 1874), p. 283; "Our Arid Regions and the Rainfall," *Popular Science Monthly*, 36 (Feb. 1890), p. 572; T. S. Van Dyke, "Fertilizing with Irrigation," *Irrigation Age*, 1 (May 30, 1891), p. 64; I. W. Hart, "Exhaustion of Our Soil," *Irrigation Age*, 2 (Nov. 15, 1891), p. 291; J. W. Sanborn, "Fertilizing Powers of Waters," *Irrigation Age*, 2 (Jan. 15, 1892), p. 379; "Both Food and Drink," *Irrigation Age*, 14 (May 1900), p. 260.

16.   The Platte Land Company sold land under the High Line Canal near Denver. The untitled, undated circular is in a collection of bound pamphlets entitled *Land Companies in Colorado*, at the Bancroft Library, University of California, Berkeley.

17.   "The East and the West," *Irrigation Age*, 14 (Jan. 1900), p. 138.

18.   Donald J. Pisani, "Forests and Conservation, 1865–1890," *Journal of American History*, 72 (Sept. 1985), pp. 340–59.

19.   Chicago *Tribune*, March 1, 1880, as reprinted in the San Francisco

Argonaut, March 13, 1880. For similar statements see the *Reno Evening Gazette,* Jan. 6, 1881; George W. Haight, "Riparian Rights," *Overland Monthly,* 5 (June 1885), p. 568; Richard J. Hinton, *Irrigation in the United States* (Washington, D.C., 1887), pp. 71, 82, 134; *Kansas Farmer* (Topeka), Sept. 25, 1889; "Our Arid Regions and the Rainfall, p. 572; James Realf, "The Irrigation Problem in the Northwest," *Arena,* 4 (June 1891), pp. 70–71; A. B. Wyckoff, "Irrigation," *Journal of the Franklin Institute,* 140 (Oct. 1895), p. 248.

20.   McAllister, "Irrigation by the Use of Windmills," p. 20.

21.   *Report of the Commissioner of Agriculture, 1887* (Washington, D.C., 1888), p. 44.

22.   Richard J. Hinton, *Irrigation in the United States: Progress Report for 1890* (Washington, D.C., 1891), p. 15.

23.   See, for example, John Wesley Powell, "The Lesson of Conemaugh," *North American Review,* 149 (Aug. 1889), p. 152.

24.   Truman G. Palmer, "Irrigation and Beet Sugar," in *Official Proceedings of the Fourteenth National Irrigation Congress Held at Boise, Idaho, Sept. 3–8, 1906,* p. 208. Also see the statement of T. S. Van Dyke, as reprinted in the *Daily Territorial Enterprise* (Virginia City, Nev.), Feb. 14, 1889.

25.   T. Evans, "Orange Culture in California," *Overland Monthly,* 11 (March 1874), pp. 241–42.

26.   Robert C. Nesbit and Charles M. Gates, "Agriculture in Eastern Washington, 1890–1910," *Pacific Northwest Quarterly,* 37 (Oct. 1946), p. 290.

27.   "Census Figures on Irrigation," *Irrigation Age,* 3 (Nov. 1892), p. 193; F. H. Newell, "Water Supply for Irrigation," in *Thirteenth Annual Report of the United States Geological Survey [1891–92],* Part 3: Irrigation (Washington, D.C., 1893), pp. 30–31; C. A. Gregory, "The Social, Economic and Financial Phases of Irrigation," *Irrigation Age,* 6 (April 1894), p. 155; "Progress of Irrigation," *Scientific American,* 72 (Jan. 19, 1895), p. 38; "Progress of Irrigation," *Journal of the Franklin Institute,* 139 (April 1895), p. 311.

28.   Timothy Paige Dictation, p. 11, in the Hubert Howe Bancroft Collection, Bancroft Library, University of California, Berkeley; *Report of the Special Committee of the United States Senate on the Irrigation and Reclamation of Arid Lands* (Washington, D.C., 1890), vol. 2, p. 198; *Irrigation Age,* 1 (June 15, 1891), p. 73; Charles M. Gates, "A Historical Sketch of Economic Development of Washington since Statehood," *Pacific Northwest Quarterly,* 39 (July 1948), p. 223; Nesbit and Gates, "Agriculture in Eastern Washington, 1890–1910," pp. 286–87; E. S. Nettleton, "The Successes and Failures of Canal Building and the Causes Thereof," in *Proceedings of the Seventh Annual Session, National Irrigation Congress [1898]* (Cheyenne, 1899), p. 55.

29.   *Twelfth Census of the United States, 1900* (Washington, D.C., 1901), vol. 1, p. 11; Hinton, *Irrigation in the United States: Progress Report for 1890,* pp. 21, 52, 54; *Annual Report of the State Board of Horticulture of the State of California for 1892* (Sacramento, 1893), pp. 44–45.

30.   See, for example, John N. Irwin, "A Great Domain by Irrigation," *Forum,* 12 (Feb. 1892), pp. 740–50; and Charles H. Brough, "Advantages of Reclaiming the Remaining Irrigable Land," *Irrigation Age,* 14 (Feb. 1900), pp. 159–64.

31.   *Report of the Secretary of Agriculture, 1890* (Washington, D.C., 1890),

p. 486; William Ellsworth Smythe, "A Trinity of Forces," *Irrigation Age,* 1 (July 1, 1891), pp. 97–98.

32.   Leo Marx, *The Machine in the Garden: Technology and the Pastoral Ideal in America* (New York, 1964), pp. 106–44.

33.   George D. Clyde, "History of Irrigation in Utah," *Utah Historical Quarterly,* 27 (1959), p. 29; *Irrigation Age,* 1 (May 1, 1891), p. 19. On early irrigation in Utah, also see George Thomas, *The Development of Institutions under Irrigation: With Special Reference to Early Utah Conditions* (New York, 1920); Leonard Arrington and Dean May, "'A Different Mode of Life': Irrigation and Society in Nineteenth-Century Utah," *Agricultural History,* 49 (Jan. 1975), pp. 3–20; and George L. Strebel, "Irrigation as a Factor in Western History, 1847–1890" (Ph.D. diss., University of California, Berkeley, 1965). Despite its broad title, Strebel's study is limited to Utah.

34.   Leonard J. Arrington, "Economic History of a Mormon Valley," *Pacific Northwest Quarterly,* 46 (Oct. 1955), p. 99. Also see Arrington, "Early Mormon Communitarianism: The Law of Consecration and Stewardship," *Western Humanities Review,* 7 (Autumn 1953), pp. 341–69; and A. F. Doremus, "Irrigation in Utah," in *Official Proceedings of the Eleventh National Irrigation Congress Held at Ogden, Utah, September 15–18, 1903* (Ogden, 1904), pp. 269–72.

35.   Ray P. Teele, *Irrigation in the United States* (New York, 1915), pp. 194–95; J. Ulrich, "Conditions Favorable and Unfavorable to Irrigation," *Irrigation Age,* 15 (Jan. 1901), pp. 117–18; *Report of the Special Committee of the United States Senate on the Irrigation and Reclamation of Arid Lands,* pp. 44–46.

36.   William Ellsworth Smythe devoted a chapter to the Greeley Colony in *The Conquest of Arid America;* see pp. 77–91. Also see Donald Worster, *Rivers of Empire: Water, Aridity and the Growth of the American West* (New York, 1985), pp. 83–88, 93–96; Frank Hall, *History of Colorado* (Chicago, 1889), vol. 1, pp. 531–49; Robert G. Athearn, *The Coloradans* (Albuquerque, 1976), pp. 106–27; Alvin T. Steinel, *History of Agriculture in Colorado* (Fort Collins, 1926), pp. 384–90; David Boyd, *A History: Greeley and the Union Colony of Colorado* (Greeley, 1890); James F. Willard, *The Union Colony at Greeley, Colorado* (Boulder, 1918); "Ralph Meeker Tells of Early Days in [Greeley] Colony," in Nathan Meeker Collection, Box 6, Colorado Historical Society, Denver, Colorado; *Report of the Commissioner of Agriculture, 1870* (Washington, D.C., 1871), pp. 569–72; William E. Smythe, "Real Utopias in the Arid West," *Atlantic,* 79 (May 1897), pp. 599–609; Smythe, "The Colony Builders," *Irrigation Age,* 14 (Nov. 1899), pp. 60–66; and Hinton, *Irrigation in the United States,* pp. 129–32.

37.   William E. Pabor, *Farmers' Guide to Northern Colorado* (Denver, 1882), p. 4; David Boyd, "Greeley's Irrigation Methods," *Irrigation Age,* 2 (Jan. 1, 1892), p. 353; Boyd, *Greeley and the Union Colony of Colorado,* pp. 59–60; Boyd discussed irrigation extensively in chapter 7 and noted that "upon this rock the whole enterprise came near splitting" (p. 88).

38.   R. A. Cameron to N. C. Meeker, May 7, 1871, Box 6, Meeker Collection. In the same box see Charles E. Thompson to Horace Greeley, May 23, 1870; H. T. West to N. C. Meeker, April 30 and May 7, 1870; James L. Lee to N. C. Meeker, May 23, 1870; and R. A. Cameron to N. C. Meeker, May 5, 1870.

39.   Pisani, *From the Family Farm to Agribusiness*, pp. 121–28; Smythe, *Conquest of Arid America*, pp. 92–105; Virginia E. Thickens, "Pioneer Agricultural Colonies of Fresno County," *California Historical Quarterly*, 25 (March and June 1946), pp. 17–38, 168–77; Arthur Maass and Raymond Anderson, ". . . *and the Desert Shall Rejoice": Conflict, Growth, and Justice in Arid Environments* (Cambridge, Mass., 1978), pp. 146–70; Oscar O. Winther, "The Colony System of Southern California," *Agricultural History*, 27 (July 1953), pp. 94–102; Frederick D. Kershner, Jr., "George Chaffey and the Irrigation Frontier," *Agricultural History*, 27 (Oct. 1953), pp. 115–22; Merlin Stonehouse, *John Wesley North and the Reform Frontier* (Minneapolis, 1965), pp. 211–32; R. Lois Gentilcore, "Ontario, California and the Agricultural Boom of the 1880s," *Agricultural History*, 34 (April 1960), pp. 77–87.

40.   Smythe, *Conquest of Arid America*, pp 191–93; Stanley Roland Davison, *The Leadership of the Reclamation Movement, 1875–1902* (New York, 1979), pp. 223–30; *Irrigation Age*, 8 (March 1895), pp. 70–71, 76–81; Smythe, "Eight Years Afterward," *Out West*, 19 (Sept. 1903), pp. 335–36.

41.   *New York Times*, April 7, 1895.

42.   "The Progress of Western America," *Irrigation Age*, 7 (Dec. 1894), pp. 245–50; "Mass Meetings in Boston and Chicago," *Irrigation Age*, 8 (April 1895), p. 110; "Plymouth Colony," *Irrigation Age*, 8 (June 1895), pp. 186–87; *Reno Evening Gazette*, May 11, 1895.

43.   Frederick Booth-Tucker, "Farm Colonies of the Salvation Army," in *The Salvation Army in America: Selected Reports, 1899–1903* (New York, 1972), pp. 1004–5.

44.   Ibid., p. 988.

45.   Edward H. McKinley, *Marching to Glory: The History of the Salvation Army in the United States of America, 1880–1980* (San Francisco, 1980), pp. 91–93.

46.   Clark C. Spence, *The Salvation Army Farm Colonies* (Tucson, 1985), pp. 42–68.

47.   Ibid., pp. 25–41.

48.   Ibid., pp. 69–76.

49.   Ibid., p. 93.

50.   Spence, *Salvation Army Farm Colonies*, pp. 103–10; McKinley, *Marching to Glory*, pp. 90–91.

51.   Frederick Booth-Tucker, "Colonization on Irrigated Lands," in *The Official Proceedings of the Tenth National Irrigation Congress Held at Colorado Springs, Colorado* (Colorado Springs, 1902), pp. 162–67; Booth-Tucker, "The Relation of Colonization to Irrigation," *Forestry and Irrigation*, 9 (Oct. 1903), pp. 499–505; USGS, "Proceedings of the First Conference of Engineers of the Reclamation Service," *Water Supply and Irrigation Paper 93* (Washington, D.C., 1904), pp. 122–26; Official Proceedings of the Twelfth National Irrigation Congress Held at El Paso, Texas, Nov. 15–16–17–18, 1904 (El Paso, 1905), pp. 134–36.

52.   W. H. Mills, "Salvation Army Colonization of the Arid Lands," *Rural Californian*, 20 (June–July 1897), p. 252.

53.   Stuart Bruchey, *The Wealth of the Nation: An Economic History of the United States* (New York, 1988), p. 72.
54.   *Report of the Special Committee of the United States Senate on the Irrigation and Reclamation of Arid Lands,* vol. 1, p. 40.
55.   Robert G. Dunbar, *Forging New Rights in Western Waters* (Lincoln, 1983), p. 20.
56.   Gates, "Historical Sketch of Economic Development of Washington since Statehood," p. 214.
57.   Rose M. Boening, "A History of Irrigation in the State of Washington," *Washington Historical Quarterly,* 10 (Jan. 1919), pp. 22–23; Calvin B. Coulter, "The Victory of National Irrigation in the Yakima Valley, 1902–1906," *Pacific Northwest Quarterly,* 42 (April 1951), pp. 101–2; Click Relander, "The Battleground of National Irrigation," *Pacific Northwest Quarterly,* 52 (Oct. 1961), p. 145; *Forestry and Irrigation,* 8 (Feb. 1902), pp. 49–50; *New York Times,* March 11, 1894.
58.   Collis P. Huntington to Leland Stanford, June 1, 1874, in Timothy Hopkins Transportation Collection, Green Library (Special Collections), Stanford University.
59.   The depression of 1873 prompted a wide array of schemes to use the western lands to alleviate industrial distress. See Albert V. House, Jr., "Proposals of Government Aid to Agricultural Settlement During the Depression of 1873–1879," *Agricultural History,* 12 (Jan. 1938), pp. 46–66; *Congressional Record,* 45th Cong., 3d sess., Jan. 27, 1879, pp. 768–71.
60.   "Report of the Commissioner of the General Land Office [1875]," in *Report of the Secretary of the Interior [1875]* (Washington, D.C., 1875), pp. 6–9. The quotations are on pp. 6, 8, and 9.
61.   *Congressional Record,* 44th Cong., 2d sess., Senate, Dec. 5, 1876, p. 32.
62.   The 1875 legislation permitted claims to 640 acres—four times the amount of land available to an individual under the 1862 Homestead Act—*if* the claimant irrigated all the land within two years. Once two witnesses swore that the land was actually desert, it could be acquired for $1.25 an acre. The measure elicited very little debate, even though a proponent described it on the floor of Congress as "an experiment," suggesting that the law might find wider use later (*Congressional Record,* 43d Cong., 2d sess., Senate, Feb. 26, 1875, pp. 1786–87).
63.   The *Scientific American,* in an editorial entitled "The Migration of the Great American Desert" (42 [April 24, 1880], p. 256), commented: "The desert was a reality; but agriculture has practically abolished it."
64.   President Rutherford B. Hayes, in his second message to Congress in 1878, noted that it was a good idea, "especially in times of depression and uncertainty in other business pursuits, with a vast area of uncultivated and hence unproductive territory, wisely opened to homestead settlement, to encourage by every proper and legitimate means the occupation and tillage of the soil." See James D. Richardson, ed., *A Compilation of the Messages and Papers of the Presidents, 1789–1897* (Washington, D.C., 1900), vol. 6, pp. 4457–58.

65.   Paul Gates, in his *History of Public Land Law Development* (Washington, D.C., 1968), pp. 642–43, maintained that the Desert Land Act was of "minor importance" compared to the Homestead Act, in that the latter allowed for the transfer of 270,216,874 acres while the former permitted only 10,601,334 acres to pass from the public domain. In states like Wyoming and Arizona, however, there were far more desert land than homestead entries, and because these entries usually adjoined streams and lakes, they often conferred monopoly control over water. See Ray P. Teele, "Land Reclamation Policies in the United States," USDA Bulletin 1257 (Washington, D.C., 1924), p. 5.

66.   By the end of the nineteenth century, the phrase *desert lands* had a very specific meaning, at least in the General Land Office. They were lands that could not produce sufficient native grasses to yield a hay crop in an ordinary year and would not produce trees or agricultural crops without irrigation.

67.   Michael P. Malone and Richard B. Roeder, *Montana: A History of Two Centuries* (Seattle, 1976), p. 123. Desert land claimants could also "parlay" entries under different laws. In many parts of the arid West it was possible to file for preemption, homestead, and timber claims of 160 acres each along with a desert land entry for an additional 640 acres, thus legally securing an estate of 1,120 acres.

68.   Gates, *History of Public Land Law Development*, p. 640.

69.   John Ganoe, "The Desert Land Act in Operation, 1877–1891," p. 147; Everett Dick, *The Lure of the Land* (Lincoln, 1970), pp. 312–13.

70.   In 1890 and 1891, amendments to the 1877 act eliminated some of its obvious flaws, but left others intact. The 1890 law reduced the size of desert land entries from 640 acres to 320 acres (*U.S. Statutes at Large*, vol. 25 [1890], p. 527). The 1891 legislation, part of the omnibus land reform law (which included the forest reserve provision), required that formal irrigation plans be filed with the land office at the time of entry, that one dollar per acre be expended on irrigation in each of the three years following entry, that 80 of the 320 acres be reclaimed within that period, that entrymen swear that they were filing for themselves, not as surrogates, and that they reside within the state that contained their claim. However, the new law did not require residence on the land (as the Homestead Act did), nor did it prevent cattlemen from entering the land, paying the twenty-five-cent-an-acre down payment, and tying it up for years. Moreover, it still permitted individuals to parlay different claims. Desert Land Act entries reached their peak in 1910, when 15,620 applicants were filed on 2,899,730 acres. See Gates, *History of Public Land Law Development*, p. 643. The 1891 law is *U.S. Statutes at Large*, vol. 26 (1891), p. 1095.

71.   Rodman Paul, *California Gold: The Beginnings of Mining in the Far West* (Cambridge, Mass., 1947), p. 345; *Ninth Census of the United States, 1870* (Washington, D.C., 1872), vol. 3, p. 820.

72.   *Report of the Commissioner of Agriculture for the Year 1862* (Washington, D.C., 1863), p. 577; *Report . . . 1868* (Washington, D.C., 1869), pp. 30–31; *Report . . . 1869* (Washington, D.C., 1870), p. 31; *Report . . . 1873* (Washington, D.C., 1874), p. 24; *Report . . . 1874* (Washington, D.C., 1875), p. 29; *Report . . . 1878* (Washington, D.C., 1879), p. 264.

73.   *Twelfth Census of the United States Taken in the Year 1900; Agriculture: Part II, Crops and Irrigation* (Washington, D.C., 1902) estimated that no more than twenty thousand acres were under irrigation in the entire United States in 1870 (p. 801). However, other authors have given substantially higher figures. See, for example, Benjamin F. Rhodes, Jr., "Thirsty Land: The Modesto Irrigation District, a Case Study of Irrigation under the Wright Law" (Ph.D. diss., University of California, Berkeley, 1943), pp. 3–4; and Lawrence J. Jelinek, *Harvest Empire: A History of California Agriculture* (San Francisco, 1979), p. 57.

74.   Pisani, *From the Family Farm to Agribusiness*, pp. 85–89.

75.   Ibid., pp. 89–91. This proposed land grant reappeared in the 1870s. See "The Proposed Irrigation of the Colorado Desert," *Scientific American*, 30 (March 28, 1874), p. 193; "The Reclamation of the Colorado Desert," *Scientific American*, 30 (May 16, 1874), p. 309; and "Another Raid on 'Desert' Lands," *Scientific American*, 38 (Feb. 9, 1878), p. 84.

76.   Pisani, *From the Family Farm to Agribusiness*, pp. 93–97.

77.   Daryl V. Gease, "William N. Byers and the Case for Federal Aid to Irrigation in the Arid West," *Colorado Magazine*, 45 (Fall 1968), pp. 340–45.

78.   *Sacramento Daily Union*, June 9, 1870. Land subsidies were only one of the reasons for seeking federal aid. By incorporating under national as well as state laws—much as the land grant railroads had—companies hoped to secure more dependable rights to water. Outside California, the company that most often requested federal aid tapped the Bear River, a much-fought-over interstate stream shared by Idaho and Utah. See S. 1035, 41st Cong., 3d sess. (1870); H.R. 583, 42d Cong., 2d sess. (1871); H.R. 1523, 42d Cong., 2d sess. (1872); S. 386, 42d Cong., 2d sess. (1871); S. 387, 42d Cong., 2d sess. (1871); S. 348, 42d Cong., 2d sess. (1872); and S. 679, 42d Cong., 2d sess. (1872).

79.   Maass and Anderson, *". . . and the Desert Shall Rejoice,"* pp. 146–274, esp. the chart on p. 147; John T. Ganoe, "The Beginnings of Irrigation in the United States," *Mississippi Valley Historical Review*, 25 (June 1938), p. 65. The best newspaper on San Joaquin Valley irrigation developments in these years is the *Fresno Weekly Expositor*, available at the California State Library, Sacramento. For example, see the *Expositor* for Dec. 7, 1870; April 5, June 21, and Sept. 20, 1871; Oct. 29, 1873; May 13 and Dec. 2, 1874; May 5, 1875; May 15, 1876; Feb. 28 and May 16, 1877.

80.   I have told the story of the San Joaquin and Kings River Canal and Irrigation Company at greater length in *From the Family Farm to Agribusiness*, pp. 102–29.

81.   Typescript biography of John Bensley prepared by George H. Morrison, in the Hubert Howe Bancroft Collection, Bancroft Library, University of California, Berkeley.

82.   The best biography of William Ralston is David Lavender's *Nothing Seemed Impossible: William C. Ralston and Early San Francisco* (Palo Alto, Calif., 1975). However, Cecil G. Tilton's *William Chapman Ralston: Courageous Builder* (Boston, 1935) and George D. Lyman's *Ralston's Ring: California Plunders the Comstock Lode* (New York, 1947) are still useful. On Ralston's

far-reaching business ventures, see Tilton, *William Chapman Ralston*, pp. 160, 166–69.

83.   Robert Glass Cleland, *From Wilderness to Empire: A History of California, 1542–1900* (New York, 1944), p. 330; Willian Lilley III, "The Early Career of Francis G. Newlands, 1848–1897" (Ph.D. diss., Yale University, 1965), p. 44; Tilton, *William Chapman Ralston*, p. 171.

84.   *Commercial Herald & Market Review* (San Francisco), Jan. 12, 1872.

85.   J. Ross Browne to William C. Ralston, Nov. 25, 1871, William Ralston Collection, Bancroft Library, University of California, Berkeley, and William Ralston Collection, Special Collections, Stanford University; J. Ross Browne, "Reclamation and Irrigation," in *Transactions of the California State Agricultural Society During the Year 1872* (Sacramento, 1874), pp. 390–425; Browne, "Agricultural Capacity of California—Overflows and Droughts," *Overland Monthly*, 20 (April 1873), pp. 297–314.

86.   Robert M. Brereton, *Reminiscences of Irrigation-Enterprise in California* (Portland, 1903). The quotation is from p. 72. Also see Robert Brereton's statement reprinted in Ezra S. Carr, *The Patrons of Husbandry on the Pacific Coast* (San Francisco, 1875), pp. 310–13; *Pacific Rural Press*, 1 (May 20, 1871), p. 316; *Sacramento Daily Union*, Jan. 13, 1872.

87.   E. F. Treadwell, *The Cattle King* (Boston, 1950), p. 67; William D. Lawrence, "Henry Miller and the San Joaquin Valley" (M.A. thesis, University of California, Berkeley, 1933), pp. 133–34.

88.   See Robert M. Brereton to George Davidson, Sept. 3, 1910, and April 14, 1911, in the George Davidson Collection, Bancroft Library, University of California, Berkeley; Treadwell, *The Cattle King*, pp. 65–66.

89.   Apparently John Bensley had also asked for an eight-hundred-thousand-acre land grant in the late 1860s. See the Visalia *Delta* (Visalia, Calif.), March 27, 1869.

90.   *Sacramento Daily Union*, Jan. 13, 1872; *Stockton Daily Independent* (Stockton, Calif.), Jan. 30, 1872; *Memorial of the California Legislature to Congress*, introduced Jan. 23, 1872 (Sacramento, 1872), p. 4.

91.   Gates, *History of Public Land Law Development*, pp. 376, 380, 390–91, 455.

92.   Robert M. Brereton to William C. Ralston, July 17, 1872, and C. J. F. Stuart (president, Oriental Bank of London) to William Ralston, July 27 and Aug. 15, 1872, William Ralston Collection.

93.   *Report of the Committee on Land Monopoly* (Sacramento, 1874), pp. 196–97.

94.   *Fresno Weekly Expositor*, June 25, 1873. For other antimonopoly statements see the *Expositor* of Nov. 12, 1873; *Sacramento Daily Union*, Jan. 29, 1872, July 19, 1873, and October 18, 1873; *Stockton Daily Independent*, Feb. 1, 1873; *Pacific Rural Press*, July 12, 1873, p. 24; and *Daily Bee* (Sacramento, Calif.), May 23, 1873.

95.   *San Francisco Chronicle*, Feb. 12, 1873; *Stockton Daily Independent*, Feb. 14, 1873; *Sacramento Daily Union*, March 1, 1873.

96.   *Sacramento Daily Union*, July 2 and 19, 1873; *Stockton Daily Independent*, July 2, 4, and 10, 1873.

97. *Stockton Daily Independent,* Dec. 20, 1873; *Weekly Colusa Sun* (Colusa, Calif.), Dec. 20, 1873; *Pacific Rural Press,* 7 (April 4, 1874), p. 210.

98. Robert M. Brereton to George Davidson, Sept. 29, 1911, George Davidson Collection; *Evening Bulletin* (San Francisco), May 18, 1874; *San Francisco Post,* May 18, 1874.

99. Robert M. Brereton to George Davidson, Sept. 3, 1910, George Davidson Collection.

100. *Fresno Weekly Expositor,* Feb. 28, 1877, Sept. 25 and Dec. 18, 1878. As early as 1874, Miller and Lux began to subdivide the land they owned adjoining the canal into 160-acre farms, which sold for twenty dollars an acre. They also offered prospective settlers five-year leases for 20 percent of the crops raised (*Fresno Weekly Expositor,* May 27, 1874).

101. Treadwell, *The Cattle King,* p. 77.

102. C. S. Kinney, *A Treatise on the Law of Irrigation and Water Rights and the Arid Region Doctrine of Appropriation of Waters,* 4 vols. (San Francisco, 1912), pp. 2634–58, 2679–2714.

103. *Cal. Stats.* (1858), p. 218; (1862), p. 541.

104. Pisani, *From the Family Farm to Agribusiness,* pp. 157–61; William Hammond Hall, *Irrigation in [Southern] California* (Sacramento, 1888), pp. 212, 221, 228–32.

105. Pisani, *From the Family Farm to Agribusiness,* pp. 356–57.

106. Ray P. Teele, "The Organization of Irrigation Companies," *Journal of Political Economy,* 12 (March 1904), p. 168.

107. Elwood Mead, *Irrigation Institutions* (New York, 1903), p. 187.

108. These rules, of course, grew not only from the California experience but from the common law principle of private property vested with a public interest, as interpreted in *Munn* v. *Illinois,* 94 U.S. 113 (1877), which reaffirmed public control over common carriers. See Harry N. Scheiber, "The Road to *Munn:* Eminent Domain and the Concept of Public Purpose in the State Courts," *Perspectives in American History,* 5 (1971), pp. 327–402.

109. Samuel C. Wiel, "Public Control of Irrigation," *Columbia Law Review,* 10 (June 1910), pp. 506–19.

110. As in California, Colorado's judges refined common law principles rather than making new law. They held that water companies engaged voluntarily in their activity; that their decisions had an impact on entire communities; that they usually held a monopoly on service within a certain area; and that they clearly served a public interest, and hence a public trust. Leonard P. Fox, "State Regulation of the Canal Corporation in Colorado," *Michigan Law Review,* 16 (1917–18), pp. 158–78.

111. Kinney, *Treatise on the Law of Irrigation and Water Rights,* pp. 2659–78; Richard Moss Alston, *Commercial Irrigation Enterprise: The Fear of Water Monopoly and the Genesis of Market Distortion in the Nineteenth Century American West* (New York, 1978), p. 81; Teele, *Irrigation in the United States,* pp. 186–88.

112. For a lengthy discussion of the irrigation district in the nineteenth century, see Pisani, *From the Family Farm to Agribusiness,* pp. 129–282.

113. For a concise summary of the Wright Act, see Herbert M. Wilson,

"American Irrigation Engineering," in *Thirteenth Annual Report of the United States Geological Survey [1891–92]* Part 3 (Washington, D.C., 1893), pp. 145–46.

114.   Ray P. Teele, "Notes on the Irrigation Situation," *Journal of Political Economy,* 13 (March 1905), p. 241; C. C. Wright, "Irrigation on Popular Principles," *Irrigation Age,* 2 (Feb. 1, 1892), pp. 446–47; "A Creation of the California District Law: Editorial Study of the Turlock-Modesto Works," *Irrigation Age,* 6 (Jan. 1895), pp. 12–15.

115.   *Ceding the Arid Lands to the States and Territories,* H.R. 3767, 51st Cong., 2d sess., serial 2888, p. 189; Richard J. Hinton, *Irrigation in the United States: Progress Report for 1890,* p. 67.

116.   F. C. Finkle, "The Wright Law in California," *Irrigation Age,* 8 (Dec. 1895), pp. 227–30, compared two irrigated areas within seven miles of each other in southern California, one served by an irrigation district, the other by a private water company. He found that the water cost $1 an acre in the district (72 cents an acre for interest on the $12-an-acre bonded debt at 6 percent and 28 cents an acre for maintenance) as opposed to $9.40 an acre in the private project (including $6.40 for interest on the $90-an-acre water stock at 6 percent and a $3-an-acre assessment for other expenses). In 1894, the head of the irrigation office in the USDA, Charles Irish, suggested that the cost of irrigation provided by private water companies ran over twenty times that provided by irrigation districts, though he was comparing irrigation within one of the few successful early districts in northern California with the cost of water rights under private ditches in southern California, where even water districts charged much more for water. Districts undoubtedly did lower the cost of water in many parts of the state, but some mutual companies did just as well. See Charles Irish to H. E. Carter, Oct. 27, 1894, RG 16, Press Copies of Letters Sent by the Office of Irrigation Inquiry, June 11–Nov. 20, 1894, National Archives.

117.   Pisani, *From the Family Farm to Agribusiness,* pp. 268–70, 281–82; Roy E. Huffman, *Irrigation Development and Public Water Policy* (New York, 1953), p. 75.

118.   For the twentieth-century story, see Donald J. Pisani, "The Irrigation District and the Federal Relationship," in Gerald D. Nash and Richard W. Etulain, eds., *The Twentieth-Century West: Historical Interpretations* (Albuquerque, 1989), pp. 257–92.

119.   F. H. Newell, *Report on Agriculture by Irrigation in the Western Part of the United States at the Eleventh Census, 1890* (Washington, D.C., 1894), pp. 2, 3, 6, 10, 33.

120.   Alston, *Commercial Irrigation Enterprise,* pp. 179–80.

121.   Samuel Fortier, "The Greatest Need of Arid America," in *Official Proceedings of the Fifteenth National Irrigation Congress* (Sacramento, 1907), p. 120; Alston, *Commercial Irrigation Enterprise,* p. 104.

122.   Frank C. Goudy, "Benefits and Dangers of Private Irrigation," in *Official Proceedings of the Eighteenth National Irrigation Congress Held at Pueblo, Colorado, Sept. 26–30, 1910* (Pueblo, Colo., n.d.), p. 40. Also see A. G. Allen, "Unprofitable Irrigation Projects in Western America," *Engineering Magazine,* 15 (June 1898), p. 440.

123.   Norman E. Webster, "Irrigation Finance," in *Official Proceedings of the Nineteenth National Irrigation Congress Held at Chicago, Illinois, December 5–9, 1911* (Chicago, 1912), p. 228; F. H. Newell, "Development of Water Resources," *The Forester*, 7 (Aug. 1901), pp. 193, 196; Teele, "Water Rights in the Arid West," pp. 524–34.

124.   Hubert Howe Bancroft, *History of Arizona and New Mexico, 1530–1888* (San Francisco, 1889), pp. 535, 767; Herbert M. Wilson, "American Canal Works," *Irrigation Age*, 2 (Dec. 15, 1891), p. 331; William E. Smythe, "The New Era in Arizona," *Irrigation Age*, 3 (Feb. 1893), pp. 282–90; "A Gigantic Irrigation Project," *Scientific American*, 69 (July 8, 1893), p. 24; B. W. Thompson, "Immigration and Irrigation," *Irrigation Age*, 10 (Oct. 1896), p. 135; "Why the Arizona Company Failed," *Irrigation Age*, 12 (Dec. 1897), pp. 54–55, 76; Christine Lewis, "The Early History of the Tempe Canal Company," *Arizona and the West*, 7 (Autumn 1965), pp. 227–38.

125.   Alston, *Commercial Irrigation Enterprise*, pp. 94, 134.

126.   James Wilson (secretary of agriculture), untitled speech, in *Official Proceedings of the Eleventh National Irrigation Congress Held at Ogden, Utah, September 15–18, 1903* (Ogden, 1904), p. 164; Herbert M. Wilson, "American Irrigation Engineering," in *Thirteenth Annual Report of the United States Geological Survey [1891–92]*, Part 3 (Washington, D.C., 1893), p. 149; Herbert M. Wilson, "The Irrigation Problem in Montana," *National Geographic Magazine*, 2 (1890), pp. 225–26.

Chapter 5

1.   *Congressional Globe*, 40th Cong., 2d sess., House, May 7, 1868, pp. 2379–80.

2.   Various letters from the commissioner of the General Land Office relating to irrigation are reprinted in "Irrigation of Public Lands," H. Ex. Doc. 293, 40th Cong., 2d sess. (Washington, D.C., 1868), serial 1343.

3.   *First, Second and Third Annual Reports of the United States Geological Survey of the Territories for the Years 1867, 1868 and 1869* (Washington, D.C., 1873), pp. 229–51.

4.   Jerome C. Smiley, *Semi-Centennial History of the State of Colorado* (Chicago, 1913), vol. 1, pp. 574–75; *Stockton Daily Independent* (Stockton, Calif.), July 11, 1873; James E. Sherow, "Watering the Plains: An Early History of Denver's Highline Canal," *Colorado Heritage*, 4 (1988), p. 2.

5.   *Congressional Record*, 43d Cong., 1st sess., app., pp. 37–38.

6.   Robert M. Brereton, *Reminiscences of an Old English Civil Engineer, 1858–1908* (Portland, 1908), pp. 25–26; Robert M. Brereton to George Davidson, April 14 and Sept. 29, 1911, George Davidson Collection, Bancroft Library, University of California, Berkeley.

7.   The William Morris Stewart Collection is at the Nevada Historical Society, Reno. Unfortunately, the correspondence from his first two terms in the Senate (1864–75) has been lost or destroyed. However, see the Stewart Collection, Box 9, Letterbook, April 30, 1888–Sept. 19, 1889, esp. Stewart's letter

to Brereton dated April 26, 1889. Also see Stewart to R. R. Bigelow, Jan. 19, 1889, in Letterbook, Dec. 12, 1888–Feb. 17, 1889, in the same box.

8.   Grant Rothwell Brown, ed., *Reminiscences of Senator William M. Stewart of Nevada* (New York, 1908), pp. 250, 251; Russell R. Elliott, *Servant of Power: A Political Biography of Senator William M. Stewart* (Reno, 1983), pp. 74–75.

9.   Senator Cornelius Cole introduced a land grant bill (S. 1396) on behalf of the company on January 17, 1873, but by the end of February concluded that the legislation did not have a chance. See the *Congressional Globe*, 42d Cong., 3d sess., Senate, Jan. 17, 1873, p. 660, and Feb. 27, 1873, p. 1846.

10.   George Gorham to William C. Ralston, Feb. 16, 1873, in Box 2, Ralston Collection, Green Library, Stanford University. In a letter to Ralston dated Jan. 30, 1873, Gorham promised to "promote an early conference between him [Brereton] and all our friends. . . . and there we can discuss modes [strategies]. You may rely on my best efforts in the matter." Also see Cornelius Cole to Ralston, Feb. 2, 1873, in Box 1, Ralston Collection, Stanford University. The same letter is contained in the Ralston Collection, Bancroft Library, University of California, Berkeley. Ralston outlined the nature of his project in his letter to "My Dear Lawton," May 5, 1873, in Box 10, "Unidentified Repository" file, Ralston Collection, Stanford University.

11.   *Congressional Globe*, 42d Cong., 3d sess., Senate, Feb. 28, 1873, pp. 1930, 2130. The Stewart Bill (S. 1584) is reprinted in the appendix to the *Globe*, p. 305.

12.   The act itself is reprinted in the commission's final report, H. Ex. Doc. 290, 43d Cong., 1st sess., 1873–74 (Washington, D.C., 1974), serial 1615, pp. 3–4.

13.   For specific activities of the commission, see the letters of George Davidson to Superintendent, U.S. Coast Geodetic Survey, June 23, July 10, August 6, and November 24, 1873, in Letterbook, vol. 26 (1873), Davidson Collection. Also see Office of the Chief of Engineers, U.S. Army, "Letters Received, 1871–1886" (1873: 927), RG 77, National Archives.

14.   *Stockton Daily Independent*, April 21, June 6, 1873. For other newspaper opposition to the survey, see the *Sacramento Daily Union*, March 12, 1873, and the *Fresno Weekly Expositor*, June 25, 1873.

15.   *New York Times*, July 5, Oct. 29, 1873.

16.   H. Ex. Doc. 290, 43d Cong., 1st sess. (Washington, D.C., 1874), serial 1615. The commission's conclusions are summarized on pp. 77–80. For a lengthy discussion of the report, see W. Turrentine Jackson, Rand F. Herbert, and Stephen R. Wee, *Engineers and Irrigation: Report of the Board of Commissioners on the Irrigation of the San Joaquin, Tulare, and Sacramento Valleys of the State of California, 1873* (Fort Belvoir, Va., 1990).

17.   H. Ex. Doc. 290, 43d Cong., 1st sess., p. 39.

18.   Ibid., p. 78.

19.   Ibid., p. 38.

20.   For an excellent summary of the report and its implications, see *Report of the Commissioner of Agriculture for the Year 1874* (Washington, D.C., 1875), pp. 352–62.

21.   H. Ex. Doc. 290, 43d Cong., 1st sess., p. 31.

22.   Letterbook, vol. 26, Davidson Collection.

23.   Apparently, the only offshoot of the commission's investigation was an appeal from Nevada's representative to Congress, C. W. Kendall, who introduced H.R. 759 at the end of 1873 calling for a special commission to investigate the water resources of Nevada in the interest of mining as well as agriculture. The bill called for an appropriation of twenty thousand dollars to bore for underground water as well as to examine the surface supply. The legislation never got out of committee. See Office of the Chief of Engineers, U.S. Army, Letters Received 1871–1886 (1873: 2414), RG 77, National Archives.

24.   As reported in Alvin T. Steinel, *History of Agriculture in Colorado* (Fort Collins, 1926), p. 196.

25.   *Tenth Annual Report of the U.S. Geological and Geographical Survey [1876]* (Washington, D.C., 1878), p. 342.

26.   "Report of the Commissioner of the General Land Office," in *Report of the Secretary of the Interior, 1875* (Washington, D.C., 1875), p. 7; *Report of the Secretary of the Interior, 1878* (Washington, D.C., 1878), p. XLII.

27.   Oscar Lewis, *George Davidson: Pioneer West Coast Scientist* (Berkeley, 1954); Michael L. Smith, *Pacific Visions: California Scientists and the Environment, 1850–1915* (New Haven, 1987), pp. 18–27; George Davidson, "The Pacific Coast and Geodetic Surveys," *The Californian*, 1 (Jan. 1880), pp. 60–65; Alonzo Phelps, *Contemporary Biography of California's Representative Men* (San Francisco, 1881), pp. 97–104; Charles B. Davenport, *Biographical Memoir of George Davidson, 1825–1911* (Washington, D.C., 1937); Charles Gregory Yale, *Brief Sketch of the Public Services of George Davidson* (n.p., 1885); Rockwell D. Hunt, *California's Stately Hall of Fame* (Stockton, Calif.), pp. 404–8; and Henry R. Wagner, "George Davidson, Geographer of the Northwest Coast of America," *California Historical Quarterly*, 11 (Dec. 1932), pp. 299–320.

28.   See Davidson's outline of his career in the "Irrigation" folder, Carton 17, Davidson Collection.

29.   H. J. Shepstone, "The Irrigation Works of India," *Scientific American Supplement*, 80 (Sept. 11, 1915), pp. 154–65; Charles D. Poston, "Irrigation," in *Report of the Commissioner of Agriculture, 1867* (Washington, D.C., 1868), p. 198; *Country Gentleman*, 24 (Nov. 3, 1864), p. 285.

30.   The federal irrigation commission discussed irrigation in Europe, India, and the Middle East in H. Ex. Doc. 290, 43d Cong., 1st sess. (Washington, D.C., 1874), pp. 40–73. For the story of the Madras and East India irrigation companies, see pp. 55–57.

31.   Ibid., p. 63.

32.   George Davidson, "Irrigation and Reclamation of Land for Agricultural Purposes as Now Practiced in India, Egypt, Italy, Etc., 1875," in S. Ex. Doc. 94, 44th Cong., 1st sess. (Washington, D.C., 1875), serial 1664, pp. 5–6.

33.   William Morris Stewart to R. R. Bigelow, Jan. 19, 1889, Box 9, Letterbook, Dec. 12, 1888–Feb. 17, 1889, Stewart Collection; George Davidson to William C. Ralston, May 15, 1875, Ralston Collection, Bancroft Library.

34.   Davidson, "Irrigation and Reclamation of Land for Agricultural Pur-

poses as Now Practiced in India, Egypt, Italy, Etc., 1875," pp. 38–39. *Scientific American* closely followed irrigation in the British Empire and Europe. See the following *Scientific American* articles: "The Irrigation Works of India," 33 (Aug. 28, 1875), p. 128; "Irrigation in Egypt," 47 (Sept. 16, 1882), p. 177; "An Extensive Irrigating Project," 48 (Jan. 27, 1883), p. 50; "Irrigation in India," 49 (Nov. 3, 1883), p. 279; "Irrigation Works in Italy," 49 (Dec. 15, 1883), p. 371; and "Irrigation in India," 69 (Aug. 5, 1893), pp. 89–90.

35.   Davidson, "Irrigation and Reclamation of Land for Agricultural Purposes as Now Practiced in India, Egypt, Italy, Etc., 1875," p. 7 (quotation), 8–9, 38–40).

36.   See the series of lectures presented to the California Academy of Sciences as published in the San Francisco *Daily Evening Bulletin,* April 7, May 3, May 19, June 10, Dec. 8, and Dec. 20, 1876, and Jan. 17, Feb. 8, and Feb. 24, 1877. Also see his lecture to the Sacramento Literary Institute in the *Sacramento Daily Record,* Feb. 17, 1877, and "Two Lectures on Irrigation" delivered to the California legislature on Jan. 15 and 16, 1878, in Carton 17, Davidson Collection. For an excellent summary of Davidson's thinking, see his "Application of Irrigation to California," in Phelps, ed., *Contemporary Biography of California's Representative Men,* pp. 105–23.

37.   "Lectures on Irrigation to California Legislature, Jan. 15 & 16, 1878," Irrigation Folder, Davidson Collection.

38.   "Report of the Commissioner of the General Land Office," in *Report of the Secretary of the Interior, 1885* (Washington, D.C., 1885), p. 231; John N. Irwin, "A Great Domain by Irrigation," *Forum,* 12 (Feb. 1892), p. 749; "Report of the Commissioner of the General Land Office," in *Report of the Secretary of the Interior, 1891* (Washington, D.C., 1891), p. 49.

39.   *Report of the Secretary of the Interior, 1896* (Washington, D.C., 1896), p. vi; S. A. Cochran, "Irrigation a Sociological Question," in *Proceedings of the Seventh Annual Session, National Irrigation Congress [1898]* (Cheyenne, 1899), p. 110.

40.   T. A. Larson, *History of Wyoming* (Lincoln, 1978), p. 191; Michael P. Malone and Richard B. Roeder, *Montana: A History of Two Centuries* (Seattle, 1976); *Denver Republican,* Feb. 22, 1887.

41.   Charles Irish to Isa S. Richards, Feb. 5, 1895, Press Copies of Letters Sent by the Office of Irrigation Inquiry, Nov. 20, 1894–Feb. 7, 1895, RG 16, National Archives.

42.   For example, in 1890 the governor of Idaho noted that in 1889 more money had been invested in irrigation works in his state than during the entire previous decade. See "Report of the Governor of Idaho," in *Report of the Secretary of the Interior, 1890* (Washington, D.C., 1890), vol. 3, p. 564.

43.   Among the vast number of bills calling for government surveys, see H.R. 125, 48th Cong., 1st sess., Dec. 10, 1883 (Belford); H.R. 6730, 49th Cong., 1st sess., March 16, 1886 (Hanback); H.R. 7937, 50th Cong., 1st sess., March 1, 1888 (Joseph); H.R. 9054, 50th Cong., 1st sess., April 2, 1888 (Symes); H.R. 3916, 52st Cong., 1st sess., Jan. 6, 1890 (Pickler); H.R. 3924, 51st Cong., 1st sess., Jan. 6, 1890 (Lanham); H.R. 8459, 51st Cong., 1st sess., March 20, 1890 (Clunie); H.R. 8979, 51st Cong., 1st sess., April 3, 1890 (Hansbrough); H.R.

11503, 51st Cong., 1st sess., July 23, 1890 (Townsend); H.R. 11727, 51st Cong., 1st sess., Aug. 12, 1890 (Pickler); H.R. 514, 52d Cong., 1st sess., Jan. 7, 1892 (Joseph); H.R. 7154, 53d Cong., 2d sess., May 21, 1894 (Sweet); H.R. 7558, 53d Cong., 2d sess., June 23, 1894 (Sweet); H.R. 7950, 53d Cong., 2d sess., Aug. 11, 1894 (Pickler); H.R. 286, 54th Cong., 1st sess., Dec. 6, 1895 (Gamble); H.R. 333, 54th Cong., 1st sess., Dec. 6, 1895 (Doolittle); H.R. 6246, 54th Cong., 1st sess., Feb. 17, 1896 (Hermann); S. 2899, 52d Cong., 1st sess., April 12, 1892 (Dolph); S. 1450, 53d Cong., 2d sess., Jan. 17, 1894 (White); S. 1763, 53d Cong., 2d sess., March 13, 1894 (Allen); S. 2248, 53d Cong., 2d sess., July 23, 1894 (Power); S. 1078, 54th Cong., 1st sess., Dec. 19, 1895 (Pettigrew); S. 1749, 54th Cong., 1st sess., Jan. 24, 1896 (Allen); S. 1762, 54th Cong., 1st sess., Jan. 24, 1896 (Pettigrew); and S. 86, 55th Cong., 1st sess., March 16, 1897 (Allen). For complete lists of survey bills introduced in Congress, see the indexes to the *Congressional Record* under "irrigation," "public lands," "arid lands," and "national irrigation congress."

44.   Everett E. Sterling, "The Powell Irrigation Survey, 1888–1893," *Mississippi Valley Historical Review*, 27 (Dec. 1940), p. 421.

45.   *Congressional Record*, Senate, July 30, 1888, pp. 7014, 7015–16.

46.   L. Carl Brandhorst, "The North Platte Oasis: Notes on the Geography and History of an Irrigated District," *Agricultural History*, 51 (Jan. 1977), p. 167.

47.   "Report of the Governor of Dakota," in *Report of the Secretary of the Interior, 1888* (Washington, D.C., 1889), vol. 2, p. 701.

48.   "Report of the Commissioner of the General Land Office," in *Report of the Secretary of the Interior, 1885*, p. 79; "Report of the Governor of Dakota," in *Report of the Secretary of the Interior, 1881* (Washington, D.C., 1881), vol. 2, p. 946; *Denver Republican*, June 28, 1889.

49.   James Realf, "The Irrigation Problem in the Northwest," *Arena*, 4 (June 1891), pp. 69–76.

50.   James Edward Wright, *The Politics of Populism: Dissent in Colorado* (New Haven, 1974), p. 34; John A. Garraty, *The New Commonwealth, 1877–1890* (New York, 1968), p. 56; Fred A. Shannon, *The Farmer's Last Frontier* (New York, 1945), pp. 307–8; A. Bower Sageser, *Joseph L. Bristow: Kansas Progressive* (Lawrence, 1968), p. 16; David M. Emmons, *Garden in the Grasslands: Boomer Literature of the Central Great Plains* (Lincoln, 1971), p. 170; A. P. Davis, "The Public Domain in Its Social Aspect," *Irrigation Age*, 7 (July 1894), p. 16.

51.   As reprinted in the "Report of the Governor of Utah," in the *Report of the Secretary of the Interior, 1891* (Washington, D.C., 1892), vol. 3, p. 364. Also see the *Kansas Farmer* (Topeka), Dec. 17, 1890, and the *Rocky Mountain News* (Denver, Colo.), Jan. 4, 1891.

52.   In addition to the Davison, Stegner, and Darrah studies cited elsewhere, readers interested in the Irrigation Survey should see A. Hunter Dupree, *Science in the Federal Government: A History of Policies and Activities to 1940* (Cambridge, Mass., 1957), pp. 195–214; and Thomas G. Manning, *Government in Science: The U.S. Geological Survey, 1867–1894* (Lexington, Ky., 1967), pp.

168–203. For background to the survey see the *Report of the Secretary of the Interior, 1890* (Washington, D.C., 1891), pp. IX–XIV.

53.   *U.S. Statutes at Large*, vol. 25, March 20, 1888, pp. 618–19, and Oct. 2, 1888, p. 526.

54.   The first extended discussion of the reclamation of arid lands in Congress took place on this day. See *Congressional Record*, 50th Cong., 1st sess., pp. 7012–33.

55.   Ibid., pp. 8475, 8479, 8505, 8509, 8511.

56.   Ibid., pp. 8462, 8471, 8511; *Congressional Record*, 50th Cong., 2d sess., House, Jan. 26, 1889, pp. 1226–30.

57.   For the irrigation survey in Congress, see the *Congressional Record*, 50th Cong., 1st sess., pp. 8460–82, 8504–18; 50th Cong., 2d sess., pp. 1224–31; 51st Cong., 1st sess., pp. 7341–60, 7393–7417; and 53d Cong., 2d sess., pp. 8079–86.

58.   *Congressional Record*, Senate, July 30, 1888, pp. 7016, 7018.

59.   *Report of the Secretary of the Interior, 1888* (Washington, D.C., 1888), p. XIII.

60.   *Report of the Secretary of the Interior, 1889* (Washington, D.C., 1889), p. XXIV; Lewis H. Groff (commissioner of the General Land Office) to Secretary of the Interior John W. Noble, Feb. 11, 1890, Records of General Land Office, Division A, Press Copies of Letters Sent Relating to Congressional Bills, vol. 8, Sept. 3, 1888–March 13, 1890, RG 49, National Archives.

61.   *Official Report of the Fifth National Irrigation Congress Held at Phoenix, Arizona, December 15, 16, and 17, 1896* (Phoenix, 1897), p. 30.

62.   *Report of the Secretary of the Interior, 1899* (Washington, D.C., 1899), p. XV. Many periodical writers also assumed that the Irrigation Survey was the prelude to full-scale federal reclamation. As early as 1884, *Science* magazine published an article by Lester F. Ward, "Irrigation in the Upper Missouri and Yellowstone Valleys," 4 (Aug. 29, 1884), p. 168, which called for a national program. Also see the editorials in the same journal, 12 (Aug. 10, 1888), p. 61, and 12 (Oct. 12, 1888), p. 169; "Editor's Table," *American Naturalist*, 22 (Sept. 1888), pp. 821–22; *Garden and Forest*, 1 (Dec. 12, 1888), p. 494; John Bonner, "The Present Stage of the Irrigation Question," *Overland Monthly*, 13 (June 1889), p. 607.

In addition, numerous state officials called for federal reclamation. For example, see "Report of the Governor of Washington," in *Report of the Secretary of the Interior, 1889* (Washington, D.C., 1890), vol. 2, pp. 525–26; "Report of the Governor of Utah," in *Report of the Secretary of the Interior, 1890* (Washington, D.C., 1890), vol. 3, p. 642; and "Report of the Governor of New Mexico," in *Report of the Secretary of the Interior, 1893* (Washington, D.C., 1893), vol. 3, p. 372. There were also bills calling for federal construction of reservoirs, though for specific localities. See, for example, H.R. 1975 (Joseph), 50th Cong., 1st sess., introduced Jan. 4, 1888; H.R. 972 (Joseph), 51st Cong., 1st sess., introduced Dec. 18, 1889; and H.R. 9756 (Vandever), 51st Cong., 1st sess., introduced April 26, 1890. The first two bills pertained to New Mexico, the third to the San Joaquin River in California.

63.   William Culp Darrah, *Powell of the Colorado* (Princeton, 1951); Wal-

lace Stegner, *Beyond the Hundreth Meridian: John Wesley Powell and the Second Opening of the West* (Boston, 1953); Stanley R. Davison, *The Leadership of the Reclamation Movement, 1875–1902* (New York, 1979); Carroll Lane Fenton and Mildred Adams Fenton, *The Story of the Great Geologists* (Garden City, N.Y., 1945), pp. 232–50.

64.   John Wesley Powell, untitled, undated memorandum (probably early 1890s), in Powell Irrigation Survey, Box 1, D-121, RG 57, National Archives.

65.   John Wesley Powell, *Report on the Lands of the Arid Region of the United States: With a More Detailed Account of the Lands of Utah* (Cambridge, Mass., 1962); "Report of the Public Lands Commission," H. Ex. Doc. 46, 46th Cong., 2d sess. (Washington, D.C., 1880), serial 1923. All references to the 1878 report are to the 1962 edition cited here. The original was published as H. Ex. Doc. 73, 45th Cong., 2d sess. (Washington, D.C., 1878), serial 1805.

66.   Powell, *Report on the Lands of the Arid Region of the United States*, pp. 37–57; "Report of the Public Lands Commission," pp. XVI–XXI.

67.   Powell, untitled, undated memorandum (probably early 1890s), in Records of the U.S. Geological Survey, Powell Irrigation Survey, Box 1, D-121, RG 57, National Archives; Darrah, *Powell of the Colorado*, pp. 252–53; John Wesley Powell to Secretary of the Interior, Feb. 15, 1888, Outgoing Correspondence, Feb. 18–Oct. 2, 1888, RG 57, National Archives.

68.   *Colorado Farmer and Live Stock Journal*, April 19, 1888; "Prevention of Floods in the Lower Mississippi," *Science*, 12 (Aug. 24, 1888), pp. 85–86; J. W. Powell to the Secretary of the Interior, March 13, 1888, and Powell to D. L. Mitchell, Aug. 10, 1888, Outgoing Correspondence, Feb. 18–Oct. 2, 1888, RG 57, National Archives; *Tenth Annual Report of the United States Geological Survey [1888–89]*, Part 2, "Irrigation" (Washington, D.C., 1890), pp. 2, 7.

69.   J. W. Powell to Secretary of the Interior, March 13, 1888, Outgoing Correspondence, Feb. 18–Oct. 2, 1888, RG 57, National Archives.

70.   *Congressional Record*, Senate, July 30, 1888, p. 7017.

71.   J. W. Powell to Secretary of the Interior, May 31, 1890, USGS, Outgoing Correspondence, April 14–Sept. 1, 1890, RG 57, National Archives; "Preliminary Report on the Organization and Prosecution of the Survey of Arid Lands for Purposes of Irrigation," S. Ex. Doc. 43, 50th Cong., 2d sess. (Washington, D.C., 1889), serial 2610; and "Sundry Civil Appropriation Bill," S. Rep. 2613, 50th Cong., 2d sess. (Washington, D.C., 1889), serial 2619, pp. 106–16.

72.   J. W. Powell to C. E. Dutton, May 28, 1889, Outgoing Correspondence, Mar. 30–July 15, 1889, RG 57, National Archives.

73.   J. W. Powell to Secretary of the Interior, March 13 and May 3, 1888, and Powell to Herbert Myrick, April 26, 1888, Outgoing Correspondence, Feb. 18–Oct. 2, 1888; Powell to Secretary of the Interior, Dec. 31, 1888, Outgoing Correspondence, Oct. 2, 1888–Mar. 30, 1889; C. E. Dutton to Powell, Feb. 20, 1890, Letters Received, Jan.–March 1890, all in RG 57, National Archives.

74.   F. E. Warren to Elwood Mead, Jan. 30, 1891, Warren Letterbook, Nov. 28, 1890–Feb. 6, 1891, Francis E. Warren Collection, University of Wyoming. Also see Warren to Mead, Jan. 26 and 27, 1891, and Warren to "Slack," Jan. 30, 1891, in the same letterbook. In July 1888, Powell argued that reservoir sites

designated by the Irrigation Survey should not be reserved from entry because having them taken up by private parties was "the very purpose" of the survey (Davison, *Leadership of the Reclamation Movement*, p. 81).

75.   J. W. Powell to Secretary of the Interior, July 26, 1888, Outgoing Correspondence, July 15–Dec. 11, 1889, and Powell to Secretary of the Interior, March 15, 1890, Outgoing Correspondence, Dec. 10, 1889–April 15, 1890, both in RG 57, National Archives; Sterling, "The Powell Irrigation Survey," p. 424.

76.   J. W. Powell to Secretary of the Interior, Dec. 31, 1888, Outgoing Correspondence, Oct. 2, 1888–Mar. 30, 1889, RG 57, National Archives.

77.   J. W. Powell to C. E. Dutton, May 28, 1889, Outgoing Correspondence, Mar. 30–July 15, 1889, RG 57, National Archives; C. E. Dutton, undated memorandum (probably early 1889), directed to USGS engineers, in "Elwood Mead, State Engineer: Correspondence, Observations of River Heights; Various Reports, 1889–1897," Elwood Mead Collection, Wyoming State Archives, Cheyenne.

78.   For example, see W. J. Murphy to J. W. Powell, Oct. 27, 1888; L. P. Bradley (Pecos Irrigation and Investment Co.) to Powell, Nov. 13, 1888; R. W. Waterman (governor of California) to W. F. Vilas (secretary of the interior), Dec. 10, 1888; Crone & Blatchford to Powell, Dec. 11, 1888; and Edgar Gray (United States Land and Investment Company, New York) to Powell, Dec. 19, 1888: all in Incoming Correspondence, Oct. 26–Dec. 29, 1888, RG 57, National Archives. Also C. P. Huntington (president, S.P. Railway Co.) to Powell, Mar. 24, 1889, and Charles F. Adams (president, U.P. Railway Co.) to Powell, Mar. 27, 1889, in Letters Received, Jan. 2–April 11, 1889; and the Report of the Executive Committee Meeting of the California State Board of Trade, April 2, 1889, in Letters Received, Apr. 11–June 17, 1889, both in RG 57, National Archives.

79.   On December 21, 1888, C. E. Dutton wrote to Powell that "the average western citizen naturally conceives the notion that the Gov't ought to & will, undertake the construction of vast irrigation works. It is of little use to converse with these men." See Letters Received, Jan. 2–April 11, 1889, RG 57, National Archives. Also see G. P. White to Grover Cleveland, Aug. 12, 1888, in Letters Received, Aug. 1–Oct. 26, 1888, RG 57, National Archives.

80.   While the Powell survey was under way, many bills to grant land and other privileges to irrigation companies came before Congress. See, for example, S. 2351 (Teller) and H.R. 8058 (Joseph), 50th Cong., 1st sess., March 14, 1888; H.R. 12412 (Joseph), 50th Cong., 2d sess., Jan. 28, 1889; S. 1375 (Reagan), 51st Cong., 1st sess., Dec. 17, 1889; H.R. 3370 (Joseph), 50th Cong., 2d sess., Dec. 20, 1889; H.R. 3371 (Joseph), 51st Cong., 1st sess., Dec. 20, 1889; H.R. 3971 (Joseph), 51st Cong., 1st sess., Jan. 6, 1890; S. 2261 (Cockrell), 51st Cong., 1st sess., Jan. 23, 1890; H.R. 5823 (Peters), 51st Cong., 1st sess., Jan. 24, 1890; and S. 3403 (Stewart), 51st Cong., 1st sess., April 5, 1890. Most of the legislation pertained to Arizona and New Mexico.

81.   The bills to implement Powell's irrigation district scheme were S.B. 2837, introduced by Senator J. P. Reagan of Texas on February 25, 1890, and an amended version, S.B. 3769, introduced by Reagan on May 8, 1890. The legislation was much more detailed than Powell's 1878 proposal—for example, it contained provisions for an irrigation court to settle water disputes—but the

basic features remained the same. The amended bill is reprinted in *Report of the Special Committee of the United States Senate on the Irrigation and Reclamation of Arid Lands* (Washington, D.C., 1890), serial 2707, pp. 178–82. For a section-by-section discussion of the bill, see pp. 140–43. Also see pp. 97, 135–36.

82. "Report of the Governor of Idaho," in *Report of the Secretary of the Interior, 1888*, vol. 2, p. 767. The Mormons had become increasingly unpopular among non-Mormons in southern Idaho. For example, in Brigham County, on the Snake, they claimed a vast quantity of irrigable land and constructed small ditches which permitted them to block the construction of a much more efficient highline canal. See C. E. Dutton to J. W. Powell, Sept. 22, 1889, Letters Received, Aug. 5–Oct. 30, 1889, RG 57, National Archives.

83. See, for example, the Fred T. Dubois Dictation, pp. 46–48, in the Dubois Collection, Special Collections, Idaho State University, Pocatello.

84. Thomas G. Alexander, "John Wesley Powell, the Irrigation Survey, and the Inauguration of the Second Phase of Irrigation Development in Utah," *Utah Historical Quarterly*, 37 (Spring 1969), pp. 203–6. Alexander pointed out that this struggle was not just between Mormons and non-Mormons, it also pitted small farmers against corporate monopoly.

85. *Cheyenne Daily Leader*, July 30, 1889.

86. *Rocky Mountain News*, Jan. 21, 1889.

87. Stegner, *Beyond the Hundredth Meridian*, pp. 303, 318–20; *Second Annual Report of the Territorial Engineer to the Governor of Wyoming, for the Year 1889* (Cheyenne, 1890), p. 49; Powell, untitled, undated memorandum (early 1890s) in USGS, Powell Irrigation Survey, Box 1, D-121, RG 57, National Archives; *Report of the General Land Commissioner, 1890* (Washington, D.C., 1891), pp. 59–78.

88. Antonio Joseph's speech of July 26, 1890, is reprinted in *Congressional Record*, 51st Cong., 1st sess., app., pp. 503–4.

89. Elwood Mead to W. J. Clarke, Feb. 6, 1892, Mead Letterbook, Jan. 16–Dec. 10, 1892, Mead Collection.

90. C. E. Dutton to J. W. Powell, June 19, 1889; John W. Noble to Powell, Aug. 5, 1889; and John R. Bothwell to Secretary of the Interior, August 8, 1889: Letters Received, Aug. 5–Oct. 30, 1889, RG 57, National Archives. *Report of the Secretary of the Interior, 1889*, p. XXV; *Report of the Secretary of the Interior, 1890*, pp. X–XII; *Report of the General Land Commissioner, 1890*, pp. 70–71; S. Ex. Doc. 136, 51st Cong., 1st. sess. (Washington, D.C., 1890), serial 2688, pp. 4–8.

91. J. W. Powell to Elwood Mead, June 9, 1890, in "Elwood Mead, Territorial & State Engineer: Incoming Correspondence from Federal Government Officials, 1888–1890," Mead Collection.

92. Stegner, *Beyond the Hundredth Meridian*, p. 304.

93. Elliott, *Servant of Power*, pp. 74, 87–88.

94. Initially, Stewart embraced many of Powell's ideas, including relatively autonomous water districts; see William Morris Stewart, "Reclaiming the Western Deserts," *Forum*, 7 (April 1889), pp. 201–8, esp. p. 208. However, he quickly backed away from this position and within a year proposed a bill (S.B. 2104)

to reserve the "unappropriated waters of the lakes and rivers on the public lands for such beneficial uses as shall be determined by the States and Territories in which such waters are situated." His bill, which was adopted by his special committee on irrigation, would have restricted federal control to interstate streams and lakes (*Report of the Special Committee of the United States Senate on the Irrigation and Reclamation of Arid Lands,* p. 13).

95.   As quoted in Darrah, *Powell of the Colorado,* p. 304.

96.   W. M. Stewart to William Hammond Hall, May 26, 1890, Box 10, Letterbook, Dec. 3, 1889–May 26, 1890, Stewart Collection; *Congressional Record,* Senate, May 26, 1890, 51st Cong., 1st sess., pp. 5373, 5590. Also see Stewart to M. L. Power, May 29, 1890, in Letterbook, May 26, 1890–Feb. 2, 1891, Stewart Collection. Stewart went to great lengths to distort the historical record. His autobiography, published in 1908, incorrectly blamed Powell entirely for the withdrawal of public land from settlement. (In 1889 he had attributed the decision to easterners who "go so far as to say that they want to reserve all public lands for future generations.") Stewart also insisted that after the Irrigation Survey had been shut down, Powell spitefully "planted" anti-irrigation articles in eastern journals in an effort to block all future appropriations for the study of irrigation agriculture by the Department of Agriculture. See Brown, *Reminiscences of Senator William M. Stewart of Nevada,* pp. 350–51; and Stewart to Thomas Gaman, Dec. 23, 1889, Box 10, Letterbook, Dec. 3, 1889–May 26, 1890, Stewart Collection.

97.   William M. Stewart to Oren B. Taft, June 9, 1890, and Stewart to Samuel Purdy, June 24, 1890, in Box 10, Letterbook, May 26, 1890–Feb. 2, 1891, Stewart Collection.

98.   William M. Stewart to John Conness, Aug. 29, 1890, Box 10, Letterbook, May 26, 1890–Feb. 2, 1891, Stewart Collection. Stewart's most thorough discussion of his charges and grievances against Powell is in his Sept. 6, 1890, letter to T. C. Friedlander in the same letterbook.

99.   John Townley, *Alfalfa Country* (Reno, 1981), p. 95. Also see Barbara Richnak, *A River Flows: The Life of Robert Lardin Fulton* (Incline, Nev., 1983), p. 79.

100.   *Morning Appeal* (Carson, City), Jan. 13, 1887.

101.   William Morris Stewart to George F. Turrintin, March 29, 1888, Box 9, Letterbook, Mar. 29–June 13, 1888, Stewart Collection. Also see Stewart to H. J. Pratt, March 11, 1889, Box 10, Letterbook, Feb. 17–April 11, 1889, Stewart Collection.

102.   William Morris Stewart to Andrew Maute, Feb. 8, 1889; also see Stewart to J. H. Crossman, Feb. 4, 1889: both letters in Box 9, Letterbook, Dec. 12, 1888–Feb. 17, 1889, Stewart Collection. Stewart's letter in the *San Francisco Chronicle,* Feb. 19, 1889, contained the same message.

103.   On the cessation of the Irrigation Survey see *Congressional Record,* 51st Cong., 1st sess., July 16–22, July 26, and August 26–27, 1890.

104.   John Wesley Powell to Secretary of the Interior, May 18, 1889, Outgoing Correspondence, Mar. 30–July 15, 1889; J. C. Pilling (chief clerk, USGS) to M. A. Smith, Aug. 2, 1889, and Pilling to H. E. Kemp, Aug. 6, 1889, in Outgoing Correspondence, July 15–Dec. 11, 1889: all in RG 57, National Archives.

105.   *Kansas Farmer* (Topeka), Dec. 17, 1890.

106.   *Irrigation Age,* 2 (Jan. 1, 1892), p. 361. William Ellsworth Smythe, in an editorial entitled "The Problem of Settlement" in *Irrigation Age,* 1 (Aug. 1, 1891), p. 116, remarked that the prime source of new settlers for the arid West was the "Old West" of Nebraska, Kansas, Illinois, Indiana, and other states "where the farmers are tired of being burned out one year and drowned out the next."

107.   *Twelfth Census of the United States* (Washington, D.C., 1902), vol. 6, pt. 2 (agriculture), p. 867. The census did not include eastern Colorado as part of the Great Plains. There were 20,818 acres irrigated in Kansas, 18,241 in Texas, 15,717 in South Dakota, 11,744 in Nebraska, and only 445 in North Dakota.

108.   See, for example, the *Denver Republican,* March 13 and 26, and June 18, 1889.

109.   As reprinted in Cyrus Thomas, "Agricultural Resources of the Territories," in *Preliminary Report of the United States Geological Survey of Montana and Portions of Adjacent Territories; Being a Fifth Annual Report of Progress* (Washington, D.C., 1872), p. 273.

110.   *Congressional Record,* 46th Cong., 2d sess., March 11, 1880, pp. 1471–72. "Report of the Commissioner of the General Land Office," in *Report of the Secretary of the Interior, 1883* (Washington, D.C., 1883), p. 29.

111.   For example, in the 47th Congress, 1st session, 1881–82, see H.R. 3365 (Nevada), H.R. 4416 (Arizona), and H.R. 5187 (New Mexico); and in the 48th Congress, 1st session, 1882–83, see S. 818 (Nevada), H.R. 950 (Nevada), H.R. 1665 (Arizona), and H.R. 1698 (Arizona).

112.   H.R. 571 (Peters), 48th Cong., 1st sess., introduced Dec. 10, 1883.

113.   H.R. 4450 (Hanback), 48th Cong., 1st sess., introduced Feb. 4, 1884.

114.   See H.R. 2853 (Joseph), 49th Cong., 1st sess., introduced Jan. 7, 1886; H.R. 6939 (Bean), 49th Cong., 1st sess., March 16, 1886; H.R. 8545 (Toole), 49th Cong., 1st sess., May 3, 1886; H. Rep. 3118, 49th Cong., 1st sess. (Washington, D.C., 1886), serial 2444; *Congressional Record,* 50th Cong., 1st sess., House, Dec. 12, 1887, p. 43; H.R. 1964 (Toole), 50th Cong., 1st sess., Jan. 4, 1888; H.R. 1980 (Joseph), 50th Cong., 1st sess., Jan. 4, 1888; *Congressional Record,* 50th Cong., 1st sess., Senate, Jan. 30, 1888, pp. 825, 826; H. Rep. 1340, 50th Cong., 1st sess. (Washington, D.C., 1888), serial 2601.

115.   "The Artesian Wells of the James River Valley, Dakota," *Scientific American,* 60 (April 6, 1889), p. 207.

116.   The quotation from the *Aberdeen Daily News* is as reprinted in Realf, "The Irrigation Problem in the Northwest," p. 76. The proposal to sink wells is recounted in the *Daily News,* Jan. 8, 1890, as quoted in Marc M. Cleworth, "Artesian-Well Irrigation: Its History in Brown County, South Dakota, 1889–1900," *Agricultural History,* 15 (Oct. 1941), p. 197.

117.   The USGS *Fifth Annual Report, 1883–84* (Washington, D.C., 1885), pp. 131–80, included a perceptive article by Thomas C. Chamberlin that argued that "artesian wells do not manufacture water. They do not even bring to the surface more than goes down from the surface. . . . They merely pour out at one point what has fallen and sunk elsewhere. If the total fall is inadequate

to the agricultural wants of the total region, artesian wells cannot make it adequate" (p. 148).

118.   *Report of the Special Committee of the United States Senate on the Irrigation and Reclamation of Arid Lands*, vol. 3, p. 220.

119.   Ibid., vol. 1, p. 87.

120.   Ibid., vol. 4, p. 95; *Eleventh Annual Report of the Director of the United States Geological Survey [1889–90]* Part 2, "Irrigation" (Washington, D.C., 1891), pp. 260–76; "Ceding the Arid Lands to the States and Territories," H. Rep. 3767, 51st Cong., 2d sess. (Washington, D.C., 1891), serial 2888, p. 138; J. W. Powell to A. W. Wilson, Feb. 13, 1891, in Outgoing Correspondence, Jan. 20–May 18, 1891, and Powell to George E. Bunning, Nov. 4, 1893, in Outgoing Correspondence, June 15–Dec. 30, 1893, RG 57, National Archives.

121.   J. W. Powell to The Senators from North and South Dakota, March 4, 1890, Outgoing Correspondence, Dec. 10, 1889–April 15, 1890, RG 57, National Archives.

122.   Darrah, *Powell of the Colorado*, pp. 286, 309; E. S. Nettleton to Elwood Mead, Feb. 24, 1890, in "Elwood Mead, Territorial & State Engineer: Incoming Correspondence from Federal Government Officials, 1888–1890," Mead Collection; Richard J. Hinton to George Nicholl, Nov. 3, 1890, and Hinton to Lyman Bridges, Dec. 24, 1890, in Press Copies of Letters Sent by the Office of Irrigation Inquiry, vol. 2, Oct. 14, 1890–Feb. 28, 1891, RG 16, National Archives.

123.   Walter Rusinek, "Western Reclamation's Forgotten Forces: Richard J. Hinton and Groundwater Development," *Agricultural History*, 61 (Summer 1987), p. 23; Dupree, *Science in the Federal Government*, pp. 234–35; Richard J. Hinton, undated newspaper interview, in Press Copies of Letters Sent by the Office of Irrigation Inquiry, vol. 3, Feb. 28–Aug. 26, 1891, RG 16, National Archives.

124.   *Report of the Secretary of Agriculture, 1890* (Washington, D.C., 1890), p. 41.

125.   "A Report on the Preliminary Investigation to Determine the Proper Location of Artesian Wells Within the Area of the Ninety-Seventh Meridian and East of the Foot-Hills of the Rocky Mountains," S. Ex. Doc. 222, 51st Cong., 1st sess. (Washington, D.C., 1890), the quotation is from pp. 19–20; *Report of the Secretary of Agriculture, 1890*, pp. 471–88.

126.   The latter appropriation suggests how quickly enthusiasm for artesian wells cooled in Congress. The ten-thousand-dollar grant was the same amount allotted to the Weather Bureau to test the effect of explosives on rainfall.

127.   *Report of the Secretary of Agriculture, 1891* (Washington, D.C., 1892), pp. 53–55, 439–50. In his 1891 report, Nettleton reduced the amount of land that could be served by artesian wells to "at least" 1,500,000 acres, a far cry from the 7,000,000 acres he had claimed were irrigable within the James River basin alone in 1890 (p. 449). The final reports of the Artesian and Underflow Investigation, written by E. S. Nettleton, Robert Hay, and James Gregory—each covering a different part of the West—were published in Richard J. Hinton, *Report on Irrigation* (Washington, D.C., 1893), serial 2899.

128.   *Irrigation Age*, 1 (May 1, 1891), p. 20; 1 (May 15, 1891), p. 36; and 1 (June 15, 1891), p. 72.

129.   F. H. Newell, "Artesian Wells," *Irrigation Age*, 3 (May 1, 1892), pp. 27–28.
130.   For example, see the following bills pertaining to artesian wells: S. 441 (Pettigrew), 52d Cong., 1st sess., introduced Dec. 10, 1891; S. 1305 (Kyle), 52d Cong., 1st sess., Jan. 5, 1892; H.R. 2784 (Smith), 52d Cong., 1st sess., Jan. 11, 1892; S. 135 (Pettigrew), 53d Cong., 1st sess., Aug. 8, 1893; H.R. 3652 (Smith), 53d Cong., 1st sess., Oct. 3, 1893; H.R. 5245 (Joseph), 53d Cong., 2d sess., Jan. 16, 1894; and H.R. 4451 (Pickler), 54th Cong., 1st sess., Jan. 21, 1896. Great Plains residents petitioned Congress repeatedly for relief from drought and depression. See, for example, the *Congressional Record*, 53d Cong., 1st sess. (1893–94), pp. 2017, 2077, 2117, 2613, 3440, 3490, 3718, 7230, and 8633. Although Congress refused to extend the Artesian Survey beyond 1891, there was much activity at the state level. For the activities of the state government in Kansas, see Sageser, *Joseph L. Bristow: Kansas Progressive*, pp. 23–25; for North Dakota's policies, see W. W. Barrett, "Irrigation in North Dakota," *Irrigation Age*, 9 (June 1896), pp. 231–32.
131.   J. W. Powell to Secretary of the Interior, Jan. 28, 1891, Outgoing Correspondence, Jan. 20–May 18, 1891, RG 57, National Archives.
132.   Stegner, *Beyond the Hundredth Meridian*, p. 338.
133.   As reprinted in Davison, *Leadership of the Reclamation Movement*, pp. 115–16. Also see Dupree, *Science in the Federal Government*, pp. 195–214; Stegner, *Beyond the Hundredth Meridian*, pp. 324–28; and Darrah, *Powell of the Colorado*, p. 319.
134.   Donald J. Pisani, "Forests and Conservation, 1865–1890," *Journal of American History*, 72 (Sept. 1985), pp. 340–59.
135.   "A National Forest Preserve," *Nation*, 37 (Sept. 6, 1883), p. 201.
136.   Abbot Kinney, "Forest Culture," in *Annual Report of the State Board of Horticulture of the State of California for 1890* (Sacramento, 1891), p. 149. For similar statements, see *Fourth Biennial Report of the California State Board of Forestry for the Years 1891–92* (Sacramento, 1893), pp. 6–7; George H. Maxwell, "Nature's Storage Reservoirs," *Forester*, 5 (Aug. 1899), pp. 183–85; James D. Schuyler, "The Influence of Forests upon Storage Reservoirs," *Forester*, 5 (Dec. 1899), pp. 285–88; and J. W. Toumey, "Forests as Sources of Water Supply," *Proceedings of the Ninth Annual Session of the National Irrigation Congress, Held at Central Music Hall, Chicago, Ill., November 21, 22, 23, 24, 1900* (St. Louis, n.d.), pp. 183–92. *Forester* published many articles on forests and agriculture in the years 1898–1903. See especially the series by Abbot Kinney in the February, April, and May 1898 issues.
137.   Gordon B. Dodds, "The Stream-Flow Controversy: A Conservation Turning Point," *Journal of American History*, 56 (June 1969), pp. 59–69.
138.   J. B. Harrison to President Benjamin Harrison, Sept. 18, 1889, Letters Received, Aug. 5–Oct. 30, 1889, RG 57, National Archives.
139.   B. E. Fernow, chief of the Forestry Division in the Department of Agriculture and one of the leading figures in American forestry in the late nineteenth century, maintained in 1889 that the drought on the Great Plains was due more to the evaporation of moisture caused by the unremitting winds than to any absolute shortage of water. He advised "checking or reducing this

evaporation by the planting of wind-breaks and timber belts," but said nothing about either storage reservoirs or artesian wells. Government—the level did not matter—could end the drought by simply planting trees. See *Report of the Secretary of Agriculture, 1889* (Washington, D.C., 1889), p. 276. Two years later he declared: "Once let woods be spread over the now arid plains of the West and there would be rain in plenty there" ("Forests," *Scientific American*, 65 [Sept. 19, 1891], p. 181).

140.   The adoption on March 3, 1891, of legislation authorizing the creation of forest reserves prompted Powell to suggest that the new reserves conform to natural drainage basins and extend no farther than the timber at the headwaters of the West's major rivers. The remainder would be left for use by district residents. See Powell to Secretary of the Interior, March 21, 1891, Outgoing Correspondence, Jan. 20–May 18, 1891, RG 57, National Archives.

141.   C. S. Sargent, "Irrigation Problems in the Arid West," *Garden and Forest*, 1 (Aug. 8, 1888), pp. 277–78; "Trees on Arid Lands" (letter from John Wesley Powell to Kansas City *Times*), as reprinted in *Science*, 12 (Oct. 12, 1888), pp. 170–71.

142.   Henry Gannett, "The Influence of Forests on the Quantity and Frequency of Rainfall," *Science*, 12 (Nov. 23, 1888), p. 244.

143.   C. S. Sargent, "The Danger from Mountain Reservoirs," *Garden and Forest*, 2 (June 19, 1889), p. 289; and Sargent, "Mountain Reservoirs and Irrigation," *Garden and Forest*, 2 (July 13, 1889), pp. 313–314. Also see Charles H. Shinn, "California Forests and Irrigation," *Garden and Forest*, 3 (Sept. 3, 1890), pp. 426–27. On the Johnstown flood see David G. McCullough, *The Johnstown Flood* (New York, 1968).

144.   John Wesley Powell, "The Lesson of Conemaugh," *North American Review*, 149 (Aug. 1889), p. 156.

145.   John Wesley Powell, "The Non-Irrigable Lands of the Arid Region," *Century*, 39 (April 1890), p. 920.

146.   *Garden and Forest*, 2 (Sept. 4, 1889), p. 422, and 3 (June 18, 1890), p. 293. Also see Sargent's editorial in 3 (March 5, 1890), p. 110, and 6 (April 26, 1893), pp. 181–82.

147.   J. B. Harrison, "Forests and Civilization: The North Woods, VII," *Garden and Forest*, 2 (Sept. 11, 1889), pp. 441–42.

148.   *Twelfth Annual Report [1891] of the Director of the United States Geological Survey: Part 2—Irrigation* (Washington, D.C., 1892), p. xvi; *Report of the Secretary of the Interior, 1891* (Washington, D.C., 1891), p. XCI; J. W. Powell to Secretary of the Interior, March 15, 1890, Outgoing Correspondence, Dec. 10, 1889–April 15, 1890, RG 57, National Archives. The *Report of the Secretary of the Interior, 1892* (Washington, D.C., 1893), p. V, claimed that these reservoirs could serve about 4 million acres.

149.   *U.S. Statutes at Large*, vol. 26, p. 1095 (March 3, 1891).

150.   *U.S. Statutes at Large*, vol. 29, p. 599 (Feb. 26, 1897).

151.   Morris Bien, "Right of Way for Canals and Reservoirs for Irrigation Purposes," *Official Proceedings of the Third National Irrigation Congress, Held at Denver, Colorado, Sept. 3rd to 8th, 1894* (Denver, n.d.), p. 48.

152.   *Reno Evening Gazette*, Oct. 7, 1889; Stuart Bruchey, *The Wealth of*

the Nation: An Economic History of the United States (New York, 1988), p. 133.

153.   An acre-foot of water is the quantity of water sufficient to cover an acre of land to a depth of one foot. Even in western Nevada, one of the driest regions in the West, Powell maintained that an acre-foot would "abundantly irrigate an acre of land through one season." Time has shown that most land in western Nevada requires four to five times that amount. See J. W. Powell to Secretary of the Interior, Dec. 31, 1888, Outgoing Correspondence, Oct. 2, 1888–March 30, 1889, and J. W. Powell to E. Bach, Sept. 29, 1890, Outgoing Correspondence, Sept. 1, 1890–Jan. 21, 1891, RG 57, National Archives; John Wesley Powell, untitled, undated memorandum (probably early 1890s), USGS, Powell Irrigation Survey, Box 1, D-121, RG 57, National Archives; Powell, "Institutions for the Arid Lands," *Century,* 40 (May 1890), pp. 111–16; *Irrigation Age,* 1 (May 30, 1891), p. 61; "Ceding the Arid Lands to the States and Territories," H. Rep. 3767, 51st Cong., 2d sess. (Washington, D.C., 1891), serial 2888, pp. 129–30.

154.   Davison, *Leadership of the Reclamation Movement.*

155.   Paul Wallace Gates, *History of Public Land Law Development* (Washington, D.C., 1968), p. 420.

156.   See for example, Powell's description of his "colony system" in *Report on the Lands of the Arid Region,* pp. 40–41.

157.   C. S. Sargent, in "The Forests on the Public Domain," *Garden and Forest,* 3 (Jan. 8, 1890), pp. 13–14, recounted Powell's address to the New York City Chamber of Commerce on December 5, 1889, in which Powell reiterated his plan for river-basin development. Powell referred to his proposed districts as "each little kingdom."

158.   Two other irrigation engineers enamored of European irrigation institutions were William Hammond Hall, California's state engineer from 1878 to 1889, and Herbert M. Wilson, one of Powell's assistants in the USGS. See particularly Hall, *Irrigation Development: History, Customs, Laws and Administrative Systems Relating to Irrigation, Water-Courses, and Waters in France, Italy, and Spain* (Sacramento, 1886); and Wilson, "American Irrigation Engineering," in *Thirteenth Annual Report of the United States Geological Survey [1891–92],* Part 3, Irrigation (Washington, D.C., 1893), pp. 109–349. Also see "Irrigation in India," *Scientific American,* 69 (Aug. 5, 1893), pp. 89–90; H. M. Wilson, "American and Indian Irrigation Works," *Irrigation Age,* 6 (March 1894), pp. 107–9; and Richard J. Hinton, *Report on Irrigation* (Washington, D.C., 1893), serial 2899, pp. 391–401.

159.   Donald Worster, *Rivers of Empire: Water, Aridity, and the Growth of the American West* (New York, 1985), pp. 147, 150, 169. Worster discusses the European influence on American irrigation on pp. 146–56. Powell, according to Worster, was one of the few real "democrats" among water planners. "Was it [the West] to be run by capitalists or by the people? Powell's answer, given as emphatically as anyone in government service has ever given it, was that the people should be in charge. And the West presented a grand opportunity, he believed, to plot that technological democracy, whereas the older industrial centers were already firmly under capitalism's control" (p. 134). I have found

little evidence to suggest that Powell was more of a "democrat" than other scientists, or that he rejected capitalism, or that he thought the West was less "firmly under capitalism's control."

160.   L. B. Lee, "The Canadian-American Irrigation Frontier, 1884–1914," *Agricultural History,* 40 (Oct. 1966), p. 280; Fred Bond, J. S. Dennis, and J. M. Wilson, "Irrigation Laws of the Northwest Territories of Canada and of Wyoming," USDA Office of Experiment Stations Bulletin 96 (Washington, D.C., 1901).

161.   J. M. Powell, *Watering the Garden State: Water, Land, and Community in Victoria, 1834–1988* (Sydney, 1989); Lewis R. East, "Parallel Irrigation Development—United States and Australia," American Society of Civil Engineers, *Centennial Transactions* (New York, 1953); Alfred Deakin, *Irrigation in Western America* (Melbourne, 1885).

162.   *Third Annual Report of the State Engineer to the Governor of Wyoming, 1895 and 1896* (Cheyenne, 1897), p. 37; Elwood Mead, "Irrigation in Victoria," *Engineering Record,* 60 (Aug. 14, 1909), p. 176. Also see Mead, "What Australia Can Teach America," *Independent,* 71 (Aug. 17, 1911), pp. 368–69.

Chapter 6

1.   Harry N. Scheiber is the preeminent student of the history of American federalism. See his "Federalism and the American Economic Order, 1789–1910," *Law & Society Review,* 10 (Fall 1975), pp. 57–118; "Federalism and Legal Process: Historical and Contemporary Analysis of the American System," *Law & Society Review,* 14 (Spring 1980), pp. 663–723; "Federalism and the Diffusion of Power: Historical and Contemporary Perspectives," *University of Toledo Law Review,* 9 (Summer 1978), pp. 619–80; and "Some Realism about Federalism: Historical Complexities and Current Challenges," in Advisory Commission on Intergovernmental Relations, *Emerging Issues in American Federalism* (Washington, D.C., 1985), pp. 41–63. Still very useful for understanding federalism is James Bryce, *American Commonwealth* (New York, 1915), vol. 1, pp. 341–64. Also see Martin Shapiro, "American Federalism," in Ronald K. L. Collins, ed., *Constitutional Government in America* (Durham, N.C., 1980), pp. 359–71; and Samuel H. Beer, "The Modernization of American Federalism," *Publius,* 3 (Fall 1973), pp. 49–95.

2.   William Appleman Williams, *The Contours of American History* (Cleveland, 1961), pp. 41–42, 70, 159–60; R. W. K. Hinton, "The Mercantile System in the Time of Thomas Mun," *Economic History Review,* 7 (April 1955), pp. 277–90.

3.   Charles Haar, ed., *The Golden Age of American Law* (New York, 1965), p. 372.

4.   Gerald D. Nash, *State Government and Economic Development: A History of Administrative Policies in California, 1849–1933* (Berkeley, 1964), pp. 91–94, 183; Spencer L. Kimball, *Insurance and Public Policy: A Study in the Legal Implementation of Social and Economic Public Policy, Based on Wisconsin Records, 1835–1959* (Madison, 1960), pp. 250–70; Joseph G. Blandi, *Maryland Business Corporations, 1783–1852* (Baltimore, 1934), p. 90.

5.   Tony Freyer, *Forums of Order: The Federal Courts and Business in American History* (Greenwich, Conn., 1979), p. 11; Harry N. Scheiber, "Xenophobia and Parochialism in the History of American Legal Process: From the Jacksonian Era to the Sagebrush Rebellion," *William & Mary Law Review,* 23 (Summer 1982), pp. 652, 657; Harold J. Graham, "Acres for Cents: The Economic and Constitutional Significance of Frontier Tax Titles, 1800–1890," in *Everyman's Constitution* (Madison, 1968), pp. 504, 511, 513; Lawrence M. Friedman, *A History of American Law* (New York, 1973), p. 397.

6.   Fred T. Dubois Dictation, Box 1, Fred T. Dubois Collection, Special Collections, Idaho State University, Pocatello; *Idaho Tri-Weekly Statesman,* March 4 and 9, 1886; *Coeur d'Alene Record,* Dec. 31, 1887; *Idaho World,* March 20, 1888; *Evening Inter-Idaho,* March 2, 14, 16, 27, 1888; *Boise City Republican,* Feb. 4 and March 13, 1888.

7.   *Field and Farm* (Denver), Feb. 23, 1889; *Rocky Mountain News* (Denver), Jan. 31 and March 3, 1889; *Cheyenne Daily Leader,* Oct. 22 and 23, 1901.

8.   *Third Biennial Report of the State Engineer of the State of Colorado, for the Years 1885–86* (Denver, 1887), pp. 233–34; *Second Biennial Report of the State Engineer to the Governor of Wyoming, 1893 and 1894* (Cheyenne, 1894), pp. 158–59; *Cheyenne Daily Leader,* Sept. 27, 1894; *Genoa Weekly Courier* (Nev.), Jan. 11, 1889; Nov. 21, 1890; Feb. 27, March 13, Oct. 2, and Dec. 25, 1891; D. W. Ross, "Home Making in Idaho," *Irrigation Age,* 7 (Dec. 1894), p. 255.

9.   Robert Kelley, *Gold vs. Grain: The Hydraulic Mining Controversy in California's Sacramento Valley, a Chapter in the Decline of Laissez-Faire* (Glendale, Calif., 1959), p. 69; *Reports of the Joint Committees of the Assembly on Mines and Mining Interests, and Agriculture, Relative to the Injury Now Being Done to Lands and Streams in This State by the Deposit of Detritus from the Gravel Mines,* 21st sess., vol. 4, 1875–76 (Sacramento, 1876); *Majority Report of the [Assembly] Committee on Mining Debris,* 22d sess., vol. 4, 1877–78 (Sacramento, 1878).

10.   Kelley, *Gold vs. Grain,* pp. 86, 87, 116–17, 121.

11.   Ibid., pp. 59, 79–81.

12.   *Sacramento Daily Record-Union,* Jan. 6, 1881. For examples of editorial support for state reclamation, see the *Tulare Times* (Tulare, Calif.), Nov. 25, 1871; *Fresno Weekly Expositor,* May 14, 1873; *Daily Alta California* (San Francisco), April 21, 1881; and *Weekly Visalia Delta,* April 9, 1885.

13.   *Cal. Stats.* (1878), p. 634. "Multiple use" was the idea that all water problems—including flooding, swampland drainage, irrigation, navigation, and later hydroelectric power generation—were related and could not be solved independently.

14.   For William Hammond Hall's career, see Donald J. Pisani, *From the Family Farm to Agribusiness: The Irrigation Crusade in California and the West, 1850–1931* (Berkeley, 1984), pp. 167–90.

15.   William Hammond Hall, *Report of the State Engineer to the Legislature of the State of California, Session of 1880* (Sacramento, 1880), p. 121 (quotation) and passim.

16.   *Marysville Daily Appeal,* Feb. 19, 1880. Also see Kelley, *Gold vs. Grain,*

pp. 99–100; the *Sacramento Daily Record-Union,* Dec. 24 and 28, 1875, Jan. 17 and 29, March 4, April 1, 1876.

17.   Kelley, *Gold v. Grain,* pp. 136, 150–52; *Report of the State Engineer to the Legislature of the State of California—Session of 1881* (Sacramento, 1881), pp. 3–13.

18.   See "An Account of the State Drainage and Debris Work of 1878–1881," dated Dec. 1904, pp. 33 (quotation), 79, in the State Engineer's File, California State Archives, Sacramento. Also see Hall to Governor George Stoneman, Nov. 19, 1882, in the same file.

19.   Kelley, *Gold vs. Grain,* pp. 154, 239; *Report of the Assembly Committee on Claims, Twenty-Fifth Session, on Assembly Bill No. 207* (Sacramento, 1885), pp. 11, 16–17.

20.   *Sacramento Daily Record-Union,* Sept. 4 and Nov. 17, 1880.

21.   William Hammond Hall to Governor George Perkins, Oct. 15, 1881, State Engineer's File, California State Archives; *Report of the State Engineer . . . 1881,* pp. 15–65; *Report of the Board of Directors of Drainage District No. 1, Showing Progress of Work to January 1, 1881* (Sacramento, 1881); *Pacific Rural Press,* 20 (Nov. 20, 1880), p. 330, and 20 (Nov. 27, 1880), p. 346.

22.   *Sacramento Daily Record-Union,* Jan. 14, 1881.

23.   "An Account of the State Drainage and Debris Work of 1878–1881," Dec. 1904, p. 81.

24.   *Weekly Colusa Sun* (Colusa, Calif.), Jan. 22, 1881; *Sacramento Daily Record-Union,* Oct. 24 and 26, Nov. 10, 1881.

25.   *Stockton Daily Independent,* Jan. 28, 31, and Feb. 10, 1881; *Sacramento Daily Record-Union,* Jan. 8, Feb. 16, 21, 25, 26, and March 2, 1881; *Kern County Californian* (Bakersfield, Calif.), March 19, 1881.

26.   It was significant that Camron came from Alameda County, home of Oakland, across the bay from San Francisco. Oakland and San Francisco engaged in a fierce competition to develop port facilities and dominate the oceanic trade. Anything that hurt investors in San Francisco was assumed to benefit Oakland.

27.   Kelley, *Gold vs. Grain,* pp. 198–99; *Kern County Californian,* March 19, April 19, 1881; *Tulare County Times,* Oct. 8, 1881; *Sacramento Daily Record-Union,* Sept. 28, Oct. 24, 1881.

28.   *Pacific Rural Press,* 21 (Jan. 1, 1881), p. 1; Feb. 5, 1881, p. 89; and Feb. 12, 1881, p. 104. *Weekly Butte Record* (Chico, Calif.), Jan. 22, 1881; *Kern County Californian,* July 15, 1880; *Sacramento Daily Record-Union,* Feb. 14, 1881.

29.   *Sacramento Daily Record-Union,* April 9 and 28, Nov. 13, 1880 (quotation). Also see the *Visalia Weekly Delta,* Dec. 10, 1880. Not surprisingly, the *Record-Union* supported state construction of a coordinated irrigation system in the hope that it would generate far more wealth than the initial cost to the state. See the issues of Dec. 13 and 28, 1880.

30.   *Los Angeles Daily Herald,* April 8, 11, and 15, 1880. Also see the *Herald* for March 21, 1880, and the *Weekly Express* (Los Angeles), April 17 and 24, 1880; *Kern County Californian,* Feb. 26, 1881; *Fresno Weekly Expositor,* Feb. 9, 1881.

31.   *Kern County Weekly Courier* (Bakersfield, Calif.), Oct. 30, 1875; *Sacramento Daily Record-Union*, June 2, 4, and 12, 1880, and Feb. 9, 1881.

32.   The letter to the *Bear River News* was reprinted in the *Pacific Rural Press*, 20 (July 31, 1880), p. 116. Also see the *Press*, 21 (Jan. 15, 1881), p. 41; *Fresno Weekly Expositor*, April 14, 1880; and *Daily Alta California* (San Francisco), April 21, 1881.

33.   Kelley, *Gold vs. Grain*, pp. 214–15, 278; *Pacific Rural Press*, 23 (April 1, 1882), p. 240. Also see *Los Angeles Daily Herald*, March 21, 1880; and *Stanislaus County Weekly News* (Modesto, Calif.), Jan. 21, 1881.

34.   William Hammond Hall to "My dear Yorke," July 17, 1881, Box 1, MS 915, Corresp. 1880–1885, Hall Collection, California Historical Society, San Francisco. The *Sacramento Daily Record-Union*, April 16, 1881, published verbatim legislative debate over the appropriation for the office of state engineer.

35.   Kelley, *Gold vs. Grain*, p. 245.

36.   Pisani, *From the Family Farm to Agribusiness*, pp. 293–99, 350–51.

37.   *Genoa Weekly Courier* (Nev.), Jan. 2, 1885.

38.   *Morning Appeal* (Carson City, Nev.), Feb. 7, 1889; *Daily Territorial Enterprise* (Virginia City, Nev.), Feb. 6, 1889.

39.   James G. Schrugham, *Nevada: A Narrative of the Conquest of a Frontier Land* (Chicago and New York, 1935), vol. 1, pp. 153–54, 209–12, 223, 225–26, 250, 272–73, 287, 301; Thomas Wren, ed., *A History of the State of Nevada: Its Resources and People* (New York, 1904), pp. 138–46; Myron Angel, *History of Nevada* (Oakland, 1881), pp. 122–30. Also see the long debate over taxation in the *Official Report of the Debate and Proceedings in the Constitutional Convention of the State of Nevada [1864]* (San Francisco, 1866), pp. 222–30, 318–87, 405–47, 499–501, 513–21. Delegates from the mining counties argued that the value of mines was much harder to determine than that of farms or livestock; that farming and ranching could not exist in Nevada without the markets provided by mining communities; and that the mining population contributed greatly to the state's tax base by paying property taxes on town lots. The proponents of equal assessment argued that taxing the mines at a lower rate was inherently unfair because it undermined respect for institutions of state government, diverted money into California, and created a privileged economic class, and also because the need to litigate mining claims was the single most important reason for creating the state's expensive court system. In other words, the legal interests of the mining industry cost far more to protect than those of the stock industry.

40.   *Reno Evening Gazette*, Aug. 11, 1890, Feb. 15, 1892, and June 26 and 27, 1894.

41.   John J. Powell, *Nevada, The Land of Silver* (San Francisco, 1876), p. 201.

42.   Russell R. Elliott, *History of Nevada* (Lincoln, 1973), pp. 115–16, 118.

43.   John Townley, *Alfalfa Country: Nevada Land, Water & Politics in the 19th Century* (Reno, 1981), p. 26; Elliott, *History of Nevada*, p. 119.

44.   Angel, *History of Nevada*, p. 133.

45.   Townley, *Alfalfa Country*, pp. 28–29, 34.

46.   In his report for 1874, Nevada's surveyor general reported that there

were 561 irrigation ditches in the state, which watered 100,699 acres. The largest block of irrigated land was in Washoe County, adjoining the Truckee River. In addition, there were 19,000 acres watered from the Carson River in Douglas County, and the Humboldt River served 18,000 acres in Elko County and 14,000 in Humboldt County. Almost all this land was pasture. See Angel, *History of Nevada*, p. 135.

47.   *Nevada State Journal* (Reno, Nev.), June 9, 1886; *Reno Evening Gazette*, July 9, 1886. The *Reno Evening Gazette* challenged Powning's gloomy appraisal in editorials published on June 15 and June 22, 1886. Also see Hubert Howe Bancroft and Frances Fuller Victor, *History of Nevada, 1540–1888* (San Francisco, 1890), p. 252; and Townley, *Alfalfa Country*, p. 254.

48.   *Reno Evening Gazette*, Sept. 10, 1881.

49.   *Reno Evening Gazette*, Oct. 17, 1881, and Feb. 19, 1883; *Morning Appeal*, Feb. 7, 1882, and Feb. 22, 1885; *Eureka Sentinel* (Eureka, Nev.), March 3, 1883; Townley, *Alfalfa Country*, pp. 73–74, 82–83.

50.   H. M. Yerington to W. M. Stewart, March 7, 1889, vol. 5, Private Correspondence, Letterbook 1884–1893; Yerington to "My dear Newlands," Feb. 14, 1891, vol. 25, Private Correspondence, 1890–97; and Yerington to William F. Herrin, Feb. 23, 1901, vol. 26, Private Correspondence, 1897–1903: all in the H. M. Yerington Collection, Bancroft Library, University of California, Berkeley.

51.   *Morning Appeal*, March 1, 4, 5, and 9, 1887. Also see the *Reno Evening Gazette*, Feb. 18, 1887; *Daily Territorial Enterprise* (Virginia City), Feb. 25, 1887; *Nevada State Journal* (Reno), Feb. 27, 1887; *Truckee Republican* (Truckee, Calif.), March 23 and 26, 1887.

52.   *Genoa Weekly Courier*, Feb. 18, April 8, 1887, and May 11, 1888; *Daily Territorial Enterprise*, Jan. 9 and 28, Feb. 3, March 1, 8, and 23, 1887.

53.   In 1886 and 1887, some southern California land appreciated by 1,000 percent. Why could not the same thing happen in western Nevada, where the state still had 1 million acres to sell and required only twenty-five cents an acre down payment and as much as twenty-five years to pay the balance? See Townley, *Alfalfa Country*, pp. 107, 166–67; *Genoa Weekly Courier*, Sept. 30, 1887, March 2, and May 25, 1888.

54.   *Reno Evening Gazette*, Sept. 3, 1888.

55.   *Morning Appeal*, Sept. 21, 1889.

56.   *Reno Evening Gazette*, Sept. 9, 1887, Feb. 3 and May 25, 1888, and Jan. 10, 1890; *Morning Appeal*, June 30, 1889. In the October 17, 1892, issue of the Reno *Gazette*, a prominent Nevada hydraulic engineer, L. H. Taylor, estimated that claims to the modest Humboldt aggregated more than the volume of the Mississippi—and were increasing every day.

57.   *Genoa Weekly Courier*, May 25, 1888.

58.   Townley, *Alfalfa Country*, pp. 149–64; Grace Dangberg, *Conflict on the Carson* (Minden, Nev., 1975), pp. 10–71.

59.   *Silver State* (Winnemucca, Nev.), March 14, 1889.

60.   *Silver State*, Jan. 19, 1889; *Daily Territorial Enterprise*, Jan. 9, 1887.

61.   H. M. Yerington to F. G. Newlands, March 4, 1889, Outgoing Correspondence, vol. 17, Yerington Collection; *Silver State*, Jan. 14 and Feb. 9, 1889;

Morning Appeal, Jan. 3, Feb. 7, 8, 9, 10, 14, 15, 16, 17, 19, 1889; *Daily Territorial Enterprise,* Feb. 6, 9, 13, 1889.

62.   *Genoa Weekly Courier,* July 27, Sept. 7, and Nov. 30, 1888; *Morning Appeal,* Jan. 30, 1889.

63.   H. M. Yerington to F. G. Newlands, Feb. 26 and March 3, 1889, and Yerington to D. O. Mills, March 8, 1889, vol. 17, Outgoing Correspondence, Yerington Collection. Yerington and others responsible for drafting the bill knew it was a "put up job." He notified U.S. senator William Morris Stewart that the dam would be constructed above Genoa and that construction would begin "at once." See Yerington to Stewart, Feb. 26 and March 7, 1889, vol. 5, Private Correspondence, Letterbook, 1884–1893, Yerington Collection.

64.   The entire water bill was reprinted in the *Genoa Weekly Courier,* March 15, 1889.

65.   *Reno Evening Gazette,* Feb. 6, 1889; *Silver State,* March 11 and 15, 1889; *Morning Appeal,* Jan. 26, Feb. 13, March 14, 31, April 3, Sept. 5, 1889; *Daily Territorial Enterprise,* March 9 and 16, 1889; Donald J. Pisani, "Storm over the Sierra: A Study in Western Water Use" (Ph.D. diss., University of California, Davis, 1975), pp. 104–6; Townley, *Alfalfa Country,* pp. 106, 114–15, 117–18. The 1889 legislature also approved legislation to pay bounties to those who bored artesian wells that provided twenty thousand or more gallons of water daily for at least a month. No more than one well could be sunk in each county. The bill set aside ten thousand dollars from the general fund to pay for these subsidies. Although some wells were sunk, there is no evidence that any well produced sufficient water to allow the driller to claim the prize. *Morning Appeal,* Jan. 24, 27, 31, March 5, 1889; *Genoa Weekly Courier,* March 29, 1889; *Report of the Special Committee of the United States Senate on the Irrigation and Reclamation of Arid Lands* (Washington, D.C., 1890), vol. 2, serial 2707, pp. 514–24.

66.   *Morning Appeal,* April 7, 1889.

67.   H. M. Yerington to "My dear Newlands," Feb. 14, 1891, vol. 25, Private Correspondence, 1890–1897, Yerington Collection; *Morning Appeal,* May 22, Sept. 5, and Dec. 31, 1889; *Reno Evening Gazette,* Oct. 21, 1889, and Jan. 12, 1891; *Report of the Special Committee of the United States Senate on the Irrigation and Reclamation of Arid Lands,* vol. 2, serial 2707, p. 511.

68.   *Daily Territorial Enterprise,* Feb. 7, 1889; *Genoa Weekly Courier,* July 12, 19, 26, Aug. 16, Sept. 13, 1889; *Morning Appeal,* July 6 and 21, 1889.

69.   C. E. Dutton to J. W. Powell, Sept. 29, 1889, USGS, Letters Received, Aug. 5–Oct. 30, 1889, RG 57, National Archives.

70.   *Genoa Weekly Courier,* June 22, 1888, and July 5, 1889.

71.   Townley, *Alfalfa Country,* pp. 106, 122–25; Dangberg, *Conflict on the Carson,* pp. 90–91; A. E. Chandler, "The Irrigation Laws of Nevada," *Forestry and Irrigation,* 9 (Nov. 1903), pp. 541–43; *Genoa Weekly Courier,* June 27, July 4, and 25, 1890.

72.   Although garbled and disorganized in places, the best account of this suit is in Dangberg, *Conflict on the Carson,* pp. 71–81. Also see H. M. Yerington to D. O. Mills, Sept. 1 and Oct. 11, 1889, Outgoing Correspondence, vol. 17,

Yerington Collection; *Morning Appeal*, Sept. 12, 1889; *Genoa Weekly Courier*, Sept. 13 and 20, 1889.

73.   *Reno Evening Gazette*, July 13 and 18, 1889; *Genoa Weekly Courier*, July 19 and 26, 1889; H. M. Yerington to D. O. Mills, July 28 and 30, Aug. 14 and 30, 1889, Outgoing Correspondence, vol. 17, Yerington Collection.

74.   *Reno Evening Gazette*, Sept. 30, 1889; *Genoa Weekly Courier*, Oct. 4 and 18, 1889.

75.   *Reno Evening Gazette*, Oct. 19, 1889.

76.   *Reno Evening Gazette*, Oct. 16 and 18, 1889; *Morning Appeal*, Oct. 15, 1889; H. M. Yerington to D. O. Mills, Oct. 28, 1889, Outgoing Correspondence, vol. 17, Yerington Collection.

77.   F. G. Newlands to W. E. Sharon, Jan. 20 and 31, 1891, Fulton Family Papers, in possession of John Fulton, Lake Tahoe, California. Also see Newlands's speech in *Report of the Proceedings of the Nevada State Irrigation Convention Held in the Opera House, Carson City, Nevada, October 9th, 1891* (Carson City, 1891), esp. pp. 13, 14, 19.

78.   See the interview with Newlands in the *Morning Appeal*, Dec. 20, 1889. Newlands's judgment was shared by most other Nevada newspapers. For example, on March 7, 1890, the *Genoa Weekly Courier* predicted that "Nevada will receive no aid from Congress for storage purposes for some time to come if ever." Most important, the winter of 1889–90 was very wet in western Nevada; there was no longer the urgency to build reservoirs. Henry Yerington informed Newlands on Feb. 22, 1890, that "from present appearances storage reservoirs during the next ten years would be like bringing Coals to Newcastle. It has been an awful winter, wholly unprecedented & there seems to be no end to it" (Outgoing Correspondence, vol. 17, Yerington Collection).

79.   William Hammond Hall went to work for Powell's Irrigation Survey after his stormy career as California's first state engineer ended. He provided Newlands with invaluable "inside" information as to the best reservoir sites and irrigable land. Fulton acted as Newlands's paid agent in acquiring the land and also served as his chief political lieutenant. Newlands spent so much time in California, the East, and Europe that he could not attend to day-to-day details.

80.   As reprinted in Dangberg, *Conflict on the Carson*, p. 81.

81.   *Reno Evening Gazette*, Oct. 14 and Nov. 25, 1889; *Morning Appeal*, Oct. 16, 1889; Lyman Bridges to J. W. Powell, Oct. 24, 1889, Letters Received, Aug. 5–Oct. 30, 1889, and F. G. Newlands to J. W. Powell, Aug. 17, 1890, USGS, Letters Received, March–September 1890, RG 57, National Archives; F. G. Newlands to R. L. Fulton, Dec. 24, 1889, Fulton Family Papers; William Lilley III and Lewis L. Gould, "The Western Irrigation Movement, 1878–1902: A Reappraisal," in Gene Gressley, ed., *The American West: A Reorientation* (Laramie, 1966), p. 60.

82.   Francis G. Newlands, *An Address to the People of Nevada on Water Storage and Irrigation* (Reno, 1890); *Reno Evening Gazette*, Oct. 7, 8, 9, 10, 11, 12, and 13, 1890.

83.   In an October 1889 speech, Newlands attributed the backward economy of Nevada to "the mining character of the country, and . . . the general belief

that life here is temporary and conditional" (*Reno Evening Gazette*, Oct. 7, 1889).

84. Newlands, *An Address to the People of Nevada*, p. 4.
85. Ibid., p. 15 (quotation). The 1890 census revealed that there were about five hundred thousand acres of irrigated land in Nevada. Most was pasture, and much of the remainder was planted to forage crops, such as alfalfa and clover. Since census figures were compiled from records kept by county and state officials, the figure of five hundred thousand acres—about half the land irrigated in Colorado in 1890—is probably inflated. *Genoa Weekly Courier*, March 4, 1892; *Reno Evening Gazette*, Oct. 17, 1892.
86. Newlands, *An Address to the People of Nevada*, p. 15.
87. F. G. Newlands to R. L. Fulton, Dec. 24, 1889, Fulton Family Papers. The ambitious charter of the Occidental Land and Improvement Company, and Newlands's frequent speculations in California during the 1880s, raise doubts that he was motivated entirely by either altruism or political ambition. The 6 percent interest he demanded on his investment was a fair rate of return, and since some of the land he purchased had been obtained through second parties—including the Carson Valley rancher H. H. Springmyer as well as Fulton—the exact size of Newlands's Nevada empire in 1890 is not known. In fairness to Newlands, he ultimately sold most of his land within the Carson basin to the federal government for five dollars an acre, not an exorbitant price (though in order to polish his image as "father of the Reclamation Act," he could scarcely do otherwise).
88. *Reno Evening Gazette*, Jan. 6 and 13, Dec. 24, 1890, and Jan. 10, 1891.
89. F. G. Newlands to R. L. Fulton, Dec. 24, 1889, Fulton Family Papers.
90. *Report of the Special Committee of the United States Senate on the Irrigation and Reclamation of Arid Lands*, vol. 2, serial 2707, p. 509.
91. Both the *Reno Evening Gazette*, Oct. 21, 1889, and the *Territorial Enterprise* (Virginia City, Nev.), Oct. 29, 1889, reprinted the correspondence between Newlands and officials of the railroad. Also see *Report of the Special Committee of the United States Senate on the Irrigation and Reclamation of Arid Lands*, vol. 2, serial 2707, pp. 507–14.
92. The letter was reprinted in the *Reno Evening Gazette*, Nov. 23, 1889.
93. *Reno Evening Gazette*, July 14, 1890. Also see the *Gazette* for Oct. 21, Dec. 13, 16, and 23, 1889.
94. *Reno Evening Gazette*, Aug. 11, 1890.
95. William H. Mills to William M. Stewart, Mar. 30, 1899, Box 3, Folder 90, William Morris Stewart Collection, Nevada Historical Society, Reno; *Reno Evening Gazette*, Sept. 1, 1890, and June 11, 1891.
96. The report was reprinted in the *Territorial Enterprise*, Feb. 14, 1891, and the *Genoa Weekly Courier*, Feb. 20, 1891. The board had spent only $888 of the $100,000 appropriated by the 1889 legislature.
97. Governor R. K. Colcord's address to the legislature on Jan. 19, 1891, was published in the *Morning Appeal*, Jan. 21, 1891.
98. Barbara Richnak, *A River Flows: The Life of Robert Lardin Fulton* (Incline Village, Nev., 1983), p. 90; *Daily Territorial Enterprise*, Jan. 25, 27, 28, and 29, 1891.

99.   Townley, *Alfalfa Country*, p. 125.

100.   *Reno Evening Gazette*, Feb. 25, 1889.

101.   See Francis G. Newlands to Nevada State Board of Trade, Jan. 6, 1891, reprinted in *Storage and Reclamation* (Reno, 1891).

102.   *Morning Appeal*, Jan. 3, 4, 5, 9, 1891; *Silver State*, Jan. 24, 1891. Newlands favored slashing the cost of government by consolidating or abolishing state and county offices and cutting salaries. For example, he proposed combining the duties of the state printer and state controller. He estimated that 9 percent of the $416,000 state budget could be saved through such reforms. See *Reno Evening Gazette*, March 5, 1891.

103.   R. L. Fulton to F. G. Newlands, March 15, 1891, Fulton Family Papers.

104.   *Silver State*, Feb. 19, 1891; also March 4, 1891.

105.   On the drafting of the 1891 district law, see H. M. Yerington to "My dear Newlands," March 8, 1891, vol. 25, Private Correspondence, 1890–1897, Yerington Collection.

106.   R. L. Fulton to F. G. Newlands, Jan. 18, 1891, Fulton Family Papers. Fulton was wrong. On March 20, 1891, he incredulously informed Newlands that the bill had gone through "without costing a cent."

107.   H. M. Yerington to "My dear Newlands," Feb. 14, 1891, vol. 25, Private Correspondence, 1890–1897, Yerington Papers. Also see Yerington to Newlands, March 9, 1891, in the same file.

108.   The district act was reprinted in full serially in the *Reno Evening Gazette*, Oct. 1, 3, 5, 6, and 7, 1891.

109.   Newlands outlined his plans in a long letter to John Mackay, Jan. 14, 1891, Fulton Family Papers. Also see the *Reno Evening Gazette*, March 4, 1891.

110.   *Reno Evening Gazette*, June 11, 1891.

111.   *Report of the Proceedings of the Nevada State Irrigation Convention Held in the Opera House, Carson City, Nevada, October 9th, 1891; Reno Evening Gazette*, Oct. 9 and 10, 1891. L. H. Taylor to R. L. Fulton, April 26, 1891; C. E. Grunsky to Fulton, April 18, 1891; Fulton to F. G. Newlands, May 26, and August 28, 1891; Newlands to Fulton, June 12 and July 4, 1891; J. E. Jones (Nevada surveyor general) to Fulton, July 2, 1891: all in Fulton Family Papers. *Irrigation Age*, 1 (Aug. 1, 1891), p. 113, and 2 (Oct. 15, 1891), pp. 238–39.

112.   R. L. Fulton to H. L. Wright, Dec. 29, 1893, Fulton Family Papers. On the formation of districts, also see Fulton to Newlands, February 24, March 20, and June 23, 1891; Fulton to W. F. Herrin, June 12, 1891; Fulton to the State Board of Trade, July 7, 1891; Fulton to A. E. Wright, July 27, 1891; and Fulton to Lem Allen, Aug. 29, 1891: all in Fulton Family Papers.

113.   Fulton to Newlands, April 16, 1892, and Newlands to Fulton, April 22, 1891, Fulton Family Papers; *Reno Evening Gazette*, March 31, 1892.

114.   Newlands to J. W. Powell, Sept. 6 and Oct. 24, 1893, and Trenmore Coffin to Chief Clerk, USGS, Oct. 16, 1893, in USGS, Letters Received, July–December 1893, RG 57, National Archives.

115.   Mills to R. L. Fulton, April 14, 1892, and Newlands to Fulton, July 29, 1893, Fulton Family Papers. *Irrigation Age*, 3 (May 15, 1892), p. 52; 3 (June

15, 1892), p. 81; 3 (Aug. 1, 1892), p. 143. Richard J. Hinton, *A Report on Irrigation* (Washington, D.C., 1893), serial 2899, p. 21; Richnak, *A River Flows*, pp. 94–96.

116.   Roswell K. Colcord, "Biennial Message of the Governor of Nevada," in appendix to the *Journals of the Nevada Legislature, 1891–92* (Carson City, 1892), p. 12; *Reno Evening Gazette*, Feb. 2 and 10, 1893; *Morning Appeal*, Jan. 8, Feb. 4, 5, 18, and 19, 1893; *Genoa Weekly Courier*, March 3, 10, and 17, 1893.

117.   H. M. Yerington to F. G. Newlands, May 16, 1895, Yerington File, Box 1, Newlands Papers, within the William Sharon Collection, Bancroft Library, University of California, Berkeley.

118.   De Quille's letter is as reprinted in the *Morning Appeal*, March 9, 1893. No state suffered more from the depression of the 1890s than Nevada. During the 1890s, the value of taxable property continued to decline until, in the fiscal year 1896–97, it fell to the level of 1872. The mines, which had paid an average of eighty thousand dollars per year in state taxes from the middle of the 1860s through the mid-1880s, paid less than one thousand dollars in state taxes in 1897. See Wren, *History of Nevada*, p. 90. On Nov. 17, 1902, William F. Sharon wrote to his brother Fred: "The old Comstock is on its *last legs* & with silver at less than 50 cts per oz I see no future for this particular section of Nevada" (William E. Sharon Folder, Box 12, Sharon Family Papers, Bancroft Library, University of California, Berkeley).

119.   *Reno Evening Gazette*, June 26, 1894.

120.   Daniel W. Working, "Agriculture," in James H. Baker, ed., *History of Colorado* (Denver, 1927), pp. 587–91; Wilbur Fiske Stone, *History of Colorado* (Chicago, 1918), vol. 1, pp. 478–505; Eva Ida Jernigan, "Early Development of Agriculture in Colorado" (M.A. thesis, University of California, Berkeley, 1928), pp. 7, 15.

121.   Alvin T. Steinel, *History of Agriculture in Colorado* (Fort Collins, Colo., 1926), p. 66; Bancroft, *History of Nevada, Colorado, and Wyoming, 1540–1888*, pp. 534, 535.

122.   Le Roy Hafen, *Colorado: The Story of a Western Commonwealth* (Denver, 1933), pp. 221–24; Stone, *History of Colorado*, vol. 1, p. 480.

123.   *Colorado Farmer and Live Stock Journal*, Feb. 13, 1890; *Field and Farm*, Jan. 12, 1889; Roger Clements, "British-Controlled Enterprise in the West Between 1870 and 1900, and Some Agrarian Reactions," *Agricultural History*, 27 (Oct. 1953), p. 137; Joseph O. Van Hook, "Development of Irrigation in the Arkansas Valley," *Colorado Magazine*, 10 (Jan. 1933), pp. 3–11; Robert G. Dunbar, "History of Agriculture," in Le Roy Hafen, ed., *Colorado and Its People* (New York, 1948), vol. 2, p. 123; Steinel, *History of Agriculture in Colorado*, p. 204; Hafen, *Colorado: The Story of a Western Commonwealth*, pp. 228–30; Bancroft, *History of Nevada, Colorado, and Wyoming, 1540–1888*, pp. 538–40.

124.   See Governor Routt's address to the legislature in *Denver Republican*, Jan. 14, 1891, and Governor Waite's address in the *Rocky Mountain News*, Jan. 5, 1895.

125.   *Denver Republican*, Jan. 1, 1887. Also see the *Republican* for Jan. 12, 1887, and the *Rocky Mountain News*, Jan. 23, 1887.
126.   Hafen, *Colorado: The Story of a Western Commonwealth*, map of creation of counties from 1861 to 1932 facing p. 234; *Denver Republican*, Jan. 1, 1887, Jan. 5, Feb. 10, and April 4, 1889; *Rocky Mountain News*, Jan. 1, 1889, and Jan. 12, 1891.
127.   Steinel, *History of Agriculture in Colorado*, p. 233; *Denver Republican*, Jan. 1 and 8, 1891; *Rocky Mountain News*, Jan. 14, 1891.
128.   *Colorado Farmer and Live Stock Grower*, July 3, 1890; *Denver Republican*, Feb. 8, 1887.
129.   James Edward Wright, *The Politics of Populism: Dissent in Colorado* (New Haven, 1974), pp. 39–40, 92, 97–102.
130.   *Rocky Mountain News*, Jan. 4, 1887; *Denver Republican*, Feb. 24, 1887.
131.   Steinel, *History of Agriculture in Colorado*, p. 208; William E. Pabor, *Colorado as an Agricultural State* (New York, 1883), pp. 38–39; *Colorado Farmer and Live Stock Journal*, Jan. 12 and 19, Feb. 16, March 22, and April 5 and 12, 1888. Mead's lecture entitled "Ownership of Water" was delivered at the Farmers' Institute in Fort Collins, in February 1887. It was reprinted in the *Denver Republican*, Feb. 21, 1887.
132.   *Rocky Mountain News*, Dec. 31, 1890. Also see the issues of Jan. 2, 3, 7, 9, 11, 12, and 24, Feb. 24 and 28, 1891.
133.   *Pueblo Chieftain* (Colo.), Feb. 23 and 25, 1891.
134.   See Governor Alva Adams's address to the legislature as reprinted in the *Rocky Mountain News*, Jan. 5, 1889, and *Weekly Gazette* (Colorado Springs), Jan. 5, 1889.
135.   *Rocky Mountain News*, Dec. 30, 1888, Jan. 21, Feb. 24 and 28, March 3, 1889; *Colorado Farmer and Live Stock Journal*, Jan. 17, 1889; *Denver Republican*, Feb. 22, 1889.
136.   *Rocky Mountain News*, Jan. 25, 1889; *Denver Republican*, Feb. 4, 7, and 22, 1889.
137.   *Rocky Mountain News*, March 20 and 30, 1889; *Denver Republican*, March 20, 1889; *Field and Farm*, March 16, 1889. The *News* repeatedly suggested that the "treasury ring" had been responsible for blocking a comprehensive reservoir construction program. There was no requirement in Colorado that the state treasurer account for interest paid on state funds. Hence, according to the *News*, members of the "ring" pocketed twenty or thirty thousand dollars each year in interest on state funds. The more money it could keep in the bank, the more interest it earned. Hence the "ring" opposed large-scale state public works, hoping that smaller works would deplete the fund at a slower rate. See the issues of March 8, 9, and 11, 1889.
138.   *Denver Republican*, April 2, 1889.
139.   *Biennial Report of the Commissioners, Warden, Chaplain and Physician of the State Penitentiary of Colorado for the Two Years Ending November 30, 1890* (Denver, 1890), pp. 9–11; *Denver Republican*, Jan. 26, Feb. 2, 7, and 8, 1889; *Rocky Mountain News*, Jan. 9, 1887; *Weekly Gazette* (Colorado Springs), Feb. 2, 1889; *Field and Farm*, March 30, 1889; *Pueblo Chieftain*, March 1, 1891.

140.   *Rocky Mountain News*, Jan. 11 and April 8, 1893.

141.   *Fifth Biennial Report of the State Engineer to the Governor of Colorado, for the Years 1889 and 1890* (Denver, 1891), pp. 613–14; *Sixth Biennial Report of the State Engineer to the Governor of Colorado for the Years 1891 and 1892* (Denver, 1893), pp. 402–5; *Rocky Mountain News*, Jan. 11 and April 11, 1891; *Pueblo Chieftain*, Feb. 28, March 14 and 21, 1891, Jan. 22, March 8 and 21, 1893; "Irrigation in Colorado," *Irrigation Age*, 5 (May 1893), p. 7, and 5 (June 1893), p. 32.

142.   The major threat to state water projects was not the construction of new ditches but the extension of old ones. The *Rocky Mountain News* reported on March 17, 1895, that the largest private canal on the Arkansas River served sixty thousand acres and had originally cost two hundred thousand dollars. It was being expanded at a projected cost of half a million dollars. At the time, the Arkansas River served ten major canals and watered 172,000 acres.

143.   *Rocky Mountain News*, Jan. 11, March 27 and 28, 1893.

144.   Donald A. MacKendrick, "Before the Newlands Act: State-Sponsored Reclamation Projects in Colorado, 1888–1903," *Colorado Magazine*, 52 (Winter 1975), pp. 1–21; *Ninth Biennial Report of the State Engineer to the Governor of Colorado, for the Years 1897 and 1898* (Denver, 1899), p. 27; Lilley and Gould, "The Western Irrigation Movement, 1878–1902: A Reappraisal," pp. 66–67; Oliver Knight, "Correcting Nature's Error: The Colorado–Big Thompson Project," *Agricultural History*, 30 (Oct. 1956), pp. 157–69; *Pueblo Chieftain*, March 30, April 5, 1893, Jan. 21 and 28, Feb. 3, March 23 and 24, 1895.

145.   See, for example, the *Rocky Mountain News*, Feb. 5, 1891.

146.   *Field and Farm*, March 2, 1895.

147.   *Field and Farm*, May 9, 1891, and Feb. 18, 1893.

148.   *Rocky Mountain News*, March 7 and 17, 1893.

149.   *Rocky Mountain News*, March 15, 1893.

150.   *Rocky Mountain News*, Jan. 25, Feb. 14 and 20, March 7, 9, 17, 1893; *Field and Farm*, March 11 and 25, April 1, 1893.

151.   *Rocky Mountain News*, March 27, 29, and 31, 1893.

152.   *Rocky Mountain News*, April 2 and 8, 1893. *Field and Farm*, April 1, 1893, provided a breakdown of the public works projects approved by the 1893 legislature.

153.   Steinel, *History of Agriculture in Colorado*, pp. 148–49; *Rocky Mountain News*, April 2, 1895.

154.   *Rocky Mountain News*, Jan. 21 and 28, Feb. 12, 1895; *Field and Farm*, Jan. 26 and March 23, 1895.

155.   In 1901, Colorado's economy revived to the point that the legislature authorized construction of State Canal Number Three to tunnel through a mountain range separating the Gunnison and Uncompahgre valleys so that water from the Gunnison could be diverted onto land in Montrose and Delta counties, south of Grand Junction. The state completed about a thousand feet of tunnel before the project was absorbed into the U.S. Reclamation Service's Uncompahgre Project. See *Eleventh Biennial Report of the State Engineer to the Governor of Colorado, for the Years 1901 and 1902* (Denver, 1902), pp.

45–46; MacKendrick, "Before the Newlands Act," p. 19; *Forestry and Irrigation,* 9 (April 1903), p. 168.

156.   "Irrigation in Colorado," *Irrigation Age,* 5 (May 1893), p. 7; Field, "Development of Irrigation," in *History of Colorado,* vol. 1, p. 500; *Sixth Biennial Report of the State Engineer to the Governor of Colorado for the Years 1891 and 1892,* pp. 380–97; *Ninth Biennial Report of the State Engineer to the Governor of Colorado, for the Years 1897 and 1898* (Denver, 1899), p. 27; *Thirteenth Biennial Report of the State Engineer to the Governor of Colorado for the Years 1905–1906* (Denver, 1907), pp. 25–28; *Preliminary Examination of Reservoir Sites in Wyoming and Colorado,* H. Doc. 141, 55th Cong., 2d sess. (Washington, D.C., 1897), pp. 94–96.

157.   *Pueblo Chieftain,* April 3, 1893, and March 17, 1895.

158.   *Denver Republican,* March 26 and April 5, 1889; *Weekly Gazette* (Colorado Springs), April 6, 1889; *Rocky Mountain News,* March 26, 1889; *Colorado Farmer and Live Stock Journal,* March 27, 1890.

159.   *Rocky Mountain News,* Jan. 11, 1891; *Fifth Biennial Report of the State Engineer to the Governor of Colorado, for the Years 1889 and 1890* (Denver, 1891), p. 612. For some of the projects rejected by the state engineer during 1889 and 1890, see pp. 596–98, 599, 603.

160.   *Ninth Biennial Report of the State Engineer to the Governor of Colorado, for the Years 1897 and 1898,* pp. 21–22. Also see the *Eleventh Biennial Report of the State Engineer to the Governor of Colorado for the Years 1901 and 1902,* p. 46.

161.   *Sixth Biennial Report of the State Engineer to the Governor of Colorado for the Years 1891 and 1892,* pp. 401–2.

162.   *Weekly San Joaquin Republican* (Stockton, Calif.), March 15, 1856.

163.   Lawrence W. Larson, *The Urban West at the End of the Frontier* (Lawrence, Kans., 1978), p. 118.

Chapter 7

1.   Lewis L. Gould, *Wyoming: A Political History, 1868–1896* (New Haven, 1968), pp. 9–11, 49, 63–64; T. A. Larson, *History of Wyoming* (Lincoln, 1978), pp. 108, 113, 119–20.

2.   Gould, *Wyoming,* pp. 64–66, 76 (Carey quotation); Ernest S. Osgood, *The Day of the Cattleman* (Minneapolis, 1929), pp. 85–87, 94–95, 97, 112; "Report of the Governor of Wyoming Territory," in *Report of the Secretary of the Interior, 1878* (Washington, D.C., 1878), pp. 1160, 1163; "Report of the Governor of Wyoming," in *Report of the Secretary of the Interior, 1881* (Washington, D.C., 1881), vol. 2, pp. 1052–53; "Report of the Governor of Wyoming," in *Report of the Secretary of the Interior, 1883* (Washington, D.C., 1884), vol. 2, p. 582; Francis E. Warren, "Reminiscences of the Range," December 1903, in Warren Letterbook, July 29, 1903–Feb. 13, 1904, Francis E. Warren Collection, American Heritage Center, University of Wyoming, Laramie.

3.   Warren, "Reminiscences of the Range;" *Report of the Secretary of the Interior, 1888* (Washington, D.C., 1888), p. CXXXV; "Report of the Governor of Wyoming," in *Report of the Secretary of the Interior, 1888,* vol. 2, p. 929;

"Report of the Governor of Wyoming," in *Report of the Secretary of the Interior,* 1889 (Washington, D.C., 1890), vol. 2, p. 563; *Third Biennial Report of the State Engineer to the Governor of Wyoming, 1895 and 1896* (Cheyenne, 1897), p. 32; Frances B. Beard, ed., *Wyoming: From Territorial Days to the Present* (Chicago, 1933), vol. 1, pp. 401–3.

4.   *Third Biennial Report of the State Engineer to the Governor of Wyoming, 1895 and 1896*, p. 20; *Cheyenne Daily Leader*, May 15 and Aug. 1, 1889.

5.   I. S. Bartlett, ed., *History of Wyoming* (Chicago, 1918), vol. 1, pp. 412–15; Fenimore Chatterton, ed., *The State of Wyoming* (Laramie, 1904), pp. 133–34.

6.   As reprinted in Beard, *Wyoming*, vol. 1, p. 511. Also see Chatterton, *State of Wyoming*, pp. 15–16. Leasing state lands did bring in a substantial amount of revenue. In 1902, the Wyoming Board of Land Commissioners leased 2,302,501.47 acres, which returned $95,925.30 in fees. That amount paid for the state's schools, university, asylum, and other institutions. Joseph A. Breckons, "Wyoming's Use of Its Lands," *Official Proceedings of the Eleventh National Irrigation Congress Held at Ogden, Utah, September 15–18, 1903* (Ogden, 1904), pp. 404–7.

7.   *First Biennial Report of the State Engineer to the Governor of Wyoming, 1891 and 1892* (Cheyenne, 1892), pp. 30–31.

8.   Julian Ralph, "Wyoming—Another Pennsylvania," *Harper's Magazine,* 87 (June 1893), p. 63.

9.   Gould, *Wyoming*, p. 129; Larson, *History of Wyoming*, p. 195; Osgood, *The Day of the Cattleman*, pp. 228, 230, 232–33; *Third Biennial Report of the State Engineer to the Governor of Wyoming, 1895 and 1896*, p.19. Gould notes that 13.5 percent of Wyoming's residents raised stock; 12.4 percent farmed; 10.4 percent engaged in mining; 9.1 percent worked in manufacturing; and 7.2 percent toiled for the railroad (p. 129).

10.   *First Biennial Report of the State Engineer to the Governor of Wyoming, 1891 and 1892*, p. 14.

11.   *Register of Debates in Congress* (Washington, D.C., 1826), vol. 2, pp. 719–50 (quotation p. 750). Also see Benton's April 9, 1828, address in *Register of Debates in Congress* (Washington, D.C., 1828), vol. 4, pp. 610–29; Roy M. Robbins, *Our Landed Heritage: The Public Domain, 1776–1970* (Lincoln, 1976), pp. 39–41; Benjamin Hibbard, *A History of Public Land Policies* (Madison, 1965), pp. 290–95.

12.   Paul W. Gates, *History of Public Land Law Development* (Washington, D.C., 1968), pp. 11–12.

13.   *Register of Debates in Congress*, vol. 4, p. 494.

14.   For John C. Calhoun's Senate speech of January 12, 1841, see *The Papers of John C. Calhoun* (Columbia, S.C., 1983), vol. 15, pp. 423–43. The quotation is from p. 425. Also see the *Congressional Globe*, 26th Cong., 2d sess., Jan. 11 and 12, 1841, pp. 91, 95–96, 120, and app., pp. 52–56; Hibbard, *History of Public Land Policies*, pp. 193–94; Robbins, *Our Landed Heritage*, pp. 93–94.

15.   *Preliminary Report of the United States Geological Survey of Montana and Portions of Adjacent Territories; Being a Fifth Annual Report of Progress* (Washington, D.C., 1872), pp. 226–27.

16.   *Rocky Mountain News*, Oct. 15, 1873.

17.   *Rocky Mountain News*, June 12, 1873; *New York Times*, Oct. 17, 1873; *Official Proceedings of the Tenth National Irrigation Congress Held at Colorado Springs, Colorado* (Colorado Springs, 1902), p. 270.

18.   For accounts of the convention, see the *Rocky Mountain News*, Oct. 12, 14, 16, and 17, 1873; and Frank Hall, *History of Colorado* (Chicago, 1890), vol. 2, pp. 177–79. Also see *Speech of Gov. S. H. Elbert of Colorado Before the Convention of Trans-Missouri States and Territories Held at Denver, Colorado, October 15, 1873* (Denver, 1873), pp. 3, 10–11; H.R. 749 (Phillips), introduced Dec. 15, 1873; and *Congressional Record*, 43d Cong., 1st sess., House, Dec. 15, 1873, pp. 207–8.

19.   For example, in 1888 the Wyoming legislature unanimously adopted one of many memorials calling for cession. See the *Cheyenne Daily Leader*, Oct. 28, 1894; and the *Colorado Farmer and Live Stock Journal*, Jan. 12 and 19, 1888. For statements of support for cession, see "Report of the Governor of Montana," in *Report of the Secretary of the Interior, 1889*, vol. 2, p. 447; the governor of Idaho's recommendations in *Report of the Secretary of the Interior, 1890* (Washington, D.C., 1891), p. XCI; the governor of Utah's recommendations in the same report, p. CIII; and the governor of Arizona's recommendations in the same report, pp. XCVI–XCVII. Congress considered a handful of cession bills during the 1870s and 1880s, but none reached the floor. See, for example, S. 768 (Hill), introduced December 8, 1879, *Congressional Record*, 46th Cong., 2d sess., pp. 30, 802; and H.R. 7443 (Bean), introduced March 29, 1886, 49th Cong., 1st sess.

20.   For example, in 1888 Congressman Symes of Colorado asked for half a million acres to help his state construct storage reservoirs. See H.R. 9053, 50th Cong., 1st sess., introduced April 2, 1888; S. 4250, 51st Cong., 1st sess., introduced July 21, 1890. Bills providing for land grants to individual states to underwrite reclamation, education, and other public services remained popular throughout the 1890s. See S. 1440 (Kyle), 52d Cong., 1st sess., introduced Jan. 7, 1892; H.R. 627 (Sweet), 52d Cong., 1st sess., Jan. 7, 1892; H.R. 2648 (Caminetti), 52d Cong., 1st sess., Jan. 11, 1892; H.R. 4203 (Caminetti), 53d Cong., 1st sess., Oct. 21, 1893; S. 2447 (Manderson), 53d Cong., 3d sess., Dec. 18, 1894; S. 794 (Thurston), 54th Cong., 1st sess., Dec. 12, 1895; S. 2604 (Carter), 54th Cong., 1st sess., March 23, 1896; H.R. 282 (Andrews), 54th Cong., 1st sess., Dec. 6, 1895; S. 4925 (Stewart), 55th Cong., 3d sess., Dec. 8, 1898; S. 315 (Warren), 57th Cong., 1st sess., Dec. 4, 1901; H.R. 4400 (Mondell), 57th Cong., 1st sess., Dec. 10, 1901.

21.   Gould, *Wyoming*, pp. 80–81, 109–10, 264, 268; Anne C. Hansen, "The Congressional Career of Senator Francis E. Warren from 1890–1902," *Annals of Wyoming*, 20 (Jan. 1948), pp. 3–49; Bartlett, *History of Wyoming*, vol. 3, pp. 5–9; Beard, *Wyoming*, vol. 2, pp. 25–30.

22.   James R. Kluger, "Elwood Mead: Irrigation Engineer and Social Planner" (Ph.D. diss., University of Arizona, 1970), pp. 6, 10, 14. Kluger discusses Mead's early life on pp. 1–18. Also see Paul. K. Conkin, "The Vision of Elwood Mead," *Agricultural History*, 34 (April 1960), pp. 88–97.

23.   Donald J. Pisani, *From the Family Farm to Agribusiness: The Irrigation Crusade in California and the West, 1850–1931* (Berkeley, 1984), pp. 154–90.

24.   On February 3, 1897, Warren wrote to one of his confidants in Wyoming: "Mead's reappointment [as state engineer] is desirable from every point of view, except that he has not been a very strong man politically, though he promises better things in this line, saying that he is beginning to appreciate more and understand better the desirability, in fact necessity, of keeping politics always in view" (Warren to Willis Van Devanter, Box 40, Willis Van Devanter Collection, Library of Congress, Washington, D.C.).

25.   In the nineteenth century, the line between public and private, and official and unofficial was far more indistinct than today. For example, the bill creating the office of Wyoming territorial engineer permitted Mead to serve as a consultant to private companies at a salary not to exceed ten dollars a day and actual expenses. The legislator who drafted the measure informed Mead that he could easily add at least one thousand dollars to his fifteen-hundred-dollar annual salary. Legislators saw consulting fees as a way to pay part of Mead's salary and reduce the cost of government. See Gibson Clark to Elwood Mead, Jan. 17 and March 3, 1888, in "Elwood Mead: Territorial and State Engineer, Incoming Correspondence, 1887–1890," Mead Papers, Wyoming State Archives, Cheyenne.

26.   F. H. Newell to Elwood Mead, Oct. 11, 1890, in "Elwood Mead, Territorial & State Engineer: Incoming Correspondence from Federal Government Officials, 1888–1890," and Mead to Newell, Oct. 31, 1890, in Mead Letterbook, Aug. 18, 1890–May 27, 1891, Mead Papers. The Mead Papers at the Wyoming State Archives contain several file folders that document his consulting work from 1887 to 1890.

27.   Lawrence B. Lee, "William Ellsworth Smythe and the Irrigation Movement: A Reconsideration," *Pacific Historical Review*, 41 (Aug. 1972), pp. 287–311; Patricia Nelson Limerick, *Desert Passages: Encounters with the American Deserts* (Albuquerque, 1985), pp. 77–90; Martin E. Carlson, "William E. Smythe: Irrigation Crusader," *Journal of the West*, 7 (Jan. 1968), pp. 41–47; Harriet Smythe, "Biographical Sketch [of William E. Smythe]," *Irrigation Age*, 14 (Oct. 1899), pp. 3–5; William E. Smythe, *The Conquest of Arid America* (New York, 1905), pp. 265–68; *Denver Republican*, Jan. 29, 1891.

28.   "Growth of Irrigation," *Irrigation Age*, 3 (July 15, 1892), p. 112.

29.   See unpublished "Report of the Wyoming Territorial Engineer, November 10, 1888," p. 20, in the State Engineer's Records, Wyoming State Archives, Cheyenne; *Second Annual Report of the Territorial Engineer to the Governor of Wyoming, for the Year 1889* (Cheyenne, 1890), pp. 47–48.

30.   *Cheyenne Daily Leader*, July 18, 1889.

31.   In addition to the July 18 and 28, 1889, issues of the *Cheyenne Daily Leader*, see the issues for July 23, Aug. 17, 21, and 27, 1889, July 8, Oct. 1 and 3, 1890, and March 21, 1891; as well as the *Rocky Mountain News*, July 23 and 24, 1889.

32.   *Cheyenne Daily Leader*, July 28, 1889.

33.   For example, see S. 326 (Cullom), 51st Cong., 1st sess., introduced Dec. 4, 1889; S. 2743 (Stewart), 51st Cong., 1st sess., February 19, 1890; H.R. 223

(Springer), 51st Cong., 1st sess., Dec. 18, 1889; H.R. 10589 (Vandever), 51st Cong., 1st sess., May 28, 1890; H.R. 11356 (Carey), 51st Cong., 1st sess., July 10, 1890.

34.　See the *New York Sun* editorial reprinted in *Field and Farm* (Denver), May 30, 1891; and the *New Orleans Times-Democrat* editorial in the *New York Times*, Jan. 10, 1892.

35.　*Cheyenne Daily Leader*, March 5, 6, 7, 8, 18, and 28, 1891; *Buffalo Bulletin*, May 28, 1891.

36.　S. 5087 (Warren), 51st Cong., 2d sess., introduced Feb. 16, 1891. Mead had already written a cession bill for Wyoming's congressman Joseph M. Carey. See H.R. 11356, 51st Cong., 1st sess., introduced July 10, 1890 (soon after Wyoming achieved statehood).

37.　Elwood Mead to Francis E. Warren, Dec. 26, 1890, in "Elwood Mead, Territorial and State Engineer: Incoming Correspondence from U.S. Representatives and Senators, 1888–1890," and Mead to Jonas M. Cleland, Feb. 23, 1891, Mead Letterbook, Aug. 18, 1890–May 27, 1891, both in Mead Papers; typescript copy of bill dated May 18, 1891, Warren Letterbook, Sept. 22, 1890–June 3, 1891, and Warren to Joseph Nimmo, Feb. 25, 1891, Warren Letterbook, Feb. 6, 1891–June 11, 1891, both in Warren Collection; *Congressional Record*, 51st Cong., 2d sess., Senate, Feb. 16, 1891.

38.　Also see S. 5086 (McConnell), 51st Cong., 2d sess., introduced Feb. 16, 1891; H.R. 12210 (Vandever), 51st Cong., 2d sess., Dec. 1, 1890; H.R. 12709 (Herbert), 51st Cong., 2d sess., Dec. 16, 1890; and "Ceding the Arid Lands to the States and Territories," H. Rep. 3767, 51st Cong., 2d sess. (Washington, D.C., 1891), serial 2888, pp. 1–8. Arizona's governor recognized that cession alone would do little for the poorest states and territories. In 1891, he proposed that after ceding the arid lands the federal government should loan the states and territories sufficient money to build canals and reservoirs, taking their bonds as security. See "Report of the Acting Governor of Arizona," in *Report of the Secretary of the Interior, 1891* (Washington, D.C., 1892), vol. 3, pp. 315–16, 319.

39.　*Report of the Commissioner of the General Land Office, 1891* (Washington, D.C., 1891), p. 51. Also see Carter's letter to the editor of the *Cheyenne Sun*, as reprinted in the *Cheyenne Weekly Sun*, Sept. 17, 1891, and the *Buffalo Bulletin* (Buffalo, Wyo.) of the same date. Carter was one of the few federal officials who supported cession. John Wesley Powell and Richard J. Hinton were strenuous opponents.

40.　For example, the Trans-Mississippi Commercial Convention, which met in Denver in May 1890, adopted a resolution calling for cession on condition that no ceded land could be taken by aliens and that individual purchasers should be limited to 320 acres at a price of not less than $1.25 an acre. The resolution is reprinted in "Report of the Governor of Utah," in *Report of the Secretary of the Interior, 1891*, vol. 3, p. 364.

41.　*Irrigation Age*, 1 (Sept. 15, 1891), p. 175.

42.　*Irrigation Age*, 1 (Oct. 1, 1891), p. 193.

43.　Lee, "William Ellsworth Smythe and the Irrigation Movement," p. 295.

44.　The *Irrigation Age*, 1 (Oct. 1, 1891), devoted many pages to the Salt

Lake City conference. Also see "Progress of Irrigation," *Scientific American,* 65 (Oct. 31, 1891), p. 272.

45. *Irrigation Age,* 1 (Oct. 1, 1891), pp. 197–98, 204. One resolution rejected by the Salt Lake City convention called for construction of reservoirs at the headwaters of the Missouri and Arkansas rivers as flood control structures, and a second asked Congress to issue $150 million in thirty-year, 2 percent bonds to pay for boring artesian wells on the plains and for building reservoirs and canals in the mountains.

46. *Congressional Record,* 52d Cong., 1st sess., House, Feb. 5, 1892, pp. 868–69; "Memorial of a Convention Held at Salt Lake City, Utah Territory, to Consider Matters Pertaining to the Reclamation of the Arid Lands of the West," S. Misc. Doc. 61, 52d Cong., 1st sess. (1892), serial 2904; *Report of the Secretary of the Interior, 1891,* p. XII; *Irrigation Age,* 1 (Oct. 1, 1891), p. 208.

47. The memorial of the Idaho legislature is reprinted in *Congressional Record,* 51st Cong., 2d sess., Senate, Feb. 13, 1891, pp. 2597–98. The Wyoming appeal was presented on February 23, 1891, pp. 3108–9.

48. F. E. Warren to Joseph Nimmo, April 29, 1891, Warren Letterbook, Feb. 6, 1891–June 11, 1891, Warren Collection.

49. *Irrigation Age,* 1 (May 30, 1891), pp. 61–62; *Pueblo Chieftain* (Pueblo, Colo.), Feb. 18 and 21, 1891; *Cheyenne Daily Leader,* Feb. 22 and 25, March 3 and 5, 1891; *Buffalo Bulletin,* March 12, 1891.

50. For example, see the *Congressional Record,* 52d Cong., 1st sess. (1891–92), pp. 530, 786, 830, 867, 913, 954, 955, 997, 1094, 1128, 1166, 1223, 1224, 1265, 1308, 1359, 1381–82, 1505, 1532, 1534, 1581, 1799, 1803, 1857, 2033, 2180, 2299, 2300, 2559, 3403, 3464, 4161, 4306, 4454, 4590.

51. Ibid., pp. 1843, 2179, 2384, 2559, 2581, 2596, 2633, 2634, 2889–90, 3154, 3464, 3690.

52. *Field and Farm,* Jan. 3, 1891.

53. *Reno Evening Gazette,* Oct. 31, 1893.

54. John D. Hicks, *The Populist Revolt: A History of the Farmers' Alliance and the People's Party* (Minneapolis, 1931), p. 268; Richard Hofstadter, *The Age of Reform: From Bryan to F.D.R.* (New York, 1955), p. 50; Lawrence Goodwyn, *Democratic Promise: The Populist Movement in America* (New York, 1976), pp. 184–86, 215–16, 319.

55. Karel D. Bicha, *Western Populism: Studies in an Ambivalent Conservatism* (Lawrence, Kans., 1976), p. 14, 16–17, 25, 78–79, 116; Robert W. Larson, *Populism in the Mountain West* (Albuquerque, 1986), pp. 7, 12–13, 60. Larson discusses Populism in Wyoming on pp. 44–61. The best state study of Populism in the Mountain West is James E. Wright, *The Politics of Populism: Dissent in Colorado* (New Haven, 1974). Also see Mary Ellen Glass, *Silver and Politics in Nevada: 1892–1902* (Reno, 1969); David B. Griffiths, "Populism in Wyoming," *Annals of Wyoming,* 40 (April 1968), pp. 57–71; David B. Griffiths, "Far Western Populist Thought: A Comparative Study of John R. Rogers and Davis H. Waite," *Pacific Northwest Quarterly,* 60 (Oct. 1969), pp. 183–92; and G. Michael McCarthy, "The People's Party in Colorado: A Profile of Populist Leadership," *Agricultural History,* 47 (April 1973), pp. 146–55.

56. *Cheyenne Daily Leader,* Aug. 21, 1890.

57.   *New York Times*, April 14, 1889.

58.   *Cheyenne Daily Leader*, July 29, 1890.

59.   For example, the *Cheyenne Daily Leader* of August 3, 1890, reported that De Forest Richards, a Douglas Republican and critic of the Cheyenne Ring, had been guaranteed a state senatorship from Converse County if he agreed to vote for Warren as senator. The offer was made even before Warren's nomination for the governorship.

60.   *Cheyenne Daily Leader*, Sept. 30, 1892.

61.   For example, see Warren's interview in the *Washington Post*, Dec. 21, 1891, and "The Hope of the West," *Irrigation Age*, 2 (Jan. 1, 1892), p. 362.

62.   F. E. Warren to W. E. Smythe, March 5, 1892, Warren Letterbook, Feb. 20, 1892–March 31, 1892, Warren Collection. Also see William Morris Stewart to Samuel B. P. Pierce, March 5, 1892, Box 10, Stewart Letterbook, Feb. 10, 1892–July 26, 1892, Stewart Collection, Nevada Historical Society, Reno.

63.   F. E. Warren to W. A. Richards, March 15, 1892. Also see Warren to E. E. Lonabaugh, March 4, 1892, and Warren to Mead, March 5, 12, and 15, 1892, in Warren Letterbook, Feb. 20, 1892–Mar. 31, 1892, Warren Collection, and Elwood Mead to F. H. Harvey, March 14, 1892, Mead Letterbook, Jan. 16, 1892–Dec. 10, 1892, Mead Papers.

64.   Warren to Mead, March 30, 1892, Incoming Correspondence, 1880–1902, Mead Papers.

65.   S. 2529 (Warren), 52d Cong., 1st sess., introduced March 9, 1892. A second bill, H.R. 6790 (Lanham), 52d Cong., 1st sess., March 2, 1892, competed for attention with Warren's. It provided for the cession of *all* nonmineral land west of the ninety-seventh meridian with the restriction that the land could not be sold or leased in parcels larger than 160 acres. Elwood Mead to F. H. Harvey, March 14, 1892, Mead Letterbook, Jan. 16, 1892–Dec. 10, 1892, Mead Papers. Also see H.R. 74 (Townsend), 52d Cong., 1st sess., Jan. 5, 1892; H.R. 512 (Joseph), 52d Cong., 1st sess., Jan. 7, 1892; H.R. 653 (Springer), 52d Cong., 1st sess., Jan. 7, 1892; H.R. 2648 (Caminetti), 52d Cong., 1st sess., Jan. 11, 1892; and H.R. 5811 (Busey), 52d Cong., 1st sess., Feb. 11, 1892.

66.   See Mead's description of the bill in the *Cheyenne Daily Leader*, March 17, 1892, and the letter from Mead's assistant, J. A. Johnston, in the *Leader*, March 18, 1892. Also see "Irrigation and Reclamation of Arid Lands," S. Rep. 1069, 52d Cong., 1st sess., 1891–92, serial 2915.

67.   "Arid Lands of the United States," H. Rep. 569, 52d Cong., 1st sess. (1892), serial 3043, pp. 1–9 (majority report), and 10–12 (minority report). The quotations are from pp. 2, 11, 12.

68.   *Congressional Record*, Senate, July 21, 1892, pp. 6485–6506.

69.   *New York Times*, Jan. 11, 1892; "Montana's Convention," *Irrigation Age*, 2 (Jan. 15, 1892), p. 384, and 2 (Feb. 15, 1892), p. 483; Robert G. Dunbar, *Forging New Rights to Western Waters* (Lincoln, 1983), p. 49.

70.   Elwood Mead to F. E. Warren, Jan. 22, 1892, Mead Letterbook, Jan. 16, 1892–Dec. 10, 1892, Mead Papers.

71.   F. E. Warren to W. A. Richards, March 15, 1892; Warren to Elwood Mead, March 5, 12, and 15, 1892; and Warren to W. E. Smythe, March 17, 1892, all in Warren Letterbook, Feb. 20, 1892–Mar. 31, 1892, Warren Collection.

72. *Cheyenne Daily Leader,* Aug. 21, 1892.
73. For a balanced account of the Johnson County War, see Larson, *History of Wyoming,* pp. 268–84. Also see Osgood, *The Day of the Cattleman,* pp. 238–58; and Robert A. Murray, *Johnson County: 175 Years at the Foot of the Big Horn Mountains* (Buffalo, Wyo., 1981), pp. 77–83.
74. *Cheyenne Daily Leader,* Sept. 9, 1892.
75. In 1906, a Department of the Interior investigation revealed that the Warren Livestock Company had unlawfully enclosed 46,330 acres of public land in Laramie County, Wyoming, and another 1,120 acres in Weld County, Colorado, and that the land had been locked up at least since 1885, when a law prohibiting the fencing of government land took effect (Larson, *History of Wyoming,* p. 381).
76. *Cheyenne Daily Leader,* March 16, 1892. Also see the issues of Sept. 4 and Dec. 15, 1890, April 9, 1891, Oct. 1, 9, 12, 20, 21, and Nov. 3, 1892; Beard, *Wyoming,* vol. 1, pp. 369–70.
77. *Cheyenne Daily Leader,* Sept. 30 and Oct. 2, 1892.
78. *Buffalo Bulletin,* March 10, 1892.
79. *Buffalo Bulletin,* Feb. 4, 1892. Also see the *Bulletin* for Feb. 18, 25, March 3, July 21, Oct. 13, 20, 27, and Nov. 3, 1892; and the *Cheyenne Daily Leader,* Jan. 14, 30, March 15, Sept. 24, and Oct. 9, 1892. The judgment of Wyoming newspapers was shared by many western journals. For example, on March 18, 1892, the *Leader* reprinted a *San Francisco Chronicle* editorial that concluded: "The vultures are gathering so fast that they must scent the feast from afar and are making ready to fatten on the loathsome food as soon as it has reached the proper stage of decomposition. There can be no serious question but that there is a fully developed ring of land grabbers who are waiting with eager and hungry eyes the cession of these lands."
80. "An Unexpected Triumph," *Irrigation Age,* 3 (June 15, 1892), p. 78.
81. The plank read: "We favor the cession of government lands to the states only under such constitutional or congressional restrictions as will prevent final disposal of them by the states until they are fully reclaimed; and prevent the control of large tracts by corporations or individuals and that all unreclaimed grazing lands shall forever remain unleased, an open common upon which all citizens may graze their flocks and herds" (*The Daily Boomerang* [Laramie], Sept. 7, 1894). Also see Hansen, "The Congressional Career of Senator Francis E. Warren from 1890–1902," p. 40.
82. On the depression of 1893, see Samuel Rezneck, "Unemployment, Unrest, and Relief in the United States During the Depression of 1893–1897," *Journal of Political Economy,* 61 (Aug. 1953), pp. 324–45; Charles Hoffman, "The Depression of the Nineties," *Journal of Economic History,* 16 (June 1956), pp. 137–64; William J. Lauck, *The Causes of the Panic of 1893* (New York, 1907); Frank P. Weberg, *The Background of the Panic of 1893* (Washington, D.C., 1929); O. M. W. Sprague, *History of Crisis under the National Banking System* (Washington, D.C., 1910), pp. 153–216.
83. *Daily Boomerang,* Aug. 7, 1894.
84. On September 13, 1894, Laramie's *Daily Boomerang* reported that the federal budget for fiscal year 1892 had been $541,223,861. In fiscal year 1894

it declined to $519,509,300 and in 1895 to $490,668,370. Of course, this did not prevent western politicians from seeking federal aid. For example, a bill introduced in the Senate on August 8, 1893, called for the federal government to loan money to the states and territories to help them construct hydraulic works—up to a yearly maximum of $2,500,000 for an individual state and $10,000,000 for the entire West. The states would then issue bonds, the proceeds from which would be paid into the U.S. treasury to retire the debt. See S. 70 (Dolph), 53d Cong., 1st sess.

85. *Reno Evening Gazette,* Nov. 22, 1897.

86. *Reno Evening Gazette,* April 28, 1893.

87. As quoted in Glass, *Silver and Politics in Nevada: 1892–1902,* p. 9.

88. "Why the Times Are Out of Joint," *Irrigation Age,* 8 (Jan. 1895), p. 9.

89. Smythe arranged a subsequent conference, held at Las Vegas, New Mexico, on March 16, 1892. He predicted it would be even bigger than the Salt Lake City convention, but almost all the three hundred delegates were employees and investors in several dozen New Mexico land and water companies. *Irrigation Age,* 2 (April 1, 1892), p. 545; H. C. Hovey, "The Las Vegas Irrigation Convention," *Scientific American,* 66 (April 9, 1892), p. 225.

90. *Official Report of the International Irrigation Congress Held at Los Angeles, California, October, 1893* (Los Angeles, n.d.), pp. 9, 106–7, 114–15, 149; Lee, "William Ellsworth Smythe and the Irrigation Movement," pp. 305–6. For an account of the 1893 irrigation meeting, see A. Bower Sageser, "Los Angeles Hosts an International Irrigation Congress," *Journal of the West,* 4 (July 1965), pp. 411–24.

91. Elwood Mead to Fred Bond, Sept. 11, 1894, Mead Letterbook, Dec. 10, 1892–Oct. 20, 1893, and Mead to W. H. Code, Nov. 11, 1893, Mead Letterbook, Oct. 20, 1893–Apr. 17, 1894, Mead Papers. Stanley Roland Davison, in his perceptive "Leadership of the Reclamation Movement, 1875–1902" (Ph.D. diss., University of California, Berkeley, 1952), p. 164, characterized the Los Angeles meeting as "the triumph of the emotional over the intellectual elements in the irrigation movement."

92. See *Official Report of the International Irrigation Congress Held at Los Angeles, California, October, 1893,* p. 61.

93. Ibid., p. 151; Carlson, "William E. Smythe: Irrigation Crusader," p. 43.

94. J. Rogers Hollingsworth, *The Whirligig of Politics* (Chicago, 1963), pp. 21–23.

95. "The Unemployed and the Public Lands," *Irrigation Age,* 6 (June 1894), p. 229; "Irrigation Scrip Proposed," *Irrigation Age,* 7 (July 1894), p. 2; "The Progress of Western America," *Irrigation Age,* 8 (Feb. 1895), p. 35.

96. George W. Paulson, "The Congressional Career of Joseph Maull Carey," *Annals of Wyoming,* 35 (April 1963), pp. 21–81; Bartlett, *History of Wyoming,* vol. 2, pp. 5–7.

97. *Irrigation Age,* 1 (May 1, 1891), p. 18; "Wyoming Colonization," *Irrigation Age,* 6 (April 1894), p. 166; *Cheyenne Daily Leader,* Oct. 29, 1890; "Report of the Governor of Wyoming," in *Report of the Secretary of the Interior, 1887* (Washington, D.C., 1887), p. 1025; *Second Annual Report of the Territorial Engineer to the Governor of Wyoming, for the Year 1889,* p. 22; Larson,

History of Wyoming, p. 304; Paulson, "The Congressional Career of Joseph Maull Carey," p. 25; Hansen, "The Congressional Career of Senator Francis E. Warren from 1890–1920," p. 38; Bartlett, *History of Wyoming,* vol. 3, p. 5.

98. Coffeen portrayed the Carey Act as a watered-down version of Warren's 1892 bill. He argued that federal reclamation was a far better alternative because powerful cattlemen could not influence Congress as they did state legislatures. See the *Congressional Record,* 53d Cong., 2d sess., August 11, 1894, pp. 8419–36, 7612–13, 7751, 8542–43, 8622; August 15, 1894 (appendix), pp. 1419–21, 1423. Also see Coffeen's speech to the Trans-Mississippi Commercial Congress, as reprinted in the *Cheyenne Daily Leader,* Sept. 6, 1894.

99. H.R. 7152 (Sweet), 53d Cong., 2d sess., May 21, 1894; *Daily Boomerang,* June 26, 1894; *Rocky Mountain News,* July 4, 1894. Also see S. 2447, 53d Cong., 3d sess., Dec. 18, 1894 (Manderson).

100. *U.S. Statutes at Large,* vol. 28, pp. 422–23; J. A. Breckons, "A View of the Carey Law," *Irrigation Age,* 7 (Oct. 1894), pp. 184–87; *Denver Sun,* Aug. 20, 1894; *Denver Republican,* Sept. 2, 1894; *Buffalo Bulletin,* May 16, Aug. 30, and Nov. 22, 1894; *Sheridan Post,* May 16, 1895; *Third Biennial Report of the State Engineer to the Governor of Wyoming, 1895 and 1896,* pp. 21–22; Chatterton, *The State of Wyoming,* pp. 16–21; Ray P. Teele, *Irrigation in the United States* (New York, 1915), pp. 123–39.

101. Years ago, John T. Ganoe, in "The Origin of a National Reclamation Policy," *Mississippi Valley Historical Review,* 18 (June 1931), pp. 34–52, argued that "prior to the passage of the Carey Act the sentiment in favor of construction [of storage reservoirs] by the national government was comparatively insignificant" (p. 38). This both misinterprets the meaning of the Carey Act and ignores the strong support for federal reclamation present in many parts of the West in the late 1880s and early 1890s.

102. *New York Sun,* Sept. 29, 1894. Joseph Carey made the same prediction. See his statements in the *Cheyenne Daily Leader,* Sept. 6, 1894, and the *Buffalo Bulletin,* Nov. 22, 1894.

103. Support for federal reclamation cannot always be taken at face value. For example, Congressman William P. Hepburn of Iowa announced that he opposed the Carey Act because the central government could do a more efficient job of reclaiming the arid West. He maintained that all reclamation should be guided by a systematic plan to serve the largest acreage. Yet, given the concern of farmers in his state for crop surpluses and "farm flight," his remarks were disingenuous. Federal reclamation was a safe haven in a storm. Before any construction could begin, a new irrigation survey would be necessary. That would take years to complete. By the time it was finished, the depression would have passed, along with much of the eastern "sympathy" for federal reclamation and cession. See Hepburn's remarks in the *Congressional Record,* August 11, 1894, pp. 8420–21.

104. Ibid.

105. The Wyoming state legislature ratified the Carey Act in February 1895. See the *Cheyenne Daily Leader,* Jan. 13 and Feb. 27, 1895, and the *Buffalo Bulletin,* Jan. 17, 24, 31, and Feb. 21, 1895. The state legislation was reprinted in the Jan. 24 issue of the *Bulletin.*

106.   Elwood Mead to G. W. Holdredge, Feb. 13, 1895, Mead Letterbook, Dec. 20, 1894–Mar. 5, 1895 and William H. Richards to Hoke Smith (secretary of the interior), Sept. 23, 1895, Mead Letterbook, July 5, 1895–Oct. 24, 1895, Mead Papers. Also see Mead to F. H. Newell, March 6, 1895, Mead Letterbook, Dec. 20, 1894–Sept. 23, 1895, and Mead to Richard J. Hinton, Oct. 9, 1895, Mead Letterbook, July 5, 1895–Oct. 24, 1895, Mead Papers; F. E. Warren to Thomas Sturgis, Jan. 15, 1895, Warren Collection; and *Third Biennial Report of the State Engineer to the Governor of Wyoming, 1895 and 1896*, p. 21.

107.   Nellie Snyder Yost, *Buffalo Bill: His Family, Friends, Fame, Failures, and Fortunes* (Chicago, 1979), p. 258.

108.   R. F. Walter and W. H. Code, "Elwood Mead," American Society of Civil Engineers, *Transactions*, 102 (1937), pp. 1611–18.

109.   "Report of the Wyoming Territorial Engineer, November 10, 1888," p. 16.

110.   Charles Lindsay, *The Big Horn Basin* (Lincoln, 1930), pp. 163–64, 166; Tacetta B. Walker, *Stories of Early Days in Wyoming: Big Horn Basin* (Casper, 1936), pp. 129–33.

111.   James D. McLaird, "Building the Town of Cody: George T. Beck, 1894–1943," *Annals of Wyoming*, 40 (April 1968), pp. 73–105.

112.   George T. Beck, "Personal Reminiscences of the Beginning of Cody, 1895–1896," January 1936, typescript in George Beck biographical file (B-B388-gt); report of Elwood Mead, consulting engineer, dated Aug. 14, 1894, unidentified folder and box; Margaret Hayden, transcript of undated interview with Beck, in Box 19, "Reports" folder: all in the George T. Beck Collection, American Heritage Center, University of Wyoming, Laramie.

113.   Ralph, "Wyoming—Another Pennsylvania," p. 63; William H. Richards to Hoke Smith, Sept. 23, 1895, Mead Letterbook, July 5, 1895–Oct. 24, 1895, Mead Papers; Mead, "The Cody Canal in Wyoming," *Irrigation Age*, 9 (Jan. 1896), p. 14; *Wyoming Tribune* (Cheyenne), Jan. 10, 1896; *Cheyenne Sun-Leader*, July 24, 1896.

114.   Mead to Cody, March 12, 1896, in Mead Letterbook, Jan. 30, 1896–April 16, 1896, Mead Papers.

115.   Mead, "The Cody Canal in Wyoming," p. 13. Mead to G. E. Girling, Dec. 5, 1895, Mead Letterbook, Oct. 24, 1895–Jan. 30, 1896; Mead to A. C. Campbell, April 13, 1896, Mead Letterbook, Jan. 30, 1896–April 16, 1896; and Mead to Shoshone Irrigation Company, Dec. 22, 1896, in Letterbook, Nov. 23, 1896–July 26, 1897: all in Mead Papers.

116.   F. E. Warren to William Ellsworth Smythe, Feb. 10, 1896, and Warren to Elwood Mead, Feb. 28, 1896, Warren Letterbook, Sept. 13, 1895–June 13, 1896, Warren Collection.

117.   *Buffalo Bulletin*, Jan. 30, April 2, and May 14, 1896; *Wyoming Tribune*, Feb. 14, March 24, May 6, and Aug. 6, 1896; *Sheridan Post*, May 28, 1896; *Third Biennial Report of the State Engineer of Wyoming, 1895 and 1896*, p. 22.

118.   *Cheyenne Daily Sun-Leader*, Nov. 16, 1895; H. C. Alger to Elwood Mead, Oct. 30, 1895, in Incoming General Correspondence, 1880–1902, "A-Carey," Wyoming State Engineer's Records; and Elwood Mead to W. F. Cody,

Oct. 11 and Nov. 4, 1895, in Mead Letterbook, July 5, 1895–Oct. 24, 1895, Mead Papers.

119.   Elwood Mead to George H. Keeney, Dec. 16, 1895, Mead Letterbook, Oct. 24, 1895–Jan. 30, 1896, Mead Papers.

120.   Mead gave many optimistic newspaper interviews describing the company's plans; see, for example, the *Rocky Mountain News*, June 21, 1897, and the *Denver Republican*, July 27, 1897. The company also planted articles in eastern newspapers, including the *New York Journal*, May 23, 1897. Privately, Mead was less sanguine and even asked Warren if the federal government could do anything to bail out the abortive project. See Mead to Francis E. Warren, July 23, 1897, in Mead Letterbook, Nov. 23, 1896–July 26, 1897, Mead Papers; and Warren to Mead, July 27, 1897, Warren Letterbook, Feb. 27, 1897–Jan. 27, 1898, Warren Collection.

121.   *Homes in the Big Horn Basin* (Buffalo, N.Y., 1897), in Records of the General Land Office, Carey Act Files, Box #3, RG 49, National Archives.

122.   D. H. Elliott to George T. Beck, July 8, 1897, and Elliott to W. F. Cody, Aug. 2, 1897, in "Correspondence: 1897," Beck Collection.

123.   "Minutes of the Board of Directors Meeting, Shoshone Irrigation Company," dated Feb. 9, 1897, no folder or box, and Directors, Shoshone Irrigation Co., to George T. Beck, July 20, 1897, in "Correspondence: 1897," Beck Collection.

124.   W. F. Cody to George T. Beck, March 24, July 5, Aug. 10, 24, Oct. 9, 11, 1899, in "Correspondence: W. F. Cody, 1899," Beck Collection. Cody had a very sharp tongue. "Am ever so much obliged for all your kindness to my family & friends," he noted in his letter of August 24. "How I wish you would take the same interest in business affairs." Not surprisingly, Beck often threatened to resign.

125.   Eliza R. Lythgoe, "Colonization of the Big Horn Basin by the Mormons," *Annals of Wyoming*, 14 (Jan. 1942), pp. 39–50; Yost, *Buffalo Bill*, p. 292; Larson, *History of Wyoming*, pp. 304, 349.

126.   *Cheyenne Daily Leader*, Oct. 26 and Dec. 26, 1901.

127.   Bronson Rumsey to George T. Beck, May 4, 1904, "Correspondence: Bronson Rumsey," Beck Collection.

128.   *Cheyenne Daily Sun-Leader*, Feb. 23, 1900.

129.   McLaird, "Building the Town of Cody," p. 84; Harry Weston to George Bleistein, Aug. 20, 1909, in "Correspondence: 1909," Beck Collection. In fairness to the farmers, when Wyoming state engineer Fred Bond inspected the Cody Canal after the completion of a new section of ditch in 1901, he informed the company that the canal was "totally inadequate to carry the water required [promised to farmers]." The work was "neither substantial nor durable in character" (Bond to George T. Beck, Dec. 26, 1901, in "Correspondence: 1901," Beck Collection).

130.   A. P. Davis, *Irrigation Works Constructed by the United States Government* (New York, 1917), pp. 277–90; George Wharton James, *Reclaiming the Arid West: The Story of the United States Reclamation Service* (New York, 1917), pp. 351–65; H. H. Johnson, "Forty-Three Years on the Shoshone Project," *Reclamation Era*, 33 (June 1947), pp. 124–27; *Third Annual Report of the Reclamation Service, 1903–4*, pp. 114–16, 507–10.

131.   Yost, *Buffalo Bill*, p. 403. Apparently at the insistence of his wife, Buffalo Bill is buried not at Cody, but on the top of Lookout Mountain near Denver.

132.   W. F. Cody, *An Autobiography of Buffalo Bill* (New York, 1920), p. 327.

133.   The first formal applications for land under the Carey Act came from the Yellowstone Park Land & Irrigation Association (16,000 acres), the Burlington Canal Company (28,000 acres), the Shoshone Land and Irrigation Company (28,000 acres), the Black's Fork Canal Company (30,000 acres), and the Fort Bridger Canal Company (30,000 acres). See the report of the Wyoming Land Board reprinted in the *Cheyenne Daily Sun-Leader*, March 19, 1897. Minutes of the meetings of the State Arid Land Board, created to administer the Carey Act projects, are available at the Wyoming State Archives, Cheyenne.

134.   Elwood Mead and F. J. Mills to S. W. Lamoreux (commissioner, General Land Office), June 13, 1895, in "Elwood Mead, State Engineer, Incoming Correspondence, Arid Land Claims, Big Horn Basin Development Co., 1895–1896," Mead Papers; *Cheyenne Daily Leader*, June 18, 1895, and Feb. 1, 1896; *Wyoming Tribune*, June 28, 1895, and April 2, 1896.

135.   Hoke Smith to Commissioner of the General Land Office, Feb. 19, April 17, and July 15, 1896, Carey Act Files, Box 6 (Wyoming), RG 49, National Archives.

136.   *Report of the Secretary of the Interior [1895]* (Washington, D.C., 1895), serial 3381, pp. XIX–XXI; *Report of the Secretary of the Interior [1896]* (Washington, D.C., 1896), serial 3488, pp. XVIII–XIX; *Cheyenne Daily Sun-Leader*, Nov. 28, 1895.

137.   Elwood Mead to S. S. Wiley, Aug. 15, 1895, Letterbook, Dec. 20, 1894–Mar. 5, 1895; Mead to F. E. Warren, Sept. 14, 1895, and Mead to F. J. Mills, Sept. 25, 1895, Letterbook, July 5, 1895–Oct. 24, 1895; Mead to H. A. Sumner (Colorado state engineer), Nov. 2, 1895, and Mead to F. W. Mondell, Dec. 21, 1895, in Letterbook, Oct. 24, 1895–Jan. 30, 1896: all in Mead Papers. The quotations are from the Mead letters of August 15 and December 21. Also see F. E. Warren to Elwood Mead, and Warren to E. F. Best (commissioner of the General Land Office), Aug. 9, 1895, and Warren to Mead, Dec. 19, 1895, in Warren Letterbook, April 10, 1895–Jan. 8, 1895; and Warren to R. J. Hinton, Feb. 10, 1896, in Warren Letterbook, Sept. 13, 1895–June 13, 1896: all in Warren Collection.

138.   Elwood Mead to F. J. Mills, Feb. 1, 1896, Mead Letterbook, Jan. 30, 1896–April 16, 1896, Mead Papers.

139.   Robert Foote to Hoke Smith, August 1895 (no specific date indicated), Records of the General Land Office, Carey Act Files, Box #6 (Wyoming), RG 49, National Archives.

140.   William H. Richards (and other state officials) to Hoke Smith, Sept. 23, 1895, Mead Letterbook, July 5, 1895–Oct. 24, 1895, Mead Papers. The letter was reprinted in the *People's Voice* (Buffalo, Wyo.), Sept. 14, 1895; *Cheyenne Daily Sun-Leader*, Sept. 24, 1895; and the *Buffalo Bulletin*, Oct. 3, 1895. Also see Richards to Frank Mondell, Oct. 28, 1895, in the William Richards Let-

terbook, Jan. 12, 1895–Dec. 31, 1895, W. A. Richards Papers, Wyoming State Archives, Cheyenne.

141.   *Big Horn Basin Savior*, Nov. 12 and 15, 1894, in Mead Scrapbook, Mead Papers. Also see the *Cheyenne Daily Leader*, Sept. 13, 1894.

142.   Intense criticism also came from Colorado, where retiring Populist governor Davis H. Waite repeated the familiar charge that the Carey Act was "in the interest of private corporations who desire to gobble up the arid lands for cattle ranges and speculative purposes." Waite favored cession only if Colorado retained title to the land, reclaimed it using proceeds from its internal improvement fund, and leased the improved tracts in parcels no larger than one hundred acres for five-year renewable terms (*Rocky Mountain News*, Jan. 5, 1895).

143.   *Cheyenne Daily Sun-Leader*, Sept. 9, 24, and Oct. 4, 1895; *Buffalo Bulletin*, Sept. 19 and Oct. 3, 1895. The *Denver Republican* editorial was reprinted in the Oct. 4 issue of the *Leader*.

144.   Both quotations are from Elwood Mead to F. W. Mondell (assistant commissioner, General Land Office), March 2, 1898, Mead Letterbook, July 27, 1897–March 11, 1898, Mead Papers. Also see *Fourth Biennial Report of the State Engineer to the Governor of Wyoming for the Years 1897 and 1898* (Cheyenne, 1898), pp. 143–44.

The Carey Act was amended many times, but never radically revised. Initially, Carey Act promoters expected to finance the construction of hydraulic works by selling water rights. But when settlers failed to appear, some projects issued bonds, like private ditch companies. Unfortunately, settlers could not acquire clear title to their land until they irrigated it, so these companies had no way to guarantee the bonds until 1896. In that year, Congress granted the states power to create liens against the lands for the cost of reclamation, and in 1901 it provided that the ten-year period allowed for reclamation—due to elapse in 1904—would not begin until the secretary of interior approved each individual application to reserve land. The same law also permitted the secretary to grant extensions. The most important *proposed* amendment, a bill to allow each state to choose up to 1 million acres without having lined up a company to reclaim it at the time of withdrawal, failed of adoption. See *Report of the Commissioner of the General Land Office, 1896* (Washington, D.C., 1896), pp. 59–60; H.R. 6465, 55th Cong., 2d sess., Jan. 13, 1898 (Jenkins); Fenimore Chatterton (Wyoming secretary of state) to F. E. Warren, Jan. 17, 1900, Warren Letterbook, Dec. 1, 1899–April 30, 1900, Warren Collection.

145.   Francis E. Warren, "What Congress Is Doing in Aid of Irrigation," *Proceedings of the Seventh Annual Session, National Irrigation Congress [1898]* (Cheyenne, 1899), p. 79.

146.   Lesley M. Heathcote, "The Montana Arid Land Grant Commission, 1895–1902," *Agricultural History*, 38 (April 1964), pp. 111–12,116, 117; *Cheyenne Daily Leader*, Feb. 1, 1895.

147.   Washington and Oregon also accepted the Carey Act. See Rose M. Boening, "History of Irrigation in the State of Washington," *Washington Historical Quarterly*, 10 (Jan. 1919), pp. 21–45; and *Official Proceedings of the*

Tenth National Irrigation Congress Held at Colorado Springs, Colorado (Colorado Springs, 1902), p. 188.

After 1902, the Carey Act—freed from the baneful influence of the depression and touted as an alternative to federal reclamation—enjoyed considerable success in the Mountain West, particularly in Idaho. See *New York Times,* March 29, 1903; James D. Schuyler, "New Irrigation Construction on Snake River, Idaho," *Official Proceedings of the Eleventh National Irrigation Congress Held at Ogden, Utah, September 15–18, 1903* (Ogden, 1904), pp. 354–62; F. R. Gooding, "Development of Idaho under the Carey Act," *Official Proceedings of the Seventeenth National Irrigation Congress [1909]* (Spokane, n.d.), pp. 314–22; Hugh T. Lovin, "A 'New West' Reclamation Tragedy: The Twin Falls Oakley Project in Idaho," *Arizona and the West,* 20 (Spring 1978), pp. 5–24; Bruce L. Schmaltz, "Headgates and Headaches: The Powell Tract," *Idaho Yesterdays,* 9 (Winter 1965–66), pp. 22–25.

148.   F. H. Newell to Charles D. Walcott (director of the USGS), Feb. 2, 1903, Records of the Bureau of Reclamation, General File, 1902–1919, Box 100, "131: Corres. re Administration: Policies and Organization thru 1905," RG 115, National Archives.

149.   "The Carey Bill Obnoxious," *Irrigation Age,* 6 (May 1894), pp. 186–87. Stanley Roland Davison notes that Smythe's self-appointed role as chief publicist of the irrigation crusade required him to lead the parade, even though his followers often made abrupt turns, leaving him to march on alone. He had many changes of heart during his career, but none greater than toward the Carey Act. Six months after Smythe wrote the words quoted in the text, he said that the new law "offers to the men of the West the most important opportunity for progress they have ever had . . . the more the law is studied the better it looks, and before this country is one year older we may be able to see that the passage of the law just at this time was providential." See "The Carey Law," *Irrigation Age,* 7 (Nov. 1894), p. 213, and in the same issue, "Labor and Homes for the Idle," pp. 214–15; and Davison, "Leadership of the Reclamation Movement," pp. 195–96, 201–2.

150.   *Denver Republican,* Sept. 5, 1894; *Rocky Mountain News,* Sept. 4, 5, 8, and 10, 1894; *Cheyenne Daily Leader,* Sept. 9, 1894; *Chicago Tribune,* Sept. 1 and 2, 1894.

151.   *Daily Boomerang,* Aug. 14 and Sept. 7, 1894; *Cheyenne Daily Sun-Leader,* Sept. 26, 1894; *New York Sun,* Sept. 29, 1894.

152.   *Irrigation Age,* 6 (Feb. 1894), pp. 74–75; *Official Proceedings of the Third National Irrigation Congress, Held at Denver, Colorado, Sept. 3rd to 8th, 1894* (Denver, n.d.), pp. 5–7; Elwood Mead to Fred Bond, September 11, 1894, Mead Letterbook, Dec. 10, 1892–Oct. 20, 1893, Mead Papers.

153.   *Cheyenne Daily Leader,* Sept. 8, 1894.

154.   *Official Proceedings of the Third National Irrigation Congress, Held at Denver, Colorado, Sept. 3rd to 8th, 1894,* p. 20; *New York Times,* Sept. 5 and 8, 1894.

155.   Charles Irish to Edward R. Chore, Dec. 5, 1894, Press Copies of Letters Sent by the Office of Irrigation Inquiry, Nov. 20, 1894–Feb. 7, 1895, RG 16,

National Archives. Also see Irish to J. W. Gregory in the Nov. 2, 1893–June 11, 1894 Letterbook.

156.   Denver's *Field and Farm*, March 9, 1895, reported that a Colorado millionaire named Hagerman had purchased *Irrigation Age* for four thousand dollars to boom his properties in the Pecos Valley. Although paid subscribers numbered two thousand, Smythe often printed as many as forty-five hundred copies and distributed the extras free.

157.   *Reno Evening Gazette*, May 11, 1895.

158.   *Boston Herald*, Feb. 17, 20, and 26, 1895; *Chicago Daily Tribune*, April 12, 1895; "The Lines of Thought Presented," *Irrigation Age*, 6 (Feb. 1894), p. 50, and 8 (March 1895), pp. 70–71; "The New Plymouth," *Irrigation Age*, 8 (March 1895), pp. 76–81; "Plymouth Colony," *Irrigation Age*, 6 (June 1895), pp. 186–87; "The Homeseekers' Convention," *Irrigation Age*, 12 (Oct. 1897), p. 8; "Eight Years Afterward," *Out West*, 19 (Sept. 1903), pp. 335–36; *Reno Evening Gazette*, April 20, 1895.

159.   Nevertheless, Smythe continued to publish articles in national journals on arid land reclamation. See, for example, his "Stepchild of the Republic," *North American Review*, 63 (July 1896), pp. 37–46.

160.   The 1895 irrigation congress met in Albuquerque, but the proceedings were never published. The resolutions called for public control over the construction of irrigation works and the cost of water, extension of the Carey Act to the territories of New Mexico and Arizona, creation of a national irrigation commission to coordinate the activities of federal agencies interested in water, and the appropriation of $250,000 to resume irrigation surveys (*New York Times*, Sept. 20, 1895).

161.   "The Northwest Overlooked," *Irrigation Age*, 10 (Aug. 1896), p. 60.

162.   *Official Report of the Fifth National Irrigation Congress Held at Phoenix, Arizona, December 15, 16, and 17, 1896* (Phoenix, 1897), p. 28.

163.   George Maxwell, who is discussed at length in the next chapter, emerged as the chief publicist for federal reclamation in the late 1890s. At this time he called for federal construction of the largest storage reservoirs, leasing of federal grazing lands, and granting the revenue from those leases to the states to pay for the construction of irrigation projects. See *Official Report of the Fifth National Irrigation Congress Held at Phoenix, Arizona, December 15, 16, and 17, 1896*, pp. 40–44.

164.   George H. Maxwell, "Irrigation and Prosperity," *Official Proceedings of the Nineteenth National Irrigation Congress Held at Chicago, Illinois, December 5–9, 1911* (Chicago, 1912), p. 126.

165.   "The Irrigation Congress," *Irrigation Age*, 12 (Nov. 1897), pp. 27–28.

166.   Elwood Mead to S. M. Emery, Oct. 12, 1897, Mead Letterbook, July 27, 1897–March 11, 1898, Mead Papers.

167.   *Cheyenne Sun-Leader*, Jan. 26 and March 5, 1898; *Third Biennial Report of the State Engineer to the Governor of Wyoming, 1895 and 1896*, p. 33; George W. Rollins, "The Struggle of the Cattleman, Sheepman, and Settler for Control of Lands in Wyoming, 1867–1919" (Ph.D. diss., University of Utah, 1951).

168.   *Buffalo Bulletin*, Feb. 3, 1898.

169.   The irrigation congress that met at Cheyenne at the beginning of September 1898 also favored outright cession. *Buffalo Bulletin*, Sept. 16, 1898.

170.   The swampland acts of 1849 and 1850 required that revenue derived from the sale of floodlands be used to build levees and drainage canals to reclaim the land. Instead, most states simply sold the unimproved land and used the money to build roads, bridges, and public buildings. The states had never appropriated the funds needed to administer the ceded lands, and they consistently used them as a form of currency rather than as the source of homes for small farmers.

171.   For example, see the Wyoming legislature's appeal in the *Congressional Record*, 55th Cong., 1st sess. (1897), pp. 67, 1915.

172.   *Congressional Record*, May 3, 1897, Senate, pp. 853–59; *Cheyenne Daily Sun-Leader*, May 8, 1897. This scheme made little headway. Senator Ben Tillman of South Carolina and others complained that it favored new states over old.

173.   The Wyoming Republican Party's platform adopted in August 1896 called for federal reclamation works along with a rebate to the states of all money paid for land under the Desert Land Act. *Buffalo Bulletin*, Aug. 27, 1896.

174.   Elwood Mead to Alva Adams (governor of Colorado), Feb. 15, 1897, in Outgoing Correspondence, Mead Letterbook, Sept. 5, 1896–March 18, 1897, Mead Papers.

175.   S. 846 (Warren), 55th Cong., 1st sess., March 19, 1897; S. 1984 (Warren), 55th Cong., 1st sess., May 17, 1897; S. 1985 (Warren), 55th Cong., 1st sess., May 17, 1897; *Cheyenne Daily Sun-Leader*, April 15, May 14, 17, 20, and 21, 1897; *Buffalo Bulletin*, April 29 and May 20, 1897. The most discussed comprehensive cession bill introduced in the Fifty-fifth Congress was H.R. 3291 (Hartman), 55th Cong., 1st sess., May 20, 1897.

176.   F. E. Warren to Elwood Mead, May 12 and 29, 1897, Letterbook, Apr. 12, 1896–Feb. 27, 1897, Warren Collection. Mead thought that Warren's obsession with squeezing every acre he could out of Congress reduced the chances for comprehensive legislation. "Noticing your criticism on my normal school bill," Warren responded to a troubled Mead in the following year, "we do not differ at all on that, except knowing the great demand for land I have felt like obtaining grants under almost every pretence—no that is not the word—for any legitimate use that we can get sufficient votes for. Land is the apple of the eastern people's eyes and it is hard to [w]ring out a few much less many acres unless it is for some sentimental use and education you know always sentimentally effects [*sic*] the cultured east" (F. E. Warren to Elwood Mead, March 4, 1898). Also Warren to J. C. Davis, March 21, 1898, Warren Letterbook, Jan. 27, 1898–Dec. 6, 1898, and Warren to George H. Maxwell, April 19, 1898, Letterbook, April 19, 1898–Jan. 3, 1899: all in Warren Collection; *Cheyenne Daily Sun-Leader*, Feb. 26 and March 24, 1900.

177.   S. 4016 and S. 4017, 55th Cong., 2d sess., March 2, 1898.

178.   For example, Congressman Shafroth of Colorado not only sponsored several bills to amend the Carey Act, he also proposed an unconditional 1-million-acre grant as well as a comprehensive cession bill. See H.R. 3585

(Shafroth), 55th Cong., 1st sess., June 17, 1897; H.R. 8488 (Shafroth), 55th Cong., 2d sess., Feb. 22, 1898; H.R. 9244 (Shafroth), 55th Cong., 2d sess., March 16, 1898; *Congressional Record,* 55th Cong., 3d sess., June 20, 1898, p. 6931; "Our Arid Public Lands," *Irrigation Age,* 12 (May 1898), pp. 233–35; *Rocky Mountain News,* March 6, 1898. Other important cession bills include S. 4195 (Pettigrew), 55th Cong., 2d sess., March 22, 1898; S. 6448 (Vandiver), 55th Cong., 2d sess., Jan. 12, 1898; H.R. 9332 (Rixey), 55th Cong., 2d sess., March 21, 1898.

179.   Binger Hermann to Secretary of the Interior, Dec. 28, 1897, and Jan. 3, 1898, Division A, Press Copies of Letters Sent Relating to Congressional Bills, vol. 16, Feb. 6, 1896–Dec. 31, 1896, RG 49, National Archives. Hermann remained a staunch opponent of new cession legislation. For example, see Hermann to Secretary of Interior, March 28, 1900, the same files, in vol. 18, Dec. 28, 1899–April 5, 1900.

180.   S. 4925, 55th Cong., 3d sess., introduced Dec. 8, 1898; *Congressional Record,* 55th Cong., 3d sess., Feb. 28, 1899, Senate, pp. 2550, 2834.

181.   Charles J. Kappler to Reinhold Sadler, March 10, 1899, Box 12, Letterbook, Feb. 25, 1898–April 14, 1899, Stewart Collection. Warren apparently reintroduced the 5-million-acre bill at the end of 1899 at the next session of Congress. See F. E. Warren to Fred Bond, Dec. 14, 1899, Warren Letterbook, Dec. 1, 1899–April 30, 1900, Warren Collection.

The most common argument against limited grants was that they were creatures of private companies or towns that sought to develop themselves at the expense of their rivals and the commonwealth. Such schemes could paralyze a legislature by raising the specter of mercantilism discussed in the last chapter.

182.   *Cheyenne Daily Sun,* Jan. 15 and 26, Feb. 5, 1900; F. E. Warren to Fred Bond, Dec. 14, 1899, Warren Letterbook, Dec. 1, 1899–April 30, 1900, Warren Collection.

183.   H.R. 5481 (Mondell), 56th Cong., 1st sess., Jan. 8, 1900; *Cheyenne Daily Sun-Leader,* Jan. 15, 1900. For another leading cession bill introduced in 1900 see H.R. 5022 (Shafroth), 56th Cong., 1st sess., Jan. 3, 1900.

The champions of cession contributed to public skepticism and anxiety by refusing to frame legislation that limited the states to *proceeds* from the use of public lands rather than ownership. Mondell's bill would have permitted Wyoming to grant leases to 2 million acres of public lands while the nation retained the rights of ownership and supervision. The land could be rented only after potential leases had been advertised—to alert claimants to agricultural land—and it would remain open to entry under all existing land laws even while under lease. Proceeds were dedicated to public schools and irrigation works.

184.   This fear was often expressed by Richard J. Hinton. See his "Waters of State and Nation," *Irrigation Age,* 2 (Dec. 1891), pp. 311–12, 328; Hinton, "A Continental Issue," *The Arena,* 8 (Oct. 1893), pp. 618–29; *Official Report of the International Irrigation Congress Held at Los Angeles, California, October, 1893,* pp. 81–82; *Official Proceedings of the Third National Irrigation*

Congress, Held at Denver, Colorado, Sept. 3rd to 8th, 1894, p. 45; and Richard J. Hinton to Elwood Mead, Sept. 30, 1895, "Incoming Correspondence: Arid Land Claims, Big Horn Development Co., 1895–1896," Mead Papers.

Chapter 8

1. F. L. Dana, *The Great West: A Vast Empire* (Denver, 1889), pp. 11–12. Also see Herbert J. Philpott, "Irrigation of Arid Lands," *Popular Science Monthly*, 36 (Jan. 1890), p. 368.

2. Richard Franklin Bensel, *Sectionalism and American Political Development, 1880–1980* (Madison, 1984), pp. 75–81; Russell R. Elliott, *Servant of Power: A Political Biography of Senator William M. Stewart* (Reno, 1983), p. 127 (quotation); George Rothwell Brown, ed., *Reminiscences of Senator William M. Stewart of Nevada* (New York, 1908), pp. 351–52.

3. Wallace Stegner, *Beyond the Hundredth Meridian: John Wesley Powell and the Opening of the West* (Boston, 1953), p. 341.

4. John Bonner, "The Present Stage of the Irrigation Question," *Overland Monthly*, 13 (June 1889), pp. 602–10.

5. "Reservoirs to Promote the Navigation of the Mississippi River," H. Ex. Doc. 49, 45th Cong., 2d sess. (Washington, D.C., 1878), serial 1806.

6. "Reservoirs of Upper Mississippi," H. Rep. 1701, 46th Cong., 2d sess. (Washington, D.C., 1880), serial 1938, p. 1. Also see "Surveys and Examinations for Establishment of Reservoirs at Headwaters of Mississippi River," S. Ex. Doc. 48, 46th Cong., 3d sess. (Washington, D.C., 1881), serial 1943.

7. *Congressional Record*, Senate, March 3, 1899, 55th Cong., 3d sess., pp. 2817, 2820; *Annual Report of the Chief of Engineers, 1892* (Washington, D.C., 1893), pp. 1817, 1818–19; Hiram Martin Chittenden, "Preliminary Examination of Reservoir Sites in Wyoming and Colorado," H. Doc. 141, 55th Cong., 2d sess. (1897), serial 3666, p. 37.

8. John Wesley Powell to J. P. Thomson, April 26, 1893, USGS, Outgoing Correspondence, Jan. 3–June 16, 1893, RG 57, National Archives.

9. *Congressional Record*, 54th Cong., 1st sess., Senate, May 12, 1896, p. 5115.

10. *Congressional Record*, 54th Cong., 1st sess., Senate, May 12, 1896, p. 5116; *Sheridan Post* (Sheridan, Wyo.), May 21, 1896.

11. F. E. Warren to W. P. Keays, May 27, 1896, in Letterbook, April 12, 1896–Feb. 27, 1897, Warren Collection, American Heritage Center, University of Wyoming. The River and Harbor Act of June 3, 1896, called for a "report upon the practicability and durability of constructing reservoirs, and other hydraulic works necessary for the storage and utilization of water, to prevent floods and overflows, erosion of river banks and breaks of levees, and to reenforce the flow of streams during drought and low-water seasons."

12. F. E. Warren to Elwood Mead, May 12 and 27, 1896, in Letterbook, April 12, 1896–Feb. 27, 1897, Warren Collection.

13. Warren to Mead, May 12, 1897, Letterbook, Apr. 12, 1896–Feb. 27, 1897, Warren Collection.

14. Chittenden is one of the few figures in the reclamation movement who

has a biography. See Gordon B. Dodds, *Hiram Martin Chittenden: His Public Career* (Lexington, Ky., 1973), esp. pp. 29–41, a chapter entitled, "Pioneer in Reclamation, 1896–1902."

15.   F. E. Warren to Hiram Martin Chittenden, Aug. 15, 1896; Warren to Joseph M. Carey, Aug. 15, 1896; and Warren to Elwood Mead, Aug. 15, 1896: all in Warren Letterbook, Apr. 12, 1896–Feb. 27, 1897, Warren Collection. Mead to Chittenden, Aug. 20 and 27, 1896, and Mead to E. Gillette, Aug. 31, 1896, Mead Letterbook, April 16–Nov. 23, 1896; Mead to Chittenden, March 17, 1897, Letterbook, Nov. 23, 1896–July 26, 1897: Mead Papers, Wyoming State Archives, Cheyenne. Apparently, Wyoming had already begun reservoir surveys of its own on Piney Creek. See the *Third Biennial Report of the State Engineer to the Governor of Wyoming, 1895 and 1896* (Cheyenne, 1897), p. 165.

Fred Bond, a Buffalo engineer who later became Wyoming state engineer, surveyed about half the reservoir sites reported on by Chittenden and apparently wrote about one quarter of the report. See C. H. Johnston to Elwood Mead, July 20, 1901, Records of the Bureau of Agricultural Engineering; Office of Experiment Stations; General Correspondence, 1898–1912, Box 1, General Correspondence, 1898–1902, RG 8, National Records Center, Suitland, Md. (hereafter cited as RG 8, National Records Center).

16.   Lt. Col. Amos Stickney to Gen. W. P. Craighill, Aug. 8, 1896, Office of the Chief of Engineers Correspondence, 1894–1923, #16519, RG 77, National Archives.

17.   Chittenden, "Preliminary Examination of Reservoir Sites in Wyoming and Colorado," p. 6; Elwood Mead to Hiram Martin Chittenden, July 26 and 27, and November 5, 1897, and Mead to B. F. Fowler, Aug. 4, 1897, Mead Letterbook, July 27, 1897–March 11, 1898, Mead Papers.

18.   Chittenden, "Preliminary Examination of Reservoir Sites in Wyoming and Colorado," pp. 40, 47, 48. Also see Chittenden's Aug. 26, 1898, letter to Joseph M. Carey, president of the National Irrigation Congress, in *Proceedings of the Seventh Annual Session, National Irrigation Congress [1898]* (Cheyenne, 1899), p. 26.

19.   By 1885, there were about 10,000 acres irrigated from Clear Creek, another 6,000 acres from Rock Creek, and 3,300 from North and South Piney creeks. The irrigation boom around Buffalo occurred in part because nearby Fort McKinney provided a market for hay, small grains, cattle, butter, eggs, and green vegetables. See Robert A. Murray, *Johnson County: 175 Years of History at the Foot of the Big Horn Mountains* (Buffalo, Wyo., 1981), pp. 72–73, 100–102.

20.   Chittenden, "Preliminary Examination of Reservoir Sites in Wyoming and Colorado," pp. 20–23, 70; H. M. Chittenden, "The Relation of the Government to the Construction of Storage Reservoirs in the Arid Regions of the West," in *Proceedings of the Ninth Annual Session of the National Irrigation Congress, Held at Central Music Hall, Chicago, Ill., November 21, 22, 23, 24, 1900* (St. Louis, n.d.), pp. 31–44; *Wyoming Tribune* (Cheyenne), Dec. 17, 1896; *Fourth Biennial Report of the State Engineer to the Governor of Wyoming for the Years 1897 and 1898* (Cheyenne, 1898), p. 74.

21.   Chittenden, "Preliminary Examination of Reservoir Sites in Wyoming

and Colorado," pp. 52, 56, 57, 58, 64. Chittenden summarized his conclusions in a letter to Joseph M. Carey, Aug. 26, 1898, reprinted in *Proceedings of the Seventh Annual Session, National Irrigation Congress [1898]*, pp. 21–22. See also Hiram M. Chittenden, "The Irrigation Problems and Possibilities of Northern Wyoming," *Irrigation Age*, 13 (March 1899), pp. 195–202; Elwood Mead, "The Irrigation Problems and Possibilities of Northern Wyoming," *Irrigation Age*, 13 (Jan. 1899), pp. 109–15, and 13 (Feb. 1899), pp. 149–57; "To Build Reservoirs," *Irrigation Age*, 13 (Feb. 1899), p. 184; E. S. Nettleton, "The Irrigation Problems and Possibilities of Northern Wyoming," *Irrigation Age*, 13 (April 1899), pp. 235–38; and Clarence T. Johnson, "The Irrigation Possibilities of Northern Wyoming," *Irrigation Age*, 13 (May 1899), pp. 263–67.

22.   See for example, Lester F. Ward, "Irrigation in the Upper Missouri and Yellowstone Valleys," *Science*, 4 (Aug. 29, 1884), pp. 166–68; John Bonner, "The Present Stage of the Irrigation Question," *Overland Monthly*, 13 (June 1889), pp. 602–10; and Herbert J. Philpott, "Irrigation of Arid Lands," *Popular Science Monthly*, 36 (Jan. 1890), pp. 364–71.

23.   Congress had been inundated with appeals for federal reclamation. For example, see the *Congressional Record*, Dec. 11, 1889, p. 142; Dec. 21, 1889, p. 353; Jan. 6, 1890, p. 383; Jan. 6, 1890, p. 413; Jan. 23, 1889, p. 1118; Jan. 23, 1890, p. 823; Feb. 5, 1890, p. 1077; Feb. 19, 1890, p. 1471; July 25, 1890, p. 7688; Sept. 5, 1890, p. 9777; Jan. 27, 1891, p. 1893; Jan. 28, 1891, p. 1943; Jan. 31, 1891, p. 1995; Feb. 9, 1891, p. 2373; Feb. 10, 1891, p. 2477; Feb. 10, 1891, p. 2478; Dec. 10, 1891, p. 21; Dec. 16, 1891, pp. 67–68; Jan. 18, 1892, p. 354; Feb. 8, 1892, p. 912; April 20, 1892, p. 3464.

24.   S. 624 (Dolph), 52d Cong., 1st sess., Dec. 14, 1891; S. 2544 (Dolph), 52d Cong., 1st sess., March 10, 1892; H.R. 5146 (Stockdale), 52d Cong., 1st sess., Feb. 1, 1892; S. 70 (Dolph), 53d Cong., 1st sess., Aug. 8, 1893; S. 2279 (Peffer), 53d Cong., 2d sess., Aug. 3, 1894; H.R. 7242 (Joseph), 53d Cong., 2d sess., May 28, 1894; H.R. 7887 (Baker), 53d Cong., 2d sess., Aug. 3, 1894; H.R. 7896 (Davis), 53d Cong., 2d sess., Aug. 3, 1897; S. 2541 (Kyle), 53d Cong., 3d sess., Jan. 10, 1895; H.R. 279 (Baker), 54th Cong., 1st sess., Dec. 6, 1895; H.R. 3635 (Bell), 54th Cong., 1st sess., Jan. 10, 1896.

25.   *Congressional Record*, 55th Cong., 3d sess., Senate, Feb. 4 and 10, 1899, pp. 1445, 1595, 1597, 1678, 1730.

26.   *Congressional Record*, 55th Cong., 3d sess., Senate, Feb. 24, 1899, p. 2282; *Cheyenne Daily Sun-Leader*, Feb. 4, 20, 25, and 28, 1899.

27.   *Congressional Record*, 55th Cong., 3d sess., Senate, Feb. 24 and March 3, 1899, pp. 2273, 2275–76, 2281, 2817, 2825, 2829, 2834.

28.   Ibid., pp. 2279, 2280.

29.   Ibid., p. 2277.

30.   Ibid., pp. 2278, 2817.

31.   Ibid., pp. 2269, 2271, 2272, 2276.

32.   *Congressional Record*, 55th Cong., 3d sess., Senate, March 3, 1899, p. 2821.

33.   *Washington Post*, March 4, 1899.

34.   *Congressional Record*, 55th Cong., 3d sess., Senate, March 3, 1899, p. 2843.

35.   Warren to Mead, March 6, 1899, March 6, 1899, Warren Letterbook, Jan. 2–May 4, 1899, Warren Collection.

36.   *Dictionary of American Biography* (New York, 1929), vol. 2, p. 545. Also see Richard B. Roeder, "Thomas H. Carter, Spokesman for Western Development," *Montana, the Magazine of Western History,* 39 (Spring 1989), pp. 23–29.

37.   Hiram Sapp (F. E. Warren's private secretary) to George H. Maxwell, Oct. 24, 1900, Letterbook, May 12–Dec. 17, 1900; Warren to E. Gillette (superintendent, Burlington and Missouri Railroad), Feb. 26, 1901, Warren to Charles G. Weir, Feb. 27, 1901, and Warren to H. G. Burt (president, Union Pacific Railroad), March 6, 1901, Warren Letterbook, Feb. 24–May 6, 1901: all in Warren Collection.

In the House, Wyoming's sole congressman, Frank Mondell, also introduced legislation calling for the construction of the Piney Creek reservoirs, using the old flood control and navigation justification. See the *Cheyenne Daily Leader,* Dec. 10, 1900, and Jan. 16, 1901; *Denver Republican,* Jan. 16 and 27, 1901; *Congressional Record,* 56th Cong., 2d sess., House, Jan. 15, 1901, p. 1052, and Jan. 21, 1901, p. 1247; *National Irrigation,* 6 (March 1901), pp. 34–35.

38.   *Congressional Record,* 56th Cong., 2d sess., Senate, March 2, 1901, pp. 3544–46.

39.   *New York Times,* March 5, 1901. For other newspaper accounts see the *Washington Post, Philadelphia Inquirer,* and *Chicago Daily Tribune* of the same date.

40.   *Congressional Record,* 56th Cong., 2d sess., Senate, March 2, 1901, p. 3521. For the filibuster see pp. 3519–62.

41.   Ibid., pp. 3521, 3523.

42.   Ibid., pp. 3525, 3552.

43.   George H. Maxwell, "One and Indivisible: Forestry, Irrigation, Drainage, Navigation; The Rivers Are the Greatest Assets of the Nation When Regulated for All Beneficial Uses," *Official Proceedings of the Nineteenth National Irrigation Congress Held at Chicago, Illinois, December 5–9, 1911* (Chicago, 1912), p. 89.

44.   *Congressional Record,* 56th Cong., 2d sess., Senate, March 2, 1901, p. 3545.

45.   F. H. Newell to Theodore Roosevelt, Feb. 26, 1913, Roosevelt Papers, Library of Congress, Washington, D.C. Also see Newell's typescript "Memoirs" for the year 1902, Box #1, F. H. Newell Collection, American Heritage Center, University of Wyoming.

46.   Andrew Hudanick, Jr., "George Hebard Maxwell: Reclamation's Militant Evangelist," *Journal of the West,* 14 (July 1975), pp. 108–19. The largest collection of Maxwell papers is at the Louisiana State Museum in New Orleans. Unfortunately, it is concentrated in the period from 1896–1900 and contains little correspondence for 1901 and 1902.

47.   George H. Maxwell to Woodrow Wilson, Sept. 23, 1917, Records of the National Reclamation Association within the Records of the Bureau of Rec-

lamation, Box 25, file "Special Correspondence with Presidents, Senators, etc.," RG 115, National Archives.

48.   George H. Maxwell to Walter Parker, Feb. 17, 1935, in the Records of the American Homecroft Society, "General Records, 1920–1921," RG 115, National Archives; Maxwell, "The Irrigation District: The Inherent Defects Which Have Caused Its Failure Can Only Be Remedied by a State System," *Irrigation Age*, 12 (June 1898), pp. 250–53; *The Citrograph* (Redlands, Calif.), July 2, 30, and Aug. 20, 1898.

49.   Nevertheless, many politicians probably shared F. E. Warren's judgment—made after he had asked Maxwell to draft a practical reclamation bill in 1898—that the publicist was "a very bright, entertaining fellow" but not "entirely practical and sound in his propositions or perhaps I should say he does not follow out his ideas to their logical conclusion" (F. E. Warren to Elwood Mead, June 1, 1898, Warren Letterbook, April 19, 1898–Jan. 3, 1899, Warren Collection). Also see Warren to Mead, June 24, 1898, in the same place.

50.   *Los Angeles Express*, Sept. 5, 1902.

51.   *Rocky Mountain News* (Denver), Dec. 17, 1896; *Maxwell's Talisman*, 6 (Dec. 1906), p. 3; F. H. Newell, "A Man's Life," pp. 55–65, typescript copy in Box #1, Newell Collection.

52.   George H. Maxwell, "Nature's Storage Reservoirs," *Forester*, 5 (Aug. 1899), p. 185.

53.   George H. Maxwell, "Reclamation of Arid America," *Irrigation Age*, 13 (Sept. 1899), pp. 407–9.

54.   "Labor Unions Favor National Irrigation," *Forestry and Irrigation*, 8 (Feb. 1902), pp. 50–51; "Forestry and Irrigation in Congress," *Forestry and Irrigation*, 8 (March 1902), pp. 134–36; *Forestry and Irrigation*, 10 (Feb. 1904), p. 84; *National Homemaker*, 7 (Jan. 1902), pp. 1–2, and 7 (Feb. 1902), pp. 43–44; *Congressional Record*, 57th Cong., 1st sess., Senate, Feb. 6, 1902, p. 1383; *National Advocate*, 5 (Oct. 1900), p. 8. Maxwell printed extensive excerpts from eastern newspapers that supported federal reclamation in *National Homemaker*, 7 (Jan. 1902), pp. 12–23. For examples of newspaper support in other parts of the country, see the *St. Louis Globe Democrat*, July 26, 1901; *Houston Post*, Dec. 25, 1901; and *San Francisco Chronicle*, Jan. 30, 1902.

55.   For example, on August 21, 1900, Maxwell wrote to U.S. senator T. R. Bard of California: "The commercial interests of Chicago are ready to put their shoulder to the wheel in the national irrigation movement. . . . They see no reason why the government should not begin immediately and appropriate $15,000,000 a year and complete the work in ten years. But they must be satisfied that the west is in earnest and wants it done. I will be in Los Angeles on Monday the 27th instant. Will you not assist actively to secure the attendance at the meeting on that day of every business man and property owner in Los Angeles?" Maxwell became a master at playing off section against section, state against state, and city against city. See Box 9-A, file "Irrigation, National, I," Thomas Bard Collection, Huntington Library, San Marino, California.

56.   John T. Ganoe, "The Origin of a National Reclamation Policy," *Mississippi Valley Historical Review*, 18 (June 1931), p. 41. Ganoe discusses Max-

well's role in the irrigation crusade on pp. 39–42. Also see Maxwell's speech in *Proceedings of the Seventh Annual Session, National Irrigation Congress [1898]*, pp. 144–49; *National Advocate*, 5 (Oct. 1900), p. 2.

57. *Citrograph*, Jan. 7, 1899; George H. Maxwell, "Annex Arid America," *Irrigation Age*, 13 (Nov. 1898), pp. 51–55.

58. *News and Courier* (Charleston, S.C.), March 7, 1913; also see the Charleston *Evening Post* of the same date.

59. Michael P. Malone and Richard B. Roeder, *Montana: A History of Two Centuries* (Seattle, 1976), pp. 184–85. On the Asian trade, see Hill's comments in the Chicago *Tribune*, July 7, 1901; and his "Federal Aid to Irrigators," *Irrigation Age*, 16 (Oct. 1901), pp. 17–18. During House debate over the Reclamation Act, Representative Charles Q. Tirrell of Massachusetts noted that wheat exports from the Puget Sound had increased 5,000 percent in twenty years while British exports to Japan were falling. Climate and terrain placed strict limits on the crops Asia could grow, so trade with Asia was bound to expand as the Asian population grew. *Congressional Record*, 57th Cong., 1st sess., House, June 12, 1902, p. 6699. Also see "Increase of Our Export Trade," *Irrigation Age*, 15 (June 1900), p. 297; *National Irrigation*, 6 (Nov. 1901), p. 148; James Wilson, "Irrigation Creates Home Markets," *Forestry and Irrigation*, 8 (Jan. 1902), pp. 10–11; and *National Homemaker*, 7 (May 1902), pp. 91, 103.

60. "Address Delivered by Mr. James J. Hill before the Farmers' National Congress, Madison, Wisconsin, September 24, 1908," Box 519, Gifford Pinchot Collection, Library of Congress, Washington, D.C.

61. James J. Hill to Jacob Schiff, June 13, 1901, Hill Letterbook, Oct. 11, 1895–May 29, 1902, James J. Hill Collection, Hill Library, St. Paul, Minnesota.

62. James J. Hill to Paris Gibson, May 23, 1897, and Hill to Mark Hanna, April 19, 1900, Hill Letterbook, Oct. 11, 1895–May 29, 1902; and Hill to Hanna, Jan. 5, 1901, Hill Letterbook, April 28–Aug. 14, 1900: in Hill Collection.

63. Malone and Roeder, *Montana*, p. 183. At least partly in anticipation of a federal reclamation program, the land grant railroads showed an increasing interest in securing formal titles to their lands after 1899. In fiscal year 1899, 504,651 acres were patented to the railroads; in fiscal year 1900, 1,272,572; in fiscal year 1901, 2,470,804; in 1902, 5,008,131; and in 1903, 3,864,182 acres. See Commissioner of the General Land Office to Theodore Roosevelt, Sept. 3, 1903, Warren Letterbook, July 29, 1902–Feb. 13, 1904, Warren Collection. Also see Senator Thomas R. Bard to William Collier, Nov. 15, 1902, Box 7-C, file "Irrigation and Arid Lands, April–Dec. 1902," Bard Collection.

64. James J. Hill to Cyrus Happy (chairman, Spokane Chamber of Commerce), Oct. 1, 1904, General Correspondence, Hill Collection.

65. James J. Hill to Jonathan S. Kennedy, May 18, 1902, General Correspondence, Hill Collection; Malone and Roeder, *Montana*, p. 180.

66. J. M. Hannaford to C. S. Mellen, April 18, 1899, President's Office Subject Files, 1. C. 1. 4F, file 19-D (George Maxwell correspondence), Northern Pacific Papers, Minnesota Historical Society, St. Paul. Maxwell supplemented his railroad subsidy with revenue generated by the National Irrigation Association's five-dollar-a-year membership charge, which bore heavily on eastern merchants and manufacturers.

67.   Maxwell's experience in Arizona and his growing friendship with F. H. Newell were also responsible for this change. Maxwell had moved to Arizona at the end of the 1890s and subsequently helped organize water users in the Salt River Valley, which won one of the first five reclamation projects authorized under the 1902 legislation. Virtually all the land in that valley was privately held. Karen L. Smith, *The Magnificent Experiment: Building the Salt River Reclamation Project, 1890–1917* (Tucson, 1986), pp. 17–24; Hudanick, "George Hebard Maxwell," p. 116.

68.   Charles F. Manderson to Elwood Mead, Aug. 3, 1901, RG 8, National Records Center; C. P. Huntington to C. S. Mellen, Feb. 15, 1900, and Mellen to Huntington, Feb. 20, 1900, President's Office Subject Files, 1. C. 1. 4F, file 19-D (George Maxwell correspondence), Northern Pacific Papers. Also see C. M. Hays to C. S. Mellen, Feb. 7, 1901; Mellen to Hays, Feb. 21, 1901; J. M. Hannaford to Mellen, Oct. 5, 1901; H. A. Fabian to Hannaford, Oct. 3, 1902; Hannaford to Mellen, Oct. 6, 1902; and Mellen to J. Kruttschnitt, April 13, 1903, in the same file; as well as James J. Hill to Hays, Feb. 9, 1901, President's Letterbooks, vol. 55, Jan. 17–April 1, 1901, Great Northern Collection, Minnesota Historical Society, St. Paul, Minnesota.

69.   *San Francisco Call*, Dec. 3, 1898.

70.   *Genoa Weekly Courier* (Gardnerville, Nev.), Jan. 25, 1901. U.S. senator Wesley A. Stuart remarked that an empire overseas would not provide new homes because most potential colonies and dependencies were already heavily populated. Moreover, "the law of natural selection and survival of the fittest has decreed that the Mongolian and the Malay are the only human types that can survive and thrive in the Orient, while the Anglo-Saxon, whose very energy he owes to the cold of the North, must make his home in a Northern zone." See "What the National Irrigation Association Stands For," *Proceedings of the Ninth Annual Session of the National Irrigation Congress, Chicago [1900]*, p. 128.

71.   William E. Smythe, "Real Utopias in the Arid West," *Atlantic*, 79 (May 1897), p. 608; Smythe, *Conquest of Arid America* (New York, 1900), pp. xiii, 297; *Rural Californian*, 23 (Nov. 1900), p. 437; F. H. Newell, "Development of Water Resources," *Forester*, 7 (Aug. 1901), p. 194; H. C. Hansbrough, "A National Irrigation Policy," *Forestry and Irrigation*, 8 (March 1902), p. 104. Also see the speeches collected in S. Doc. 446, 57th Cong., 1st sess. (Washington, D.C., 1902), esp. those of F. W. Mondell and H. C. Hansbrough, pp. 7–9.

72.   See the Maxwell editorials in *California—A Journal of Rural Industry*, 1 (Feb. 1890), p. 4, and 1 (March 1890), p. 2.

73.   Thomas F. Walsh, "Humanitarian Aspect of National Irrigation," *Forestry and Irrigation*, 8 (Dec. 1902), p. 506; Frederick Booth-Tucker, "The Relation of Colonization to Irrigation," *Forestry and Irrigation*, 9 (Oct. 1903), pp. 503–4.

74.   Stuart, "What the National Irrigation Association Stands For," p. 127.

75.   *Official Proceedings of the Tenth International Irrigation Congress, 1902* (Colorado Springs, 1902), pp. 34–35; Lawrence B. Lee, "The Mormons Come to Canada, 1877–1902," *Pacific Northwest Quarterly*, 59 (Jan. 1968), pp.

11–22. The quotation is from James J. Hill to William B. Dean, April 8, 1902, Personal and Private Correspondence, Hill Letterbook, Mar. 13, 1899–May 29, 1902, Hill Collection. Also see Hill to J. P. Heatwole, Feb. 21, 1901, President's Letterbooks, vol. 55, Jan. 17–April 1, 1901, Great Northern Collection; Hill to George H. Maxwell, April 16, 1902, in Personal and Private Correspondence, Hill Letterbook, Mar. 13, 1899–May 29, 1902, and Hill to Charles Steele, May 14, 1902, and Hill to Jonathan S. Kennedy, May 16 and 18, 1902, in the same letterbook, Hill Collection.

76.   Truman G. Palmer, "Irrigation and Beet Sugar," *Official Proceedings of the Eleventh National Irrigation Congress Held at Ogden, Utah, September 15–18, 1903* (Ogden, 1904), p. 310. A Department of Interior memorandum dated August 4, 1909, estimated that over the previous decade an average of forty-five to sixty thousand American families migrated each year to Canada, "carrying with them over $70,000,000 in property. This statement is checked [confirmed] by the reports of the Canadian Immigration Commission. This drain upon our resources must be stopped" (in file "Reclamation Service: Publicity Department," Box 1706, Records of the Office of the Secretary of the Interior, Central Files, 1907–1936, RG 48, National Archives).

77.   "National Board of Trade," *Forestry and Irrigation*, 10 (Feb. 1904), p. 86; Nelson A. Miles, "Our Unwatered Empire," *North American Review*, 150 (March 1890), pp. 371–72; A. P. Davis, "The Public Domain in Its Social Aspect," *Irrigation Age*, 7 (July 1894), pp. 15–17; *Proceedings of the International Irrigation Congress, Los Angeles, October, 1893* (Los Angeles, 1893), pp. 22, 145; A. B. Wyckoff, "Irrigation," *Journal of the Franklin Institute*, 140 (Oct. 1895), p. 244; *Official Proceedings of the Fourth National Irrigation Congress Held at Albuquerque, New Mexico, September 16–19, 1895* (Santa Fe, 1896), pp. 27, 66; A. J. Wells, *Government Irrigation and the Settler* (San Francisco, n.d.), p. 9; "Irrigation: Existing Conditions and Needs," in *Final Report of the Industrial Commission, 1902* (Washington, D.C., 1902), vol. 19, pp. 1071, 1073; F. H. Newell, "Reclamation of Arid Public Lands," *Independent*, 54 (May 22, 1902), p. 1243.

78.   W. V. Doyle, "What Can Be Accomplished by Irrigation," *Proceedings of the Seventh Annual Session, National Irrigation Congress [1898]* (Cheyenne, 1899), pp. 134–35.

79.   *Congressional Record*, 50th Cong., 1st sess., Senate, July 30, 1888, p. 7027.

80.   *Congressional Record*, 57th Cong., 1st sess., Senate, March 1, 1902, pp. 2276–85, and House, June 13, 1902, p. 6751; James J. Hill to Elwood Mead, Oct. 20, 1902, RG 8, National Records Center.

81.   *Congressional Record*, 57th Cong., 1st sess., House, June 12, 1901, p. 6672; Paul W. Gates, *History of Public Land Law Development* (Washington, D.C., 1968), p. 496.

82.   Alvin T. Steinel, "The Range Livestock Industry," in James H. Baker, ed., *History of Colorado* (Denver, 1927), pp. 645–93; Agnes Wright Spring, *Seventy Years: A Panoramic History of the Wyoming Stock Growers Association* (n.p., 1942), pp. 87–88; T. A. Larson, *History of Wyoming* (Lincoln, 1978), pp. 176–77. On the history of grazing and grazing legislation, see Frank Bell,

"Federal Legislation Concerning the Disposition of Grazing Land" (Ph.D. diss., Indiana University, 1959); Ernest Staples Osgood, *The Day of the Cattleman* (Minneapolis, 1929), pp. 176–215; William D. Rowley, *U.S. Forest Service Grazing and Rangelands: A History* (College Station, Tex., 1985), pp. 3–21; Samuel P. Hays, *Conservation and the Gospel of Efficiency: The Progressive Conservation Movement, 1890–1920* (Cambridge, Mass., 1959), pp. 49–60; and Gates, *History of Public Land Law Development*, pp. 466–94.

83.   "Leasing Arid and Desert Lands in Colorado, with Minority Report," H. Rep. 197, 47th Cong., 1st sess. (Washington, D.C., 1882), serial 2065; Acting Commissioner of the General Land Office to Henry M. Teller (secretary of the interior), March 11, 1884, Division A, Press Copies of Letters Sent Relating to Congressional Bills, vol. 4, Feb. 4–July 3, 1884, RG 49, National Archives.

84.   William A. Richards (and many other state officials) to F. E. Warren, C. D. Clark, and J. E. Osborne, March 17, 1897, Mead Letterbook, Nov. 23, 1896–July 26, 1897, Mead Papers. Coville estimated the value of all cattle in Wyoming in 1886 as $32,022,900 and gave the figure for 1895 as $10,562,332. He listed the total number of beef cattle in the territory as 1,280,916 in 1886, but only 688,092 in 1898. See his article, "Our Public Grazing Lands," *Forum*, 26 (Sept. 1898), pp. 109–10.

85.   The quotation from Mead's report is as given in Larson, *History of Wyoming*, p. 306; "Our Arid Public Lands," *Irrigation Age*, 12 (May 1898), pp. 233–35; Elwood Mead, "The Arid Public Lands—Their Reclamation, Management, and Disposal," in S. Doc. 130, 55th Cong., 1st sess. (Washington, D.C., 1897), serial 3562, p. 13; Elwood Mead to Alva Adams (Colorado governor), and Mead to F. J. Cannon, Feb. 15, 1897, Mead Letterbook, Nov. 23, 1896–July 26, 1897, and the undated statement (probably February 1898), in Letterbook, July 27, 1897–March 11, 1898, Mead Papers; "Grazing Lands in Wyoming," April 13, 1897, S. Doc. 31, 55th Cong., 1st sess.

86.   Elwood Mead to John Minto, March 22, 1898, Mead Letterbook, Mar. 11, 1898–Jan. 21, 1899, Mead Papers. As mentioned earlier, George Maxwell initially supported Mead's ideas, though the two men eventually became bitter enemies. See Maxwell, "Nature's Storage Reservoirs," pp. 183–85; Maxwell, "Let's Hang Together," *Irrigation Age*, 13 (May 1899), pp. 279–81; and Maxwell, "Reclamation of Arid America," pp. 407–9. Francis G. Newlands also favored Mead's scheme. See his letter to Mead, Nov. 4, 1899, Box 2, F. G. Newlands Collection, Sterling Library, Yale University.

87.   *Cheyenne Daily Sun-Leader*, Feb. 24, March 1, and April 20, 1900.

88.   Coville, "Our Public Grazing Lands," pp. 108–18. Coville wanted leases that could be terminated at any time by state officials with reimbursement for improvements, such as fences, or compensation through the grant of equivalent grazing lands elsewhere. He argued that a termination provision would discourage lessees from overgrazing the land. However, Coville did not regard leasing as a permanent solution. Once the public lands had been classified, the federal government and states could consider other options, including outright sale.

89.   Elwood Mead to Ray Stannard Baker, Jan. 20, 1902, RG 8, National Records Center.

90.   *Cheyenne Daily Leader,* April 7, 1902.
91.   H.R. 7212 (Bowersock), 57th Cong., 1st sess., introduced Dec. 18, 1901. A twin bill was introduced in the Senate on Jan. 28, 1902. See S. 3311 (Millard). Also see *Cheyenne Daily Leader,* April 21, 1902.
92.   E. Louise Peffer, *The Closing of the Public Domain: Disposal and Reservation Policies, 1900–1950* (Stanford, 1951), pp. 75–77; Binger Hermann (commissioner of the General Land Office) to Secretary of the Interior, April 14, 1902, and his undated letter to the secretary of May 1902, General Land Office, Division A, Press Copies of Letters Sent Relating to Congressional Bills, vol. 21, April 4–Aug. 20, 1902, RG 49, National Archives; Hermann's letter to the secretary concerning S. 3311, dated April 14, 1902, was reprinted in *Congressional Record,* 57th Cong., 1st sess., Senate, May 2, 1902, pp. 4960–62; *Report of the Secretary of the Interior, 1902* (Washington, D.C., 1902), pp. 167–74; F. G. Newlands to Charles F. Manderson, Dec. 27, 1901, Newlands to A. W. Riley, Newlands to J. W. Dorsey, and Newlands to D. C. Wheeler, all Jan. 23, 1902, in Correspondence, Box 5, Newlands Collection. The resolutions from Montana and Colorado are reprinted in *Congressional Record,* 57th Cong., 1st sess., Senate, Dec. 5, 1901, p. 135, and Jan. 14, 1902, p. 645.
93.   Besides the Bowersock measure, the most important grazing bills introduced in the Fifty-seventh Congress were H.R. 6246 (Stephens), Dec. 13, 1901; H.R. 7954 (Stephens), Jan. 7, 1902; and H.R. 14108 (Lacey), April 30, 1902.
94.   The most important bills were S. 2341 (Allen), introduced Jan. 11, 1900; S. 5833 (Hansbrough), Jan. 31, 1901; H.R. 12230 (Shafroth), Dec. 3, 1900; H.R. 13779 (Barham), Jan. 23, 1901; H.R. 13847 (Mondell), Jan. 26, 1901; H.R. 13993 (Mondell), Feb. 2, 1901; H.R. 14165 (Mondell), Feb. 12, 1901; H.R. 14192 (Wilson), Feb. 14, 1901; H.R. 14203 (Wilson), Feb. 15, 1901; H.R. 14241 (Reeder), Feb. 20, 1901; H.R. 14250 (Needham), Feb. 21, 1901; and H.R. 14280 (Mondell), Feb. 25, 1901.
95.   William Lilley III, "The Early Career of Francis G. Newlands, 1848–1897" (Ph.D. diss., Yale University, 1965); H. H. Bancroft, *Chronicles of the Builders of the Commonweath* (San Francisco, 1892), vol. 4, pp. 80–102.
96.   Barbara Richnak, *A River Flows: The Life of Robert Lardin Fulton* (Incline Village, Nev., 1983), pp. 74–75; Russell R. Elliott, *History of Nevada* (Lincoln, 1973), pp. 175, 203; John Townley, *Alfalfa Country: Nevada Land, Water & Politics in the 19th Century* (Reno, 1981), pp. 130–32; Grace Dangberg, *Conflict on the Carson* (Minden, Nev., 1975), p. 74; H. M. Yerington to D. O. Mills, Dec. 26, 1888, and Feb. 12, 1889, Outgoing Correspondence, vol. 17, H. M. Yerington Collection, Bancroft Library, University of California, Berkeley.
97.   On Newlands's activities in the San Joaquin Valley, see the E. B. Perrin Dictation, pp. 44–45, dated Jan. 15, 1890, in the Hubert Howe Bancroft Collection, and William Hammond Hall to Francis G. Newlands, March 26, 1887, in the Sharon Family Papers, both at the Bancroft Library, University of California, Berkeley. On Newlands's involvement in the Owens Valley, see the long series of letters written in 1888 by H. M. Yerington to D. O. Mills, in Outgoing Correspondence, vol. 17, Yerington Collection. Newlands apparently

had no *immediate* political plans when he moved to Nevada. "I have no idea at present of contesting [U.S. senator J. P.] Jones' seat," he wrote to Fred Sharon on Jan. 10, 1889. "I simply intend to hold myself in line and wait" (Newlands Papers, within the Sharon Family Papers, Box 2).

98.   Bancroft, *Chronicles of the Builders of the Commonwealth*, vol. 4, pp. 90, 97; Lilley, "The Early Career of Francis G. Newlands, 1848–1897," p. iv. Newlands's desire to build a planned suburban community in Chevy Chase, Maryland, is discussed in Kenneth T. Jackson, *Crabgrass Frontier: The Suburbanization of the United States* (New York, 1985), pp. 122–24.

99.   *Reno Evening Gazette,* June 13, 1894.

100.   *Congressional Record,* 53d Cong., 2d sess., House, Aug. 11, 1894, p. 8427.

101.   *Reno Evening Gazette,* Aug. 6 and Sept. 13, 1898, July 17 (quotation) and 20, 1900.

102.   H.R. 9080, which Newlands introduced on May 14, 1898, called for a $250,000 appropriation for reservoir surveys on major western streams. H.R. 9376, which he introduced on March 22, 1898, provided for surveys of damsites at the headwaters of the Truckee, Carson, Walker, and Humboldt rivers. Elliott, *History of Nevada,* pp. 201–9; Townley, *Alfalfa Country,* pp. 174–75; "First Steps," *Irrigation Age,* 12 (May 1898), p. 216.

103.   H.R. 4751, 56th Cong., 1st sess., Dec. 19, 1899; H.R. 12844, 56th Cong., 2d sess., Dec. 17, 1900. Apparently, this bill was designed to pacify the Southern Pacific and large stockmen, both of which owned large tracts of land in the Humboldt country, and whose help Newlands needed to gain election to the U.S. Senate. Newlands's 1900 bill provided that surplus water would be sold at the same price to established farmers and ranchers as to new settlers.

104.   The Mondell dinner set a precedent. The congressmen agreed to hold regular conferences to discuss reclamation and forge a united front. See the *Denver Republican* and *Denver News,* Dec. 21, 1899; *Salt Lake Tribune* and *Salt Lake Herald,* Dec. 25, 1899; and *Rawlins Republican* (Rawlins, Wyo.), Jan. 13, 1900.

105.   R. J. Laws to F. G. Newlands, Feb. 10, 1899, E. E. Copeland to Newlands, Feb. 15, 1899, and Newlands to Laws, Feb. 16, 1899, Box 2, Newlands Collection. "We favor an intelligent system of improving the arid lands of the West," the Democratic plank read, "storing the waters for the purposes of irrigation, and the holding of the lands for actual settlers." Not to be outdone, the Republican party adopted the following plank: "In further pursuance of the constant policy of the Republican party to provide free homes on the public domain, we recommend adequate national legislation to reclaim the arid lands of the United States, reserving control of the distribution of water for irrigation to the respective States and Territories." For the platform statements, see *First Annual Report of the Reclamation Service from June 17 to December 1, 1902* (Washington, D.C., 1903), pp. 40–41.

106.   *Proceedings of the Ninth Annual Session of the National Irrigation Congress, Held at Central Music Hall, Chicago, Ill., November 21, 22, 23, 24, 1900.*

107.   For example, the Chicago congress asked Congress to reserve all water

that had not yet been claimed in the West for the perpetual use of the federal government. See "Great Irrigation Enterprises," *World's Work*, 1 (Dec. 1900), p. 252.

108.   As of the middle of 1900, Congress had appropriated about $1,800,000 for previous irrigation investigations, including artesian well surveys. The USGS had spent about $700,000, the Department of Agriculture about $200,000, the Indian Office $850,000, and the Army Corps of Engineers less than $100,000. The USGS enjoyed a great advantage over the Army Corps of Engineers and the USDA in its efforts to manage federal reclamation. It had conducted the Powell survey from 1888 to 1890, had gauged western streams since the middle 1890s, and had assembled a talented group of engineers, including Newell and Arthur P. Davis. The Army Corps of Engineers had shown little inclination to follow Chittenden's lead. Its leaders questioned the value of dams and worried that if they supported western demands for reservoirs, they might alienate eastern political support. Newell's most likely rival was Elwood Mead, who headed the Office of Irrigation Inquiry in the USDA. *Congressional Record*, 56th Cong., 2d sess., House, Feb. 19, 1901, p. 2659; J. C. Needham to J. B. Lippincott, June 12, 1900, Needham Papers, Special Collections, Green Library, Stanford University.

109.   See entry for 1901, F. H. Newell, "Memoirs," Box #1, Frederick H. Newell Collection, University of Wyoming. Newell summarized his views on reclamation in his "Development of Water Resources," *Forester*, 7 (Aug. 1901), pp. 193–99.

Although he did not attract the public attention Maxwell and Newlands enjoyed, Newell contributed greatly to the formation of the reclamation coalition in 1901–2. For example, he had long been active in the American Forestry Association and helped win the support of that organization for federal reclamation. See "The American Forestry Association," *Forester*, 5 (Aug. 1899), pp. 171–76.

110.   See F. H. Newell's testimony in House Irrigation of Arid Lands Committee, "Hearings, Feb. 1–11, 1909 relating to present condition of reclamation projects . . . ," pp. 64–68. Also see *First Annual Report of the Reclamation Service*, pp. 34–75; the typescript copy of F. G. Newlands's speech at Sheridan, Wyoming, June 30, 1905, in Box 94, Newlands collection; Francis G. Newlands to Members of the House Public Lands Committee, Feb. 18, 1901, in Box 5, Correspondence Jan. 21–Feb. 23, 1901, Newlands Collection; and Ganoe, "The Origin of a National Reclamation Policy," pp. 43–44.

111.   One of the two bills Newlands introduced on March 1 (H.R. 14338) stipulated that the secretary of the interior "may decline to let any contract for the construction of any proposed reservoir or irrigation works in any State until under the laws of such State the rights to the use of water from such reservoir or irrigation works . . . shall be assured under the laws of such State." The problem, of course, was that some of the arid states had virtually no laws regulating the acquisition or distribution of water.

112.   H.R. 13846, 56th Cong., 2d sess., Jan. 26, 1901; H.R. 14088, Feb. 6, 1901; H.R. 14326 and H.R. 14338, March 1, 1901. Initially, Newlands left the

question of how the cost of works would be recovered to the secretary of the interior. Also see S. 5833, 56th Cong., 2d sess., Jan. 31, 1901 (Hansbrough).

113.   F. G. Newlands to Henry C. Hansbrough, Feb. 1 and 4, 1901, Box 94, file "Irrigation and Reclamation: Democratic Measure," Newlands Collection. For Newlands's description of his January 26 bill, see *Congressional Record*, 56th Cong., 2d sess., Senate, Jan. 30, 1901, pp. 1700–1701. Reclamation was discussed before the House on January 9, 15, 30, and February 19, 1901.

114.   See F. G. Newlands to Members of the House Public Lands Committee, Feb. 18, 1901; Newlands to Charles Harrison Tweed, Feb. 24, 1901; Newlands to Henry Hansbrough, Feb. 26, 1901; and Newlands to Joseph Cannon, Feb. 26, 1901: all in Box 5, Correspondence Feb. 24–June 30, 1901, Newlands Collection; *Congressional Record*, 57th Cong., 2d sess., House, Feb. 19, 1901, p. 2665.

115.   The *Country Gentleman*, probably the most widely read farm journal in the nation, had been at the vanguard of the opposition press since the days of the Powell Irrigation Survey. See, for example, these issues: 55 (Nov. 6, 1890), p. 882; 55 (Nov. 13, 1890), p. 902; 64 (March 2, 1899), p. 164; 65 (June 8, 1899), p. 450; 64 (June 22, 1899), p. 490; 66 (Jan. 10, 1901), p. 25; 66 (Jan. 24, 1901), p. 65; 66 (June 31, 1901), p. 90; 67 (Jan. 16, 1902), p. 43; 67 (Jan. 23, 1902), p. 64; 67 (Feb. 6, 1902), pp. 105–6; 67 (Feb. 20, 1902), pp. 149–50; 67 (March 6, 1902), pp. 193–95; 67 (March 20, 1902), pp. 237–39; 67 (April 3, 1902), pp. 281–83; 67 (April 17, 1902), pp. 325–26; 67 (April 24, 1902), p. 348.

116.   Richard Hinton to E. S. Willits, Acting Secretary of Agriculture, April 29, 1891, RG 16, Department of Agriculture, Copies of Letters Sent by the Office of Irrigation Inquiry, Feb. 28, 1891 to Aug. 26, 1891, National Archives. For a brief sketch of Hinton's life see Harwood P. Hinton, "Richard J. Hinton and the American Southwest," in Donald C. Dickinson et al., eds., *Voices from the Southwest: A Gathering in Honor of Lawrence Clark Powell* (Flagstaff, 1976), pp. 82–91.

117.   True to his section, Senator William A. Peffer of Kansas was no friend of Powell or the USGS. He introduced several bills to increase the appropriations and responsibilty of the irrigation office. See, for example, S. 1267, 52d Cong., 1st sess., introduced Jan. 5, 1892; S. 1168, 53d Cong., 2d sess., introduced Dec. 4, 1893; and S. 234, 54th Cong., 1st sess., introduced Dec. 3, 1895.

118.   Richard J. Hinton, "Irrigation Surveys," *Science*, 21 (Jan. 6, 1893), p. 10; Charles W. Irish to J. W. Gregory, May 18, 1894, RG 16, Records of the Department of Agriculture, "Copies of Letters Sent by the Office of Irrigation Inquiry, Nov. 2, 1893 to June 11, 1894," National Archives.

119.   *New York Times*, March 27 and Dec. 22, 1895; *Board of Irrigation, Executive Departments*, S. Doc. 36, 54th Cong., 1st sess. (Washington, D.C., 1896), serial 3349. The 1894 irrigation congress which met at Denver called for the creation of a national irrigation commission to supervise the construction of irrigation works by the federal government and to investigate and resolve interstate water conflicts. See *Official Proceedings of the Third National Irrigation Congress, Held at Denver, Colorado, Sept. 3rd to 8th, 1894* (Denver: Local Committee of Arrangements, n.d.), p. 91.

120.   *Sixteenth Annual Report of the United States Geological Survey* (Washington, D.C., 1896), p. 70; *New York Times,* Dec. 22, 1895.
121.   F. E. Warren to Elwood Mead, March 20, 1898, Warren Letterbook, Jan. 27–Dec. 6, 1898. Also see Elwood Mead to H. W. Wiley, Nov. 22, 1897, Mead Letterbook, July 27, 1897–March 11, 1898.
122.   F. E. Warren, "Reasons for Creating Division of Irrigation," undated memorandum (probably January 1898), in Warren Letterbook, Jan. 7–April 18, 1898.
123.   *Congressional Record,* 55th Cong., 2d sess., Senate, pp. 1349, 1395, 1396, 1401; F. E. Warren to Mead, Feb. 4 and March 20, 1898, Warren Letterbook, Jan. 7–April 18, 1898. Also see Warren to Mead, Jan. 23, 26, and Feb. 1, 1898 in the same letterbook.
124.   F. E. Warren to Elwood Mead, Feb. 12, March 4, March 16 (quotation), March 20, and April 8, 1898, and Warren to James Wilson (secretary of agriculture), April 11, 1898, Warren Letterbook, Jan. 7–April 18, 1898.
125.   C. E. Dutton to Elwood Mead, March 14, 1889, in Warren Letterbook, Jan. 27–Dec. 6, 1898; Mead to Dutton, March 25, 1889, Mead Letterbook, April 23, 1888–Aug. 16, 1890.
126.   Elwood Mead to F. H. Newell, Aug. 5, 1892, Mead Letterbook, Jan. 16–Dec. 10, 1892; Governor William A. Richards, et al. to F. E. Warren, C. D. Clark, and J. E. Osborne, March 17, 1897, Mead Letterbook, Nov. 23, 1896–July 26, 1897.
127.   Elwood Mead to John Wesley Powell and Mead to F. E. Warren, both Jan. 12, 1891, and Mead to F. H. Newell, Dec. 9, 1890, in Mead Letterbook, Aug. 18, 1890–May 27, 1891. Also see Mead's unpublished "Report of the State Engineer," dated Oct. 30, 1890, in "Elwood Mead, State Engineer: Correspondence, Observation of River Heights, Various Reports, 1889–1897," Wyoming State Archives, Cheyenne. Mead was not completely honest with Powell. He noted in his January 12 letter to Warren that the first legislature had "appropriated more money for the [state engineering] department than I asked for on account of the anxiety felt in having these water right disputes settled, but I am anxious to complete the work with as little expense as possible and if we can perfect this arrangement we can turn back a goodly sum into the Treasury." In short, initially Mead hoped to win political support by using federal aid to reduce the cost of his work.
128.   Elwood Mead to F. H. Newell, March 27, 1891, Mead Letterbook, Aug. 18, 1890–May 27, 1891, and Mead to Newell, Oct. 16, Dec. 8, and Dec. 17, 1891, in Mead Letterbook, May 26, 1891–Jan. 16, 1892.
129.   Elwood Mead to F. E. Warren, May 13, 1892, Mead Letterbook, Jan. 16–Dec. 10, 1892.
130.   Elwood Mead to Edwin Willits (assistant secretary of agriculture), Dec. 27, 1892, Mead Letterbook, Dec. 10, 1892–Oct. 20, 1893.
131.   Elwood Mead to J. M. Carey, Oct. 17, 1890, Mead Letterbook, Aug. 18, 1890–May 27, 1891.
132.   Elwood Mead to C. D. Clark, Feb. 13, 1895, and Mead to F. H. Newell, Feb. 14, 1895, Mead Letterbook, Dec. 20, 1894–Mar. 5, 1895.
133.   Elwood Mead to F. H. Newell, Feb. 11, 1898 and Mead to Willard

Young (Utah state engineer), Feb. 21, 1898, Mead Letterbook, July 27, 1897–March 11, 1898.

134.   Elwood Mead to F. H. Newell, June 14 and 20, 1898, Mead Letterbook, Mar. 11, 1898–Jan 21, 1899; F. E. Warren to Mead, Jun 24, 1898, Warren Letterbook, April 19, 1898–Jan. 3, 1899.

135.   For a good summary of Mead's work in California, see his article, "Irrigation in California," *Irrigation Age*, 14 (Jan. 1900), pp. 121–24.

136.   *The Forester*, 6 (July 1900), p. 170.

137.   *Report of Irrigation Investigations, 1900* (Washington, D.C., 1902), p. 14.

138.   F. E. Warren to Elwood Mead, May 20, June 1, July 15, and Aug. 20, 1901; Warren Letterbook, May 6–Oct. 26, 1901; Elwood Mead to Frank Adams, May 28, 1901, RG 8; Gates, *History of Public Land Law Development*, p. 650. Gifford Pinchot, a close friend of F. H. Newell, headed the Forestry Division. By the end of Theodore Roosevelt's second administration, he yearned to be czar of conservation—head of a new cabinet department that would unify water, forest, grazing, and other natural resource policies. In 1901, however, he was probably simply trying to weaken Mead's influence to help Newell.

139.   Elwood Mead, "Problems of Irrigation Legislation," *Forum*, 32 (Jan. 1902), p. 581; Elwood Mead to H. G. Burt (president, Union Pacific Railroad), undated memorandum on water rights, probably 1899, in Outgoing Correspondence, Elwood Mead Collection, California Water Resources Archives, University of California, Berkeley; Mead, "Irrigation Legislation," *Outlook*, 70 (April 12, 1902), pp. 907–10. The secretary of agriculture echoed Mead's sentiments. See *Report of the Secretary of Agriculture, 1901* (Washington, D.C., 1901), pp. XCI–XCII. Also see Clarence T. Johnston and Joseph A. Breckons, *Water-Right Problems of Bear River*, USDA, Office of Experiment Stations Bulletin 70 (Washington, D.C., 1899), p. 39; *Denver Republican*, June 8 and 11, 1900, March 2, 1901; *Proceedings of the Ninth Annual Session of the National Irrigation Congress, Held at Central Music Hall, Chicago, Ill., November 21, 22, 23, 24, 1900*, pp. 36–37; W. E. Smythe, "State and National Irrigation Policies," *Land of Sunshine*, 15 (July 1901), pp. 66–67; Smythe, "20th Century West," *Land of Sunshine*, 15 (Nov. 1901), pp. 381–82.

140.   Elwood Mead to Robert Gauss (editor, Denver *Republican*), Dec. 18, 1901, and Mead to D. W. Ross, Dec. 28, 1901, RG 8, National Records Center.

141.   Mead, "Irrigation Legislation," pp. 907–8; D. W. Ross to Fred Dubois, Jan. 27, 1901, Box 2, Folder 4, and Ross to Dubois, Dec. 17, 1901, Box 2, Folder 16, Dubois Collection, Special Collections, Idaho State University, Pocatello; D. W. Ross to Elwood Mead, Dec. 17, 1901, Ross to Mead, Sept. 5, 1901, Fred Bond to Elwood Mead, Dec. 3, 1901, and Elwood Mead to D. W. Ross, Dec. 9, 1901, all in RG 8, National Records Center. As late as 1918, Colorado's state engineer noted that "almost without exception" the reservoirs built in neighboring Wyoming impounded water needed "to supply differences in the water supply during the periods of small flow . . . especially in the months of July, August and September," not to open new land to cultivation. See Wilbur Fiske Stone, *History of Colorado* (Chicago, 1918), vol. 1, p. 497.

142.   *Denver Republican*, March 2, 1902; also Feb. 21, 1902.

143.　　J. A. Breckons to Elwood Mead, June 28, 1901, RG 8, National Records Center.

144.　　*Cheyenne Daily Leader*, Aug. 23, 1901; Fred Bond to Elwood Mead, June 21, 1901; Clarence Johnston to Elwood Mead, June 21, 1901; and Clarence Johnston to Elwood Mead, June 25, 1901: all in RG 8, National Records Center. F. E. Warren to Elwood Mead, July 1, 1901, Letterbook, May 6–Oct. 26, 1901, Warren Collection; Warren to Theodore Roosevelt, Oct. 26, 1901, RG 8, National Records Center; George H. Maxwell to Thomas R. Bard, Nov. 27, 1901, "Irrigation, National, I," Box 9-A, Bard Collection; Hays, *Conservation and the Gospel of Efficiency*, p. 19.

145.　　Theodore Roosevelt, *Autobiography* (New York, 1926), p. 384; *Forester*, 6 (Dec. 1900), pp. 289–90.

146.　　Theodore Roosevelt, *Autobiography* (New York, 1913), p. 429. Also see Roosevelt to Gifford Pinchot, Feb. 24, 1909, Box 714, Pinchot Collection, Library of Congress, Washington, D.C.

147.　　Theodore Roosevelt, *State Papers as Governor and President, 1899–1909* (New York, 1926), pp. 106, 108; Elwood Mead to Benjamin Ide Wheeler, Nov. 12, 1901, Wheeler Papers, Bancroft Library, University of California Archives, Berkeley; A. Hunter Dupree, *Science in the Federal Government: A History of Policies and Activities to 1940* (Cambridge, Mass., 1957), p. 248.

148.　　Fred Dubois, untitled and undated memorandum or speech, Box 39, Folder 9, Dubois Collection.

149.　　Shafroth had introduced two major reclamation bills: H.R. 12230, 56th Cong., 2d sess., Dec. 3, 1900, and H.R. 125, 57th Cong., 1st sess., Dec. 2, 1901. The latter provided for reclamation from land sale proceeds, at a cost to settlers of no more than five dollars an acre. According to the *Cheyenne Daily Leader* of December 16, 1901, the drafting committee initially used the Shafroth bill as a model rather than the Newlands or Hansbrough legislation.

150.　　F. E. Warren to Charles F. Manderson, Dec. 15, 1901, Warren Letterbook, Oct. 26, 1901–Mar. 17, 1902, Warren Collection. Also see Warren to Fred Bond, Dec. 6, 1901, in the same place; F. G. Newlands to Manderson, Dec. 27, 1901, in Box 5, Correspondence, Dec. 21–27, 1901, and Newlands to "My dear Herrin," Feb. 5, 1902, Box 6, Newlands Collection; Fred Dubois to Edward J. Murray, Dec. 25, 1901, Dubois to Hugh McElroy, Jan. 2, 1902, Dubois to D. W. Ross, Jan. 11, 1902, Dubois to Frank T. Hunt, Jan. 11, 1902, and Dubois to Frank W. Harris, Jan. 21, 1902, Dubois Letterbook, Nov. 23, 1901–April 19, 1902, Dubois Collection; *Forestry and Irrigation*, 8 (Jan. 1902), pp. 2–3; *Cheyenne Daily Leader*, Dec. 4, 10, 16, and 18, 1901; *Genoa Weekly Courier*, Jan. 24, 1902.

151.　　H.R. 9676, 57th Cong., 1st sess. (Newlands); S. 3057, 57th Cong., 1st sess. (Hansbrough).

152.　　*San Francisco Call*, Jan. 16, 1902; *Denver Republican*, Jan. 22, 1902.

153.　　H.R. 7676, 57th Cong., 1st sess., Jan. 6, 1902; Binger Hermann to Secretary of the Interior, Feb. 15, 1902, Division A, Press Copies of Letters Sent Relating to Congressional Bills, vol. 20, Dec. 20, 1901–Apr. 2, 1902, RG 49, National Archives; *Forestry and Irrigation*, 8 (Feb. 1902), pp. 56–58; *National Homemaker*, 7 (March 1902), p. 57; "National Works in Aid of Irrigation," H. Rep. 2954, 56th Cong., 2d sess. (Washington, D.C., 1901), serial 4214, p. 8; *Washington Post*, Jan. 31, 1902; *Cheyenne Leader*, April 1, 1902.

154.   Fred Bond, Wyoming state engineer, complained to John Lacey on Feb. 17, 1902, that Colorado and Wyoming would be automatically excluded from benefits of the act because their constitutions proclaimed water to be the property of the state. He feared that if the bill passed, the secretary of the interior would simply pick a state or territory with no water laws because that would give the central government undisputed control over water. See RG 8, National Records Center.

155.   I have taken the liberty here of amplifying points in Ray's minority report with comments made by Ray and his allies during floor debate in the House and Senate on June 12 and 13, 1902. See *Congressional Record*, 57th Cong., 1st sess., Senate, pp. 1383–86, 2218–24, 2276–85; and House, pp. 835–42, 6668–6708, 6722–78. Excerpts from the most important speeches were reprinted in S. Doc. 446, 57th Cong., 1st sess. (Washington, D.C., 1902), serial 4249.

156.   The *Louisville Courier Journal* editorialized on March 4, 1902, following passage of the Newlands Act's twin in the Senate: "The Hansbrough act is about the most paternalistic measure that has yet come before Congress with such a prospect of becoming legislation. It is the finest tribute possible to the political influence of the West. . . . The Government under the most favorable conditions, pays 15 to 25 per cent. more for work than private enterprise. . . . Once the work has been begun, its friends may be trusted to keep it going, no matter what the cost." The editorial also warned that if the bill became law it would serve as a precedent for "numberless other instances of expensive paternalism." The *New York Sun* of March 7, 1902, commented: "River and harbor improvements, federal buildings extravagence [*sic*], war pensions, new navies and interoceanic canals become petty items in comparison with the unknown possibilities of irrigation as a channel for a continuous flow of money from the United States Treasury." Also see the *New York Mail and Express*, March 4, 1902.

157.   On the same day the Newlands bill was introduced in the House, Congressman Sibley of Pennsylvania claimed that in the preceding three decades, the value of the farmland in the eastern, middle, and southern states had declined by 50 percent, about the same loss as in the value of crops. New England was filled with abandoned farms. Westerners in Congress argued that the nation's population growth ensured that the reclaimed land would soon be needed, but since it could not be used in the short run, critics of federal reclamation feared that it would inevitably fall into the hands of speculators. *Congressional Record*, 57th Cong., 1st sess., House, Jan. 21, 1902, p. 836. Also see *Congressional Record*, 55th Cong., 3d sess., Senate, Feb. 24, 1899, p. 2271.

158.   *Congressional Record*, 57th Cong., 1st sess., House, June 13, 1902, pp. 6723, 6730.

159.   "Irrigation and Reclamation of Arid Lands," H. Rep. 794, March 8, 1902, 57th Cong., 1st sess., serial 4402; "Irrigation and Reclamation of Arid Lands," H. Rep. 1468, April 7, 1902, 57th Cong., 1st sess., serial 4404. The quotation is from p. 6 of the minority report in H. Rep. 794. George Ray also

wrote the minority report on the Newlands Act in 1901. See "Reclamation and Irrigation of Arid Lands, with Minority Report and Views," H. Rep. 2927 dated Feb. 23, 1901, 56th Cong., 2d sess., serial 4214. Also see *Congressional Record*, 57th Cong., 1st sess., House, June 12, 1902, pp. 6687–88, 6696, and June 13, 1902, p. 6766.

160.   *Report of the Secretary of Agriculture, 1901* (Washington, D.C., 1901), pp. LXXXIX–XCVI. The quotation is on p. XC.

161.   Thomas H. Tongue, chairman of the House Committee on Irrigation of Arid Lands, noted in a letter to Elwood Mead in November that "Mr. Maxwell's action in reference to irrigation has at least been very peculiar. . . . I have been disposed to regard his attitude towards irrigation at all times as inspired by the land grant railroads" (Tongue to Mead, Nov. 13, 1902, RG 8, National Records Center).

162.   For Maxwell's views see *National Irrigation*, 6 (Oct. 1901), p. 128, and 6 (Nov. 1901), p. 142; *National Homemaker*, 7 (Jan. 1902), pp. 3–4; *Cheyenne Daily Leader*, March 11, 1902. Maxwell's fullest critique of the legislation was contained in a March 1902 supplement to *National Homemaker*. Also see Newlands to "My dear Herrin," Feb. 5, 1902, Box 6, Newlands Collection. Maxwell's criticisms were not entirely self-serving. His fear of land speculation was shared in the General Land Office. See, for example, the review of the Newlands/Hansbrough bills in Binger Hermann (commissioner, General Land Office) to Secretary of the Interior, Jan. 13, Feb. 8, and Feb. 15, 1902, all in Division A, Press Copies of Letters Sent Relating to Congressional Bills, vol. 20, Dec. 20, 1901–Apr. 2, 1902, RG 49, National Archives.

163.   "He intends to suggest that one or two large reservoirs be built," F. H. Newell informed Charles D. Walcott, head of the USGS, after meeting with Roosevelt in late September 1901, "or possibly several small ones, and he thinks that Congress should permit the experiment to be made of selling the lands benefitted at a price sufficient to return the cost of the outlay." Roosevelt insisted that the reservoirs be located by "impartial experts." See Newell to Walcott, Sept. 23, 1901, Charles Walcott Collection, Incoming Correspondence, Smithsonian Institution Archives, Washington, D.C.

164.   William E. Smythe, *The Conquest of Arid America* (New York, 1905), p. 292.

165.   *Washington Evening Star*, April 2, 1902; *Worcester Evening Post*, April 10, 1902; *Cheyenne Daily-Leader*, March 31 and April 11, 1902; *Boston Morning Journal*, April 21, 1902; *San Francisco Chronicle*, March 30, 1902, and Sept. 16, 1904; Smythe, *Conquest of Arid America*, p. 286; *Forestry and Irrigation*, 8 (April 1902), p. 141; J. A. Breckons to F. E. Warren, April 3, 1902, Warren Letterbook, Oct. 26, 1901–Mar. 17, 1902, and Warren to A. J. Parshall, April 21, 1902, Warren Letterbook, Mar. 17–July 24, 1902, Warren Collection; C. E. Wantland to Clarence Johnston, April 18, 1902, RG 8, National Records Center.

166.   Elwood Mead to Benjamin Ide Wheeler, Feb. 6 and April 24, 1902, Wheeler Correspondence, Wheeler Papers; Thomas Carter to Ellen Carter, Feb. 16, 1902, Reel 2, Thomas Carter Collection, Library of Congress, Washington, D.C.; George Maxwell to William M. Stewart, Feb. 24, 1902, Box 6, Folder 40,

Stewart Collection, Nevada Historical Society, Reno, Nevada. Also see D. W. Ross to Fred T. Dubois, Feb. 11, 1902, Box 3, Folder 12, Dubois Collection.

167.   *Cheyenne Daily Leader,* March 10, April 1, 11, 22, 25, May 6 and 8, 1902.

168.   Newlands's remarks are from *Congressional Record,* 57th Cong., 1st sess., House, Jan. 21, 1902, pp. 839–40. Also see the statements of Oscar Underwood, Frank Mondell, and Thomas L. Glenn on June 12, 1902, pp. 6672, 6681, 6748. For good summaries of these arguments, see Guy Elliott Mitchell (George Maxwell's aide-de-camp), "Light Out of Darkness," *Forestry and Irrigation,* 8 (March 1902), p. 127; and "Effect of Western Development on the East," 9 (April 1903), pp. 205–7. The *Chicago Tribune* estimated that the Reclamation Act would increase the amount of arable land by less than one tenth of one percent annually, "while population will increase twenty times as fast." H. C. Hansbrough pointed out that while more than 13 million acres of public land had been disposed of in 1900, the average December crop prices in 1901 were far above the average prices for any year since 1892. In any case, as had been argued so many times in the past, market pressures, along with the high cost of land under ditch, would force the West to concentrate either on crops that could be consumed locally, such as forage, or high value crops not produced in the East, such as citrus fruits. *Chicago Tribune,* June 16, 1902; Hansbrough, "A National Irrigation Policy," p. 103; *Los Angeles Times,* July 13, 1901; *Boston Transcript,* July 26, 1901.

169.   *Congressional Record,* 57th Cong., 1st sess., House, June 13, 1902, p. 6740.

170.   Theodore Roosevelt to Joseph G. Cannon, June 13, 1902, Series 2, vol. 35 (June 2–14, 1902), Reel 328, Theodore Roosevelt Papers.

171.   During the Senate debate over the Hansbrough/Newlands bill, Senator Tillman of South Carolina suggested that the South and West would soon join forces "to secure drainage for the swamps of the South and a proper expediture of money for irrigation in the West." Many members of Congress expected that in the future the USGS—which had begun to study eastern streams during the 1890s—would be given the responsibility for reclaiming wetlands as well as arid lands (*Congressional Record,* 57th Cong., 1st sess., Senate, March 1, 1902, p. 2279).

172.   *Congressional Record,* 57th Cong., 1st sess., House, June 13, 1902, p. 6778; *Cheyenne Daily Leader,* May 17, 19, and 24, June 11 and 12, 1902; Daniel McCool, *Command of the Waters: Iron Triangles, Federal Water Development, and Indian Water* (Berkeley, 1987), p. 23.

173.   "The Status of the Irrigation Idea," *Harper's Weekly,* 46 (Aug. 30, 1902), p. 1192; *Christian Work* (New York), Aug. 16, 1902; *Philadelphia Inquirer,* June 16, 1902. The *New York Times* editorial was reprinted in the *Cheyenne Daily Leader,* June 26, 1902. Also see the *Chicago Inter-Ocean,* June 15, 1902; "Government Irrigation," *Scientific American,* 86 (June 28, 1902), pp. 44–45; and *National Geographic Magazine,* 13 (Oct. 1902), p. 388.

174.   *Daily Progress* (Charlottesville, Va.), June 26, 1902; *Lawrence Daily Journal* (Lawrence, Kans.), July 3, 1902; *Denver Republican,* July 21, 1902; *Salt Lake Tribune,* June 14, 1902. The *New York Sun* editorial was reprinted in the

Genoa Weekly Courier, July 4, 1902, the same issue that contained the *Courier* editorial quoted above.

175. F. G. Newlands to George S. Nixon, Dec. 27, 1901, and Newlands to William Sharon, Dec. 28, 1901, Box 5, Newlands Collection.

176. F. G. Newlands to George S. Nixon, June 17, 1902, Box 7, Newlands Collection.

177. George H. Maxwell to F. G. Newlands, July 20, 1902, Box 7, Newlands Collection.

178. Theodore Roosevelt to James Wilson and Ethan Allen Hitchcock, July 2, 1902, Theodore Roosevelt Papers.

179. For basic interpretations of the meaning of the Reclamation Act, see William Lilley III and Lewis L. Gould, "The Western Irrigation Movement, 1878–1920: A Reappraisal," in Gene Gressley, ed., *The American West: A Reorientation* (Laramie, 1966), pp. 57–74; Stanley R. Davison, *The Leadership of the Reclamation Movement, 1875–1902* (New York, 1979), pp. 238–59; Hays, *Conservation and the Gospel of Efficiency*, pp. 5–26; and Gates, *History of Public Land Law Development*, pp. 652–56.

180. R. P. Teele, "Magnitude of Irrigation Interests," *Official Proceedings of the Nineteenth National Irrigation Congress Held at Chicago, Illinois, December 5–9, 1911*, pp. 36–42; and in the same volume, Samuel Fortier, "The Present Stage of Irrigation Development and a Forecast of the Future," pp. 141–47.

181. C. F. Emerick, "Government Loans to Farmers," *Political Science Quarterly*, 14 (Sept. 1899), p. 461.

182. Gates, *History of Public Land Law Development*, pp. 28–30. The Mineral Leasing Act (1920) provided that 52½ percent of income from the mining of coal, oil, gas, and sodium on the public lands should go into the Reclamation Fund, with another 37½ percent dedicated to the states in which the lands were found. The Water Power Act (1920) promised 50 percent of licensing fees to the Reclamation Fund and 37½ percent to the states. The Taylor Grazing Act (1934) promised the states 50 percent of the revenue from leases.

183. *Genoa Weekly Courier*, June 20, 1902.

184. A congressional report issued early in 1901, "Construction of Reservoirs, Etc.," S. Rep. 2308, 56th Cong., 2d sess. (Washington, D.C., 1901), serial 4065, concluded that the interest-free provision of the Reclamation Act was justified because interest amounted to as much as 50 percent of the cost of irrigation projects. Defenders of the interest-free provision argued that the high cost of money encouraged private companies to build shoddy and inefficient hydraulic systems as promoters rushed to complete works as quickly as possible to cut interest costs and bring about early returns. Also see "Reclamation of Arid Lands," H. Rep. 2927, 56th Cong., 2d sess. (Washington, D.C., 1901), serial 4214, p. 6.

185. *Congressional Record*, 57th Cong., 1st sess., House, June 12, 1902, p. 6670.

186. William Henry Harbaugh, *Power and Responsibility: The Life and Times of Theodore Roosevelt* (New York, 1961), p. 318. Also see Michael C.

Robinson, *Water for the West: The Bureau of Reclamation, 1902–1977* (Chicago, 1979), p. 32; Lilley, "The Early Career of Francis G. Newlands, 1848–1897," pp. 325, 327–29.

187.   Donald J. Pisani, "Reclamation and Social Engineering in the Progressive Era," *Agricultural History*, 57 (Jan. 1983), pp. 46–63.

188.   *Kansas* v. *Colorado*, 206 U.S. 46 (1907).

189.   Donald J. Pisani, "State vs. Nation: Federal Reclamation and Water Rights in the Progressive Era," *Pacific Historical Review*, 51 (Aug. 1982), pp. 265–82.

Chapter 9

1.   John T. Ganoe, "The Origin of a National Reclamation Policy," *Mississippi Valley Historical Review*, 28 (Dec. 1931), pp. 34–52. For overviews of the historiography of reclamation, see Lawrence B. Lee, *Reclaiming the Arid West: An Historiography and Guide* (Santa Barbara, 1980); Lee, "Water Resource History: A New Field of Historiography?" *Pacific Historical Review*, 57 (Nov. 1988), pp. 457–67; and Donald J. Pisani, "Deep and Troubled Waters: A New Field of Western History?" *New Mexico Historical Review*, 63 (Oct. 1988), pp. 311–31.

2.   Stanley Roland Davison, *The Leadership of the Reclamation Movement, 1875–1902* (New York, 1979). Davison's book is identical to his 1952 University of California, Berkeley, doctoral dissertation in history.

3.   Ibid., pp. 23–24.

4.   Ibid., p. 254.

5.   Ibid., p. 25.

6.   Samuel P. Hays, *Conservation and the Gospel of Efficiency: The Progressive Conservation Movement, 1890–1920* (Cambridge, Mass., 1959).

7.   Robert Wiebe, *The Search for Order, 1877–1920* (New York, 1967).

8.   Samuel P. Hays, "The New Organizational Society," in Jerry Israel, ed., *Building the Organizational Society: Essays on Associational Activities in Modern America* (New York, 1972), p. 5.

9.   For examples of these older interpretations, see J. Leonard Bates, "Fulfilling American Democracy: The Conservation Movement, 1907–1921," *Mississippi Valley Historical Review*, 43 (June 1957), pp. 29–57; and Roy Robbins, *Our Landed Heritage: The Public Domain, 1776–1936* (Princeton, N.J., 1942).

10.   Hays, *Conservation and the Gospel of Efficiency*, p. 3.

11.   Ibid., pp. 5–26. The quotations are from p. 5.

12.   William Lilley III and Lewis L. Gould, "The Western Irrigation Movement, 1878–1902," in Gene M. Gressley, ed., *The American West: A Reorientation* (Laramie, 1966), pp. 57–74.

13.   Lilley and Gould, "The Western Irrigation Movement, 1878–1902," pp. 57, 58, 72, 73–74.

14.   Donald Worster, *Rivers of Empire: Water, Aridity, and the Growth of the American West* (New York, 1985), p. 64.

15.   Worster, *Rivers of Empire*, pp. 64, 130–31. In addition, see Worster's "Hydraulic Society in California: An Ecological Interpretation," *Agricultural*

History, 56 (July 1982), pp. 503–16; and his "New West, True West: Interpreting the Region's History," *Western Historical Quarterly,* 18 (April 1987), pp. 141–56.

16.   Patricia Nelson Limerick, *The Legacy of Conquest: The Unbroken Past of the American West* (New York, 1987), p. 87, claims that "the Reclamation Act of 1902 put the national government in the center of the control and development of water, the West's key resource." It is easy to forget that until the construction of Boulder Dam—and in many parts of the West long thereafter—most reclamation projects were locally controlled and financed. By 1922, there were 598 irrigation districts in the 17 western states and they covered about 16 million acres—several times the amount of land within the two dozen federal water projects. The irrigation district, not federal reclamation, accounted for most of the growth in irrigated acreage from 1900 to 1920, particularly during the war years. Until the middle 1920s, most districts were formed by amalgamating unsuccessful private projects or mutual water companies. Donald J. Pisani, "The Irrigation District and the Federal Relationship: Neglected Aspects of Water History," in Gerald Nash and Richard W. Etulain, eds., *The Twentieth-Century West: Historical Interpretations* (Albuquerque, 1989), pp. 270–71.

17.   Political scientists are much more sensitive to the ways in which local interests manage to have their way in Congress. For example, see Arthur Maass and Raymond L. Anderson, *". . . and the Desert Shall Rejoice": Conflict, Growth, and Justice in Arid Environments* (Cambridge, Mass., 1978); Daniel McCool, *Command of the Waters: Iron Triangles, Federal Water Development, and Indian Water* (Berkeley, 1987); and Stephen Skowronek, *Building a New American State: The Expansion of National Administrative Capacities, 1877–1920* (Cambridge, 1982).

18.   Morton Keller, "Social Policy in Nineteenth-Century America," in Donald T. Critchlow and Ellis W. Hawley, eds., *Federal Social Policy: The Historical Dimension* (University Park, Pa., 1988), pp. 99–115.

19.   F. H. Newell to D. C. Henny, May 11, 1908, Records Group 115, Records of the Bureau of Reclamation, General Administrative and Project Records, 1902–1919, "Sacramento, 340–991," Box 831; Harry Riesenberg, "A Plea for Nationalization of Our Natural Resources," *Forestry and Irrigation,* 14 (Aug. 1908), pp. 414–24; Hays, *Conservation and the Gospel of Efficiency,* p. 72.

20.   Gifford Pinchot, *Breaking New Ground* (New York, 1947), p. 321.

21.   The new Reclamation Service tried, but failed, to persuade the western states to draft a model water code drafted in Washington. See Donald J. Pisani, "State vs. Nation: Federal Reclamation and Water Rights in the Progressive Era," *Pacific Historical Review,* 51 (Aug. 1982), pp. 265–82.

22.   See, for example, David P. Thelen, *Paths of Resistance: Tradition and Dignity in Industrializing Missouri* (New York, 1986).

Bibliography

I. Archival Materials

A. National Archives, Washington, D.C., and Federal Records Center, Suitland, Md.
   Record Group 8: Records of the Bureau of Agricultural Engineering, Suitland, Md.
   Record Group 16: Records of the Office of Irrigation Inquiry.
   Record Group 48: Records of the Office of the Secretary of the Interior.
   Record Group 49: Records of the General Land Office.
   Record Group 57: Records of the United States Geological Survey.
   Record Group 77: Records of the Office of Chief of Engineers, United States Army.
   Record Group 115: Records of the Bureau of Reclamation.
B. California State Archives, Sacramento.
   Office of the State Engineer.
   Papers of the Governors.
C. Wyoming State Archives, Cheyenne.
   Office of the State Engineer.
   Papers of the Governors.

II. Manuscript Collections

Bancroft, Hubert Howe. Bancroft Library, University of California, Berkeley, Calif.
Bard, Thomas R. Huntington Library, San Marino, Calif.
Beck, George T. American Heritage Center, University of Wyoming, Laramie, Wyo.
Carter, Thomas. Library of Congress, Washington, D.C.
Davidson, George. Bancroft Library, Berkeley, Calif.
Davis, Arthur Powell. American Heritage Center, University of Wyoming, Laramie, Wyo.

Dubois, Fred T. Special Collections, Idaho State University, Pocatello, Idaho.
Fulton, Robert Lardin. In possession of John Fulton, Lake Tahoe, California.
Grunsky, C. E. Bancroft Library, Berkeley, Calif.
Hall, William Hammond. California Historical Society, San Francisco, Calif.
Hill, James J. James Jerome Hill Library, St. Paul, Minn.
Hopkins, Timothy, Green Library (Special Collections), Stanford University, Stanford, Calif.
Lippincott, Joseph Barlow. California Water Resources Center Archives, University of California, Berkeley, Calif.
Maxwell, George. Louisiana Historical Center (Louisiana State Museum), New Orleans, La.
Maxwell, George. Records of the National Irrigation Association, Record Group 115, Records of the Bureau of Reclamation, National Archives, Washington, D.C.
Mead, Elwood, California Water Resources Center Archives, Berkeley, Calif.
Mead, Elwood. Wyoming State Archives, Cheyenne, Wyo.
Meeker, Nathan. Colorado Historical Society, Denver, Colo.
Needham, J. C. Special Collections, Green Library, Stanford University, Stanford, Calif.
Newell, Frederick Haynes. American Heritage Center, University of Wyoming, Laramie, Wyo., and Library of Congress.
Newlands, Francis G. Sterling Library, Yale University, New Haven, Conn.
Pardee, George C. Bancroft Library, Berkeley, Calif.
Pinchot, Gifford. Library of Congress, Washington, D.C.
Ralston, William. Bancroft Library, Berkeley, Calif., and Green Library (Special Collections), Stanford University, Stanford, Calif.
Roosevelt, Theodore. Library of Congress, Washington, D.C.
Sharon, William. Bancroft Library, Berkeley, Calif.
Shorb, James De Barth. Huntington Library, San Marino, Calif.
Stewart, William Morris. Nevada Historical Society, Reno, Nev.
Walcott, Charles D. Smithsonian Institution Archives, Washington, D.C.
Warren, Francis E. American Heritage Center, University of Wyoming, Laramie, Wyo.
Waterman, Robert W. Bancroft Library, Berkeley, Calif.
Wheeler, Benjamin Ide. University of California Archives, Bancroft Library, Berkeley, Calif.
Van Devanter, Willis. Library of Congress, Washington, D.C.
Yerington, H. M. Bancroft Library, University of California, Berkeley, Calif.

III. Dissertations and Theses

Beach, Frank. "The Transformation of California, 1900–1920: The Effects of the Westward Movement on California's Growth and Development in the Progressive Period." Ph.D. dissertation, University of California, Berkeley, 1963.

Bell, Frank. "Federal Legislation Concerning the Disposition of Grazing Land." Ph.D. dissertation, Indiana University, 1959.

Carothers, Alice L. "The History of the Southern Pacific Railroad in the San Joaquin Valley." M.A. thesis, University of Southern California, Los Angeles, 1934.

Davison, Stanley Roland. "The Leadership of the Reclamation Movement, 1875–1902." Ph.D. dissertation, University of California, Berkeley, 1951.

Gidney, Ray M. "The Wright Irrigation Act in California." M.A. thesis, University of California, Berkeley, 1912.

Graff, Leo W., Jr. "The Senatorial Career of Fred T. Dubois of Idaho, 1890–1907." Ph.D. dissertation, University of Idaho, 1968.

Jernigan, Eva Ida. "Early Development of Agriculture in Colorado." M.A. thesis, University of California, Berkeley, 1928.

Jewell, Marion Nielson. "Agricultural Development in Tulare County, 1870–1900." M.A. thesis, University of Southern California, Los Angeles, 1950.

Kenny, William R. "History of the Sonora Mining Region of California, 1848–1860." Ph.D. dissertation, University of California, Berkeley, 1955.

Kluger, J. R. "Elwood Mead: Irrigation Engineer and Social Planner." Ph.D. dissertation, University of Arizona, 1970.

Lawrence, William D. "Henry Miller and the San Joaquin Valley." M.A. thesis, University of California, Berkeley, 1933.

Lilley, William III. "The Early Career of Francis G. Newlands, 1848–1897." Ph.D. dissertation, Yale University, 1965.

Mack, Effie Mona. "Life and Letters of William Morris Stewart, 1827–1909." Ph.D. dissertation, University of California, Berkeley, 1930.

Malone, Thomas E. "The California Irrigation Crisis of 1886: Origins of the Wright Act." Ph.D. dissertation, Stanford University, 1965.

Marten, Effie E. "The Development of Wheat Culture in the San Joaquin Valley, 1846–1900." M.A. thesis, University of California, Berkeley, 1924.

More, Rosemary McDonald. "The Influence of Water-Rights Litigation upon Irrigation Farming in Yolo County, California." M.A. thesis, University of California, Berkeley, 1960.

Pisani, Donald J. "Storm over the Sierra: A Study in Western Water Use." Ph.D. dissertation, University of California, Davis, 1975.

Quastler, Imre E. "American Images of California Agriculture, 1800–1890." Ph.D. dissertation, University of Kansas, 1971.

Rhodes, Benjamin F., Jr. "Thirsty Land: The Modesto Irrigation District, a Case Study of Irrigation Under the Wright Law." Ph.D. dissertation, University of California, Berkeley, 1943.

Rollins, George W. "The Struggle of the Cattleman, Sheepman, and Settler for Control of Lands in Wyoming, 1867–1919." Ph.D. dissertation, University of Utah, 1951.

Strebel, George L. "Irrigation as a Factor in Western History, 1847–1890." Ph.D. dissertation, University of California, Berkeley, 1965.

Thickens, Virginia E. "Pioneer Colonies of Fresno County." M.A. thesis, University of California, Berkeley, 1939.

Wallace, Thomas D. "The Status of Irrigation Companies in California." J.D. thesis, University of California, Berkeley, 1917.

Walters, Donald E. "Populism in California, 1889–1900." Ph.D. dissertation, University of California, Berkeley, 1952.

Wheaton, Donald W. "The Political History of California, 1887–1898." Ph.D. dissertation, University of California, Berkeley, 1924.

IV. Published Government Documents: United States

Congressional Globe.

Congressional Record.

Congress, House. *Irrigation of Public Lands.* 40th Cong., 2d sess., 1868. H. Ex. Doc. 293. Serial 1343.

———. *U.S. Board of Commissioners on the Irrigation of the San Joaquin, Tulare and Sacramento Valleys of the State of California.* 43d Cong., 1st sess., 1874. H. Ex. Doc. 290. Serial 1615.

———. *Irrigation of San Joaquin, Tulare, and Sacramento Valleys, California.* 43rd Cong., 1st sess., 1874. H. Ex. Doc. 290. Serial 1615.

———. *Geographical Surveys West of the One Hundredth Meridian in California, Nevada, Utah, Colorado, Wyoming, New Mexico, Arizona, and Montana.* 44th Cong., 2d sess., 1876. H. Ex. Doc. 1, pt. 2. Serial 1745.

———. *Report on the Lands of the Arid Region of the United States, with a More Detailed Account of the Lands of Utah.* 45th Cong., 2d sess., 1878. H. Ex. Doc. 73. Serial 1805.

———. *Reservoirs to Promote the Navigation of the Mississippi River.* 45th Cong., 2d sess., 1878. H. Ex. Doc. 49. Serial 1806.

———. *Report of the Public Lands Commission.* 46th Cong., 2d sess., 1880. H. Ex. Doc. 46. Serial 1923.

———. *Reservoirs of Upper Mississippi.* 46th Cong., 2d sess., 1880. H. Rep. 1701. Serial 1938.

———. *Leasing Arid and Desert Lands in Colorado, with Minority Report.* 47th Cong., 1st sess., 1882. H. Rep. 197. Serial 2065.

———. *Ceding the Arid Lands to the States and Territories.* 51st Cong., 2d sess., 1891. H. Rep. 3767. Serial 2888.

———. *Report on the Climate of California and Nevada with Particular Reference to Questions of Irrigation and Water Storage in the Arid Region.* 51st Cong., 2d sess., 1891. H. Ex. Doc. 287. Serial 2868.

———. *Arid Lands of the United States.* 52d Cong., 1st sess., 1892. H. Rep. 569. Serial 3043.

———. *Report on Agriculture by Irrigation in the Western Part of the United States at the Eleventh Census, 1890.* by F. H. Newell. 52d Cong., 1st sess., 1896. H. Misc. Doc. 340. Serial 3021.

———. *Preliminary Examination of Reservoir Sites in Wyoming and Colorado.* By Hiram Martin Chittenden. 55th Cong., 2d sess., 1897. H. Doc. 141. Serial 3666.

———. *National Works in Aid of Irrigation*. 56th Cong., 2d sess., 1901. H. Rep. 2954. Serial 4214.

———. *Reclamation and Irrigation of Arid Lands, with Minority Reports and Views*. 56th Cong., 2d sess., 1901. H. Rep. 2927. Serial 4214.

———. *Irrigation*. By Elwood Mead. 57th Cong., 1st sess., 1901. H. Doc. 179. Serial 4340.

———. *Irrigation and Reclamation of Arid Lands*. 57th Cong., 1st sess., 1902. H. Rep. 794. Serial 4402.

———. *Irrigation and Reclamation of Arid Lands*. 57th Cong., 1st sess., 1902. H. Rep. 1468. Serial 4404.

———. *Fund for Reclamation of Arid Lands*. 61st Cong., 3d sess., 1911. H. Doc. 1262. Serial 6022.

Congress. Senate. *Irrigation: Its Evils, the Remedies, and the Compensations*. 43d Cong., 1st sess., 1874. S. Misc. Doc. 55. Serial 1584.

———. *Irrigation and Reclamation of Land for Agricultural Purposes as Now Practiced in India, Egypt, Italy, Etc*. 44th Cong., 1st sess., 1875. S. Ex. Doc. 94. Serial 1664.

———. *Surveys and Examinations for Establishment of Reservoirs at Headwaters of Mississippi River*. 46th Cong., 3d sess., 1881. S. Ex. Doc. 48. Serial 1943.

———. *Irrigation in the United States*. 49th Cong., 2d sess., 1887. S. Misc. Doc. 15. Serial 2450.

———. *Preliminary Report on the Organization and Prosecution of the Survey of Arid Lands for Purposes of Irrigation*. 50th Cong., 2d sess., 1889. S. Ex. Doc. 43. Serial 2610.

———. *Sundry Civil Appropriation Bill*. 50th Cong., 2d sess., 1889. S. Rep. 2613. Serial 2619.

———. *Irrigation of Arid Lands*. 51st Cong., 1st sess., 1890. S. Ex. Doc. 136. Serial 2688.

———. *A Report on the Preliminary Investigation to Determine the Proper Location of Artesian Wells Within the Area of the Ninety-Seventh Meridian and East of the Foot-Hills of the Rocky Mountains*. 51st Cong., 1st sess., 1890. S. Ex. Doc. 222. Serial 2689.

———. *Report of the Special [Stewart] Committee of the United States Senate on the Irrigation and Reclamation of Arid Lands*. 51st Cong., 1st sess., 1890. S. Rept. 928. Serial 2707.

———. *Irrigation in the United States: Progress Report for 1890*. 51st Cong., 2d sess., 1890. S. Ex. Doc. 53. Serial 2818.

———. *Irrigation and Reclamation of Arid Lands*. 52nd Cong., 1st sess., 1891–92. S. Rep. 1069. Serial 2915.

———. *Memorial of a Convention Held at Salt Lake City, Utah Territory, to Consider Matters Pertaining to the Reclamation of the Arid Lands of the West*. 52d Cong., 1st sess., 1892. S. Misc. Doc. 61. Serial 2904.

———. *Report on Irrigation, 1891*. 52d Cong., 1st sess., 1892. S. Ex. Doc. 41, pt. 1. Serial 2899.

———. *An Address to the People of the United States by the National Irri-*

gation Congress, Fourth Annual Session, at Albuquerque, N. Mexico, September 16–19, 1895. 54th Cong., 1st sess., 1896. S. Doc. 253. Serial 3354.
———. The Arid Public Lands—Their Reclamation, Management, and Disposal. 55th Cong., 1st sess., 1897. S. Doc. 130. Serial 3562.
———. Cession of the Public Lands, etc. 55th Cong., 1st sess., 1897. S. Doc. 130. Serial 3562.
———. Memorial of Wyoming State Board of Control for grant of grazing lands. 55th Cong., 2d sess., 1897. S. Doc. 31. Serial 3559.
———. Equitable Distribution of the Waters of the Rio Grande. 55th Cong., 2d sess., 1898. S. Doc. 229. Serial 3610.
———. Surveys of Reservoir Sites. 55th Cong., 3d sess., 1899. S. Doc. 116. 1899. Serial 3735.
———. Irrigation Investigations in California. 56th Cong., 2d sess., 1901. S. Doc. 108. Serial 4033.
———. Report of Irrigation Investigations in California. U.S.D.A. Office of Experiment Stations Bulletin #100. 57th Cong., 1st sess., 1902. S. Doc. 356. Serial 4246.
Department of Agriculture. Annual Reports of the Commissioner and Secretary.
———. Irrigation in Arizona. By R. H. Forbes. Office of Experiment Stations Bulletin no. 235. Washington, D.C., 1911.
———. Irrigation Laws of the Northwest Territories of Canada and of Wyoming. By Fred Bond, J. S. Dennis, and J. M. Wilson. Office of Experiment Stations Bulletin no. 96. Washington, D.C., 1901.
———. Land Reclamation Policies in the United States. By Ray P. Teele. Bulletin no. 1257. Washington, D.C., 1924.
———. Mutual Water Companies. By Wells A. Hutchins. Technical Bulletin no. 82. Washington, D.C., 1929.
———. Report on the Climatic and Agricultural Features and the Agricultural Practice and Needs of the Arid Regions of the Pacific Slope, with Notes on Arizona and New Mexico. By E. W. Hilgard, T. C. Jones, and R. W. Furnas. Department Report no. 20. Washington, D.C., 1882.
———. Water-Right Problems of Bear River. By Clarence T. Johnston and Joseph A. Breckons. Office of Experiment Stations Bulletin no. 70. Washington, D.C., 1899.
Department of Commerce. Bureau of the Census. Censuses of the United States.
———. Irrigation: Existing Conditions and Needs. Final Report of the Industrial Commission. Washington, D.C., 1902.
———. Mining Laws. (Washington, D.C., 1885).
———. Precious Metals. (Washington, D.C., 1885).
———. Report on Agriculture by Irrigation in the Western Part of the United States at the Eleventh Census, 1890. By F. H. Newell. (Washington, D.C., 1894).
———. Agriculture: Part II, Crops and Irrigation. (Washington, D.C., 1902).
Department of the Interior. Annual Reports of the Secretary.
———. General Land Office. Annual Reports.
———. Geological Survey. Annual Reports.

———. Patent Office. *Annual Reports* of the Commissioner.

———. Reclamation Bureau. *Annual Reports.*

———. Territorial Governors. *Annual Reports.*

———. *California Hydrography.* By J. B. Lippincott. Geological Survey Water Supply and Irrigation Paper no. 81. Washington, D.C., 1903.

———. *Irrigation in Mesilla Valley, New Mexico.* By F. C. Barker. Geological Survey Water Supply and Irrigation Paper no. 10. Washington, D.C., 1898.

———. *Irrigation Systems in Texas.* By William F. Hutson. Geological Survey Water Supply and Irrigation Paper no. 13. Washington, D.C., 1898.

———. *Proceedings of the First Conference of Engineers of the Reclamation Service.* Geological Survey Water Supply and Irrigation Paper no. 93. Washington, D.C., 1904.

V. Published Government Documents: California

Board of Agriculture. *Reports.*

Board of Forestry. *Biennial Reports.*

Board of Horticulture. *Reports.*

Senate and Assembly. *Journals of the California Assembly and Senate.*

———. *Annual Message of George C. Perkins to the [California] Legislature, December, 1880.* (Sacramento, 1881).

———. *Majority Report of the [Assembly] Committee on Mining Debris.* (Sacramento, 1878).

———. *Memorial of the California Legislature to Congress.* (Sacramento, 1872).

———. *Report of the Board of Directors of Drainage District No. 1, Showing Progress of Work to January 1, 1881.* (Sacramento, 1881).

———. *Report of the Committee on Land Monopoly.* (Sacramento, 1874).

———. *Reports of the Joint Committees of the Assembly on Mines and Mining Interests, and Agriculture, Relative to the Injury now being done to Lands and Streams in this State by the Deposit of Detritus from the Gravel Mines.* (Sacramento, 1876).

State Engineer. *Reports.*

———. *The Irrigation Question in California: Appendix to the Report of the State Engineer to His Excellency George C. Perkins, Governor of California.* By William Hammond Hall. (Sacramento, 1881).

State Surveyor-General. *Reports.*

———. *The View of the State Engineer as Contrasted with those of the Surveyor General.* By William Hammond Hall. (Sacramento, 1883).

VI. Published Government Documents: Colorado

Commissioners, Warden, Chaplin and Physician of the State Penitentiary. *Biennial Reports.*

Proceedings of the Constitutional Convention of Colorado, 1875 and 1876 (Denver, 1906).
Report of the Commission Appointed by his Excellency the Governor of the State of Colorado to Revise the Laws of the State.
Regulating the Appropriation, Distribution and Use of Water (Denver, 1890).
State Engineer. *Biennial Reports.*

VII. Published Government Documents: Nevada

Nevada Constitutional Convention of 1864. *Official Report of the Debate and Proceedings in the Constitutional Convention of the State of Nevada* [1864] (San Francisco, 1866).
Report of the Proceedings of the Nevada State Irrigation Convention Held in the Opera House, Carson City, Nevada, October 9th, 1891 (Carson City, 1891).
State Surveyor General. *Biennial Reports.*

VIII. Published Government Documents: Wyoming

Wyoming Constitutional Convention of 1889. *Journals and Debates of the Constitutional Convention of the State of Wyoming* (Cheyenne, 1893).
State Engineer. *Biennial Reports.*

IX. Court Cases

Basey v. *Gallagher.* 87 U.S. 670 (1874).
Benton v. *Johncox.* 17 Wash. 277 (1897).
Boggs v. *Merced Mining Co.* 14 Cal. 279 (1859).
Bradley v. *Fallbrook Irrigation District.* 68 Fed. 948 (1895).
Brown v. *'49 and '56 Quartz Mining Co.* 15 Cal. 152 (1860).
Central Irrigation District v. *De Lappe.* 79 Cal. 351 (1889).
Coffin v. *Left Hand Ditch Company.* 6 Colo. 443 (1882).
Conger v. *Weaver.* 6 Cal. 548 (1856).
Crall v. *Poso Irrigation District.* 87 Cal. 140 (1890).
Crandall v. *Woods.* 8 Cal. 136 (1857).
Creighton v. *Evans.* 53 Cal. 55 (1878).
Drake v. *Earhart.* 2 Ida. 750 (1890).
Eddy v. *Simpson.* 3 Cal. 249 (1853).
Fallbrook Irrigation District v. *Bradley.* 164 U.S. 112 (1896).
Ferrea v. *Knipe.* 28 Cal. 340 (1865).

Hicks v. *Bell.* 3 Cal. 219 (1853).
Hill v. *King.* 8 Cal. 336 (1857).
Hill v. *Newman.* 5 Cal. 445 (1855).
Hill v. *Smith.* 27 Cal. 476 (1865).
Hoffman v. *Stone.* 7 Cal. 47 (1857).
Irwin v. *Phillips.* 5 Cal. 140 (1855).
Jones v. *Adams.* 19 Nev. 78 (1885).
Kansas v. *Colorado.* 206 U.S. 46 (1907).
Kelly v. *Natoma Water Company.* 6 Cal. 105 (1856).
Lux v. *Haggin.* 69 Cal. 255 (1886); 4 Pac. 919 (1884); 10 Pac. 674 (1886).
McDonald & Blackburn v. *Bear River and Auburn Water and Mining Company.* 13 Cal. 220 (1859).
Maeris v. *Bicknell.* 7 Cal. 261 (1857).
In the Matter of the Bonds of the Madera Irrigation District. 92 Cal. 296 (1891).
In the Matter of the Organization and Bonds of the Central Irrigation District. 117 Cal. 382 (1897).
Mettler v. *Ames Realty Co.* 61 Mont. 152 (1921).
Monroe v. *Ivri.* 2 Utah 535 (1880).
Munn v. *Illinois.* 94 U.S. 113 (1877).
Ortman v. *Dixon.* 13 Cal. 33 (1859).
Palmer v. *Railroad Commission.* 167 Cal. 163 (1914).
Pope v. *Kinman.* 54 Cal. 3 (1879).
Rupley v. *Welch.* 23 Cal. 452 (1863).
Smith v. *Denniff.* 24 Mont. 20 (1900).
Sowards v. *Meagher.* 37 Utah 212 (1910).
Sparrow v. *Strong.* 70 U.S. 97 (1865).
Stoaks v. *Barrett.* 5 Cal. 39 (1855).
Tartar v. *Spring Creek Water and Mining Company.* 5 Cal. 395 (1855).
Thompson v. *Lee.* 8 Cal. 275 (1857).
Thorp v. *Freed.* 1 Mont. 651 (1872).
Thorp v. *Woolman.* 1 Mont. 168 (1870).
Turlock Irrigation District v. *Williams.* 76 Cal. 360 (1888).
Union Mill & Mining Co. v. *Ferris.* 2 Sawy. 176 (1872).
Vansickle v. *Haines.* 7 Nev. 249 (1872).
Yunker v. *Nichols.* 1 Colo. 551 (1872).

X. Newspapers and Periodicals

Aberdeen *News* (et seq.: *Aberdeen Daily News, Daily News*)
American Agriculturalist (New York City)
Auburn *Placer Herald* (Auburn, Calif.)
Bakersfield *Californian* (Bakersfield, Calif.)
Big Horn Basin Savior (Cheyenne, Wyo.)
Boise City *Republican* (Boise, Ida.)
Boston *Evening Transcript* (et seq.: *Boston Transcript, Transcript*)

Boston *Herald*
Boston *Journal*
Buffalo *Bulletin* (Buffalo, Wyo.)
Buffalo *Voice* (Buffalo, Wyo.)
California Farmer (San Francisco)
California Mining Journal (Grass Valley, Calif.)
Carson City *Appeal* (Carson City, Nev.)
Charleston *News and Courier* (Charleston, S.C.)
Charleston *Evening Post* (Charleston, S.C.)
Charlottesville *Progress* (Charlottesville, Va.)
Cheyenne *State Leader* (et seq.: *Cheyenne Daily Leader, Daily Leader, Leader,
     Cheyenne Sun-Leader, Cheyenne Daily Sun-Leader, Cheyenne Daily Sun,
     Cheyenne Leader*) (Cheyenne, Wyo.)
Cheyenne *Weekly Sun* (Cheyenne, Wyo.)
Chicago *Inter Ocean*
Chicago *Tribune* (et seq.: *Chicago Tribune, Chicago Daily Tribune*)
Chico *Record* (Chico, Calif.)
Christian Work and Evangelist (New York City)
Colorado Farmer and Live Stock Grower (Denver, Colo.)
Colorado Springs *Gazette* (Colorado Springs, Colo.)
Columbia *Gazette* (Columbia, Calif.)
Colusa *Sun* (Colusa, Calif.)
Commercial Herald and Market Review (San Francisco)
Country Gentleman (Philadelphia)
Cour d'Alene *Record* (Cour d'Alene, Ida.)
Denver *News*
Denver *Republican*
Denver *Sun*
Eureka *Sentinel* (Eureka, Nev.)
Field and Farm (Denver)
Forest and Stream (New York City)
Forestry and Irrigation (Washington, D.C.)
Fresno *Weekly Expositor* (et seq.: *Fresno Weekly Expositor, Expositor*)
Genoa *Weekly Courier* (Genoa, Nev.)
Harper's Weekly
Houston *Post*
Idaho Statesman (Boise, Ida.)
Idaho World (Idaho City, Ida.)
Irrigation Age (Chicago, Salt Lake City)
Kansas Farmer (Topeka, Kansas)
Kern County Californian (Bakersfield, Calif.)
Kern County Weekly Courier (Bakersfield, Calif.)
Laramie *Boomerang* (Laramie, Wyo.)
Lawrence *Journal* (Lawrence, Kan.)
Los Angeles *Daily Commercial*
Los Angeles *Express (et seq.: Weekly Express, Los Angeles Express*)
Los Angeles *Herald*

Los Angeles Star
Los Angeles Times
Louisville *Courier Journal* (Louisville, Ky.)
Marysville *Appeal* (Marysville, Calif.)
Maxwell's Talisman (Chicago, Washington, New Orleans)
Mining and Scientific Press (San Francisco)
National Advocate (San Francisco)
National Homemaker (Washington, D.C.)
National Irrigation Journal (Chicago)
Nevada Journal (Nevada City, Calif.)
Nevada State Journal (Reno, Nev.)
New Orleans *Times-Democrat* (New Orleans, La.)
New York *Journal* (New York City)
New York Mail and Express (New York City)
New York *Sun* (New York City)
New York Times (New York City)
Out West (Los Angeles)
Overland Monthly (San Francisco)
Pacific Rural Press (San Francisco)
Philadelphia *Inquirer*
Pueblo *Chieftain* (Pueblo, Colo.)
Rawlins *Republican* (Rawlins, Wyo.)
Redlands *Citrograph* (Relands, Calif.)
Reno *Evening Gazette*
Rocky Mountain News (Denver)
Rural Californian (Los Angeles)
Sacramento *Bee*
Sacramento Daily Record (et seq.: *Sacramento Daily Record-Union, Record-Union, Sacramento Daily Record*)
Sacramento *Union*
St. Louis Globe-Democrat
Salt Lake Herald Republican
Salt Lake *Tribune*
San Francisco *Alta California* (et seq.: *Daily Alta California*)
San Francisco *Argonaut*
San Francisco *Bulletin* (et seq.: *Evening Bulletin, Daily Evening Bulletin*)
San Francisco *Call* (et seq.: *San Francisco Call*)
San Francisco *Chronicle*
San Francisco *Evening Post*
San Francisco *Herald*
San Francisco *News*
Scientific American (New York City)
Shasta *Courier* (Shasta, Calif.)
Sheridan *Post* (Sheridan, Wyo.)
Stanislaus County News (Modesto, Calif.)
Stockton *Democrat* (Stockton, Calif.)
Stockton *Journal* (Stockton, Calif.)

Stockton *Independent* (Stockton, Calif.)
Sunset (San Francisco)
Truckee *Republican* (Truckee, Calif.)
Tulare County Times (Visalia, Calif.)
Virginia City Territorial Enterprise (Virginia City, Nev.)
Visalia *Delta* (Visalia, Calif.)
Washington Post
Water and Forest (San Francisco)
Weekly San Joaquin Republican (Stockton, Calif.)
Winnemucca *Silver State* (Winnemucca, Nev.)
Worcester Evening Post (Worcester, Mass.)
Wyoming Tribune (Cheyenne, Wyo.)

XI. Articles

Anon. "The American Forestry Association." *Forester* 5 (Aug. 1899): 171–76.
———. "Another Raid on 'Desert' Lands." *Scientific American* 38 (Feb. 9, 1878): 84.
———. "The Artesian Wells of the James River Valley, Dakota." *Scientific American* 60 (April 6, 1889): 207.
———. "Both Food and Drink." *Irrigation Age* 14 (May 1900): 260.
———. "The Carey Bill Obnoxious." *Irrigation Age* 6 (May 1894): 186–87.
———. "The Carey Law." *Irrigation Age* 7 (Nov. 1894): 213–14.
———. "Census Figures on Irrigation." *Irrigation Age* 3 (Nov. 1892): 193.
———. "A Creation of the California District Law: Editorial Study of the Turlock-Modesto Works." *Irrigation Age* 6 (Jan. 1895): 12–15.
———. "The East and the West." *Irrigation Age* 14 (Jan. 1900): 138.
———. "Editor's Table." *American Naturalist* 22 (Sept. 1888): 821–22.
———. "Eight Years Afterward." *Out West* 19 (Sept. 1903): 335–36.
———. "An Extensive Irrigating Project." *Scientific American* 48 (Jan. 27, 1883): 50.
———. "Forestry and Irrigation in Congress." *Forestry and Irrigation* 8 (March 1902): 134–36.
———. "A Gigantic Irrigation Project." *Scientific American* 69 (July 8, 1893): 24.
———. "Government Irrigation." *Scientific American* 86 (June 28, 1902): 444–45.
———. "Great Irrigation Enterprises." *World's Work* 1 (Dec. 1900): 252–53.
———. "The Homeseekers' Convention." *Irrigation Age* 12 (Oct. 1897): 8.
———. "The Hope of the West." *Irrigation Age* 2 (Jan. 1, 1892): 362.
———. "Increase of Our Export Trade." *Irrigation Age* 15 (June 1900): 297.
———. "The Irrigation Congress." *Irrigation Age* 12 (Nov. 1897): 27–28.
———. "Irrigation in Egypt." *Scientific American* 47 (Sept. 16, 1882): 177.
———. "Irrigation in India." *Scientific American* 69 (Aug. 5, 1893): 89–90.
———. "Irrigation Scrip Proposed." *Irrigation Age* 7 (July 1894): 2.

————. "The Irrigation Works of India." *Scientific American* 33 (Aug. 28, 1875): 128.

————. "Irrigation Works in Italy." *Scientific American* 49 (Dec. 15, 1883): 371.

————. "Labor and Homes for the Idle." *Irrigation Age* 7 (Nov. 1894): 214–15.

————. "Labor Unions Favor National Irrigation." *Forestry and Irrigation* 8 (Feb. 1902): 50–51.

————. "The Lines of Thought Presented." *Irrigation Age* 6 (Feb. 1894): 50.

————. "Mass Meetings in Boston and Chicago." *Irrigation Age* 8 (April 1895): 110.

————. "The Migration of the Great American Desert." *Scientific American* 42 (April 24, 1880): 256–57.

————. "Montana's Convention." *Irrigation Age* 2 (Jan. 15, 1892): 384.

————. "National Board of Trade." *Forestry and Irrigation* 10 (Feb. 1904): 86.

————. "A National Forest Preserve." *Nation* 37 (Sept. 6, 1883): 201.

————. "The New Plymouth." *Irrigation Age* 8 (March 1895): 76–81.

————. "The Northwest Overlooked." *Irrigation Age* 10 (Aug. 1896): 60.

————. "Our Arid Public Lands." *Irrigation Age* 12 (May 1898): 233–35.

————. "Our Arid Regions and the Rainfall." *Popular Science Monthly* 36 (Feb. 1890): 572.

————. "Our Rapidly Growing Irrigation Areas." *Scientific American* 82 (March 3, 1900): 131.

————. "Plymouth Colony." *Irrigation Age* 6 (June 1895): 186–87.

————. "Progress of Irrigation." *Scientific American* 65 (Oct. 31, 1891): 272.

————. "Progress of Irrigation." *Scientific American* 72 (Jan. 19, 1895): 38.

————. "Progress of Irrigation." *Journal of the Franklin Institute* 139 (April 1895): 310–12.

————. "The Progress of Western America." *Irrigation Age* 7 (Dec. 1894): 245–50.

————. "The Progress of Western America." *Irrigation Age* 8 (Feb. 1895): 35.

————. "The Proposed Irrigation of the Colorado Desert." *Scientific American* 30 (March 28, 1874): 193.

————. "The Protection of Irrigation Works." *Forester* 5 (Feb. 1899): 44–46.

————. "The Reclamation of the Colorado Desert." *Scientific American* 30 (May 16, 1874): 309.

————. "The Status of the Irrigation Idea." *Harper's Weekly* 46 (August 30, 1902): 1192.

————. "Texas." *Irrigation Age* 3 (Jan. 1893): 247.

————. "The Unemployed and the Public Lands." *Irrigation Age* 6 (June 1894): 229.

————. "An Unexpected Triumph." *Irrigation Age* 3 (June 15, 1892): 78.

————. "What the National Irrigation Association Stands For." In *Proceedings of the Ninth Annual Session of the National Irrigation Congress, Chicago* [*1900*] (St. Louis, n.d.).

————. "Why the Arizona Company Failed." *Irrigation Age* 12 (Dec. 1897): 54–55, 76.

————. "Why the Times are Out of Joint." *Irrigation Age* 8 (Jan. 1895): 7–10.

————. "Wyoming Colonization." *Irrigation Age* 6 (April 1894): 166.

Adams, Frank. "The Historical Background of California Agriculture." In *California Agriculture*, ed. Claude B. Hutchinson, 1–50. Berkeley, 1946.

———. "Irrigation Development Through Irrigation Districts." *American Society of Civil Engineers Transactions* 90 (1927): 773–90.

Alexander, Thomas G. "John Wesley Powell, the Irrigation Survey, and the Inauguration of the Second Phase of Irrigation Development in Utah." *Utah Historical Quarterly* 37 (Spring 1969): 190–206.

———. "The Powell Irrigation Survey and the People of the Mountain West." *Journal of the West* 7 (Jan. 1968): 48–54.

Allen, R. H. "The Spanish Land-Grant System as an Influence in the Agricultural Development of California." *Agricultural History* 9 (July 1935): 127–42.

Arneson, Edwin P. "Early Irrigation in Texas." *Southwestern Historical Quarterly* 25 (Oct. 1921): 121–30.

Arrington, Leonard J. "Early Mormon Communitarianism: The Law of Consecration and Stewardship." *Western Humanities Review* 7 (Autumn 1953): 341–69.

———. "Economic History of a Mormon Valley." *Pacific Northwest Quarterly* 46 (Oct. 1955): 97–107.

Arrington, Leonard J., and May, Dean. "'A Different Mode of Life': Irrigation and Society in Nineteenth-Century Utah." *Agricultural History* 49 (Jan. 1975): 3–20.

Baade, Hans W. "The Historical Background of Texas Water Law—A Tribute to Jack Pope." *St. Mary's Law Journal* 18 (Number 1, 1986): 1–98.

Bakken, Gordon M. "The English Common Law in the Rocky Mountain West." *Arizona and the West* 11 (Summer 1969): 109–28.

Barrett, W. W. "Irrigation in North Dakota." *Irrigation Age* 9 (June 1896): 231–32.

Bateman, Richard Dale. "Anaheim Was an Oasis in a Wilderness." *Journal of the West* 4 (Jan. 1965): 1–20.

Bates, J. Leonard."Fulfilling American Democracy: The Conservation Movement, 1907–1921." *Mississippi Valley Historical Review* 43 (June 1957): 29–57.

Beattie, George William. "San Bernardino Valley before the Americans Came." *California Historical Quarterly* 12 (March 1933): 111–24.

Beer, Samuel H. "The Modernization of American Federalism." *Publius* 3 (Fall 1973): 49–95.

Bell, Daniel. "The End of American Exceptionalism." *The Public Interest* 41 (Fall 1975): 193–224.

Bernstein, Harry. "Spanish Influence in the United States: Economic Aspects." *The Hispanic American Historical Review* 18 (Feb. 1938): 46–65.

Boening, Rose M. "History of Irrigation in the State of Washington." *Washington Historical Quarterly* 10 (Jan. 1919): 21–45.

Bonner, John. "The Present Stage of the Irrigation Question." *Overland Monthly* 13 (June 1889): 602–10.

Booth-Tucker, Frederick. "Colonization on Irrigated Lands." In *The Official*

Proceedings of the Tenth National Irrigation Congress Held at Colorado Springs, Colorado, 162–67. Colorado Springs, 1902.

———. "Farm Colonies of the Salvation Army." In *Salvation Army in America: Selected Reports, 1899–1903,* 983–1005. New York, 1972.

———. "The Relation of Colonization to Irrigation." *Forestry and Irrigation* 9 (Oct. 1903): 499–505.

Boyd, David. "Greeley's Irrigation Methods." *Irrigation Age* 2 (Jan. 1, 1892): 353.

Brandhorst, L. Carl. "The North Platte Oasis: Notes on the Geography and History of an Irrigated District." *Agricultural History* 51 (Jan. 1977): 166–72.

Breckons, Joseph A. "A View of the Carey Law." *Irrigation Age* 7 (Oct. 1894): 184–87.

———. "Wyoming's Use of Its Lands." In *Official Proceedings of the Eleventh National Irrigation Congress Held at Ogden, Utah, September 15–18, 1903,* 404–7. Ogden, 1904.

Bright, Charles C. "The State in the United States During the Nineteenth Century." In *Statemaking and Social Movements: Essays in History and Theory,* ed. by Charles Bright and Susan Harding, 121–58. Ann Arbor, 1984.

Brough, Charles H. "Advantage of Reclaiming the Remaining Irrigable Land." *Irrigation Age* 14 (Feb. 1900): 159–64.

Browne, J. Ross. "Agricultural Capacity of California—Overflows and Droughts." *Overland Monthly* 20 (April 1873): 297–314.

———. "Reclamation and Irrigation." In *Transactions of the California State Agricultural Society during the Year 1872,* 390–425. Sacramento, 1874.

Burcham, L. T. "Cattle and Range Forage in California: 1770–1880." *Agricultural History* 35 (July 1961): 140–49.

Carlson, Martin E. "William E. Smythe: Irrigation Crusader." *Journal of the West* 7 (Jan. 1968): 41–47.

Chandler, Alfred E. "The Appropriation of Water in California." *California Law Review* 4 (March 1916): 206–15.

———. "The Irrigation Laws of Nevada." *Forestry and Irrigation* 9 (Nov. 1903): 541–43.

———. "The 'Water Bill' Proposed by the Conservation Commission of California." *California Law Review* 1 (1912–1913): 148–68.

Chaplin, W. E. "Reminiscences of a Member of the Wyoming Constitutional Convention." *Annals of Wyoming* 12 (July 1940): 176–77, 191–92, 196.

Chittenden, Hiram Martin. "Government Construction of Reservoirs in Arid Regions." *North American Review* 174 (Feb. 1902): 245–58.

———. "The Irrigation Problems and Possibilities of Northern Wyoming." *Irrigation Age* 13 (March 1899): 195–202.

———. "The Relation of the Government to the Construction of Storage Reservoirs in the Arid Regions of the West." In *Proceedings of the Ninth Annual Session of the National Irrigation Congress, Held at Central Music Hall, Chicago, Ill., November 21, 22, 23, 24, 1900,* 31–44. St. Louis, n.d.

Clark, Ira. "The Elephant Butte Controversy: A Chapter in the Emergence of

Federal Water Law." *Journal of American History* 61 (March 1975): 1006–33.

Clark, Robert E. "The Pueblo Rights Doctrine in New Mexico." *New Mexico Historical Review* 35 (Oct. 1960): 265–83.

Clements, Roger. "British-Controlled Enterprise in the West between 1870 and 1900, and Some Agrarian Reactions." *Agricultural History* 27 (Oct. 1953): 132–41.

Cleworth, Marc M. "Artesian-Well Irrigation: Its History in Brown County, South Dakota, 1889–1900." *Agricultural History* 15 (Oct. 1941): 195–201.

Clyde, George D. "History of Irrigation in Utah." *Utah Historical Quarterly* 27 (Jan. 1959): 27–36.

Cochran, S. A. "Irrigation a Sociological Question." In *Proceedings of the Seventh Annual Session, National Irrigation Congress* [1898], 109–12. Cheyenne, 1899.

Coville, F. V. "Our Public Grazing Lands." *Forum* 26 (Sept. 1898): 108–18.

Conkin, Paul K. "The Vision of Elwood Mead." *Agricultural History* 34 (April 1960): 88–97.

Coulter, Calvin B. "The Victory of National Irrigation in the Yakima Valley, 1902–1906." *Pacific Northwest Quarterly* 42 (April 1951): 99–122.

Davidson, George. "The Application of Irrigation to California." In *Contemporary Biography of California's Representative Men*, ed. by Alonzo Phelps, 105–23. San Francisco, 1881.

———. "The Pacific Coast and Geodetic Surveys." *The Californian* 1 (Jan. 1880): 60–65.

Davis, A. P. "The Public Domain in its Social Aspect." *Irrigation Age* 7 (July 1894): 15–17.

Dodds, Gordon B. "The Stream-Flow Controversy: A Conservation Turning Point." *Journal of American History* 56 (June 1969): 59–69.

Donaldson, Orren M. "Irrigation and State Boundaries: A Problem of the Arid West and Its Solution." *Irrigation Age* 8 (Feb. 1895): 47–53.

Doremus, A. F. "Irrigation in Utah." In *Official Proceedings of the Eleventh National Irrigation Congress Held at Ogden, Utah, September 15–18, 1903*, 269–72. Ogden, 1904.

Doyle, W. V. "What Can Be Accomplished by Irrigation." In *Proceedings of the Seventh Annual Session, National Irrigation Congress* [1898], 131–35. Cheyenne, 1899.

Dunbar, Robert G. "History of Agriculture." In *Colorado and Its People*, ed. by Le Roy Hafen, vol. 2:121–57. New York, 1948.

———. "The Origins of the Colorado System of Water Right Control." *Colorado Magazine* 27 (Oct. 1950): 241–62.

———. "Pioneering Groundwater Legislation in the United States: Mortgages, Land Banks, and Institution-Building in New Mexico." *Pacific Historical Review* 47 (November 1978): 565–84.

———. "The Significance of the Colorado Agricultural Frontier." *Agricultural History* 34 (July 1960): 119–26.

———. "Water Conflicts and Controls in Colorado." *Agricultural History* 22 (1948): 180–86.

East, Lewis R. "Parallel Irrigation Development—United States and Australia." American Society of Civil Engineers, *Centennial Transactions* (New York, 1953): 400–411.

Eastman, Philip. "Windmill Irrigation in Kansas." *Review of Reviews* 29 (Feb. 1904): 183–87.

Emerick, C. F. "Government Loans to Farmers." *Political Science Quarterly* 14 (Sept. 1899): 444–69.

Evans, T. "Orange Culture in California." *Overland Monthly* 12 (1874): 235–44.

Farnham, Wallace D. "Railroads in Western History: The View from the Union Pacific." In *The American West: A Reorientation*, ed. by Gene M. Gressley, 95–109. Laramie, 1966.

———. "'The Weakened Spring of Government': A Study in Nineteenth-Century American History." *American Historical Review* 68 (April 1963): 662–80.

Finkle, F. C. "The Wright Law in California." *Irrigation Age* 8 (Dec. 1895): 227–30.

Fitzsimmons, W. C. "The Wind-Mill in Irrigation." *Irrigation Age* 11 (Jan. 1897): 15–16.

Foley, Doris, and Morley, S. Griswold. "The 1883 Flood on the Middle Yuba River." *California Historical Quarterly* 28 (Sept. 1949): 233–42.

Follett, W. W. "The Interstate Uses of Water." In *Official Proceedings of the Eighteenth International Irrigation Congress, 1910*, 315–25. Pueblo, Colo., n.d.

———. "Irrigation on the Rio Grande." In *Proceedings of the Sixteenth National Irrigation Congress [1908]*, 136–52. Albuquerque, n.d.

———. "The Greatest Need of Arid America." *Official Proceedings of the Fifteenth National Irrigation Congress*, 118–23. Sacramento, Calif., 1907.

———. "The Present Stage of Irrigation Development and a Forecast of the Future." In *Official Proceedings of the Nineteenth National Irrigation Congress Held at Chicago, Illinois, December 5–9, 1911*, 141–47. Chicago, 1912.

Fox, Leonard P. "State Regulation of the Canal Corporation in Colorado." *Michigan Law Review* 16 (1917–1918): 158–78.

Freyfogle, Eric T. "*Lux* v. *Haggin* and the Common Law Burdens of Modern Water Law." *University of Colorado Law Review* 57 (Spring 1986): 485–525.

Gannett, Henry. "The Influence of Forests on the Quantity and Frequency of Rainfall." *Science* 12 (Nov. 23, 1888): 242–44.

Ganoe, John T. "The Beginnings of Irrigation in the United States." *Mississippi Valley Historical Review* 25 (June 1938): 59–78.

———. "The Desert Land Act in Operation, 1877–1891." *Agricultural History* 11 (Jan. 1937): 142–57.

———. "The Desert Land Act Since 1891." *Agricultural History* 11 (Oct. 1937): 266–77.

———. "The Origin of a National Reclamation Policy." *Mississippi Valley Historical Review* 18 (June 1931): 34–52.

Gates, Charles M. "A Historical Sketch of Economic Development of Washington since Statehood." *Pacific Northwest Quarterly* 39 (July 1948): 214–32.

Gates, Paul W. "Adjudication of Spanish-Mexican Land Claims in California." *Huntington Library Quarterly* 21 (May 1958): 213–36.

———. "The California Land Act of 1851." *California Historical Quarterly* 50 (December 1971): 395–430.

———. "California's Agricultural College Lands." *Pacific Historical Review* 30 (May 1961): 103–22.

———. "California Embattled Settlers." *California Historical Quarterly* 41 (June 1962): 99–130.

———. "Pre-Henry George Land Warfare in California." *California Historical Quarterly* 46 (June 1967): 121–48.

———. "Public Land Disposal in California." *Agricultural History* 49 (Jan. 1975): 158–78.

———. "The Role of the Land Speculator in Western Development." *Pennsylvania Magazine of History and Biography* 64 (July 1942): 314–33.

———. "The Suscol Principle, Preemption, and California Latifundia." *Pacific Historical Review* 39 (Nov. 1970): 453–72.

Gease, Daryl V. "William N. Byers and the Case for Federal Aid to Irrigation in the Arid West." *Colorado Magazine* 45 (Fall 1968): 340–45.

Gentilcore, R. Louis. "Ontario, California and the Agricultural Boom of the 1880s." *Agricultural History* 34 (April 1960): 77–87.

Gooding, F. R. "Development of Idaho under the Carey Act." In *Official Proceedings of the Seventeenth National Irrigation Congress* [1909], 314–22. Spokane, n.d.

Goodrich, Carter. "Internal Improvements Reconsidered." *Journal of Economic History* 30 (June 1970): 289–311.

Gopalakrishnan, Chennat. "The Doctrine of Prior Appropriation and Its Impact on Water Development: A Critical Survey." *American Journal of Economics and Sociology* 32 (January 1973): 61–72.

Goudy, Frank C. "Benefits and Dangers of Private Irrigation." In *Official Proceedings of the Eighteenth National Irrigation Congress Held at Pueblo, Colorado, Sept. 26–30, 1910*, 39–49. Pueblo, Colo., n.d.

Graham, Harold J. "Acres for Cents: the Economic and Constitutional Significance of Frontier Tax Titles, 1800–1890." In *Everyman's Constitution*, 494–518. Madison, 1968.

Gregory, C. A. "The Social, Economic and Financial Phases of Irrigation." *Irrigation Age* 6 (April 1894): 153–56.

Gregory, J. W. "Irrigation in Southwest Kansas: Experience Teaches Practicability of Pump Irrigation." *Irrigation Age* 8 (Jan. 1895): 13–17.

Greenleaf, Richard E. "The Founding of Albuquerque, 1706: An Historical-Legal Problem." *New Mexico Historical Review* 39 (Jan. 1964): 1–15.

———. "Land and Water in Mexico and New Mexico, 1700–1821." *New Mexico Historical Review* 47 (April 1972): 85–112.

Gressley, Gene M. "Arthur Powell Davis, Reclamation and the West." *Agricultural History* 42 (July 1968): 241–57.

Griffiths, David B. "Anti-Monopoly Movements in California, 1873–1898." *Southern California Quarterly* 52 (March 1970): 93–121.

———. "Far-Western Populist Thought: A Comparative Study of John R. Rogers and Davis H. Waite." *Pacific Northwest Quarterly* 60 (Oct. 1969): 183–92.

———. "Populism in Wyoming." *Annals of Wyoming* 40 (April 1968): 57–71.

Guest, Francis F. "Municipal Government in Spanish California." *California Historical Quarterly* 47 (Dec. 1967): 307–36.

Guinn, J. M. "The Great Real Estate Boom of 1887." *Annual Publication of the Historical Society of Southern California, 1890* 1 (1890): 13–21.

———. "A History of California Floods and Drought." *Annual Publication of the Historical Society of Southern California, 1890* 1 (1890): 33–39.

Haas, Charles E. "Early California Courts." *The State Bar Journal* (California) 10 (May, July 1935): 126–30, 172–75.

Haight, George W. "Riparian Rights." *Overland Monthly* 2d ser., 5 (June 1885): 561–69.

Hansbrough, H. C. "A National Irrigation Policy." *Forestry and Irrigation* 8 (March 1902): 102–4.

Hansen, Anne C. "The Congressional Career of Senator Francis E. Warren from 1890–1902." *Annals of Wyoming* 20 (Jan. 1948): 3–49.

Hardy, Osgood. "Agricultural Changes in California, 1860–1900." *Proceedings of the American Historical Association, Pacific Coast Branch, 1929*, 216–30. Eugene, Oreg., 1930.

Hargreaves, Mary. "The Dry-Farming Movement in Retrospect." *Agricultural History* 51 (Jan. 1977): 149–65.

Harrison, J. B. "Forests and Civilization: The North Woods, VII." *Garden and Forest* 2 (Sept. 11, 1889): 441–42.

Harrison, Robert. "The 'Weakened Spring of Government' Revisited: The Growth of Federal Power in the Late Nineteenth Century." In *The Growth of Federal Power in American History*, ed. by Rhondri Jeffreys Jones and Bruce Collins, 62–75. Dekalb, Ill., 1983.

Hart, I. W. "Exhaustion of Our Soil." *Irrigation Age* 2 (Nov. 15, 1891): 291.

Hays, Samuel P. "The New Organizational Society." In *Building the Organizational Society: Essays on Associational Activities in Modern America*, ed. by Jerry Israel, 1–15. New York, 1972.

Heathcote, Lesley M. "The Montana Arid Land Grant Commission, 1895–1902." *Agricultural History* 38 (April 1964): 108–17.

Hess, Ralph H. "An Illustration of Legal Development—The Passing of the Doctrine of Riparian Rights." *American Political Science Review* 2 (Nov. 1907): 15–31.

Hicks, L. E. "Storage of Storm-Waters on the Great Plains." *Science* 19 (April 1, 1892): 183–84.

Hill, James J. "Federal Aid to Irrigators." *Irrigation Age* 16 (Oct. 1901): 17–18.

Hinton, Richard J. "A Continental Issue." *Arena* 8 (Oct. 1893): 618–29.

———. "Waters of State and Nation." *Irrigation Age* 2 (Dec. 1891): 311–12, 328.

Hinton, R. W. K. "The Mercantile System in the Time of Thomas Mun." *Economic History Review* 7 (April 1955): 277–90.

Hobson, J. B. "Nevada County." *Tenth Annual Report of the [California] State Mineralogist* (Sacramento, 1890).

Hoffman, Charles."The Depression of the Nineties." *Journal of Economic History* 16 (June 1956): 137–64.

Hollingsworth, J. Rogers. "The United States." In *Crises of Political Development in Europe and the United States,* ed. by Raymond Grew, 163–95. Princeton, N.J., 1978.

House, Albert V., Jr. "Proposals of Government Aid to Agricultural Settlement During the Depression of 1873–1879." *Agricultural History* 12 (Jan. 1938): 46–66.

Hovey, H. C. "The Las Vegas Irrigation Convention." *Scientific American* 66 (April 9, 1892): 225.

Hudanick, Andrew, Jr. "George Hebard Maxwell: Reclamation's Militant Evangelist." *Journal of the West* 14 (July 1975): 108–19.

Hughes, Charles J. "The Evolution of Mining Law." In *Report of the Twenty-Fourth Annual Meeting of the American Bar Association Held at Denver, Colorado, August 21, 22, and 23, 1901,* 320–50. Philadelphia, 1901.

Hutchins, Wells A. "The Community Acequia: Its Origin and Development." *The Southwestern Historical Quarterly* 31 (Jan. 1928): 261–84.

Hutchins, Wells A., and Steele, Harry A. "Basic Water Rights Doctrines and Their Implications for River Basin Development." *Law and Contemporary Problems* 22 (Spring 1957): 276–300.

———. "Pumping Water for Irrigation." *Forestry and Irrigation* 8 (March 1902): 130–33.

Irwin, John N. "A Great Domain by Irrigation." *Forum* 12 (Feb. 1892): 740–50.

Jenkins, W. W. "History of the Development of Placer Mining in California." In *Publications of the Historical Society of Southern California, 1906,* 69–77. Los Angeles, 1907.

Johnson, H. H. "Forty-Three Years on the Shoshone Project." *Reclamation Era* 33 (June 1947): 124–27.

Johnston, Clarence T. "The Irrigation Possibilities of Northern Wyoming." *Irrigation Age* 13 (May 1899): 263–67.

———. "State Progress in Irrigation, Wyoming." In *Official Proceedings of the Eleventh National Irrigation Congress Held at Ogden, Utah, September 15–18, 1903,* 402–4.

Keller, Morton. "Social Policy in Nineteenth-Century America." In *Federal Social Policy: The Historical Dimension,* ed. by Donald T. Critchlow and Ellis W. Hawley, 99–115. University Park, Pa., 1988.

Kelley, Robert. "Taming the Sacramento: Hamiltonianism in Action." *Pacific Historical Review* 34 (February 1965): 21–49.

Kent, F. L. "Value of Drought Resistant Crops." In *Official Proceedings of the Fourteenth National Irrigation Congress Held at Boise, Idaho, Sept. 3–8, 1906,* 198–203. Boise, 1906.

Kershner, Frederick D., Jr. "George Chaffey and the Irrigation Frontier." *Agricultural History* 27 (Oct. 1953): 115–22.

Knight, Oliver. "Correcting Nature's Error: The Colorado-Big Thompson Project." *Agricultural History* 30 (Oct. 1956): 157–69.

Lasky, Moses. "From Prior Appropriation to Economic Distribution of Water by the State—Via Irrigation Administration." *Rocky Mountain Law Review* 1 (April 1929): 161–216.

Lee, Lawrence B. "The Canadian-American Irrigation Frontier, 1884–1914." *Agricultural History* 40 (Oct. 1966): 271–83.

———. "Environmental Implications of Governmental Reclamation in California." *Agricultural History* 49 (Jan. 1975): 223–29.

———. "The Mormons Come to Canada, 1887–1902." *Pacific Northwest Quarterly* 59 (Jan. 1968): 11–22.

———. "Water Resource History: A New Field of Historiography?" *Pacific Historical Review* 57 (Nov. 1988): 457–67.

———. "William Ellsworth Smythe and the Irrigation Movement: A Reconsideration." *Pacific Historical Review* 41 (Aug. 1972): 289–311.

Lewis, Christine. "The Early History of the Tempe Canal Company." *Arizona and the West* 7 (Autumn 1965): 227–38.

Lilley, William III, and Gould, Lewis L. "The Western Irrigation Movement, 1878–1902: A Reappraisal." In *The American West: A Reorientation*, ed. by Gene M. Gressley, 57–74. Laramie, Wyo., 1966.

Littlefield, Douglas R. "Water Rights during the California Gold Rush: Conflicts over Economic Points of View." *Western Historical Quarterly* 14 (Oct. 1983): 415–34.

Lively, Robert A. "The American System: A Review Article." *Business History Review* 29 (March 1955): 81–96.

Lovin, Hugh T. "A 'New West' Reclamation Tragedy: The Twin Falls Oakley Project in Idaho." *Arizona and the West* 20 (Spring 1978): 5–24.

Lowi, Theodore J. "Party, Policy, and Constitution in America." In *The American Party Systems: Stages of Political Development*, ed. by William Nisbet Chambers and Walter Dean Burnham, 238–76. New York, 1967.

Lythgoe, Eliza R. "Colonization of the Big Horn Basin By the Mormons." *Annals of Wyoming* 14 (Jan. 1942): 39–50.

MacKendrick, Donald A. "Before the Newlands Act: State-Sponsored Reclamation Projects in Colorado, 1888–1903." *Colorado Magazine* 52 (Winter 1975): 1–21.

McAllister, B. A. "Irrigation By the Use of Windmills." *Irrigation Age* 6 (Jan. 1894): 18–20.

McCarthy, G. Michael. "The People's Party in Colorado: A Profile of Populist Leadership." *Agricultural History* 47 (April 1973): 146–55.

McConnell, Grant. "The Conservation Movement—Past and Present." *Western Political Quarterly* 7 (September 1954): 463–78.

McCormick, Richard L. "The Party Period and Public Policy: An Exploratory Hypothesis." *Journal of American History* 66 (Sept. 1979): 279–98.

McCurdy, Charles. "Stephen J. Field and Public Land Law Development in California, 1850–1866: A Case Study of Judicial Resource Allocation in Nineteenth-Century America." *Law and Society Review* 10 (Fall 1975): 235–66.

McLaird, James D. "Building the Town of Cody: George T. Beck, 1894–1943." *Annals of Wyoming* 40 (April 1968): 73–105.

Maxwell, George H. "Annex Arid America." *Irrigation Age* 13 (Nov. 1898): 51–55.

———. "Editorial." *California—A Journal of Rural Industry* 1 (Feb. 1890): 4.

———. "Editorial." *California—A Journal of Rural Industry* 1 (March 1890): 2.

———. "Irrigation and Prosperity." In *Official Proceedings of the Nineteenth Irrigation Congress Held at Chicago, Illinois, December 5–9, 1911*, 125–42. Chicago, 1912.

———. "The Irrigation District: The Inherent Defects Which Have Caused Its Failure Can Only Be Remedied By a State System." *Irrigation Age* 12 (June 1898): 250–53.

———. "Let's Hang Together." *Irrigation Age* 13 (May 1899): 279–81.

———. "Nature's Storage Reservoirs." *Forester* 5 (Aug. 1899): 183–85.

———. "One and Indivisible: Forestry, Irrigation, Drainage, Navigation: The Rivers are the Greatest Asset of the Nation When Regulated for all Beneficial Uses." In *Official Proceedings of the Nineteenth National Irrigation Congress Held at Chicago, Illinois, December 5–9, 1911*, 87–90. Chicago, 1912.

———. "Reclamation of Arid America." *Irrigation Age* 13 (Sept. 1899): 407–9.

Mead, Elwood. "The Cody Canal in Wyoming." *Irrigation Age* 9 (Jan. 1896): 12–14.

———. "The Influence of State Borders on Water-Right Controversies." *Independent* 57 (Dec. 8, 1904): 1302–1303.

———. "Irrigation in Victoria." *Engineering Record* 60 (Aug. 14, 1909): 175–76.

———. "Irrigation Legislation." *Outlook* 70 (April 12, 1902): 907–10.

———. "The Irrigation Problems and Possibilities of Northern Wyoming." *Irrigation Age* 13 (Jan. 1899): 109–15.

———. "Problems of Irrigation Legislation." *Forum* 32 (Jan. 1902): 573–81.

———. "To Build Reservoirs." *Irrigation Age* 13 (Feb. 1899): 184.

———. "What Australia Can Teach America." *Independent* 71 (Aug. 17, 1911): 367–70.

Meinig, Donald W. "The Growth of Agricultural Regions in the Far West: 1850–1910." *The Journal of Geography* 54 (May 1955): 223–32.

Miles, Nelson A. "Our Unwatered Empire." *North American Review* 150 (March 1890): 370–81.

Miller, Gordon R. "Shaping California Water Law, 1781 to 1928." *Southern California Quarterly* 55 (Spring 1973): 9–42.

Mills, W. H. "Salvation Army Colonization of the Arid Lands." *Rural Californian* 20 (June–July, 1897): 252–53.

Mitchell, Guy Elliott. "Effects of Western Development on the East." *Forestry and Irrigation* 9 (April 1903): 205–7.

———. "Light Out of Darkness." *Forestry and Irrigation* 8 (March 1902): 126–29.

Moorhead, Dudley T. "Sectionalism and the California Constitution of 1879." *Pacific Historical Review* 12 (September 1943): 287–93.

Morgan, Dale. "The State of Deseret." *Utah Historical Quarterly* 8 (April, July, Oct. 1940): 66–239.

Morris, Ralph C. "The Notion of a Great American Desert East of the Rockies." *Mississippi Valley Historical Review* 13 (June 1926): 190–200.

Moses, Raphael J. "Irrigation Corporations." *Rocky Mountain Law Review* 32 (1959–1960): 527–33.

Murphy, Paul L. "Early Irrigation in the Boise Valley." *Pacific Northwest Quarterly* 44 (Oct. 1953): 177–84.

Nash, Gerald D. "The California State Land Office, 1858–1898." *Huntington Library Quarterly* 27 (August 1964): 347–56.

———. "Henry George Reexamined: William S. Chapman's Views on Land Speculation in Nineteenth Century California." *Agricultural History* 33 (July 1959): 133–37.

———. "Problems and Projects in the History of Nineteenth Century California Land Policy." *Arizona and the West* 2 (Winter 1960): 327–40.

Nesbit, Robert C., and Gates, Charles M. "Agriculture in Eastern Washington, 1890–1910." *Pacific Northwest Quarterly* 37 (Oct. 1946): 279–302.

Nettleton, E. S. "The Irrigation Problems and Possibilities of Northern Wyoming." *Irrigation Age* 13 (Apr. 1899): 235–38.

———. "The Successes and Failures of Canal Building and the Causes Thereof." In *Proceedings of the Seventh Annual Session, National Irrigation Congress* [1898], 54–60. Cheyenne, 1899.

Newell, Frederick H. "Artesian Wells." *Irrigation Age* 3 (May 1,1892): 27–28.

———. "Development of Water Resources." *Forester* 7 (Aug. 1901): 193–99.

———. "Irrigation." In *U.S. Smithsonian Institution, Annual Report, 1901*, 407–28. Washington, D.C., 1902.

———. "Reclamation of Arid Public Lands." *Independent* 54 (May 22, 1902): 1243–44.

———. "Water Supply for Irrigation." In *Thirteenth Annual Report of the United States Geological Survey* [1891–92], Part III, Irrigation, 7–99. Washington, D.C., 1893.

Orsi, Richard J. "*The Octopus* Reconsidered: The Southern Pacific and Agricultural Modernization in California, 1865–1915." *California Historical Quarterly* 54 (Fall 1975): 197–220.

Palmer, Truman G. "Irrigation and Beet Sugar." In *Official Proceedings of the Eleventh National Irrigation Congress Held at Ogden, Utah, September 15–18, 1903*, 308–14. Ogden, 1904.

———. "Irrigation and Beet Sugar." In *Official Proceedings of the Fourteenth National Irrigation Congress Held at Boise, Idaho, Sept. 3–8, 1906*, 208. Boise, 1906.

Palmer, William R. "Utah's Water Courts." *Reclamation Era* 33 (Nov. 1947): 233–40, 246.

Paludan, Phillip S. "John Norton Pomeroy, States Rights Nationalist." *American Journal of Legal History* 12 (July 1968): 275–93.

Paul, Rodman. "The Beginnings of Agriculture in California: Innovation vs. Continuity." *California Historical Quarterly* 52 (Spring 1973): 16–27.

———. "The Great California Grain War: The Grangers Challenge the Wheat King." *Pacific Historical Review* 27 (November 1958): 331–50.

Paulson, George W. "The Congressional Career of Joseph Maull Carey." *Annals of Wyoming* 35 (April 1963): 21–81.

Peterson, Richard H. "The Failure to Reclaim: California State Swamp Land Policy and the Sacramento Valley, 1850–1866." *Southern California Quarterly* 56 (Spring 1974): 45–60.

Philpott, Herbert J. "Irrigation of Arid Lands." *Popular Science Monthly* 36 (Jan. 1890): 364–71.

Pisani, Donald J. "Conflict over Conservation: The Reclamation Service and the Tahoe Contract." *Western Historical Quarterly* 10 (April 1979): 167–90.

———. "Deep and Troubled Waters: A New Field of Western History?" *New Mexico Historical Review* 63 (Oct. 1988): 311–31.

———. "Enterprise and Equity: A Critique of Western Water Law in the Nineteenth Century." *Western Historical Quarterly* 18 (Jan. 1987): 15–37.

———. "Federal Reclamation and Water Rights in Nevada." *Agricultural History* 51 (July 1977): 540–58.

———. "Forests and Conservation, 1865–1890." *Journal of American History* 72 (Sept. 1985): 340–59.

———. "The Irrigation District and the Federal Relationship: Neglected Aspects of Water History." In *The Twentieth-Century West: Historical Interpretations*, ed. by Gerald D. Nash and Richard W. Etulain, 257–92. Albuquerque, 1989.

———. "The Origins of Western Water Law: Case Studies from Two California Mining Districts." *California History* 70 (Fall 1991): 242–57, 324–25.

———. "Promotion and Regulation: Constitutionalism and the American Economy." *Jorunal of American History* 74 (Dec. 1987): 740–68.

———. "Reclamation and Social Engineering in the Progressive Era." *Agricultural History* 57 (Jan. 1983): 46–63.

———. "State vs. Nation: Federal Reclamation and Water Rights in the Progressive Era." *Pacific Historical Review* 51 (August 1982): 265–82.

———. "Water Law Reform in California, 1900–1913." *Agricultural History* 54 (April 1980): 295–317.

Pomeroy, Earl. "California, 1846–1860: Politics of a Representative Frontier State." *California Historical Quarterly* 32 (Dec. 1953): 291–302.

———. "Toward a Reorientation of Western History: Continuity and Environment." *Mississippi Valley Historical Review* 41 (March 1955): 579–600.

Poston, Charles D. "Irrigation." In *Report of the Commissioner of Agriculture, 1867*, 193–200. Washington, D.C., 1868.

Powell, John Wesley. "Institutions for the Arid Lands." *Century* 40 (May 1890): 111–16.

———. "The Lesson of Conemaugh." *North American Review* 149 (Aug. 1889): 150–56.

———. "The New Lake in the Desert." *Scribner's Magazine* 12 (Oct. 1891): 463–68.

———. "The Non-Irrigable Lands of the Arid Region." *Century* 39 (April 1890): 915–22.

———. "Trees on Arid Lands." *Science* 12 (Oct. 12, 1888): 170–71.

Prescott, Gerald L. "Farm Gentry vs. the Grangers: Conflict in Rural America." *California Historical Quarterly* 56 (Winter 1977): 328–45.

Ralph, Julian. "Wyoming—Another Pennsylvania." *Harper's Magazine* 87 (June 1893): 63–77.

Raup, H. F. "Transformation of Southern California to a Cultivated Land." *Annals of the Association of American Geographers, Supplement* 49 (Sept. 1959): 58–78.

Realf, James. "The Irrigation Problem in the Northwest." *Arena* 4 (June 1891): 69–76.

Relander, Click. "The Battleground of National Irrigation." *Pacific Northwest Quarterly* 52 (Oct. 1961): 144–51.

Ressler, John B. "Indian and Spanish Water-Control on New Spain's Northwest Frontier." *Journal of the West* 7 (Jan. 1968): 10–17.

Rezneck, Samuel. "Unemployment, Unrest, and Relief in the United States During the Depression of 1893–1897." *Journal of Political Economy* 61 (Aug. 1953): 324–45.

Riesenberg, Harry. "A Plea for Nationalization of Our Natural Resources." *Forestry and Irrigation* 14 (Aug. 1908): 414–24.

Roeder, Richard B. "Thomas H. Carter, Spokesman for Western Development." *Montana, the Magazine of Western History* 39 (Spring 1989): 23–29.

Ross, D. W. "Home Making in Idaho." *Irrigation Age* 7 (Dec. 1894): 254–56.

Rusinek, Walter. "Western Reclamation's Forgotten Forces: Richard J. Hinton and Groundwater Development." *Agricultual History* 61 (Summer 1987): 18–35.

Sageser, A. Bower. "Editor Bristow and the Great Plains Irrigation Revival of the 1890s." *Journal of the West* 3 (Jan. 1964): 75–89.

———. "Los Angeles Hosts an International Irrigation Congress." *Journal of the West* 4 (July 1965): 411–24.

———. "Windmill and Pump Irrigation on the Great Plains, 1890–1910." *Nebraska History* 48 (Summer 1967): 107–18.

Sanborn, J. W. "Fertilizing Powers of Water." *Irrigation Age* 2 (Jan. 15, 1892): 379.

Sargent, A. A. "Irrigation and Drainage." *Overland Monthly*, 2d ser., 8 (July 1886): 19–32.

Sargent, C. S. "The Danger from Mountain Reservoirs." *Garden and Forest* 2 (June 19, 1889): 289.

———. "The Forests on the Public Domain." *Garden and Forest* 3 (Jan. 8, 1890): 13–14.

———. "Irrigation Problems in the Arid West." *Garden and Forest* 1 (Aug. 8, 1888): 277–78.

———. "Mountain Reservoirs and Irrigation." *Garden and Forest* 2 (July 13, 1889): 313.

Scheiber, Harry N. "American Constitutional History and the New Legal History." *Journal of American History* 68 (Sept. 1981): 337–50.

———. "Federalism and the American Economic Order, 1789–1910." *Law & Society Review* 10 (Fall 1975): 57–118.

———. "American Federalism and the Diffusion of Power: Historical and Contemporary Perspectives." *University of Toledo Law Review* 9 (Summer 1978): 619–80.

———. "Federalism and Legal Process: Historical and Contemporary Analysis of the American System." *Law & Society Review* 14 (Spring 1980): 663–723.

———. "Government and the Economy: Studies of the 'Commonwealth' Policy in Nineteenth-Century America." *Journal of Interdisciplinary History* 3 (Summer 1972): 135–51.

———. "Law and the Imperatives of Progress: Private Rights and Public Values in American Legal History." In *Ethics, Economics, and the Law,* ed. J. Roland Pennock and John W. Chapman, 303–20. New York, 1982.

———. "Public Rights and the Rule of Law in American Legal History." *California Law Review* 72 (March 1984): 217–51.

———. "Regulation, Property Rights, and Definition of 'The Market': Law and the American Economy." *Journal of Economic History* 41 (March 1981): 103–11.

———. "The Road to *Munn:* Eminent Domain and the Concept of Public Purpose in the State Courts." *Perspectives in American History* 5 (1971): 327–40.

———. "Some Realism about Federalism: Historical Complexities and Current Challenges." In *Emerging Issues in American Federalism,* Advisory Committee on Intergovernmental Relations, 41–63. Washington, D.C., 1985.

———. "Xenophobia and Parochialism in the American Legal Process: From the Jacksonian Era to the Sagebrush Rebellion." *William & Mary Law Review* 23 (Summer 1982): 625–61.

Scheiber, Harry N. and Charles W. McCurdy. "Eminent-Domain Law and Western Agriculture, 1849–1900." *Agricultural History* 49 (Jan. 1975): 112–30.

Schmaltz, Bruce L. "Headgates and Headaches: The Powell Tract." *Idaho Yesterdays* 9 (Winter 1965–66): 22–25.

Schuyler, James D. "The Influence of Forests Upon Storage Reservoirs." *Forester* 5 (Dec. 1899): 285–88.

———. "New Irrigation Construction on Snake River, Idaho." In *Official Proceedings of the Eleventh National Irrigation Congress Held at Ogden, Utah, September 15–18, 1903,* 354–62. Ogden, 1904.

Shapiro, Martin. "American Federalism." In *Constitutional Government in America,* ed. by Ronald K. L. Collins, 359–71. Durham, N.C., 1980.

Shaw, John A. "Railroads, Irrigation, and Economic Growth: The San Joaquin Valley of California." *Explorations in Economic History* 10 (Winter 1973): 211–27.

Shaw, Lucien. "The Development of the Law of Waters in the West." *California Law Review* 10 (September 1922): 443–60.

———. "The Development of Water Law in California." *California Bar As-*

sociation, Proceedings of the Thirteenth Annual Convention 13 (1913): 154–73.

Shepstone, H. J. "The Irrigation Works of India." *Scientific American Supplement* 80 (Sept. 11, 1915): 164–65.

Sherow, James E. "Watering the Plains: An Early History of Denver's Highline Canal." *Colorado Heritage* (Issue 4, 1988): 2–13.

Shinn, Charles Howard. "California Forests and Irrigation." *Garden and Forest* 3 (Sept. 3, 1890): 426–27.

———. "Irrigation in the United States." *Popular Science Monthly* 43 (June 1893): 145–62.

Simmons, Marc. "Spanish Irrigation Practices in New Mexico." *New Mexico Historical Review* 47 (April 1972): 135–50.

Smith, E. Goodrich. "Irrigation." In *Report of the Commissioner of Patents, For the Year 1860*, 166–224. Washington, D.C., 1861.

Smith, Henry Nash. "Rain Follows the Plow: The Notion of Increased Rainfall for the Great Plains, 1844–1860." *Huntington Library Quarterly* 10 (Feb. 1947): 169–93.

Smythe, Harriet. "Biographical Sketch [of William E. Smythe]." *Irrigation Age* 14 (Oct. 1899): 3–5.

Smythe, William Ellsworth. "The Colony Builders." *Irrigation Age* 14 (Nov. 1899): 60–66.

———. "Eight Years Afterward." *Out West* 19 (Sept. 1903): 335–36.

———. "The Failure of the Water and Forest Commission." *Out West* 17 (Dec. 1902): 751–57.

———. "The New Era in Arizona." *Irrigation Age* 3 (Feb. 1893): 282–90.

———. "The Problem of Settlement." *Irrigation Age* 1 (Aug. 1, 1891): 116.

———. "A Program for California." *Land of Sunshine* 15 (Dec. 1901): 487–98.

———. "Real Utopias in the Arid West." *Atlantic* 79 (May 1897): 599–609.

———. "State and National Irrigation Policies." *Land of Sunshine* 15 (July 1901): 65–72.

———. "Stepchild of the Republic." *North American Review* 63 (July 1896): 37–46.

———. "The Struggle for Water in the West." *Atlantic* 86 (Nov. 1900): 646–54.

———. "A Trinity of Forces." *Irrigation Age* 1 (July 1, 1891): 97–98.

———. "20th Century West." *Land of Sunshine* 15 (Nov. 1901): 377–82.

Steinel, Alvin T. "The Range Livestock Industry." In *History of Colorado*, ed. by James H. Baker, 645–93. Denver, 1927.

Sterling, Everett W. "The Powell Irrigation Survey, 1888–1893." *Mississippi Valley Historical Review* 27 (Dec. 1940): 421–34.

Stewart, William Morris. "Reclaiming the Western Deserts." *Forum* 7 (April 1889): 201–8.

Strong, Douglas H. "The Sierra Forest Reserve: The Movement to Preserve the San Joaquin Valley Watershed." *California Historical Quarterly* 45 (March 1967): 3–18.

Sunseri, Alvin R. "Agricultural Techniques in New Mexico at the Time of the Anglo-American Conquest." *Agricultural History* 47 (Oct. 1973): 329–37.

Teele, Ray P. "Magnitude of Irrigation Interests." In *Official Proceedings of the Nineteenth National Irrigation Congress Held at Chicago, Illinois, December 5–9, 1911*, 36–42. Chicago, 1912.

———. "Notes on the Irrigation Situation." *Journal of Political Economy* 13 (March 1905): 237–45.

———. "The Organization of Irrigation Companies." *Journal of Political Economy* 12 (March 1904): 161–78.

———. "Water Rights in the Arid West." *Journal of Political Economy* 8 (Sept. 1900): 524–34.

Teilman, Hendrick. "The Role of Irrigation Districts in California's Water Development." *American Journal of Economics and Sociology* 22 (July 1963): 409–15.

Thickens, Virginia E. "Pioneer Agricultural Colonies of Fresno County." *California Historical Quarterly* 25 (March and June 1946): 17–38, 169–77.

Thompson, Kenneth, and Eigenheer, Richard A. "The Agricultural Promise of the Sacramento Valley: Some Early Views." *Journal of the West* 18 (Oct. 1979): 33–41.

Thompson, Kenneth. "Historic Flooding in the Sacramento Valley." *Pacific Historical Review* 29 (November 1960): 349–60.

———. "Insalubrious California: Perception and Reality." *Annals of the Association of American Geographers* 59 (1969): 50–64.

———. "Irrigation as a Menace to Health in California: A Nineteenth Century View." *The Geographical Review* 59 (April 1969): 195–214.

Tilly, Charles. "Reflections on the History of European State-Making." In *The Formation of National States in Western Europe*, ed. by Charles Tilly, 3–83. Princeton, N.J., 1975.

Toumey, J. W. "Forests as Sources of Water Supply." In *Proceedings of the Ninth Annual Session of the National Irrigation Congress, Held at Central Music Hall, Chicago, Ill., November 21, 22, 23, 1900*, 183–92. St. Louis, n.d.

Trelease, Frank J. "Uneasy Federalism—State Water Laws and National Water Uses." *Washington Law Review* 55 (Nov. 1980): 751–75.

Tucker, Frederick Booth. "The Relation of Colonization to Irrigation." *Forestry and Irrigation* 9 (Oct. 1903): 499–505.

Ulrich, J. "Conditions Favorable and Unfavorable to Irrigation." *Irrigation Age* 15 (Jan. 1901): 112–20.

Van Dyke, T. S. "Fertilizing with Irrigation." *Irrigation Age* 1 (May 30, 1891): 64.

Van Hook, Joseph O. "Development of Irrigation in the Arkansas Valley." *Colorado Magazine* 10 (Jan. 1933): 3–11.

Vinovskis, Maris A. "Have Social Historians Lost the Civil War? Some Preliminary Demographic Speculations." *Journal of American History* 76 (June 1989): 51–55.

Wagner, Henry R. "George Davidson, Geographer of the Northwest Coast of America." *California Historical Quarterly* 11 (Dec. 1932): 299–320.

Walsh, Thomas F. "Humanitarian Aspect of National Irrigation." *Forestry and Irrigation* 8 (Dec. 1902): 505–9.

Walter, R. F. and W. H. Code. "Elwood Mead." *American Society of Civil Engineers Transactions,* 102 (1937): 1611–18.

Ward, Lester F. "Irrigation in the Upper Missouri and Yellowstone Valleys." *Science* 4 (Aug. 29, 1884): 166–68.

Warren, Francis E. "What Congress is Doing in Aid of Irrigation." In *Proceedings of the Seventh Annual Session, National Irrigation Congress [1898],* 77–82. Cheyenne, 1899.

Webb, Walter Prescott. "The West: A Plundered Province." *Harper's* 169 (Aug. 1934): 355–64.

Webster, Norman E. "Irrigation Finance." In *Official Proceedings of the Nineteenth National Irrigation Congress Held at Chicago, Illinois, December 5–9, 1911,* 225–30. Chicago, 1912.

Whitaker, Arthur P. "The Spanish Contribution to American Agriculture." *Agricultural History* 3 (Jan. 1929): 1–14.

Wiel, Samuel C. "Fifty Years of Water Law." *Harvard Law Review* 50 (Dec. 1936): 252–304.

———. "Origin and Comparative Development of the Law of Watercourses in the Common Law and Civil Law." *California Law Review* 6 (May, July 1918): 245–67, 342–71.

———. "'Priority' in Western Water Law." *Yale Law Journal* 18 (Jan. 1909): 189–98.

———. "Public Control of Irrigation." *Columbia Law Review* 10 (June 1910): 506–19.

———. "Theories of Water Law." *Harvard Law Review* 27 (April 1914): 530–44.

———. "The Water Law of the Public Domain." *American Law Review* 43 (July–Aug. 1909): 481–515.

———. "Waters: American Law and French Authority." *Harvard Law Review* 33 (Dec. 1919): 133–67.

Wilson, Herbert M. "American and Indian Irrigation Works." *Irrigation Age* 6 (March 1894): 107–9.

———. "American Canal Works." *Irrigation Age* 2 (Dec. 15, 1891): 331.

———. "American Irrigation Engineering." In *Thirteenth Annual Report of the United States Geological Survey [1891–92],* Part III, 109–349. Washington, D.C., 1893.

———. "The Irrigation Problem in Montana." *National Geographic Magazine* 2 (No. 3, 1890): 212–29.

Wilson, James. "Irrigation Creates Home Markets." *Forestry and Irrigation* 8 (Jan. 1902): 10–11.

———. "Untitled Speech." In *Official Proceedings of the Eleventh National Irrigation Congress Held at Ogden, Utah, September 15–18, 1903,* 164. Ogden, 1904.

Wilson, James Q. "The Rise of the Bureaucratic State." *The Public Interest* 41 (Fall 1975): 77–103.

Winther, Oscar O. "The Colony System of Southern California." *Agricultural History* 27 (July 1953): 94–102.

Wooster, Clarence M. "Building the Railroad Down the San Joaquin in 1871."
    California Historical Quarterly 18 (March 1939): 22–31.
Working, Daniel W. "Agriculture." In *History of Colorado*, ed. by James H.
    Baker, 573–643. Denver, 1927.
Works, John D. "Irrigation Laws and Decisions of California." In *History of
    the Bench and Bar in California*, by Oscar T. Shuck, 101–72. Los Angeles,
    1901.
Worster, Donald. "Hydraulic Society in California: An Ecological Interpreta-
    tion." *Agricultural History* 56 (July 1982): 503–16.
———. "New West, True West: Interpreting the Region's History." *Western
    Historical Quarterly* 18 (April 1987): 141–56.
Wright, C. C. "Irrigation on Popular Principles." *Irrigation Age* 2 (Feb. 1, 1892):
    446–47.
Wyckoff, A. B. "Irrigation." *Journal of the Franklin Institute* 140 (Oct. 1895):
    241–62.

XII. Books and Pamphlets

Ackerman, E. A., and Lof, George, O. G., *Technology in American Water De-
    velopment* (Baltimore, Md., 1959).
Alexander, J. A., *The Life of George Chaffey* (Melbourne, Australia, 1928).
Alexander, Thomas G., *A Clash of Interests: Interior Department and the
    Mountain West, 1863–1896* (Provo, Utah, 1977).
Alston, Richard Moss, *Commercial Irrigation Enterprise: The Fear of Water
    Monopoly and the Genesis of Market Distortion in the Nineteenth Century
    American West* (New York, 1978).
Anderson, David B., *Riparian Water Rights in California* (Sacramento, Calif.,
    1977).
Angel, Myron, *History of Nevada* (Oakland, 1881).
Angell, Joseph K., *A Treatise on the Law of Watercourses* (Boston, 1847).
Archibald, Marybelle D., *Appropriative Water Rights in California* (Sacra-
    mento, Calif., 1977).
Arrington, Leonard, *Great Basin Kingdom: An Economic History of the Latter-
    Day Saints, 1830–1900* (Cambridge, Mass., 1958).
Athearn, Robert G., *The Coloradans* (Albuquerque, 1976).
Bakken, Gordon, *The Development of Law on the Rocky Mountain Frontier:
    Civil Law and Society, 1850–1912* (Westport, Conn., 1983).
Bancroft, Hubert Howe, *California Pastoral, 1769–1848* (San Francisco, 1888).
———, *Chronicles of the Builders of the Commonwealth* (7 vols., San Fran-
    cisco, 1892).
———, *History of Arizona and New Mexico, 1530–1888* (San Francisco, 1889).
———, *History of California, 1860–1890* (San Francisco, 1890).
———, *History of Nevada, Colorado, and Wyoming, 1540–1888* (San Fran-
    cisco, 1889).

Bancroft, Hubert Howe, and Victor, Frances Fuller, *History of Nevada, 1540–1888* (San Francisco, 1890).

Bartlett, I. S., ed., *History of Wyoming* (3 vols., Chicago, 1918).

Beard, Frances B., ed., *Wyoming: From Territorial Days to the Present* (3 vols., Chicago & New York, 1933).

Beattie, George William, and Beattie, Helen P., *Heritage of the Valley: San Bernardino's First Century* (Pasadena, Calif., 1939).

Bensel, Richard Franklin, *Sectionalism and American Political Development, 1880–1980* (Madison, 1984).

Bentley, Arthur F., *The Process of Government* (Cambridge, Mass., 1967).

Berg, Norman, *A History of Kern County Land Company* (Bakersfield, Calif., 1971).

Beth, Loren P., *The Development of the American Constitution, 1877–1917* (New York, 1971).

Bicha, Karel D., *Western Populism: Studies in an Ambivalent Conservatism* (Lawrence, Kansas, 1976).

Billington, Ray A., *America's Frontier Heritage* (Albuquerque, 1974).

Black, George, *Report on the Middle Yuba Canal and Eureka Lake Canal, Nevada County, California* (San Francisco, 1864).

Blandi, Joseph G., *Maryland Business Corporations, 1783–1852* (Baltimore, 1934).

Boyd, David, *A History: Greeley and the Union Colony of Colorado* (Greeley, Colo., 1890).

———, *Irrigation Near Greeley, Colorado* (Washington, D.C., 1897).

Brace, Charles Loring, *The New West: Or, California in 1867–1868* (New York, 1869).

Brereton, Robert M., *Reminiscences of Irrigation-Enterprise in California* (Portland, Oreg., 1903).

———, *Reminiscences of an Old English Civil Engineer, 1858–1908* (Portland, Oreg., 1908).

Brock, William R., *Investigation and Responsibility in the United States, 1865–1900* (Cambridge, 1984).

Brown, George Rothwell, ed., *Reminiscences of Senator William M. Stewart of Nevada* (New York, 1908).

Brown, John Jr., and Boyd, James, *History of San Bernardino and Riverside Counties* (Chicago, 1922).

Browne, J. Ross, *Resources of the Pacific Slope* (San Francisco, 1869).

Brownlee, W. Elliott, *Dynamics of Ascent: A History of the American Economy* (New York, 1979).

Bruchey, Stuart, *The Wealth of the Nation: An Economic History of the United States* (New York, 1988).

Bryant, Edwin, *What I Saw in California* (New York, 1848).

Bryce, James, *The American Commonwealth* (New York, 1915).

Buck, Solon J., *The Granger Movement: A Study of Agricultural Organization and Its Political, Economic and Social Manifestations, 1870–1880* (Cambridge, Mass., 1913).

Burnley, James, *Millionaires and Kings of Enterprise* (Philadelphia, 1901).

Carr, Ezra S., *The Patrons of Husbandry on the Pacific Coast* (San Francisco, 1875).

Caughey, John Walton, *The California Gold Rush* (Berkeley, 1948).

Chandler, Alfred E., *Elements in Western Water Law* (San Francisco, 1913).

Chatterton, Fenimore, ed., *The State of Wyoming* (Laramie, 1904).

Christman, Enos, *One Man's Gold: The Letters & Journal of a Forty-Niner* (New York, 1930).

Clapp, Louise Amelia Knapp Smith, *The Shirley Letters* (Santa Barbara, Calif., 1970).

Clark, Ira G., *Water in New Mexico: A History of Its Management and Use* (Albuquerque, 1987).

Cleland, Robert Glass, *The Cattle on a Thousand Hills: Southern California, 1850–1880* (San Marino, Calif., 1951).

————. *From Wilderness to Empire: A History of California, 1542–1900* (New York, 1944).

Cody, W. F., *An Autobiography of Buffalo Bill* (New York, 1920).

Comfort, Herbert G., *Where Rolls the Kern* (Moorpark, Calif., 1934).

Crenson, Matthew A., *The Federal Machine: Beginnings of Bureaucracy in Jacksonian America* (Baltimore, 1975).

Cronise, Titus Fey, *The Agricultural and other Resources of California* (San Francisco, 1870).

Dana, F. L., *The Great West: A Vast Empire* (Denver, 1889).

Dangberg, Grace, *Conflict on the Carson* (Minden, Nev., 1975).

Darrah, William Culp, *Powell of the Colorado* (Princeton, 1951).

Davenport, Charles B., *Biographical Memoir of George Davidson, 1825–1911* (Washington, D.C., 1937).

Davis, Arthur P., *Irrigation Works Constructed by the United States Government* (New York, 1917).

Davis, John F., *Historical Sketch of the Mining Law in California* (Los Angeles, 1902).

Davison, Stanley Roland, *The Leadership of the Reclamation Movement, 1875–1902* (New York, 1979).

Deakin, Alfred, *Irrigation in Western America* (Melbourne, 1885).

Delano, A., *Life on the Plains and Among the Diggings* (Buffalo, 1854).

Dick, Everett, *The Lure of the Land* (Lincoln, 1970).

Dobkins, Betty Eakle, *The Spanish Element in Texas Water Law* (Austin, 1959).

Dodds, Gordon B., *Hiram Martin Chittenden: His Public Career* (Lexington, Ky., 1973).

Dumke, Glenn, *The Boom of the Eighties in Southern California* (San Marino, Calif., 1944).

Dunbar, Robert G., *Forging New Rights in Western Waters* (Lincoln, 1983).

Dupree, A. Hunter, *Science in the Federal Government: A History of Policies and Activities to 1940* (Cambridge, Mass., 1957).

Dwinelle, John W., *The Colonial History, City of San Francisco* (San Francisco, 1867).

Elliott, Russell, R., *History of Nevada* (Lincoln, 1973).

————, *Servant of Power: A Political Biography of Senator William M. Stewart* (Reno, 1983).

Elliott, Wallace W., *History of San Bernardino and San Diego Counties* (San Francisco, 1883).

————, *History of Tulare County* (San Francisco, 1883).

Ellison, Joseph, *California and the Nation, 1850–1869: A Study of the Relations of a Frontier Community with the Federal Government* (Berkeley, 1927).

Ellison, William E., *A Self-Governing Dominion: California, 1849–1860* (Berkeley, 1950).

Emmons, David M., *Garden in the Grasslands: Boomer Literature of the Central Great Plains* (Lincoln, 1971).

Fabian, Bentham, *The Agricultural Lands of California* (San Francisco, 1869).

Fenton, Carroll Lane and Fenton, Mildred Adams, *The Story of the Great Geologists* (Garden City, N.Y., 1945).

Fine, Sidney, *Laissez-Faire and the General Welfare State: A Study of Conflict in American Thought, 1865–1901* (Ann Arbor, 1956).

Fite, Gilbert C., *The Farmer's Frontier, 1865–1900* (New York, 1966).

Fogelson, Robert M., *The Fragmented Metropolis: Los Angeles, 1850–1930* (Cambridge, Mass., 1967).

Freyer, Tony, *Forums of Order: The Federal Courts and Business in American History* (Greenwich, Conn., 1979).

Friedman, Lawrence M., *A History of American Law* (New York, 1973).

Garraty, John, *The New Commonwealth, 1877–1890* (New York, 1968).

Gates, Paul W., ed., *California Ranchos and Farms, 1846–1862* (Madison, 1967).

————, *The Farmers' Age: Agriculture, 1815–1860* (New York, 1960).

————, *History of Public Land Law Development* (Washington, D.C., 1968).

George, Henry, *Our Land and Land Policy* (San Francisco, 1871).

Giffen, Helen S., ed., *The Diaries of Peter Decker: Overland to California in 1849 and Life in the Mines, 1850–1851* (Georgetown, Calif., 1966).

Glass, Mary Ellen, *Silver and Politics in Nevada: 1892–1902* (Reno, 1969).

Glick, Thomas F., *The Old World Background of the Irrigation System of San Antonio, Texas* (El Paso, 1972).

Golze, Alfred R., *Reclamation in the United States* (New York, 1952).

Goodwyn, Lawrence, *Democratic Promise: The Populist Movement in America* (New York, 1976).

Gould, Lewis L., *Wyoming: A Political History, 1868–1896* (New Haven, 1968).

Grabhorn, Jane Bissell, *A California Gold Rush Miscellany* (San Francisco, 1934).

Gregory, Tom, et al., *History of Yolo County, California* (Los Angeles, 1913).

Gressley, Gene, ed., *The American West: A Reorientation* (Laramie, Wyo., 1966).

Guice, John D. W., *The Rocky Mountain Bench: The Territorial Supreme Courts of Colorado, Montana, and Wyoming, 1861–1890* (New Haven, 1972).

Guinn, J. M., *Historical and Biographical Record of Los Angeles and Vicinity* (Chicago, 1901).

Haar, Charles, ed., *The Golden Age of American Law* (New York, 1965).

Hafen, Le Roy, *Colorado: The Story of a Western Commonwealth* (Denver, 1933).

Haggin, James B., et al., *Desert Lands of Kern County, California: Affidavits of Various Residents of Said County* (San Francisco, 1877).

Haines, Charles G., *The American Doctrine of Judicial Supremacy* (New York, 1914).

Hall, Frank, *History of Colorado* (2 vols., Chicago, 1889).

Hall, Kermit, *The Magic Mirror: Law in American History* (New York, 1989).

Hall, William Hammond, *Irrigation in [Southern] California* (Sacramento, 1888).

———, *Irrigation Development: History, Customs, Laws and Administrative Systems Relating to Irrigation, Water-Courses, and Waters in France, Italy, and Spain* (Sacramento, 1886).

Hamilton, Leonidas, *Hamilton's Mexican Law* (San Francisco, 1882).

Harbaugh, William Henry, *Power and Responsibility: The Life and Times of Theodore Roosevelt* (New York, 1961).

Hargreaves, Mary, *Dry Farming in the Northern Great Plains, 1900–1925* (Cambridge, Mass., 1957).

Harlow, Neal, *California Conquered: War and Peace on the Pacific, 1846–1850* (Berkeley, 1982).

Hartz, Louis, *Economic Policy and Democratic Thought: Pennsylvania, 1776–1860* (Cambridge, Mass., 1948).

———, *The Founding of New Societies: Studies in the History of the United States, Latin America, South Africa, Canada, and Australia* (New York, 1964).

Hazen, W. B., *Our Barren Lands: The Interior of the United States* (Cincinnati, 1875).

Hays, Samuel P., *Conservation and the Gospel of Efficiency: The Progressive Conservation Movement, 1890–1920* (Cambridge, Mass., 1959).

Hibbard, Benjamin H., *A History of the Public Land Policies* (Madison, 1965).

Hine, Robert V., *The American West: An Interpretive History* (Rev. ed., Boston, 1984).

Hittell, John S., *Commerce and Industries of the Pacific Coast* (San Francisco, 1882).

———, *Mining in the Pacific States of North America* (San Francisco, 1861).

———, *The Resources of California* (San Francisco, 1863).

Hittell, Theodore H., *History of California* (San Francisco, 1897).

Hofstadter, Richard, *The Age of Reform: From Bryan to F.D.R.* (New York, 1955).

Holcombe, Arthur N., *State Government in the United States* (New York, 1916).

Holliday, J. S., *The World Rushed In: The California Gold Rush Experience* (New York, 1981).

Hollingsworth, J. Rogers, *The Whirligig of Politics* (Chicago, 1963).

Hollon, Eugene, *The Great American Desert: Then and Now* (New York, 1966).

Horwitz, Morton, *The Transformation of American Law, 1780–1860* (Cambridge, Mass., 1977).

Howe, Daniel Walker, *The Political Culture of the American Whigs* (Chicago, 1979).

Huffman, Roy E., *Irrigation Development and Public Water Policy* (New York, 1953).

Hundley, Norris, Jr., *The Great Thirst: Californians and Water, 1770s–1990s* (Berkeley, 1992).

Hunt, Rockwell D., *California's Stately Hall of Fame* (Stockton, Calif., 1950).

Huntington, Samuel P., *Political Order in Changing Societies* (New Haven, 1968).

Hurst, James Willard, *Law and the Conditions of Freedom in the Nineteenth-Century United States* (Madison, 1967).

Hutchins, Wells A., *The California Law of Water Rights* (Sacramento, 1956).

Hutchinson, Claude B., *California Agriculture* (Berkeley, 1946).

Ingersoll, L. A., *Ingersoll's Century Annals of San Bernardino County, 1769 to 1904* (Los Angeles, 1904).

Irving, Washington, *The Adventures of Captain Bonneville, U.S.A., in the Rocky Mountains and the Far West* (Norman, Okla., 1961).

Jackson, Kenneth T., *Crabgrass Frontier: The Suburbanization of the United States* (New York, 1985).

Jackson, W. Turrentine, Rand F. Herbert, and Stephen R. Wee, *Engineers and Irrigation: Report of the Board of Commissioners on the Irrigation of the San Joaquin, Tulare, and Sacramento Valleys of the State of California, 1873* (Fort Belvoir, Va., 1990).

James, George Wharton, *Reclaiming the Arid West: The Story of the United States Reclamation Service* (New York, 1917).

Jelinek, Lawrence J., *Harvest Empire: A History of California Agriculture* (San Francisco, 1979).

Keller, Morton, *Affairs of State: Public Life in Late Nineteenth Century America* (Cambridge, Mass., 1977).

———, *The Life Insurance Enterprise, 1885–1910: A Study in the Limits of Corporate Power* (Cambridge, Mass., 1963).

Kelley, Robert L., *Battling the Inland Sea: American Political Culture, Public Policy, & the Sacramento Valley, 1850–1986* (Berkeley, 1989).

———, *The Cultural Pattern in American Politics: The First Century* (New York, 1979).

———, *Gold vs. Grain: The Hydraulic Mining Controversy in California's Sacramento Valley, A Chapter in the Decline of Laissez-Faire* (Glendale, Calif., 1959).

Kimball, Spencer L., *Insurance and Public Policy: A Study in the Legal Implementation of Social and Economic Public Policy, Based on Wisconsin Records, 1835–1959* (Madison, 1960).

Kinney, Clesson S., *A Treatise on the Law of Irrigation and Water Rights and the Arid Region Doctrine of Appropriation of Waters* (4 vols., San Francisco, 1912).

Kirkland, E. C., *A History of American Economic Life* (New York, 1969).

LaFuze, Pauliena B., *Saga of the San Bernardinos* (San Bernardino, Calif., 1971).

Lamar, Howard R., *Dakota Territory, 1861–1889: A Study of Frontier Politics* (New Haven, 1956).

———, *The Far Southwest, 1846–1912: A Territorial History* (New Haven, 1966).

Larson, Lawrence W., *The Urban West at the End of the Frontier* (Lawrence, Kansas, 1978).

Larson, Robert W., *Populism in the Mountain West* (Albuquerque, 1986).

Larson, T. A., *History of Wyoming* (Lincoln, 1978).

Lauck, William J., *The Causes of the Panic of 1893* (New York, 1907).

Lavender, David, *Nothing Seemed Impossible: William C. Ralston and Early San Francisco* (Palo Alto, Calif., 1975).

Layne, J. Gregg, *Annals of Los Angeles* (San Francisco, 1935).

Lee, Lawrence B., *Reclaiming the Arid West: An Historiography and Guide* (Santa Barbara, 1980).

Levy, Leonard, *The Law of the Commonwealth and Chief Justice Shaw: The Evolution of American Law, 1830–1860* (Cambridge, Mass., 1954).

Lewis, Oscar, *George Davidson: Pioneer West Coast Scientist* (Berkeley, 1954).

Lewis Publishing Company, *An Illustrated History of Los Angeles County, California* (Chicago, 1889).

Limerick, Patricia Nelson, *Desert Passages: Encounters with the American Deserts* (Albuquerque, 1985).

———, *The Legacy of Conquest: The Unbroken Past of the American West* (New York, 1987).

Lindsay, Charles, *The Big Horn Basin* (Lincoln, 1930).

Lipson, Leslie, *The American Governor from Figurehead to Leader* (Chicago, 1939).

Lowitt, Richard, *The New Deal and the West* (Bloomington, 1984).

Lyman, George D., *Ralston's Ring: California Plunders the Comstock Lode* (New York, 1947).

Maass, Arthur, and Anderson, Raymond, *. . . and the Desert Shall Rejoice: Conflict, Growth, and Justice in Arid Environments* (Cambridge, Mass., 1978).

Maass, Arthur, *Muddy Waters: The Army Engineers and the Nation's Rivers* (Cambridge, Mass., 1951).

———, *Water Law and Institutions in the Western United States* (Boulder, Colo., 1990).

MacArthur, Mildred Yorba, *Anaheim: "The Mother Colony"* (Los Angeles, 1959).

McCarthy, Michael G., *Hour of Trial: The Conservation Conflict in Colorado and the West, 1891–1907* (Norman, Okla., 1977).

McCool, Daniel, *Command of the Waters: Iron Triangles, Federal Water Development, and Indian Water* (Berkeley, 1987).

McCullough, David G., *The Johnstown Flood* (New York, 1968).

McKinley, Edward H., *Marching to Glory: The History of the Salvation Army in the United States of America, 1880–1980* (San Francisco, 1980).

Malin, James C., *The Grassland of North America: Prolegomena to its History with Addenda and Postscript* (Gloucester, Mass., 1967).

Malone, Michael P., and Roeder, Richard B., *Montana: A History of Two Centuries* (Seattle, 1976).

Mann, Ralph, *After the Gold Rush: Society in Grass Valley and Nevada City, California, 1849–1870* (Stanford, Calif., 1982).

Manning, Thomas G., *Government in Science: The U.S. Geological Survey, 1867–1894* (Lexington, Ky., 1967).

Marsh, George Perkins, *Man and Nature: or Physical Geography as Modified by Human Action* (New York, 1864).

Marx, Leo, *The Machine in the Garden: Technology and the Pastoral Ideal in America* (New York, 1964).

May, Philip Ross, *Origins of Hydraulic Mining in California* (Oakland, Calif., 1970).

Mead, Elwood, *Irrigation Institutions* (New York, 1903).

Menefee, Eugene L., *History of Tulare and Kings Counties, California* (Los Angeles, 1913).

Meriwether, Robert L., ed., *The Papers of John C. Calhoun* (18 vols., Columbia, South Carolina, 1959).

Meyer, Michael C., *Water in the Hispanic Southwest: A Social and Legal History, 1550–1850* (Tucson, 1984).

Miller, Thelma B., *History of Kern County, California* (Chicago, 1929).

Morgan, Arthur E., *Dams and Other Disasters: A Century of the Army Corps of Engineers in Civil Works* (Boston, 1971).

Morgan, Wallace T., *History of Kern County, California* (Los Angeles, 1914).

Murray, Robert A., *Johnson County: 175 Years at the Foot of the Big Horn Mountains* (Buffalo, Wyo., 1981).

Nadeau, Remi A., *The Water Seekers*, rev. ed. (Santa Barbara, Calif., 1974).

Nash, Gerald D., *State Government and Economic Development: A History of Administrative Policies in California, 1849–1933* (Berkeley, 1964).

Nash, Gerald D., and Etulain, Richard W., *The Twentieth Century West: Historical Interpretations* (Albuquerque, 1989).

Nelson, William E., *Americanization of the Common Law: The Impact of Legal Change on Massachusetts Society, 1760–1830* (Cambridge, Mass., 1975).

Newell, Frederick H., *Irrigation in the United States* (New York, 1902).

Newlands, Francis G., *An Address to the People of Nevada on Water Storage and Irrigation* (Reno, 1890).

Osgood, Ernest S., *The Day of the Cattleman* (Minneapolis, 1929).

Ostrom, Vincent, *Water and Politics: A Study of Water Policies and Administration in the Development of Los Angeles* (Los Angeles, 1953).

Pabor, William E., *Colorado as an Agricultural State* (New York, 1883).

———, *Farmer's Guide to Northern Colorado* (Denver, 1882).

Patterson, Lauson B., *Twelve Years in the Mines of California* (Cambridge, Mass., 1862).

Paul, Rodman W., *California Gold: The Beginning of Mining in the Far West* (Cambridge, Mass., 1947).

———, *Mining Frontiers of the Far West, 1848–1880* (New York, 1963).

Peffer, E. Louise, *The Closing of the Public Domain: Disposal and Reservation Policies, 1900–1950* (Stanford, 1951).

Phelps, Alonzo, *Contemporary Biography of California's Representative Men* (San Francisco, 1881).

Pinchot, Gifford, *Breaking New Ground* (New York, 1947).

Pisani, Donald J., *From the Family Farm to Agribusiness: The Irrigation Crusade in California and the West, 1850–1931* (Berkeley, 1984).

Pocock, J. G. A., *The Machiavellian Movement: Florentine Political Thought and the Atlantic Republican Tradition* (Princeton, 1975).

Pomeroy, Earl, *The Pacific Slope* (New York, 1965).

Pomeroy, John Norton, *A Treatise on the Law of Water Rights* (St. Paul, Minn., 1893).

Powell, J. M., *Watering the Garden State: Water, Land and Community in Victoria, 1834–1988* (Sydney, 1989).

Powell, John J., *Nevada: The Land of Silver* (San Francisco, 1876).

Powell, John Wesley, *Report on the Lands of the Arid Region of the United States: With a More Detailed Account of the Lands of Utah* (Cambridge, Mass., 1962).

Powers, Stephen, *Alone and Afoot: A Walk from Sea to Sea* (Hartford, Conn., 1872).

Preston, William L., *Vanishing Landscapes: Land and Life in the Tulare Lake Basin* (Berkeley, 1981).

Proceedings of the Third National Irrigation Congress, Held at Denver, Colorado, Sept. 3rd to 8th, 1894 (Denver, n.d.)

Proceedings of the Fourth National Irrigation Congress Held at Albuquerque, New Mexico, September 16–19, 1895 (Santa Fe, 1896).

Proceedings of the Seventh Annual Session, National Irrigation Congress [1898] (Cheyenne, 1899).

Proceedings of the Ninth Annual Session of the National Irrigation Congress, Chicago [1900] (St. Louis, n.d.).

Proceedings of the Tenth National Irrigation Congress Held at Colorado Springs, Colorado [1902] (Colorado Springs, 1902).

Proceedings of the Eleventh National Irrigation Congress Held at Ogden, Utah, September 15–18, 1903 (Ogden, 1904).

Proceedings of the Twelfth National Irrigation Congress Held at El Paso, Texas, Nov., 15–16–17–18, 1904 (El Paso, 1905).

Ratner, Sidney, *American Taxation: Its History as a Social Force in Democracy* (New York, 1942).

Raymond, Rossiter W., *Mining Industry of the States and Territories of the Rocky Mountains* (New York, 1874).

Report of the Fifth National Irrigation Congress Held at Phoenix, Arizona, December 15, 16, and 17, 1896 (Phoenix, 1897).

Report of the International Irrigation Congress Held at Los Angeles, California, October, 1893 (Los Angeles, n.d.).

Richardson, Elmo R., *The Politics of Conservation: Crusades and Controversies, 1897–1913* (Berkeley, 1962).

Richardson, James D., *A Compilation of the Messages and Papers of the Presidents, 1789–1897* (20 vols., Washington, 1900).

Richnak, Barbara, *A River Flows: The Life of Robert Lardin Fulton* (Incline Village, Nev., 1983).

Robbins, Roy M., *Our Landed Heritage: The Public Domain, 1776–1970* (Lincoln, 1976).

Robinson, Michael C., *Water for the West: The Bureau of Reclamation, 1902–1977* (Chicago, 1979).

Rockwell, John A., ed., *A Compilation of Spanish and Mexican Law in Relation to Mines, and Titles to Real Estate in Force in California, Texas and New Mexico* (New York, 1851).

Roosevelt, Theodore, *Autobiography* (New York, 1926).

———, *State Papers as Governor and President, 1899–1909* (New York, 1926).

Rothman, David, *Politics and Power: The United States Senate, 1869–1901* (Cambridge, Mass., 1966).

Rowley, William D., *U.S. Forest Service Grazing and Rangelands: A History* (College Station, Tex., 1985).

Royce, Josiah, *California: From the Conquest in 1846 to the Second Vigilance Committee in San Francisco, A Study in American Character* (Boston, 1886).

Sageser, A. Bower, *Joseph L. Bristow: Kansas Progressive* (Lawrence, 1968).

Scheiber, Harry N., *Ohio Canal Era: A Case Study of Government and the Economy, 1820–1860* (Athens, Ohio, 1969).

Schlesinger, Arthur M., Jr., *The Cycles of American History* (Boston, 1986).

Schrugham, James G., ed., *Nevada: A Narrative of the Conquest of a Frontier Land* (2 vols., Chicago and New York, 1935).

Seavoy, Ronald E., *The Origins of the American Business Corporation, 1784–1855* (Westport, Conn., 1982).

Shannon, Fred A., *The Centennial Years: A Political and Economic History of America from the Late 1870s to the Early 1890s* (New York, 1967).

———, *The Farmer's Last Frontier* (New York, 1945).

Shaw, Ronald E., *Erie Water West: A History of the Erie Canal, 1792–1854* (Lexington, Ky., 1990).

Shaw, William, *Golden Dreams and Waking Realities: Being the Adventures of a Gold-Seeker in the California and Pacific Islands* (London, 1851).

Sherow, James E., *Watering the Valley: Development along the High Plains Arkansas River, 1870–1950* (Lawrence, Kansas, 1990).

Shinn, Charles H., *Land Laws of the Mining Camps* (Baltimore, 1884).

———, *Mining Camps: A Study in American Frontier Government* (New York, 1885).

Skowronek, Stephen, *Building a New American State: The Expansion of National Administrative Capacities, 1877–1920* (Cambridge, Mass., 1982).

Small, Kathleen Edwards, *History of Tulare County, California* (Chicago, 1926).

Smiley, Jerome C., *Semi-Centennial History of the State of Colorado* (2 vols., Chicago & New York, 1913).

Smith, Duane A., *Mining America: The Industry and the Environment, 1800–1980* (Lawrence, Kansas, 1987).

Smith, Karen L., *The Magnificent Experiment: Building the Salt River Reclamation Project, 1890–1917* (Tucson, 1986).

Smith, Michael L., *Pacific Visions: California Scientists and the Environment, 1850–1915* (New Haven, 1987).

Smith, Wallace, *Garden of the Sun* (Los Angeles, 1939).

Smythe, William Ellsworth, *The Conquest of Arid America* (New York, 1900).

Spence, Clark C., *The Rainmakers: American 'Pluviculture' to World War II* (Lincoln, 1980).

———, *The Salvation Army Farm Colonies* (Tucson, 1985).

Sprague, O. M. W., *History of Crisis Under the National Banking System* (Washington, D.C., 1910).

Spring, Agnes Wright, *Seventy Years: A Panoramic History of the Wyoming Stock Growers Association* (n.p., 1942).

Steele, John, *In Camp and Cabin: Mining Life and Adventure in California During 1850 and Later* (Lodi, Wisc., 1901).

Stegner, Wallace, *Beyond the Hundredth Meridian: John Wesley Powell and the Second Opening of the West* (Boston, 1953).

Steinberg, Theodore, *Nature Incorporated: Industrialization and the Waters of New England* (Cambridge, Mass., 1991).

Steinel, Alvin T., *History of Agriculture in Colorado* (Fort Collins, 1926).

Stone, Wilbur Fiske, ed., *History of Colorado* (4 vols., Chicago, 1918).

Stonehouse, Merlin, *John Wesley North and the Reform Frontier* (Minneapolis, 1965).

Stourzh, Gerald, *Alexander Hamilton and the Idea of Republican Government* (Stanford, Calif., 1970).

Taylor, Paul S., *Essays on Land, Water, and Law in California* (New York, 1979).

Teele, Ray P., *Irrigation in the United States* (New York, 1915).

Teilman, I., and Shafer, W. H., *The Historical Story of Irrigation in Central California* (Fresno, Calif., 1943).

Thelen, David P., *Paths of Resistance: Tradition and Dignity in Industrializing Missouri* (New York, 1986).

Thomas, George, *The Development of Institutions under Irrigation: With Special Reference to Early Utah Conditions* (New York, 1920).

Tilton, Cecil G., *William Chapman Ralston: Courageous Builder* (Boston, 1935).

Townley, John, *Alfalfa Country: Nevada Land, Water and Politics in the 19th Century* (Reno, 1981).

Treadwell, Edward F., *The Cattle King* (Boston, 1950).

Tyler, Daniel, *The Mythical Pueblo Rights Doctrine: Water Administration in Hispanic New Mexico* (El Paso, 1990).

Umbeck, John R., *A Theory of Property Rights with Application to the California Gold Rush* (Ames, Iowa, 1981).

Vandor, Paul E., *History of Fresno County California* (Los Angeles, 1919).

Walker, Tacetta B., *Stories of Early Days in Wyoming: Big Horn Basin* (Casper, Wyo., 1936).

Warne, William E., *The Bureau of Reclamation* (New York, 1973).

Warner, Juan Jose, *An Historical Sketch of Los Angeles County, California* (Los Angeles, 1876).

Webb, Walter Prescott, *Divided We Stand: The Crisis of a Frontierless Democracy* (New York, 1937).

———, *The Great Plains* (Boston, 1931).

Weberg, Frank P., *The Background of the Panic of 1893* (Washington, D.C., 1929).

Wells, A. J., *Government Irrigation and the Settler* (San Francisco, n.d.)

Werth, John J., *A Dissertation on the Resources and Policy of California* (Benicia, Calif., 1851).

Weston, S., *Four Months in the Mines of California: or, Life in the Mountains* (Providence, 1854).

White, Leonard D., *The Jacksonians: A Study in Administrative History, 1829–1861* (New York, 1954).

———, *The Republican Era, 1869–1901* (New York, 1958).

Widtsoe, John A., *Dry-Farming* (New York, 1911).

Wiel, Samuel C., *Water Rights in the Western States* (San Francisco, 1905).

———, *Waters: French Law and Common Law* (San Francisco, n.d.).

Willard, James F., *The Union Colony at Greeley, Colorado* (Boulder, 1918).

Williams, William Appleman, *The Contours of American History* (Cleveland, 1961).

Wilson, Warren, *History of San Bernardino County* (San Francisco, 1883).

Winchell, Lilbourne A., *History of Fresno County and the San Joaquin Valley* (Fresno, Calif., 1933).

Wood, Gordon S., *The Creation of the American Republic, 1776–1787* (Chapel Hill, 1969).

Woods, Daniel B., *Sixteen Months at the Gold Diggings* (New York, 1851).

Worster, Donald, *Rivers of Empire: Water, Aridity & the Growth of the American West* (New York, 1985).

Wren, Thomas, ed., *A History of the State of Nevada: Its Resources and People* (New York, 1904).

Wright, James Edward, *The Politics of Populism: Dissent in Colorado* (New Haven, 1974).

Wyckoff, Robert M., *Hydraulicking: A Brief History of Hydraulic Mining in Nevada City, California* (Nevada City, Calif., 1962).

Yale, Charles Gregory, *Brief Sketch of the Public Services of George Davidson* (n.p., 1885).

Yale, Gregory, *Legal Titles to Mining Claims and Water Rights in California, Under the Mining Laws of Congress of July, 1866* (San Francisco, 1867).

Yost, Nellie Snyder, *Buffalo Bill: His Family, Friends, Fame, Failures, and Fortunes* (Chicago, 1979).

Young, Otis, *Western Mining* (Norman, 1970).

Zainaldin, Jamil, *Law in Antebellum Society: Legal Change and Economic Growth* (New York, 1983).

Zonlight, Margaret Aseman Cooper, *Land, Water and Settlement in Kern County California, 1850–1890* (New York, 1979).

Index

477